Juvenile Delinquency
The Core

Larry J. Siegel, Ph.D.
University of Massachusetts—Lowell

W9-CHS-691

WADSWORTH

THOMSON LEARNING

Australia • Canada • Mexico • Singapore • Spain • United Kingdom • United States

Executive Editor, Criminal Justice: Sabra Horne
Development Editor: Terri Edwards
Assistant Editor: Dawn Mesa
Editorial Assistant: Lee McCracken
Marketing Manager: Jennifer Somerville
Marketing Assistant: Neena Chandra
Project Manager, Editorial Production: Jennie Redwitz
Print/Media Buyer: Mary Noel
Permissions Editor: Bob Kauser
Technology Project Manager: Susan DeVanna
Production Service: Linda Jupiter, Jupiter Productions

Text Designer: Carolyn Deacy
Photo Researcher: Linda Rill
Copy Editor: Judy Johnstone
Proofreader: Andy Joron
Indexer: Paula C. Durbin-Westby
Illustrator: Scientific Illustrators
Cover Designer: Yvo Riezebos
Cover Image: James Yang/© SIS
Cover Printer: Phoenix Color Corp.
Compositor: Thompson Type
Printer: Quebecor/SIS © World

For permission to use material from this text, contact us by
Web: http://www.thomsonrights.com **Fax:** 1-800-730-2215
Phone: 1-800-730-2214

ExamView® and ExamView Pro® are registered trademarks of FSCreations, Inc. Windows is a registered trademark of the Microsoft Corporation used herein under license. Macintosh and Power Macintosh are registered trademarks of Apple Computer, Inc. Used herein under license.

COPYRIGHT 2002 Thomson Learning, Inc. All Rights Reserved. Thomson Learning WebTutor™ is a trademark of Thomson Learning, Inc.

Library of Congress Catalog-in-Publication Data

Siegel, Larry J.
   Juvenile delinquency : the core / Larry J. Siegel.
      p. cm.
   Includes bibliographical references and index.
   ISBN 0-534-51932-6
   1. Juvenile delinquency—United States. 2. Juvenile justice, Administration of—United States—States. 3. Juvenile corrections—United States. I. Title.

HV9104 .S52 2001
364.36'0973—dc21

Wadsworth/Thomson Learning
10 Davis Drive
Belmont, CA 94002-3098
USA

For more information about our products, contact us:
Thomson Learning Academic Resource Center
1-800-423-0563
http://www.wadsworth.com

International Headquarters
Thomson Learning
International Division
290 Harbor Drive, 2nd Floor
Stamford, CT 06902-7477
USA

UK/Europe/Middle East/South Africa
Thomson Learning
Berkshire House
168-173 High Holborn
London WC1V 7AA
United Kingdom

Asia
Thomson Learning
60 Albert Street, #15-01
Albert Complex
Singapore 189969

Canada
Nelson Thomson Learning
1120 Birchmount Road
Toronto, Ontario M1K 5G4
Canada

To my children, Eric, Andrew, Julie, and
Rachel and her new husband, Mace
and to Therese J. Libby,
my wife, confidante, and best friend

Brief Contents

Contents

CHAPTER FOUR

Sociological Views of Delinquency 78

CHAPTER FIVE

Developmental Views of Delinquency 106

CHAPTER SIX

Gender and Delinquency 130

CHAPTER SEVEN

The Family and Delinquency 155

CHAPTER EIGHT

Peers and Delinquency: Juvenile Gangs and Groups 184

CHAPTER TWELVE

Police Work with Juveniles 291

CHAPTER THIRTEEN

Juvenile Court Process: Pretrial, Trial, and Sentencing 311

CHAPTER FOURTEEN

Juvenile Corrections: Probation, Community Treatment, and Institutionalization 343

Preface

On April 20, 1999 two students, Eric Harris, 18, and Dylan Klebold, 17, members of a cult-like group called the "Trenchcoat Mafia," went on a shooting spree at Columbine High School in Littleton, Colorado that claimed the lives of at least twelve students and one teacher and wounded 24 others, many seriously. Before they could be captured, the boys committed suicide in the school library, leaving authorities to puzzle over the cause of their deadly outburst. How can their bizarre, violent incident be explained? The Columbine shooting and others like it have shocked the nation and highlighted the immediacy and gravity of the problem of youth crime and violence.

Considering the national concern with the problems of youth, it is not surprising that courses on juvenile delinquency have become popular in colleges and universities. *Juvenile Delinquency: The Core* is designed to help students understand the nature of juvenile delinquency, its causes and correlates, as well as the current strategies being used to control or eliminate it. This new text succinctly reviews some of the major issues in delinquency: What is the effect of divorce on children? Can children be required to submit to drug testing in school? Can teachers search suspicious students or use corporal punishment as a method of discipline? Can children testify on closed-circuit TV in child abuse cases? Can a minor be given a death penalty sentence?

Juvenile Delinquency: The Core reflects the changes that have taken place in the study of delinquent behavior during the past few years. It includes a review of recent legal cases, research studies, and policy initiatives. It addresses the nature and extent of delinquency, the suspected causes of delinquent behavior, and the environmental influences on youthful misbehavior. It also covers what most experts believe are the critical issues in juvenile justice, including the use of pretrial detention, waiver to adult court, and restorative justice programs.

GOALS AND OBJECTIVES

The primary goals and objectives of *Juvenile Delinquency: The Core* are as follows:

1. To present a wide variety of material concisely.

2. To be objective in presenting the many diverse views and perspectives that characterize the study of juvenile delinquency and reflect its interdisciplinary nature.

3. To maintain a balance of theory, law, policy, and practice. A text on delinquency must concern itself with theories and at the same time look pragmatically at the juvenile justice system; it must look at current policies and also examine legal issues and cases.

4. To be thorough and up-to-date. I have included the most recent data available.

To make the study of delinquency interesting as well as informative. I want my readers to decide to pursue this study further, either on an undergraduate or a graduate level.

It has been my intention to provide a text that is informative, interesting, well organized, to the point, objective, provocative, and thought provoking.

ORGANIZATION OF THE TEXT

Chapter 1, on childhood and delinquency, contains extensive material on the history of childhood and the legal concept of delinquency and status offending. This material enables the reader to understand how the concept of adolescence evolved over time and how that evolution influenced the development of the juvenile court and the special status of delinquency.

Chapter 2 covers the measurement of delinquent behavior, along with trends and patterns in teen crime, and discusses the correlates of delinquency, including race, gender, class, age, and chronic offending.

Chapter 3 covers views of delinquency causation that emphasize the individual offender. It focuses on choice, biological, and psychological theories.

Chapter 4 looks at sociological theories of delinquency, which hold that economic, cultural and environmental influences control delinquent behavior.

Chapter 5 reviews developmental theories, which find that events that occur during the adolescent's life course influence and control behavior.

Chapter 6, on gender and delinquency, explores the sex-based differences that are thought to account for the gender patterns in the delinquency rate.

Chapter 7 reviews the family's influence on delinquency and pays special attention to child abuse and its control.

Chapter 8 reviews gang and group delinquency. It covers the development of gangs, the nature of gangs, and efforts to reduce gang delinquency.

Chapter 9, on schools and delinquency, looks at three issues: the effect of the school experience on delinquent behavior, delinquency within schools, and school-based delinquency prevention efforts.

Chapter 10, on drug use and delinquency, reviews the effect that substance abuse has on delinquent behavior. Is drug use increasing? Does substance abuse cause delinquency? What is being done to control drugs?

Chapter 11 gives extensive coverage to the emergence of state control over children in need and the development of the juvenile justice system. It also covers the contemporary juvenile justice system, the major stages in the justice process, the role of the federal government in the juvenile justice system, and an analysis of the differences between the adult and juvenile justice system.

Chapter 12, on police work with juveniles, discusses the role of police in delinquency prevention. It covers legal issues such as *Miranda* rights of juveniles. It also contains material on race and gender effects on police discretion.

Chapter 13 reviews the juvenile court process and contains information on plea bargaining in juvenile court, the use of detention, and transfer to the adult system. It also contains an analysis of the juvenile trial and sentencing.

Chapter 14, on juvenile corrections, looks at community-based treatment, including probation and other community dispositions, as well as secure corrections, including juvenile training schools and boot camps.

LEARNING TOOLS

Juvenile Delinquency: The Core contains the following features, which are designed to help students learn and comprehend the material:

- **Chapter outline** Each chapter has an outline of its main topics.
- **Chapter-opening vignette** Every chapter begins with a scenario that describes an issue or event with intriguing implications for delinquency policy or processes. The scenario is followed by critical thinking questions that help students conceptualize problems of concern within juvenile delinquency.

- **Focus on Delinquency** These boxed inserts focus attention on topics of special importance and concern. For example, in Chapter 7 a new and important book, "The Unexpected Legacy of Divorce," is discussed in some detail.

- **Juvenile Law in Review** These boxes include major Supreme Court cases (for example, *In re Gault*, which defines the concept of due process for youthful offenders) that influence and control the juvenile justice system.

- **Policy and Practice** These boxes discuss major initiatives and programs that are now being used in juvenile justice. In Chapter 2, for example, a box entitled "Helping Prevent Serious and Violent Juvenile Crime" discusses some of the most important and effective delinquency prevention techniques now being used.

- **Checkpoints** These lists are placed at strategic points throughout each chapter to help students retain key concepts.

- **Web links** Easily visible in the margins of every chapter, these inserts guide students to current, topic-related Internet sites. Students not only enrich their understanding of key topics but also fine-tune their Web research skills.

- **Running glossary** Glossary terms appear in the margins where the terms are first mentioned in the text. This immediately reinforces understanding of key terms. These terms are also listed at the end of the chapter in a **Key Terms** section as an additional reinforcement and study aid. A **Glossary,** which defines key terms used in the text, is included at the end of the book.

- **Summaries and discussion questions** Located at the end of each chapter, carefully constructed summaries and probing questions for discussion offer students still another opportunity to reinforce their knowledge and to study more effectively for exams.

- Each chapter closes with a **Viewpoint.** This feature provides an overview of the main themes of the chapter and an excerpt from an article found in the InfoTrac® College Edition online library. Readers are given the full-length article citation.

SUPPLEMENTS

A number of supplements are provided by Wadsworth to help instructors use *Juvenile Delinquency: The Core* in their courses and to aid students in preparing for exams. These include:

Instructor's Manual

The manual includes lecture outlines, learning objectives, discussion topics, key terms, student activities, relevant Web sites, media resources, and a test bank that will not only help time-pressed teachers communicate more effectively with their students but also strengthen the coverage of course material. Each chapter has multiple choice, true/false, and fill-in-the-blank test items, as well as sample essay questions.

Student Study Guide

An extensive student study guide has been developed for this edition. Because students learn in different ways, a variety of pedagogical aids are included in the guide. The guide outlines each chapter, includes major terms, and provides learning objectives and practice tests.

ExamView®

This computerized testing software helps instructors to create and customize exams in minutes. Instructors can easily edit and import their own questions and graphics, change test layouts, and reorganize questions. This software also offers the ability to test and grade online. It is available for both Windows and Macintosh.

WebTutor™ on WebCT and Blackboard

Designed specifically for *Juvenile Delinquency: The Core, WebTutor* is an online resource that gives both instructors and students a virtual environment that is rich with study and communication tools. For instructors, *WebTutor* can provide virtual office hours, post syllabi, set up threaded discussions, and track student progress. *WebTutor* can also be customized in a variety of ways, such as uploading images and other resources and adding Web links to create customized practice materials. For students, *WebTutor* offers real-time access to many study aids, including flash cards, practice quizzes, online tutorials, and Web links.

Web Site for *Juvenile Delinquency: The Core*

This text-specific Web site, located at http://cj.wadsworth.com, offers a variety of online resources for students and instructors. Students can enhance their learning experience with book-specific and chapter-based resources. Web links, periodicals, and InfoTrac College Edition offer valuable and reliable sources for researching specific topics. Projects and quizzing activities provide immediate feedback and can be emailed to instructors. Online homework assignments integrate Web site research with textbook activities. Student study tips provide a well-developed guide to encourage student success. Instructor downloads and Web links for professionals offer an array of resources for curriculum development.

The Wadsworth Criminal Justice Video Library

The Wadsworth Criminal Justice Video Library offers an exciting collection of videos to enrich lectures. Qualified adopters may select from a wide variety of professionally prepared videos covering various aspects of policing, corrections, and other areas of the criminal justice system. The selections include videos from CNN, *Films for the Humanities & Sciences*, CourtTV, the *A&E American Justice Series*, the *National Institute of Justice's Crime File*, ABC News, and *MPI Home Videos*.

InfoTrac® College Edition

Students receive four months of real-time access to InfoTrac College Edition's online database of continually updated, full-length articles from hundreds of journals and periodicals. By doing a simple key word search, users can quickly generate a list of related articles, then select relevant articles to explore and print out for reference or further study.

Crime Scenes: An Interactive Criminal Justice CD-ROM

This highly visual and interactive program casts students as the decision makers in various roles as they explore all aspects of the criminal justice system. Exciting videos and supporting documents put students in the midst of a juvenile murder trial, a prostitution case that turns to manslaughter, and several other scenarios. This product received the gold medal in higher education and a silver medal for video interface from *NewMedia Magazine's Invision Awards*.

Mind of a Killer CD-ROM

Based on Eric Hickey's book *Serial Murderers and Their Victims*, this award-winning CD-ROM offers viewers a look at the psyches of the world's most notorious killers. Students can view confessions of and interviews with serial killers, and they can examine famous cases through original video documentaries and news footage.

Included are 3-D profiling simulations that seek to find out what motivates these killers.

Careers in Criminal Justice Interactive CD-ROM

This engaging self-exploration CD-ROM provides interactive discovery of the wide range of careers in criminal justice. The self-assessment helps steer students to suitable careers based on their personal profile. Students can gather information on various careers from the job descriptions, salaries, employment requirements, and sample tests, as well as view video profiles of criminal justice professionals on this valuable tool.

Seeking Employment in Criminal Justice and Related Fields

Written by J. Scott Harr and Kären Hess, this practical book, now in its third edition, helps students develop a search strategy for finding employment in criminal justice and related fields. Each chapter includes "insiders' views," written by individuals in the field, and addresses promotions and career planning.

Guide to Careers in Criminal Justice

This 60-page booklet provides a brief introduction to the exciting and diverse field of criminal justice. Students can learn about opportunities in law enforcement, courts, and corrections, and how they can go about getting these jobs.

The Criminal Justice Internet Investigator III

This handy brochure lists the most useful criminal justice links on the World Wide Web. It includes the most popular criminal justice and criminology sites, featuring current topics and research information, statistics, fun sites, and more.

Internet Guide for Criminal Justice

Developed by Daniel Kurland and Christina Polsenberg, this easy-reference text helps newcomers as well as experienced Web surfers to use the Internet for criminal justice research.

Internet Activities for Criminal Justice

This 60-page booklet shows how best to utilize the Internet for research via searches and activities.

ACKNOWLEDGMENTS

The preparation of this text would not have been possible without the aid of my colleagues, who helped by reviewing the manuscript and making important suggestions for improvement. These colleagues include: Bruce Berg, California State University, Long Beach; Sue Bourke, University of Cincinnati; Jerald C. Burns, Alabama State University; Ann Butzin, Owens State Community College; John R. Cross, Oklahoma State University; Brendan Maguire, Western Illinois University; Jane Kravitz Munley, Luzerne County Community College; Rebecca D. Petersen, University of Texas, San Antonio; Cheryl Tieman, Radford University.

My colleagues at Wadsworth did their usual outstanding job of aiding in the preparation of the text. Sabra Horne, my wonderful editor, is always there for me when I need her. Terri Edwards is a terrific developmental editor who has become a good friend. Linda Rill did her usual thorough, professional job in photo research and is an honorary family member. Linda Jupiter, who managed the book's production, has been great to work with, as was copyeditor Judith Johnstone. Dawn Mesa, assistant editor, and Susan DeVanna, technology project manager, were invaluable in developing the book's supplemental package and text-specific Web site. Jennie Redwitz, project manager, somehow pulls everything together. Jennifer Somerville, marketing manager and friend, is terrific at explaining what the book is all about.

Larry Siegel
Bedford, NH

Chapter 1

Childhood and Delinquency

© D. R. M. News/CORBIS-Sygma

ou have just been appointed by the governor as chairperson of a newly formed group charged with overhauling the state's juvenile justice system. One primary concern is the treatment of *status offenders*—kids who have been picked up and charged with being runaways, sexually active, truant from school, or unmanageable at home. Under existing status offense statutes, these youth can be sent to juvenile court and stand trial for their misbehaviors. If the allegations against them are proven valid, they may be removed from the home and placed in foster care or even in a state or private custodial institution.

Recently, a great deal of media attention has been given to the plight of runaway children who live on the streets, take drugs, and engage in prostitution. At an open hearing, advocates of the current system argue that many families cannot provide the care and control needed to keep kids out of trouble and that the state must maintain control of "at risk" youth. They contend that many status offenders have histories of drug and delinquency problems and are little different from kids arrested on criminal charges; control by the juvenile court is necessary if the youths are ever to get needed treatment.

Another vocal group argues that it is a mistake for a system that deals with criminal youth also to handle troubled adolescents, whose problems usually are the result of child abuse and neglect. They believe that the current statute should be amended to give the state's department of social welfare (DSW) jurisdiction over all noncriminal youths who are in need of assistance. These opponents of the current law point out that, even though status offenders and delinquents are held in separate facilities, those who run away or are unmanageable can be transferred to more secure correctional facilities that house criminal youths. Furthermore, the current court-based process, where troubled youths are involved with lawyers, trials, and court proceedings, helps convince them that they are "bad kids" and social outcasts.

- Should status offenders be treated differently than juvenile delinquents?

- Should distinctions be made between different types of status offenders? That is, are runaways different from truants?

- Are these behavioral problems better handled by a social service or mental health agency than a juvenile court?

- What recommendations would you make to the governor?

How to deal effectively with troubled adolescents is a critical element of contemporary social policy. There are about 70 million adolescents in the United States and the number is projected to rise (Figure 1.1). The present generation of adolescents has been described as cynical, preoccupied with material acquisitions, and uninterested in creative expression.[1] By age 18 they have spent more time in front of a TV set than in the classroom; each year they may see up to one thousand rapes, murders, and assaults on TV.

In the 1950s youths were reading comic books, but today teens are listening to rap CDs such as Eminem's "The Real Slim Shady," whose lyrics routinely praise violence and substance abuse. They watch TV shows and movies that rely on graphic scenes of violence as their main theme, and cyberspace has exposed youth to images that their parents could not imagine. How will this exposure affect them? Should we be concerned?

Figure 1.1
Adolescent Population Trends

Number of children under age 18 in the United States, 1950–98 and projected 1999–2020

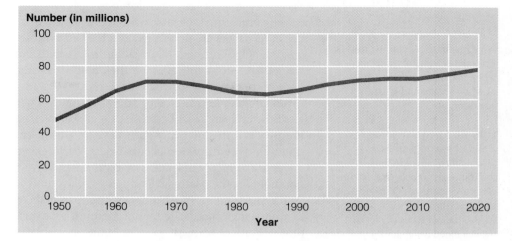

Number of children under age 18 in the United States, 1950–2020 (projected)

Number (in millions)

- In 1998, there were 69.9 million children in the United States, 0.3 million more than in 1997. This number is projected to increase to 77.6 million in 2020.
- The number of children under 18 has grown during the last half-century, increasing about half again in size since 1950.
- During the "baby boom" (1946 to 1964), the number of children grew rapidly.
- During the 1970s and 1980s, the number of children declined and then grew slowly.
- Beginning in 1990, the rate of growth in the number of children increased, although not as rapidly as during the baby boom.
- In 1998, there were approximately equal numbers of children—between 23 and 24 million—in each age group 0–5, 6–11, and 12–17 years of age.

THE ADOLESCENT DILEMMA

The problems of American society have had a significant effect on our nation's youth. Adolescence is a time of trial and uncertainty, a time when youths experience anxiety, humiliation, and mood swings. During this period, the personality is still developing and is vulnerable to a host of external factors.[2] Adolescents also undergo a period of rapid biological development. Over a period of a few years, their height, weight, and sexual characteristics change dramatically. A hundred and fifty years ago girls

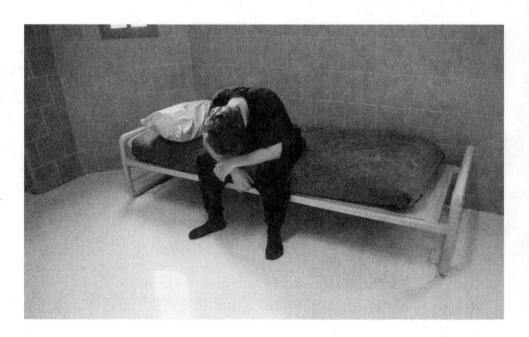

An adolescent sits in a juvenile detention cell in Austin, Texas. Should noncriminal youth who have run away from home or broken curfew be kept in secure detention before trial? Some experts believe that many status offenders have histories of drug and delinquency problems and are little different from kids arrested on criminal charges. Consequently, such confinement may be warranted. Do you agree? (© Bob Daemmrich/The Image Works)

matured sexually at age 16, but today they do so at 12.5 years of age. Although they may be capable of having children as early as age 14, many youngsters remain emotionally immature long after reaching biological maturity.[3] At age 15 a significant number of teenagers are unable to meet the responsibilities of the workplace, the family, and the neighborhood. Many suffer from health problems, are underachievers in school, and are skeptical about their ability to enter the workforce and become productive members of society.[4]

In later adolescence (ages 16 to 18) youths may experience a crisis that psychologist Erik Erikson described as a struggle between ego identity and role diffusion. **Ego identity** is formed when youths develop a firm sense of who they are and what they stand for; **role diffusion** occurs when youths experience uncertainty and place themselves at the mercy of leaders who promise to give them a sense of identity they cannot mold for themselves.[5] Psychologists also find that late adolescence is dominated by the yearning for independence from parental control.[6] Given this mixture of biological change and desire for autonomy, it isn't surprising that the teenage years are a time of conflict with authority at home, at school, and in the community.

ego identity According to Erik Erikson, ego identity is formed when persons develop a firm sense of who they are and what they stand for.

role diffusion According to Erik Erikson, role diffusion occurs when youths spread themselves too thin, experience personal uncertainty, and place themselves at the mercy of leaders who promise to give them a sense of identity they cannot develop for themselves.

Youth in Crisis

Problems in the home, the school, and the neighborhood have placed a significant portion of American youth at risk. Youths considered at risk are those who engage in dangerous conduct such as drug abuse, alcohol use, and precocious sexuality. Although it is impossible to determine precisely the number of **at-risk youths** in the United States, one estimate is that 25 percent of the population under age 17, or about 17 million youths, are in this category. Of these, 7 million are extremely vulnerable to delinquency and gang activity.[7] An additional 7 million adolescents can be classified as at moderate risk.[8] The most pressing problems facing American youth revolve around four issues.

at-risk youths Young people who are extremely vulnerable to the negative consequences of school failure, substance abuse, and early sexuality.

Poverty Though the number of American children living in poverty is dropping, the U.S. Census Bureau finds that there are still more than 12 million indigent children (the Census Bureau defines poverty as an income below $13,290 a year, or the equivalent of $1,108 a month for a family of three).[9] While the percentage of children living in poverty in America is at its lowest level since 1979, the percentage of poor children in working families continues to climb, with 77 percent of poor children living in families where someone is working; this indicates that many working families are still struggling to stay afloat.

Family Problems Divorce strikes about half of all new marriages, and many families sacrifice time with each other to afford more affluent lifestyles. Research shows that children are being polarized into two distinct economic groups: those in affluent, two-earner, married-couple households and those in poor, single-parent households.[10]

Formed in 1985, the Children's Rights Council (CRC) is a national nonprofit organization based in Washington, D.C. that works to assure children meaningful and continuing contact with both their parents and extended family regardless of the parents' marital status. For more information, go to

http://www.gocrc.com/

For an up-to-date list of Web links, go to www.wadsworth.com/product/0534573053s.

Urban Decay Adolescents living in deteriorated urban areas are prevented from having productive and happy lives. Many die from random bullets and drive-by shootings. Some are homeless and living on the street, where they are at risk of drug addiction and sexually transmitted diseases (STDs) including AIDS. One study of street kids in New York City found that 37 percent earned money through prostitution and almost one-third had contracted an STD.[11]

Inadequate Education The U.S. educational system seems to be failing many young people. We are lagging behind other developed nations in critical areas such as science and mathematics. The rate of *retention* (being forced to repeat a grade) is far higher than it should be. Retention rates are associated with another major problem:

Although it is impossible to precisely determine the number of at-risk youth in the United States, one estimate is that 25 percent of the population under 17, or more than 7 million youths, are extremely vulnerable to the negative consequences of school failure, substance abuse, and early sexuality. This teen prostitute is at extreme risk of violent crime and victimization. (© Catherine Leroy/Sipa Press)

www

There are, in fact, a number of organizations dedicated to improving educational standards in the United States. The Eisenhower National Clearinghouse's mission is to identify effective curriculum resources, create high-quality professional development materials, and disseminate useful information and products to improve K–12 mathematics and science teaching and learning. For more information, go to

http://www.enc.org/

For an up-to-date list of Web links, go to www.wadsworth.com/product/0534573053s.

dropping out. It is estimated that about 14 percent of all eligible youths do not finish high school.[12] In addition, poor and minority-group children attend the most underfunded schools, receive inadequate educational opportunities, and have the fewest opportunities to achieve conventional success. Some of the social problems faced by American youth are detailed in Table 1.1.

Considering that youth are at risk during the most tumultuous time of their lives, it comes as no surprise that they are willing, as the Focus on Delinquency box ("Risky Business") suggests, to engage in risky, destructive behavior.

Are There Reasons for Hope?

Despite the many hazards faced by teens, there are some bright spots on the horizon. Teenage birthrates nationwide have declined substantially during the past decade, with the sharpest declines being experienced by African American girls.[13] These data indicate that more young girls are using birth control and practicing safe sex. Fewer children with health risks are being born today than in 1990. This probably means that fewer women are drinking or smoking during pregnancy and that fewer are receiving late or no prenatal care. In addition, since 1990 the number of children immunized against disease has increased.[14] And, due largely to improved medical technology, the infant mortality rate (the number of children who die before their first birthday) declined about 30 percent during the past decade (from 10.6 to 7.6 per 1,000 births).[15]

TABLE 1.1	The State of America's Children

1 in 2 preschoolers has a mother in the labor force.

1 in 2 will live in a single-parent family at some point in childhood.

1 in 2 never completes a single year of college.

1 in 3 is born to unmarried parents.

1 in 3 will be poor at some point in their childhood.

1 in 3 is behind a year or more in school.

1 in 4 lives with only one parent.

1 in 4 was born poor.

1 in 5 is poor now.

1 in 5 lives in a family receiving food stamps.

1 in 5 is born to a mother who did not graduate from high school.

1 in 5 has a foreign-born mother.

1 in 6 is born to a mother who did not receive prenatal care in the first 3 months of pregnancy.

1 in 6 has no health insurance.

1 in 7 has a worker in their family but still is poor.

1 in 8 never graduates from high school.

1 in 8 is born to a teenage mother.

1 in 12 lives at less than half the poverty level.

1 in 12 has a disability.

1 in 13 was born with low birth weight.

1 in 24 lives with neither parent.

1 in 26 is born to a mother who received late, or no, prenatal care.

1 in 60 sees parents divorce in any year.

1 in 138 will die before their first birthday.

1 in 910 will be killed by guns before age 20.

Source: Children's Defense Fund, *The State of America's Children, Yearbook 2000.*

www

The mission of the Children's Defense Fund is to "Leave No Child Behind" and to ensure every child a Healthy Start, a Head Start, a Fair Start, a Safe Start, and a Moral Start in life and a successful passage to adulthood with the help of caring families and communities. The CDF tries to provide a strong, effective voice for kids who cannot vote, lobby, or speak for themselves. Visit their Web site at

http://www.childrensdefense.org/

For an up-to-date list of Web links, go to www.wadsworth.com/ product/0534573053s.

Education is still a problem area, but more parents are reading to their children, and math achievement is rising in grades 4 through 12. More students are receiving degrees in math and science than were doing so in the 1970s and 1980s.[16] There are also indications that youngsters may be rejecting hard drugs. Teen smoking and drinking rates remain high, but fewer kids are using heroin and crack cocaine and the numbers of teens who report cigarette use is declining.[17]

Although these signs are encouraging, many problem areas remain, and the improvement of adolescent life continues to be a national goal.

THE STUDY OF JUVENILE DELINQUENCY

juvenile delinquency Participation in illegal behavior by a minor who falls under a statutory age limit.

The problems of youth in modern society are an important subject for academic study. This text focuses on one area of particular concern: **juvenile delinquency,** or criminal behavior engaged in by minors. The study of juvenile delinquency is important both because of the damage suffered by its victims and the problems faced by its perpetrators.

Almost 1.5 million youths are arrested each year for crimes ranging from loitering to murder.[18] Though most juvenile law violations are minor, some young offenders are extremely dangerous and violent. More than 700,000 youths belong to street

RISKY BUSINESS

The Centers for Disease Control and Prevention (CDC) report that, in the United States, 73 percent of all deaths among youth and young adults from 10 to 24 years of age result from only four causes: motor vehicle crashes, other unintentional injuries, homicide, and suicide. The reason may be that many high school students engage in risky behaviors that increase their likelihood of death from violence, accident, or self-destruction. A survey conducted by the CDC found that about 20 percent of youths rarely or never wore a seat belt; 37 percent had ridden with a driver who had been drinking alcohol; 18 percent had carried a weapon; 50.8 percent had drunk alcohol; and 26 percent had used marijuana. About 8 percent had attempted suicide during the 12 months preceding the survey. The survey found that about half of all high school students had sexual intercourse; 43 percent of sexually active students had not used a condom; and about 36 percent of high school students had smoked cigarettes during the previous month.

Why do youths take such chances? Criminologist Nanette Davis suggests there is a potential for "risky" behavior among youth in all facets of American life. *Risky* describes behavior that is emotionally edgy, dangerous, exciting, hazardous, challenging, volatile, and potentially emotionally, socially, and financially costly—even life threatening. Youths commonly become involved in risky behavior as they negotiate the hurdles of adolescent life, learning to drive, date, drink, work , relate, and live. Davis finds that social developments in the United States have increased the risks of growing up for all children. The social, economic, and political circumstances that increase adolescent risk-taking include:

1. The uncertainty of contemporary social life. Planning a future is problematic in a society where job elimination and corporate downsizing are accepted business practices and divorce and family restructuring are epidemic.

2. Politicians who opt for short-term solutions while ignoring long-term consequences. For example, they may find that fighting minimum wage increases pleases their constituents. Yet, a low minimum wage reinforces the belief that economic advancement cannot be achieved through conventional means; the politicians' actions may undermine the working poor's belief in the American Dream of economic opportunity. Lack of legitimate opportunity may lead to delinquent alternatives such as drug dealing or theft.

3. Emphasis on consumerism. In high schools, peer respect is bought through the accumulation of material goods. Underprivileged youth are driven to illegal behavior in an effort to engage in conspicuous consumption. Drug deals and theft may be a short cut to getting coveted name-brand clothes and athletic shoes.

4. Racial, class, age, and ethnicity inequalities discourage kids from believing in a better future. Children are raised to be skeptical that they can receive social benefits from any institution beyond themselves or their immediate family.

5. The lack of adequate childcare has become a national emergency. Lower-class women cannot afford adequate childcare. New welfare laws that require single mothers to work put millions of kids in high-risk situations. Children in low-quality care can have delayed cognition and language development. They behave more aggressively toward others and react poorly to stress.

6. For some, access to dominant social institutions and persons in authority is barred. The inability to have access—most often a function of social class and occupation—decreases the ability to manage risk.

7. The "cult of individualism" makes people self-centered and hurts collective and group identities. Children are taught to put their own interests above those of others.

As children mature into adults, the uncertainty of modern society may prolong their risk-taking behavior. Jobs have become unpredictable, and many under-educated and undertrained youths find themselves competing for the same low-paying job with hundreds of applicants; they are a "surplus product." They may find their only alternative for survival is to return to their childhood bedroom and live off their parents. Under these circumstances, risk-taking may be a plausible alternative for fitting in our consumer-oriented society.

Davis calls for a major national effort to restore these troubled youth using a holistic, nonpunitive approach that recognizes the special needs of children.

Sources: Laura Kann et al., *Youth Risk Behavior Surveillance— United States, 1997* (Atlanta: CDC, August 14, 1998); Nanette Davis, *Youth Crisis: Growing Up in the High-Risk Society* (New York: Praeger, Greenwood, 1998).

chronic delinquents Youths who have been arrested five or more times during their minority; this small group of offenders is believed to engage in a significant portion of all delinquent behavior.

gangs. Youths involved in multiple serious criminal acts, referred to as *repeat*, or **chronic delinquent** offenders, are considered a serious social problem. State juvenile authorities must deal with these offenders, while responding to a range of other social problems, including child abuse and neglect, school crime and vandalism, family crises, and drug abuse.

Clearly, there is an urgent need for strategies to combat juvenile delinquency. But formulating effective strategies demands a solid understanding of delinquency's causes. Is delinquency a function of psychological abnormality? A reaction against destructive social conditions? The product of a disturbed home life? Does serious delinquent behavior occur only in urban areas among lower-class youths? Or is it spread throughout the social structure? What are the effects of family life, substance abuse, school experiences, and peer relations?

juvenile justice system The segment of the justice system, including law enforcement officers, the courts, and correctional agencies, designed to treat youthful offenders.

The study of delinquency also involves the analysis of the **juvenile justice system,** the law enforcement, court, and correctional agencies designed to treat youthful offenders. How should police deal with minors who violate the law? What are the legal rights of children? What kinds of correctional programs are most effective with delinquent youths? How useful are educational, community, counseling, and vocational development programs? Is it true, as some critics claim, that most efforts to rehabilitate young offenders are doomed to failure?[19] The reaction to juvenile delinquency frequently divides the public. People want to insulate young people from a life of crime and drug abuse. Research suggests that a majority still favors policies mandating rehabilitation of offenders.[20] Evidence also exists that many at-risk youths can be helped successfully with the proper treatment.[21] However, many Americans are wary of teenage hoodlums and gangs. How can we control their behavior? Should we embrace a *get tough* policy in which violent teens are locked up? Or should we continue to treat delinquents as troubled teens who need a helping hand? Many juvenile court judges today base their sentencing decisions on the need to punish offenders and are more concerned about protecting the rights of victims of crime than rehabilitating juveniles.[22] Similarly, the Supreme Court has legalized the death penalty for children once they reach age 16.[23] Should the juvenile justice system be more concerned about the long-term effects of punishment? Can even the most violent teenager one day be rehabilitated?

In summary, the scientific study of delinquency requires understanding the nature, extent, and cause of youthful law violations and the methods devised for their control. We also need to study environmental and social issues, including substance abuse, child abuse and neglect, education, and peer relations. All of these aspects of juvenile delinquency will be discussed in this text. We begin, however, with a look back to the development of the concept of *childhood* and how children were first identified as a unique group with their own special needs and behaviors.

THE DEVELOPMENT OF CHILDHOOD

The treatment of children as a distinct social group with special needs and behavior is a relatively new concept. Only for the past 350 years has any formal mechanism existed to care for even the neediest children. In Europe during the Middle Ages (A.D. 700–1500), the concept of childhood as we know it today did not exist. In the **paternalistic family** of the time, the father exercised complete control over his wife and children.[24] Children who did not obey were subject to severe physical punishment, even death.

paternalistic family A family style wherein the father is the final authority on all family matters and exercises complete control over his wife and children.

Custom and Practice in the Middle Ages

During the Middle Ages, as soon as they were physically capable, children of all classes were expected to engage in adult roles. Males engaged in farming or learning a skilled trade such as masonry or metalworking; females aided in food preparation or household maintenance.[25] Some peasant youths went into domestic or agricultural service on the estates of powerful landowners or in trades or crafts.[26] Children of the landholding classes also assumed adult roles at an early age. At age 7 or 8, boys born to landholding families were either sent to a monastery or cathedral school or sent to serve as squires, or assistants, to experienced knights. At age 21, young men of the

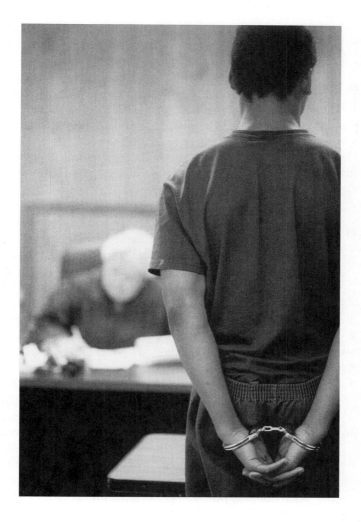

Many juvenile court judges today base their sentencing decisions on the need to punish offenders and are more concerned about protecting the rights of victims of crime than rehabilitating juvenile offenders. Antwuan Burton stands handcuffed during a bond hearing, Feb. 23, 2001, at the Multi-County Juvenile Attention Center in Canton, Ohio. Magistrate Connie Butera ordered Burton, who is charged with aggravated murder in the death of 3-year-old Shay K. Williams, to be held without bond. (© *The Repository,* photo by Joy Newcomb)

knightly classes received their own knighthood and returned home to live with their parents. Girls were educated at home and married in their early teens. A few were taught to read, write, and do sufficient mathematics to handle household accounts in addition to typical female duties such as supervising servants.

Childrearing and Discipline The harshness of medieval life influenced childrearing practices. Newborns were handed over to *wet nurses* who fed and cared for them during the first two years of life. Parents had little contact with their children. Discipline was severe. Young children of all classes were subjected to stringent rules and regulations. Children were beaten severely for any sign of disobedience or ill temper, and many would be considered abused by today's standards. Children were expected to undertake responsibilities early in their lives, sharing in the work of siblings and parents. Those thought to be suffering from disease or retardation were often abandoned to churches, orphanages, or foundling homes.[27]

The impersonal relationship between parent and child can be traced to high mortality rates. Parents were reluctant to invest emotional effort in relationships that could so easily end due to violence, accidents, or disease. Many believed children must be toughened to ensure their survival, and close family relationships were viewed as detrimental to this process. Also, since the oldest male child was the essential player in a family's well-being, younger male and female siblings were considered liabilities.

The Development of Concern for Children

Throughout the seventeenth and eighteenth centuries, a number of developments in England heralded the march toward the recognition of children's rights. Among them were changes in family style and childcare, the English Poor Laws, the apprenticeship movement, and the role of the chancery court.[28]

Changes in Family Structure Family structure began to change after the Middle Ages. Extended families, which were created over centuries, gave way to the nuclear family structure with which we are familiar today. It became more common for marriage to be based on love rather than on parental consent and paternal dominance. This changing concept of marriage from an economic arrangement to an emotional commitment also began to influence the way children were treated. Although parents still rigidly disciplined their children, they formed closer ties and had greater concern for their offsprings' well-being.

Grammar and boarding schools were established in many large cities during this time.[29] Children studied grammar, Latin, law, and logic. Teachers often ruled by fear. Students were beaten for academic mistakes as well as for moral lapses. Such brutal treatment fell on both the rich and the poor throughout all levels of educational life, including boarding schools and universities. This treatment abated in Europe with the rise of the Enlightenment, but it remained in full force in Great Britain until late in the nineteenth century.

Toward the close of the eighteenth century, the work of such philosophers as Voltaire, Rousseau, and Locke launched a new age for childhood and the family.[30] Their vision produced a period known as the Enlightenment, which stressed a humanistic view of life, freedom, family, reason, and law. These new beliefs influenced the family. The father's authority was tempered, discipline became more relaxed, and the expression of affection became more commonplace. Upper- and middle-class families began to devote attention to childrearing, and the status of children was advanced.

As a result of these changes, children began to emerge as a distinct group with independent needs and interests. Serious questions arose over the treatment of children in school. Restrictions were placed on the use of the whip, and in some schools academic assignments or the loss of privileges replaced corporal punishment. Despite such reforms, punishment was still primarily physical, and schools continued to mistreat children.

Poor Laws English statutes that allowed the courts to appoint overseers over destitute and neglected children, who then placed them in families, workhouses, or apprenticeships.

Poor Laws As early as 1535, the English passed statutes known as **Poor Laws**.[31] These laws allowed for the appointment of overseers to place destitute or neglected children as servants in the homes of the affluent, where they were trained in agricultural, trade, or domestic services. The Elizabethan Poor Laws of 1601 created a system of church wardens and overseers who, with the consent of justices of the peace, identified vagrant, delinquent, and neglected children and put them to work. Often this meant placing them in poorhouses or workhouses or apprenticing them to masters.

The Apprenticeship Movement Apprenticeship existed throughout almost the entire history of Great Britain.[32] Under this practice, children were placed in the care of adults who trained them in specific skills. *Voluntary apprentices* were bound out by parents or guardians. *Involuntary apprentices* were compelled by the authorities to serve until they were 21 or older. The master-apprentice relationship was similar to the parent-child relationship in that the master had complete authority over the apprentice. If an apprentice was unruly, he could be punished. Incarcerated apprentices were often kept separate from other prisoners and treated differently. Even at this early stage, the conviction was growing that the criminal law should be applied differently to children.

chancery courts Court proceedings created in fifteenth-century England to oversee the lives of high-born minors who were orphaned or otherwise could not care for themselves.

Chancery Court Throughout Great Britain in the Middle Ages, **chancery courts** were established to protect property rights, although their authority also extended to the welfare of children. The major issues in cases that came before the chancery

As soon as they were physically capable, children of the Middle Ages were expected to engage in adult roles. Among the working classes, males engaged in peasant farming or learned a skilled trade, such as masonry or metalworking; females aided in food preparation or household maintenance. Some peasant youth went into domestic or agricultural service on the estate of a powerful landowner or into trades or crafts, such as blacksmith or farrier (horseshoer). (The Pierpont Morgan Library/Art Resource, NY)

parens patriae Power of the state to act in behalf of the child and provide care and protection equivalent to that of a parent.

courts concerned guardianship of orphans. This included safeguarding their property and inheritance rights and appointing a guardian to protect them until they reached the age of majority.

Chancery courts were founded on the proposition that children were under the protective control of the king; thus, the Latin phrase **parens patriae** was used, which refers to the role of the king as the father of his country. The concept was first used by English kings to establish their right to intervene in the lives of the children of their vassals.[33] In the famous 1827 case *Wellesley v. Wellesley,* a duke's children were taken away from him in the name and interest of *parens patriae* because of his scandalous behavior.[34] Thus, the concept of *parens patriae* became the theoretical basis for the protective jurisdiction of the chancery courts acting as part of the crown's power. As time passed, the monarchy used *parens patriae* more and more to justify its intervention in the lives of families and children.[35]

The chancery courts did not have jurisdiction over children charged with criminal conduct. Juveniles who violated the law were handled within the regular criminal court system. Nonetheless, the concept of *parens patriae* grew to refer primarily to the responsibility of the courts and the state to act in the best interests of the child.

Work in the newly developing factories taxed young laborers, placing demands on them they were often too young to endure. To alleviate a rapidly developing problem, the Factory Acts of the early nineteenth century limited the hours children were permitted to work and the age at which they could begin work. It also prescribed a minimum amount of schooling to be provided by factory owners. (Stock Montage, Inc.)

Childhood in America

While England was using its chancery courts and Poor Laws to care for children in need, the American colonies were developing similar concepts. The colonies were a haven for people looking for opportunities denied them in England and Europe. Along with early settlers, many children came not as citizens but as indentured servants, apprentices, or agricultural workers. They were recruited from workhouses, orphanages, prisons, and asylums that housed vagrant and delinquent youths.[36]

At the same time, the colonists themselves produced illegitimate, neglected, and delinquent children. The initial response to caring for such children was to adopt court and Poor Law systems similar to those in England. Poor Law legislation requiring poor and dependent children to serve apprenticeships was passed in Virginia in 1646 and in Massachusetts and Connecticut in 1673.[37]

The master in colonial America acted as a surrogate parent, and in certain instances apprentices would actually become part of the family. If they disobeyed their masters, they were punished by local tribunals. If masters abused apprentices, courts would make them pay damages, return the children to the parents, or find new guardians. Maryland and Virginia developed an orphan's court that supervised the treatment of youths placed with guardians. These courts did not supervise children living with their natural parents, leaving intact parents' rights to care for their children.[38]

By the beginning of the nineteenth century, the apprenticeship system gave way to the factory system, and the problems of how to deal with dependent youths increased. Early settlers believed hard work, strict discipline, and education were the only reliable methods for salvation. A child's life was marked by work alongside parents, some schooling, prayer, more work, and further study. Work in the factories, however, often placed demands on child laborers that they were too young to endure. To alleviate this problem, the *Factory Act* of the early nineteenth century limited the hours children were permitted to work and the age at which they could begin to work. It also prescribed a minimum amount of schooling to be provided by factory owners.[39] This and related statutes were often violated, and conditions of work and school remained troublesome issues well into the twentieth century. Nevertheless, the statutes were a step in the direction of reform.

Controlling Children

www

For more information on the early history of childhood and the development of education, go to the Web site of The History of Education and Childhood at Nijmegen University, the Netherlands:

http://www.socsci.kun.nl/ped/whp/histeduc/

For an up-to-date list of Web links, go to www.wadsworth.com/product/0534573053s.

In the United States, as in England, moral discipline was rigidly enforced. Stubborn child laws were passed that required children to obey their parents.[40] It was not uncommon for children to be whipped if they were disobedient or disrespectful to their families. Children were often required to attend public whippings and executions because these events were thought to be important forms of moral instruction. Parents referred their children to published writings on behavior and expected them to follow their precepts carefully. The early colonists, however, viewed family violence as a sin, and child protection laws were passed as early as 1639 (in New Haven, Connecticut). These laws expressed the community's commitment to God to oppose sin, but offenders usually received lenient sentences.[41]

Although most colonies adopted a protectionist stance, few cases of child abuse were actually brought before the courts. This neglect may reflect the nature of life in extremely religious households. Children were productive laborers and respected by their parents. In addition, large families provided many siblings and kinfolk who could care for children and relieve the burden on parents.[42] Another view is that although many children were harshly punished, in early American families the acceptable limits of discipline were so high that few parents were charged with assault. Any punishment that fell short of maiming or permanently harming a child was considered within the sphere of parental rights.[43]

✔ Checkpoints

✔ The problems of American youth have become a national concern and an important subject of academic study.

✔ There are 70 million youth in the United States and the number is expected to rise.

✔ American youth are under a great deal of stress. They face poverty, family problems, urban decay, inadequate education, teen pregnancy, and social conflict.

✔ The concept of a separate status of "childhood" has developed slowly over the centuries.

✔ Early family life was controlled by parents. Punishment was severe and children were expected to take on adult roles early in their lives.

✔ With the start of the seventeenth century came greater recognition of the needs of children. In Great Britain, the chancery court movement, the Poor Laws, and the apprenticeship programs greatly affected the lives of children.

✔ In colonial America, many of the characteristics of English family living were adopted.

✔ In the nineteenth century, neglected, delinquent, and dependent or runaway children were treated no differently than criminal defendants. Children were often charged and convicted of crimes.

THE CONCEPT OF DELINQUENCY

Prior to the twentieth century, little distinction was made between adult and juvenile offenders. Although judges considered the age of an offender when deciding on punishment, both adults and children were eligible for prison, corporal punishment, and even the death penalty. In fact, children were treated with extreme cruelty at home, at school, and by the law.[44]

child savers Nineteenth-century reformers who developed programs for troubled youth and influenced legislation creating the juvenile justice system; today some critics view them as being more concerned with control of the poor than with their welfare.

Over the years this treatment changed as society became sensitive to the special needs of children. Beginning in the mid-nineteenth century, there was official recognition that children formed a separate group with their own special needs. In New York, Boston, and Chicago, groups known as **child savers** were formed to assist children. They created community programs to service needy children and lobbied for a separate legal status for children, which ultimately led to development of a formal juvenile justice system. The child-saving movement will be discussed more fully in Chapter 9.

Delinquency and *Parens Patriae*

delinquent Juvenile who has been adjudicated by a judicial officer of a juvenile court as having committed a delinquent act.

best interests of the child A philosophical viewpoint that encouraged the state to take control of wayward children and provide care, custody, and treatment to remedy delinquent behavior.

The current treatment of juvenile delinquents is a byproduct of this developing national consciousness of children's needs. The designation **delinquent** became popular at the onset of the twentieth century when the first separate juvenile courts were instituted. The child savers believed treating minors and adults equally violated the humanitarian ideals of American society. Consequently, the emerging juvenile justice system operated under the *parens patriae* philosophy. Minors who engaged in illegal behavior were viewed as victims of improper care at home. Illegal behavior was a sign that the state should step in and take control of the youths before they committed more serious crimes. The state should act in the **best interests of the child**. Children should not be punished for their misdeeds but instead should be given the care necessary to control wayward behavior. It makes no sense to find children guilty of specific crimes, such as burglary or petty larceny, because that stigmatizes them as thieves or burglars. Instead, the catchall term *juvenile delinquency* should be used because it indicates that the child needs the care and custody of the state.

The Legal Status of Delinquency

The child savers fought hard for a legal status of juvenile delinquent, but the concept that children could be treated differently before the law can actually be traced to the British legal tradition. Early British jurisprudence held that children under the age of 7 were legally incapable of committing crimes. Children between the ages of 7 and 14 were responsible for their actions, but their age might be used to excuse or lighten their punishment. Our legal system still recognizes that many young people are incapable of making mature judgments and that responsibility for their acts should be limited. Children can intentionally steal cars and know that the act is illegal, but they may be incapable of fully understanding the consequences of their behavior. Therefore, the law does not punish a youth as it would an adult, and it sees youthful misconduct as evidence of impaired judgment.

Today, the legal status of *juvenile delinquent* refers to a minor child who has been found to have violated the penal code. Most states define *minor child* as an individual who falls under a statutory age limit, most commonly 17 or 18 years of age. Juveniles are usually kept separate from adults and receive different treatment under the law. Most large police departments employ officers whose sole responsibility is delinquency. Every state has some form of juvenile court with its own judges, probation department, and other facilities. Terminology is also different: Adults are *tried* in court; children are *adjudicated.* Adults can be *punished;* children are *treated.* If treatment is mandated, children can be sent to secure detention facilities, but they cannot normally be committed to adult prisons.

Children also have a unique legal status. A minor apprehended for a criminal act is usually charged with being a juvenile delinquent regardless of the offense. These charges are confidential, and trial records are kept secret. The purpose of these safeguards is to shield children from the stigma of a criminal conviction and to prevent youthful misdeeds from becoming a lifelong burden.

Legal Responsibility of Youths

In our society the actions of adults are controlled by two types of law: criminal law and civil law. Criminal laws prohibit activities that are injurious to the well-being of society, such as drug use, theft, and rape; criminal legal actions are brought by state authorities against private citizens. In contrast, civil laws control interpersonal or private activities, and legal actions are usually initiated by individual citizens. Contractual relationships and personal conflicts (torts) are subjects of civil law. Also covered under civil law are provisions for the care of people who cannot care for themselves—for example, the mentally ill, the incompetent, and the infirm.

Those who favor removing status offenders from juvenile court authority charge that their experience with the legal system further stigmatizes these already troubled youths, exposes them to the influence of "true" delinquents, and enmeshes them in a system that cannot really afford to help or treat their needs. Will the youth in this photo suffer from his experience with the police or might his behavior improve? (© Sherman Zent/*Palm Beach Post*)

need for treatment The criteria on which juvenile sentencing is based. Ideally, juveniles are treated according to their need for treatment and not the seriousness of the delinquent act they committed.

Today juvenile delinquency falls somewhere between criminal and civil law. Under *parens patriae,* delinquent acts are not considered criminal violations. The legal action against them is similar (though not identical) to a civil action that, in an ideal situation, is based upon their **need for treatment.** This legal theory recognizes that children who violate the law are in need of the same treatment as are law-abiding citizens who cannot care for themselves.

Delinquent behavior is treated more leniently than adult misbehavior because the law considers juveniles to be less responsible for their behavior than adults. Compared to adults, adolescents are believed to (1) have a stronger preference for risk and novelty; (2) be less accurate in assessing the potential consequences of risky conduct; (3) be more impulsive and more concerned with short-term consequences; (4) have a different appreciation of time and self-control; and (5) be more susceptible to peer pressure.[45]

Even though youths have a lesser degree of legal responsibility, they, like adults, are subject to arrest, trial, and incarceration. Their legal predicament has prompted the courts to grant children many of the same legal protections conferred on adults accused of criminal offenses. These include the right to consult an attorney, to be free from self-incrimination, and to be protected from illegal searches and seizures.

waiver (also known as bindover or removal) Transferring legal jurisdiction over the most serious and experienced juvenile offenders to the adult court for criminal prosecution.

While most children who break the law are considered salvageable and worthy of community treatment efforts, there are also violent juvenile offenders whose behavior requires a firmer response. Some state authorities have declared that these hard-core offenders cannot be treated as children and must be given more secure treatment that is beyond the resources of the juvenile justice system. This recognition has prompted the policy of **waiver** (also known as **bindover** or **removal**), that is, transferring legal jurisdiction over the most serious juvenile offenders to the adult court for criminal prosecution. So although the *parens patriae* concept is still applied to children whose law violations are considered not to be serious, the more serious juvenile offenders can be declared legal adults.

STATUS OFFENDERS

status offense Conduct that is illegal only because the child is under age.

A child can become subject to state authority for committing actions that would not be considered illegal if perpetrated by an adult. Conduct that is illegal only because the child is under age is known as a **status offense.** (Table 1.2 illustrates some typical status offenses.) Eleven states classify these youths using the term *child in need of*

TABLE 1.2

Status Offense Laws: Wisconsin and Louisiana

Louisiana

"Child in need of supervision" means a child who needs care or rehabilitation because:

1. Being subject to compulsory school attendance, he is habitually truant from school or willfully violates the rules of the school;
2. He habitually disobeys the reasonable and lawful demands of his parents, and is ungovernable and beyond their control;
3. He absents himself from his home or usual place of abode without the consent of his parent;
4. He purposefully, intentionally and willfully deceives, or misrepresents the true facts to any person holding a retail dealer's permit, or his agent, associate, employee or representative, for the purposes of buying or receiving alcoholic beverages or beer, or visiting or loitering in or about any place where such beverages are the principal commodities sold or handled;
5. His occupation, conduct, environment or associations are injurious to his welfare; or
6. He has committed an offense applicable only to children.

Wisconsin

The court has exclusive original jurisdiction over a child alleged to be in need of protection or services which can be ordered by the court, and:

1. Who is without a parent or guardian;
2. Who has been abandoned;
3. Who has been the victim of sexual or physical abuse including injury which is self-inflicted or inflicted by another by other than accidental means;
4. Whose parent or guardian signs the petition requesting jurisdiction and states that he or she is unable to care for, control or provide necessary special care or special treatment for the child;
5. Who has been placed for care or adoption in violation of law;
6. Who is habitually truant from school, *after evidence is provided by the school attendance officer that the activities under s. 118.16(5) have been completed;*
7. Who is habitually truant from home and either the child or a parent, *guardian or a relative in whose home the child resides signs* the petition requesting jurisdiction and attests in court that reconciliation efforts have been attempted and have failed;
8. Who is receiving inadequate care during the period of time a parent is missing, incarcerated, hospitalized or institutionalized;
9. Who is at least age 12, signs the petition requesting jurisdiction and attests in court that he or she is in need of special care and treatment which the parent, guardian or legal custodian is unwilling to provide;
10. Whose parent, guardian or legal custodian neglects, refuses or is unable for reasons other than poverty to provide necessary care, food, clothing, medical or dental care or shelter so as to seriously endanger the physical health of the child;
11. Who is suffering emotional damage for which the parent or guardian is unwilling to provide treatment, which is evidenced by one or more of the following characteristics, exhibited to a severe degree: anxiety, depression, withdrawal or outward aggressive behavior;
12. Who, being under 12 years of age, has committed a delinquent act as defined in s. 48.12;
13. Who has not been immunized as required by s. 140.05(16) and not exempted under s. 140.05(16)(c); or
14. Who has been determined, under s. 48.30(5)(c), to be not responsible for a delinquent act by reason of mental disease or defect.

Source: LA. Code Juv. Proc. Ann. art. 13 § 12 (West 1979, amended 1987) and Wis. Stat. Ann. § 48.13 (West 1979, amended 1987).

supervision, whereas the remainder use terms such as *unruly child, incorrigible child,* or *minor in need of supervision.*[46] The court can also exercise control over dependent children who are not being properly cared for by their parents or guardians.[47]

State control over a child's noncriminal behavior supports the *parens patriae* philosophy because it is assumed to be in the best interests of the child. Usually, status offenders are directed to the juvenile court when it is determined that their parents are unable or unwilling to care for or control them and that the adolescent's behavior is self-destructive or harmful to society.

A historical basis exists for status offense statutes. It was common practice early in the nation's history to place disobedient or runaway youths in orphan asylums, residential homes, or houses of refuge.[48] When the first juvenile courts were established in Illinois, the Chicago Bar Association described part of their purpose as follows:

> *The whole trend and spirit of the [1889 Juvenile Court Act] is that the State, acting through the Juvenile Court, exercises that tender solicitude and care over its neglected, dependent wards that a wise and loving parent would exercise with reference to his own children under similar circumstances.*[49]

Until relatively recently, however, almost every state treated status offenders and juvenile delinquents alike, referring to them either as **wayward minors** or delinquent children. A trend begun in the 1960s has resulted in the creation of separate status offense categories that vary from state to state: children, minors, persons, youths, or juveniles in need of supervision (CHINS, MINS, PINS, YINS, or JINS). The purpose was to shield noncriminal youths from the stigma attached to the label juvenile delinquent and to signify that they had special needs and problems. Table 1.2 shows the differences in these laws in two states. Wisconsin law is more oriented toward protective services than Louisiana law and encompasses more areas of child neglect.

Even where there are separate legal categories for delinquents and status offenders, the distinction between them has become blurred. Some noncriminal conduct may be included in the definition of delinquency, and some less serious criminal offenses occasionally may be labeled as status offenses.[50] In some states the juvenile court judge may substitute a status offense for a delinquency charge.[51] This possibility can be used to encourage youths to admit to the charges against them in return for less punitive treatment.

The Status Offender in the Juvenile Justice System

Separate status offense categories may avoid some of the stigma associated with the delinquency label, but they have little effect on treatment. Youths in either category can be picked up by the police and brought to a police station. They can be petitioned to the same juvenile court, where they have a hearing before the same judge and come under the supervision of the probation department, the court clinic, and the treatment staff. At a hearing, status offenders may see little difference between the treatment they receive and the treatment of the delinquent offenders sitting across the room. Although status offenders are usually not detained or incarcerated with delinquents, they can be transferred to secure facilities if they are considered uncontrollable.

Aiding the Status Offender

Efforts have been ongoing to reduce the penalties and stigma borne by status offenders. The federal **Office of Juvenile Justice and Delinquency Prevention (OJJDP)** has long encouraged the removal of status offenders from secure lockups, detention centers, and postdisposition treatment facilities that also house delinquent offenders. This has been a highly successful policy, and the number of status offenders kept in secure pretrial detention has dropped significantly during the past two decades. Nevertheless, juvenile court judges in many states can still detain status offenders in secure lockups if the youths are found in contempt of court. The act that created the

Status offender statutes typically include behavior that is "unmanageable," "unruly," and "in danger of leading to an idle, dissolute, lewd, or immoral life." Sometimes these definitions are so broad that they have been challenged in court for being unconstitutionally vague and indefinite. However, most statutes have been upheld because of their overall concern for the welfare of the child. (© Mike Mazzachi/ Stock, Boston)

www

To learn more about the efforts
to remove status offenders from secure lockups, go to Gwen A. Holden and Robert A. Kapler, "Deinstitutionalizing Status Offenders: A Record of Progress":

http://www.ncjrs.org/txtfiles/ jjjf95.txt

For an up-to-date list of Web links, go to www.wadsworth.com/ product/0534573053s.

OJJDP was amended in 1987 to allow status offenders to be detained for violations of valid court orders.[52] Children have been detained for behavior such as wearing shorts to court, throwing paper on the floor, and, in one Florida case involving a pregnant teenager, for not keeping a doctor's appointment.[53] Activists have attempted to outlaw this practice, and the Florida State Supreme Court forbade it in *A.A. v. Rolle* (1992).[54] It remains to be seen whether other jurisdictions will follow suit.

Changes in the treatment of status offenders reflect the current attitude toward children who violate the law. On the one hand, there appears to be a movement to severely sanction youths who commit serious offenses and transfer them to the adult court. On the other hand, a great effort has been made to remove nonserious cases from the official agencies of justice and place these youths in community-based treatment programs.

Reforming Status Offense Laws

For more than 20 years national crime commissions have called for limiting control over status offenders. More than 20 years ago the National Council on Crime and Delinquency, a nonprofit organization dedicated to reducing criminal activity, recommended removing status offenders from the juvenile court.[55] In 1976 the National Advisory Commission on Criminal Justice Standards and Goals, created by the federal government to study the crime problem, opted for the nonjudicial treatment of status offenders by arguing that the only conduct that should warrant family court intervention is conduct that is clearly self-destructive or otherwise harmful to the child. The commission suggested that juvenile courts confine themselves to controlling five status offenses: habitual truancy, repeated disregard for parental authority, repeated running away, repeated use of intoxicating beverages, and delinquent acts by youths under the age of 10.[56]

These calls for reform prompted a number of states to experiment with community-based treatment programs for status offenders.[57] A few states, including Maine, Delaware, Idaho, and Washington, have attempted to eliminate status offense laws and treat these youths as neglected or dependent children, giving child protective services the primary responsibility for their care. However, juvenile court judges believe that reducing judicial authority over children will limit juvenile court jurisdiction to

INCREASING SOCIAL CONTROL OVER JUVENILES AND THEIR PARENTS

Those in favor of retaining the status offense category point to society's responsibility to care for troubled youths. Others maintain that the status offense should remain a legal category so that juvenile courts can force a youth to receive treatment. Although it is recognized that a court appearance can produce a stigma, the taint may be less important than the need for treatment. Many state jurisdictions, prompted by concern over serious delinquency, have enacted laws that actually expand social control over juveniles.

Curfew Laws

Beginning in 1990 there has been an explosion in the passage of curfew laws aimed at restricting the opportunity kids have for getting in trouble. A survey of 77 large U.S. cities found that 59 of them have such laws. Each year about 60,000 youths are arrested for curfew violations. As of yet, there is little conclusive evidence that curfews have a significant impact on youth crime rates. Contrary to expectations, victimizations, juvenile victimizations, and juvenile arrests do not seem to decrease significantly during curfew hours. Some research efforts have even found that, after curfews were implemented, victimizations increased significantly during noncurfew hours. This indicates that, rather than suppressing delinquency, curfews merely shift the time of occurrence of the offenses.

Disciplining Parents

Since the early twentieth century, there have been laws aimed at disciplining parents for *contributing to the delinquency of a minor.* The first of these was enacted in Colorado in 1903, and today 42 states and the District of Columbia maintain similar laws. Such laws allow parents to be sanctioned in juvenile courts for behaviors associated with their child's misbehavior. Some states (Florida, Idaho, Virginia) require parents to reimburse the government for the costs of detention or care of their children. Others (Maryland, Missouri, Oklahoma) demand that parents make restitution payments, for example, paying for damage caused by their children who vandalized a school. All states except New Hampshire have incorporated parental liability laws within

their statutes, though most recent legislation places limits on recovery somewhere between $250 (Vermont) and $15,000 (Texas); the average is $2,500. Other states (Colorado, Texas, Louisiana) require parents as well as children to participate in counseling and community service activities.

Parents may also be held civilly liable, under the concept of *vicarious liability,* for the damages caused by a child. In some states, parents are responsible for up to $300,000 damages; in others the liability cap is $3,500 (sometimes homeowner's insurance covers at least some of liability). Parents can also be charged with civil negligence if they should have known of the damage a child was about to inflict but did nothing to stop them—for example, when they give a weapon to an emotionally unstable youth. Juries have levied awards of up to $500,000 in such cases.

An extreme form of discipline for parents makes them criminally liable for the illegal acts of their children. Since 1990 there have been more than 18 cases in which parents have been ordered to serve time in jail because their children have been truant from school. Civil libertarians charge that these laws violate the constitutional right to due process and seem to be used only against lower-class parents. They find little evidence that punishing parents can deter delinquency. State laws of this kind have been successfully challenged in the lower courts.

Sources: Mike Reynolds, Ruth Seydlitz, and Pamela Jenkins, "Do Juvenile Curfew Laws Work? A Time-Series Analysis of the New Orleans Law," *Justice Quarterly* (2000); Mike Males and Dan Macallair, "An Analysis of Curfew Enforcement and Juvenile Crime in California," *Western Criminology Review* (Sept. 1999); Joannie M. Schrof, "Who's Guilty?" *U.S. News & World Report* 126:60 (May 17, 1999); William Ruefle and Kenneth Mike Reynolds, "Curfews and Delinquency in Major American Cities," *Crime and Delinquency* 41:347–63 (1995); *Federal Bureau of Investigation Uniform Crime Report, 1999* (Washington, DC: FBI, 2000) p. 213; *Juvenile Justice Reform Initiatives in the States* (Washington, DC: Office of Juvenile Justice and Delinquency Prevention, 1997); Gilbert Geis and Arnold Binder, "Sins of Their Children: Parental Responsibility for Juvenile Delinquency," *Notre Dame Journal of Law, Ethics, and Public Policy* 5:303–322 (1991).

hard-core offenders and constrain its ability to help youths before they commit serious antisocial acts.[58] Legislative changes may be more cosmetic than practical; when efforts to remedy the child's problems through a social welfare approach fail, the case can be referred to the juvenile court.[59]

Those who favor removing status offenders from juvenile court authority charge that their experience with the legal system further stigmatizes these already troubled youths, exposing them to the influence of true delinquents and enmeshing them

Do curfew laws work in reducing the rate of youth crime? To find out, visit the following site at the Justice Policy Institute:

http://www.cjcj.org/jpi/curfewex.html

For an up-to-date list of Web links, go to www.wadsworth.com/product/0534573053s.

in a system that cannot really afford to help them.[60] Reformer Ira Schwartz argues that status offenders should be removed from the jurisdiction of the courts altogether.[61] Status offenders would best be served by dispute resolution programs designed to strengthen family ties because status offense cases are often rooted in family problems.[62]

Though this debate will not end soon, we cannot lose sight of the fact that a majority of youths engage in some status offenses.[63] Illegal acts such as teen sex and substance abuse have become commonplace. Does it make sense, then, to have the juvenile court intervene in cases when no criminal act occurred? The predominant view today is that many status offenders and delinquents share similar problems, and that both categories should fall under the jurisdiction of the juvenile court. (See Policy and Practice box on the previous page.)

Checkpoints

✔ The concept of *parens patriae* meant that the state had to take responsibility for children under the criminal law in both Great Britain and the United States.

✔ The concept of delinquency was developed in the early twentieth century. Before that, criminal youths and adults were treated in almost the same fashion.

✔ A group of reformers, referred to as *child savers*, helped create a separate delinquency category to insulate juvenile offenders from the influence of adult criminals.

✔ The separate status of juvenile delinquency is based on the *parens patriae* philosophy, which holds that children have the right to care and custody and that, if parents are not capable of providing that care, the state must step in to take control.

✔ Delinquents are given greater legal protection than adult criminals and are shielded from stigma and labels.

✔ More serious juvenile cases may be transferred or waived to the adult court.

✔ Juvenile courts also have jurisdiction over noncriminal, status offenders. Status offenses are illegal only because of the minority status of the offender. They include such misbehavior as truancy, running away, and sexual misconduct.

✔ Some experts believe that status offenders are harmed by juvenile court processing. Other efforts indicate that status offenders and delinquents are actually quite similar.

SUMMARY

The study of delinquency is concerned with the nature and extent of the criminal behavior of youths, the causes of youthful law violations, the legal rights of juveniles, and with prevention and treatment. The problems of American youths have become an important subject of academic study.

The concept of a separate status of childhood has developed slowly. In earlier times relationships between children and parents were remote. Punishment was severe, and children were expected to take on adult roles early in their lives. With the start of the seventeenth century came greater recognition of the needs of children. In Great Britain, the chancery court movement, the Poor Laws, and apprenticeship programs helped reinforce the idea of children as a distinct social group. In colonial America, many of the characteristics of English family living were adopted.

In the nineteenth century, delinquent and runaway children were treated no differently than criminal defendants. During this time, however, increased support for the concept of *parens patriae* resulted in steps to reduce the responsibility of children under the criminal law. The concept of delinquency was developed in the early twentieth century.

Before that time, criminal youths and adults were treated in almost the same fashion. A group of reformers, referred to as *child savers,* helped create a separate delinquency category to insulate juvenile offenders from the influence of adult criminals. The status of juvenile delinquency is still based on the *parens patriae* philosophy, which holds that children have the right to care and custody and that if parents are not capable of providing that care the state must step in to take control.

Juvenile courts also have jurisdiction over noncriminal status offenders, whose offenses (truancy, running away, sexual misconduct) are illegal only because of their minority status. Some experts have called for an end to juvenile court control over status offenders, charging that it further stigmatizes already troubled youths. Some research indicates that status offenders are harmed by juvenile court processing. Other research indicates that status offenders and delinquents are quite similar.

The treatment of juveniles is an ongoing dilemma. Still uncertain is whether young law violators respond better to harsh punishments or to benevolent treatment.

KEY TERMS

ego identity

role diffusion

at-risk youths

juvenile delinquency

chronic delinquents

juvenile justice system

paternalistic family

Poor Laws

chancery courts

parens patriae

child savers

delinquent

best interests of the child

need for treatment

waiver, bindover, removal

status offense

wayward minors

Office of Juvenile Justice and Delinquency Prevention (OJJDP)

QUESTIONS FOR DISCUSSION

1. Is it fair to have a separate legal category for youths? Considering how dangerous young people can be, does it make more sense to group offenders on the basis of what they have done rather than on their age?

2. At what age are juveniles truly capable of understanding the seriousness of their actions?

3. Is it fair to institutionalize a minor simply for being truant or running away from home? Should the jurisdiction of status offenders be removed from juvenile court and placed with the state's department of social services or some other welfare organization?

4. Should delinquency proceedings be secretive? Does the public have a right to know who juvenile criminals are?

5. Can a *get tough* policy help control juvenile misbehavior, or should *parens patriae* remain the standard?

6. Should juveniles who commit felonies such as rape or robbery be treated as adults?

VIEWPOINT

Children in the colonial period were seen as beings who should adopt adult behavior and assume adult responsibilities as soon as possible. They were dressed as adults as early as 7 or 8. By age 10, children often lived with other families and worked for them as hired laborers or servants.

 Analysis of the history of childhood provides an important glimpse into the forces that shape contemporary culture. To read more about this fascinating topic go to InfoTrac® College Edition. Elizabeth H. Pleck, *The Reader's Companion to American History,* 3rd ed. (1991):163.

Chapter 2

The Nature and Extent of Delinquency

© Bruce Davidson/
Magnum Photos

s a juvenile court judge you are forced to make a tough decision during a hearing to decide whether a juvenile should be waived to the adult court. It seems that gang activity has become a way of life for residents living in local public housing projects. The "Bloods" sell crack, and "Wolfpack" controls the drug market. When the rivalry between the two gangs explodes, 16-year-old Shatiek Johnson, a Wolfpack member, shoots and kills a member of the Bloods; in retaliation the Bloods put out a contract on his life. While in hiding, Shatiek is confronted by two undercover detectives who recognize the young fugitive. Fearing for his life, Shatiek pulls a pistol and begins firing, fatally wounding one of the officers. During the hearing you learn that Shatiek's story is not dissimilar from that of many other children raised in tough housing projects. With an absent father and a single mother who could not control her five sons, Shatiek lived in a world of drugs, gangs, and shootouts long before he was old enough to vote. By age 13, Shatiek had been involved in the gang beating death of a homeless man in a dispute over ten dollars, for which he was given a 1-year sentence at a youth detention center and released after 6 months. Now charged with a crime that could be considered first-degree murder if committed by an adult, Shatiek could—if waived to the adult court—be sentenced to life in prison or even face the death penalty.

At the hearing, Shatiek seems like a lost soul. He claims he thought the police officers were killers out to collect the bounty put on his life by the Bloods. He says that killing the rival gang boy was an act of self-defense. The DA confirms that the victim was in fact a known gang assassin with numerous criminal convictions. Shatiek's mother begs you to consider the fact that her son is only 16 years old, that he has had a very difficult childhood, and that he is a victim of society's indifference to the poor.

■ Would you treat Shatiek as a juvenile and see if a prolonged stay in a youth facility could help this troubled young man?

■ Would you bind him over to the adult system?

■ Does a 16-year-old like Shatiek deserve a second chance?

■ Is Shatiek's behavior common among adolescent boys?

■ Is this case just the tip of a rising tide of juvenile violence?

Cases like that of Shatiek Johnson are all too common today—and, in fact, the scenario is based loosely on an actual case that occurred in New York City in 1998.[1] Is it accurate to say that these cases are common? Just how common *are* serious acts of juvenile delinquency? Who commits delinquent acts, and where are they most likely to occur? Is the juvenile crime rate increasing or decreasing? Are juveniles more likely than adults to become the victims of crime?[2] To understand the causes of delinquent behavior and to devise effective means to reduce their occurrence, we must seek answers to these questions.

Delinquency experts have devised a variety of methods to measure the nature and extent of delinquency. We begin with a description of the most widely used sources of data on crime and delinquency. We also examine the information these resources furnish on juvenile crime rates and trends. These data sources will then be used to provide information on the characteristics of adolescent law violators.

Federal Bureau of Investigation (FBI) Arm of the U.S. Department of Justice that investigates violations of federal law, gathers crime statistics, runs a comprehensive crime laboratory, and helps train local law enforcement officers.

OFFICIAL STATISTICS

ach year the U.S. Justice Department's **Federal Bureau of Investigation (FBI)** compiles information gathered by police departments on the number of criminal acts reported by citizens and the number of persons arrested. This information is published

Juveniles commit a garden variety of criminal acts, ranging from using a false ID to buying alcohol to murder. Here John Ronald Espie, 17, sits in 10th Judicial Circuit Court in Saginaw, Michigan, while awaiting the start of his felony murder trial, July 20, 1999. Espie is accused of murdering Nathan Nover, a Shiawassee County probate court transport officer, while being transported to a juvenile detention center in Bay City, Michigan, November 15, 1998. (AP/Wide World Photos)

To get the UCR online, as well as to access other important information, go to

http://www.fbi.gov/

For an up-to-date list of Web links, go to www.wadsworth.com/ product/0534573053s.

Uniform Crime Report (UCR) Compiled by the FBI, the UCR is the most widely used source of national crime and delinquency statistics.

Part I offenses, index crimes Offenses include homicide and non-negligent manslaughter, forcible rape, robbery, aggravated assault, burglary, larceny, arson, and motor vehicle theft; recorded by local law enforcement officers, arrests for these crimes are tallied quarterly and sent to the FBI for inclusion in the UCR.

Part II offenses All crimes other than Part I offenses; recorded by local law enforcement officers, arrests for these crimes are tallied quarterly and sent to the FBI for inclusion in the UCR.

in the **Uniform Crime Report (UCR),** which is the most widely used source of national crime and delinquency statistics.

The UCR is compiled from statistics sent to the FBI from more than 16,000 police departments. It groups offenses into two categories. **Part I offenses,** also known as **index crimes,** include homicide and non-negligent manslaughter, forcible rape, robbery, aggravated assault, burglary, larceny, arson, and motor vehicle theft. Police record every reported incident of these offenses and report them on a quarterly basis to the FBI. Data are broken down by city, county, metropolitan area, and geographical divisions. In addition, the UCR provides information on individuals who have been arrested for these and all other criminal offenses, including vandalism, liquor law violations, and drug trafficking. These are known as **Part II offenses.** The arrest data are presented by age, sex, and race.

The UCR expresses crime data in three ways. First, the number of crimes reported to the police and the arrests made are given as raw figures (for example, 15,533 murders occurred in 1999). Second, crime rates per one hundred thousand people are computed. That is, when the UCR indicates that the murder rate was 5.7 in 1999, it means that about 6 people in every 100,000 were murdered between January 1 and December 31 of 1999.

Crime Trends in the United States

The U.S. crime rate skyrocketed between 1960 (3.3 million crimes reported to police agencies) and 1981 (13.4 million crimes recorded). Then, after four years of decline, the rate went up in 1985 and continued to increase for the remainder of the decade.

Figure 2.1
**Crime Rate Trends,
1960–2000**

Figure 2.1
Crime Rate Trends, 1960–2000

Source: *Uniform Crime Report,*
1999, updated.

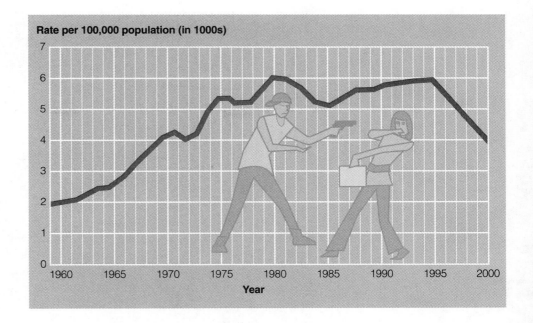

Rate per 100,000 population (in 1000s)

The crime rate then began to decline in the 1990s. The 1999 Crime Index total was 16 percent less than 1995 and 20 percent less than 1990. Nevertheless, the FBI estimates that about 11 million serious crimes currently are reported to police annually, more than 4,000 per 100,000 inhabitants (Figure 2.1).[3] So, while the number and rate of crime has undergone a dramatic decline, millions of serious criminal incidents still occur each year.

Measuring Official Delinquency

disaggregated Analyzing the relationship between two or more variables (such as murder convictions and death sentence) while controlling for the influence of a third variable (such as race).

Because the UCR arrest statistics are **disaggregated** (broken down) by suspect's age, they can be used to estimate adolescent crime. Juvenile arrest data must be interpreted with caution, however. First, the number of teenagers arrested does not represent the actual number of youths who have committed delinquent acts. Some offenders are never counted because they are never caught. Others are counted more than once because multiple arrests of the same individual for different crimes are counted separately in the UCR. Consequently, the total number of arrests does not equal the number of people who have been arrested. Put another way, if 2 million arrests of youths under 18 years of age were made in a given year, we could not be sure if 2 million individuals had been arrested once or if 500,000 chronic offenders had been arrested four times each. In addition, when an arrested offender commits multiple crimes, only the most serious one is recorded. Therefore, if 2 million juveniles are arrested, the number of crimes committed is at least 2 million, but it may be much higher.

Despite these limitations, the nature of arrest data remains constant over time. Consequently, arrest data can provide some indication of the nature and trends in juvenile crime. What does the UCR tell us about delinquency?

Official Delinquency In 1999 (the latest data available), 14 million arrests were made, or about 5,000 per 100,000 population. Of these, about 2.3 million were for serious Part I crimes and 12 million for less serious Part II crimes. About 19 percent of all arrests were juveniles under age 18 (1.6 million); about 420,000 (28 percent) of these arrests were for the more serious Part I crimes.[4] A disproportionate number of violent crime arrests involve young people. The under-18 population is about one-twelfth, or 8 percent, of the U.S. population but is responsible for about 16 percent of the violent crime arrests and about one-third of the property crime arrests (Table 2.1).[5]

TABLE 2.1	Persons Arrested, by Age		
	Under 15	Under 18	Over 18
Index violent crime	5%	16%	84%
Index property crime	13%	32%	68%
Index total	11%	28%	72%
Total all crimes	6%	17%	83%

Source: FBI, *Crime in the United States, 1999*, p. 222.

About 1.1 million juvenile arrests were made in 1999 for Part II offenses. Included in this total were 96,000 arrests for running away from home, 113,000 for disorderly conduct, 128,000 for drug-abuse violations, and 114,000 for curfew violations.

It comes as no surprise, then, that crime is a young person's game. As Figure 2.2 shows, most serious property crime activity peaks at age 16, and the peak for violent crime arrests is age 18. Age-level crime rates decline after these years, and by age 24 violent crime arrests are about 64 percent and property crime arrests 31 percent of what they were at their peak. Even though most juvenile arrests are for petty crimes, more than 400 youths under 12 years of age were arrested for rape in 1999; of these, 40 were less than 10 years old.

Juvenile Crime Trends Juvenile crime continues to have a significant influence on the nation's overall crime statistics. As Figure 2.3 shows, arrests for violent juvenile crime began to increase in 1989, peaked in 1994, and then began to fall. Juvenile murder rates more than doubled between the early 1980s and their peak in 1993; they have since been in decline. Even the teen murder rate, which had remained stubbornly high, has undergone a decline during the past few years.[6] For example, 1,700 youths were arrested for murder in 1997, a number which by 1999 had declined by almost half to 919. Similarly, 3,800 juveniles were arrested for rape in 1997, and 3,100 in 1999. This decline in juvenile violence is especially welcome considering that its rate was approaching epidemic proportions.

Figure 2.2
The Relationship between Age and Serious Crime Arrests

Source: FBI, *Uniform Crime Report*, 1999, pp. 232–33.

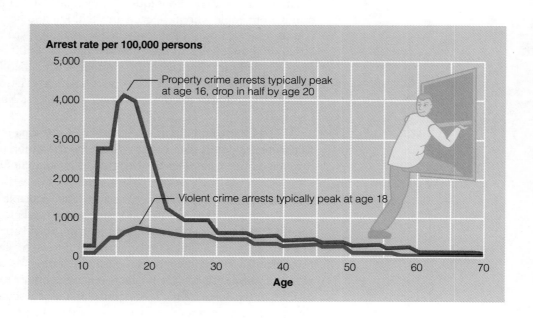

Arrest rate per 100,000 persons

Property crime arrests typically peak at age 16, drop in half by age 20

Violent crime arrests typically peak at age 18

Age

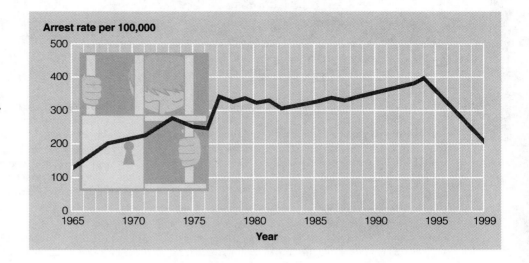

Figure 2.3
Juvenile Violent Crime Arrest Rates: United States, 1965–1999

Source: FBI, *Uniform Crime Report,* 1999, p. 280.

The official data tell us that juvenile crime rates ebb and flow. What factors account for change in the juvenile crime rate? This is the topic of the accompanying Focus on Delinquency box entitled "The Rise and Fall of Juvenile Crime Rates."

What the Future Holds Some experts, such as criminologist James A. Fox, predict a significant increase in teen violence if current population trends persist. The nation's teenage population will increase by 15 percent, or more than 9 million, between now and 2010; the number in the high-risk ages between 15 and 17 will increase by more than 3 million, or 31 percent. There are approximately 50 million school-age children in the United States, many under age 10—more than we have had for decades. While many come from stable homes, others lack stable families and adequate supervision; these are some of the children who will soon enter their prime crime years. As a result, Fox predicts a wave of youth violence even greater than that of the past 10 years.[7]

While Fox's predictions may be persuasive, not all delinquency experts believe that we are in for an age-driven crime wave. Some, like Steven Levitt, dispute the fact that the population's age makeup contributes as much to the crime rate as suggested by Fox and others.[8] Levitt finds that, even if the rising number of teens will contribute heavily to the total crime rate, their effect will be offset by the equally growing number of senior citizens, a group with a relatively low crime rate. The crime rate effect of these two growing segments of the population should neutralize one another, creating a more stable crime rate. While such prognostication is reassuring, there is no accurate way to foretell the factors that influence crime rates to go either up or down.

IS THE UCR DATA VALID?

uestions have been raised about the validity and accuracy of UCR's "official" crime data. Victim surveys show that less than half of all victims report the crime to police. Because official data is derived entirely from police records, we can assume that a significant number of crimes are not accounted for in the UCR. There are also concerns that police departments make systematic errors in recording crime data. In addition, some police commanders may manipulate crime data.[9] In New York, Atlanta, and Boca Raton, Florida, charges of falsely reporting crime statistics have resulted in the resignation or demotion of police commanders.

Using official arrest data to measure delinquency rates is particularly problematic. Arrest records only count adolescents who have been *caught,* and these youths may

THE RISE AND FALL OF JUVENILE CRIME RATES

rime rates climb and fall, reflecting a variety of social and economic conditions. While there is still disagreement over what causes crime rate fluctuations, the following factors are considered to play a major role in determining patterns and trends.

Age

Change in the age distribution of the population deeply influences crime and delinquency rates. Since juvenile males commit more crime than any other population segment, as a general rule the crime rate follows the proportion of young males in the population. The postwar baby-boom generation reached their teenage years in the 1960s, just as the crime rate began a sharp increase. With the "graying" of society and a decline in the birthrate, it is not surprising that the overall crime rate began to decline in the mid-1990s. Some criminologists fear crime rates will begin to climb when (and if) the number of juveniles in the population begins to increase.

Economy

In the short term, a poor economy may actually help lower crime rates. Unemployed parents are at home to supervise children and guard their homes. Because there is less to spend, a poor economy means that there are actually fewer valuables worth stealing. However, long-term periods of economic weakness and unemployment eventually lift crime rates. Chronic teenage unemployment rates may produce a perception of hopelessness that leads to crime and delinquency. Violence may be a function of urban problems and the economic deterioration in the nation's inner cities. Our nation's economy is now fueled by the service and technology industries. Youths who at one time might have obtained low-skill jobs in factories and shops find these legitimate economic opportunities no longer exist. Low-skill manufacturing jobs have been dispersed to overseas plants; most

new jobs that don't require specialized skills are in the low-paying service area. Lack of real economic opportunity may encourage drug dealing, theft, and violence. Experts fear that a long-term economic downturn coupled with a relatively large number of teens in the population will produce the high delinquency rates of the late eighties and early nineties.

Drugs

Drug use has been linked to fluctuations in the crime and delinquency rate. Abusers are particularly crime-prone, so as drug use levels increase, so too do crime rates. When teen violence skyrocketed in the 1980s, it was no coincidence that this period also witnessed increases in drug trafficking and arrests for drug crimes. Teenage substance abusers commit a significant portion of all serious crimes and inner-city drug-abuse problems may account in part for the persistently high violent-crime rate. Groups and gangs that are involved in the urban drug trade recruit juveniles because they work cheaply, are immune from heavy criminal penalties, and are daring and willing to take risks. Arming themselves for protection, these youthful dealers pose a threat to neighborhood adolescents, who in turn arm themselves for self-protection. The result is an "arms race" that produces an increasing spiral of violence.

Drug abuse may also have a more direct influence on teen crime patterns—for example, when alcohol-abusing kids engage in acts of senseless violence. Users may turn to theft and violence for money to purchase drugs and support drug habits. Increases in teenage drug use may be a precursor to higher violence rates in the future.

Ongoing Social Problems

As the level of social problems increase—divorce, school dropout, teen pregnancy, and racial conflict—so do crime and delinquency rates. For example, cross-

be different from those who evade capture. In addition, victimless crimes such as drug and alcohol use are significantly undercounted using this measure.

Arrest decision criteria vary between police agencies. Some police agencies may practice full enforcement, arresting all teens who violate the law, whereas others may follow a policy of discretion that encourages unofficial handling of juvenile matters through social service agencies.

While these questions are troubling, the problems associated with collecting and verifying the official UCR data are consistent and stable over time. This means that, while the absolute accuracy of the data can be questioned, the trends and patterns they show are probably reliable. While we cannot be absolutely sure about the actual number of adolescents who commit crime, it is likely that the teen crime rate has been in a significant decline.

national research indicates that child homicide rates are greatest in those nations, including the United States, that have the highest rates of children born out of wedlock and teenage mothers. Children living in single-parent homes are twice as likely to be impoverished than those in two-parent homes, and are consequently at greater risk for juvenile delinquency.

Abortion

In a controversial work, John J. Donohue III and Steven D. Levitt found empirical evidence that the recent drop in the crime rate can be attributable to the availability of legalized abortion. In 1973, *Roe v. Wade* legalized abortion nationwide. Within a few years of *Roe v. Wade*, more than 1 million abortions were being performed annually, or roughly 1 abortion for every 3 live births. Donohue and Levitt suggest that decrease in the crime rate that began approximately eighteen years later, in 1991, can be related to the fact that the first group of potential offenders affected by the abortion decision began reaching the peak age of criminal activity. It is possible that the link between crime rates and abortion is the result of two mechanisms: (1) selective abortion on the part of women most at risk to have children who would engage in delinquent activity, and (2) improved childrearing or environmental circumstances caused by better maternal, familial, or fetal circumstances because women are having fewer children. If abortion were illegal, they find, crime rates might be 10 to 20 percent higher than they currently are with abortion.

Guns

Another important influence on violence rates is the number of weapons in the hands of teens. In 1999, 28,000 kids were arrested on weapons related charges. More than 60 percent of the homicides committed by juveniles involve firearms. Guns can turn a schoolyard fight into a homicide. Their presence creates a climate in which kids who would otherwise shun firearms begin to carry them to "protect" themselves. As the number of guns in the hands of children increases, so does juvenile violence rates.

Gangs

The explosive growth in teenage gangs has also contributed to teen violence rates. Surveys indicate that there are about one-half million gang members in the United States. A large and growing number of juveniles who kill do so in groups of two or more; multiple-offender killings have doubled since the mid-1980s. Gang-related violence is frequently compounded by the use of firearms. Research indicates that in major cities about one-third of kids who are gang members carry a gun all or most of the time.

Juvenile Justice Policy

Some law-enforcement experts have suggested that a reduction in crime rates may be attributed to a recent "get tough" attitude toward delinquency and drug abuse. Police have become more aggressive. New laws call for mandatory incarceration for juvenile offenders. Juveniles may even be eligible for the death penalty. Putting potentially high-rate offenders behind bars may help to stabilize crime rates.

Sources: John J. Donohue III and Steven D. Levitt, "Legalized Abortion and Crime" (June 24, 1999, unpublished paper, University of Chicago); Donald Green, Dara Strolovitch, and Janelle Wong, "Defended Neighborhoods, Integration, and Racially Motivated Crime," *American Journal of Sociology* 104:372–403 (1998); Robert O'Brien, Jean Stockard, and Lynne Isaacson, "The Enduring Effects of Cohort Characteristics on Age-Specific Homicide Rates, 1960–1995," *American Journal of Sociology* 104:1061–1095(1999); Darrell Steffensmeier and Miles Harer, "Making Sense of Recent U.S. Crime Trends, 1980 to 1996/1998: Age Composition Effects and Other Explanations," *Journal of Research in Crime and Delinquency* 36:235–74 (1999);Rosemary Gartner, "Family Structure, Welfare Spending, and Child Homicide in Developed Democracies," *Journal of Marriage and the Family* 53:231–40(1991); Scott Decker and Susan Pennell, *Arrestees and Guns: Monitoring the Illegal Firearms Market* (Washington, DC: National Institute of Justice, 1995); G. David Curry, Richard Ball, and Scott Decker, "Estimating the National Scope of Gang Crime from Law Enforcement Data," in C. Ronald Huff, ed., *Gangs in America*, 2nd ed. (Newbury Park, CA: Sage, 1996).

SELF-REPORTED DELINQUENCY

Official statistics are useful for examining general trends, but they cannot tell us how many youth commit crime but are never arrested. Nor do they reveal much about the personality, attitudes, and behavior of individual delinquents. To get information at this level, criminologists have developed alternative sources of delinquency statistics, the most commonly used source being **self-reports** of delinquent behavior.

self-reports Questionnaire or survey technique that asks subjects to reveal their own participation in delinquent or criminal acts.

Self-report studies are designed to obtain information from youthful subjects about their violations of the law. Youths arrested by police may be interviewed at the station house; an anonymous survey can be distributed to every student in a high school; boys in a detention center may be asked to respond to a survey; or, youths randomly selected from the population of teenagers can be questioned in their

Please indicate how often in the past twelve months you did each act. (Check the best answer.)

	Never Did Act	One Time	2–5 Times	6–9 Times	10+ Times
Stole something worth less than $50	___	___	___	___	___
Stole something worth more than $50	___	___	___	___	___
Used cocaine	___	___	___	___	___
Been in a fistfight	___	___	___	___	___
Carried a weapon such as a gun or knife	___	___	___	___	___
Fought someone using a weapon	___	___	___	___	___

homes. Self-report information can be collected in one-to-one interviews or through a self-administered questionnaire, but more commonly this information is gathered through a mass distribution of anonymous questionnaires.

Self-report surveys can include all segments of the population. They provide information on offenders who have never been arrested and are therefore not part of the official data. They also measure behavior that is rarely detected by police, such as drug abuse, because their anonymity allows youths freely to describe their illegal activities. Surveys can also include items measuring personality characteristics, behavior, and attitudes.

Table 2.2 shows one format for asking self-report questions. Youths are asked to indicate how many times they have participated in illegal or deviant behavior. Other formats allow subjects to record the precise number of times they engaged in each delinquent activity. Note that the reporting period is limited to the previous twelve months; some surveys question lifetime activity.

Questions not directly related to delinquent activity are often included on self-report surveys. Information on self-image; intelligence; personality; attitudes toward family, friends, and school; leisure activities; and school activities may be collected. Self-report surveys also gather information on family background, social status, race, and sex. Reports of delinquent acts can be correlated with this information to create a much more complete picture of delinquent offenders than official statistics can provide.

Criminologists have used self-report studies of delinquency for more than 40 years.[10] They are a valuable source of information on the activities of youths who have had contact with the juvenile justice system as well as on the **dark figures of crime**—that is, those who have escaped official notice.

dark figures of crime Incidents of crime and delinquency that go undetected by police.

Self-Report Data

Most self-report studies indicate that the number of children who break the law is far greater than official statistics would lead us to believe.[11] In fact, when truancy, alcohol consumption, petty theft, and recreational drug use are included in self-report scales, delinquency appears to be almost universal. The most common offenses are truancy, drinking alcohol, using a false ID, shoplifting or larceny under five dollars, fighting, using marijuana, and damaging the property of others. In Chapter 10, self-report data will be used to gauge trends in adolescent drug abuse.

Researchers at the University of Michigan's Institute for Social Research (ISR)[12] conduct an annual national self-report survey, called Monitoring the Future (MTF), that involves a sample of about 3,000 youths. Table 2.3 contains some of the data

TABLE 2.3

Self-Reported Delinquent Activity

Percent of High School Seniors, Class of 1999, Engaging in Offenses during the Past 12 Months

Crime Category	At Least One Offense	Multiple Offenses
Serious fight	9	6
Gang fight	10	8
Hurt someone badly	8	6
Used a weapon to steal	2	2
Stole less than $50	13	18
Stole more than $50	5	8
Shoplift	11	16
Breaking and entering	11	13
Arson	1	2
Damaged school property	6	7

Source: *Monitoring the Future, 1999* (Ann Arbor, MI: Institute for Social Research, 2000)

To find out more about the Institute for Social Research, go to their Web site at

http://monitoringthefuture.org/

For an up-to-date list of Web links, go to www.wadsworth.com/ product/0534573053s.

from the 1999 MTF survey. A surprising number of these *typical* teenagers reported involvement in serious criminal behavior: about 14 percent reported hurting someone badly enough that the victim needed medical care (6 percent said they did it more than once); about 31 percent reported stealing something worth less than $50, and another 13 percent stole something worth more than $50; 24 percent reported shoplifting; 13 percent had damaged school property.

If the ISR data are accurate, the juvenile crime problem is much greater than official statistics would lead us to believe. There are approximately 14 million youths between the ages of 14 and 17. Extrapolating from the MTF findings, this group accounts for more than 100 percent of all theft offenses reported in the UCR (about 8 million). More than 3 percent of the students said they used a knife or a gun in a robbery. At this rate, high school students commit 1.05 million armed robberies per year. In comparison, the UCR tallies about 400,000 armed robberies for all age groups annually.

Although these statistics show that the delinquency problem is far greater than indicated by the national arrest statistics, self-reports rarely show the delinquency rate climbing. Over the past decade, the MTF surveys indicate that teenager participation in theft, violence, and damage-related crimes seems to be stable. Indeed, these trends may have originated more than 30 years ago, as self-report statistics are little changed from similar data obtained in the 1960s.[13]

✔ Checkpoints

✔ The FBI's Uniform Crime Report is an annual tally of crime reported to local police departments. It is the nation's official crime data.

✔ Crime rates peaked in the early 1990s and have been in sharp decline ever since.

✔ The murder rate has undergone a particularly steep decline.

✔ A number of factors influence crime rate trends, including the economy, drug use, gun availability, and crime control policies.

✔ The number of youth arrested for delinquent behavior has also declined, including a significant decrease in violent offenses.

✔ Self-report surveys ask respondents about their criminal activity. They are useful in measuring crimes such as drug usage that are rarely reported to police.

✔ Self-reports show us that a significant number of kids engage in criminal acts, far more than is measured by the arrest data. It is difficult to gauge future trends. Some experts forecast an increase in juvenile crime while others foresee a long-term decline in the crime rate.

Although males maintain a significant edge in arrests for most illegal acts, one relationship does reverse this general pattern: girls are more likely than boys to be arrested for being runaways. It is possible that police hold paternalistic attitudes and are more likely to arrest female runaways and process them through the official justice channels? These two runaway girls comfort each other on the streets of New York. (© Catherine Leroy/Sipa Press)

CORRELATES OF DELINQUENCY

An important aspect of delinquency research is measurement of the personal traits and social characteristics associated with adolescent misbehavior. If, for example, a strong association exists between delinquent behavior and family income, then poverty and economic deprivation must be considered in any explanation of the onset of adolescent criminality. If the delinquency–income association is not present, than other forces may be responsible for producing antisocial behavior. It would be fruitless to concentrate delinquency control efforts in areas such as job creation and vocational training if social status were found to be unrelated to delinquent behavior. Similarly, if only a handful of delinquents are responsible for most serious crimes, crime control policies might be made more effective by identifying and treating these offenders. The next sections discuss the relationship between delinquency and the characteristics of gender, race, social class, and age.

Gender and Delinquency

Official arrest statistics, victim data, and self-reports indicate that males are significantly more criminal than females. The teenage gender ratio for serious violent crime is approximately 6 to 1, and for property crime approximately 2.5 to 1, male to female.

One relationship reverses this general pattern: Girls are more likely than boys to be arrested as runaways. There are two possible explanations for this. Girls could be more likely than boys to run away from home, or police may view the female runaway as the more serious problem and therefore be more likely to process females through official justice channels. This may reflect paternalistic attitudes toward girls, who are viewed as likely to "get in trouble" if they are on the street.[14]

Similar findings have been observed in self-report and official record studies in Great Britain. A Home Office study found that the overall male–female offense ratio was about 5 to 1 at ages 10–13, and 4 to 1 at ages 14–16. The ratio was much higher for serious crimes.[15]

In recent years arrests of female delinquents have been increasing faster than those for males. Between 1990 and 1999, the number of arrests of male delinquents increased about 5 percent, whereas the number of female delinquents arrested in-

TABLE 2.4	Delinquent Acts	
		Percentage of High School Seniors Admitting to at Least One Offense during the Past 12 Months, by Gender
Crime Category	Males	Females
Serious fight	23	14
Gang fight	27	15
Hurt someone badly	21	4
Used a weapon to steal	7	4
Stole less than $50	41	25
Stole more than $50	15	5
Shoplift	32	23
Breaking and entering	31	17
Arson	4	1
Damaged school property	20	6

Source: *Monitoring the Future, 1999* (Ann Arbor, MI: Institute for Social Research, 2000).

creased almost 32 percent. The change in serious violent crime arrests was even more striking: Males actually decreased 11 percent, while females' violent-crime arrests increased about 40 percent.

Self-report data also seem to show that the incidence of female delinquency is much higher than believed earlier, and that the most common crimes committed by males are also the ones most female offenders commit.[16] Table 2.4 shows the percentages of males and females who admitted engaging in delinquent acts during the past 12 months in the latest MTF survey. As Table 2.4 indicates, about 32 percent of boys and 23 percent of girls admit to shoplifting, 15 percent of boys and 5 percent of girls said they stole something worth more than $50, and 21 percent of boys and 6 percent of girls said they hurt someone badly enough that they required medical care. Although self-report studies indicate that the content of girls' delinquency is similar to boys', the few adolescents who reported engaging frequently in serious violent crime are still predominantly male.[17] Because the relationship between gender and delinquency rate is so apparent, this topic will be discussed further in chapter 6.

Racial Patterns in Delinquency

There are approximately 38 million white and 7.5 million African American youths ages 5 to 17, a ratio of about 5 to 1. Yet racial minorities are disproportionately represented in the arrest statistics. African Americans make up about 12.5 percent of the population, but they account for about 25 percent of all arrests and 40 percent of index crime violence arrests. African American youths are arrested for a disproportionate number of murders, rapes, robberies, and assaults, while white youths are arrested for a disproportionate share of arsons. Among Part II crimes, white youths are disproportionately arrested for alcohol-related violations.

The racial gap in the juvenile arrest rate has widened during the past decade. African American youths have experienced a steady increase in their arrest rates, whereas rates for other groups have remained stable.

Self-Report Differences Official statistics show that minority youths are much more likely than white youths to be arrested for serious criminal behavior. To many delinquency experts, this pattern reflects discrimination in the juvenile justice system. In other words, African American youths are more likely to be formally arrested by the police, who, in contrast, will treat white youths informally. One way to examine this issue is to compare the racial differences in self-reported data with those found in the official delinquency records. Given the disproportionate numbers of African Americans arrested, charges of racial discrimination would be supported if we found little difference between the number of self-reported minority and white crimes.

Early researchers found that the relationship between race and self-reported delinquency was virtually nonexistent.[18] This suggests that racial differences in the official crime data may reflect the fact that African American youths have a much greater chance of being arrested and officially processed.[19] Self-report studies also suggest that the delinquent behavior rates of African American and white teenagers are generally similar and that differences in arrest statistics may indicate discrimination by police.[20] The MTF survey, for example, generally shows that offending differences between African American and white youths are marginal.[21] However, some experts warn that African American youths may underreport more serious crimes, limiting the ability of self-reports to be a valid indicator of racial differences in the crime rate.[22]

Are the Data Valid? The view that the disproportionate amount of African American official delinquency is a result of bias has found some support in research studies. For example, recent research shows that juvenile suspects who belong to ethnic minorities who are male, and are poor, are more likely to be formally arrested than suspects who are white, female, and affluent.[23]

Juvenile court judges may see the offenses committed by African American youths as more serious than those committed by white offenders.[24] Judges seem more willing to give white defendants lenient sentences if, for example, they show strong family ties or live in two-parent households.[25] Any form of racial bias is crucial because possession of a prior record increases the likelihood that, upon subsequent contact, police will formally arrest a suspect rather than release the individual with a warning.[26]

Although evidence of racial bias does exist in the justice system, there is enough correspondence between official and self-report data to conclude that racial differences in the crime rate are real.[27] Samuel Walker, Cassia Spohn, and Miriam DeLone found that African American youths are arrested at a disproportionately high rate and that for crimes such as robbery and assault this is a result of offending rates rather than bias on the part of the criminal justice system.[28]

Explaining Racial Patterns If, in fact, the racial differences in the delinquency rate recorded by official data are valid, one view is that they are a function of the institutionalized racism that is present in the United States. African Americans have suffered through a long history of discrimination, which has produced lasting emotional scars.[29] Racism is still an element of daily life in the African American community, a factor that undermines faith in social and political institutions and weakens confidence in the justice system. These learned attitudes are supported by empirical evidence that, in at least some jurisdictions, young African American males are treated more harshly by the justice system than members of any other group.[30] There is evidence that in some legal jurisdictions African Americans, especially those who are indigent or unemployed, receive longer sentences than whites. It is possible that some judges view poor blacks as antisocial, considering them more dangerous and likely to recidivate than white offenders.[31] Yet when African Americans are the victims of crime, their predicament receives less public concern and media attention than that afforded white victims.[32]

Racial differentials in the crime rate may also be tied to frustrations over perceived racism, discrimination, and economic disparity. Even during times of economic growth, many economically disadvantaged African Americans believe they are being left out of the mainstream and feel a growing sense of frustration.[33] Such frustration may be magnified by frequent exposure to violence. African Americans who live in poor areas with

Some experts believe that racial differences in the juvenile arrest rate are a function of police officer bias. While African-American and Caucasian juveniles commit crimes at the same rate, the former are much more likely to get arrested and maintain an official record. Here, Lonnell McGhee of Oakland, California, listens to speakers at a rally against racial profiling at the state capitol in Sacramento, California, on Thursday, April 27, 2000. Hundreds of others were there to show support for SB1389, the so-called "DWB Bill," or "Driving While Black/Brown Bill." (AP/Wide World Photos)

If you want to learn more about race-related issues in America, check out the NAACP Web site at

http://www.naacp.org/

For an up-to-date list of Web links, go to www.wadsworth.com/ product/0534573053s.

high crime rates may be disproportionately violent because they are exposed to more violence in their daily lives than other racial and economic groups. Research has shown that such exposure is a significant risk factor for violent behavior.[34]

The burden of social and economic marginalization may be compounded by the weakening of the African American family structure. Family dissolution is tied to low employment rates among minority males, which places a strain on marriages. When families are weakened or disrupted, their ability to act as social control agents is compromised. It is not surprising that divorce and separation rates are significantly associated with homicide rates in the African American community.[35]

In summary, official data indicate that African American youths are arrested for more serious crimes than whites. However, self-report studies show that the differences in the rate of delinquency between the races is insignificant and that official differences are an artifact of bias in the justice system: Police are more likely to arrest and courts are more likely to convict young African Americans.[36] To those who believe that the official data has validity, the participation of African American youths in serious criminal behavior is generally viewed as a function of their socioeconomic position and the racism they face.

Social Class and Delinquency

Defining the relationship between economic status and delinquent behavior is a key element in the study of delinquency. If youth crime is purely a lower-class phenomenon, its cause must be rooted in the social forces that are found solely in lower-class areas: poverty, unemployment, social disorganization, culture conflict, and alienation.[37] However, if delinquent behavior is spread throughout the social structure, its cause must be related to some noneconomic factor: intelligence, personality, socialization, family dysfunction, educational failure, or peer influence. According to this line of reasoning, providing jobs or economic incentives would have little effect on the crime rate.

At first glance, the relationship between class and crime seems clear. Youths who lack wealth or social standing are the most likely to use criminal means to achieve their goals. Communities that lack economic and social opportunities produce high levels of frustration. Kids who live in these areas believe that they can never compete socially or economically with adolescents being raised in more affluent areas. They may turn to criminal behavior for monetary gain and psychological satisfaction.[38] Family life is disrupted in these low-income areas and law-violating youth groups thrive in a climate that undermines and neutralizes adult supervision.[39]

Research on Social Class and Delinquency The social class–delinquency relationship was challenged by pioneering self-report studies, specifically those that revealed no direct relationship between social class and the commission of delinquent acts.[40] Instead, socioeconomic class was related to the manner of official processing by police, court, and correctional agencies.[41] In other words, while both poor and affluent kids get into fights, shoplift, and take drugs, only the indigent are likely to be arrested and sent to juvenile court.[42]

Those who fault self-report studies point to the inclusion of trivial offenses, for example, using a false ID, in most self-report instruments. Although middle- and upper-class youths may appear to be as delinquent as those in the lower class, it is because they engage in significant amounts of status offenses. Lower-class youths are more likely to engage in serious delinquent acts.[43]

In sum, there are those experts who believe that antisocial behavior occurs at all levels of the social strata. Other experts argue that, while some middle- and upper-class youths engage in some forms of minor illegal activity and theft offenses, it is members of the underclass who are responsible for the majority of serious delinquent acts.[44] The prevailing wisdom is that kids who engage in the most serious forms of delinquency (for example, gang violence) are more likely to be members of the lower class.

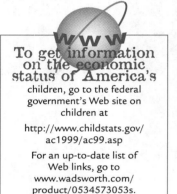

To get information on the economic status of America's children, go to the federal government's Web site on children at

http://www.childstats.gov/ ac1999/ac99.asp

For an up-to-date list of Web links, go to www.wadsworth.com/ product/0534573053s.

Age and Delinquency

Age is inversely related to criminality:[45] As youthful offenders age, the likelihood that they will commit offenses declines. Official statistics tell us that young people are arrested at a disproportionate rate to their numbers in the population, and this finding is supported by victim surveys. Youths, 17 and under, make up about 10 percent of the total U.S. population, but they account for 27 percent of the index crime arrests and 16 percent of the arrests for all crimes. In contrast, adults, 50 and older, who make up 32 percent of the population, account for only about 10 percent of arrests.

The results of a six-year nationwide survey of high school seniors found that the self-reported rates for crimes such as assault, robbery, and trespass decline substantially between the ages of 17 and 23.[46] Although there is a general decline in criminal activity as youths mature, the incidence of some illegal acts, such as substance abuse, may increase.[47] In addition, some delinquent youths continue to engage in criminal behavior as adults. Chronic offending is discussed later in this chapter.

Why Age Matters Why do people commit less crime as they age? One view is that the relationship is constant: regardless of race, sex, social class, intelligence, or any other social variable, people commit less crime as they age.[48] This is referred to as the **aging-out process,** sometimes called **desistance from crime,** or **spontaneous remission.** According to some experts, even the most chronic juvenile offenders will commit less crime as they age.[49]

aging out, desistance, spontaneous remission Frequency of offending or delinquent behavior diminishes as youths mature; occurs among all groups of offenders.

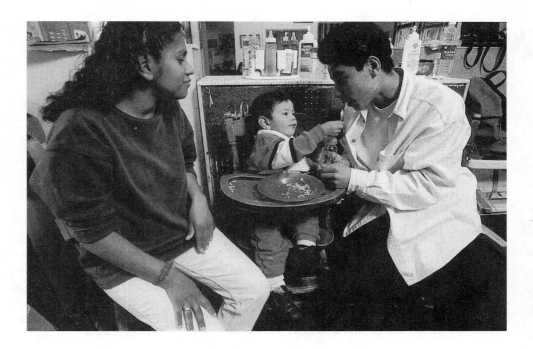

Delinquency rates tend to go down as people mature. Increasing levels of responsibility result in lower levels of criminality. Young people who marry, enlist in the armed services, and enroll in vocational training courses are less likely to pursue criminal activities. Although having a baby will place great stress upon them, this teen couple will simply have less time to get in trouble than before their child was born. (© A. Ramey/Stock, Boston)

age of onset Age at which youths begin their delinquent careers; early onset is believed to be linked with chronic offending patterns.

developmental view The view that factors present at birth and events that unfold over a person's lifetime influence behavior; developmental theory focuses on the onset, escalation, desistance, and amplification of delinquent behaviors.

There are also those experts who disagree with the concept of spontaneous remission. They suggest that age is one important determinant of crime but that other factors directly associated with a person's lifestyle, such as peer relations, also affect offending rates.[50] The probability that a person may become a persistent career criminal is influenced by a number of personal and environmental factors.[51] Evidence exists, for example, that the **age of onset** of a delinquent career has an important effect on its length: Those who demonstrate antisocial tendencies at a very early age are more likely to commit more crime for a longer duration. In sum, this is referred to as the **developmental view** of delinquency.

In summary, some criminologists believe youths who get involved with delinquency at a very early age are most likely to become career criminals. These researchers believe age is a key determinant of delinquency.[52] Those opposed to this view find that all people commit less crime as they age and that because the relationship between age and crime is constant it is therefore irrelevant to the study of delinquency.[53]

Why Does Crime Decline with Age? While there is certainly disagreement about the nature of the aging out process, there is no question that people commit less crime as they grow older. Delinquency experts have developed a number of reasons for the aging-out process:

- Growing older means having to face the future. Young people, especially the indigent and antisocial, tend to "discount the future."[54] Why should they delay gratification when faced with an uncertain future?

- With maturity comes the ability to resist the "quick fix" to their problems.[55] Research shows that some kids may turn to crime as a way to solve the problems of adolescence, loneliness, frustration, and fear of peer rejection. As they mature, conventional means of problem solving become available. Life experience helps former delinquents seek out nondestructive solutions to their personal problems.[56]

- Maturation coincides with increased levels of responsibility. Petty crimes are a risky and exciting social activity that provides adventure in an otherwise boring world. As youths grow older, they take on new responsibilities that are inconsistent with criminality.[57] For example, young people who marry, enlist in the armed services, or enroll in vocational training courses are less likely to pursue criminal activities.[58]

- Personalities can change with age. As youths mature, rebellious youngsters may develop increased self-control and be able to resist antisocial behavior.[59]

- Young adults become more aware of the risks that accompany crime. As adults, they are no longer protected by the kindly arms of the juvenile justice system.[60]

Of course, not all juvenile criminals desist as they age; some go on to become chronic adult offenders. Yet, even they slow down as they age. Crime is too dangerous, physically taxing, and unrewarding, and punishments too harsh and long-lasting, to become a way of life for most people.[61]

Checkpoints

✔ Official arrest statistics, victim data, and self-reports indicate that males are significantly more criminal than females.

✔ In recent years arrests of female delinquents have been increasing faster than those for males.

✔ African American youths are arrested for a disproportionate number of crimes such as robbery and assault, while white youths are arrested for a disproportionate share of lesser crimes such as arson and alcohol-related violations.

✔ Racial differences may be a function of institutionalized racism that is still present in the United States.

✔ Kids who engage in the most serious forms of delinquency, for example, gang violence, are more likely to be members of the lower class.

✔ Delinquency rates decline with age. As youthful offenders mature, the likelihood that they will commit offenses declines.

✔ Not all juvenile criminals desist as they age; some go on to become chronic adult offenders.

✔ Age of onset has an important effect on a delinquent career: those who demonstrate antisocial tendencies at a very early age are more likely to commit more crimes for a longer duration.

CHRONIC OFFENDING: CAREERS IN DELINQUENCY

chronic delinquent offenders Youths who start their delinquent careers at a young age, have serious and repeated brushes with the law, and build a career in crime; these youths do not age out of crime but continue their criminal behavior into adulthood.

early onset The outbreak of deviant or delinquent behavior in preadolescence generally viewed as a precursor of chronic offending in adolescence and usually continues into adulthood.

Although most adolescents age out of crime, a relatively small number of youths begin to violate the law early in their lives (early onset) and continue at a high rate well into adulthood (persistence).[62] The association between early onset and high-rate persistent offending has been demonstrated in samples drawn from a variety of cultures, time periods, and offender types.[63] These offenders are resistant to change and seem immune to the effects of punishment. Arrest, prosecution, and conviction do little to slow down their offending careers. These so-called chronic offenders are responsible for a significant amount of all delinquent and criminal activity.

Current interest in the delinquent life cycle was also prompted by the "discovery" in the 1970s of the **chronic delinquent offender.** According to this view, a relatively small number of youthful offenders commit a significant percentage of all serious crimes, and many of these same offenders grow up to become chronic adult criminals.

Chronic offenders can be distinguished from other delinquent youths. Many youthful law violators are apprehended for a single instance of criminal behavior such as shoplifting or joyriding. Chronic offenders begin their delinquent careers at a young age (under 10 years old, referred to as **early onset**), have serious and persistent brushes with the law, and may be excessively violent and destructive. They do not age out of crime but continue their law-violating behavior into adulthood.[64] Most research shows that early and repeated delinquent activity is the best predictor of future adult criminality.

A number of research efforts have set out to chronicle the careers of serious delinquent offenders. The next sections describe these initiatives.

Delinquency in a Birth Cohort The concept of the chronic career offender is most closely associated with the research efforts of Marvin Wolfgang.[65] In 1972, Wolfgang, Robert Figlio, and Thorsten Sellin published a landmark study, *Delinquency in a Birth Cohort*. They followed the delinquent careers of a cohort of 9,945 boys born in Philadelphia from birth until they reached age 18. Data were obtained from police files and school records. Socioeconomic status was determined by locating the residence of each member of the cohort and assigning him the median family income for that area. About one-third of the boys (3,475) had some police contact. The remaining two-thirds (6,470) had none. Those boys who had at least one contact with the police committed a total of 10,214 offenses.

The most significant discovery of Wolfgang and his associates was that of the so-called chronic offender. The data indicated that 54 percent (1,862) of the sample's delinquent youths were repeat offenders. The repeaters could be further categorized as nonchronic recidivists and **chronic recidivists.** Nonchronic recidivists had been arrested more than once but fewer than five times. The 627 boys labeled chronic recidivists had been arrested five times or more. Although these offenders accounted for only 18 percent of the delinquent population (6 percent of the total sample), they were responsible for 52 percent of all offenses. Known today as the "chronic 6 percent," this group perpetrated 71 percent of the homicides, 82 percent of the robberies, and 64 percent of the aggravated assaults.

Arrest and juvenile court experience did little to deter chronic offenders. In fact, the greater the punishment, the more likely they were to engage in repeat delinquent behavior. Strict punishment also increased the probability that further court action would be taken. Two factors stood out as encouraging recidivism: the seriousness of the original offense and the severity of the punishment. The researchers concluded that efforts of the juvenile justice system to eliminate delinquent behavior may be futile.

Wolfgang and his colleagues conducted a second cohort study with children born in 1958 and substantiated the finding that a relatively few chronic offenders are responsible for a significant portion of all delinquent acts.[66] Wolfgang's results have been duplicated in a number of research studies conducted in locales across the United States and also in Great Britain.[67] Some have used the records of court-processed youths and others have employed self-report data.

chronic recidivists Youths who have been arrested five or more times and perpetuate a striking majority of serious criminal acts; this small group, known as the "chronic 6 percent," is believed to engage in a significant portion of all delinquent behavior.

Stability in Crime: From Delinquent to Criminal

Do chronic juvenile offenders grow up to become chronic adult criminals? One study that followed a 10 percent sample of the original Pennsylvania cohort (974 subjects) to age 30 found that 70 percent of the "persistent" adult offenders had also been chronic juvenile offenders. Chronic juvenile offenders had an 80 percent chance of becoming adult offenders and a 50 percent chance of being arrested four or more times as adults.[68] Paul Tracy and Kimberly Kempf-Leonard conducted a follow-up study of all subjects in the second 1958 cohort. By age 26, Cohort II subjects were displaying the same behavior patterns as their older peers. Kids who started their delinquent careers early, committed a violent crime, and continued offending throughout adolescence were most likely to persist in criminal behavior as adults. Delinquents who began their offending careers with serious offenses or who quickly increased the severity of their offending early in life were most likely to persist in their criminal behavior into adulthood. Severity of offending rather than frequency of criminal behavior had the greatest impact on later adult criminality.[69]

HELPING PREVENT SERIOUS AND VIOLENT JUVENILE CRIME

The Office of Juvenile Justice and Delinquency Prevention, the federal agency responsible for dealing with the problems of youth, has sponsored a group of experts, led by distinguished scholars Rolf Loeber and David P. Farrington, to investigate the most efficient and effective methods of reducing the incidence of serious and violent delinquency. According to studies conducted by these researchers, we now know that the most successful delinquency prevention programs involve multiple and simultaneous interventions in the home, in the school, in the community, and through public health approaches that target at-risk youth.

The public health approach can be effective with violent offenders because preventive actions often work best when implemented at the community level. For example, centrally mobilized police officers who use community policing strategies and coordinate their efforts with school nurses and other social service and mental health workers can be effective in identifying and targeting violent offenders. School-based strategies are also useful, especially those focused on school organization or on classroom curriculums emphasizing the reinforcement of pro-social and academic skills. The community can also intervene by reducing the availability of firearms and drugs and encouraging norms and laws favorable to pro-social behaviors (see following table).

The study group has found that to be effective, the prevention of violent juvenile offending must involve:

- Effective screening for children who are exposed to adverse circumstances or who exhibit behaviors that place them at high risk of becoming violent offenders.

- Access by families, children, and adolescents to early intervention services, programs, and opportunities that have been determined to be effective in preventing or reducing the likelihood of violent offending or in mediating associated risk factors. Effective interventions include home visitation of pregnant teenagers, parent training, preschool intellectual enrichment programs, interpersonal skills training, and medication for neurological disorders or mental illness.

- Preventive interventions based on public health approaches and implemented within a comprehensive, community-based program that targets risk factors in disadvantaged neighborhoods.

- Integration of services, including those provided by the juvenile justice system, mental health system, medical system, schools, and child protection agencies.

- Prevention of gang formation and involvement, drug dealing, drug markets, and violent victimization.

continuity of crime The idea that chronic juvenile offenders are likely to continue violating the law as adults.

These studies indicate that chronic juvenile offenders continue their law-violating careers as adults, a concept referred to as the **continuity of crime**. Kids who are disruptive as early as age 5 or 6 are most likely to exhibit disruptive behavior throughout adolescence.[70] They have measurable behavior problems in learning and motor skills, cognitive abilities, family relations, and other areas.[71] Apprehension and punishment seem to have little effect on their offending behavior. Youths who have long juvenile records will most likely continue their offending careers into adulthood.

Policy Implications

Efforts to chart the life cycle of crime and delinquency will have a major influence on both theory and policy. Rather than simply asking why youths become delinquent or commit antisocial acts, theorists are charting the onset, escalation, frequency, and cessation of delinquent behavior. Research on delinquent careers has also influenced policy. If a relatively few offenders commit a great proportion of all delinquent acts and then persist as adult criminals, it follows that steps should be taken to limit their criminal opportunities.[72] One approach is to identify persistent offenders at the beginning of their offending careers and provide early treatment.[73] This might be facilitated by research aimed at identifying traits (for example, impulsive personalities) that can be used to classify high-risk offenders.[74] Because many of these youths suffer from a variety of problems, treatment must be aimed at a broad range of educational, family, vocational, and psychological problems. Focusing on a single problem, such as a lack of employment, may be ineffective.[75] (See Policy and Practice box above.)

Effective Early Intervention Programs to Mediate Risk Factors Known to Predict Serious and Violent Juvenile Offending

Involving parents:

- Parent management training
- Functional family therapy
- Family preservation

Involving children:

- Home visitation of pregnant teenagers
- Social competence training
- Peer mediation and conflict resolution
- Medication for neurological disorders and mental illness

Involving schools:

- Early intellectual enrichment (preschools)
- School organization interventions

Involving the community:

- Comprehensive community mobilization
- Situational crime prevention
- Intensive police patrolling, especially crime "hot spots"
- Legal and policy changes restricting availability and use of guns, drugs, and alcohol
- Mandatory laws for crimes involving firearms

The Study Group identified a number of promising prevention and intervention programs to reduce gang involvement and gang violence. Three such programs are:

The Little Village Gang Violence Reduction Program, operated by the Chicago Police Department, which employed targeted control of violent gang members through increased surveillance by probation and law enforcement agents, along with a wide range of social services and opportunities for targeted gang members to transition out of gangs.

The Gang Resistance Education and Training (G.R.E.A.T.) Program, developed by the Bureau of Alcohol, Tobacco and Firearms, is a prevention program being tested and evaluated in 42 schools across the country with very promising results. It uses a structured curriculum provided by trained law enforcement officers to discourage adolescents from joining gangs.

A third promising strategy under way in Boston and Chicago involves a multiple-component program to target youth gang homicides. This program maintains an online, geocoded information system to track gang violence, restricts access to firearms, enhances prosecution of gang crimes, and provides increased multi-agency sanctioning and hospital emergency room intervention.

Sources: Rolf Loeber and David Farrington, *Serious and Violent Juvenile Offenders* (Washington, DC: Office of Juvenile Justice and Delinquency Prevention, 1998).

✔ Checkpoints

✔ There are stable and enduring patterns in the delinquency rate.

✔ Males have a higher crime rate than females. The female delinquency rate, however, appears to be expanding at a faster pace.

✔ While the true association between class and crime is still unknown, the official data tell us that crime rates are highest in areas with high rates of poverty.

✔ Self-reports show that delinquency is spread through every level of the social structure.

✔ Minority teens have a higher arrest rate for most delinquent acts than whites.

✔ Some criminologists suggest that institutional racism, such as police profiling, accounts for the racial differences in the crime rate. Others believe that high African American crime rates are a function of living in a racially segregated society.

✔ Young people have the highest crime rates. People commit less crime as they mature.

✔ Chronic offenders commit a significant portion of all delinquent acts.

JUVENILE VICTIMIZATION

Juveniles are also victims of crime, and data from victim surveys can help us understand the nature of juvenile victimization. Most of what is known about juvenile victimization comes from an ongoing cooperative effort of the Bureau of Justice Statistics of the U.S. Department of Justice and the U.S. Census Bureau, called the National Crime Victimization Survey (NCVS). The NCVS is a household survey of victims of criminal behavior that measures the nature of the crime and the characteristics of victims.

TABLE 2.5	Number of Violent Crimes per 1,000 Persons Age 12 or Older	
	1998	1999
12–15 years	82.4	74.4
16–19 years	91.1	77.4
20–24 years	67.3	68.5
25–34 years	41.5	36.3
35–49 years	29.9	25.2
50–64 years	15.4	14.4
65+ years	2.8	3.8

Source: Callie Marie Rennison, *Criminal Victimization 1999, Changes 1998–99, with Trends 1993–99* (Washington, DC: Bureau of Justice Statistics, 2000).

To read the latest victimization data, go to

http://www.ojp.usdoj.gov/bjs/abstract/cv99.htm

For an up-to-date list of Web links, go to www.wadsworth.com/product/05345730s.

The total annual sample size of the NCVS has been about 43,000 households containing about 80,000 individuals. The sample is broken down into sub-samples of 10,000 households, and each group is interviewed twice a year. The NCVS has been conducted annually for more than 15 years.

Victimization in the United States

victimizations The number of people who are victims of criminal acts; young teens are fifteen times more likely than older adults (age 65 and over) to be victims of crimes.

The NCVS provides estimates of the total number of personal contact crimes (assault, rape, robbery) and household **victimizations** (burglary, larceny, vehicle theft). The survey indicates that currently about 30 million criminal incidents occur each year. Being the target or victim of rape, robbery, or assault is a terrible burden and one that can have considerable long-term consequences. If we translate the value of pain, emotional trauma, disability, and risk of death into dollar terms, the cost is $450 billion, or $1,800 for every person in the United States.[76] At first glance these figures seem overwhelming, but victimization rates are stable or declining for most crime categories.

Many of the differences between NCVS data and official statistics can be attributed to the fact that victimizations are frequently not reported. About 57 percent of the crimes of violence, 72 percent of the personal crimes of theft, and 66 percent of household crimes go unreported.

Young Victims NCVS data indicate that young people are much more likely to be the victims of crime than adults (Table 2.5).[77] The chance of victimization declines with age. The difference is particularly striking when we compare teens under age 19 with people over age 65—in 1999, teens were more than 20 times as likely to become victims than their grandparents! As Table 2.6 shows, kids ages 17 and under make up about 10 percent of the population and are the victims of more than 20 percent of all violent crimes. In contrast, people over age 50—more than 30 percent of the population—account for about 7 percent of all victimization.

The data also show that male teenagers have a significantly higher chance than females of becoming victims of violent crime, and that African American youth have a greater chance of becoming victims of violent crimes than white teenagers of the same age.[78]

As part of their Monitoring the Future program, the Institute for Social Research also collects data on teen victimization. The most recent data available (1999) indicate that each year a significant number of adolescents become crime victims (Table 2.7). This and other self-report surveys reveal that the NCVS seriously *underreports* juvenile victimization, and that the true rate of juvenile victimization may actually be several times higher.[79]

		Percent of Victims, by Age		
TABLE 2.6				
Age of victim	Percent of population	All violent crime	Rape/sexual assault	Robbery
Total	100	100	100	100
12 to 14	5	10	8	11
15 to 17	5	12	12	10
18 to 21	7	17	21	14
22 to 24	5	11	14	9
25 to 29	9	13	9	12
30 to 34	11	11	13	12
35 to 39	10	8	9	8
40 to 49	17	12	10	12
50 to 64	16	5	2	6
65 or older	15	2	1	4

Source: Craig A. Perkins, *Age Patterns of Victims of Serious Violent Crime* (Washington, DC: Bureau of Justice Statistics, 1997).

Checkpoints

✔ The National Crime Victimization Survey (NCVS) samples more than 50,000 people annually in order to estimate the total number of criminal incidents, including those not reported to police.

✔ Males are more often the victims of delinquency than females.

✔ Younger people are more often targets than older people.

✔ African-American rates of violent victimization are much higher than white rates. Crime victimization tends to be intraracial.

✔ Self-report data shows that a significant number of adolescents become crime victims. The NCVS may underreport juvenile victimization

The Victims and Their Criminals

NCVS data can also tell us something about the relationship between victims and offenders. This information is available because victims of violent personal crimes, such as assault and robbery, can identify the age, sex, and race of their attackers.

	Juvenile Self-Reported Victimization, Class of 1999		
TABLE 2.7			
		Once	More than once
Something stolen < $50		27%	18%
Something stolen > $50		18%	7.5%
Damaged your property		20%	11%
Injured you with a weapon		2.5%	2%
Threatened with a weapon but no injury		9%	6.5%

Source: *Monitoring the Future, 1999* (Ann Arbor, MI: Institute for Social Research, 2000).

Juveniles are much more likely to become crime victims than adults. They have a more dangerous lifestyle, which places them at risk for crime. One reason is that they spend a great deal of time in one of the most dangerous areas in the community, the local school. (© Joel Gordon)

In general, teens tend to be victimized by their peers. A majority of teens were shown to have been victimized by other teens, whereas victims age 20 and over identified their attackers as being 21 or older. However, people in almost all age groups who were victimized by *groups* of offenders identified their attackers as teenagers. Violent crime victims report that a disproportionate number of their attackers are young, ranging in age from 16 to 25.

The data also tell us that victimization is intraracial (within race). White teenagers tend to be victimized by white teens, and African American teenagers tend to be victimized by African American teens.

Most teens are victimized by people with whom they are acquainted, and their victimization is more likely to occur during the day. In contrast, adults are more often victimized by strangers, and at night. One explanation for this pattern is that youths are at greatest risk from their own family and relatives. (Chapter 8 deals with the issue of child abuse and neglect.) Another possibility is that many teenage victimizations occur at school. About 13 percent of all crimes of violence take place in school buildings or on school grounds.

Despite some sensational cases, the number of children seriously harmed (abducted or murdered) by strangers is less than commonly thought.[80] Each year there are about 50 cases in which it can be verified that a child was abducted and killed by a stranger; in another 100 cases the circumstances remain unknown, except that a child was killed by a stranger. Although stranger victimizations may be less common than once thought, the fact that as many as three children are abducted and killed by strangers every week is extremely disturbing.

SUMMARY

Official delinquency refers to youths who are arrested. What is known comes from the FBI's *Uniform Crime Report* (UCR), an annual tally of crimes reported to police by citizens. In addition, the FBI gathers arrest statistics from local police departments. From these, it is possible to determine the number of youths who are arrested each year, along with their age, race, and gender.

About 2 million youths are arrested annually. There has been an increase in the number of juveniles arrested for violent crimes. Though it is not certain why this trend has developed, possible explanations include involvement in gang activity, drug abuse, and teen gun ownership.

Dissatisfaction with the UCR prompted criminologists to develop other means of measuring delinquent behavior.

Self-reports are surveys in which subjects are asked to describe their misbehavior. Although self-reports indicate that many more crimes are committed than are known to the police, they also show that the delinquency rate is rather stable.

The third method of gathering information on delinquency involves victim surveys. The National Crime Victimization Survey (NCVS) is an annual national survey of the victims of crime conducted by agencies of the federal government. Teenagers are much more likely to become victims of crime than are people in other age groups. All three sources of crime statistics agree that young people commit more crimes than adults.

Delinquents are disproportionately male, although female delinquency rates are rising faster. Minority youth are over-represented in the delinquency rate, especially for violent crime. Experts are split on the cause of racial differences. Some believe they are a function of system bias; others see them as representing actual differences in the delinquency rate. Disagreement also exists over the rela-

tionship between class position and delinquency. Some hold that adolescent crime is a lower-class phenomenon, whereas others see it throughout the social structure. Problems in methodology have obscured the true class–crime relationship. However, official statistics indicate that lower-class youths are responsible for the most serious criminal acts.

There is general agreement that delinquency rates decline with age. Some experts believe this phenomenon is universal, whereas others believe a small group of offenders persists in crime at a high rate. The age–crime relationship has spurred research on the nature of delinquency over the life course. One discovery is the chronic persistent offender, who begins his or her offending career early in life and persists as an adult. Wolfgang and his colleagues identified chronic offenders in a series of cohort studies conducted in Philadelphia. Ongoing research has identified the characteristics of persistent offenders as they mature, and both personality and social factors help us predict long-term offending patterns.

KEY TERMS

Federal Bureau of
  Investigation (FBI)
Uniform Crime Report (UCR)
Part I offenses, index crimes
Part II offenses

disaggregated
self-reports
dark figures of crime
aging out, desistance,
  spontaneous remission

age of onset
developmental view
chronic delinquent offenders
early onset
chronic recidivists

continuity of crime
victimizations

QUESTIONS FOR DISCUSSION

1. What factors contribute to the aging-out process?

2. Why are males more delinquent than females? Is it a matter of lifestyle, culture, or physical properties?

3. Discuss the racial differences found in the crime rate. What factors account for differences in the African American and white crime rates?

4. Should kids who have been arrested more than three times be given mandatory incarceration sentences?

5. Do you believe that self-reports are an accurate method of gauging the nature and extent of delinquent behavior?

VIEWPOINT

Kids are also victimized at a higher rate than adults—most are attacked by acquaintances. Such statistics on youth violence and media portrayals of the incidents they represent have produced a tremendous climate of fear in our nation and a super-predator mentality that is changing the way policies are made and the way people live.

I think it's time for us to shift how we are framing the problem of juvenile violence. While it is true that we need to be vigilant in ensuring our immediate safety through our law enforcement and correctional efforts, it is also true that if we are to find long-lasting solutions, we must explore the predator theme from a different vantage point.

So says Shay Bilchick, director of the Office of Juvenile Justice and Delinquency Prevention. To learn more, go to InfoTrac® College Edition, and look at: Shay Bilchik, "Prevention and teamwork key to fighting juvenile crime." *Corrections Today* 59:42 (1997). To see more on this topic, use *juvenile violence* as a key term.

Chapter 3

Individual Views of Delinquency

© Catherine Leroy/Sipa Press

ou are a state legislator who is a member of the subcommittee on juvenile justice. Your committee has been asked to redesign the state's juvenile code because of public outrage over serious juvenile crime.

At an open hearing, a professor from the local university testifies that she has devised a sure-fire test to predict violence-prone delinquents. The procedure involves brain scans, DNA testing, and blood analysis. Used with samples of incarcerated adolescents, her procedure has been able to distinguish with 90 percent accuracy between youths with a history of violence and those who are exclusively property offenders. The professor testifies that, if each juvenile offender were tested with her techniques, the violence-prone career offender could easily be identified and given special treatment.

Opponents argue that this type of testing is unconstitutional because it violates the Fifth Amendment protection against self-incrimination and can unjustly label non-violent offenders. Any attempt to base policy on biosocial makeup seems inherently wrong and unfair. Those who favor the professor's approach maintain that it is not uncommon to single out the insane or mentally incompetent for special treatment and that these conditions often have a biological basis. It is better that a few delinquents be unfairly labeled than that seriously violent offenders be ignored until it is too late.

- Is it possible that some kids are born to be delinquents? Or, do kids "choose" crime?

- Is it fair to test kids to see if they have biological traits related to crime even if they have never committed a single offense?

- Should special laws be created to deal with the "potentially" dangerous offender?

- Should offenders be typed on the basis of their biological characteristics?

choice theory Holds that youths will engage in delinquent and criminal behavior after weighing the consequences and benefits of their actions; delinquent behavior is a rational choice made by a motivated offender who perceives that the chances of gain outweigh any possible punishment or loss.

trait theory Holds that youths engage in delinquent or criminal behavior due to aberrant physical or psychological traits that govern behavioral choices; delinquent actions are impulsive or instinctual rather than rational choices.

Some experts believe that delinquent behavior is a function of individual traits: selfish temperament, impulsive personality, abnormal hormones, genetic characteristics, and so on. They reject the notion that delinquents are a "product of their environment." If social and economic factors alone determine behavior, how is it that many youths residing in dangerous neighborhoods live law-abiding lives? Conversely, why are so many middle-class youths involved in delinquency? Research indicates that relatively few youths in any population, even the most economically disadvantaged, actually become hard-core, chronic delinquents.[1] The quality of neighborhood and family life may have little impact on the choices individuals make.[2] To some theorists, delinquency is rooted in the individual. This sentiment was first expressed by William Healy in 1915: "The dynamic center of the whole problem of delinquency and crime will ever be the individual offender."

Views of delinquency that focus on the individual can be divided into two categories. One position, referred to as **choice theory**, suggests that offenders are rational decision makers who choose to engage in antisocial activity because they believe their actions will be beneficial. Whether they join a gang, steal cars, or sell drugs, their delinquent acts are motivated by the belief that crime can be a relatively risk-free way to better their situation. They have little fear of getting caught. Some have fantasies of riches, and others may enjoy the excitement produced by criminal acts such as beating up an opponent or stealing a car.

The second and opposing view, referred to as **trait theory**, suggests that delinquent acts, especially violent ones, are actually uncontrollable, irrational behaviors. Many forms of delinquency, such as substance abuse and vandalism, appear more impulsive than rational, and these behaviors may be inspired by aberrant physical or psychological traits. Although some youths may choose to commit crime because they desire conventional luxuries and power, others may be driven by abnormalities such as hyperactivity, low intelligence, biochemical imbalance, or genetic defects.

Choice and trait theories are linked because they both focus on an individual's mental processes and behavioral reactions. They suggest that each person reacts to environmental and social circumstances in a unique fashion. Faced with the same set of conditions, one person will live a law-abiding life while another will use antisocial or violent behavior to satisfy his or her needs. Choice theorists suggest that the delinquent freely chooses antisocial behaviors to satisfy needs, while trait theorists argue that the choice of antisocial behavior is shaped by mental and physical traits.

free will View that youths are in charge of their own destinies and are free to make personal behavior choices unencumbered by environmental factors.

CHOICE THEORY AND CLASSICAL CRIMINOLOGY

utilitarian Those who believe that people weigh the benefits and consequences of their future actions before deciding on a course of behavior.

classical criminology Holds that decisions to violate the law are weighed against possible punishments and to deter crime the pain of punishment must outweigh the benefit of illegal gain; led to graduated punishments based on seriousness of the crime (let the punishment fit the crime).

The first formal explanations of crime held that human behavior is a matter of choice. It was assumed that people had **free will** to choose their behavior and that those who violated the law were motivated by greed, revenge, survival, or hedonism. More than 200 years ago, **utilitarian** philosophers Cesare Beccaria and Jeremy Bentham argued that people weigh the consequences of their actions before deciding on a course of behavior.[3] Their writings formed the core of **classical criminology.**

The classical view holds that the decision to violate the law comes after a careful weighing of the benefits and costs of criminal behaviors. Most potential law violators would cease their actions if the pain associated with a behavior outweighed the gain; conversely, law-violating behavior seems attractive if the rewards seem greater than the punishment.[4]

According to the classical view, youths who decide to become drug dealers compare the benefits, such as cash to buy cars and other luxury items, with the penalties, such as arrest followed by a long stay in a juvenile facility. If they believe drug dealers are rarely caught and even when caught avoid severe punishments, youths are more likely to choose to become dealers than if they believe dealers are almost always caught and punished by lengthy prison terms. They may know or hear about criminals who make a significant income from their illegal activities and want to follow in their footsteps.[5] Put simply, to prevent crime, the pain of punishment must outweigh the benefit of illegal gain.[6]

Classical criminologists argued that punishment should be graded according to the seriousness of particular crimes: "Let the punishment fit the crime." For example, Beccaria argued that it would be foolish to punish pickpockets and murderers in a similar fashion because this would encourage thieves to kill victims or witnesses.[7] The popularity of the classical approach was responsible, in part, for the development of prisons as an alternative to physical punishment and the creation of sentences geared to the seriousness of crimes.[8] The choice approach dominated the U.S. justice system for about 150 years.

www
To read a selection from Beccaria's
"On Crime and Punishment," go to http://www.fordham.edu/halsall/mod/18beccaria.html

For an up-to-date list of Web links, go to www.wadsworth.com/product/0534573053s.

THE RATIONAL DELINQUENT

The view that delinquents *choose* to violate the law remains a popular approach to the study of delinquency. It is argued that delinquency is not merely a function of social ills, such as lack of economic opportunity or family dysfunction. In reality, many youths from affluent families choose to break the law, and most indigent adolescents are law abiding. For example, at first glance drug abuse appears to be a senseless act motivated by grinding poverty and a sense of desperation. However, a sense of economic hopelessness cannot be the motivating force behind the substance abuse of millions of middle-class users, many of whom plan to finish high school and go on to college. These kids are more likely to be motivated by the desire for physical gratifi-

cation, peer group acceptance and other social benefits. They choose to break the law because, despite the inherent risks, they believe that taking drugs and drinking provides more pleasure than pain. Their entry into substance abuse is facilitated by their perception that valued friends and family members endorse and encourage drug use and abuse substances themselves.[9] Subscribers to the rational choice model believe the decision to commit a specific type of crime is a matter of personal decision making; hence, the term *rational choice.*

The emergence of gangs, and their involvement in the drug trade, strengthens the case for rational choice: these young, well-armed entrepreneurs are seeking to cash in on a lucrative, albeit illegal, "business enterprise." (See Chapter 9 for more on gangs.) Gang leaders are surely "rational decision makers," constantly processing information: Who are my enemies? What are the chances of getting caught? Where can I find a good lawyer?[10] Gang members have been found to act like employers, providing their associates with security and the know-how to conduct "business deals." Like legitimate business enterprises, some gangs recruit new personnel and cut deals with rivals over territory.[11] Similarly, drug dealers have been observed to evaluate the desirability of their "sales area" before getting ready to deal.[12] Dealers usually choose the middle of a long street to conduct transactions because of the good visibility in both directions; police raids can then be spotted before they occur.[13]

Choosing Delinquent Acts

The focus of choice theory is on the *act,* not the offender. In rational choice theory, the concepts of crime and criminality are separate. *Criminality* is the propensity to engage in criminal acts; *crimes* are events that are in violation of the criminal law.[14] There will always be criminally motivated adolescents, but if they do not have the opportunity to commit crime they will not be able to act on their inclinations. Similarly, given an opportunity for illegal gain, even the least criminally inclined youths may be motivated to act. Why a child has the propensity to commit delinquent acts is an issue quite distinct from the reasons a delinquent decides to break into a particular house one day or to sell narcotics the next.

The decision to "choose" crime occurs when an offender decides to take the chance of violating the law after considering his or her situation (e.g., need for money, opportunities for conventional success), values (e.g., conscience, need for peer approval), and situational factors (e.g., the likelihood of getting caught, the punishment if apprehended). Conversely, the decision to forgo law-violating behavior may be based on the perception that the benefits are no longer good or the probability of successfully completing a crime is less than the chance of being caught. For example, aging-out may occur because as delinquents mature they begin to realize that the risks of crime are greater than the potential profits. The solution to crime, therefore, may be formulating policies that will cause the potential criminal to choose conventional behaviors.[15]

Routine Activities

routine activities theory View that crime is a "normal" function of the routine activities of modern living; offenses can be expected if there is a motivated offender and a suitable target that is not protected by capable guardians.

predatory crimes Violent crimes against persons and crimes in which an offender attempts to steal an object directly from its holder.

If the motivation to commit delinquent acts is a constant, why do crime rates rise and fall? Why are some areas more crime ridden than others? To answer these questions, attention must be paid to the *opportunity to commit crimes.*[16] Crime may occur not only because a criminal decides to break the law but also because victims place themselves at risk.[17]

According to the **routine activity** view, developed by Lawrence Cohen and Marcus Felson, the volume and distribution of **predatory crimes** (violent crimes against persons and crimes in which an offender attempts to steal an object directly from its holder) are influenced by the interaction of three variables: the availability of *suitable targets* (such as homes containing easily salable goods), the absence of *capable guardians* (such as homeowners, police, and security guards), and the presence of *motivated offenders* (such as unemployed teenagers) (Figure 3.1).[18]

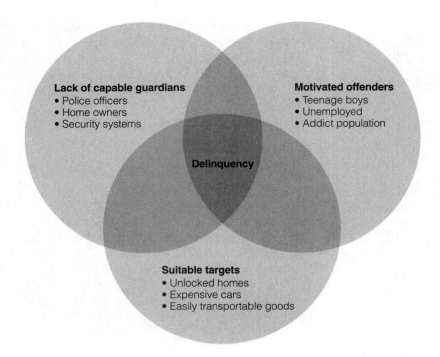

Figure 3.1
Routine Activities Theory Posits the Interaction of Three Factors

Lack of capable guardians
- Police officers
- Home owners
- Security systems

Motivated offenders
- Teenage boys
- Unemployed
- Addict population

Delinquency

Suitable targets
- Unlocked homes
- Expensive cars
- Easily transportable goods

This approach gives equal weight to the roles of the victim and the offender. Criminal opportunity is influenced by the victim's behavior; the greater the opportunity for criminals and victims to interact, the greater the probability of crime.[19]

Lack of Capable Guardians Kids will commit crime when they believe their actions will go undetected by guardians such as police, security guards, neighbors, teachers, or homeowners. They choose what they consider safe places to commit crimes and to buy and sell drugs.[20]

According to the routine activities approach, general social change can influence delinquency rates and patterns. Research shows that robbery levels are relatively low in neighborhoods where residents keep a watchful eye on their neighbor's property.[21] Delinquency rates may trend upward as the number of adult caretakers (guardians) who are at home during the day decreases. With mothers at work and children in day care, homes are left unguarded and become "suitable targets." Similarly, in our highly transient society, the traditional neighborhood, in which streets are monitored by familiar guardians such as family members, neighbors, and friends, has been vanishing and replaced by anonymous housing developments.[22] Burglars appear to monitor car and pedestrian traffic and avoid selecting targets on heavily traveled streets.[23]

Suitable Targets The availability of suitable targets, such as easily transportable commodities, will increase crime rates. Research has generally supported the fact that, the more wealth a home contains, the more likely it is to be a crime target.[24] Burglary rates should rise as easily transportable but expensive items become commonplace: notebook computers, DVD players, and digital cameras.[25]

People do not like to travel to commit crimes, and targets are generally found close to their homes.[26] Familiarity with an area gives kids a ready knowledge of escape routes; this is referred to as their "awareness space." This behavior routine also influences the risk of victimization: People who routinely go out to public places are most likely to be victimized by strangers; stay-at-homes are most likely to be harmed by family or friends.[27] Frequenting dangerous hot spots, such as bars and taverns, increases the likelihood of victimization.[28]

Why are some areas more crime ridden than others? It may be because of variations in the opportunity to commit crimes. Places that are unguarded may be more vulnerable to criminal activities. Crime may occur not only because a criminal decides to break the law, but also because victims place themselves at risk and no one is around to protect them from harm. (© Nick Lacy/Stock, Boston)

Motivated Offenders Routine activities theory also links delinquency rates to the number of kids in the population who are motivated to commit crime. For example, if the number of teenagers in a given population exceeds the number of available part-time and after-school jobs, the supply of motivated offenders may be increased simply because many potential offenders are competing for a limited number of legitimate economic resources.[29]

Lifestyle also affects criminal motivation. Adolescents who spend a lot of time socializing with peers in the absence of authority figures are more likely to engage in deviant behaviors.[30] In the presence of motivated peers, the lack of structure and guardianship leaves more opportunity for antisocial behaviors. Participation in unstructured activities helps explain the association between crime rates and gender, age, and status. Teenage boys have the highest crime rates because they are most likely to engage in unsupervised socialization. Even for adolescents who engage in "character building" activities—such as a part-time job after school—the opportunity to socialize with deviant peers combined with lack of parental supervision increases criminal motivation.[31]

PREVENTING DELINQUENCY

If delinquency is a rational choice and a routine activity, delinquency prevention is a matter of convincing potential delinquents that they will be punished for committing delinquent acts, punishing them so severely that they never again commit crimes, or making it so difficult to commit crimes that the potential gain is not worth the risk. The first of these strategies is called *general deterrence*, the second *specific deterrence*, and the third *situational crime prevention*. Let's look at each of these strategies in more detail.

General Deterrence

general deterrence Crime control policies that depend on the fear of criminal penalties, such as long prison sentences for violent crimes; aim is to convince law violator that the pain outweighs the benefit of criminal activity.

The **general deterrence** concept holds that the choice to commit delinquent acts can be controlled by the threat of punishment. If people believe illegal behavior will result in severe sanctions, they will choose not to commit crimes.[32] A guiding principle of deterrence theory is that the more severe, certain, and swift the punishment, the greater its deterrent effect will be.[33] Even if a particular crime carries a severe punishment, there will be relatively little deterrent effect if most people do not believe they will be caught.[34] Conversely, even a mild sanction may deter crime if people believe punishment is certain. And even the most severe sanctions will have little deterrent effect if they are delayed or easily put off.

Traditionally, juvenile justice authorities have been reluctant to incorporate deterrence-based punishments on the ground that they interfere with its *parens patriae* philosophy. Children are punished less severely than adults, limiting the power of the law to deter juvenile crime. However, the increase in teenage violence, gang activity, and drug abuse has prompted a reevaluation of deterrence strategies. Some juvenile courts have shifted from an emphasis on treatment to concerns with public safety.[35] Police are more willing to use aggressive tactics to deter membership in drug-trafficking gangs, and officers have been sent into high schools undercover to identify and arrest student drug dealers.[36]

Many courts have also attempted a deterrence strategy. Juvenile court judges have become more willing to waive youths to adult courts; prior record may outweigh need for services in making this decision.[37] In addition, legislators have passed more restrictive juvenile codes, and the number of incarcerated juveniles continues to increase. Not even adolescents are spared capital punishment; the U.S. Supreme Court has upheld the use of the death penalty for youths 16 years of age.[38]

Can Delinquency Be Deterred? The effectiveness of deterrence strategies is a topic of considerable debate. A number of studies have contributed data supportive of deterrence concepts. Evidence indicates that the threat of arrest can deter property crimes, and areas in which punishment is more certain seem to have lower delinquency rates.[39] The more likely people are to anticipate punishment, the less likely they are to commit crimes.[40] But although these findings are persuasive, there is little conclusive evidence that the threat of arrest and punishment alone can bring down delinquency rates.[41]

Because deterrence strategies are based on the idea of a "rational" offender, they may not be effective when applied to young people. Minors tend to be less capable of making mature judgments, and many younger offenders are unaware of the content of juvenile legal codes. A deterrence policy (for example, mandatory waiver to the adult court for violent crimes) will have little effect on delinquency rates of kids who are not even aware these statutes exist.[42] It seems futile, therefore, to try to deter delinquency through fear of legal punishment. Teens seem more fearful of being punished by their parents or of being the target of disapproval from their friends than they are of the police.[43]

It is also possible that for the highest-risk group of young offenders—teens living in economically depressed neighborhoods—the deterrent threat of formal sanctions may be irrelevant. Inner-city youngsters may not have internalized the norms that hold that getting arrested is wrong. They have less to lose if arrested; they have a limited stake in society and are not worried about their future. They also may not connect their illegal behavior with punishment because they see many people committing crimes and not getting caught or being punished.

Research also shows that many juvenile offenders are under the influence of drugs or alcohol, a condition that might impair their decision-making ability.[44] Similarly, juveniles often commit crimes in groups, a process called **co-offending**, and peer pressure can outweigh the deterrent effect of the law.

In summary, deterring delinquency through the fear of punishment may be of limited value because children may not fully comprehend either the seriousness of their acts or their consequences.[45] On the surface, deterrence appears to have benefit, but there is reason to believe that the benefit is limited.

co-offending Committing criminal acts in groups.

Specific Deterrence

It stands to reason that if delinquents truly are rational and commit crimes because they see them as beneficial, they will stop offending if they are caught and severely

Can delinquency and drug abuse be deterred when so many teens consider it fun and socially acceptable? High school student Cathy, left, parties with other rave fans at an abandoned warehouse in Portland, Oregon, Sept. 4, 2000. Oregon's rave scene is an escape for teens, a worry for parents, and a worrisome new challenge to law enforcement officials. (AP/Wide World Photos)

specific deterrence Sending convicted offenders to secure incarceration facilities so that punishment is severe enough to convince offenders not to repeat their criminal activity.

punished. What rational person would recidivate after being exposed to an arrest, court appearance, and incarceration in an unpleasant detention facility, with the promise of more to come? According to the concept of **specific deterrence**, if young offenders are punished severely the experience will convince them not to repeat their illegal acts. Juveniles are punished by state authorities with the understanding that their ordeal will deter future misbehavior.

Though admissions to confinement facilities have increased sharply during the past decade, there is little evidence that punitive measures alone will deter future delinquency. Research shows that arrest and punishment may in fact increase the likelihood that first-time offenders will commit new crimes (recidivate).[46] Kids who are placed in a juvenile justice facility are just as likely to become adult criminals as those treated with greater leniency.[47] In fact, a history of prior arrests, convictions, and punishments has proven to be the best predictor of re-arrest among young offenders released from correctional institutions. Rather than deterring future offending, punishment may in fact encourage re-offending.[48]

Why does punishment encourage rather than reduce delinquency? According to some experts, institutionalization cuts youths off from pro-social supports in the community, making them more reliant on deviant peers. Incarceration may also diminish chances for successful employment, reducing access to legitimate opportunities. This might help explain why delinquency rates are increasing at the same time that incarceration rates are at an all-time high.

Rather than deter future crimes, the experience of punishment may actually motivate some adolescents to re-offend. For example, the use of mandatory sentences for some crimes means that all youths who are found to have committed those crimes must be institutionalized; first offenders may then be treated the same as chronic recidivists. These novice offenders may be packed into overcrowded facilities with experienced violent juveniles and consequently suffer significant and irrevocable harm from their experience. While some researchers have found that punishment may reduce the frequency of future offending, the weight of the evidence suggests that time served has little impact on recidivism.[49]

Situational Crime Prevention

situational crime prevention A crime prevention method that relies on reducing the opportunity to commit criminal acts by (1) making them more difficult to perform, (2) reducing their reward, and (3) increasing their risks.

According to choice theory, rational offenders weigh the potential gains of delinquent acts and balance them with the potential losses (getting arrested, punished). It stands to reason that if we can convince these rational decision makers that their illegal activities are risky, that the potential gain is minimal, and that the opportunity for success is limited, then they will choose not to commit crime. This is the logic behind the measures that have become known collectively as **situational crime prevention**. These strategies are designed to make it so difficult to commit delinquent acts that would-be offenders will be convinced the risks are greater than the rewards.[50] Rather than deterring or punishing individuals, they aim to reduce opportunities to commit delinquent acts. This can be accomplished by increasing the effort or the risks of delinquent activity or by reducing the rewards attached to delinquent acts.

Increasing the effort of delinquency might involve *target-hardening techniques,* such as placing steering locks on cars and unbreakable glass on storefronts. *Access control* can be maintained by locking gates and fencing yards.[51] The *facilitators of crime* can be controlled by banning the sale of spray paint to adolescents in an effort to cut down on graffiti or having a photo put on credit cards to reduce their value if stolen. Increasing the risks of delinquency might involve improving lighting, creating neighborhood watch programs, controlling building exits, installing security systems, or increasing the number of security officers and police patrols.

Reducing the rewards of delinquency could include strategies such as making car radios removable so they can be kept in the home at night, marking property so it is more difficult to sell when stolen, and having gender-neutral phone listings to discourage obscene phone calls. Tracking systems help police locate and return stolen vehicles.

hot spot A particular location or address that is the site of repeated and frequent criminal activity.

crack down A law enforcement operation designed to reduce or eliminate a particular criminal activity through the application of aggressive police tactics, typically involving a larger than usual contingent of police officers.

Hot Spots and Crackdowns One type of situational crime prevention effort targets locales that are known to be the scene of repeated delinquent activity. By focusing on a **hot spot**—for example, a shopping mall, public park, or housing project—law enforcement efforts can be used to **crack down** on crime. For example, a police task force might target gang members who are street-level drug dealers by using undercover agents and surveillance cameras in known drug-dealing locales. Unfortunately, these efforts have not often proven to be successful mechanisms for lowering crime and delinquency rates.[52] Crackdowns seem to be an effective short-term strategy, but their effect begins to decay once the initial shock effect wears off.[53] Crackdowns also may displace illegal activity to areas where there are fewer police.

While these results are discouraging, crime rates seem to be reduced when police officers combine the use of aggressive problem solving with community improvement techniques (increased lighting, cleaned vacant lots) to fight particular crimes in selected places.[54] For example, a recent initiative by the Dallas Police Department to aggressively pursue truancy and curfew enforcement resulted in lower rates of gang violence.[55]

Do Delinquents Choose Crime?

All the control methods based on choice theory assume delinquents to be motivated offenders who break the law because they perceive an abundance of benefits and an absence of threat. Increase the threat and reduce the benefits, and the delinquency rate should decline. This logic is hard to refute. Nonetheless, to say that delinquents choose their crimes is logical, yet several questions remain unanswered. First, why do some people choose to break the law even after suffering its consequences whereas others live law-abiding lives?[56] Conversely, why do affluent youths break the law when they have everything to lose and little to gain?

Choice theorists also have difficulty explaining seemingly irrational crimes such as vandalism, arson, and even drug abuse. To say a teenager painted swastikas on a synagogue after making a "rational choice" seems inadequate. The relationships observed by rational choice theorists can be explained in other ways. For example, even though the high victimization rates in lower-class neighborhoods can be explained by an oversupply of motivated offenders, other factors, such as social disorganization, may also explain this phenomenon.[57]

In summary, choice theories help us understand criminal events and victim patterns. However, the question remains, why are some adolescents motivated to commit crime whereas others in similar circumstances remain law abiding? Why do some kids choose crime over legal activities? The remaining sections of this chapter present some possible explanations.

✔ Checkpoints

✔ Choice theory maintains that delinquency is rational and can be prevented by punishment that is sufficiently severe and certain.

✔ Delinquents who choose crime must evaluate the characteristics of a target to determine its suitability.

✔ Routine activities theory suggests that delinquent acts are a function of motivated offenders, capable guardians, and the availability of suitable targets.

✔ General deterrence models are based on the fear of punishment. If punishments are severe, swift, and certain, would-be delinquents would choose not to risk breaking the law.

✔ Specific deterrence aims at reducing crime through the application of severe punishments. Once offenders experience these punishments they will be unwilling to repeat their delinquent activities.

✔ Situational crime prevention efforts are designed to reduce or redirect crime by making it more difficult to profit from illegal acts.

TRAIT THEORIES: BIOSOCIAL AND PSYCHOLOGICAL VIEWS

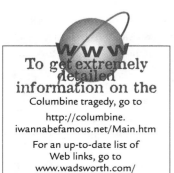

To get extremely detailed information on the Columbine tragedy, go to http://columbine. iwannabefamous.net/Main.htm

For an up-to-date list of Web links, go to www.wadsworth.com/product/0534573053s.

Choice theorists would have us believe that young people select crime after weighing the benefits of delinquent over legal behavior. For example, youths decide to commit a robbery if they believe they will make a good profit, have a good chance of getting away, and, even if caught, stand little chance of being severely punished. But a number of experts think this model is incomplete. They believe it is wrong to infer that all youths choose crime simply because the advantages outweigh the risks. If that were the case, how could profitless crimes such as violence or vandalism be explained? These experts argue that behavioral choices are a function of an individual's mental and physical makeup. Most law-abiding youths have traits that keep them within conventional society. In contrast, youths who choose to engage in antisocial behavior manifest abnormal traits that influence their choices.[58] Impulsive behavior patterns place some youths at odds with society, and they soon find themselves in trouble with the law. Although delinquents may choose their actions, some researchers believe these decisions are byproducts of mental and physical traits. Is it possible that violent adolescents—such as Dylan Klebold and Eric Harris, who on April 20, 1999 killed 13 and wounded 21 classmates at Columbine High school—were "rational" decision makers, or was their behavior the product of twisted minds?

The idea that delinquents are "abnormal" is not a new one. Some of the earliest theories of criminal behavior stressed that crime is a product of personal traits, and that measurable conditions, such as IQ and body build, determine behavior. This view is referred to as *positivism*. Positivists believe the scientific method can be used to measure the causes of behavior and that behavior is a function of often-uncontrollable factors, such as mental illness.

The *source* of behavioral control is one difference between trait and choice theories. To a choice theorist, reducing the benefits of crime by increasing the likelihood of punishment will lower the crime rate. Because trait theorists question whether delinquents are rational decision makers, they focus more on the treatment of abnormal mental and physical conditions as a method of delinquency reduction. In the next sections, the primary components of trait theory are reviewed.

The Origins of Trait Theory

criminal atavism The idea that delinquents manifest physical anomalies that make them biologically and physiologically similar to our primitive ancestors, savage throwbacks to an earlier stage of human evolution.

For a complete list of the crime-producing physical traits identified by Lombroso, go to

http://www.d.umn.edu/
~jhamlin1/lombroso.html

For an up-to-date list of Web links, go to www.wadsworth.com/ product/0534573053s.

inheritance school An early form of biological theory that held that deviant behavior was inherited and therefore ran in families, being passed on from generation to generation.

somatotype school Argued that delinquents manifest distinct physiques that make them susceptible to particular types of delinquent behavior.

The first attempts to discover why criminal tendencies develop focused on biological traits present at birth. The origin of this school of thought is generally credited to the Italian physician Cesare Lombroso (1835–1909).[59] Known as the father of criminology, Lombroso developed the theory of **criminal atavism**.[60] He found that delinquents manifest physical anomalies that make them similar to our primitive ancestors. These individuals are throwbacks to an earlier stage of human evolution. Because of this link, the "born criminal" has such traits as enormous jaws, strong canines, a flattened nose, and supernumerary teeth (double rows, as in snakes). Lombroso made statements such as: "[I]t was easy to understand why the span of the arms in criminals so often exceeds the height, for this is a characteristic of apes, whose forelimbs are used in walking and climbing."[61]

Contemporaries of Lombroso refined the notion of a physical basis of crime. Raffaele Garofalo (1851–1934) shared Lombroso's belief that certain physical characteristics indicate a criminal nature.[62] Enrico Ferri (1856–1929), a student of Lombroso, accepted the biological approach to explaining criminal activity, but he attempted to interweave social factors into his explanation.[63] The English criminologist Charles Goring (1870–1919) challenged the validity of Lombroso's research and claimed instead that delinquent behaviors bore a significant relationship to "defective intelligence."[64] Consequently, he advocated that criminality could best be controlled by regulating the reproduction of families exhibiting abnormal traits such as "feeble-mindedness."[65]

Some early criminologists believed that criminality was an inherited trait passed down from one generation to the next. Advocates of the **inheritance school** traced the activities of several generations of families believed to have an especially large number of criminal members. The most famous of these studies involved the Jukes and the Kallikaks. Richard Dugdale's *The Jukes: A Study in Crime, Pauperism, Disease, and Heredity* (1875) and Arthur Estabrook's later work, *The Jukes in 1915,* traced the history of the Jukes, a family responsible for a disproportionate amount of crime.[66]

Advocates of the **somatotype school,** or body build school, argued that criminals manifest distinct physiques that made them crime prone.[67] William H. Sheldon linked body type to delinquency.[68] *Mesomorphs* have well-developed muscles and an athletic appearance. They are active, aggressive, and the most likely to become delinquents. *Endomorphs* have heavy builds and are lethargic. *Ectomorphs* are tall and thin, and less social and more intellectual than the other types.[69]

The early views that portrayed delinquent behavior as a function of a single biological trait had a significant impact on American criminology; bio-criminologists helped develop a science of "criminal anthropology."[70] Eventually, these views evoked criticism for their unsound methodology. Many trait studies used captive offender populations and failed to compare experimental subjects with control groups.[71] These methodological flaws make it impossible to determine if biological traits produce delinquency. It is equally plausible that police are more likely to arrest the mentally and physically abnormal. By the middle of the twentieth century, biological theories had fallen out of favor.

Contemporary Biosocial Theory

For most of the twentieth century, most delinquency research focused on social factors such as poverty and family life. However, a small group of researchers kept alive the biological approach.[72] Some embraced sociobiology, a perspective suggesting that behavior will adapt to the environment in which it evolved.[73] Creatures of all species

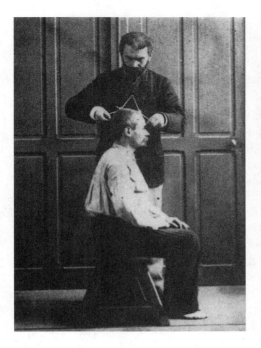 

Early biocriminologists believed that the physical makeup of offenders controlled their behavior. Biological traits present at birth were thought to predetermine whether people would live a life of crime. Here the skull of a criminal is measured in a study to determine if brain size and shape are related to violent behavior. (© Collection Viollet/Liaison Agency)

equipotentiality View that all people are equal at birth and are thereafter influenced by their environment.

biosocial theory The view that both thought and behavior have biological and social bases.

are influenced by their innate need to survive and dominate others. Sociobiology revived interest in a biological basis for crime. If biological (genetic) makeup controls all human behavior, it follows that a person's genes should determine whether he or she chooses law-violating or conventional behavior.[74]

Today, those who embrace trait theory reject the assumptions that all humans are born with equal potential (**equipotentiality**) and that thereafter their behavior is controlled by social forces in the environment.[75] Sociological criminologists suggest that all people are born equal and that parents, schools, neighborhoods, and friends control subsequent development. But trait theorists argue that no two people (with rare exceptions, such as identical twins) are alike and therefore that each will react to environmental stimuli in a distinct way. They assert that a combination of personal traits and environmental influences produce individual behavior patterns. People with pathological traits, such as abnormal personality or a low IQ, may have a heightened risk for crime. People may develop physical or mental traits at birth or soon after that effect their social functioning over the life course and influence their behavior choices. For example, low-birth-weight babies have been found to suffer poor educational achievement later in life; academic deficiency has been linked to delinquency and drug abuse.[76] This risk is elevated by environmental stresses such as poor family life, educational failure, and exposure to delinquent peers. The reverse may also apply: a supportive environment may counteract adverse biological and psychological traits.[77]

The interaction between a child's predisposition and his or her environment produces delinquency. Children born into disadvantaged environments often do not get the social support they need to overcome their handicaps. Lack of family support can have long-term consequences. For example, neural pathways may be damaged by neglect or abuse, and a pattern of electrochemical activation may be established that remains across the lifespan.[78] The relatively small number of youths who suffer both physical and social handicaps and also lack social supports are the ones who become early offenders and persist in a life of crime.[79]

Contemporary **biosocial theory** explains the onset of antisocial behaviors by focusing on physical qualities.[80] The majority of research efforts are concentrated in three areas: biochemical reactions, neurological dysfunction, and genetic influences.

Biochemical Factors

This area of research concerns the suspected relationship between antisocial behavior and biochemical makeup.[81] One view is that body chemistry can govern behavior and personality, including levels of aggression and depression.[82]

You Are What You Eat? There is evidence that diet may influence behavior through its impact on body chemistry. Of particular concern is an unusually high intake of artificial food coloring, milk, and sweets. Some scientists believe chronic under- or over-supply of vitamins C, B3, and B6 may be related to antisocial behavior. Evidence also exists that allergies to foods can influence mood, resulting in swings between hyperactivity and depression.[83] High intake or excessive exposure to certain common minerals has also been linked to aggression.[84] Overexposure to lead, for example, has been traced to learning disabilities and lower IQ, which are considered risk factors for delinquency.[85]

Evidence exists that institutionalized youths have a history of poor nutrition, with diets low in protein and high in sugar and other carbohydrates.[86] Antisocial youths who are given a diet balanced in nutrients have significantly reduced episodes of antisocial behavior and improved scores on psychological inventories.[87] A high-protein, low-carbohydrate, sugarless diet, supplemented by megavitamins, has been found to improve behavior problems, including hyperactivity and aggression. Diets containing lower levels of sugar and preservatives have been linked to improved scores on national achievement tests. Research shows that persistent abnormality in the way the brain metabolizes glucose can be linked to substance abuse.[88]

Stephen Schoenthaler, a well known biocriminologist, has conducted a number of studies which substantiate his belief that there is a significant association between a person's diet and their aggressive behavior patterns. In one study of 803 New York City public schools, Schoenthaler found academic performance of 1.1 million school children rose 16 percent after the diets were modified. The number of children classified as "learning-disabled" fell from 125,000 to 74,000 in one year. The improvements in behavior and academic performance was attributed to diets containing more vitamins and minerals as compared with the old diets. The greater amounts of these essential nutrients in the new diets were believed to have corrected impaired brain function caused by poor nutrition.

More recently, Schoenthaler conducted three randomized controlled studies in which 66 elementary school children, 62 confined teenage delinquents, and 402 confined adult felons received dietary supplements meant to be the equivalent of a diet providing more fruit, vegetables, and whole grains. In each study, the subjects receiving the dietary supplement demonstrated significantly less violent, and nonviolent, antisocial behavior when compared to the control subjects who received placebos. Schoenthaler finds that vitamins, minerals, and other nutrients from a diet rich in fruits, vegetables, and whole grains can improve brain function, basic intelligence, and academic performance. These are all variables that have been linked to delinquent behavior.[89]

Dissenting Views The relationship between biochemical intake and abnormal behavior is far from settled. A number of controlled experiments have failed to substantiate any link between the two variables.[90] In one study, researchers had 25 preschool and 23 school-age children described as sensitive to sugar follow a different diet for three consecutive 3-week periods. One diet was high in sucrose (a form of sugar), the second substituted aspartame (Nutrasweet) for a sweetener, and the third relied on saccharin (another artificial sweetener). The researchers found little evidence of cognitive or behavioral differences that could be linked to diet. If anything, sugar seemed to have a calming effect on the children.[91] Despite these criticisms, the relationship between diet and delinquency remains unresolved. As the recent Schoenthaler research indicates, further studies are certainly warranted.

Hormonal Levels Antisocial behavior allegedly peaks in the teenage years because hormonal activity is then at its greatest level. It is argued that increased levels of testosterone are responsible for excessive violence among teenage boys. Adolescents who experience more intense moods, anxiety, and restlessness also have the highest crime rates.[92] Research has shone that hormonal sensitivity may begin very early in life if the fetus is exposed to abnormally high levels of testosterone. This may trigger a heightened response to the release of testosterone at puberty. Although testosterone levels may appear normal, the young male is at risk for overaggressive behavior.[93] Hormonal activity as an explanation of gender differences in delinquency will be discussed further in Chapter 6.

Neurological Dysfunction

minimal brain dysfunction (MBD) Damage to the brain itself that causes antisocial behavior injurious to the individual's lifestyle and social adjustment.

Another focus of biosocial theory is the neurological, or brain and nervous system, structure of offenders. Studies measure indicators of system functioning such as arousal levels, attention span, and cognitive ability and compare them to measures of antisocial behavior.

One view is that the neuro-endocrine system, which controls brain chemistry, is the key to understanding aggression. Imbalance in this system has been linked to antisocial behavior.[94] Another view is that neurological dysfunction is the key factor. Children who manifest behavior disturbances may have neurological deficits, such as damage to the hemispheres of the brain; this is sometimes referred to as **minimal brain dysfunction (MBD)**.[95] (See Focus on Delinquency, "Aftermath of Abuse.") Impairment is produced by factors such as low birth weight, brain injury, birth complications, and inherited abnormalities.[96] Research indicates that children exhibiting neurological impairment also have an increased risk for developmental problems, such as low IQ scores and cognitive impairment, that have been associated with delinquency.[97]

Research efforts to substantiate a link between neurological impairment and crime found that this relationship can be detected quite early in life. Children who suffer from measurable neurological deficits at birth are more likely to become criminals as adults.[98] Low birth weight is highly correlated with neurological impairment, and low-birth-weight children are also likely to be early-onset delinquents.[99] Clinical analysis of death-row inmates found that a significant number had suffered head injuries as children that resulted in neurological impairment.[100] Measurement of the brain activity of antisocial youths has revealed impairments that might cause them to experience outbursts of anger, hostility, and aggression.[101] Evidence has also been found linking brain damage to mental disorders such as depression.[102]

A number of studies have used an electroencephalogram (EEG) to measure the brainwaves of delinquents and then compared them with those of law-abiding adolescents. In the most significant of these studies, 335 violent delinquents were classified on the basis of their antisocial activities and measured by EEG.[103] Youths who committed a single violent act had a 12 percent abnormality rate (the same as the general population), but the habitually aggressive youths tested at a 57 percent abnormality rate—almost five times normal. Behaviors believed to be highly correlated with abnormal EEG functions include poor impulse control, inadequate social ability, hostility, temper tantrums, destructiveness, and hyperactivity.[104]

learning disability (LD) Neurological dysfunction that prevents an individual from learning to his or her potential.

The Learning Disabilities One type of MBD that has generated considerable interest is **learning disability (LD)**, which usually involves problems in understanding or using spoken or written languages. Some LD kids have problems in reading and writing, or may suffer perceptual handicaps.[105]

ATTENTION DEFICIT HYPERACTIVITY DISORDER

Many parents have noticed that their children do not pay attention to them—they run around and do things in their own way. Sometimes this inattention is a function of age; in other instances it is a symptom of a common learning disability referred to as attention deficit hyperactivity disorder (ADHD), a condition in which a child shows a developmentally inappropriate lack of attention, distractibility, impulsivity, and hyperactivity. The various symptoms of ADHD are listed in the table below.

No one is really sure how ADHD develops, but some psychologists believe it is tied to dysfunction in a section

Symptoms of ADHD

Lack of Attention

- Frequently fails to finish projects
- Does not seem to pay attention
- Does not sustain interest in play activities

- Cannot sustain concentration on schoolwork or related tasks
- Is easily distracted

Impulsivity

- Frequently acts without thinking
- Often "calls out" in class
- Does not want to wait his or her turn

- Shifts from activity to activity
- Cannot organize tasks or work
- Requires constant supervision in line or games

Hyperactivity

- Constantly runs around and climbs on things
- Shows excessive motor activity while asleep
- Cannot sit still; is constantly fidgeting
- Does not remain in his or her seat in class

- Is constantly on the go like a "motor"
- Difficulty regulating emotions
- Difficulty getting started
- Difficulty staying on track
- Difficulty adjusting to social demands

The relationship between learning disabilities and delinquency has been highlighted by studies showing that arrested and incarcerated children have a far higher LD rate than do children in the general population.[106] Although approximately 10 percent of all youths have some form of learning disorder, estimates of LD among adjudicated delinquents range from 26 to 73 percent.[107] There are two possible explanations of the link between learning disabilities and delinquency.[108] One view, known as the *susceptibility rationale,* argues that the link is caused by side effects of learning disabilities, such as impulsiveness and inability to take social cues. In contrast, the *school failure rationale* assumes that the frustration caused by poor school performance will lead to a negative self-image and acting-out behavior.

Psychologist Terrie Moffitt has evaluated the literature on the connection between LD and delinquency and concludes that it is a significant correlate of persistent antisocial behavior (or conduct disorders).[109] She finds that neurological symptoms, such as LD and MBD, correlate highly with early onset of deviance, hyperactivity, and aggressiveness.[110] There is also new evidence that the factors that cause learning disabilities are also highly related to substance abuse, which may help explain and LD–JD connection. The National Center on Addiction and Substance Abuse at Columbia University recently released findings that show how learning disabilities are linked to substance abuse:

- Risk factors for adolescent substance abuse are very similar to the behavioral effects of learning disabilities—reduced self-esteem, academic difficulty, loneli-

of the lower portion of the brain known as the reticular activating system. This area keeps the higher brain centers alert and ready for input. There is some evidence that this area is not working properly in ADHD kids and that their behavior is really the brain's attempt to generate new stimulation to maintain alertness. Other suspected origins are neurological damage to the frontal lobes of the brain, prenatal stress, and even food additives and chemical allergies. Some experts suggest that the condition might be traced to the neurological effects of abnormal levels of the chemicals dopamine and norepinephrine.

Children from any background can develop ADHD, but it is five to seven times more common in boys than girls. It does not affect intelligence, and ADHD children often show considerable ability with artistic endeavors. More common in the United States than elsewhere, ADHD tends to run in families, and there is some suggestion of an association with a family history of alcoholism or depression.

Estimates of ADHD in the general population range from 3 to 12 percent, but it is much more prevalent in adolescents, where some estimates reach as high as one-third of the population. ADHD children are most often treated by giving them doses of stimulants, most commonly Ritalin and Dexedrine (or dextroamphetamine), which, ironically, help these children control their emotional and behavioral outbursts. The antimanic, anticonvulsant drug Tegretol has also been used effectively.

ADHD usually results in poor school performance, including a high dropout rate, bullying, stubbornness, mental disorder, and a lack of response to discipline; these conditions are highly correlated with delinquent behavior. A series of research studies now link ADHD to the onset and continuance of a delinquent career and increased risk for antisocial behavior and substance abuse in adulthood. ADHD children are more likely to be arrested, to be charged with a felony, and to have multiple arrests than non-ADHD youths. There is also evidence that ADHD youths who also exhibit early signs of MBD and conduct disorder (for example, fighting) are the most at risk for persistent antisocial behaviors continuing into adulthood. Of course many, if not most, children who are diagnosed ADHD do not engage in delinquent behavior, and new treatment techniques featuring behavior modification and drug therapies are constantly being developed to help children who have attention or hyperactivity problems.

Sources: Kimberly Barletto, "Who's at Risk: Delinquent Trajectories of Children with Attention and Conduct Problems," paper presented at the American Society of Criminology Meeting, San Diego, Calif., 1997; Harry Wexler, "Attention Deficit Disorder, Drugs and Crime: The Dangerous Mixture," paper presented at the American Society of Criminology Meeting, Boston, Mass., November 1995; Terrie Moffitt and Phil Silva, "Self-Reported Delinquency, Neuropsychological Deficit, and History of Attention Deficit Disorder," *Journal of Abnormal Child Psychology* 16:553–69 (1988); American Psychiatric Association, *Diagnostic and Statistical Manual of the Mental Disorders,* 4th ed. (Washington, DC: American Psychiatric Press, 1994), pp. 60-64.

ness, depression, and the desire for social acceptance. Thus, learning disabilities may indirectly lead to substance abuse by generating the types of behavior that typically lead adolescents to abuse drugs.

- A child with a learning disability is twice as likely to suffer Attention Deficit Disorder (ADD) as a member of the general population, and there is a high incidence of ADD among individuals who abuse alcohol and drugs. It is known that as many as half of those suffering ADD self-medicate with drugs and alcohol.

- Children who are exposed to alcohol, tobacco, and illicit drugs in the womb are at higher risk for various developmental disorders, including learning disabilities. A mother who uses drugs while pregnant may be a predictor that the child will grow up in a home with a parent who is a substance abuser. This will also increase the risk that the child will abuse drugs or alcohol himself. [111]

Despite this evidence, the LD–JD link has always been controversial. It is possible that the LD child may not be more susceptible to delinquent behavior than the non-LD child and that the link may be an artifact of bias in the way LD children are treated at school and/or by the police.[112] LD youths are more likely to be arrested and, if petitioned to juvenile court, they bring with them a record of school problems and low grades and a history of frustrating efforts to help them. In the Focus on Delinquency, "Attention Deficit Hyperactivity Disorder," a neurological condition associated with antisocial behavior is discussed in some detail.

AFTERMATH OF ABUSE: THE LONG-TERM PHYSICAL EFFECTS OF CHILD ABUSE

Can harsh words, brutal beatings, or sexual abuse by a parent cause brain deformities in a child and lead to significant long-term emotional problems? According to research conducted by Dr. Martin Teicher, of the McLean Hospital in Massachusetts, emotional trauma such as child abuse can actually cause adverse physical changes in the brain, and these deformities can lead to depression, anxiety, and other serious emotional conditions. Teicher's research focused primarily on serious abuse cases involving sexual and physical assault. He finds that four types of brain abnormalities are linked to child abuse and neglect.

Limbic Irritability

The limbic system is a network of brain cells sometimes known as the "emotional brain." It controls many of the most fundamental emotions and drives important for survival. The McLean researchers found evidence that abuse may cause disturbances in electrical impulses as limbic nerve cells communicate, resulting in seizures or significant abnormalities on an EEG, a diagnostic test that measures brain waves. The researchers studied adults who reported being physically and/or sexually abused as children. They found that patients who experienced abuse scored much higher, suggesting an underlying disturbance in the limbic system. Patients with a history of abuse were twice as likely as nonabused patients to have an abnormal EEG. All of the extra EEG abnormalities affected the left hemisphere of the brain, an area associated with self-destructive behavior and aggression.

Arrested Development of the Left Hemisphere

The brain is divided into two hemispheres, with the left controlling language and the right responsible for visual-spatial ability, perception, and expression of negative affect. In a number of separate analyses, the researchers examined the results of magnetic resonance imaging (MRI) scans to provide pictures of the brain at work, and studied the results of sophisticated EEG coherence tests, which provide information on brain structure as well as function. These studies indicated deficient development of the left brain hemisphere in abused patients, so that

the right hemisphere may be more active than in healthy individuals. The left hemisphere deficits seen in abused patients may contribute to the development of depression and increase the risk of memory impairments.

Deficient Integration between the Left and Right Hemispheres

The corpus callosum is a major information pathway connecting the two hemispheres of the brain. When they compared MRI brain scans from 51 abuse patients with those from healthy children they found that the corpus callosum was smaller. Neglect was associated with a 24–42 percent reduction in the size of various regions of the corpus callosum in boys, but sexual abuse had no effect. In girls, sexual abuse was associated with an 18–30 percent smaller size in the corpus callosum, but neglect had no effect. It is possible that a smaller corpus callosum leads to less integration of the brain hemispheres, which in turn can result in dramatic shifts in mood or personality.

Increased Vermal Activity

The cerebellar vermis is a part of the brain that is involved in emotion, attention, and the regulation of the limbic system. When the McLean team used sophisticated devices that provide information about blood flow to the brain during a resting state, they found that abused patients displayed higher vermal activity. It is possible that the cerebellar vermis helps to maintain emotional balance, and that the trauma of abuse may impair this ability.

The McLean team theorizes that the stress caused by child abuse and neglect may also trigger the release of some hormones and neurotransmitters while inhibiting others, in effect remolding the brain so that the individual is "wired" to respond to a hostile environment. Research has shown that animals exposed to stress and neglect early in life develop a brain that is wired to experience fear, anxiety, and stress, and the same process may be true of people.

Source: "McLean Researchers Document Brain Damage Linked to Child Abuse and Neglect." Information provided by newsletter of McLean's Hospital, Belmont, MA, December 14, 2000.

Arousal Theory It has long been suspected that adolescents may engage in crimes such as shoplifting and vandalism because they offer the thrill of "getting away with it."[113] Is it possible that thrill seekers have some form of abnormal brain functioning? Arousal theorists believe that some people's brains function differently in response to environmental stimuli. All of us seek to maintain an optimal level of arousal: too

Arousal theorists believe that, for a variety of genetic and environmental reasons, some people's brains function differently in response to environmental stimuli. All of us seek to maintain a preferred or optimal level of arousal. Too much stimulation may leave us anxious and stressed out; too little may make us bored and weary. Some kids may need the rush that comes from getting into scrapes and conflicts in order to feel relaxed and at ease. (© Frank Siteman/Stock, Boston)

much stimulation leaves us anxious, and too little makes us feel bored. However, there is variation in the way children's brains process sensory input. Some nearly always feel comfortable with little stimulation, whereas others require a high degree of environmental input to feel comfortable. The latter group become "sensation seekers," who seek out stimulating activities that may include aggressive behavior.[114] The factors that determine a person's level of arousal are not fully understood. Suspected sources include brain chemistry and brain structure. Another view is that adolescents with low heart rates are more likely to commit crimes because they seek out stimulation to increase their arousal to normal levels.[115]

Genetic Influences

It has been hypothesized that some youths inherit a genetic configuration that predisposes them to aggression.[116] In the same way that people inherit genes that control height and eye color, biosocial theorists believe antisocial behavior characteristics and mental disorders also may be passed down.[117] Early theories suggested that delinquency proneness ran in families. However, most families share a similar lifestyle as well as a similar gene pool, making it difficult to determine whether behavior is a function of heredity or the environment.

Interest in a genetic basis of crime was given new life in 1966 when Richard Speck killed eight Chicago nurses. It was reported that Speck possessed an extra male chromosome; instead of the normal 46XY chromosomal structure, his was 47XYY. Though numerous studies failed to find proof that males with an extra Y chromosome were disproportionately violent, interest brought about by the Speck case boosted research on genetic influences on delinquency (it was later revealed that Speck's genetic structure had been misidentified).[118]

Biosocial theorists have once again taken up the study of family transmission of delinquent traits. Some research shows that brothers and sisters seem to share antisocial lifestyles.[119] Siblings share the same environment, so it is not surprising that their behavior co-varies. To establish the influence of environment and genetics independently, criminologists have studied twins and adopted children.

To learn more about twin research, go to

University of Minnesota–Twin Cities Department of Psychology, Minnesota Twin Family Study, What's Special About Twins to Science?

http://www.psych.umn.edu/ psylabs/mtfs/special.htm

For an up-to-date list of Web links, go to www.wadsworth.com/ product/0534573053s.

Twin Studies One method of studying the genetic basis of delinquency is to compare twins to non-twin siblings. If crime is an inherited trait, identical twins should be quite similar in their behavior because they share a common genetic makeup. Because twins are usually brought up in the same household, however, any similarity in their delinquent behavior might be a function of environmental influences and not genetics. To guard against this, biosocial theorists have compared the behavior of identical, monozygotic (MZ) twins with fraternal, dizygotic (DZ) twins; the former have an identical genetic makeup, but the latter share only about 50 percent of their genes. Research has shown that MZ twins are significantly closer in characteristics such as intelligence than DZ twins.[120] Reviews of twin studies found that in almost all cases MZ twins have more similar antisocial behavior patterns than DZ twins.[121]

Although this seems to support a connection between genetic makeup and delinquency, it is also true that MZ twins are more likely to look alike and to share physical traits than DZ twins, and they are more likely to be treated similarly. Shared behavior patterns may therefore be a function of socialization and not heredity.

Against this interpretation is research evidence that identical twins reared apart are as similar in many traits as twins who live in the same household.[122] The Minnesota study of twins reared apart found that MZ twins who were separated at birth shared many similarities in behavior; in contrast, the DZ twins reared apart seldom produced similar behavior patterns.[123] Such findings support a genetic basis of behavior.

Adoption Studies Another way to determine whether delinquency is an inherited trait is to compare the behavior of adopted children with that of their biological parents. If the criminal behavior of children is more like that of their biological parents (whom they have never met) than that of their adoptive parents (who brought them up), it would indicate that the tendency toward delinquency is inherited.

Studies of this kind have generally supported the hypothesis that there is a link between genetics and behavior.[124] Adoptees share many of the behavioral and intellectual characteristics of their biological parents despite the conditions found in their adoptive homes. Genetic makeup is sufficient to counteract even extreme conditions such as malnutrition and abuse.[125] Some of the most influential research in this area has been conducted by Sarnoff Mednick. In one study, Mednick and Bernard Hutchings found that, although only 13 percent of the adoptive fathers of a sample of delinquent youths had criminal records, 31 percent of their biological fathers had criminal records.[126] Analysis of a control group's background indicated that about 11 percent of all fathers have criminal records. Hutchings and Mednick were forced to conclude that genetics played at least some role in creating delinquent tendencies.[127]

In addition to a direct link between heredity and delinquency, the literature also shows that behavior traits indirectly linked to delinquency may be inherited. Biological parents of adopted hyperactive children are more likely to show symptoms of hyperactivity than the adoptive parents.[128] Several studies have reported a higher incidence of psychological problems in parents of hyperactive children when compared to control groups. All hyperactive children do not become delinquent, but the link between this condition and delinquency has long been suspected.

Similarly, there is evidence (disputed) that intelligence is related to heredity and that low intelligence is a cause of impulsive acts that are more likely to result in arrest.[129] This connection can create the appearance of a relationship between heredity and delinquency (see later sections for more on IQ and delinquency). Connecting delinquency to heredity is controversial because it implies that delinquency (1) is present at birth, (2) is "transmitted" from one generation to the next, and (3) is immune to treatment (since genes cannot be altered). Recent evaluations find that, even though a relationship can be detected, the better-designed research efforts provide less support than earlier and weaker studies.[130] If there is a genetic basis of delinquency, it is likely that genetic factors contribute to certain individual differences that interact with specific social and environmental conditions to bring about antisocial behavior.[131]

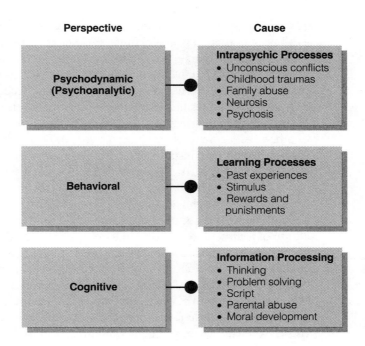

Figure 3.2
Psychological Perspectives of Delinquency

Perspective	Cause
Psychodynamic (Psychoanalytic)	**Intrapsychic Processes** • Unconscious conflicts • Childhood traumas • Family abuse • Neurosis • Psychosis
Behavioral	**Learning Processes** • Past experiences • Stimulus • Rewards and punishments
Cognitive	**Information Processing** • Thinking • Problem solving • Script • Parental abuse • Moral development

PSYCHOLOGICAL THEORIES OF DELINQUENCY

Some experts view the cause of delinquency as psychological.[132] After all, most behaviors labeled delinquent seem to be symptomatic of some psychological problem. Psychologists point out that many delinquent youths have poor home lives, destructive relationships with neighbors, friends, and teachers, and conflicts with authority figures. These relationships seem to indicate a disturbed personality. Furthermore, studies of incarcerated youths indicate that the youths' personalities are marked by antisocial characteristics. And since delinquent behavior occurs among youths in every racial, ethnic, and socioeconomic group, psychologists view it as a function of mental disturbance rather than social factors such as racism and poverty. Many delinquents do not manifest significant psychological problems, but enough do to give clinicians a powerful influence on delinquency theory.

Because psychology is a complex discipline, more than one psychological perspective on crime exists. Three prominent psychological perspectives on delinquency are psychodynamic theory, behavioral theory, and cognitive theory.[133] These are outlined in Figure 3.2.

Psychodynamic Theory

psychodynamic theory
Branch of psychology that holds that the human personality is controlled by unconscious mental processes developed early in childhood.

According to the **psychodynamic theory,** which originated with the Austrian physician Sigmund Freud (1856–1939), law violations are a product of an abnormal personality formed early in life.[134] The theory argues that the personality contains three major components. The *id* is the unrestrained, pleasure-seeking component with which each child is born. The *ego* develops through the reality of living in the world and helps restrain the id's need for immediate gratification. The *superego* develops through interactions with parents and others and represents the conscience and the moral rules that are shared by most adults.

All three segments of the personality operate simultaneously. The id dictates needs and desires, the superego counteracts the id by fostering feelings of morality, and the ego evaluates the reality of a position between these two extremes. If these components are balanced, the individual can lead a normal life. If one aspect of the personality becomes dominant at the expense of the others, however, the individual exhibits abnormal personality traits. Furthermore, the theory suggests that an imbalance in personality traits caused by a traumatic early childhood can result in long-term psychological difficulties. For example, if parents fail to help the child develop his or her superego adequately, the child's id may become dominant. The absence of a strong superego results in inability to distinguish clearly between right and wrong. Later, the youth may demand immediate gratification, lack sensitivity for the needs of others, act aggressively and impulsively, or demonstrate psychotic symptoms. Antisocial behavior may result from conflict or trauma occurring early in a child's development, and delinquent activity may become an outlet for these feelings.

Neuroses and Psychosis According to Freud's version of psychodynamic theory, people who experience anxiety and are afraid they are losing control are suffering from a form of *neurosis* and are referred to as *neurotics*. People who have lost control and are dominated by their id are known as *psychotics;* their behavior may be marked by hallucinations and inappropriate responses. Psychosis takes many forms, the most common being *schizophrenia,* a condition marked by illogical thought processes, distorted perceptions, and abnormal emotional expression. According to the classical psychoanalytic view, the most serious types of antisocial behavior might be motivated by psychosis, whereas neurotic feelings would be responsible for less serious delinquent acts and status offenses.[135] Contemporary psychologists no longer use the term *neuroses* to describe all forms of unconscious conflict. It is more common to refer to specific types of disorders, including *anxiety disorder, mood disorder, sleep disorder,* and so on.

The Psychodynamic Tradition and Delinquency A number of psychoanalysts have expanded on Freud's model. Erik Erikson speculated that many adolescents experience a life crisis in which they feel emotional, impulsive, and uncertain of their role and purpose.[136] He coined the phrase **identity crisis** to denote this period of inner turmoil. Erikson's approach might characterize the behavior of youthful drug abusers as an expression of confusion over their place in society, inability to direct their behavior toward useful outlets, and, perhaps, dependence on others to offer solutions to their problems.

Psychoanalysts view youth crime as a result of unresolved internal conflict. Some children, especially those who have been abused or mistreated, may experience unconscious feelings of fear and hatred. If these conflicts cannot be reconciled, regression occurs and the id becomes dominant. This regression accounts for a great number of mental diseases, and in many cases it may be related to criminal behavior.[137]

Another psychoanalytic view is that delinquents are unable to control their impulsive drives. Perhaps because they suffered unhappy experiences in childhood or had families who could not provide proper care, they have weak egos and are unable to cope with conventional society.[138] In its most extreme form, delinquency may be viewed as a form of psychosis that prevents delinquent youths from appreciating the feelings of victims or controlling their need for gratification. August Aichorn identified **latent delinquents** as youths whose troubled family lives lead them to seek immediate gratification without consideration of right and wrong or the feelings of others.[139] Could Dylan Klebold and Eric Harris been suffering from these symptoms when they went on their rampage at Columbine High?

Others view antisocial behavior as a consequence of inability to cope with feelings of oppression. In this instance, criminality actually produces positive psychic results: it helps youths feel independent; gives them the possibility of excitement and the chance to use their skills and imagination; provides the promise of gain; allows them to blame others (the police) for their predicament; and gives them a chance to rationalize their sense of failure ("If I hadn't gotten into trouble, I could have been a success").[140]

The psychodynamic view is supported by research that shows that a number of violent juvenile offenders suffer from some sort of personality disturbance. Violent

identity crisis Psychological state, identified by Erikson, in which youth face inner turmoil and uncertainty about life roles.

latent delinquents Youths whose troubled family life leads them to seek immediate gratification without consideration of right and wrong or the feelings of others.

youths have been clinically diagnosed as "overtly hostile," "explosive or volatile," "anxious," and "depressed."[141] As many as 75 percent of male adolescents accused of murder could be classified as having some mental illness.[142]

Family Life The psychodynamic approach places heavy emphasis on the family's role. Antisocial youths frequently come from families in which parents are unable to provide the controls that allow children to develop the personal tools to cope with the world.[143] Destructive behavior of a youth may actually be a call for help. In fact, some psychoanalysts view delinquent behaviors as motivated by an unconscious urge to be punished. These children, who feel unloved, assume the reason must be their own inadequacy; hence, they deserve punishment.

Behavioral Theory

behaviorism Branch of psychology concerned with the study of observable behavior rather than unconscious processes; focuses on particular stimuli and responses to them.

Not all psychologists agree that behavior is controlled by unconscious mental processes determined by relationships early in childhood. Behavioral psychologists argue that personality is learned throughout life during interaction with others. Based primarily on the work of the American psychologist John B. Watson (1878–1958), and popularized by Harvard professor B. F. Skinner (1904–1990), **behaviorism** concerns itself with measurable events rather than unobservable psychic phenomena.

Behaviorists suggest that individuals learn by observing how people react to their behavior. Behavior is triggered initially by a stimulus or change in the environment. If a particular behavior is reinforced by some positive reaction or event, that behavior will be continued and eventually learned. However, behaviors that are not reinforced or are punished will be extinguished. For example, if children are given a reward (dessert) for eating their entire dinner, eventually they will learn to eat successfully. Conversely, if children are punished for some misbehavior, they will associate disapproval with that act and avoid that behavior.

social learning theory The view that behavior is modeled through observation either directly through intimate contact with others or indirectly through media; interactions that are rewarded are copied, whereas those that are punished are avoided.

Social Learning Theory Some behaviorists hold that learning and social experiences, coupled with values and expectations, determine behavior. This is known as **social learning theory.** The most widely read social learning theorists are Albert Bandura, Walter Mischel, and Richard Walters.[144] They hold that children will model their behavior according to the reactions they receive from others; the behavior of adults, especially parents; and the behavior they view on television and in movies. (See Focus on Delinquency, "The Media and Delinquency.") If children observe aggression and see that it is approved or rewarded, they will likely react violently during a similar incident. Eventually, they will master the techniques of aggression and become more confident that their behavior will bring tangible rewards.[145] Social learning suggests that children who grow up in homes where violence is a way of life may learn to believe that such behavior is acceptable. Even if parents tell children not to be violent and punish them if they are, the children will model their behavior on the observed violence. Thus, children are more likely to heed what parents *do* than what they *say.* By middle childhood, some children have already acquired an association between their use of aggression against others and the physical punishment they receive at home. Often their aggressive responses are directed at other family members. The family may serve as a training ground for violence because the child perceives physical punishment as the norm during conflict situations.[146]

Adolescent aggression is a result of disrupted dependency relations with parents. This refers to the frustration a child feels when parents provide poor role models and hold back affection. Children who lack close ties to their parents may have little opportunity or desire to model themselves after them or to internalize their standards. In the absence of such internalized controls, the child's frustration is likely to be expressed in a socially unacceptable fashion such as aggression.[147]

THE MEDIA AND DELINQUENCY

One aspect of social learning theory that has received a great deal of attention is the belief that children will model their behavior after characters they observe on TV or see in movies. Many parents are concerned about the effects of their children's exposure to violence in the mass media. Often the violence is of a sexual nature, and some experts fear there is a link between sexual violence and viewing pornography.

Children are particularly susceptible to TV imagery. It is believed that many children consider television images to be real, especially if they are authoritatively presented by an adult (as in a commercial). Some children, especially those considered "emotionally disturbed," may be unable to distinguish between fantasy and reality when watching TV shows.[148] Children begin frequent TV viewing at 2.5 years of age and continue at a high level during the preschool and early school years. But what do they watch? Marketing research indicates that adolescents of ages 11 to 14 rent violent horror movies at a higher rate than any other age group; adolescents also use older peers and siblings or apathetic parents to gain access to R-rated films. More than 40 percent of U.S. households now have cable TV, which features violent films and shows. Even children's programming is saturated with violence. A well-publicized study by researchers at UCLA found that at least 10 network shows made heavy use of violence. Of the 161 television movies monitored, 23 raised concerns about their use of violence. Of the 118 theatrical films monitored, 50 raised concerns about their use of violence. Some television series may contain limited depictions of violence, each of which may be appropriate in its context. However, it was found that commercials for these programs emphasized only the violent scenes. Even some children's programs were found to feature "sinister combat." It is estimated that the average child views 8,000 TV murders before finishing elementary school.

TV and Violence

A number of methods have been used to measure the effect of TV viewing on violent behavior. One method is to expose groups of people to violent TV shows in a laboratory setting and compare them to control groups who viewed nonviolent programming; observations have also been made at playgrounds, athletic fields, and residences. Other experiments require individuals to answer attitude surveys after watching violent TV shows. Still another approach is to use aggregate measures of TV viewing; for example, the number of violent TV shows on the air during a given period is compared to crime rates during the same period.

Most evaluations of experimental data indicate that watching violence on TV is correlated with aggressive behaviors. Individuals who view violent TV shows are likely to commence aggressive behavior almost immediately. This is demonstrated by reports of copycat behavior after a particularly violent film or TV show is aired. For example, on November 27, 1995, thieves ignited flammable liquid in a New York City subway token booth, seriously injuring the clerk. Their behavior was virtually identical to a robbery scene in the film *Money Train,* which had been released a few days before.

Rethinking the Media-Violence Link

Though this evidence is persuasive, the relationship between TV viewing and violence is still uncertain. A number of critics say the evidence does not support the claim that TV viewing is related to antisocial behavior. Some assert that experimental results are short-lived. Children may have an immediate reaction to viewing violence on TV, but aggression is extinguished once the viewing ends. Experiments showing that children act aggressively after watching violent TV shows fail to link aggression to criminal behaviors such as assault.

Aggregate data are also inconclusive. Little evidence exists that areas that have high levels of violent TV viewing also have rates of violent crime that are above the norm.[149] Millions of children watch violence yet fail to become violent criminals. And even if a violent behavior–TV link could be established, it would be difficult to show that antisocial people develop aggressive traits merely from watching TV. Aggressive youths may simply enjoy watching TV shows that support their behavioral orientation, in the same way that science fiction fans flock to *Star Wars* and *Star Trek* films.

Sources: Edward Donnerstein and Daniel Linz, "The Question of Pornography," *Psychology Today* 20:56–59 (1986); Joyce Sprafkin, Kenneth Gadow, and Monique Dussault, "Reality Perceptions of Television: A Preliminary Comparison of Emotionally Disturbed and Nonhandicapped Children," *American Journal of Orthopsychiatry* 56:147–52 (1986); UCLA Center for Communication Policy, *Television Violence Monitoring Project* (Los Angeles: University of California Press, 1995); Associated Press, "Hollywood Is Blamed in Token Booth Attack," *Boston Globe,* 28 November 1995, p. 30; Wendy Wood, Frank Wong, and J. Gregory Chachere, "Effects of Media Violence on Viewers' Aggression in Unconstrained Social Interaction," *Psychological Bulletin* 109:371–83 (1991); Lynette Friedrich-Cofer and Aletha Huston, "Television Violence and Aggression: The Debate Continues," *Psychological Bulletin* 100:364–71 (1986).

Cognitive Theory

A third area of psychology that has received increasing recognition in recent years is **cognitive theory.** Psychologists with a cognitive perspective focus on mental

Some critics charge that viewing violent slasher films like "Scream" or "Scream II" causes kids to become violent and aggressive. However, millions of children watch media violence every day yet fail to become violent criminals. Does watching films such as the extremely violent "Scream" series produce antisocial behaviors? If so, why have crime rates been in decline? (Dimension Films/ Shooting Star)

cognitive theory The branch of psychology that studies the perception of reality and the mental processes required to understand the world we live in.

processes. The pioneers of this school were Wilhelm Wundt (1832–1920), Edward Titchener (1867–1927), and William James (1842–1920). This perspective contains several subgroups. Perhaps the most important of these for delinquency theory is the one that is concerned with how people morally represent and reason about the world.

Jean Piaget (1896–1980), founder of this approach, hypothesized that reasoning processes develop in an orderly fashion, beginning at birth and continuing until age 12 and older.[150] At first, during the *sensorimotor stage,* children respond to the environment in a simple manner, seeking interesting objects and developing their reflexes. By the fourth and final stage, the *formal operations stage,* they have developed into mature adults who can use logic and abstract thought.

Lawrence Kohlberg applied this concept to issues in delinquency.[151] He suggested that there are stages of moral development during which the basis for moral decisions changes. It is possible that serious offenders have a moral orientation that differs from that of law-abiding citizens. Kohlberg classified people according to the stage at which their moral development has ceased to grow. In his studies, the majority of delinquents were revealed as having a lack of respect for the law and a personality marked by self-interest; in contrast, nonoffenders viewed the law as something that benefits all of society and were willing to honor the rights of others.[152] Subsequent research has found that a significant number of nondelinquent youths displayed higher stages of moral reasoning than delinquents.[153]

Information Processing Cognitive theorists who study information processing try to explain antisocial behavior in terms of perception and analysis of data. When people make decisions, they engage in a sequence of thought processes. First they encode information so it can be interpreted. Then they search for a proper response and decide on the most appropriate action. Finally, they act on their decision.[154]

Adolescents who use information properly and can make reasoned decisions when facing emotion-laden events are best able to avoid antisocial behavior.[155] In contrast, violence-prone adolescents may be using information incorrectly when making decisions. They have difficulty making the "right" decision while under stress. One reason may be that they are relying on mental "scripts" learned in early childhood that tell them how to interpret events, what to expect, how they should react, and what the outcome of the interaction should be.[156] Hostile children may have learned improper scripts by observing how others react to events. Child-abuse victims may have had early exposure to violence, which increased their sensitivity to maltreatment. Violence becomes a stable behavior because the scripts that emphasize aggressive responses are repeatedly rehearsed as the child matures.

Violence-prone kids perceive people as more aggressive than they actually are, and they may feel threatened when there is no reason for alarm. As these children mature, they use fewer cues than most people to process information. Some use violence as a means of getting what they want; others react in a volatile fashion to the slightest provocation. When they attack victims, they may believe they are defending themselves, even though they are misreading the situation.[157] Adolescents who use violence as a coping technique are more likely to exhibit other problems such as drug abuse.[158] There is also evidence that delinquent boys who engage in theft are more likely than nondelinquent youths to exhibit cognitive deficits. For example, delinquent boys have a poor sense of time, leaving them incapable of dealing with social problems in an effective manner.[159]

Cognitive Treatment Treatment based on information processing acknowledges that people are more likely to respond aggressively to a provocation when thoughts stir feelings of anger. Cognitive therapists attempt to teach people to control aggressive impulses by experiencing provocations as problems demanding a solution rather than as insults requiring retaliation. Programs teach problem-solving skills that may include self-disclosure, listening, following instructions, and using self-control.[160] Areas for improvement include (1) coping and problem-solving skills; (2) relationships with peers, parents, and other adults; (3) conflict resolution and communication skills; (4) decision-making abilities; (5) pro-social behaviors, including cooperation with others and respecting others; and (6) awareness of feelings of others (empathy).[161]

Gerald Patterson and his colleagues at the Oregon Social Learning Center are important figures in the area of cognitive treatment. Their program seems to help parents deal with disruptive children. It stresses praising desirable behavior and punishing undesirable behavior (such as back talk) with loss of privileges and short-term isolation in the child's room.[162]

Personality and Delinquency

Personality can be defined as the stable patterns of behavior, including thoughts and emotions, that distinguish one person from another.[163] Personality reflects characteristic ways of adapting to life's demands. The way we behave is a function of how our personality enables us to interpret events and make appropriate choices.

Can Delinquency Be Linked to Personality? There has been much research on this subject and an equal amount of debate over the findings.[164] Sheldon and Eleanor Glueck identified a number of personality traits that characterize delinquents:[165]

self-assertiveness	extraversion
defiance	ambivalence
impulsiveness	feeling unappreciated
narcissism	distrust of authority
suspicion	poor personal skills
destructiveness	mental instability
sadism	hostility
lack of concern for others	resentment

Some teens may commit violent acts because they misread situations and use faulty information when making decisions. Here Hallie Gnatovich of Lexington, Mass., performs an educational play called "The Yellow Dress" during a teen dating violence workshop at Ashland High School in Ashland, Mass., June 1, 2000. She portrays a character battered to death by an abusive boyfriend. (AP/Wide World Photos)

This research is representative of the view that delinquents maintain a distinct personality whose characteristics increase the probability that they will be antisocial and that their actions will involve them with agents of social control ranging from teachers to police.

Extraversion and Neuroticism Other research has attempted to identify traits that would increase the chances for a delinquent career.[166] A common theme is that delinquents are impulsive individuals with short attention spans who frequently manifest conduct disorders, anxiety disorders, and depression.[167] Suspected traits include impulsivity, hostility, and aggressiveness.[168] These traits make them prone to problems ranging from psychopathology to drug abuse and violence.[169] Psychologist Hans Eysenck identified two traits that he associated with antisocial behavior: extraversion and neuroticism. He defines **extraverts** as impulsive individuals who lack the ability to examine their own motives. **Neuroticism** produces anxiety and emotional instability.[170] Youths who lack insight and are impulsive and emotionally unstable are likely to interpret events differently than youths who are able to make reasoned judgments. The former may act destructively, whereas the latter are able to reason that such behavior is self-defeating.

extravert A person who behaves impulsively and doesn't have the ability to examine motives and behavior.

neuroticism A personality trait marked by unfounded anxiety, tension, and emotional instability.

psychopathic personality, sociopathic personality A person lacking in warmth and affection, exhibiting inappropriate behavioral responses, and unable to learn from experience.

The Antisocial Personality It has also been suggested that delinquency may result from a syndrome interchangeably referred to as the antisocial, **psychopathic**, or **sociopathic personality**. Although no more than 3 percent of male offenders may be classified as an antisocial, it is possible that a large segment of persistent offenders share this trait.[171]

Antisocial youths exhibit low levels of guilt and anxiety and persistently violate the rights of others. Although they may exhibit charm and intelligence, these mask a disturbed personality that makes them incapable of forming enduring relationships. Frequently involved in such deviant behaviors as truancy, lying, and substance abuse, antisocial people lack the ability to empathize with others. From an early age, the antisocial person's home life was filled with frustration and quarreling. Consequently, throughout life the antisocial youth is unreliable, unstable, and demanding.

Youths diagnosed as being clinically antisocial are believed to be thrill seekers who engage in destructive behavior. Some become gang members and participate in violent sexual escapades to compensate for a fear of responsibility and an inability to maintain relationships.[172] Delinquents have been described as sensation seekers who desire an extraverted lifestyle, partying, drinking, and a variety of sexual partners.[173] Psychologists have attempted to treat antisocial youths by giving them adrenaline, which increases their arousal levels.

The Origins of an Antisocial Personality A number of factors contribute to the development of antisocial personalities. They include having an emotionally disturbed parent, parental rejection during childhood, and inconsistent discipline.[174] Another view, related to arousal theory, is that antisocial youths suffer from lower levels of arousal than the general population. Consequently, they may need greater-than-average stimulation to bring them up to comfortable levels.

Psychologist Linda Mealey suggests that there are two types of antisocial youth: **Primary sociopaths** have inherited traits that predispose them to antisocial behavior. **Secondary sociopaths** are constitutionally normal but are influenced by negative environmental factors such as poor parenting and social conflict.

The Delinquency-Personality Link Numerous attempts have been made to show that tests that measure personality can predict delinquent behavior. The most common of these is the Minnesota Multiphasic Personality Inventory (MMPI). The MMPI has subscales that measure many personality traits, including psychopathic deviation (Pd scale), schizophrenia (Sc), and hypomania (overactivity, Ma).[175] Early research found that scores on some of the MMPI subscales, especially the Pd scale, predicted delinquency.[176] But despite the time and energy put into using MMPI scales to predict delinquency (new versions have been developed over the years), the results are inconclusive.[177] Some delinquents manifest abnormal traits, but others score no differently than the general population. These conclusions must be interpreted with caution, however. Some recent research efforts have successfully classified offenders and predicted their behavioral traits on the basis of personality inventory scores.[178] Sufficient evidence exists of an association between some kinds of delinquency and personality disturbance to warrant further research on this issue.

Intelligence and Delinquency

Early criminologists thought that, if they could determine which individuals were less intelligent, they might be able to identify potential delinquents before they committed socially harmful acts.[179] Psychologists began to measure the correlation between IQ and crime by testing adjudicated juvenile delinquents. Delinquent juveniles were believed to be substandard in intelligence and thus inclined to commit more crimes than more intelligent persons. Thus, juvenile delinquents were used as a test group around which numerous theories about intelligence were built.

Nature Theory When IQ tests were administered to inmates of prisons and juvenile training schools early in the twentieth century, a large proportion of the inmates scored low on the tests. Henry Goddard found in 1920 that many institutionalized persons were "feeble-minded" and concluded that at least half of all juvenile delinquents were mental defectives.[180] In 1926, William Healy and Augusta Bronner tested a group of delinquents in Chicago and Boston and found that 37 percent were subnormal in intelligence.[181] They concluded that delinquents were 5 to 10 times more likely to be mentally deficient than nondelinquent boys. These and other early studies were embraced as proof that a correlation existed between innate low intelligence and deviant behavior. IQ tests were believed to measure genetic makeup, and many psychologists accepted the predisposition of substandard individuals toward delinquency. This view is referred to as the **nature theory** of intelligence.

Nurture Theory In the 1930s, more culturally sensitive explanations of behavior led to the **nurture theory.** Nurture theory argues that intelligence is not inherited and that low-IQ parents do not necessarily produce low-IQ children.[182] This view holds that intelligence must be viewed as partly biological but primarily sociological. Nurture theorists discredit the notion that people commit crimes because they have low IQs. Instead, they postulate that environmental stimulation from parents, schools, peer groups, and others create a child's IQ level and that low IQs result from an environment that also encourages delinquent behavior.[183] For example, if educational environments could be improved, the result might be both an elevation in IQ scores and a decrease in delinquency.[184]

Rethinking IQ and Delinquency

The relationship between IQ and delinquency is controversial because it implies that a condition is present at birth that accounts for delinquent behavior throughout the life cycle and that this condition is not easily changed. Research shows that measurements of intelligence taken in infancy are good predictors of later IQ.[185] By implication, if delinquency is not spread evenly through the social structure, neither is intelligence.

Some social scientists actively dispute that any association actually exists. As early as 1931, Edwin Sutherland evaluated IQ studies of criminals and delinquents and found evidence disputing the association between intelligence and criminality.[186] His findings did much to discredit the notion that a strong relationship exists between IQ and criminality, and for many years the IQ–delinquency link was ignored. Sutherland's research has been substantiated by a number of contemporary studies that find that IQ has a negligible influence on behavior.[187]

Those who still believe in an IQ–delinquency link refer to a study by Travis Hirschi and Michael Hindelang, who, after conducting a statistical analysis of IQ and delinquency data, concluded that "the weight of evidence is that IQ is more important than race and social class" for predicting delinquency.[188] They argued that a low IQ increases the likelihood of delinquent behavior through its effect on school performance. Youths with low IQs do poorly in school, and school failure is highly related to delinquency. Their conclusions have also been supported by a number of research efforts.[189]

Even those experts who believe that IQ influences delinquent behavior are split on the structure of the associations. Some believe IQ has an indirect influence on delinquency. For example, children with low IQs are more likely to engage in delinquent behavior because low IQ leads to school failure, and educational underachievement is associated with delinquency.[190] Even high-risk youths are less likely to become delinquents if they have relatively high IQs; low IQ increases the probability of a delinquent career.[191] The relationship between IQ and delinquency has been found to be consistent after controlling for class, race, and personality traits.[192]

Some experts believe IQ may have a direct influence on delinquency. The key linkage is the ability to manipulate abstract concepts. Low intelligence limits adolescents' ability to "foresee the consequences of their offending and to appreciate the feelings of victims."[193] Therefore, youths with limited intelligence are more likely to misinterpret events, take risks, and engage in harmful behavior.

Checkpoints

✔ According to psychodynamic theory, unconscious motivations developed early in childhood propel some people into destructive or illegal behavior.

✔ Behaviorists view aggression as a learning behavior.

✔ Some learning is direct and experiential while other types are observational, such as watching TV and movies. A link between media and violence has not been proven.

✔ Cognitive theory stresses knowing and perception. Some adolescents have a warped view of the world.

✔ There is evidence that kids with abnormal or antisocial personalities are delinquency-prone.

✔ While some experts find a link between intelligence and delinquency, others dispute any linkage between IQ level and law-violating behaviors.

CRITIQUING TRAIT THEORY VIEWS

Trait theories have been criticized on a number of grounds. One view is that the research methodologies they employ are invalid. Most research efforts use adjudicated or incarcerated offenders. It is difficult to determine whether findings represent the delinquent population or merely those most likely to be arrested. For example, some critics have described heredity studies as "poorly designed, ambiguously reported, and exceedingly inadequate in addressing the relevant issues."[194] Some critics also fear that trait-theory research can be socially and politically damaging. If an above-average number of indigent youths become delinquent offenders, can it be assumed that the less affluent are genetically inferior? This conclusion is unacceptable to many social scientists in light of what is known about race, gender, and class bias.

Defenders counter that biosocial/psychological theorists do not ignore environmental and social factors.[195] For example, some kids may have emotional and psychological problems that place them at a disadvantage, limit their chances of success, and heighten their feelings of anger and frustration. If their family is affluent, they will have the resources available to treat these problems; a less affluent family would lack the economic means and the institutional support needed to counteract these potentially destructive traits. Delinquency rate differences may then result from differential access to opportunities either to commit crime or to receive the treatment needed to correct developmental problems.

TRAIT THEORY AND DELINQUENCY PREVENTION

Trait-theory perspectives on delinquency suggest that prevention efforts should be directed at strengthening a youth's home life and relationships. If parents cannot supply proper nurturing, discipline, nutrition, and so on, the child cannot develop properly. Whether we believe that delinquency has a biosocial basis, a psychological basis, or a combination of both, it is evident that prevention efforts should be oriented to reach children early in their development.

County welfare agencies and private treatment centers offer counseling and other mental health services to families referred by schools, welfare agents, and court authorities. In some instances, intervention is focused on a particular family problem that has the potential for producing delinquent behavior, for example, alcohol and drug problems, child abuse, or sexual abuse. In other situations, intervention is oriented toward developing the self-image of parents and children or improving discipline in the family.

Some programs utilize treatment regimens based on specific theories (such as behavioral modification therapies). For example, the Decisions to Actions program in Kincheloe, Michigan is organized around cognitive-behavioral restructuring of children's personalities. Its main focus is changing attitudes and beliefs associated with improper feelings and behaviors. Youths are taught to identify poor decision making and to explore the thinking behind "bad" decisions. They also are taught

Trait theory suggests that prevention efforts should be directed at strengthening a youth's mental and physical well-being. If parents cannot supply proper nurturing, discipline, nutrition, and so on, the child cannot develop properly; consequently, the juvenile justice system is required to provide assistance. Here Lonnie Kelly climbs the rock wall at Piedmont Wilderness Institute in Clinton, S.C. Looking on are Duprie Owens, 17, Martez Rodgers, 16, and Eddie Outing (no hat), 15. At the institute the boys learn to trust their ability to overcome limits that they put on themselves. The young men in the program were at various state detention centers for nonviolent felonies before the Juvenile Justice Department assigned them to the institute. (AP/Wide World Photos)

secondary prevention, special prevention Psychological counseling, psychotropic medications, and other rehabilitation treatment programs designed to prevent repeat offenses.

relapse prevention techniques that enable them to better manage their emotions and behavior. The 10-week program includes an assessment, meetings between the youths and mentors, victim empathy sessions where convicted felons speak with the youths, and team-building exercises.[196]

In addition, individual approaches have been used to prevent adjudicated youths from engaging in further criminal activities. This is sometimes referred to as **secondary prevention,** or **special prevention.** Incarcerated and court-adjudicated youths are now almost universally given some form of mental and physical evaluation before they begin their correctional treatment. Such rehabilitation methods as psychological counseling and psychotropic medication (drugs such as Ritalin) are often prescribed. In some instances, rehabilitation programs are provided through drop-in centers that service youths who are able to remain in their homes; more intensive programs require residential care. The creation of such programs illustrates that agents of the juvenile justice system believe many delinquent youths and status offenders have psychological or physical problems and that their treatment can help reduce repeat criminal behavior. Faith in this approach suggests widespread agreement that delinquency can be traced to individual pathology.

The influence of psychological theory on delinquency prevention has been extensive, and programs based on biosocial theory have been dormant for some time. However, institutions are beginning to sponsor projects designed to study the influence of diet on crime and to determine whether regulating metabolism can affect behavior. Such efforts are relatively new and untested. Similarly, schools are making an effort to help youths with learning disabilities and other developmental problems. Delinquency prevention efforts based on biocriminological theory are still in their infancy.

Some questions remain about the effectiveness of individual treatment as a delinquency prevention technique. Little hard evidence exists that clinical treatment alone can prevent delinquency or rehabilitate delinquents. Critics still point to the failure of the Cambridge-Somerville Youth Study as evidence that clinical treatment has little value. In that effort, 325 high-risk youths were given intensive counseling, and their progress was compared with a control group that received no special attention. An evaluation of the project by Joan and William McCord found that the treated youths were more likely to become involved in law violation than the untreated controls.[197] By implication, the danger is that the efforts designed to help youths may actually stigmatize them, hindering their efforts to live conventional lives.

Critics argue that, the more we try to help youths, the more likely they will be to see themselves as different, or as troublemakers.[198] Such questions have led to prevention efforts designed to influence the social as well as the psychological world of youths (see Chapters 4 and 5).

Both choice and trait theories have been embraced by conservatives because they focus on personal characteristics and traits rather than on the social environment. Both theoretical positions agree that delinquency can be prevented by dealing with the youths who engage in crime, not by transforming the social conditions associated with youth crime. In contrast, more liberal delinquency experts view the environment as the main source of delinquency.

SUMMARY

Criminological theories that focus on the individual can be classified in two groups: choice theories and trait theories. Choice theory holds that people have free will to control their actions. Delinquency is a product of weighing the risks of crime against its benefits. If the risk is greater than the gain, people will choose not to commit crimes. One way of creating a greater risk is to make sure that the punishments associated with delinquency are severe, certain, and fast.

There are several subcategories of choice theory. Routine activities theory maintains that a pool of motivated offenders exists and that they will take advantage of suitable targets. Deterrence theory holds that if criminals are rational, an inverse relationship should exist between punishment and crime. This theory has been criticized on the grounds that it wrongfully assumes that criminals make a rational choice before committing crimes and does not take into account the social and psychological factors that may influence delinquency. Research has not indicated that deterrent measures actually reduce the delinquency rate.

Specific deterrence theory holds that the crime rate can be reduced if offenders are punished so severely that they never commit crimes again. However, there is little evidence that harsh punishments reduce the crime rate. Incapacitation theory maintains that, if deterrence does not work, the best course of action is to incarcerate offenders for long periods so they lack criminal opportunity. Research efforts have not provided clear proof that punishment will reduce crime rates.

Situational crime prevention strategies aim to reduce opportunities for crime to take place. By imposing obstacles that make it difficult to offend, such strategies strive to dissuade would-be offenders.

Choice theorists argue that delinquent behavior can be prevented if youths can be deterred from illegal acts. Consequently, they agree that the punishment for delinquency should be increased. One method is to transfer youths to the criminal courts or to grant the adult justice system jurisdiction over serious juvenile cases. Similarly, some experts advocate incapacitation for serious juvenile offenders—for example, long-term sentences for chronic delinquents.

Trait theories hold delinquents do not choose to commit crimes freely but are influenced by forces beyond their control. Two types of trait theory are: biological and psychological. One of the earliest branches of biological theory was formulated by Cesare Lombroso, who linked delinquency to inborn traits. Following his lead were theories based on genetic inheritance and body build. Although biological theory was in disrepute for many years, it has recently reemerged. Biochemical, neurological, and genetic factors have been linked to aggressiveness in youth. However, because biosocial theory has not been subjected to methodologically sound tests, the results remain problematic.

Psychological theories also fall into several categories. Some theorists rely on Freud's psychoanalytic theory and link delinquency to personality. Others use a behavioral perspective, which emphasizes behavior rather than unconscious processes. Social learning theorists hold that children imitate the behavior they observe live or on television. Children who are exposed to violence and see it rewarded may become violent as adults. Cognitive psychology is concerned with how people perceive the world. Criminality is viewed as a function of improper information processing or lack of moral development.

Psychological traits have been linked to delinquency. One area of study is the psychopath, a person who lacks concern for others. The relationship of IQ to delinquency has received new interest with the publication of studies purporting to show that delinquents have lower IQs than nondelinquents.

Many delinquency prevention efforts are based on psychological theory. Judges commonly order delinquent youths to receive counseling. Recently, some delinquent offenders have been given biochemical therapy.

KEY TERMS

choice theory
trait theory
free will
utilitarian
classical criminology
routine activities theory
predatory crimes
general deterrence
co-offending

specific deterrence
situational crime
  prevention
hot spot
crack down
criminal atavism
inheritance school
somatotype school
equipotentiality

biosocial theory
minimal brain dysfunction
  (MBD)
learning disability (LD)
psychodynamic theory
identity crisis
latent delinquents
behaviorism
social learning theory

cognitive theory
extravert
neuroticism
psychopathic personality
sociopathic personality,
  secondary prevention,
  special prevention

QUESTIONS FOR DISCUSSION

1. Are all delinquent acts psychologically abnormal? Can there be "normal" crimes?

2. How would you apply psychodynamic theory to delinquent acts such as shoplifting and breaking-and-entering a house?

3. Can delinquent behavior be deterred by the threat of punishment? If not, how can it be controlled?

4. Does watching violence on TV and in films encourage youths to be aggressive and antisocial?

5. Do advertisements for beer that feature attractive, scantily dressed young men and women encourage drinking and precocious sex? If not, why bother advertising? If suggestive advertising works for getting people to buy beer, then why shouldn't suggestive violence encourage kids to be violent?

6. Discuss the characteristics of psychopaths. Do you know anyone who fits the description?

VIEWPOINT

We now spend twice the money on video games than we do going to the movies. The core gaming audience is 8- to 14-year-old males. Eighty percent of the games produced are violent. Blood, decapitation, guns, knives, mutilation, and death are presented in color, sound, and ever-more realistic graphics. If imitation or modeling is a problem with television, as social learning research has shown, extrapolate this to the more immersible media, where visually, auditorily, and physically the audience becomes embedded in its context. Piaget has shown how learning/assimilation is enhanced with sensorimotor activity—using a joystick or mouse. These actions become habits and are further reinforced. As Jane Healy has said, "Habits of the mind become structures of the brain."

 Does playing with violent video games increase a child's chances of becoming violent? To find out, go to Michael Brody, "Playing with Death," *The Brown University Child and Adolescent Behavior Letter* 16:8 (2000), on InfoTrac®College Edition. Use *violence in the mass media* as a subject guide to learn more about the topic.

Chapter 4

Sociological Views of Delinquency

© Joel Gordon

ou have just been appointed as a presidential adviser on urban problems. The president informs you that he wants to initiate a demonstration project in a major city aimed at showing that government can do something to reduce poverty, crime, and drug abuse. The area he has chosen for development is a large inner-city neighborhood with more than 100,000 residents. The neighborhood suffers from disorganized community structure, poverty, and hopelessness. Predatory delinquent gangs run free and terrorize local merchants and citizens. The school system has failed to provide opportunities and education experiences sufficient to dampen enthusiasm for gang recruitment. Stores, homes, and public buildings are deteriorated and decayed. Commercial enterprise has fled the area, and civil servants are reluctant to enter the neighborhood. There is an uneasy truce among the various ethnic and racial groups that populate the area. Residents feel that little can be done to bring the neighborhood back to life.

You are faced with suggesting an urban redevelopment program that can revitalize the area and eventually bring down the crime rate. You can bring any element of the public and private sector to bear on this rather overwhelming problem—including the military! You can also ask private industry to help in the struggle, promising them tax breaks for their participation.

- Do you believe that living in such an area contributes to high delinquency rates? Or is poverty merely an excuse and delinquency a matter of personal choice?

- What programs do you feel could break the cycle of urban poverty?

- Would reducing the poverty rate produce a lowered delinquency rate?

- What role does the family play in creating delinquent behaviors?

Even though there may be some factors related to delinquent behavior at the individual level, the majority of delinquency researchers believe it would be a mistake to ignore social and environmental factors in trying to understand the cause of adolescent misbehavior.[1] Most delinquents are indigent and desperate, not calculating or evil. Most grew up in deteriorated parts of town and lack the social support and economic resources familiar to more affluent members of society. Understanding delinquent behavior, then, requires analyzing the influence of these destructive social forces on human behavior.

According to this view, explanations of delinquency as an individual-level phenomenon fail to account for these consistent social patterns in delinquency. If violence is related to biochemical or chromosome abnormality, then how can we explain ecological differences in delinquency rates? It is unlikely that all people with physical anomalies live in one section of town or in one area of the country. There has been a heated national debate over the effects of violent TV shows on adolescent aggression. Yet adolescents in cities and towns with widely disparate crime rates probably watch the same shows and movies, so how can crime-rate differences be explained? If violence has a biological or psychological origin, should it not be distributed more evenly throughout the social structure, as opposed to being concentrated in certain areas?

Delinquency experts who have a social or sociological orientation are concerned with social change and the dynamic aspects of human behavior. They study changing cultural norms and institutions and how they affect individual and group behavior. In our postmodern society, there has been a reduction in the influence of the family and an increased emphasis on individuality, independence, and isolation. Weakened family ties have been linked to crime and delinquency.[2] Political unrest and mistrust, economic stress, and family disintegration are social changes that have been found to precede sharp increases in crime rates. Conversely, stabilization of traditional social institutions typically precedes crime rate declines.[3]

Another important social change has been the rapid advance in technology and its influence on the social system. People who lack the requisite social and educational training have found that the road to success is almost impassable. Their lack of opportunity for upward mobility may make drug dealing and other crimes an attractive solution to socially deprived but economically enterprising people.[4]

The shape of intergroup and interpersonal relationships may also be a source of delinquent behavior. The dynamics of interactions between individuals and important social institutions—families, peers, schools, jobs, criminal justice agencies, and the like—is important for understanding the cause of delinquency.[5] The relationship of one social class or group to another or to the power structure that controls the nation's legal and economic system may also be closely related to delinquency. It seems logical that people on the lowest rung of the economic ladder will have the greatest incentive to commit crime: They may be either enraged by their lack of economic success or simply financially desperate and disillusioned. In either instance, crime, despite its inherent dangers, may appear an attractive alternative to a life of indigence.

Illegal behavior is itself an interaction, and it must be seen in the context of the interactions of all participants in a delinquent act. This includes the law violator, the victim, the law enforcers, the law makers, and social institutions.

In this chapter we will review the most prominent social theories of delinquency. They are divided into four groups: (1) *social structure theories* hold that delinquency is a function of a person's place in the economic structure; (2) *social process theories* view delinquency as a result of poor socialization or upbringing; (3) *social reaction* or *labeling theories* view delinquent careers as a function of stigma; and (4) *social conflict theories* consider delinquent behavior to be a result of economic deprivation caused by the inequities of the capitalist system of production.

SOCIAL STRUCTURE THEORIES

Social conditions have worsened in many blighted urban areas during the past decade, and a major effort is needed to revitalize those areas.[6] Recognition of this problem is not new. In 1966, sociologist Oscar Lewis coined the phrase **culture of poverty** to describe the crushing burden faced by the urban poor.[7] According to Lewis, the culture of poverty is marked by apathy, cynicism, helplessness, and mistrust of institutions such as police and government. Mistrust of authority prevents the impoverished from taking advantage of the few conventional opportunities available to them. The result is a permanent **underclass** whose members have little chance of upward mobility or improvement. This extreme level of economic and social hardship has been related to psychological adjustment: People who live in poverty are more likely to suffer low self-esteem, depression, and loneliness.[8]

Nowhere are urban problems more pressing than in the inner-city neighborhoods that experience constant population turnover as their more affluent residents move to stable communities or suburbs. As a city becomes *hollowed out*, with a deteriorated inner core surrounded by less devastated communities, delinquency rates spiral upward.[9] Those remaining are forced to live in communities with poorly organized social networks, alienated populations, and high crime.[10] Members of the urban underclass, typically minority group members, are referred to by sociologist William Julius Wilson as the **truly disadvantaged**.[11]

The impoverished are deprived of a standard of living enjoyed by most other citizens, and their children suffer from much more than financial hardship. They attend poor schools, live in substandard housing, and lack good health care. More than half of families in poverty are fatherless and husbandless; many are supported

culture of poverty View that lower-class people form a separate culture with their own values and norms, which are sometimes in conflict with conventional society.

underclass Group of urban poor whose members have little chance of upward mobility or improvement.

To read the transcript of an interview with Dr. William Julius Wilson, go to

http://www.pbs.org/newshour/forum/november96/wilson2.html

For an up-to-date list of Web links, go to www.wadsworth.com/product/0534573053s.

truly disadvantaged According to William Julius Wilson, those people who are left out of the economic mainstream and reduced to living in the most deteriorated inner-city areas.

The Northwestern University/University of Chicago Joint

Center for Poverty Research examines what it means to be poor and live in America:

http://www.jcpr.org/

For an up-to-date list of Web links, go to www.wadsworth.com/product/0534573053s.

social structure theories Explain delinquency using socioeconomic conditions and cultural values.

entirely by government aid. Instead of increasing government aid to the needy, however, in the past decade a concerted effort has been made to limit eligibility for public assistance.

Neighborhoods that provide few employment opportunities are the most vulnerable to predatory crime. Unemployment destabilizes households, and unstable families are more likely to produce children who choose aggression as a means of dealing with limited opportunity.[12] Lack of employment opportunity also limits the authority of parents, reducing their ability to influence children. Because adults cannot serve as role models, the local culture is dominated by gangs whose members are both feared and respected. Predatory crime increases to levels that cannot easily be controlled by police. Hundreds of studies have documented the association between family poverty and children's health, achievement, and behavior.[13] Children in poor families suffer many problems, including inadequate education. They are less likely to achieve in school and to complete their schooling than children with more affluent parents.[14]

Poor children are also more likely to suffer from health problems and to receive inadequate health care. Unfortunately, the number of children covered by health insurance has decreased and will continue to do so for the foreseeable future.[15] Lack of coverage almost guarantees that these children will suffer health problems that will impede their long-term development. Children who live in extreme poverty or who remain poor for extended periods exhibit the worst outcomes. Findings suggest that poverty during early childhood may have a greater detrimental impact on children than poverty during the adolescent or teen years.[16] Poor children are much more likely than the wealthy to suffer social ills ranging from low birth weight to never earning a college degree. The cycle of poverty can lead to a variety of adverse outcomes, including life- and health-endangering conditions (Figure 4.1). Providing adequate care to children under these circumstances can be an immense undertaking.

This view of delinquency is *structural* and *cultural*. It holds that delinquency is a consequence of the inequalities built into the social structure. Even youths who receive the loving support of family members are at risk of delinquency if they suffer from social disadvantage.[17]

The **social structure theories** tie delinquency rates to socioeconomic conditions and cultural values. Areas that experience high levels of poverty and social disorganization will also have high delinquency rates. Residents of such areas view prevailing social values skeptically; they are frustrated by their inability to be part of the American Dream. Structural theories are less concerned with why an individual youth becomes delinquent than with why certain areas experience high delinquency rates. There are actually a variety of structural views and we look at them next.

Social Disorganization

social disorganization Posits that delinquency is a product of the social forces existing in inner-city, low-income areas.

transitional neighborhood Area undergoing a shift in population and structure, usually from middle-class residential to lower-class mixed use.

cultural transmission Cultural norms and values that are passed down from one generation to the next.

The concept of **social disorganization** was first recognized early in the twentieth century by sociologists Clifford Shaw and Henry McKay. These Chicago-based scholars found that delinquency rates were high in what they called **transitional neighborhoods**—areas that had changed from affluence to decay. Here, factories and commercial establishments were interspersed with private residences. In such environments, teenage gangs developed as a means of survival, defense, and friendship. Gang leaders recruited younger members, passing on delinquent traditions and ensuring survival of the gang from one generation to the next, a process referred to as **cultural transmission**. While mapping delinquency rates in Chicago, Shaw and McKay noted that distinct ecological areas had developed that could be visualized as a series of concentric zones, each with a stable delinquency rate (Figure 4.2).[18] The areas of heaviest delinquency concentration appeared to be the poverty-stricken, transitional, inner-city zones. The zones farthest from the city's center were the least prone to delinquency. Analysis of these data indicated a stable pattern of delinquent activity in the ecological zones over a 65-year period.[19]

Source: Arloc Sherman, *Poverty Matters* (Washington, D.C.: Children's Defense Fund, 1997), p. 23.

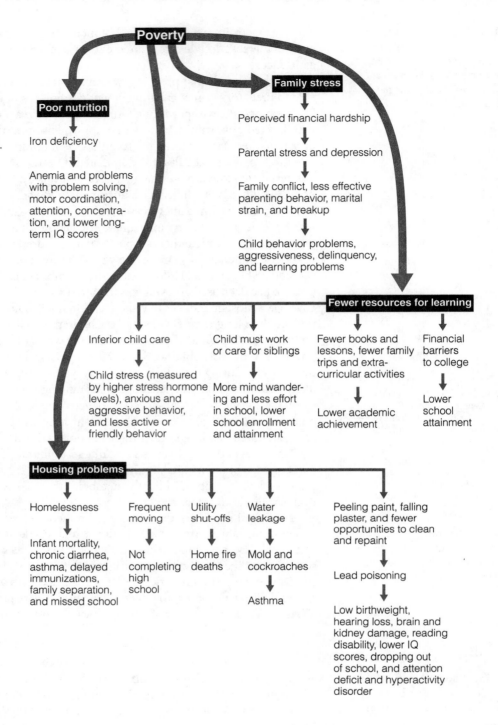

social control Ability of social institutions to influence human behavior; the justice system is the primary agency of formal social control.

According to the social disorganization view, a healthy, organized community has the ability to regulate itself so that common goals (such as living in a crime-free area) can be achieved; this is referred to as **social control**.[20] Those neighborhoods that become *disorganized* are incapable of social control because they are wracked by deterioration and economic failure; they are most at risk for crime.[21] In areas where social control remains high, children are less likely to become involved with deviant peers and engage in problem behaviors.[22] Social institutions like schools and churches cannot work effectively in the climate of alienation and mistrust that characterizes disorganized areas. The absence of political power limits access to external funding and protection; without outside resources and financial aid, the neighborhood cannot get back on its feet.[23] Children who reside in these disorganized neigh-

Figure 4.2
Shaw and McKay's Concentric Zones Map of Chicago

Source: Clifford R. Shaw et al., *Delinquency Areas* (Chicago: University of Chicago Press, 1929), p. 99. Reprinted with permission. Copyright 1929 by the University of Chicago. All rights reserved.

Note: Arabic numerals represent the rate of male delinquency.

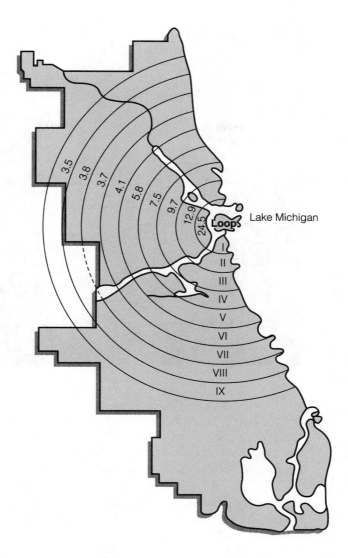

borhoods find that involvement with conventional social institutions, such as schools and afternoon programs, is either absent or blocked, which puts them at risk for recruitment into gangs.[24] These problems are stubborn and difficult to overcome. Even when an attempt is made to revitalize a disorganized neighborhood by creating institutional support programs such as community centers and better schools, the effort may be countered by the ongoing drain of deep-rooted economic and social deprivation.[25] Even in relatively crime-free rural areas, social disorganization caused by such factors as residential instability, family disruption, and changing ethnic composition is associated with high rates of delinquent behavior and youth violence.[26]

Relative Deprivation

relative deprivation Condition that exists when people of wealth and poverty live in close proximity to one another; the relatively deprived are apt to have feelings of anger and hostility, which may produce criminal behavior.

According to the concept of **relative deprivation,** a sense of injustice occurs in communities in which the poor and the wealthy live close to one another. According to the relative deprivation concept, kids who feel they are less well off than others begin to form negative self-feelings and hostility, which motivates them to engage in delinquent and antisocial behaviors.[27]

Adolescents in poor, inner-city areas experience frustration because their neighborhoods are contiguous with some of the most affluent areas in the United States. Deprived teenagers can observe wealth close up, but they have no hope of achieving riches themselves. This condition is felt most acutely by racial and ethnic minorities in low-status areas.[28] Minority group members living in these areas also suffer race-based

Delinquency is a product of the social forces existing in inner-city areas. Within these areas, the unsupervised behavior of juvenile gangs and groups overwhelms the ability of social institutions, such as the family and the school, to maintain order. The result is stable pockets of crime and deviance. Environmental and ecological factors such as substandard housing, low income, high unemployment levels, deteriorated housing, substandard schools, broken families, urban density, and overcrowding are predictive of a high incidence of gang delinquency. These young men are suspected members of a New York City Chinese gang. (© Patrick Zachman/Magnum Photos)

gentrified The process of transforming a lower-class area into a middle-class enclave through property rehabilitation.

inequality, such as income inequality and institutional racism.[29] Psychologists warn that, under these circumstances, young males will envy people they perceive as doing much better socially and financially than themselves. If they fail to take aggressive tactics, they are going to lose out in social competition.[30]

Community Change Urban areas have a life cycle during which they undergo significant change: from affluent to impoverished, from impoverished to rehabilitated or **gentrified,** from residential to commercial, from stable to transient. As communities go through these changes, levels of delinquency also change.[31] Neighborhood deterioration precedes increasing rates of delinquency.[32]

Communities on the down-swing are likely to experience increases in the number of single-parent families, changes in housing from owner- to renter-occupied units, a loss of semiskilled and unskilled jobs, and a growth in numbers of discouraged, unemployed workers who are no longer seeking jobs.[33] These communities also tend to develop mixed-use areas in which commercial and residential properties stand side by side. Areas in which retail establishments are abandoned have the highest crime rates.[34]

The changing racial makeup of communities may also influence delinquency rates. Areas undergoing change in their racial composition will experience increases in delinquency rates.[35] This may reflect fear of racial conflict. Adults may encourage teens to terrorize the newcomers; the result is conflict, violence, and disorder.

Community Fear Disorganized neighborhoods suffer social incivility—trash and litter, graffiti, burned-out buildings, drunks, vagabonds, loiterers, prostitutes, noise, congestion, angry words. This evidence of incivility convinces residents that their neighborhood is dangerous; not surprisingly, when crime rates are high in these areas, fear levels undergo a dramatic increase.[36] Perceptions of crime produce *neighborhood fear.*[37]

Fear of crime is much higher in disorganized neighborhoods than in affluent suburbs.[38] Members of the underclass fear crime and have little confidence that the government can do anything to counter the drug dealers and gangs that terrorize the

Areas with weak social controls may become deteriorated, increasing the level of community fear. Unsupervised youth groups flourish in these areas. (© Mark Richards/Sipa Press)

neighborhood.[39] People tell others of their experiences of being victimized, spreading the word that the neighborhood is dangerous.

Residents of areas with short life expectancies may alter their behavior. Why plan for the future when there is a significant likelihood that they may never see it? In such areas young boys and girls may adjust psychologically by taking risks and discounting the future. Teenage birth rates soar, and so do violence rates.[40]

When fear grips a neighborhood, people do not want to leave their homes at night, so they withdraw from community life. Fear has been related to distress, inactivity, and decline in health.[41] High levels of fear are also related to deteriorating business conditions, increased population mobility, and the domination of street life by violent gangs.

Weak Social Controls Most neighborhood residents share the goal of living in a crime-free area. Some communities rely on institutions such as families and schools to regulate behavior. When these efforts are blunted, delinquency rates increase and neighborhood cohesiveness is weakened, setting the stage for deterioration.

Neighborhoods maintain a variety of agencies of social control. Some operate on the personal level and involve peers, families, and relatives. These sources exert informal control over behavior by either awarding or withholding approval and respect. Informal control mechanisms include criticism, ridicule, ostracism, and physical punishment.[42] Communities also use local institutions to control delinquency; these include business associations, schools, churches, and voluntary organizations.[43]

Disorganized neighborhoods cannot mount an effective social control effort. Because the population is transient, interpersonal relationships tend to be superficial and cannot help reduce deviant behavior. Social institutions cannot work effectively

Strain occurs because legitimate avenues for success may be all but closed to some young people, such as these teen runaways living under a highway in California. Because legal and socially acceptable means for obtaining success do not exist, individuals may either use deviant methods to achieve their goals or reject socially accepted goals and substitute deviant ones. (© Dorothy Littell/Stock, Boston)

in a climate of mistrust. In such neighborhoods, the absence of political power brokers limits access to external funding and police protection.

Social control is also weakened because unsupervised peer groups, which flourish in disorganized areas, disrupt the influence of neighborhood control agents.[44] Children in disorganized areas report that they are unable to become involved with conventional social institutions and are therefore vulnerable to aggression and delinquency.[45]

Rage, Distrust, and Hopelessness Kids in disorganized areas are socialized in a world where adults maintain a siege mentality, sometimes believing there are government plots to undermine the neighborhood ("the AIDS virus was created to kill us off"; "the government brings drugs into the neighborhood to keep people under control").[46] Young people growing up in these areas become angry, convinced that no one cares about their plight. There is free-floating anger, which causes adolescents to strike out at the merest hint of provocation.[47]

Children living in these conditions become "crusted over"; they do not let people get close to them. Their peer relations are exploitive, and they develop a sense of hopelessness. Parents and teachers seem to focus on their failures rather than on their achievements, leaving them vulnerable to the lure of delinquent groups.[48]

Anomie/Strain

anomie Normlessness produced by rapidly shifting moral values; according to Merton, anomie occurs when personal goals cannot be achieved using available means.

According to Robert Merton, one of America's preeminent sociologists, although most people share common values and goals, the means for legitimate economic and social success are stratified by socioeconomic class. Upper-class kids have ready access to good education and prestigious jobs; kids in the lower-class rarely have such opportunities. Without acceptable means for obtaining success, individuals feel social and psychological **strain;** Merton called this condition **anomie.** Consequently, these youths may either (1) use deviant methods to achieve their goals (for example, stealing money), or (2) reject socially accepted goals and substitute deviant ones (for

Figure 4.3
Elements of General Strain Theory

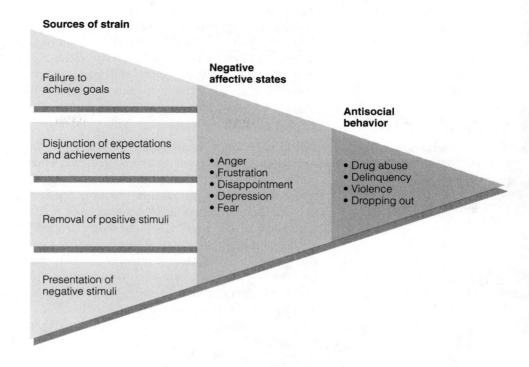

Sources of strain

- Failure to achieve goals
- Disjunction of expectations and achievements
- Removal of positive stimuli
- Presentation of negative stimuli

Negative affective states

- Anger
- Frustration
- Disappointment
- Depression
- Fear

Antisocial behavior

- Drug abuse
- Delinquency
- Violence
- Dropping out

example, becoming drug users or alcoholics). Feelings of anomie or strain are not typically found in middle- and upper-class communities, where education and prestigious occupations are readily obtainable. In lower-class areas, however, strain occurs because legitimate avenues for success are closed. Considering the economic stratification of U.S. society, anomie predicts that crime will prevail in lower-class culture, which it does.[49]

Sociologist Robert Agnew has expanded on Merton's views in his **general strain theory.** He argues that there are actually three sources of strain (Figure 4.3):[50]

1. *Strain caused by failure to achieve positively valued goals.* This type of strain will occur when youths aspire to wealth and fame but assume that such goals are impossible to achieve. Also falling within this category is the strain that occurs when individuals compare themselves to peers who seem to be doing a lot better, or when youths believe they are not being treated fairly by a parent or teacher. Such perceptions may result in reactions ranging from running away from the source of the problem to lowering the benefits of others through physical attacks or vandalism of their property. For example, the student who believes he is being "picked on" unfairly by a teacher slashes the tires on the teacher's car for revenge.

2. *Strain as the removal of positively valued stimuli.* Strain may occur because of the loss of a positively valued stimulus.[51] For example, the loss of a girl- or boyfriend can produce strain, as can the death of a loved one, moving to a new neighborhood, or the divorce or separation of parents. Loss of positive stimuli may lead to delinquency as the adolescent tries to prevent the loss, retrieve what has been lost, obtain substitutes, or seek revenge against those responsible for the loss.

3. *Strain as the presentation of negative stimuli.* Strain may also be caused by negative stimuli. Included in this category are such pain-inducing social interactions as child abuse, criminal victimization, school failure, and stressful events ranging from verbal threats to air pollution. For example, children who are abused at home may take their rage out on younger children at school or become involved in violent delinquency.[52]

According to Agnew, adolescents engage in delinquency as a result of **negative affective states,** the anger, frustration, fear, and other adverse emotions that derive

strain theory Links delinquency to the strain of being locked out of the cultural and economic mainstream, which creates the anger and frustration that lead to delinquent acts.

negative affective states Anger, depression, disappointment, fear, and other adverse emotions that derive from strain.

from strain. The greater the intensity and frequency of strain experiences, the greater their impact and the more likely they are to cause delinquency. Research supports many of Agnew's claims: kids who report feelings of stress and anger are more likely to interact with delinquent peers and engage in criminal behaviors;[53] people who fail to meet success goals are more likely to engage in illegal activities.[54]

Cultural Deviance

cultural deviance theory Links delinquent acts to the formation of independent subcultures with a unique set of values that clash with the mainstream culture.

culture conflict When the values of a subculture clash with those of the dominant culture.

Cultural deviance theory holds that delinquency is a result of youths' desire to conform to lower-class neighborhood cultural values that conflict with those of the greater society. Lower-class values include being tough, never showing fear, living for today, and disrespecting authority. In a socially disorganized neighborhood, conventional values such as honesty, obedience, and hard work make little sense to youths whose role models may include the neighborhood gun runner, drug dealer, or pimp. Those adolescents who share lower-class values and admire criminals, drug dealers, and pimps, find it difficult to impress authority figures such as teachers or employers. They experience a form of **culture conflict** and are rendered incapable of achieving success in a legitimate fashion; as a result, they join together in gangs and engage in behavior that is malicious and negativistic.[55]

Both legitimate and illegitimate opportunities are closed to youths in the most disorganized inner-city areas.[56] Consequently, they may join violent gangs to defend their turf, displaying their bravery and fighting prowess.[57] Instead of aspiring to be "preppies" or "yuppies," they want to be considered tough and street-smart.

Youths living in disorganized areas consider themselves part of an urban underclass whose members must use their wits to survive or they will succumb to poverty, alcoholism, and drug addiction.[58] Exploitation of women abounds in a culture wracked by limited opportunity. Sexual conquest is one of the few areas open to lower-class males for achieving self-respect. The absence of male authority figures contributes to the fear that marriage will limit freedom. Peers heap scorn on anyone who allows himself to get "trapped" by a female, fueling the number of single-parent households. Youths who are committed to the norms of this deviant subculture are also more likely to disparage agents of conventional society such as police and teachers.[59] By joining gangs and committing crimes, lower-class youths are rejecting the culture that has already rejected them; they may be failures in conventional society, but they are the kings and queens of the neighborhood.

Checkpoints

✔ The social structure view is that place in the socioeconomic structure influences the chances of becoming a delinquent.

✔ Poor kids are more likely to commit crimes because they are unable to achieve monetary or social success in any other way.

✔ Kids who live in socially disorganized areas commit crime because the forces of social control have broken down.

✔ Strain occurs when kids experience anger over their inability to achieve legitimate social and economic success.

✔ The best-known strain theory is Robert Merton's theory of anomie, which describes what happens when people have inadequate means to satisfy their goals.

✔ Robert Agnew found that strain has multiple sources.

✔ Cultural deviance theories hold that a unique value system develops in lower-class areas. Lower-class kids approve of behaviors such as being tough and having street smarts.

SOCIAL PROCESS, SOCIALIZATION AND DELINQUENCY

Not all sociologists believe that merely living in an impoverished, deteriorated, lower-class area is determinant of a delinquent career. Instead they argue that the root cause of delinquency may be traced to learning delinquent attitudes from peers, becoming detached from school, or experiencing conflict in the home. Although social position is

Learning theories such as differential association stress that human behavior is learned through group process and social interaction. They suggest that in order to begin a delinquent career, youthful law violators must first learn the attitudes, morals, skills, behaviors, and techniques necessary to both commit crimes and then to cope with the emotional turmoil that is the inevitable consequence of their behavior. (© Richard Hutchings/Photo Edit)

socialization Process of human development and enculturation that is influenced by key social processes and institutions.

important, **socialization** is considered to be the key determinant of behavior. If the socialization process is incomplete or negatively focused, it can produce an adolescent with a poor self-image who is alienated from conventional social institutions.

Socialization is the process of guiding people into acceptable behavior patterns through information, approval, rewards, and punishments. It involves learning the techniques needed to function in society. Socialization is a developmental process that is influenced by family and peers, neighbors, teachers, and other authority figures.

Early socialization experiences have a lifelong influence on self-image, values, and behavior. Even children living in the most deteriorated inner-city environments will not get involved in delinquency if their socialization experiences are positive.[60] After all, most inner-city youths do not commit serious crimes, and relatively few of those who do become career criminals.[61] More than 14 million youths live in poverty, but the majority do not become chronic offenders. Only those who experience improper socialization are at risk for crime.

Research consistently shows a relationship between the elements of socialization and delinquency. The primary influence is the family. When parenting is inadequate, a child's maturational processes will be interrupted and damaged. Although much debate still occurs over which elements of the parent-child relationship are most critical, there is little question that family relationships have a significant influence on behavior.[62] One view is that youths socialized in families wracked by conflict and abuse are at risk for delinquency. For example, there is now evidence that children who grow up in homes where parents use severe discipline, yet lack warmth and involvement in their lives, are prone to antisocial behavior.[63]

The literature linking delinquency to poor school performance and inadequate educational facilities is extensive. Youths who feel that teachers do not care, who consider themselves failures, and who drop out of school are more likely to become involved in a delinquent way of life than adolescents who are educationally successful.[64]

Figure 4.4
Learning Theory of Delinquency

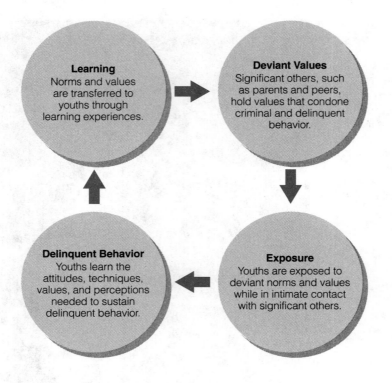

Learning
Norms and values are transferred to youths through learning experiences.

Deviant Values
Significant others, such as parents and peers, hold values that condone criminal and delinquent behavior.

Delinquent Behavior
Youths learn the attitudes, techniques, values, and perceptions needed to sustain delinquent behavior.

Exposure
Youths are exposed to deviant norms and values while in intimate contact with significant others.

learning theory Posits that delinquency is learned through close relationships with others; asserts that children are born "good" and learn to be "bad" from others.

control theory Posits that delinquency results from a weakened commitment to the major social institutions (family, peers, and school); lack of such commitment allows youths to exercise antisocial behavioral choices.

Learning Theories

differential association theory Asserts that criminal behavior is learned primarily within interpersonal groups and that youths will become delinquent if definitions they have learned favorable to violating the law exceed definitions favorable to obeying the law within that group.

Still another suspected element of deviant socialization is peer group relations. Youths who become involved with peers who engage in antisocial behavior may learn the attitudes that support delinquency and soon find themselves cut off from conventional associates and institutions.[65] Chronic offenders surround themselves with peers who share their antisocial activities, and these relationships seem to be stable over time. People who maintain close relations with antisocial peers will sustain their own criminal behavior into their adulthood. When peer influence diminishes, so does delinquent activity.[66]

Sociologists believe that the socialization process impacts delinquency in two ways. The first, **learning theory,** holds that delinquency is learned through close relationships with others. Both the techniques of crime and the attitudes necessary to support delinquency are learned. Learning theories assume that children are born "good" and then learn to be "bad."

The second, **control theory,** views delinquency as a result of a weakened commitment to family, peers, and school. Because their bonds to these institutions of informal social control are severed, some adolescents feel free to exercise antisocial behavior. Unlike learning theories, control theories assume that people are born "bad" and then must be taught to control themselves through the efforts of parents and teachers.

Learning theories hold that children living in even the most deteriorated areas can resist inducements to crime if they have learned proper values and behaviors. Delinquency, by contrast, develops by learning the values and behaviors associated with criminal activity (Figure 4.4). Kids can learn deviant values from their parents, relatives, or peers. Social learning can involve the techniques of crime (how to hot-wire a car) as well as the psychological aspects (how to deal with guilt). The former are needed to commit crimes, whereas the latter are required to cope with the emotional turmoil that follows.

The best-known learning theory is Edwin Sutherland's **differential association theory,** which he first articulated in 1939 in *Principles of Criminology*.[67] Sutherland believed that, as children are socialized, they are exposed to and learn pro-social and

Control theory holds that people who have a weakened bond to society are prone to violate the law. Kids who are attached to friends and family, involved in pro-social activities, and committed to their future are less likely to commit crimes than those who are unattached and noncommitted. Here, teens perform a comedy skit as a benefit for the Foundation for the Junior Blind in Los Angeles. According to control theory, their activities will insulate them from delinquent behaviors. (© Gregg Mancuso/Stock, Boston)

drift Idea that youths move in and out of delinquency and that their lifestyles can embrace both conventional and deviant values.

neutralization techniques A set of attitudes or beliefs that allow would-be delinquents to negate any moral apprehension they may have about committing crime so that they may freely engage in antisocial behavior without regret.

antisocial attitudes and behavior. Simply put, if the pro-delinquency definitions they have learned outweigh the anti-delinquency definitions, they will be vulnerable to choosing criminal behaviors over conventional ones.

Another prominent learning approach, identified with David Matza and Gresham Sykes, suggests that delinquents hold values similar to those of law-abiding citizens but that they learn techniques that enable them to neutralize those values and drift back and forth between legitimate and delinquent behavior.[68] **Drift** is the process by which an individual moves from one behavioral extreme to another, behaving sometimes in an unconventional manner and at other times with constraint.

Sykes and Matza suggest that juveniles develop a distinct set of justifications for their behavior when it violates accepted social rules and norms. These **neutralization techniques** allow youths to drift away from the rules of the normative society and participate in delinquent behaviors. While most adolescents accept the rules of society, they learn these techniques to release themselves temporarily from moral constraints. The most prominent techniques of neutralization are described in Table 4.1.[69]

Learning theory then portrays the delinquent as someone who, during the socialization process, has been consistently exposed to people who teach that "crime pays" and the techniques for becoming a successful criminal. Conversely, a child living in the most highly disorganized neighborhood will be able to avoid the temptations of the streets if they are socialized in a warm, supportive family and have law-abiding peers.

Control Theories

social bond Ties a person to the institutions and processes of society; elements of the bond include attachment, commitment, involvement, and belief.

Control theories suggest that the cause of delinquency lies in the strength of the relationships a child forms with conventional individuals and groups. Those who are socialized to have close relationships with their parents, friends, and teachers will develop a positive self-image and the ability to resist the lure of deviant behaviors. They develop a strong "commitment to conformity" that enables them to resist pressures to violate the law. If these bonds to society become fractured or broken, youths will feel free to violate the law; if caught, they have nothing to lose (Figure 4.5).

The most prominent control theory is the one developed by sociologist Travis Hirschi. In his classic book *Causes of Delinquency*, Hirschi linked delinquent behavior to the **social bond** an individual maintains with society. When that bond weakens, the constraints society places on its members are lifted, and the person is free to violate the law. The youthful law violator, then, is someone who lacks a real commitment to social norms. The major elements of Hirschi's argument are (1) all people have the

TABLE 4.1 Sykes and Matza's Techniques of Neutralization

Denial of responsibility   Delinquents sometimes claim that their unlawful acts were simply not their fault, that they were due to forces beyond their control or were an accident.

Denial of injury   By denying the wrongfulness of an act, delinquents are able to rationalize their illegal behavior. For example, stealing is viewed as "borrowing," vandalism is considered mischief that got out of hand. Society often agrees with delinquents, labeling their illegal behavior "pranks" and thereby reaffirming that delinquency can be socially acceptable.

Denial of victim   Delinquents sometimes rationalize their behavior by maintaining that the victim of crime "had it coming." For example, a school is vandalized because a student believes he was treated unfairly.

Condemnation of the condemners   Delinquents view the world as a corrupt place with a dog-eat-dog moral code. Police and judges are on the take, teachers show favoritism, and parents take out their frustrations on their children, so it is ironic and unfair for these authorities to turn around and condemn youthful misconduct. By shifting the blame to others, delinquents are able to repress the feeling that their own acts are wrong.

Appeal to higher loyalties   Delinquents argue that they are caught in the dilemma of being loyal to their own peer group while at the same time attempting to abide by the rules of the larger society. The needs of the group take precedence over the rules of society because the demands of the former are immediate and localized.

Sources: Gresham Sykes and David Matza, "Techniques of Neutralization: A Theory of Delinquency," *American Sociological Review* 22:664–70 (1957); and David Matza, *Delinquency and Drift* (New York: Wiley, 1964).

potential to commit crimes—for example, under-age drinking—because they are pleasurable; (2) people are kept in check by their social bonds or attachments to society; and (3) weakened social bonds free people to engage in antisocial but personally desirable behaviors. Hirschi argues that the social bond a person maintains with society is divided into four main elements (Figure 4.5):

- **Attachment** to parents, peers, and schools
- **Commitment** to the pursuit of conventional activities such as getting an education and saving for the future
- **Involvement** in conventional activities such as school, sports and religion
- **Belief** in values such as sensitivity to the rights of others and respect for the legal code

Hirschi suggests that the elements of the social bond may be interrelated. For example, boys or girls who are attached to their parents and friends are also more likely to be committed to future goals. Youths who are unattached may lack commitment to conventional goals and are more likely to be involved in unconventional activities. Hirschi's vision of delinquency causation is one of the most influential of recent times; more than 70 attempts have been made to corroborate his findings.[70] There has been significant empirical support for Hirschi's work. For example, research shows that positive attachments help control delinquency.[71] Kids who fail at school and are detached from the educational experience are at risk of criminality; those who do well and are committed to school are less likely to engage in delinquent acts.[72]

While many research efforts support Hirschi's ideas, there are also some important questions still being raised about his views. For example, Hirschi argues that commit-

Figure 4.5
Elements of the Social Bond

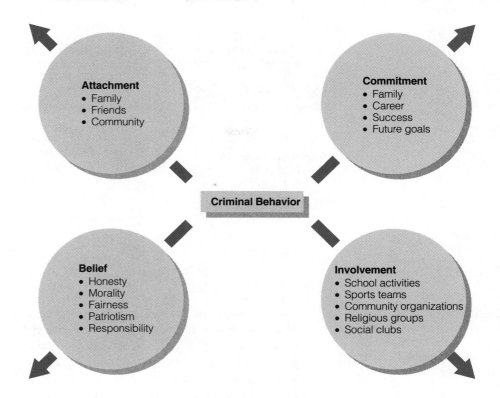

ment to future success, such as an exciting career, reduces delinquent involvement. Research indicates that kids who are committed to success but actually fail to achieve it may be crime-prone.[73] Perhaps their failures produce feelings of strain that counterbalance the control of commitment. Questions have also been raised about the social relations of delinquents. Hirschi portrays them as "lone wolves," detached from family and friends. A number of research efforts show that delinquents do maintain close peer group ties.[74] Their friendship patterns seem close to those of conventional youths.[75] In fact, there is some evidence that drug abusers maintain even more intimate relations with peers than do nonabusers.[76] Attachment to deviant peers seems to motivate the decision to commit crime; deviant friends facilitate delinquent acts.[77] While the issue of peer relations is troublesome, Hirschi's vision of control has remained one of the most influential models of delinquency for the past 25 years.

LABELING AND STIGMA

stigmatized People who have been negatively labeled because of their participation, or alleged participation, in deviant or outlawed behaviors.

Another group of sociologists believes that the way *society* reacts to individuals and the way *individuals* react to society determines behavior. Social reactions determine which behaviors are considered criminal or conventional; they also determine individual behavior and can contribute to the formation of delinquent careers. Being **stigmatized,** or labeled, by agents of social control, including official institutions such as the police and the courts, and unofficial institutions, such as parents and neighbors, is what sustains delinquent careers.[78]

The Labeling Process

According to this view, known as **labeling theory,** youths may violate the law for a variety of reasons, including poor family relationships, peer pressure, psychological abnormality, and pro-delinquent learning experiences. Regardless of the cause, if individuals' delinquent behaviors are detected, the offenders will be given a negative label that can follow them throughout life. These labels include "troublemaker," "juvenile delinquent," "mentally ill," "junkie," and many more.

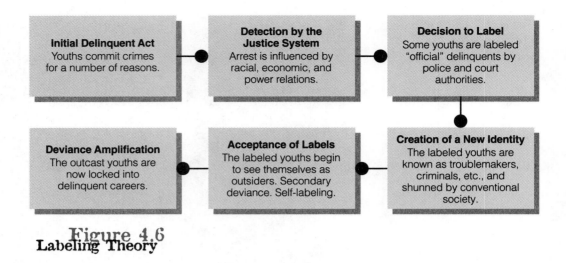

Figure 4.6
Labeling Theory

Initial Delinquent Act	Detection by the Justice System	Decision to Label
Youths commit crimes for a number of reasons.	Arrest is influenced by racial, economic, and power relations.	Some youths are labeled "official" delinquents by police and court authorities.

Deviance Amplification	Acceptance of Labels	Creation of a New Identity
The outcast youths are now locked into delinquent careers.	The labeled youths begin to see themselves as outsiders. Secondary deviance. Self-labeling.	The labeled youths are known as troublemakers, criminals, etc., and shunned by conventional society.

labeling theory Posits that society creates deviance through a system of social control agencies that designate (or label) certain individuals as delinquent, thereby stigmatizing youths and encouraging them to accept this negative personal identity.

The way labels are applied is likely to have important consequences for the delinquent. The degree to which youngsters are perceived as deviants may affect their treatment at home and at school. Parents may consider them a detrimental influence on younger brothers and sisters. Neighbors may tell their children to avoid the "troublemaker." Teachers may place them in classes reserved for students with behavior problems, minimizing their chances of obtaining higher education. The delinquency label may also affect the attitudes of society in general, and youthful offenders are subjected to sanctions ranging from mild reprimands to incarceration.

Beyond these results, and depending on the visibility of the label and the manner in which it is applied, youths will have an increasing commitment to delinquent careers. As the negative feedback of law-enforcement agencies, teachers, and other figures strengthens their commitment, delinquents may come to see themselves as "screwups." Thus, through a process of identification and sanctioning, re-identification, and increased sanctioning, young offenders are transformed. They are no longer children in trouble; they are "delinquents," and they accept that label as a personal identity—a process called **self-labeling** (Figure 4.6).[79]

self-labeling The process in which a person who has been negatively labeled accepts the label as a personal role or identity.

The Effect of Labeling

We often form opinions of others based on first impressions.[80] If interactions involve perceptions of deviance, individuals may be assigned informal labels that both harm their social relationships and damage their self-image—"loser," "slut." Kids who are suspected of harboring such behavior problems are scrutinized by those with whom they interact; people search for signs of deviance, or simply shun them.[81]

When kids who have been rejected by society violate the criminal law, they may be given official labels, applied in "ceremonies"—for example, during trials or expulsion hearings in schools—that are designed to redefine the deviant's identity.[82] The effect of this process is a *durable negative label and an accompanying loss of status*. The labeled deviant becomes a social outcast who is prevented from enjoying higher education, well-paying jobs, and other societal benefits. Because this label is "official," few question the accuracy of the assessment. People who may have been merely suspicious now feel justified in their assessments: "I always knew he was a bad kid."

A good example of the labeling ceremony occurs in juvenile courts. Here offenders find (perhaps for the first time) that authority figures consider them incorrigible outcasts who must be separated from the right-thinking members of society. To reach that decision, the judge relies on the testimony of witnesses—parents, teachers, police officers, social workers, and psychologists—who may testify that the offender is unfit to be part of conventional society.[83] As the label *juvenile delinquent* is conferred on offenders, their identities may be transformed from kids who have done something bad to "bad kids."[84]

Labeling theorists believe that negative labels create a self-fulfilling prophecy. If children continually receive negative feedback from parents, teachers, judges, and others whose opinions they take to heart, they will eventually interpret this rejection as accurate and self-defining. In contrast, children who constantly receive positive feedback, such as these champion athletes, will define themselves as successful and behave accordingly. (© McLaughlin/The Image Works)

self-fulfilling prophecy Deviant behavior patterns that are a response to an earlier labeling experience; youths act out these social roles even if they were falsely bestowed.

The Self-Fulfilling Prophecy The labeling process helps create a **self-fulfilling prophecy.**[85] If children continually receive negative feedback from parents, teachers, and others whose opinion they take to heart, they will interpret this rejection as accurate. Their behavior will begin to conform to the negative expectations; they will become the person others perceive them to be ("Teachers already think I'm stupid, so why should I bother to study"). The self-fulfilling prophecy leads to a damaged self-image and an increase in antisocial behaviors.[86]

Self-Rejection Labeling helps create a deviant identity. Those exposed to negative sanctions experience both self-rejection and lowered self-image. Self-rejecting attitudes result in both a weakened commitment to conventional values and the acquisition of motives to deviate from social norms.[87] This transformation is amplified by the bonds social outcasts form with peers.[88] Labeled delinquents will seek out others who are similarly stigmatized.[89] Associating with deviant peers helps reinforce conventional society's negative evaluations: "We were right all along about him, look who his friends are!"

Delinquent peers may help labeled youths "reject their rejectors." Teachers are "stupid"; cops are "dishonest"; parents "just don't understand."[90] Group identity enables outcast youths to show contempt for the sources of the labels and to distance themselves. These actions help solidify both the grip of deviant peers and the impact of the labels.[91]

The Juvenile Justice Process and Labeling

dramatization of evil The process of social typing that transforms an offender's identity from a doer of evil to an evil person.

The justice system has long been accused of bestowing destructive labels on children who are suspected of being delinquents. Frank Tannenbaum first suggested that social typing, which he called **dramatization of evil,** transforms the offender's identity from a doer of evil to an "evil person."[92] Delinquents, the argument goes, are the products of the juvenile justice assembly line.[93] Although youths enter as children in trouble, they emerge as bearers of criminal histories, which are likely to re-involve them in criminal activity. Authority figures anticipate that these troublemakers will continue their life of crime.[94] Labeled delinquents are assumed to engage in a full range of violence, theft, and drug abuse. Although they have not necessarily demonstrated these characteristics, they become perennial suspects.[95] The system designed to reduce delinquency may help produce young criminals.

Degradation Ceremonies According to the social reaction perspective, the actions of the juvenile justice system turn the self-perception of a youthful suspect into that of a delinquent.[96] Harold Garfinkel addressed the reason this occurs when he described what he called a **degradation ceremony,** where the public identity of an offender is transformed in a solemn ritual during which the targeted person is thrust outside the social mainstream.[97] This process may be seen in juvenile court when a youngster goes before the court, is scolded by a judge, has charges read, and is officially labeled a delinquent; this process contains all the conditions for "successful degradation." Recognizing the role stigma plays in developing a delinquent career has prompted some juvenile justice agencies to create programs designed to limit delinquent labels.

Evaluating Labeling Theory Enthusiasm for the labeling approach diminished when its validity was heavily criticized. Some critics argued that the crime-controlling effects of punishment more than made up for the crime-producing effects of stigma. In *Beyond Delinquency,* Charles Murray and Louis Cox found that youths assigned to a program designed to reduce labels were more likely later to commit delinquent acts than a comparison group who were placed in a more punitive state training school. The implication was that the threat of punishment was deterrent and that the crime-producing influence of labels was minimal.[98]

While these criticisms were damaging, other experts suggest that the labeling perspective can offer important insights:

1. It identifies the role played by social control agents in the process of delinquency causation; delinquent behavior cannot be fully understood if the agencies empowered to control it are ignored.

2. It recognizes that delinquency is not a pathological behavior; it focuses on the social interactions that shape behavior.

3. It distinguishes between delinquent acts and delinquent careers and shows that they must be treated differently.[99]

Labeling theory may help explain why some youths continue down the path of antisocial behaviors (they are labeled), whereas most are able to desist from crime (they are stigma-free).

degradation ceremony
Going to court, being scolded by a judge, or being found delinquent after a trial are examples of public ceremonies that can transform youthful offenders by degrading their self-image.

✔Checkpoints

✔ Some experts believe that delinquency is a function of socialization.

✔ People in all walks of life have the potential to become delinquents if they maintain destructive social relationships with families, schools, peers, and neighbors.

✔ Social learning theory stresses that kids *learn* both how to commit crimes and the attitudes needed to support the behavior.

✔ People learn criminal behaviors much as they learn conventional behavior.

✔ Social control theory analyzes the failure of society to control antisocial tendencies.

✔ All people have the potential to become delinquents, but their bonds to conventional society prevent them from violating the law.

✔ Labeling theory maintains that negative labels produce delinquent careers.

✔ Labels create expectations that the labeled person will act in a certain way; labeled people are always watched and suspected.

SOCIAL CONFLICT VIEW

social conflict theory Asserts that society is in a state of constant internal conflict, and focuses on the role of social and governmental institutions as mechanisms for social control.

ccording to the **social conflict theory**, society is in a constant state of internal conflict, and different groups strive to impose their will on others. Those with money and power succeed in shaping the law to meet their needs and to maintain their interests. Those adolescents whose behavior cannot conform to the needs of the power elite are defined as delinquents and criminals.

According to this view, those in power use the justice system to maintain their status while keeping others subservient: men use their economic power to subjugate women; members of the majority want to stave off the economic advancement of minorities; capitalists want to reduce the power of workers to ensure they are willing to accept low wages. Conflict theory thus centers around a view of society in which an elite class uses the law as a means of meeting threats to its status. The ruling class is a self-interested collective whose primary interest is self-gain.[100]

Law and Justice

The conflict view of delinquency is rooted in the political philosophy of Karl Marx. To learn more about his viewpoints, go to

http://www.anu.edu.au/polsci/marx/marx.html

For an up-to-date list of Web links, go to www.wadsworth.com/product/0534573053s.

Social conflict theorists view the law and the justice system as vehicles for controlling the have-not members of society; legal institutions help the powerful and rich to impose their standards of good behavior on the entire society. The law protects the property and physical safety of the haves from attack by the have-nots, and helps control the behavior of those who might otherwise threaten the status quo.[101] The ruling elite draws the lower-middle class into this pattern of control, leading it to believe it has a stake in maintaining the status quo.[102] According to social conflict theory, the poor may or may not commit more crimes than the rich, but they certainly are arrested more often. Police may act more forcefully in areas where class conflict creates the perception that extreme forms of social control are needed to maintain order.[103] It is not surprising to conflict theorists that complaints of police brutality are highest in minority neighborhoods, especially those that experience relative deprivaton. (African American residents earn significantly less money than the majority and therefore have less political and social power.[104]) Police misbehavior, which is routine in minority neighborhoods, would never be tolerated in affluent white areas. Consequently, a deep-rooted hostility is generated among members of the lower class toward a social order which they may neither shape nor share.[105]

The Conflict Concept of Delinquency

Conflict theorists view delinquency as a normal response to the conditions created by capitalism.[106] In fact, the creation of a legal category, *delinquency,* is a function of the class consciousness that occurred around the turn of the century.[107] In *The Child Savers,* Anthony Platt documented the creation of the delinquency concept and the role played by wealthy child savers in forming the philosophy of the juvenile court. Platt believed the child-saving movement's real goal was to maintain order and control while preserving the existing class system.[108] He and others have concluded that the child savers were powerful citizens who aimed to control the behavior of disenfranchised youths.[109]

Conflict theorists still view delinquent behavior as a function of the capitalist system's inherent inequity. They argue that capitalism accelerates the trend toward replacing human labor with machines so that youths are removed from the labor force.[110] From early childhood, the values of capitalism are reinforced. Social control agencies such as schools prepare youths for placement in the capitalist system by presenting them with behavior models that will help them conform to later job expectations. For example, rewards for good schoolwork correspond to the rewards a manager uses with employees. In fact, most schools are set up to reward youths who

According to conflict theory, the alienation of individuals from one another, the competitive struggle, and the absence of human feeling, all qualities of capitalism, contribute to middle-class delinquency. Because capitalism is dehumanizing, it is not surprising that even middle-class youths turn to violence, drugs, gambling, and illicit sex to find escape. Here Jayson Vreeland reads a statement in Sussex County Superior Court, Feb. 25, 2000 in Newton, N.J., before being sentenced to life plus 42 years for his role in the April 19, 1997 shooting deaths of two pizza deliverymen. (AP/Wide World Photos)

show promise in self-discipline and motivation and are therefore judged likely to perform well in the capitalist system. Youths who are judged inferior as potential job prospects become known as *losers* and *punks* and wind up in delinquent roles.[111]

Class and Delinquency The capitalist system affects youths differently at each level of the class structure. In the lowest classes youths form gangs, which can be found in the most desolated ghetto areas. These gangs serve as a means of survival in a system that offers no reasonable alternative. Lower-class youths who live in more stable areas are on the fringe of criminal activity because the economic system excludes them from meaningful opportunity.

Conflict theory also acknowledges middle-class delinquency. The alienation of individuals from one another, the competitive struggle, and the absence of human feeling, all qualities of capitalism, contribute to middle-class delinquency. Because capitalism is dehumanizing, it is not surprising that even middle-class youths turn to drugs, gambling, and illicit sex to find escape.

Controlling Delinquents Conflict theorists suggest that, rather than inhibiting delinquent behavior, the justice system may help to sustain such behavior. They claim that the capitalist state fails to control delinquents because it is in the state's interest to maintain a large number of outcast deviant youths. These youths can be employed as marginal workers, willing to work for minimum wage in jobs no one else wants. Thus, labeling by the justice system fits within the capitalist managers' need to maintain an underclass of cheap labor.

Social Structure Theory and Delinquency Prevention

Each of the various branches of social theory has had an impact on delinquency prevention activities and programs. The following sections describe a few of these efforts.

The decade of the 1960s was the heyday of delinquency prevention programs based on social structure theory. The approach seemed compatible with the policies of the Kennedy (New Frontier) and Johnson (Great Society/War on Poverty) administrations. Delinquency prevention programs received copious federal funding. The most ambitious of these was the New York City–based Mobilization for Youth (MOBY). Funded by more than $50 million, MOBY attempted an integrated approach to community development. Based on Cloward and Ohlin's concept of providing opportunities for legitimate success, MOBY created employment opportunities in the community, coordinated social services, and sponsored social action groups such as tenants' committees, legal action services, and voter registration. But MOBY died for lack of funding amid questions about its utility and use of funds. The most prominent contemporary manifestation of a program based on social structure theory is Operation Weed and Seed, the federal multi-level action plan for revitalizing communities.[112] The concept of this program is that no single approach can reduce crime rates and that social service and law enforcement agencies must cooperate to be effective. Therefore there are four basic elements in this plan: law enforcement; community policing; prevention, intervention, and treatment; and neighborhood restoration. The last element, neighborhood restoration, is the one most closely attached to the social structure theory because it is designed to revitalize distressed neighborhoods and improve the quality of life in the target communities. The neighborhood restoration element focuses on economic development activities, such as economic opportunities for residents, improved housing conditions, enhanced social services, and improved public services in the target area. Programs are being developed that will improve living conditions; enhance home security; allow for low-cost physical improvements; develop long-term efforts to renovate and maintain housing; and provide educational, economic, social, recreational, and other vital opportunities. A key feature is the fostering of self-worth and individual responsibility among community members.

Socialization and Delinquency Prevention

Social process theories suggest that delinquency can be prevented by strengthening the socialization process. One approach has been helping social institutions improve their outreach. Educational programs have been improved by expanding preschool programs, developing curricula relevant to students' lives, and stressing teacher development. Counseling and remedial services have been aimed at troubled youth.

Prevention programs have also been aimed at strengthening families in crisis. Because attachment to parents is a cornerstone of all social process theories, developing good family relations is an essential element of delinquency prevention. Programs have been developed that encourage families to help children develop the positive self-image necessary to resist the forces promoting delinquency.[113]

Prevention programs have also focused on providing services for youngsters who have been identified as delinquents or predelinquents. Such services usually include counseling, job placement, legal assistance, and more. Their aim is to reach out to troubled youths and provide them with the skills necessary to function in their environment before they get in trouble with the law. For example, New York City's Beacon Community Center Program has, since 1991, provided city youths with a variety of interrelated services. The program gives youths the tools to help them avoid crime and solve problems. Among the array of services and programs provided are mentoring, tutoring, employment training, and recreational activities. Many of these services are aimed at strengthening protective factors (such as bonding with role

Some delinquency prevention programs attempt to help kids become properly socialized. Redlands Police officer Stephen Crane, 24, jumps on one leg in Redlands, Calif., as he participates in potato sack jumping race with children during a neighborhood "Rec-On-Wheels," a community program of the police's Recreation Bureau. The weekly play dates are the latest addition to Redlands' Risked Focus Policing Program, which uses statistics compiled from school, hospital, and police records to target areas where residents, particularly children, have the highest exposure to drugs, gang violence, poverty, domestic instability, and other factors long believed to play a role in criminal behavior. (AP/Wide World Photos)

www

To read more about
the Beacon Community Program, go to
http://www.ncjrs.org/txtfiles/ beacons.txt

For an up-to-date list of Web links, go to www.wadsworth.com/ product/0534573053s.

models and developing healthy peer groups).[114] Each of the 76 Beacons are managed by community-based organizations (CBOs) working collaboratively with the community school boards, principals, and community advisory boards comprised of parents, teachers, church leaders, youth, and private and city service providers.

In addition to these local efforts, the federal government has sponsored several delinquency-prevention efforts using the principles of social process theory. These include vocational training programs, such as the Comprehensive Employment Training Act, as well as educational enrichment programs, such as Head Start for preschoolers. (See Policy and Practice on the next page.)

Labeling and Delinquency Prevention

www

To learn more about
Head Start, go to the Web site at
http://www2.acf.dhhs.gov/ programs/hsb/index.htm?/

For an up-to-date list of Web links, go to www.wadsworth.com/ product/0534573053s.

deinstitutionalization Removing juveniles from adult jails and placing them in community-based programs to avoid the stigma attached to these facilities.

As the dangers of labeling became known, a massive effort was made to limit the interface of youths with the juvenile justice system. One approach was to divert youths from official processing at the time of their initial contact with police. The usual practice is to have police refer children to treatment facilities rather than to the juvenile court. In a similar vein, children who were petitioned to juvenile court might be eligible for alternative programs rather than traditional juvenile justice processing. For example, restitution allows children to pay back the victims of their crimes for the damage (or inconvenience) they have caused instead of receiving an official delinquency label.

If a youth was found delinquent, efforts were made to reduce stigma by using alternative programs such as boot camp or intensive probation monitoring. Alternative community-based sanctions substituted for state training schools, a policy known as **deinstitutionalization**. Whenever possible, anything producing stigma was to be avoided, a philosophy referred to as *nonintervention*.

The federal government was a prime mover in the effort to divert children from the justice system. The Office of Juvenile Justice and Delinquency Prevention sponsored numerous diversion and restitution programs. In addition, it made one of its priorities the removal of juveniles from adult jails and the discontinuance of housing

HEAD START

ead Start is probably the best-known effort to help lower-class youths achieve proper socialization and, in so doing, reduce their potential for future criminality. Head Start programs were instituted in the 1960s as part of President Johnson's War on Poverty. In the beginning, Head Start was a 2-month summer program for children who were about to enter a school that was aimed at embracing the "whole child." In embracing the whole child, the school offered comprehensive programming that helped improve physical health, enhance mental processes, and improve social and emotional development, self-image, and inter-personal relationships. Preschoolers were provided with an enriched educational environment to develop their learning and cognitive skills. They were given the opportunity to use pegs and pegboards, puzzles, toy animals, dolls, letters and numbers, and other materials that middle-class children take for granted. These opportunities provided the children a leg up in the educational process.

Today, with annual funding approaching $5 billion, the Head Start program is administered by the Head Start Bureau, the Administration on Children, Youth, and Families (ACFY), the Administration for Children and Families (ACF), and the Department of Health and Human Services (DHHS). Head Start teachers strive to provide a variety of learning experiences appropriate to the child's age and development. These experiences encourage the child to read books, to understand cultural diversity, to express feelings, and to play with and relate to peers in an appropriate fashion. Students are guided in developing gross and fine motor skills, and self-confidence. Health care is also an issue, and most children enrolled in the program receive comprehensive health screening, physical and dental examinations, and appropriate follow-up. Many programs provide meals, and in so doing help children receive proper nourishment.

Head Start programs now serve parents in addition to their preschoolers. Some programs allow parents to enroll in classes, which cover parenting, literacy, nutrition/weight loss, domestic violence prevention and other social issues; social services, health, nutrition, and educational services are also available.

Considerable controversy has surrounded the success of the Head Start program. In 1970, the Westinghouse Learning Corporation issued a definitive evaluation of the Head Start effort and concluded that there was no evidence of lasting cognitive gains on the part of the participating children. Initial gains seemed to evapo-rate during the elementary school years, and by the third grade, the performance of the Head Start children was no different than their peers.

While disappointing, this evaluation focused on IQ levels and gave short shrift to improvement in social competence and other survival skills. More recent research has produced dramatically different results. One report found that, by age 5, children who experienced the enriched day care offered by Head Start averaged more than 10 points higher on their IQ scores than their peers who did not participate in the program. Other research that carefully compared Head Start children to similar youngsters who did not attend the program found that the former made significant intellectual gains. Head Start children were less likely to have been retained in a grade or placed in classes for slow learners; they outperformed peers on achievement tests; and they were more likely to graduate from high school.

Head Start kids also made strides in nonacademic areas: they appear to have better health, immunization rates, nutrition, and enhanced emotional characteristics after leaving the program. Research also shows that the Head Start program can have important psychological benefits for the mothers of participants, such as decreasing depression and anxiety and increasing feelings of life satisfaction. While findings in some areas may be tentative, they are all in the same direction: Head Start enhances school readiness and has enduring effects on social competence.

If, as many experts believe, there is a close link between school performance, family life, and crime, programs such as Head Start can help some potentially criminal youths avoid problems with the law. By implication, their success indicates that programs that help socialize youngsters can be used to combat urban criminality. While some problems have been identified in individual centers, the government has shown its faith in Head Start as a socialization agent.

Sources: Current information, personal contact, head start program, 2001; Edward Zigler and Sally Styfco, "Head Start, Criticisms in a Constructive Context," *American Psychologist 49*:127–32 (1994); Nancy Kassebaum, "Head Start, Only the Best for America's Children," *American Psychologist 49*:123–26 (1994); Faith Lamb Parker, Chaya Piorkowski, and Lenore Peay, "Head Start as Social Support for Mothers: The Psychological Benefits of Involvement," *American Journal of Orthopsychiatry 57*:220–33 (1987).

status offenders and juvenile delinquents together. These programs were designed to limit the juvenile's interaction with the justice system, to reduce stigma, and to make use of informal treatment modalities. (Diversion and deinstitutionalization are covered in more detail in Chapter 13).[115] While these programs were initially popular, critics claimed that the nonintervention movement created a new class of juvenile

Restorative programs for juveniles typically involve diversion from the formal court process and the use of programs that encourage meeting and reconciliation between offenders and victims. Programs include victim advocacy, mediation programs, and sentencing circles, in which crime victims and their families are brought together with offenders to formulate a peaceful and equitable solution to their problems. Many of these programs originate in the practices of Native American and Native Canadian people who have traditionally used restoration techniques in their justice systems. Here, Simon Roberts is shown leaving Pine Lodge Pre-Release Facility in Medical Lake, Washington, after serving time for a 1993 assault on a pizza deliveryman when he was 16 years old. He was banished to an Alaskan island, then sent to prison. (AP/Wide World Photos)

offenders who heretofore might have avoided prolonged contact with juvenile justice agencies; they referred to this phenomenon as *widening the net*.[116] Evaluation of existing programs did not indicate that they could reduce the recidivism rate of clients.[117] While these criticisms proved damaging, many nonintervention programs still operate.

Social Conflict and Delinquency Prevention

restorative justice Nonpunitive strategies for dealing with juvenile offenders that make the justice system a healing process rather than a punishment process.

If conflict is the source of delinquency, conflict resolution may be the key to its demise. This is the aim of **restorative justice,** an approach that relies on nonpunitive strategies for delinquency control.[118] Restoration involves turning the justice system into a healing process rather than a distributor of retribution. Most people involved in offender-victim relationships actually know one another or are related. Restorative justice attempts to address the issues that produced conflict between these people rather than to treat one as a victim deserving sympathy and the other as a delinquent deserving punishment. Rather than choose whom to punish, society should try to reconcile the parties.[119]

Restorative justice is based on a social rather than a legal view of delinquency. The relationships damaged by delinquent acts can only be healed in less formal and more cohesive social groups, such as families and communities.[120] Restorative justice stands in opposition to views of juvenile justice that limit consideration of the personal and social qualities of offenders. As a result of its preoccupation with the protection of society, the justice system relies on punishment to control law violating. It encourages youths to deny or excuse their actions, thereby precluding the acceptance of responsibility. In addition, the central role of trained professionals (prosecution and

TABLE 4.2 — Principles of Restorative Justice

Crime and delinquency are fundamentally a violation of people and interpersonal relationships.	Victims and the community have been harmed and are in need of restoration. Victims include the target of the offense but also include family members, witnesses, and the community at large.
	Victims, offenders, and the affected communities are the key stakeholders in justice. The state must investigate crime and ensure safety, but it is not the center of the justice process. Victims are the key, and they must help in the search for restoration, healing, responsibility, and prevention.
Violations create obligations and liabilities.	Offenders have the obligation to make things right as much as possible. They must understand the harm they have caused. Their participation should be as voluntary as possible; coercion is to be minimized.
	The community's obligations are to both victims and offenders as well as the general welfare of its members. This includes the obligation to reintegrate the offender in the community and to ensure the offender the opportunity to make amends.
Restorative justice seeks to heal and put right the wrongs.	Victims needs are the focal concern of the justice process. Safety is a top priority, and victims should be empowered to participate in determining their needs and case outcomes.
	The exchange of information between victim and offender should be encouraged; when possible, face-to-face meetings might be undertaken. There should be mutual agreement over imposed outcomes.
	Offenders' needs and competencies need to be addressed. Healing and reintegration are emphasized; isolation and removal from the community are restricted.
	The justice process belongs to the community; members are encouraged to "do justice." The justice process should be sensitive to community needs and geared at preventing similar harm in the future. Early interventions are encouraged.
	Justice is mindful of the outcomes, intended and unintended, of its responses to crime and victimization. It should monitor case outcome and provide necessary support and opportunity to all involved. The least restrictive intervention should be used, and overt social control should be avoided.

Source: Howard Zehr and Harry Mika, "Fundamental Concepts of Restorative Justice," *Contemporary Justice Review* 1:47–55 (1998).

defense attorneys) in the justice process limits the possibility of direct exchanges between victim and offender. Because the adversaries are defined as the accused and the state, little consideration can be given to community concerns. These limitations impede the effectiveness of traditional programs designed to reduce delinquent activities.

Restorative justice depends on returning law-violating youths to the community where they can resume a productive role. The effectiveness of this approach depends on the stake a person has in a particular group. If adolescents do not value their membership in the group, they will be unlikely to accept responsibility, show remorse, or repair the injuries caused by their actions. Even the most effective restorative justice programs will be unable to reach those who are disengaged from community institutions. Therefore, community involvement is an essential ingredient of the restorative justice approach. The principles of restorative justice are outlined in Table 4.2.

The restorative justice movement has a number of sources. Negotiation, mediation, and peacemaking have been part of the dispute resolution process in European and Asian communities for centuries.[121] Native American and Native Canadian people have long used participation of community members in the adjudication process (sentencing circles, panels of elders).[122] Members of the U.S. peacemaking movement have also championed the use of nonpunitive alternatives to justice. Gordon Bazemore and other policy experts helped formulate a version of restorative justice known as the balanced approach, which emphasizes that victims, offenders, and the community should all benefit from interactions with the justice system.[123] The balanced approach attempts to link community protection and victims' rights. Offenders must take responsibility for their actions, a process that can increase self-esteem and decrease recidivism.[124] In contrast, over-reliance on punishment can be counterproductive.[125] To counteract the negative effects of punishment, restorative justice programs for juveniles typically involve diversion from the court process, reconciliation between offenders and victims, victim advocacy, mediation programs, and sentencing circles, in which crime victims and their families are brought together with offenders and their families in an effort to formulate a sanction that addresses the needs of each party.

SUMMARY

Social structure theories hold that delinquent behavior is an adaptation to conditions that predominate in lower-class environments. The social disorganization view suggests that economically deprived areas lose their ability to control the behavior of residents. Gangs flourish in these areas. Delinquency is a product of the socialization mechanisms within a neighborhood: unstable neighborhoods have the greatest chance of producing delinquents. More recent ecological theories have shown how fear, unemployment, change, and attitudes influence behavior patterns.

Strain theories hold that lower-class youths may desire legitimate goals but that their unavailability causes frustration and deviant behavior. Robert Merton linked strain to anomie, a condition caused when there is a disjunction between goals and means. In his general strain theory, Robert Agnew identifies two more sources of strain: the removal of positive reinforcements and the addition of negative ones. He shows how strain causes delinquent behavior by creating negative affective states, and he outlines the means adolescents employ to cope with strain.

The third branch of structural theory is cultural deviance, or subcultural, theory. This maintains that the result of social disorganization and strain is the development of subcultures that hold values in opposition to mainstream society. Social process theories hold that improper socialization is the key to delinquency. One branch called learning theories holds that kids learn deviant behaviors and attitudes during interaction with family and peers. In contrast, control theories suggest that kids are prone to delinquent behavior when they have not been properly socialized and lack a strong bond to society. Labeling and stigma may also reinforce delinquency. Social conflict theory views delinquency as an inevitable result of the class and racial conflict that pervades society. Delinquents are members of the "have-not" class that is shut out of the mainstream. The law benefits the wealthy over the poor.

Sociological views of delinquency have had a great deal of influence on social policy. Programs have been designed to improve neighborhood conditions, help children be properly socialized, and reduce conflict.

KEY TERMS

culture of poverty	gentrified	control theory	self-fulfilling prophecy
underclass	anomie	differential association theory	dramatization of evil
truly disadvantaged	strain theory	drift	degradation ceremony
social disorganization	negative affective states	neutralization techniques	social conflict theory
transitional neighborhood	cultural deviance theory	social bond	deinstitutionalization
cultural transmission	culture conflict	stigmatized	restorative justice
social control	socialization	labeling theory	
relative deprivation	learning theory	self-labeling	

1. Is there a transitional area in your town or city?

2. Is it possible that a distinct lower-class culture exists? Do you know anyone who has the focal concerns Miller talks about?

3. Have you ever perceived anomie? What causes anomie? Is there more than one cause of strain?

4. How does poverty cause delinquency?

5. Do middle-class youths become delinquent for the same reasons as lower-class youths?

6. Does relative deprivation produce delinquency?

VIEWPOINT

Does this renewed excitement and confidence in federal early-childhood education programs in general, and Head Start in particular, reflect new information about their effectiveness? Probably not. As we have seen, major evaluation studies have repeatedly found that only modest gains at best result from these programs. Ron Haskins (1989), a developmental psychologist and congressional staff member, wrote a balanced and thoughtful summary of the impact of early childhood education. He found that, while significant gains in intellectual and socio-emotional performance do occur during the first year, most of these gains disappear over time.

 For an extremely comprehensive view of the history of federal support of education programs such as Head Start, read the following paper on InfoTrac® College Edition: Maris A. Vinovskis, "Do Federal Compensatory Education Programs Really *Work*? A Brief Historical Analysis of Title I and Head Start," *American Journal of Education* 107:18 (1999).

Chapter 5

Developmental Views of Delinquency

© Katherine McGlynn

ou are the governor of your state. In 1991, when Steven B was a 16-year-old high school wrestler, he and a teammate raped and severely beat a young girl who asked them for a ride home from a party. Though never in serious trouble before the attack, Steven was involved in an ongoing pattern of school misbehavior, substance abuse, and petty scrapes with the law. Those who knew him recognized that he had a short attention span and poor study habits, and he seemed to be impulsive and lacking in self-control.

While out on bail, Steven escaped to Europe with the help of his wealthy parents. After wandering the continent for two years, he settled in a small French town. There Steven, now known as "Paul," established a thriving wine shop, became a respected community member, married a local woman, and fathered two children. He even served on the town council. However, after more than a decade abroad, Steven's conscience began to bother him and he decided to return to the United States and voluntarily turn himself over to the police.

Steven now asks that you pardon him so he can return to his home and family. He argues that his friend, who was convicted of rape and served time in prison, was the one who actually attacked the girl. Steven claims he merely helped prevent her from escaping; his friend substantiates the story. He now realizes he was wrong but he points out that he has lived an exemplary life for the last ten years, that his family needs him, and that he poses no danger to society. He has returned to see his family and make financial restitution to the victim before returning to France. Finally, since Steven committed the act as a juvenile, state law says he must be tried in juvenile court. Even if convicted, his age and maturity make him an unsuitable candidate for the juvenile justice system.

- Do you believe that Steven is unlikely to commit another violent act as an adult even though he did so as a juvenile?

- Is it possible, now that Steven is an adult, that his impulsive personality has moderated and he has regained the ability to control his own behavior? Or do you believe that behavior patterns originating in childhood, such a lack of self control, persist into adulthood?

- Should the justice system distinguish between a young man who commits a single act of violence and a chronic offender who repeatedly is involved in criminal acts?

Cases such as Steven B, though unusual, raise important questions about young people's antisocial activities. Why do some kids become delinquents and then abandon the delinquent way of life as they mature? While most traditional views of delinquency seek to explain why kids engage in antisocial behaviors, relatively few focus on why kids discontinue their illegal acts as they mature. Yet it is now well known that crime rates peak in the teenage years and then begin to decline. The fact that most adolescents "age out of crime" has a critical bearing on our understanding of the nature and causes of delinquency. For example, some experts believe (Chapter 3) that antisocial behavior is a function of some personal trait, such as a low IQ or an impulsive personality, which is present at birth or soon afterward. If abnormally low intelligence is a cause of delinquency, as some experts claim, then how can we account for the fact that most delinquents fail to become adult criminals? It seems unlikely that intelligence increases as young offenders mature. Even if the onset of criminality can be explained by low intelligence, then some other factor must explain its termination. Delinquency experts today are concerned with both the onset of criminality and its termination.

The scenario described at the beginning of this chapter is based loosely on the case of Alex Kelly, who fled to Europe rather than face rape charges. Here Kelly is seen as he is being led out of Stamford Superior Court Wednesday, Dec. 23, 1998 in Stamford, Conn. More than a decade after fleeing his wealthy suburban home, Kelly returned to stand trial and was convicted of two rapes. He was sentenced to 16 years in prison. (AP/Wide World Photos)

www
Interested in the concept of human development? Then
access the United Nation's Web site on the topic at

http://www.undp.org/hdro/

For an up-to-date list of Web links, go to www.wadsworth.com/ product/0534573053s

developmental theory Asserts that personal characteristics guide human development and influence behavioral choices but that these choices may change over the life course.

life-course theory The view that people change as they mature and that the quality of their personal development shapes their behavior choices.

latent trait view The view that a master trait, developed at birth or soon after, influences behavior across the life course. People who have this trait are crime prone throughout their lives.

It has become important to chart the natural history of a delinquent career. Why do some offenders escalate their delinquent activities while others decrease or limit their law violations? Why do some delinquents turn away from criminal activity for a short period of time, only to resume it? Research now shows that some offenders begin their delinquent careers at a very early age, whereas others begin later. How can early- and late-onset delinquency be explained?[1] Focusing attention on these questions has produced what is known as the **developmental theory** of delinquency.

There are actually two distinct developmental views. The first, referred to as the **life-course theory,** suggests that delinquent behavior is a dynamic process, influenced by individual characteristics as well as social experiences, and that the factors that cause antisocial behaviors change dramatically over a person's life span. However, while their position is growing increasingly popular, the life course theorists are challenged by another group of scholars who suggest that human development is controlled by a "master trait" that remains stable and unchanging throughout a person's lifetime. Rather than focusing on human change and development, **latent trait view** regards the opportunities people have to commit crime at various stages of their life as critical. They believe that "people don't change, opportunities do."

In the sections below, we will review the history, basic concepts, and theoretical models of the developmental, or life course, approach. We will then turn to the latent trait view that challenges its validity.

ORIGINS OF DEVELOPMENTAL THEORY

urrent developmental research was inspired by the early efforts of Sheldon and Eleanor Glueck. Working at Harvard University in the 1930s, the Gluecks popularized research on the life cycle of delinquent careers. In a series of longitudinal research studies, making extensive use of interviews and records, they followed the careers of known delinquents to determine the factors that predicted persistent offending.[2]

The Gluecks' research focused on early onset of delinquency as a harbinger of a delinquent career: ". . . the deeper the roots of childhood maladjustment, the smaller the chance of adult adjustment."[3] They also noted the stability of offending careers. Children who are antisocial early in life are the most likely to continue their offending careers into adulthood. They identified a number of personal and social factors related to persistent offending, the most important of which was family relations. The adolescent raised in a large, single-parent family of limited economic means and educational achievement was the most vulnerable to delinquency. However, the Gluecks did not restrict their analysis to social variables but included such biological and psychological traits as body type, intelligence, and personality in their analysis. They found that physical and mental factors also played a role in determining behavior, and that children with low intelligence and a background of mental disease were the most likely to become persistent offenders. The Glueck research indicated that both physical and social factors shaped the direction of children's behavior and that these factors changed over the life course.

The Murray Research Center at Radcliffe College sponsors an ongoing Crime Causation Study: Unraveling Juvenile Delinquency 1940–1963, based on the work of the Gluecks. You can visit their site at

http://www.radcliffe.edu/murray/data/ds/ds0896.htm

For an up-to-date list of Web links, go to www.wadsworth.com/product/0534573053s

While it was popular during their lifetime, the Gluecks' research was ignored after their deaths, being replaced by the social theories described in Chapter 4. The Gluecks' efforts were attacked and disputed by social scientists who believed any effort to link physical and psychological traits to delinquency was spurious. For many years delinquency experts believed that the root cause of adolescent misbehavior could be traced to purely social constructs such as poverty and improper socialization. However, in the late 1980s, a series of research papers published by well-known criminologists John Laub and Robert Sampson rekindled interest in the Gluecks' vision of delinquency.[4] Other prominent researchers followed suit and began to call for a rethinking of the directions taken by delinquency theory.[5] It was proposed that delinquency experts devote time and effort to understanding some basic questions about the evolution of delinquent careers: Why do kids begin committing antisocial acts? Why do some stop while others continue? Why do some escalate the severity of their criminality (that is, go from shoplifting to drug dealing to armed robbery) while others de-escalate and commit less serious crimes as they mature? If some terminate their delinquent activity, what, if anything, causes them to begin again? Why do some delinquents specialize in certain types of crime, whereas others are generalists engaging in a variety of antisocial behavior?

CONTEMPORARY DEVELOPMENTAL CONCEPTS

hese pioneering efforts have produced views of delinquency causation that integrate both social and personal factors and also recognize that the factors that produce crime and delinquency are multi-dimensional and dynamic. Crime-producing elements that affect people at one point in the life cycle may not be relevant at another.[6] People may show a propensity to offend early in their lives, but the nature and frequency of their activities are affected by outside forces beyond their control.[7] While one factor may dominate, the cause of delinquency is essentially multi-dimensional. The next sections review some of the more important concepts associated with the developmental perspective.

Developmental theories focus attention on the chronic or persistent offender. Although the concept of chronic offenders, who begin their offending careers as children and persist into adulthood, is now an accepted fact, delinquency experts are still struggling to understand why this is so. They do not fully understand why, when faced with a similar set of life circumstances (poverty and family dysfunction, for example), one youth becomes a chronic offender while another may commit an occasional illegal act but later desists from crime. One possibility is that, when faced with important life transitions such as becoming a student or getting a job, some kids have what it takes to succeed while others are incapable of maturing in a reasonable and timely fashion because of family, environmental, or personal problems.

According to developmental theory, even as toddlers people begin relationships and behaviors that will determine their adult life course. At first they must learn to conform to social rules and function effectively in society. Later they are expected to begin thinking about careers, leave their parental homes, find permanent relationships, and eventually marry and begin their own families.[8] These transitions are expected to take place in order: completing education, entering the workforce, getting married, and having children. In some cases transitions can occur too early—for example, when an adolescent girl engages in precocious sex and has a child while still enrolled in school. In other cases transitions may occur too late, such as when a student fails to graduate on time because of bad grades or too many incompletes. Sometimes disruption of one trajectory can harm another. For example, teenage childbirth will most likely disrupt educational and career development.

Disruptions in life's major transitions can be destructive and, ultimately, may promote criminality. Those who are already at risk because of socioeconomic problems or family dysfunction are the most susceptible to these awkward transitions. The cumulative impact of these disruptions sustains criminality from childhood into adulthood.

Because a transition from one stage of life to another can be a bumpy ride, the propensity to commit delinquent acts is neither stable nor constant; it is a *developmental process*. A positive life experience may help some delinquents desist from crime for a while, whereas a negative one may cause them to resume their activities. Delinquent careers are also said to be developmental because people are influenced by the behavior of those around them and, in turn, influence others' behavior. For example, a youth's antisocial behavior may turn his or her more conventional friends against him; their rejection solidifies and escalates his antisocial behavior.

Changing Life Experiences As people mature, the factors that influence their behavior change.[9] At first, family relations may be most influential; in later adolescence, school and peer relations predominate; in adulthood, vocational achievement and marital relations may be the most critical influences. For example, some antisocial children who are in trouble throughout their adolescence may manage to find stable work and maintain intact marriages as adults; these life events help them desist from crime. In contrast, the less-fortunate adolescents who develop arrest records and get involved with the wrong crowd may find themselves limited to menial jobs and at risk for delinquent careers. Because people are influenced by different factors as they mature, a factor that may have an important influence at one stage of life (like delinquent peers) may have little influence later on.[10]

problem behavior syndrome (PBS) Convergence of a variety of psychological problems and family dysfunctions including substance abuse and criminality.

Problem Behavior Syndrome

Some developmental advocates believe that delinquency may best be understood as one of many social problems faced by at-risk youth. Referred to as **problem behavior syndrome (PBS)**, developmental theorists realize that crime occurs among a group

According to developmental theories, people change as they go through critical life transitions such as having a child and becoming a parent. Fifteen-month-old Brian Vides is held by his mother, Jasira Perlera, as they attend a rally March 14, 2001 at the State-house in Boston, in support of increased funding for teen parent families. Legislators and family advocate organizations say increased funding is necessary to reduce the level of homelessness among teen parents. (AP/Wide World Photos)

The Program of Research on the Causes and Correlates of Delinquency, sponsored by the federal government, comprises three coordinated longitudinal projects that are often referred to in this text. You can reach their Web site at

http://ojjdp.ncjrs.org/ccd/oview.html

For an up-to-date list of Web links, go to www.wadsworth.com/product/0534573053s

of antisocial behaviors that cluster together and typically involve family dysfunction, substance abuse, smoking, precocious sexuality and early pregnancy, educational underachievement, suicide attempts, sensation seeking, and unemployment.[11]

People who suffer from one of these conditions typically exhibit many symptoms of the others.[12] All varieties of delinquent behavior, including violence, theft, and drug offenses, may be part of a generalized PBS, indicating that all forms of antisocial behavior have similar developmental patterns (Table 5.1).[13] Those who suffer PBS are prone to more difficulties than the general population.[14] They find themselves with a range of personal dilemmas ranging from drug abuse, to being accident-prone, to requiring more health care and hospitalization, to becoming teenage parents. Problem behavior syndrome has been linked to personality problems (rebelliousness, low ego), family problems (intrafamily conflict, parental mental disorder), and educational failure.[15] Multi-site research has shown that PBS is not unique to any single area of the country and that children who suffer PBS, including drug use, delinquency, and precocious sexuality, display symptoms at an early age.[16]

PBS can manifest itself in many different ways. For example, one study of youth in Pittsburgh found that kids who became fathers before their nineteenth birthday were much more likely to get into trouble with the law (72%) compared to youths who did not have children out of wedlock (41%). About 40 percent of the fathers were involved in frequent alcohol use and drug dealing, compared to about 20 percent for nonfathers. Similarly, while 60 percent of the fathers dropped out of school, only 21 percent of the nonfathers failed to complete their education. Fathers were also more likely to use drugs and become high-rate chronic offenders. A similar study using samples of youth from Rochester, New York also found that teenage fatherhood was related to antisocial behavior, delinquency, and drug abuse.[17]

While not all delinquents have multiple social problems, kids who suffer from PBS are more likely to become delinquent. Data from these same two studies in Pittsburgh and Rochester, as well as a similar one conducted in Denver, show that kids with two or more persistent social problems (substance abuse, school failure, mental health problems) are significantly more likely to be persistent offenders than youths who are problem free.[18]

TABLE 5.1	Problem Behaviors
Social	• Family dysfunction
	• Unemployment
	• Educational underachievement
	• School misconduct
Personal	• Substance abuse
	• Suicide attempts
	• Early sexuality
	• Sensation seeking
	• Early parenthood
	• Accident-prone
	• Medical problems
	• Mental disease
	• Anxiety
	• Eating disorders (bulimia, anorexia)
Environmental	• High-crime area
	• Disorganized area
	• Racism
	• Exposure to poverty

Pathways to Crime and Delinquency

authority-conflict pathway The developmental path taken to delinquency that begins with stubborn and defiant behavior.

covert pathway The developmental path taken to delinquency that begins with sneaky, deceitful, and underhanded behavior.

overt pathway The developmental path taken to delinquency that begins with violent outbursts and bullying.

www
To read about the highlights of the Pittsburgh Youth Study, which is directed by Rolf Loeber, go to http://www.ncjrs.org/txtfiles1/ fs9995.txt

For an up-to-date list of Web links, go to www.wadsworth.com/ product/0534573053s

Developmental theorists recognize that career delinquents may travel more than a single road: some may specialize in violence and extortion; some may be involved in theft and fraud; others may engage in a variety of delinquent acts. Some offenders may begin their careers early in life, whereas others are late bloomers who begin committing crime when most people desist.

Are there different pathways to crime? Using data from a longitudinal cohort study conducted in Pittsburgh, Rolf Loeber and his associates have identified three distinct paths to a delinquent career (Figure 5.1):[19]

1. The **authority-conflict pathway** begins at an early age with stubborn behavior. This leads to defiance (doing things one's own way, disobedience) and then to authority avoidance (staying out late, truancy, running away).

2. The **covert pathway** begins with minor, underhanded behavior (lying, shoplifting) that leads to property damage (setting nuisance fires, damaging property). This behavior eventually escalates to more serious forms of criminality, ranging from joyriding, pocket picking, larceny, and fencing to passing bad checks, using stolen credit cards, stealing cars, dealing drugs, and breaking and entering.

3. The **overt pathway** escalates to aggressive acts beginning with aggression (annoying others, bullying), and leading to physical (and gang) fighting and then to violence (attacking someone, forced theft).

The Loeber research indicates that each of these paths may lead to a sustained deviant career. Some people enter two and even three paths simultaneously: they are stubborn, lie to teachers and parents, are bullies, and commit petty thefts. These adolescents are the most likely to become persistent offenders as they mature. Although some persistent offenders may specialize in one type of behavior, others engage in varied delinquent acts and antisocial behaviors as they mature. For example, they cheat on tests, bully kids in the schoolyard, take drugs, commit burglary, steal a car, and then shoplift from a store.

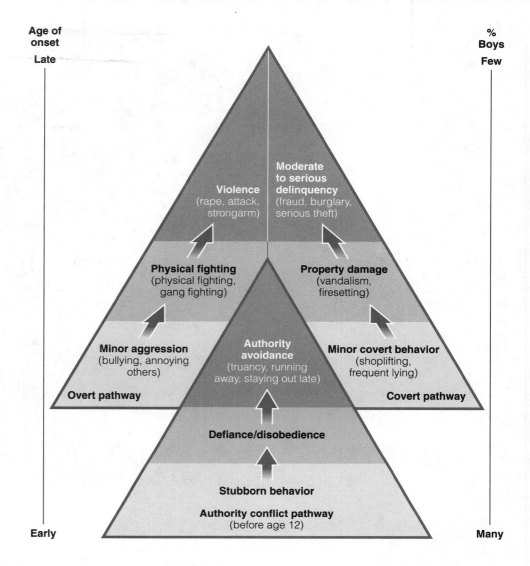

Figure 5.1
Loeber's Pathways to Crime

Source: "Serious and Violent Offenders," *Juvenile Justice Bulletin,* May 1998.

Age of onset

Late

% Boys

Few

Violence (rape, attack, strongarm)

Moderate to serious delinquency (fraud, burglary, serious theft)

Physical fighting (physical fighting, gang fighting)

Property damage (vandalism, firesetting)

Minor aggression (bullying, annoying others)

Authority avoidance (truancy, running away, staying out late)

Minor covert behavior (shoplifting, frequent lying)

Overt pathway

Covert pathway

Defiance/disobedience

Stubborn behavior

Authority conflict pathway (before age 12)

Early

Many

Delinquent Trajectories

In addition to taking different paths to criminality, people may begin their journey at different times: some are precocious, beginning their delinquent careers early, while others stay out of trouble until their teenage years. Some offenders may peak at an early age, whereas others persist into adulthood. Research shows that there are a number of categories of delinquent careers that seem to reflect changes in the life course. Some youths maximize their offending rates at a relatively early age and then reduce their delinquent activity; others persist into their twenties. Some are high-rate offenders, whereas others offend at relatively low rates.[20]

According to psychologist Terrie Moffitt, although the prevalence and frequency of antisocial behavior peak in adolescence and then diminish for most offenders (she labels these **adolescent-limiteds**), a small group of **life-course persisters** offends well into adulthood.[21] Life-course persisters combine family dysfunction with severe neurological problems that predispose them to antisocial behavior patterns. These afflictions can be the result of maternal drug abuse, poor nutrition, or exposure to toxic agents such as lead. Life-course persisters may have low verbal ability, which inhibits reasoning skills, learning ability, and school achievement. They seem to mature faster and engage is early sexuality and drug use, referred to *as pseudomaturity*.[22]

adolescent-limiteds Delinquent youth who begin their offending career in their late teens and soon desist from crime.

life-course persisters Delinquent youth who begin their offending career quite early and persist into their adulthood.

According to the trajectory concept, people may begin their journey into crime at different times: some are precocious, beginning their delinquent careers early; others stay out of trouble until their teenage years. Some offenders may peak at an early age, whereas others persist into adulthood. Here 12-year-old Michael Nichols is escorted out of the Federal Courts Building followed by his father, Thomas Paul Nichols (rear), in Fayetteville, Ark. on July 25, 2000. A juvenile court judge refused to allow a mental insanity defense for Nichols, who is accused of shooting a police officer while heading toward his school with a shotgun. (AP/Wide World Photos)

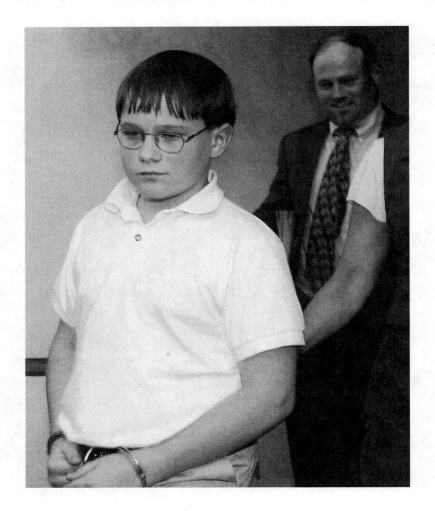

There may be more than one subset of life-course persisters. One begins acting out during the preschool years; these youths show signs of ADHD and do not outgrow the levels of disobedience typical of the preschool years. The second group shows few symptoms of ADHD but, from an early age, is aggressive, underhanded, and in constant opposition to authority.[23]

In contrast, adolescent-limited delinquents mimic the behavior of the more troubled teens, only to reduce the frequency of their offending as they mature to around age 18.[24] They are deeply influenced by the misbehavior of their friends and peers up to around age 16, then peer group influence begins to decline. Peer influence, then, has a significant influence on law-violating behavior.[25] Adolescent-limited delinquents tend to focus on a specific type of misbehavior, such as drug abuse, while life-course persisters (both males and females) are more likely to engage in a variety of antisocial behaviors.[26]

Why do some people embark on a path to crime later rather than sooner? Early starters, who begin offending before age 14, experience (1) poor parenting, which leads them into (2) deviant behaviors, and (3) involvement with delinquent groups. In contrast, late starters, who begin offending after age 14, follow a somewhat different path: (1) poor parenting leads to (2) identification with delinquent groups, and to (3) deviant involvement. By implication, adolescents who suffer poor parenting and are at risk for deviant careers can avoid criminality if they can bypass involvement with delinquent peers.[27]

Continuity of Crime and Delinquency

Another aspect of developmental theory is the continuity of crime: the best predictor of future criminality is past criminality. Children who are repeatedly in trouble during early adolescence will generally still be antisocial in their middle and late teens and as adults.[28] Early delinquent activity is likely to be sustained because these offenders seem to lack the social survival skills necessary to find work or to develop the interpersonal relationships needed to allow them to drop out of crime.[29] One explanation for this phenomenon suggests that delinquent propensity may be *contagious*: kids at risk for crime may be located in families and neighborhoods in which they are constantly exposed to deviant behavior. As they mature, having brothers, fathers, neighbors, and friends who engage in and support their activities reinforces their deviance.[30]

One of the most important studies of the continuity of crime is the Cambridge Youth Survey conducted in England by David Farrington. The results of this important project are described in the Focus on Delinquency, "The Cambridge Youth Study."

✔ Checkpoints

✔ Pioneering criminologists Sheldon and Eleanor Glueck proposed tracking the onset and termination of a criminal career.

✔ Developmental theories look at such issues as the onset of crime, escalation of offenses, continuity of crime, and desistance from crime.

✔ The concept of problem behavior syndrome (PBS) suggests that criminality may be just one of a cluster of social, psychological, and physical problems.

✔ There is more than one pathway to crime.

✔ Adolescent-limited offenders begin offending late and age out of crime. Life-course persisters exhibit early onset of crime and then persist into adulthood.

✔ The best predictor of future delinquency is past delinquency.

THEORIES OF DELINQUENT DEVELOPMENT

An ongoing effort has been made to track persistent offenders over their life course.[31] The early data seem to support what is already known about delinquent and criminal career patterns: early onset predicts more lasting crime; there is continuity in crime (juvenile offenders are likely to become adult criminals); and chronic offenders commit a significant portion of all crimes.[32] Based on these findings, a number of systematic theories that account for the onset, continuance, and desistance from crime have been formulated. The following sections discuss a number of developmental theories.

The Social Development Model (SDM)

social development model (SDM) An array of personal, psychological, and community-level risk factors that make some children susceptible to development of antisocial behaviors.

In their **social development model (SDM),** Joseph Weis, Richard Catalano, J. David Hawkins, and their associates show how different factors affecting children's social development over their life course influence their delinquent behavior patterns.[33] As children mature within their environment, elements of socialization control their developmental process. Children are socialized and develop bonds to their families through four distinct interactions and processes:

1. The perceived opportunities for involvement in activities and interactions with others

2. The degree of involvement and interaction with parents

3. The children's ability to participate in these interactions

4. The reinforcement (such as feedback) they perceive for their participation

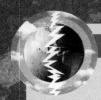

THE CAMBRIDGE YOUTH STUDY

ne of the most important longitudinal studies tracking persistent offenders is the Cambridge Study in Delinquent Development, which has followed the offending careers of 411 London boys born in 1953. This cohort study, directed since 1982 by David Farrington, is one of the most serious attempts to isolate the factors that predict lifelong continuity of criminal behavior. The study uses self-report data as well as in-depth interviews and psychological testing. The boys have been interviewed eight times over 24 years, beginning at age 8 and continuing to age 32.

The results of the Cambridge study show that many of the same patterns found in the United States are repeated in a cross-national sample: the existence of chronic offenders, the continuity of offending, and early onset of criminal activity. Each of these patterns leads to persistent criminality.

Farrington found that the traits present in persistent offenders can be observed as early as age 8. The chronic criminal begins as a property offender; is born into a large low-income family headed by parents who have criminal records; and has delinquent older siblings. The future criminal receives poor parental supervision, including the use of harsh or erratic punishment and childrearing techniques; the parents are likely to divorce or separate. The chronic offender tends to associate with friends who are also future criminals. By age 8, the child exhibits antisocial behavior, including dishonesty and aggressiveness; at school the chronic offender tends to have low educational achievement and is restless, troublesome, hyperactive, impulsive, and often truant. After leaving school at age 18, the persistent criminal tends to take a relatively well-paid but low-status job and is likely to have an erratic work history and periods of unemployment.

Farrington found that deviant behavior tends to be versatile rather than specialized. That is, the typical offender not only commits property offenses, such as theft and burglary, but also engages in violence, vandalism, drug use, excessive drinking, drunk driving, smoking, reckless driving, and sexual promiscuity—evidence of a generalized problem behavior syndrome. Chronic offenders are more likely to live away from home and have conflicts with their parents. They wear tattoos, go out most evenings, and enjoy hanging out with groups of their friends. They are much more likely than nonoffenders to get involved in fights, to carry weapons, and to use them in violent encounters. The frequency of offending reaches a peak in the teenage years (about 17 or 18) and then declines in the twenties, when the offenders marry or live with a significant other.

By the thirties, the former delinquent is likely to be separated or divorced and be an absent parent. His employment record remains spotty, and he moves often between rental units. His life is still characterized by evenings out, heavy drinking, substance abuse, and more violent behavior than his contemporaries. Because the typical offender provides the same kind of deprived and disrupted family life for his own children that he experienced, the social experiences and conditions that produce delinquency are carried on from one generation to the next. Table A, which follows, summarizes the specific risk factors that Farrington associates with forming a delinquent career.

Nonoffenders and Desisters

Farrington has also identified factors that predict the discontinuity of criminal offenses. He found that people who exhibit these factors have backgrounds that put them at risk of becoming offenders; however, either they are able to remain nonoffenders, or they begin a criminal career and then later desist. The factors that protected high-risk youths from beginning criminal careers include having a somewhat shy personality, having few friends (at age 8), having nondeviant families, and being highly regarded by their mothers. Shy children with few friends avoided damaging relationships with other adolescents (members of a high-risk group) and were therefore able to avoid criminality.

What Caused Offenders to Desist?

Holding a relatively good job helped reduce criminal activity. Conversely, unemployment seemed to be related to the escalation of theft offenses; violence and substance abuse were unaffected by unemployment. In a similar vein, getting married also helped diminish criminal activity. However, finding a spouse who was also involved in criminal activity and had a criminal record increased criminal involvement. Physical relocation also helped some offenders desist because they were forced to sever ties with co-offenders. For this reason, leaving the city for a rural or suburban area was linked to reduced criminal activity.

Although employment, marriage, and relocation helped potential offenders desist, not all desisters found success. At-risk youths who managed to avoid criminal convictions were unlikely to avoid other social problems. Rather than becoming prosperous homeowners with flourishing careers, they tended to live in unkempt homes and have large debts and low-paying jobs. They were also more likely to remain single and live alone. Youths who experienced social isolation at age 8 were also found to experience it at age 32.

Farrington's theory suggests that life experiences shape the direction and flow of behavior choices. He finds that, while there may be continuity in offending, the factors that predict criminality at one point in the life course may not be the ones that predict criminality at another. Although most adult criminals begin their careers in childhood, life events may help some children forgo criminality as they mature.

Sources: David Farrington, "The Development of Offending and Anti-Social Behavior from Childhood: Key Findings from the Cambridge Study of Delinquent Development," *Journal of Child Psychology and Psychiatry* 36:2–36 (1995); idem, "Understanding and Preventing Youth Crime" (Joseph Rowntree Foundation: London, 1996).

TABLE A

Risk Factors for a Delinquent Career

Prenatal and perinatal: Early childbearing increases the risk of such undesirable outcomes for children as low school attainment, antisocial behavior, substance use, and early sexual activity. An increased risk of offending among children of teenage mothers is associated with low income, poor housing, absent fathers, and poor childrearing methods.

Personality: Impulsiveness, hyperactivity, restlessness, and limited ability to concentrate are associated with low attainment in school and a poor ability to foresee the consequences of offending.

Intelligence and attainment: Low intelligence and poor performance in school, although important statistical predictors of offending, are difficult to disentangle from each other. One plausible explanation of the link between low intelligence and crime is its association with a poor ability to manipulate abstract concepts and to appreciate the feelings of victims.

Parental supervision and discipline: Harsh or erratic parental discipline and cold or rejecting parental attitudes have been linked to delinquency and are associated with children's lack of internal inhibitions against offending. Physical abuse by parents has been associated with an increased risk of the children themselves becoming violent offenders in later life.

Parental conflict and separation: Living in a home affected by separation or divorce is more strongly related to delinquency than when the disruption has been caused by the death of one parent. However, it may not be a "broken home" that creates an increased risk of offending so much as the parental conflict that lead to the separation.

Socioeconomic status: Social and economic deprivation are important predictors of antisocial behavior and crime, but low family income and poor housing are better measurements than the prestige of parents' occupations.

Delinquent friends: Delinquents tend to have delinquent friends. But it is not certain whether membership in a delinquent peer group leads to offending or whether delinquents simply gravitate towards each other's company (or both). Breaking up with delinquent friends often coincides with desisting from crime.

School influences: The prevalence of offending by pupils varies widely between secondary schools. But it is not clear how far schools themselves have an effect on delinquency (for example, by paying insufficient attention to bullying or providing too much punishment and too little praise), or whether it is simply that troublesome children tend to go to high-delinquency-rate schools.

Community influences: The risks of becoming criminally involved are higher for young people raised in disorganized inner city areas, characterized by physical deterioration, overcrowded households, publicly subsidized renting, and high residential mobility. It is not clear, however, whether this is due to a direct influence on children, or whether environmental stress causes family adversities which in turn cause delinquency.

Figure 5.2
The Social Development Model of Antisocial Behavior

Source: Adapted from Seattle Social Development Project.

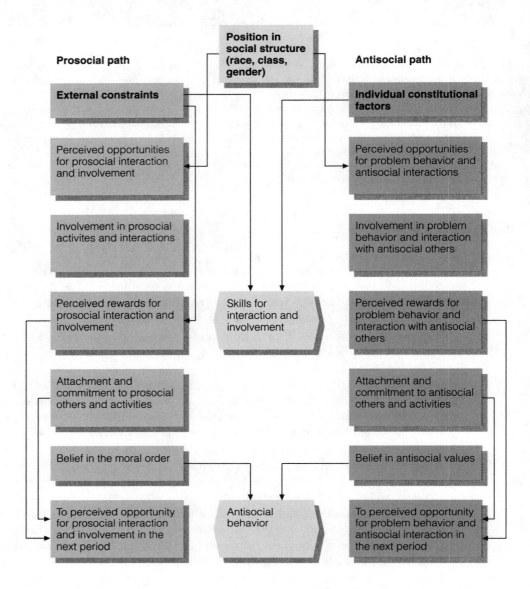

pro-social bonds The attachment a child has with positive elements of society such as schools, parents, and peers.

To control the risk of antisocial behavior, a child must maintain **pro-social bonds.** These are developed within the context of family life, which not only provides prosocial opportunities but reinforces them by consistent, positive feedback. Parental attachment affects a child's behavior for life, determining both school experiences and personal beliefs and values. For those with strong family relationships, school will be a meaningful experience marked by academic success and commitment to education. Youths in this category are likely to develop conventional beliefs and values, become committed to conventional activities, and form attachments to conventional others.

Children's antisocial behavior also depends on the quality of their attachments to parents and other influential relations. If they remain unattached or develop attachments to deviant others, their behavior may become deviant as well. The SDM suggests that interaction with antisocial peers and adults promotes participation in delinquency and substance abuse.[34]

As Figure 5.2 shows, the SDM suggests that involvement in pro-social or antisocial behavior determines the quality of attachments. Adolescents who perceive opportunities and rewards for antisocial behavior will form deep attachments to deviant peers and will become committed to a delinquent way of life. In contrast, those who perceive opportunities for pro-social behavior will take a different path, getting involved in conventional activities and forming attachments to others who share their conventional lifestyle.

Figure 5.3

Overview of the Interactional Theory of Delinquency

Source: Terence Thornberry, Margaret Farnworth, Alan Lizotte, and Susan Stern, "A Longitudinal Examination of the Causes and Correlates of Delinquency," working paper No. 1, Rochester Youth Development Study (Albany, NY: Hindelang Criminal Justice Research Center, 1987), p. 11.

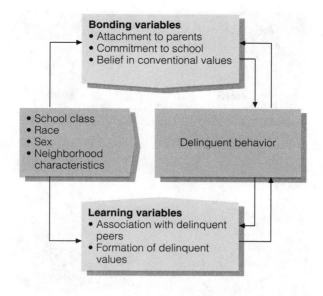

The SDM holds that commitment and attachment to conventional institutions, activities, and beliefs insulate youths from the crimogenic influences of their environment. The pro-social path inhibits deviance by strengthening bonds to pro-social others and activities. Without the proper level of bonding, adolescents can succumb to the influence of deviant others.

Interactional Theory

interactional theory Asserts that youths' interactions with institutions and events over the life course determine criminal behavior patterns and that these patterns of behavior evolve over time.

Terence Thornberry has proposed an age-graded view of crime that he calls **interactional theory** (Figure 5.3).[35] He also finds that the onset of crime can be traced to a deterioration of the social bond during adolescence, marked by weakened attachment to parents, commitment to school, and belief in conventional values. Interactional theory also holds that seriously delinquent youths form belief systems that are consistent with their deviant lifestyle. They seek out the company of other kids who share their interests and who are likely to reinforce their beliefs about the world and support their delinquent behavior. According to interactional theory, delinquents find a delinquent peer group in the same way that chess buffs look for others who share their passion for the game; hanging out with other chess players helps improve their game. Similarly, deviant peers do not turn an otherwise innocent boy into a delinquent; they support and amplify the behavior of kids who have already accepted a delinquent way of life.[36]

The key idea here is that causal influences are bi-directional. Weak bonds lead kids to develop friendships with deviant peers and get involved in delinquency. Frequent delinquency involvement further weakens bonds and makes it difficult to reestablish conventional ones. Delinquency-promoting factors tend to reinforce one another and sustain a chronic delinquent career.

Thornberry suggests that criminality is a developmental process that takes on different meaning and form as a person matures. According to Thornberry, the causal process is a dynamic one and develops over a person's life.[37] During early adolescence, attachment to the family is the single most important determinant of whether a youth will adjust to conventional society and be shielded from delinquency. By midadolescence the influence of the family is replaced by the "world of friends, school and youth culture."[38] By adulthood, individuals' behavioral choices are shaped by their place in conventional society and their own nuclear family.

In sum, interactional theory suggests that criminality is *part* of a dynamic social process and not just an outcome of that process. Although crime is influenced by

According to the Social Development Model (SDM), there are a number of personal, psychological, and community-level "risk factors" that make some children susceptible to the development of antisocial behaviors over the course of their lives. Children with pre-existing risk factors find that their antisocial behavior is either reinforced or neutralized through community and individual-level interactions. Actor/Latino activist Edward Olmos, shown here, is an example of someone who was able to overcome these risk factors and succeed in society. He now helps at-risk youths succeed and reach their potential. (PhotoEdit)

social forces, it also influences these processes and associations to create behavioral trajectories toward increasing law violations for some people.[39] Interactional theory integrates elements of social disorganization, social control, social learning, and cognitive theories into a powerful model of the development of a delinquent career.

Sampson and Laub: Age-Graded Theory

turning points According to Laub and Sampson, life events, such as marriage, that help a person desist from crime.

If there are various pathways to crime and delinquency, are there trails back to conformity? In an important 1993 work, *Crime in the Making*, Robert Sampson and John Laub identify the **turning points** in a delinquent career.[40] Laub and Sampson reanalyzed the data originally collected by the Gluecks more than 40 years ago. Using modern statistical analysis, Laub and Sampson found evidence supporting the developmental view. Their theory is age-graded because they recognize that different factors influence people as they go through the life-course.

Life's Turning Points Laub and Sampson's most important contribution is identifying the life events that enable young offenders to desist from crime as they mature (Figure 5.4). Two critical turning points are marriage and career. For example, adolescents who are at risk for crime can live conventional lives if they can find good jobs or achieve successful careers. Their success may hinge on a lucky break. Even those who have been in trouble with the law may turn from crime if employers are willing to give them a chance despite their records. When they achieve adulthood, adolescents who had significant problems with the law are able to desist from crime if they become attached to a spouse who supports and sustains them even when the spouse knows about their earlier trouble. Happy marriages are life-sustaining, and marital quality improves over time (as people work less and have fewer parental responsibilities).[41] Spending time in marital and family activities also reduces exposure to deviant peers, which in turn reduces the opportunity to become involved in delinquent activities.[42] People who cannot sustain secure marital relations are less likely to desist from crime.

Sampson and Laub's age-graded theory is also supported by research that shows children who grow up in two-parent families are likely to have happier marriages than children who are the product of divorced or never-married parents.[43] This find-

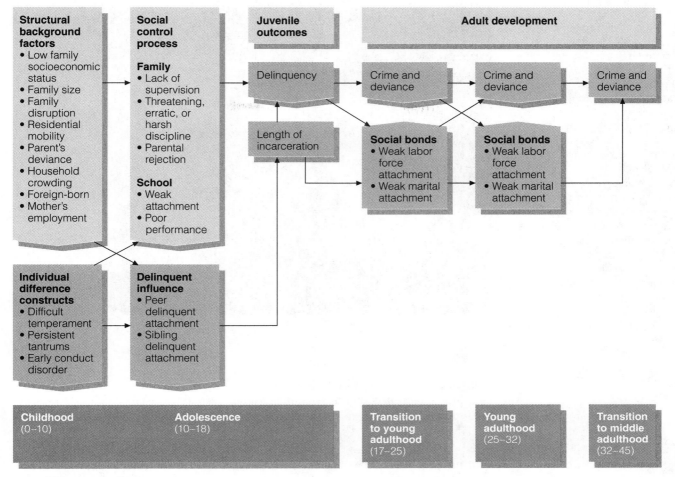

Figure 5.4
Sampson and Laub's Age-Graded Theory

Source: Robert Sampson and John Laub, *Crime in the Making: Pathways and Turning Points Through Life* (Cambridge, MA: Harvard University Press, 1993), pp. 244–45.

ing suggests that the marriage/crime association may be intergenerational: If people with marital problems are more crime-prone, their children will suffer a greater long-term risk of marital failure and antisocial activity.

social capital The positive relationships a person develops that helps him or her succeed in life and avoid criminal behaviors.

Social Capital Social scientists recognize that people build **social capital**—that is, positive relations with individuals and institutions that are life-sustaining. In the same manner that building financial capital improves the chances for personal success, building social capital supports conventional behavior and inhibits deviant behavior. For example, a successful marriage creates social capital when it improves a person's stature, creates feelings of self-worth, and encourages people to trust the individual. A successful career inhibits crime by creating a stake in conformity; why commit crime when you are doing well at your job? The relationship is reciprocal. If people are chosen to be employees, they return the favor by doing the best job possible; if they are chosen as spouses, they blossom into devoted partners. In contrast, moving to a new city reduces social capital by closing people off from long-term relationships.[44]

Sampson and Laub's research indicates that building social capital and strong social bonds reduces the likelihood of long-term deviance. This finding suggests that, in contrast to latent trait theories, events that occur in later adolescence and adulthood do in fact influence the direction of delinquent careers. Life events can either help to

According to age-graded theory, creating social capital can decrease the risk of anti-social behaviors. Calvin Whitehead, 16 (left), and Marquis Copeland, 14, unload mulch on July 1, 2000, in Newport, Va. They're both in the Youth Employment for the Summer program. Mary Cherry, director of Youth Employment for the Summer, also known as YES, has been working hard to get teenagers summer jobs. Through the YES program, Cherry serves as liaison between teenagers and home and business owners who need services, such as cleaning, mowing lawns, and baby sitting. (AP/Wide World Photos)

terminate or sustain deviant careers. For example, getting arrested and punished may have little direct effect on future criminality, but it can help sustain a delinquent career because it reduces the chances of employment and job stability, two factors that are directly related to crime.[45]

Testing Age-Graded Theory Several indicators support the validity of age-graded theory.[46] Evidence now shows that delinquent career trajectories can be reversed if life conditions improve, an outcome predicted by age-graded theory.[47] For example, employment status affects behavior—men who are unemployed or underemployed report higher delinquent participation rates than employed men. Similarly, men released from prison on parole who obtain jobs are less likely to recidivate than those who lack or lose employment.[48]

Research has been directed at identifying the sources of social capital and determining whether and how it is related to crime. For example, youths who accumulate social capital in childhood (doing well in school, having a tightly knit family) are also the most likely to maintain steady work as adults; employment may help insulate them from crime.[49] People who maintain a successful marriage in their twenties and become parents are the most likely to mature out of crime.[50] Although it is possible that marriage stabilizes people and helps them build social capital, it is also likely that marriage may discourage crime by reducing contact with delinquent peers.[51]

A number of research efforts have supported the Sampson and Laub association between social capital and crime. For example, delinquents who enter the military, serve overseas, and receive veterans' benefits enhance their occupational status (social capital) while reducing delinquent involvement.[52] In contrast, research shows that people who are self-centered and present-oriented are less likely to accumulate social capital and more prone to commit delinquent acts.[53]

In an important new study, Laub and Sampson have recontacted subjects from the original Glueck sample to find out how they fared as adults. Now in their sixties and seventies, these men provide an important source of information on what happens to former delinquents as they go throught the life cycle. Some of their findings are discussed in the Focus on Delinquency, "Five Hundred Delinquent Boys in the New Millennium."

FIVE HUNDRED DELINQUENT BOYS IN THE NEW MILLENNIUM

Why, and when, do most juvenile delinquents stop offending? Are some delinquents destined to become persistent criminals as adults? John Laub and Robert Sampson are now conducting a follow-up to their re-analysis of Sheldon and Eleanor Glueck's study, which matched 500 delinquent with 500 nondelinquents. The original sample was re-interviewed by the Gluecks at age 25 and later at age 32. Now Sampson and Laub have located the survivors, the oldest subject being 70 years old and the youngest 62!

Persistence and Desistance

Laub and Sampson find that delinquency and other forms of antisocial conduct in childhood are strongly related to adult crime and to drug and alcohol abuse. Former delinquents also suffer consequences in other areas of social life, such as school, work, and family life. For example, they are far less likely to finish high school than nondelinquents and subsequently more likely to be unemployed, receive welfare, and experience separation or divorce as adults.

In their latest research, Laub and Sampson address one of the key questions posed by developmental theories: Is it possible for former delinquents to rehabilitate themselves as adults? They found that most antisocial children do not remain antisocial as adults. Of those men who survived to age 50, 24 percent had no arrests for crimes of violence and property after age 17 (6% had no arrests for total crime); 48 percent had no arrests for these predatory crimes after age 25 (19% for total crime); 60 percent had no arrests for predatory crime after age 31 (33% for total crime); and 79 percent had no arrests for predatory crime after age 40 (57% for total crime). They conclude that desistance from crime is the norm and that most, if not all, serious delinquents eventually desist from crime.

Why Do Delinquents Desist?

Laub and Sampson's earlier research indicated that building social capital through marriage and job were key components of desistance from crime. However, in this new round of research, they were able to find out more about long-term desistance by interviewing 52 men as they approached age 70. Drawing on the men's own words, they find that one important element for going straight is "knifing off" individuals from their immediate environment and offering them a new script for the future. Joining the military can provide this "knifing-off" effect, as does marriage, and changing one's residence. One former delinquent (age 69) told them:

> I'd say the turning point was, number one, the Army. You get into an outfit, you had a sense of belonging, you made your friends. I think I became a pretty good judge of character. In the Army, you met some good ones, you met some foul balls. Then I met the wife. I'd say probably that would be the

turning point. Got married, then naturally, kids come. So now you got to get a better job, you got to make more money. And that's how I got to the Navy Yard and tried to improve myself.

Former delinquents who "went straight" were able to put structure into their lives. Structure often led the men to disassociate from delinquent peers, reducing the opportunity to get into trouble. Getting married, for example, may limit the number of nights men can "hang with the guys." As one wife of a former delinquent said, "It is not how many beers you have, it's who you drink with." Even multiple offenders who did time in prison were able to desist with the help of a stabilizing marriage.

The former delinquents who can turn their life around, who have acquired a degree of maturity by taking on family and work responsibilities, and who have forged new commitments, are the ones most likely to make a fresh start and find new direction and meaning in life. It seems that men who desisted changed their identity as well, and this in turn affected their outlook and sense of maturity and responsibility. The ability to change was not related to the type of crimes committed in their youth; violent offenders followed the same path as property offenders.

Policy Implications

Laub and Sampson find that youth problems—delinquency, substance abuse, violence, dropping out, teen pregnancy—often share common risk characteristics. Intervention strategies therefore should consider a broad array of antisocial, criminal, and deviant behaviors, and not just limit the focus to one subgroup or crime type. Because delinquency and other social problems are linked, early prevention efforts that reduce crime will probably also reduce alcohol abuse, drunk driving, drug abuse, sexual promiscuity, and family violence, and perhaps school failure, unemployment, marital disharmony, and divorce. The best way to achieve these goals is through four significant life-changing events: getting married, joining the military, getting a job, and changing one's environment or neighborhood. What appears to be important about these processes is that they all involve, to varying degrees, the following items: a knifing off of the past from the present; new situations that provide both supervision and monitoring as well as new opportunities of social support and growth; and new situations that provide the opportunity for transforming identity. Prevention of crime must therefore be a policy at all times and at all stages of life.

Source: John Laub, "Crime over the Life Course," *Poverty Research News*, the Newsletter of the Northwestern University/University of Chicago Joint Center for Poverty Research, 4(3), May-June 2000.

Checkpoints

✔ The social development model (SDM) integrates social control, social learning, and structural models.

✔ According to interactional theory, the causes of crime are bi-directional. Weak bonds lead to deviant peer relations and delinquency; delinquency weakens conventional bonds and strengthens relations with deviant peers.

✔ According to age-graded theory, building social capital and strong social bonds reduces the likelihood of long-term deviance.

THE CONCEPT OF LATENT TRAITS

Some delinquency experts question whether people constantly change and that change affects criminality over the life cycle. This model assumes that a number of people in the population have a personal attribute or latent trait that controls their inclination or propensity to commit crimes.[54] This disposition or latent trait may be either present at birth or established early in life, and it remains stable over time. Suspected latent traits include defective intelligence, impulsive personality, genetic abnormalities, the physical-chemical functioning of the brain, and environmental influences on brain function such as drugs, chemicals, and injuries.[55] Those who carry one of these latent traits are in danger of becoming career delinquents; those who lack the traits have a much lower risk. Latent traits should affect the behavioral choices of all people equally, regardless of their gender or personal characteristics.[56]

The latent trait view can be contrasted with previously discussed developmental theories on the basis of human growth and maturation. According to developmental theory, people are constantly changing, and so too is their propensity to commit crime. According to this view, there is an unchanging master trait that remains stable over time and influences all other aspects of a person's life. Consequently, the *propensity* to commit crime is actually quite stable, but other factors such as the *opportunity* to commit crime fluctuates over time. People age out of crime because, as they mature, there are simply fewer opportunities to violate the law and greater inducements to remain "straight." They may marry, have children, and obtain jobs. The former delinquents' newfound adult responsibilities leave them little time to hang out with their friends, abuse substances, and get into scrapes with the law.

Michael Gottfredson and Travis Hirschi's general theory of crime, probably the most prominent latent trait view, is discussed in some detail in the following section.

General Theory of Crime

Michael Gottfredson and Travis Hirschi's *General Theory of Crime (GTC)* is probably the most prominent latent-trait view. It modifies and redefines some of the principles articulated in Hirschi's social control theory (Chapter 4) by integrating the concepts of control with those of biosocial, psychological, routine activities, and rational choice theories.[57]

The Act and the Offender In their General Theory of Crime (GTC), Gottfredson and Hirschi consider the delinquent offender and the delinquent act as separate concepts (Figure 5.5). On the one hand, delinquent acts, such as robberies or burglaries, are illegal events or deeds that people engage in when they perceive them to be advantageous. For example, burglaries are typically committed by young males looking for cash, liquor, and entertainment; the crime provides "easy, short-term gratification."[58] Crime is rational and predictable; people commit crime when it promises

Figure 5.5
The General Theory of Crime

Impulsive personality
- Physical
- Insensitive
- Risk-taking
- Short-sighted
- Nonverbal

Low self-control
- Poor parenting
- Deviant parents
- Lack of supervision
- Active
- Self-centered

Weakening of social bonds
- Attachment
- Involvement
- Commitment
- Belief

Criminal opportunity
- Gangs
- Free time
- Drugs
- Suitable targets

Crime and deviance
- Delinquency
- Smoking
- Drinking
- Sex
- Crime

rewards with minimal threat of pain; the threat of punishment can deter crime. If targets are well guarded, crime rates diminish. Only the truly irrational offender would dare to strike under those circumstances.

On the other hand, delinquent offenders are predisposed to commit crimes. They are not robots who commit crime without restraint; their days are also filled with conventional behaviors, such as going to school, parties, concerts, and church. But given the same set of delinquent opportunities, such as having a lot of free time for mischief and living in a neighborhood with unguarded homes containing valuable merchandise, crime-prone people have a much higher probability of violating the law than do nondelinquents. The propensity to commit crimes remains stable throughout a person's life. Change in the frequency of delinquent activity is purely a function of change in criminal opportunity.

By recognizing that there are stable differences in people's propensity to commit crime, the GTC adds a biosocial element to the concept of social control. The biological and psychological factors that make people impulsive and crime-prone may be inherited or may develop through incompetent or absent parenting.

What Makes Kids Delinquency-Prone? What, then, causes kids to become excessively crime-prone? Gottfredson and Hirschi attribute the tendency to commit crimes to an adolescent's level of **self-control**. People with limited self-control tend to be impulsive; they are insensitive to other people's feelings, physical (rather than mental) risk takers, shortsighted, and nonverbal.[59] They have a here-and-now orientation and refuse to work for distant goals; they lack diligence, tenacity, and persistence. Adolescents lacking self-control tend to be adventuresome, active, physical, and self-centered. As they mature, they often have unstable marriages, jobs, and friendships.[60] They are less likely to feel shame if they engage in deviant acts and are more likely to find them pleasurable.[61] As they mature they are also more likely to engage in dangerous behaviors such as drinking, smoking, and reckless driving; all of these behaviors are associated with criminality.[62]

Because those with low self-control enjoy risky, exciting, or thrilling behaviors with immediate gratification, they are more likely to enjoy delinquent acts, which require stealth, agility, speed, and power, than conventional acts, which demand long-term study and cognitive and verbal skills. They enjoy taking risks and consequently are more likely to get involved in accidents and suffer injuries than people who maintain self-control.[63] As Gottfredson and Hirschi put it, they derive satisfaction from "money without work, sex without courtship, revenge without court delays."[64] Many of these individuals who have a propensity for committing crime also engage in other behaviors such as smoking, drinking, gambling, and immoral sexuality.[65] Although these acts are not illegal, they too provide immediate, short-term gratification. Figure 5.5 lists the elements of self-control.

Gottfredson and Hirschi trace the root cause of poor self-control to inadequate childrearing practices. Parents who refuse or are unable to monitor a child's behavior, to recognize deviant behavior when it occurs, and to punish that behavior, will produce

self-control Ability to control impulsive and often imprudent behaviors that offer immediate short-term gratification.

Capricious acts of vandalism bolster Gottfredson and Hirschi's claim that criminals are impulsive individuals who lack self-control. Is it at all possible that the people who vandalized this vehicle could be well reasoned and thoughtful? (© Joel Gordon)

children who lack self-control. Children who are not attached to their parents, who are poorly supervised, and whose parents are criminal or deviant themselves are the most likely to develop poor self-control. In a sense, lack of self-control occurs naturally when steps are not taken to stop its development.[66] Low self-control develops early in life and remains stable into and through adulthood.[67]

Self-Control and Delinquency Gottfredson and Hirschi claim that the principles of self-control theory can explain all varieties of delinquent behavior and all the social and behavioral correlates of crime. That is, such widely disparate crimes as burglary, robbery, embezzlement, drug dealing, murder, rape, and insider trading all stem from a deficiency of self-control. Likewise, gender, racial, and ecological differences in crime rates can be explained by discrepancies in self-control. Put another way, the male crime rate is higher than the female crime rate because males have lower levels of self-control. Although the delinquent activity of individuals with low self-control also declines as those individuals mature, they maintain an offense rate that remains consistently higher than those with strong self-control.

By integrating the concepts of socialization and criminality, Gottfredson and Hirschi help explain why kids who lack self-control can escape criminality and, conversely, why others who have self-control might not escape criminality. Adolescents who are at risk because they have impulsive personalities may forgo delinquent careers because there are no delinquent opportunities that satisfy their impulsive needs; instead, they may find other outlets for their impulsive personalities. In contrast, if the opportunity is strong enough, even people with relatively strong self-control may be tempted to violate the law; the incentives to commit crime may overwhelm self-control.

Evaluating the General Theory. Following the publication of a general theory of crime, dozens of research efforts have tested the validity of Gottfredson and Hirschi's theoretical views. One approach involves identifying indicators of impulsiveness and self-control to determine whether scales measuring these factors correlate with measures of delinquent activity; a number of studies conducted both in the United States and abroad have successfully showed this type of association.[68] Supporting research seems to show that young offenders, lacking in self-control, commit a garden variety of criminal acts.[69] Kids whose problems develop early in life are the most resistant to change in treatment and rehabilitation programs.[70] Conversely, delinquency can be suppressed by parents who manage their children's behavior and help them increase their self-control.[71] Having parents (or step-parents) available to control behavior may reduce the opportunity to commit crime.[72]

Although there has been quite a bit of supporting evidence, several questions and criticisms remain unanswered. Some critics argue that the theory is tautological or involves circular reasoning: How do we know when people are impulsive? When they commit crimes, are all delinquents impulsive? Of course, or else they would not have broken the law![73]

The GTC also fails to address distinct gender differences in the crime rate. For example, while the male delinquency rate is higher than the female rate, there is little evidence that males are more impulsive than females (although females and males differ in many other personality traits).[74] Similarly, Gottfredson and Hirschi explain racial differences in the crime rate as a failure of childrearing practices in the African American community.[75] In so doing, they overlook issues of institutional racism, poverty, and relative deprivation, which have been shown to significantly impact crime rate differentials.

Do Kids Change? In contrast to developmental theories, the GTC assumes that, while the opportunity to commit crime constantly fluctuates, delinquent propensity does not. This is the key difference between the two positions. Here the criticism of the GTC is most pointed: A number of research efforts show that factors that help control delinquent behavior, such as peer relations and school performance, vary over time. Consequently, the ability to exert self-control may vary with age. As people mature, they may be better able to control their impulsive behavior.[76] Social influences, which are dominant in early adolescence, may fade and be replaced by others in adulthood.[77] This finding contradicts the GTC, which suggests the influence of friends should be stable and unchanging. However, it is uncertain whether life changes affect the propensity to commit crime or merely the opportunity, as Gottfredson and Hirschi would suggest.

Although questions like these remain, the strength of the general theory lies in its scope and breadth; it attempts to explain all forms of crime and deviance, from lower-class gang delinquency to sexual harassment in the business community.[78] By integrating concepts of delinquent choice, delinquent opportunity, socialization, and personality, Gottfredson and Hirschi make a plausible argument that all deviant behaviors may originate at the same source. Continued efforts are needed to test the GTC and establish the validity of its core concepts. It remains one of the key developments of modern criminological theory.

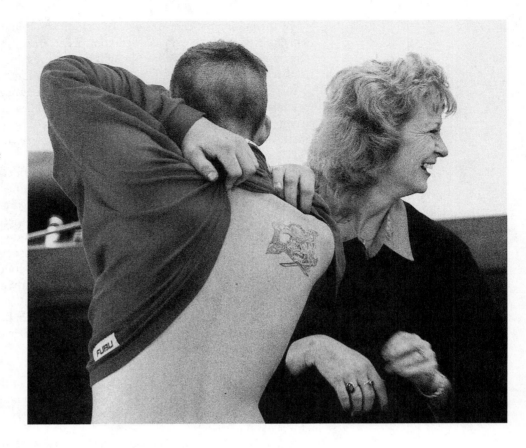

The General Theory of Crime assumes that the opportunity to commit crime constantly fluctuates while delinquent propensity remains the same. Yet treatment programs typically assume that they can help youngsters change. Lorain County Judge Paulette Lilly laughs as the first juvenile to graduate from the Lorain County Domestic Relations and Juvenile Drug Court program shows her his new tattoo, Oct. 26, 2000, in Elyria, Ohio. (AP/Wide World Photos)

✔ Checkpoint

✔ Latent-trait theories assume that some people have a physical or psychological trait that makes them crime-prone.

✔ The opportunity to commit crime varies, while latent traits remain stable.

✔ According to the general theory of crime, an impulsive personality is the key latent crime-producing trait.

✔ People who are impulsive develop low self-control, which weakens their bond to society.

✔ Impulsive people with low self-control will be unable to resist criminal opportunities.

SUMMARY

Developmental theories look at multiple factors derived from a number of structural and process theories. Examples include the social development model, interactional theory, and age-graded theory. These theories find that events that take place over the life course influence delinquent choices. The cause of crime constantly changes as people mature. At first, the nuclear family influences behavior; during adolescence, the peer group dominates; in adulthood, marriage and career are critical. There are a variety of pathways to crime: Some kids are sneaky, others hostile, and still others defiant. Crime may be part of a variety of social problems, including health, physical, and interpersonal troubles.

Latent-trait theories hold that some underlying condition present at birth or soon after controls behavior. Suspect traits include low IQ, impulsivity, and personality structure. This underlying trait explains the continuity of offending because, once present, it remains with individuals throughout their lives. The latent-trait theory developed by Gottfredson and Hirschi integrates choice theory concepts: people with latent traits choose crime over noncrime. The opportunity for crime mediates their choice.

See the book-specific Web site at www.cj.wadsworth.com for additional chapter links, discussions, and quizzes.

developmental theory
life-course theory
latent trait view
problem behavior
   syndrome (PBS)

authority-conflict pathway
covert pathway
overt pathway
adolescent-limiteds
life-course persisters

social development model
   (SDM)
pro-social bonds
interactional theory
turning points

social capital
self-control

QUESTIONS FOR DISCUSSION

1. Do you consider yourself the holder of "social capital"? If so, what form does it take?

2. A person gets 1600 on the SATs. Without knowing him or her, what personal, family, and social characteristics do you think he or she must have? Another person becomes a serial killer. Without knowing him or her, what personal, family, and social characteristics must he or she have? If "bad behavior" is explained by multiple

problems, is "good behavior" explained by multiple strengths?

3. Do you believe there is a "latent trait" that makes a person crime-prone, or is crime a function of environment and socialization?

4. Do you agree with Loeber's multiple-pathway model? Do you know people who have traveled down those paths?

VIEWPOINT

Serious and violent juvenile (SVJ) offenders comprise a troubled and often dangerous population. Although their numbers are small, they are responsible for a disproportionate amount of crime. To know what to do about this difficult problem and to garner the necessary financial, political, and public support to deal with it effectively, policymakers need a solid research foundation. To build this research base, the Office of Juvenile Justice and Delinquency Prevention (OJJDP) convened the Study Group on Serious and Violent Juvenile Offenders. The findings of this panel are hopeful and compelling. Perhaps the panel's most important findings are that it's never too early to begin efforts to prevent SVJ offending, and it's never too late to intervene with known serious and violent juvenile offenders.

 To read more about Rolf Loeber's view of the problem of serious and violent juvenile offenders and how they should be treated, read his paper on InfoTrac® College Edition: Rolf Loeber, "Early intervention can work for serious and violent juvenile offenders," *The Brown University Child and Adolescent Behavior Letter* 16:1 (May 2000).

Chapter 6

Gender and Delinquency

© Bruce Davidson/Magnum Photos

s the principal of a northeastern junior high school, you get a call from a parent who is disturbed because he has heard a rumor that the student literary digest plans to publish a story with a sexual theme. The work is written by a junior high school girl who became pregnant during the year and underwent an abortion. You ask for and receive a copy of the narrative.

The girl's story is actually a cautionary tale of young love that results in an unwanted pregnancy. The author details the abusive home life that led her to engage in an intimate relationship with another student, her pregnancy, her conflict with her parents, her decision to abort, and the emotional turmoil that the incident created. She tells students to use contraception if they are sexually active and recommends appropriate types of birth control. There is nothing provocative or sexually explicit in the work.

Some teachers argue that girls should not be allowed to read this material because it has sexual content from which they must be protected, and that in a sense it advocates defiance of parents. Also, some parents may object to a story about precocious sexuality because they fear it may encourage their children to "experiment." Such behavior is linked to delinquency and drug abuse. Those who advocate publication believe that girls have a right to read about such important issues and decide on their own course of action.

- Should you force the story's deletion because its theme is essentially sexual and controversial?

- Should you allow publication because it deals with the subject matter in a mature fashion?

- Do you think reading and learning about sexual matters encourages or discourages experimentation in sexuality?

- Should young girls be protected from such material? Would it cause them damage?

Inequalities still exist in the way boys and girls are socialized by their parents and treated by social institutions. Do these gender differences also manifest themselves in the delinquency rate? What effect do gender roles have on behavior choices?

As we saw in Chapter 2, males are much more likely than females to engage in repeat and serious offending. Official statistics show that girls are arrested far less often than boys, and then for relatively minor offenses; correctional data show that about 95 percent of incarcerated inmates are males.

Nor is this relationship recent. To early delinquency experts, the female offender was an aberration who engaged in crimes that usually had a sexual connotation—prostitution, running away (which presumably leads to sexual misadventure), premarital sex, and crimes of sexual passion (killing a boyfriend or a husband).[1] Delinquency experts often ignored female offenders, assuming that they rarely violated the law, or, if they did, that their illegal acts were status-type offenses. Female delinquency was viewed as emotional or family-related, and such problems were not an important concern of criminologists. In fact, the few "true" female delinquents were considered anomalies whose criminal activity was a function of taking on masculine characteristics, a concept referred to as the "masculinity hypothesis."[2]

Because female delinquency was considered unimportant, most early theories of delinquency focused on male misconduct. Quite often these models failed adequately to explain gender differences in the delinquency rate. For example, strain theory (Chapter 4) holds that delinquency results from the failure to achieve socially desirable goals. Using this logic, females should be more criminal than males because they face *gender discrimination* and males do not. Some delinquency experts interpret such exceptions to the rules as an indication that separate explanations for male and female delinquency are required.[3]

Interest in the association between gender and delinquency is emerging, in part fueled by observations of contemporary crime trends. Official data indicate that, although the female delinquency rate is still much lower than the male rate, it is growing at a faster pace. Female crime patterns are remarkably similar to those of males; larceny and aggravated assault, the crimes for which most males are arrested (as measured by the UCR), are also the most common offenses for which females are arrested. Although girls still commit less crime than boys, members of both sexes are similar in the onset and development of their offending careers.[4] In societies with high rates of male delinquency, there are also high rates of female delinquency. Over time, male and female arrest rates rise and fall in a parallel fashion.[5]

Another reason for the interest in gender studies is that conceptions of gender differences have changed. A feminist approach to understanding crime is now firmly established. The stereotype of the female delinquent as a sexual deviant is no longer taken seriously.[6] The result has been an increased effort to conduct research that would adequately explain differences and similarities in male and female offending patterns.

This chapter provides an overview of gender factors in delinquency. We first discuss some of the gender differences in development and offending patterns. Then we turn to some explanations for these differences: (1) the trait view, (2) the socialization view, (3) the liberal feminist view, and (4) the radical feminist view.

GENDER DIFFERENCES IN DEVELOPMENT

Research on the developmental differences between males and females is a relatively new area of study, but we know that gender differences may exist as early as infancy when boys are able to express emotions at higher rates. Infant girls show greater control over their emotions, whereas boys are more easily angered and depend more on inputs from their mothers.[7] There are indications that gender differences in socialization and development do exist and that they may have an effect on juvenile offending patterns.[8]

Socialization Differences

Psychologists believe that differences in the way females and males are socialized affect their development. Males learn to value independence, whereas females are taught that their self-worth depends on their ability to sustain relationships. Girls, therefore, run the risk of losing themselves in their relationships with others, while boys may experience a chronic sense of alienation. Because so many relationships go sour, females also run the risk of feeling alienated because of the failure to achieve relational success.[9]

Although there are few gender differences in aggression during the first few years of life, girls are socialized to be less aggressive than boys and are supervised more closely.[10] Differences in aggression become noticeable between ages 3 and 6, when children are socialized into organized groups such as the daycare center. Males are more likely to display physical aggression, whereas females display relational aggression—for example, by excluding disliked peers from play groups.[11]

As they mature, girls learn to respond to provocation by feeling anxious, unlike boys, who are encouraged to retaliate.[12] Overall, women are much more likely to feel distressed than men.[13] Although females get angry as often as males, many have been taught to blame themselves for such feelings. Females are, therefore, much more likely than males to respond to anger with feelings of depression, anxiety, and shame. Females are socialized to fear that anger will harm relationships; males are encouraged to react with "moral outrage," blaming others for their discomfort.[14]

A youth worker talks with young girls in an after-school program. Are gender differences in personality a matter of experience, or do you believe that males and females are inherently different? (© Gale Zucker/Stock, Boston)

Females are also more likely than males to be targets of sexual and physical abuse. Female victims have been shown to suffer more seriously from these attacks, sustaining damage to their self-image; victims of sexual abuse find it difficult to build autonomy and life skills.

Cognitive Differences

There are also cognitive differences between adolescent males and females. Girls have been found to be superior in verbal ability; boys test higher in visual-spatial performance. Girls learn to speak earlier and faster, with better pronunciation. Girls are far less likely than boys to have reading problems, but boys do much better on standardized math tests, which is attributed by some experts to their strategies for approaching math problems. In most cases cognitive differences are small, narrowing, and usually attributed to cultural expectations. When given training, girls can increase their visual-spatial skills.

Personality Differences

Girls are often stereotyped as talkative, but research shows that in many situations boys spend more time talking than girls do. Females are more willing to reveal their feelings and more likely to express concern for others. Females are more concerned about finding the "meaning of life" and less interested in competing for material success.[15] Males are more likely to introduce new topics and to interrupt conversations.

Adolescent females use different knowledge than males and have different ways of interpreting their interactions with others. These gender differences may have an impact on self-esteem and self-concept. Research shows that, as adolescents develop, male self-esteem and self-concept rise whereas female self-confidence is lowered.[16] However, females display more self-control than males, a factor that has been related to criminality.[17]

What Causes Gender Differences?

Why do these gender differences occur? Some experts suggest that gender differences may have a biological origin: males and females are essentially different. The reason

Adolescent females use different knowledge than males and have different ways of interpreting their interactions with others. These gender differences may have an impact on self-esteem and self-concept. Research shows that as adolescents develop, male self-esteem and self-concept rise, whereas female self-confidence is lowered. Paula Albert, 16, stands in the hallway of Bethel Regional High School in Bethel, Alaska. Albert says depression led her to abuse inhalants. She now speaks to teens about the problem. (AP/Wide World Photos)

gender-schema theory Asserts that our culture polarizes males and females, forcing them into exclusive gender roles of "feminine" or "masculine"; these gender scripts provide the basis for deviant behaviors.

The mission of the National Council for Research on Women is to enhance the connections among research, policy analysis, advocacy, and innovative programming on behalf of women and girls. Visit their site at

http://www.ncrw.org/

For an up-to-date list of Web links, go to www.wadsworth.com/product/0534573053s

may be neurological. Males and females have somewhat different brain organizations; females are more left brain–oriented and males more right brain–oriented. (The left brain is believed to control language, and the right, spatial relations.) Others point to the hormonal differences between the sexes as the key to understanding their behavior.

Another view is that gender differences are a result of the interaction of socialization, learning, and enculturation. Boys and girls may behave differently because they have been exposed to different styles of socialization, learned different values, and had different cultural experiences. It follows, then, that if members of both sexes were equally exposed to the factors that produce delinquency, their delinquency rates would be equivalent.[18] According to psychologist Sandra Bem's **gender-schema theory,** our culture polarizes males and females by forcing them to obey mutually exclusive gender roles, or "scripts." Girls are expected to be "feminine," exhibiting traits such as being sympathetic and gentle. In contrast, boys are expected to be "masculine," exhibiting assertiveness and dominance. Children internalize these scripts and accept gender polarization as normal. Children's self-esteem becomes wrapped up in how closely their behavior conforms to the proper sex role stereotype. When children begin to perceive themselves as either *boys* or *girls* (which occurs at about age 3), they search for information to help them define their role; they begin to learn what behavior is appropriate for their sex.[19] Girls are expected to behave according to the appropriate script and to seek approval of their behavior: Are they acting as girls should at that age? Masculine behavior is to be avoided. In contrast, males look for cues from their peers to define their masculinity; aggressive behavior may be rewarded with peer approval, whereas sensitivity is viewed as nonmasculine.[20]

Biology or Socialization? In her recent book, *The Two Sexes: Growing up Apart, Coming Together,* psychologist Eleanor Maccoby argues that gender differences are not a matter of individual personality or biological difference but the way kids socialize and how their relationships are structured.[21] Despite the best efforts of parents who want to break down gender boundaries, kids still segregate themselves by gender in their play groups. Thus a "boy culture" and a "girl culture" develop side by side. Kids also take on different roles depending on who they are with and who is being exposed to behavior. A boy will be all macho bravado when he is with his peers but may be a tender, loving big brother when asked to babysit for his little sister. Little girls aren't "passive" as a result of some ingrained quality; they have learned to be passive only when boys are present. According to Maccoby, gender separation has partly biological and partly social causes. While biological and cognitive differences do impact on behavior, Maccoby claims that gender distinctions arise mainly in social interactions and that peer groups are highly influential in greatly enhancing gender. Nonetheless, biological and social factors are so intertwined that it is erroneous to think of gender differences as having an independent social or physical origin.

GENDER DIFFERENCES AND DELINQUENCY

Regardless of their origin, gender distinctions may partly explain the significant gender differences in the delinquency rate. Males seem more aggressive and less likely to form attachments to others, factors that might increase their crime rates. Males view aggression as an appropriate means to gain status. Boys are also more likely than girls to socialize with deviant peers and, when they do, they display personality traits that make them more susceptible to delinquency. Boys are more interested in their own self-interest.

Girls are shielded by their moral sense, which directs them to avoid harming others. Their moral sensitivity may counterbalance the effects of family problems.[22] Females are more verbally proficient, a skill that may help them deal with conflict without resorting to violence. They are taught to be less aggressive and view belligerence as a lack of self-control.[23] When girls are aggressive, they are more likely than boys to hide their behavior from adults; girls who "bully" others are less likely than boys to admit their behavior.[24]

Cognitive and personality differences are magnified when children internalize gender-specific behaviors. Boys who aren't tough are labeled sissies. Girls are expected to form closer bonds with their friends and to share feelings. Research by Stacey Nofziger finds that grasp of one's **gender identity** is the most important predictor of intersex differences in the delinquency rate. Members of both sexes who identify with so-called masculine traits are more likely to engage in delinquent acts than those who admire "feminine" traits. Because boys are more likely to identify with masculine traits, their crime rates are higher. Sex may only have an impact on delinquency, Nofziger concludes, to the extent that females learn to be "feminine" and males "masculine."[25]

gender identity The gender characteristics individuals identify in their own behaviors; members of both sexes who identify with "masculine" traits are more likely to engage in delinquent acts.

Gender Patterns in Delinquency

Over the past decades, females have increased their participation in delinquent behaviors at a faster rate than males. Arrest data indicate that juvenile females make up a greater percentage of the arrest statistics today than they did 30 years ago. In 1967, females constituted 13 percent of all juvenile index-crime arrests; today they make up more than 25 percent. The most recent arrest data show that between 1990 and 1999 the total teenage male arrest rate increased by about 5 percent and the female rate by more than 30 percent.[26] Even more striking was the relative change in arrests for serious violent crimes—during the 1990s, teenage male arrests declined 11 percent while female arrests rose 40 percent (Figures 6.1, 6.2).

Patterns of male and female criminality appear to be converging. Self-report data indicate that the rank ordering of male and female deviant behaviors is similar. The illegal acts most common for boys—petty larceny, using a false ID, and smoking marijuana—are also the ones most frequently committed by girls.

There are a number of institutes at major universities devoted to the study of women's issues. You can visit the site of the one at the University of Michigan, http://www.umich.edu/~womenstd/ For an up-to-date list of Web links, go to www.wadsworth.com/product/0534573053s

Violent Behavior

Gender differences in the delinquency rate may be narrowing, but males continue to be overrepresented in arrests for violent crimes. For example, almost all homicide

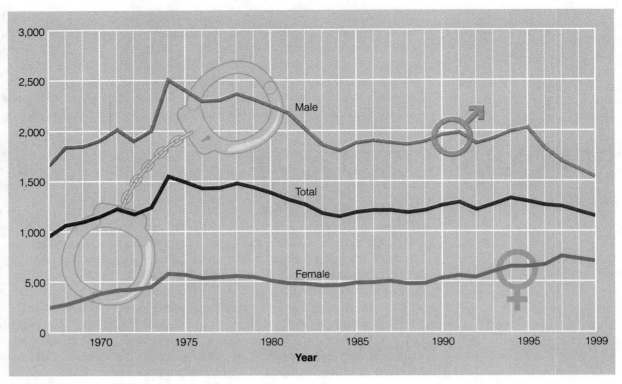

Figure 6.1

Juvenile Index Crime Arrest Rates by Sex (per 100,000)

Source: *Uniform Crime Report,* 1999.

offenders are males. In 1999, of the more than 900 juveniles arrested for murder, only 70 were female.[27]

Males and females who engage in violence show differences in the victims they target and the weapons they use. The typical male juvenile kills a friend or acquaintance with a handgun during an argument. In contrast, the typical female is as likely to kill a family member as an acquaintance and is more likely to use a knife. Both males and females tend to kill males, generally their brothers, fathers, or friends.

Why do these differences occur, and why are girls increasing their involvement in delinquent activities at a faster pace than boys? The wide range of opinions on these questions will be presented in the remaining sections of this chapter.

✔ Checkpoints

✔ Female delinquency was considered unimportant by early delinquency experts because girls rarely committed crime, and when they did it was sexual in nature.

✔ Interest in female delinquency has risen because the female crime rate has been increasing, while the male rate is in decline.

✔ There are distinct gender patterns in development that may explain crime rate differences.

✔ Girls are socialized to be less aggressive than boys.

✔ Girls read better and have better verbal skills than boys.

✔ Gender differences may have both biological and social origins.

✔ The female proportion of the delinquency rate has doubled during the past 25 years.

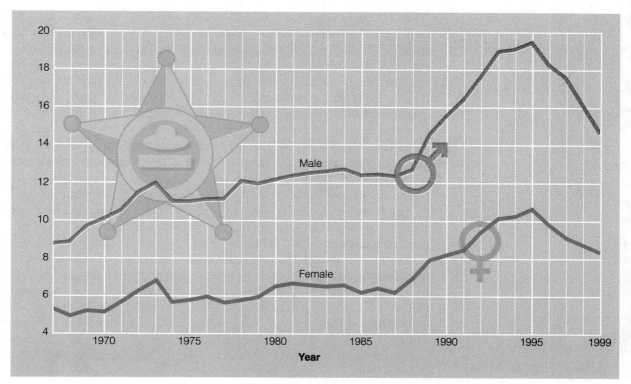

Figure 6.2
Violent Crime Arrests by Sex as a Percentage of all Index Crime Arrests for Juveniles

Source: *Uniform Crime Report,* 1999.

ARE FEMALE DELINQUENTS BORN THAT WAY?

There is a long tradition of tracing gender differences in delinquency to traits that are uniquely male or female. The argument that biological and psychological differences between males and females can explain differences in crime rates is not a new one. The earliest criminologists focused on physical characteristics believed to be precursors of crime. Cesare Lombroso's concept of the "born criminal" rested on male-oriented traits such as extraordinary strength and agility, lack of emotion, and insensitivity to pain. Female delinquents were treated as an aberration. Because the female crime rate was so low and most girls were not delinquents, those whose behavior deviated from what was considered appropriate for females were believed to be inherently evil or physically maladapted.

Biological Explanations

masculinity hypothesis View that women who commit crimes have biological and psychological traits similar to those of men.

With the publication in 1895 of *The Female Offender,* Lombroso (with William Ferrero) extended his work on criminality to females.[28] Lombroso maintained that women were lower on the evolutionary scale than men, more childlike and less intelligent.[29] Women who committed crimes could be distinguished from "normal" women by physical characteristics—excessive body hair, wrinkles, and an abnormal cranium, for example.[30] In appearance, delinquent females appeared closer to men than to other women. The **masculinity hypothesis** suggested that delinquent girls had excessive male characteristics.[31]

Lombroso's suggestion that women were lower on the evolutionary scale than men is puzzling because he viewed primitivism as the key element in producing criminal behavior, yet the crime rate of females is lower than that of males. Lombroso explained this inconsistency by arguing that most girls are restrained from committing delinquent acts by counterbalancing traits such as "piety, maternity, want of passion, sexual coldness, weakness, and undeveloped intelligence."[32] The delinquent female lacks these traits and is therefore "unrestrained in her childlike, unreasoned passions." Lombroso also believed much female delinquency is hidden.

Lombroso did recognize that there were far fewer female than male delinquents. He suggested that this was a function of the relative uniformity among females; the female "born criminal" was a rare creature. But he also believed that if a girl did become a delinquent her behavior might be more vicious than that of males.[33]

Lombroso's early work portrayed female offenders as suffering from weak egos, abnormal personalities, and other psychological problems. Another theme begun by Lombroso was that female delinquency was linked to anatomy and sexuality.

Lombrosian thought had a significant influence for much of the twentieth century. Delinquency rate differentials were explained in terms of gender-based differences. For example, in 1925 Cyril Burt linked female delinquency to menstruation.[34] Similarly, William Healy and Augusta Bronner suggested that males' physical superiority enhanced their criminality. Their research showed that about 70 percent of the delinquent girls they studied had abnormal weight and size, a finding that supported the "masculinity hypothesis."[35] In a later work, *The Criminality of Women* (1950), Otto Pollak linked female criminality to the impact of biological conditions such as menstruation, pregnancy, and menopause:[36]

> *Thefts, particularly shoplifting, arson, homicide, and resistance against public officials seem to show a significant correlation between the menstruation of the offender and the time of the offense. The turmoil of the onset of menstruation and the puberty of girls appears to express itself in the relatively high frequency of false accusations and—where cultural opportunities permit—of incendiarism. Pregnancy in its turn is a crime-promoting influence with regard to attacks against the life of the fetus and the newborn. The menopause finally seems to bring about a distinct increase in crime, especially in offenses resulting from irritability such as arson, breaches of the peace, perjury, and insults.[37]*

Pollak argued that most female delinquency goes unrecorded because the female is the instigator rather than the perpetrator.[38] Females first use their sexual charms to instigate crime and then beguile males in the justice system to obtain deferential treatment. This observation, referred to as the **chivalry hypothesis,** holds that gender differences in the delinquency rate can be explained by the fact that female criminality is overlooked or forgiven by male agents of the justice system. Those who believe in the chivalry hypothesis point to data showing that, even though women make up about 20 percent of arrestees, they account for less than 5 percent of inmates. Police and other justice system personnel may be less willing to penalize female offenders than male offenders.[39]

Psychological Explanations

Psychologists also viewed the physical differences between male and female as a basis for their behavior differentials. Sigmund Freud maintained that girls interpret their lack of a penis as a sign that they have been punished. Boys fear that they can be punished by having their penis cut off, and thus learn to fear women. From this conflict comes *penis envy,* which often produces an inferiority complex in girls, forcing them to make an effort to compensate for their "defect." One way to compensate is to identify with their mothers and accept a maternal role. Also, girls may attempt to compensate for their lack of a penis by dressing well and beautifying themselves.[40]

chivalry hypothesis View that low female crime and delinquency rates are a reflection of the leniency with which police treat female offenders.

The New York Public Library maintains a research site for those interested in conducting scholarship on gender issues. Go to

http://www.nypl.org/research/chss/grd/resguides/womhist.html

For an up-to-date list of Web links, go to www.wadsworth.com/product/0534573053s

A longitudinal study that followed children born on the Hawaiian island of Kauai in 1955 for thirty-two years found that the most reliable traits for predicting delinquency in boys included the

- Disordered care-taking

- Lack of educational stimulation in the home

- Reading problems

- A need for remedial education by age 10

- Late maturation

- An unemployed, criminal, or absent father

In addition, boys appeared to be particularly vulnerable to early childhood learning problems, leading to school failure. A combination of reaching puberty late and lack of a significant male role model also encouraged the persistence of antisocial behavior throughout adolescence.

In the same longitudinal study, researchers found that delinquent girls tend to have the following traits:

- A history of minor congenital defects

- Low development scores by age 2

- A need for mental health services by age 10

- Earlier-than-average onset of puberty

Researchers hypothesize that birth defects and slow early development could lead to poor self-esteem, whereas early sexual development may encourage sexual relationships with older males and conflict with parents.

Figure 6.3
Trait Differences in Male and Female Delinquents

Source: Felton Earls and Albert Reiss, *Breaking the Cycle: Predicting and Preventing Crime* (Washington, DC: National Institute of Justice, 1994), pp. 24–25.

Freud also claimed that "If a little girl persists in her first wish—to grow into a boy—in extreme cases she will end as a manifest homosexual, and otherwise she will exhibit markedly masculine traits in the conduct of her later life, will choose a masculine vocation, and so on."[41]

Freud's concept of penis envy has been questioned by contemporary psychologists who scoff at the notion that girls feel inferior to boys and charge that Freud's thinking was influenced by the sexist culture of his age.[42]

At mid-century, psychodynamic theorists suggested that girls are socialized to be passive, which helps explain their low crime rate. However, this condition also makes some females susceptible to being manipulated by men; hence, their participation in sex-related crimes such as prostitution. A girl's wayward behavior, psychoanalysts suggested, was restricted to neurotic theft (kleptomania) and overt sexual acts, which were symptoms of personality maladaption.[43]

According to these early versions of the psychoanalytic approach, gender differences in the delinquency rate can be traced to differences in psychological orientation. Male delinquency reflects aggressive traits, whereas female delinquency is a function of repressed sexuality, gender conflict, and abnormal socialization.

Contemporary Trait Views

Contemporary biosocial and psychological theorists have continued the tradition of attributing gender differences in delinquency to physical and emotional traits (Figure 6.3). These theorists recognize that it is the interaction of biological and psychological traits with the social environment that produces delinquency.

The adolescent girl who is growing up in a troubled home or one marked by abuse, conflict, or neglect may be prone to delinquency. If a girl grows up in an atmosphere of sexual tension, where hostility exists between her parents or where the parents are absent, she likely will turn to outside sources, such as older males, for affection and support. (© Myrleen Ferguson/Photo Edit)

precocious sexuality Sexual experimentation in early adolescence.

Precocious Sexuality Early theorists linked female delinquency to early or **precocious sexuality.** According to this view, girls who experience an early onset of physical maturity are most likely to engage in antisocial behavior.[44] Female delinquents were believed to be promiscuous and more sophisticated than male delinquents.[45] Linking female delinquency to sexuality was responsible, in part, for the view that female delinquency is symptomatic of maladjustment.[46]

Equating female delinquency with sexual activity is no longer taken seriously, but early sexuality has been linked to other problems, such as higher risk of teen pregnancy and sexually transmitted diseases.[47] Empirical evidence suggests that girls who reach puberty at an early age are at the highest risk for delinquency.[48] One reason is that "early bloomers" may be more attractive to older adolescent boys, and increased contact with this high-risk group places the girls in jeopardy for antisocial behavior. The delinquency gap between early and late bloomers narrows when the latter group reaches sexual maturity and increases their exposure to boys.[49] Biological and social factors seem to interact to postpone or accelerate female delinquent activity.

Hormonal Differences As you may recall from Chapter 3, some biosocial theorists link antisocial behavior to hormonal influences.[50] The argument is that male hormones (androgens) account for more aggressive behavior and that gender-related hormonal differences can also explain the gender gap in delinquency.[51] Females may be biologically "protected" from deviant behavior in the same way that they are immune from some diseases that strike males. Sensation seeking, aggression, and lesser verbal skills are androgen-related male traits that are linked to antisocial behaviors.

Gender differences in the crime rate may be a function of androgen levels; these hormones cause areas of the brain to become less sensitive to environmental stimuli, making males more likely to seek high levels of stimulation, such as the "rush" that accompanies crime.[52] Androgens are also linked to brain seizures, which result in greater emotional volatility. Some experts believe androgens affect the brain structure itself (the left hemisphere of the neocortex), reducing sympathetic feelings that inhibit the urge to victimize.[53]

A great deal of research has been done on the relationship between hormone levels and aggression. In general, females who test higher for testosterone (an androgen) are more likely to engage in stereotypical male behaviors.[54] Females who have low androgen levels are less aggressive than males, whereas those who have elevated levels will take on characteristically male traits, including aggression.[55]

Some females are overexposed to male hormones in utero. Females affected this way may become "constitutionally masculinized." They may develop abnormal hair growth, large musculature, low voice, irregular menstrual cycle, and hyperaggressiveness; this condition can also develop as a result of steroid use or certain medical disorders.[56] Diana Fishbein has reviewed the literature in this area and finds that, after holding constant a variety of factors (including IQ, age, and environment), females exposed to male hormones in utero are more likely to engage in aggressive behavior later in life.[57]

Premenstrual Syndrome Early biotheorists suspected that premenstrual syndrome (PMS) was a direct cause of the relatively rare instances of female violence: "For several days prior to and during menstruation, the stereotype has been that 'raging hormones' doom women to irritability and poor judgment—two facets of premenstrual syndrome."[58] The link between PMS and delinquency was popularized by Katharina Dalton, whose studies of English women led her to conclude that females are more likely to commit suicide and be aggressive and otherwise antisocial before or during menstruation.[59]

Today there is conflicting evidence on the relationship between PMS and female delinquency. Diana Fishbein, an expert on biosocial theory, concludes that there is an association between elevated levels of female aggression and menstruation. Research shows that a significant number of incarcerated females committed their crimes during the premenstrual phase and that a small percentage of women appear vulnerable to cyclical hormonal changes that make them more prone to anxiety and hostility.[60] Fishbein notes that the majority of these women do not actually engage in criminal behavior.[61]

Existing research has been criticized on the basis of methodological inadequacy.[62] A valid test of the association must consider its time-ordering: it is possible that the stress of antisocial behavior produces early menstruation and not vice versa.[63]

Aggression According to some biosocial theorists, gender differences in the delinquency rate can be explained by inborn differences in aggression; males are inherently more likely to be aggressive.[64] Some psychologists have suggested that these differences are present very early in life, appearing before socialization can influence behavior. Males seem to be more aggressive in all societies for which data is available; gender differences in aggression can even be found in nonhuman primates.[65]

Some biosocial theorists argue that gender-based differences in aggression reflect the dissimilarities in the male and female reproductive systems. Males are more aggressive because they wish to possess as many sex partners as possible to increase their chances of producing offspring. Females have learned to control their aggressive impulses because multiple mates do not increase their chances of conception. Instead they concentrate on acquiring things that will help them rear their offspring, such as a reliable mate who will supply material resources.[66]

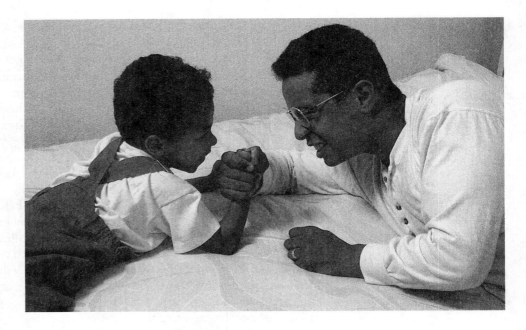

Males seem more aggressive and assertive and less likely to form attachments to others, factors that might increase their crime rates. One reason may be that sons try to emulate their fathers' macho behavior, and the fathers are then pleased when their sons act "manly." Gender-based differences in behavior may be intergenerational, passed down from father to son in an unending cycle. (© Jeffry W. Myers/Stock, Boston)

The weight of the evidence is that males are more aggressive than females. However, evidence also exists that females are more likely to act aggressively under some circumstances than others. For instance:

- Females may feel more freedom than males to express anger and aggression in the family setting.[67]

- Males are more likely than females to report physical aggression in their behavior, intentions, and dreams.

- Females are more likely to feel anxious or guilty about behaving aggressively, and these feelings tend to inhibit aggression.

- Females behave as aggressively as males when they have the means to do so and believe their behavior is justified.

- Females are more likely to empathize with the victim—to put themselves in the victim's place.

- Sex differences in aggression decrease when the victim is anonymous; anonymity may prevent females from empathizing with the victim.[68]

In summary, biosocial theorists find that biological traits make males "naturally" more aggressive than females; under some circumstances, however, females may be more aggressive than males.

SOCIALIZATION VIEWS

Socialization views are based on the idea that a child's social development may be the key to understanding delinquent behavior. If a child experiences impairment, family disruption, and so on, the child will be more susceptible to delinquent associations and criminality.

Linking crime rate variations to gender differences in socialization is not a recent discovery. In a 1928 work, *The Unadjusted Girl,* W. I. Thomas suggested that some girls who have not been socialized under middle-class family controls can become impulsive thrill seekers. According to Thomas, female delinquency is linked to the "wish" for luxury and excitement.[69] Inequities in social class condemn poor girls from demoralized families to using sex as a means to gain amusement, pretty clothes, and other luxuries. Precocious sexuality makes these girls vulnerable to older men, who lead them down the path to decadence.[70]

Socialization and Delinquency

To read about the socialization of female delinquents, go to http://ojjdp.ncjrs.org/pubs/principles/ch1_4.html

For an up-to-date list of Web links, go to www.wadsworth.com/product/0534573053s

Scholars concerned with gender differences in crime are interested in the distinction between the lifestyles of males and females. Girls may be supervised more closely than boys. If girls behave in a socially disapproved fashion, their parents may be more likely to notice. Adults may be more tolerant of deviant behavior in boys and expect boys to act tough and take risks.[71] Closer supervision restricts the opportunity for crime and the time available to mingle with delinquent peers. It follows, then, that the adolescent girl who is growing up in a troubled home and lacks supervision may be more prone to delinquency.[72]

Focus on Socialization In the 1950s, a number of researchers began to focus on gender-specific socialization patterns. They made three assumptions about gender differences in socialization: families exert a more powerful influence on girls than on boys; girls do not form close same-sex friendships but compete with their peers; and female criminals are primarily sexual offenders. First, parents are stricter with girls because they perceive them as needing control. In some families, adolescent girls rebel against strict controls. In others, where parents are absent or unavailable, girls may turn to the streets for companionship. Second, girls rarely form close relationships with female peers because they view them as rivals for males who would make eligible marriage partners.[73] Instead, girls enter into affairs with older men who exploit them, involve them in sexual deviance, and father their illegitimate children.[74] The result is prostitution, drug abuse, and marginal lives. Their daughters repeat this pattern in a never-ending cycle of exploitation.

In a classic work, *The Adolescent Girl in Conflict* (1966), Gisela Konopka suggested that female delinquency has its roots in feelings of uncertainty and loneliness.[75] During adolescence, a girl's major emotional need is to be accepted by members of the opposite sex. If normal channels (such as family and friends) for receiving such approval are impaired, she may join a "crowd" or engage in gratuitous sexual relationships. This behavior leads to "rejection by the community, general experience of having no recognized success . . . and more behavior which increases the feeling of worthlessness."[76] In fatherless homes, girls have an especially hard time because "the road to a healthy development toward womanhood through affection for the male and identification with the female simply does not exist."[77] The absence of socioeconomic mobility can also create problems. Delinquent girls are believed to suffer from lack of education. This locks them into low-paying jobs with little hope for advancement. These conditions lead girls to relieve their thwarted ambition through destructive behavior. The world presents a hostile environment to some girls; adult authority figures tell them what to do, but no one is there to listen to their needs.

Broken Homes/Fallen Women A number of experts shared Konopka's emphasis on the family as a primary influence on delinquent behavior. Male delinquents were portrayed as rebels who esteemed "toughness," "excitement," and other lower-class values. Males succumbed to the lure of delinquency when they perceived few legitimate opportunities. In contrast, female delinquents were portrayed as troubled adolescents who suffered inadequate home lives and, more often than not, were victims of sexual and physical abuse. Ruth Morris described delinquent girls as unattractive youths who reside in homes marked by family tensions.[78] In *The Delinquent Girl* (1970), Clyde Vedder and Dora Somerville suggest that female delinquency is usually a problem of adjustment to family pressure; an estimated 75 percent of institutionalized girls have family problems.[79] They also suggest that girls have serious problems in a male-dominated culture with rigid and sometimes unfair social practices.

Eleanor and Sheldon Glueck also distinguished between the causes of male and female delinquency. They linked male delinquency to muscular body type, a hostile attitude, and a poor home life.[80] Delinquent males had been reared in homes of "little understanding or affection, stability or moral fiber," by parents who were unfit to be role models.[81] In contrast, when they examined the life histories of institutionalized female offenders in *Five Hundred Delinquent Women*, they found that a majority of these women had been involved in sexual deviance that began early in their teens.[82] The Gluecks concluded that sexual delinquency and general maladjustment developed in girls simultaneously with unstable home lives.[83]

Other early efforts linked "rebellious" behavior to sexual conflicts in the home.[84] Broken or disrupted homes were found to predict female delinquency.[85] Females petitioned to juvenile court were more likely than males to be charged with ungovernable behavior and sex offenses. They also were more likely to reside in single-parent homes.[86] Studies of incarcerated juveniles found that most of the male delinquents were incarcerated for burglary and other theft-related offenses, but female delinquents tended to be involved in incorrigibility and sex offenses. The conclusion: Boys became delinquent to demonstrate their masculinity; girls were delinquent because of hostility toward parents and a consequent need to obtain attention from others.[87]

Contemporary Socialization Views

Investigators continue to support the view that female delinquents have more dysfunctional home lives than male offenders.[88] Institutionalized girls tell of lives filled with severe physical and sexual abuse. In addition to tragic home lives, delinquent girls report social experiences that were frustrating or even degrading.[89]

Girls seem to be more deeply affected than boys by child abuse, and the link between abuse and female delinquency seems stronger than it is for male delinquency.[90] A significant amount of female delinquency can be traced to abuse in the home.[91] Meda Chesney-Lind, a prominent feminist scholar, has described this association: "Young women on the run from homes characterized by sexual abuse and parental neglect are forced, by the very statutes designed to protect them, into the life of an escaped convict."[92] To further explore this theme, read the Focus on Delinquency, "Girls on the Run."

Joan Moore's analysis of gang girls in East Los Angeles found that many came from troubled homes. Sixty-eight percent of the girls she interviewed were afraid of their fathers, and 55 percent reported fear of their mothers. One girl told Moore about the abuse she received from her mother: "She would hit me, pinch me, and pull my hair, and then she'd have my brother—the oldest one—get a whip, and whip me, and then I'd have stripes all over my body like a zebra, and I went to school like that."[93]

Many of the girls reported that their parents were overly strict and controlling despite the fact that they engaged in criminality themselves. Moore also details accounts of sexual abuse; about 30 percent of the girls reported that family members had made sexual advances. Considering the restrictions placed on these girls and the high incidence of incest, it comes as no surprise that three-quarters reported having run away at least once. Moore concludes:

> . . . clearly more women than men came from troubled families. They were more likely to have been living with a chronically sick relative, one who died, one who was a heroin addict, or one who was arrested. . . . This seems on the face of it to imply that the gang represents [for girls] . . . a refuge from family problems.[94]

In summary, the socialization approach holds that family interaction is the key to understanding female delinquency. If a girl grows up in an atmosphere of sexual

GIRLS ON THE RUN

On any given night in the United States, there are at least a million adolescent runaways; about 1 in 8 American adolescents have run away at least once before the age of 18. Runaways emerge from the full range of American families: black, Hispanic, Native American, and Asian families; "broken" homes, and homes with intact marriages; and privileged, middle-class, working-class, and low-income families. Over half of teenagers who run away from home are girls.

Sociologist Laurie Schaffner studied young runaways from a variety of backgrounds who were being held in a short-term residential facility in Massachusetts. She found that, rather than being rebellious and antisocial, (1) adolescents actually resisted running away—it was actually a last option for them, and (2) each runaway had a plan of action that included "running to somebody" in search of the love and protection that they needed from other people. She also found that running away can be viewed as a "fixable" problem—that healing and reconciliation does take place and that running away was not necessarily a permanently disabling rupture for every family.

The adolescent girls in her sample actually resisted running away, resisted fighting back with their parents, and resisted breaking family rules. They seemed to struggle *against* running away, preferring instead to try to remain socially attached in intact family bonds. Runaways expressed resentment and hurt feelings at the loss of an interconnection between themselves and their parents. While many told of the rage and anger that precipitated their runs, the young women also expressed fear, hurt, and pain over their fractured family relations.

Fourteen-year-old Amy, typical of the girls interviewed by Schaffner, was an articulate dark-haired youth who had been physically abused by her mother. Amy was from a white, low-income family; her mother had dropped out of high school and was currently working as a nursing aide in a convalescent home. Her 6-year-old brother still lived at home with her mom. Amy was in the shelter awaiting her dispositional hearing on a charge of possession of a stolen vehicle. Amy said that she ran away from home because her mother didn't want her "running around" with the friends that Amy selected, because Amy had an 18-year-old boyfriend whom her mother wanted to "put statutory rape charges on," and because of the "physical fights" she constantly had with her mom:

> I ran away from home because—I have a lot of problems with my mom, we fight a lot. And we get in physical fights and I don't hit her because she's my mom, but—she—'cause I respect her for that, 'cause she's my mom, but she just—we have really different viewpoints. (Amy)

Another runaway, Gretchen, shared the disappointment and anger she felt toward physically abusive parents that motivated her to "keep running away from all my problems." Sixteen-year-old Gretchen was severely abused physically by both her father and mother. She ran away from her family home in the rural region near the shelter, leaving a younger brother still living there. Tall and slight, from a white, working-class background, Gretchen was confused about her role as a daughter. Although she believed that "daughters should not physically strike their mothers," this became an impossibility because Gretchen's parents were abusing her physically and she had to be disobedient in order to survive. She talked about the dilemma of not wanting to hit her mother back, even when her mother was choking her:

> My mother, she beat me—but I'm not afraid of my mother! The last time she beat me up—I had respect—I did not hit her back—until the day she got arrested. She was beating the s__t out of me and I would not hit her back! I cried, I felt so sorry for myself, but I didn't hit her back!

Gretchen fought back against her inclination to strike her mother back, but her angry running-away survival behavior won out in the end. Gretchen resolved her moral and emotional dilemma by initiating self-protective "last resort" behavior that consisted of running away.

According to Schaffner, the vision of runaways as incorrigible delinquents is a popular misconception. She found, instead, a much more complex picture of children who find it impossible to conform and comply with unevenly applied family rules and proscriptions; these emotionally abused girls use their running away as a desperate survival strategy. Runaway girls perceived their living arrangements as being so bad that they felt forced to run away, forced to go against what they really wished for or wanted: warm relationships with parents who could be trusted. Finally, Schaffner found that accounts of healing and reconciliation among family members of runaways indicate that, except for families where severe and persistent physical and sexual abuse has been occurring, children who have run away from home can be reunited with family members. In families where emotional and relational dynamics are deeply problematic, but not physical, youths often recounted wishful hopes for reconciliation.

Source: Laurie Schaffner, *Teenage Runaways: Broken Hearts and "Bad Attitudes"* (New York: Haworth Press, 1999).

tension, where hostility exists between her parents, or where the parents are absent, she is likely to turn to outside sources for support. Girls are expected to follow narrowly defined behavioral patterns. In contrast, it is not unusual for boys to stay out late, drive around with friends, or get involved in other unstructured behaviors linked to delinquency. If, in reaction to loneliness and parental hostility, girls engage in the same "routine activities" as boys (staying out late, partying, and riding around with friends), they run the risk of engaging in similar types of delinquent behavior.[95]

The socialization approach holds that a poor home life is likely to have an even more damaging effect on females than on males. Because girls are less likely than boys to have close-knit peer associations, they are more likely to need close parental relationships to retain emotional stability. In fact, girls may become sexually involved with boys to receive support from them, a practice that tends to magnify their problems.

LIBERAL FEMINIST VIEWS

The feminist movement has, from its origins, fought to help women break away from their traditional roles and secure economic, educational, and social advancement. There is little question that the women's movement has revised the way women perceive their roles in society, and it has altered the relationships of women to many social institutions.

liberal feminism Asserts that females are less delinquent than males because their social roles provide them with fewer opportunities to commit crimes; as the roles of girls and women become more similar to those of boys and men, so too will their crime patterns.

Liberal feminism also has influenced thinking about delinquency. A number of scholars, including Rita Simon and Freda Adler, drew attention to the changing pattern of female criminality and offered new explanations for the differences between male and female delinquency rates.[96] Their position is that economic conditions and sex role differences are a greater influence on delinquency rates than socialization. After all, improper socialization affects both males and females, and therefore cannot be the sole explanation for gender differences in the crime rate.

According to liberal feminists, females are less delinquent than males because their social roles provide fewer opportunities to commit crime. As the roles of women become more similar to those of men, so will their crime patterns. Female criminality is motivated by the same influences as male criminality. This view was spelled out in Freda Adler's book *Sisters in Crime* (1975), which explained how sex role differences influence crime.

Adler's thesis was that, by striving for independence, women have begun to alter the institutions that had protected males in their traditional positions of power.[97] Adler argued that female delinquency would be affected by the changing role of women. As females entered new occupations and participated in sports, politics, and other traditionally male endeavors, they would also become involved in crimes that had heretofore been male-oriented; delinquency rates would then converge. She noted that girls were becoming increasingly involved in traditionally masculine crimes such as gang activity and fighting.

Adler predicted that the women's movement would produce steeper increases in the rate of female delinquency because it created an environment in which the roles of girls and boys converge. She predicted that the changing female role will produce female criminals who are similar to their male counterparts.[98]

Support for Liberal Feminism

A number of studies support the feminist view of gender differences in delinquency.[99] More than 20 years ago, Rita Simon explained how the increase in female criminality is a function of the changing role of women. She claimed that, as women were empowered economically and socially, they would be less likely to feel dependent and oppressed. Consequently, women would be less likely to attack their traditional targets: their husbands, their lovers, or even their own children.[100] Instead, their new role as breadwinner might encourage women to engage in traditional male crimes such as larceny and car theft.

According to liberal feminists, females are less delinquent than males because their social roles provide them with fewer opportunities to commit crime. As the roles of girls and women become more similar to those of males, so too will their crime patterns. Female criminality is actually motivated by the same crime-producing influences as male criminality. The fact that female delinquency is rising at a faster rate than male delinquency reflects the convergence of their social roles. (© Lisa Quinones/Black Star)

Simon's view has been supported in part by research showing a significant correlation between the women's rights movement and the female crime rate.[101] If 1966 is used as a jumping-off point (because the National Organization for Women was founded in that year), there are indications that patterns of serious female crime (robbery and auto theft) correlate with indicators of female emancipation (the divorce rate and participation in the labor force). Although this research does not prove that female crime is related to social change, it identifies behavior patterns that support that hypothesis.

In addition to these efforts, self-report studies support the liberal feminist view by showing that gender differences in delinquency are fading; that is, the delinquent acts committed most and least often by girls are nearly identical to those reported most and least often by boys.[102] The pattern of female delinquency, if not the extent, is now similar to that of male delinquency,[103] and with few exceptions the factors that seem to motivate both male and female criminality seem similar.[104] For example, research shows that economic disadvantages are felt equally by both male and female residents.[105]

As the sex roles of males and females have become less distinct, their offending patterns have become more similar. Girls may be committing crimes to gain economic advancement and not because they lack parental support. Both of these patterns are predicted by liberal feminists.

Critiques of Liberal Feminism

Not all delinquency experts believe changing sex roles influence crime rates. Some argue that the delinquent behavior patterns of girls have remained static and have not been influenced by the women's movement. Females involved in violent crime more often than not have some connection to a male partner who influences their behavior. One recent study of women who kill in the course of their involvement in the drug trade found that they kill on behalf of a man or out of fear of a man.[106]

Others dispute that changes in female rates relate to the feminist movement. Self-report studies show that female participation in most crime has remained stable for the past 10 years.[107] It is possible that the women's movement has not influenced crime rates as much as previously thought.[108] Perhaps the greater participation by females in the UCR arrest data is more a function of how police are treating females than an actual change in female behavior patterns.

In summary, gender differences in crime have not changed as much as liberal feminist writers had predicted.[109] Consequently, the argument that female crime will be elevated by the women's movement has not received unqualified support.

Is Convergence Possible?

Will the gender differences in delinquency disappear as liberal feminists have predicted, or are they permanent and unchanging? Not all experts have abandoned the convergence argument, suggesting that, in the long run, male and female delinquency rates will become similar.[110] For example, female gang membership has increased, and gang activity is associated with increased levels of crime.[111]

Perhaps crime convergence has been delayed by a slower-than-expected change in gender roles; the women's movement has not yet achieved its full impact on social life.[112] Although they are expanding their economic role, women have not abandoned their conventional role as family caretakers. Women are being forced to cope with added financial and social burdens. If gender roles were truly equivalent, crime rates might converge. As our society shifts toward more balanced gender roles, there may be significant changes in female delinquency rates.

RADICAL FEMINIST VIEWS

radical feminists, Marxist feminists Hold that gender inequality stems from the unequal power of men and women and the subsequent exploitation of women by men; the cause of female delinquency originates with the onset of male supremacy and the efforts of males to control females' sexuality.

A number of writers take a more revolutionary view of gender differences in crime. These scholars can be categorized as **radical feminists.** They believe gender inequality stems from the unequal power of men and women in a capitalist society and the exploitation of females by fathers and husbands: women are a "commodity" like land or money.[113] Female delinquency originates with the onset of male supremacy (*patriarchy*), the subordination of women, male aggression, and the efforts of men to control females sexually.[114]

Radical feminists focus on the social forces that shape girls' lives.[115] They attempt to show how the sexual victimization of girls is often a function of male socialization and that young males learn to be exploitive of women. James Messerschmidt, an influential feminist scholar, has formulated a theoretical model to show how misguided concepts of "masculinity" flow from the inequities built into "patriarchal capitalism." Men dominate business in capitalist societies, and males who cannot function well within its parameters are at risk for crime. Women are inherently powerless in such a society, and their crimes reflect their limited access to both legitimate and illegitimate opportunity.[116] It is not surprising that research surveys have found that 90 percent of adolescent girls are sexually harassed in school, with almost 30 percent reporting having been psychologically pressured to "do something sexual," and 10 percent physically forced into sexual behaviors.[117]

According to the radical view, male exploitation acts as a trigger for female delinquent behavior. Female delinquents recount being so severely harassed at school that they were forced to carry knives. Some reported that boyfriends, sometimes in their thirties, who "knew how to treat a girl" would draw them into criminal activity such as drug trafficking, which eventually entangled them in the justice system.[118]

When female adolescents run away and use drugs, they may be reacting to abuse at home or at school. Their attempts at survival are then labeled delinquent.[119] Research shows that a significant number of girls who require emergency room treatment for sexual abuse later engage in violence; many of these girls actually form a romantic attachment with the abusive partner.[120] All too often, school officials ignore complaints made by female students. Young girls therefore may feel trapped and desperate.

For more than 20 years, the Center for Research on Women has been in the forefront of research in which the central questions are shaped by the experiences and perspectives of women. Their Web site can be accessed at

http://www.wellesley.edu/WCW/crwsub.html

For an up-to-date list of Web links, go to www.wadsworth.com/product/0534573053s

According to power-control theory, girls who grow up in gender-equal egalitarian households are given greater freedom and may be more assertive and crime prone than girls who are socialized in more controlling, paternalistic homes. (© David Woo/Stock, Boston)

Crime and Patriarchy

A number of theoretical models have attempted to use a radical or **Marxist feminist** perspective to explain gender differences in delinquency. For example, in *Capitalism, Patriarchy, and Crime,* Marxist James Messerschmidt argues that capitalist society is marked by both patriarchy and class conflict. Capitalists control workers, and men control women, both economically and biologically.[121] This "double marginality" explains why females in a capitalist society commit fewer crimes than males: they are isolated in the family and have fewer opportunities to engage in elite deviance (white-collar and economic crimes); they are also denied access to male-dominated street crimes. Because capitalism renders women powerless, they are forced to commit less serious crimes such as abusing drugs.

Power-Control Theory

power-control theory Holds that gender differences in the delinquency rate are a function of class differences and economic conditions that influence the structure of family life.

John Hagan and his associates have speculated that gender differences in delinquency are a function of class differences that influence family life. Hagan, who calls his view **power-control theory**, suggests that class influences delinquency by controlling the quality of family life.[122] In paternalistic families, fathers assume the role of breadwinners, and mothers have menial jobs or remain at home. Mothers are expected to control the behavior of their daughters while granting greater freedom to sons. The parent–daughter relationship can be viewed as a preparation for the "cult of domesticity," which

egalitarian families Husband and wife share power at home; daughters gain a kind of freedom similar to that of sons and their law-violating behaviors mirror those of their brothers.

makes daughters' involvement in delinquency unlikely. Hence, males exhibit a higher degree of delinquent behavior than their sisters.

In **egalitarian families**—in which the husband and wife share similar positions of power at home and in the workplace—daughters gain a kind of freedom that reflects reduced parental control. These families produce daughters whose law-violating behaviors mirror those of their brothers. Ironically, these kinds of relationships also occur in households with absent fathers. Similarly, Hagan and his associates found that when both fathers and mothers hold equally valued managerial positions the similarity between the rates of their daughters' and sons' delinquency is greatest. Therefore, middle-class girls are most likely to violate the law because they are less closely controlled than lower-class girls.

Research conducted by Hagan and his colleagues has tended to support the core relationship between family structure and gender differences in delinquency.[123] However, some of the basic premises of power-control theory, such as the relationship between social class and delinquency, have been challenged. For example, some critics have questioned the assumption that upper-class youths may engage in more petty delinquency than lower-class youths because they are brought up to be "risk takers" who do not fear the consequences of their misdeeds.[124]

Power-control theory encourages a new approach to the study of delinquency, one that addresses gender differences, class position, and family structure. It also helps explain the relative increase in female delinquency by stressing the significance of changing feminine roles. With the increase in single-parent homes, the patterns Hagan has identified may change. The decline of the patriarchal family may produce looser family ties on girls, changing sex roles, and increased delinquency.

Checkpoints

✔ There are a variety of views of why girls become delinquent and why there are gender differences in the crime rate.

✔ At one time it was believed that girls were naturally less aggressive and female criminals were a biological aberration.

✔ Some experts still believe that hormonal differences can explain why males are more aggressive.

✔ Some experts believe that males are more aggressive because they have evolved that way to secure mates.

✔ Under some circumstances females may act more aggressively than males.

✔ Some experts believe that girls have been socialized to be less violent.

✔ Female delinquents may be the product of a destructive home life who are rebelling against abusive parents.

✔ The liberal feminist view is that girls did not have the same opportunities to commit crime as boys and that rising female crime rates represent changing life circumstances.

✔ Radical feminists view female delinquency as a function of male domination and abuse.

GENDER AND THE JUVENILE JUSTICE SYSTEM

Not only do gender differences have an effect on crime patterns but they also may have a significant impact on the way children are treated by the juvenile justice system. Several feminist scholars argue that girls are not only the victims of injustice at home but also risk being victimized by agents of the justice system. In many respects, the treatment girls receive today is not too dissimilar from the "sexualization" of female delinquency found by Odem and Schlossman in 1920. (See the Policy and Practice box entitled "Guardians of Virtue" for more on this topic.) Paternalistic attitudes and the sexual double standard increase the likelihood that girls will be referred to juvenile court for status offenses.

Are girls "victims" of the juvenile justice system? More than 25 years ago, Meda Chesney-Lind's classic research found that police in Honolulu, Hawaii were likely to

Several feminist scholars believe that girls are at risk when they enter the juvenile court. They argue that girls are not only the victims of injustice at home but also risk being victimized by agents of the juvenile justice system. Paternalistic attitudes and the sexual "double standard" increase the likelihood that girls will be referred to juvenile court for status-type offenses and, after adjudication, receive a disposition involving incarceration. (© Joel Gordon)

arrest female adolescents for sexual activity and to ignore the same behavior among male delinquents.[125] Some 74 percent of the females in her sample were charged with sexual activity or incorrigibility; in comparison, only 27 percent of the males were so charged. Similar to the Los Angeles juvenile justice practices of the 1920s, the Honolulu court ordered 70 percent of the females to undergo physical examinations but required only 15 percent of the males to undergo this procedure. Girls were also more likely to be sent to a detention facility before trial, and the length of their detention averaged three times that of boys.

Chesney-Lind concluded that female adolescents are granted a much narrower range of acceptable behavior than male adolescents. Any sign of misbehavior in girls is seen as a challenge to authority and to the sexual double standard.

Are Standards Changing?

More than 20 years after the Chesney-Lind research brought attention to the gender "double standard" in juvenile court, distinctions are still being made between male and female offenders. Girls are still more likely than boys to be petitioned to court for incorrigibility and status offenses.[126] Girls are still disadvantaged if their behavior

GUARDIANS OF VIRTUE

The view that female delinquency is sexual in nature and that the great majority of female delinquents' troubles can be linked to their sexual precociousness influenced the treatment of young female offenders in the first juvenile courts. Mary Odem and Steven Schlossman explored this "sexualization" of female delinquency in their study of more than 200 girls petitioned to the Los Angeles Juvenile Court in 1920.

Odem and Schlossman argue that, in the first decades of the twentieth century, delinquency "experts" identified young female "sex delinquents" as a major social problem that required a forceful public response. These experts spoke of a rise in illicit sexual activity among young working-class females. This phenomenon was perceived in part as a product of new-found freedoms enjoyed by girls after the turn of the century. Young females were getting jobs in stores and offices where they were more likely to meet eligible young men. Recreation now included dance halls, movie theaters, beaches, and amusement parks—areas fraught with the danger of "sexual experimentation." Civic leaders concerned about immorality mounted a social hygiene campaign that identified the "sex delinquent" as a moral and sexual threat to American society and advocated a policy of *eugenics* (sterilization) to prevent these inferior individuals from having children.

The juvenile justice system also responded to this "epidemic" of sexuality by targeting Los Angeles' lower-class female population. At first, female civic leaders and social workers campaigned for special attention to be given to female delinquency in an effort to combat "moral ruin." Los Angeles responded by hiring the first female police officers in the nation to deal with girls under arrest and female judges to hear girls' cases in juvenile court. The city also developed a nationally recognized female detention center and a girl's reformatory.

The first female officer in the country was Alice Stebbins Wells, appointed on September 13, 1910.

A social worker, Wells argued that she could better serve her clients if she had full police powers. She and her fellow female officers inspected dance halls, cafes, theaters, and other public amusement places to ferret out girls who were in danger of moral ruin, sending some home and bringing the incorrigible to the detention center.

Female "referees" were appointed to hear cases involving girls, and female probation officers were assigned to supervise them. The influx of new cases prompted the county to open custodial institutions for girls, including the El Retiro School, which was considered the latest in modern rehabilitative treatment.

When Odem and Schlossman evaluated the juvenile court records of delinquent girls who entered the Los Angeles Juvenile Court in 1920, they found that the majority were petitioned for either suspected sexual activity or behavior that placed them at risk of sexual relations. Despite the limited seriousness of these charges, the majority of girls were detained prior to their trials, and while in Juvenile Hall, all were given a compulsory pelvic exam. Girls adjudged sexually delinquent on the basis of the exam were segregated from the merely incorrigible girls to prevent moral corruption. Those testing positive for venereal disease were confined in Juvenile Hall Hospital, usually for 1 to 3 months.

After trial, *29 percent* of these female adolescents were committed to custodial institutions, a high price to pay for moral transgressions. While society was undergoing a sexual revolution, the juvenile court seemed wedded to a philosophy of controlling "immoral" young women, a policy that was to last more than thirty years.

Source: Mary Odem and Steven Schlossman, "Guardians of Virtue: The Juvenile Court and Female Delinquency in Early 20th-Century Los Angeles," *Crime and Delinquency 37*:186–203 (1991).

is viewed as morally incorrect by government officials or if they are considered beyond parental control.[127] Girls who are held in contempt of court for failing to obey a judge's orders are much more likely than boys to be sentenced to incarceration in a secure detention facility.[128] This finding has been substantiated by multiple studies showing that girls are much more likely than boys to be sanctioned for status offenses.[129]

Girls may still be subject to harsh punishments if they are considered dangerously immoral. Girls arrested on status offense charges are more likely than boys to have descriptions of their physical attractiveness placed in case files. There still appears to be an association between male standards of "beauty" and sexual behavior: criminal justice professionals may look on attractive girls who engage in sexual behavior more harshly, overlooking some of the same behaviors in less attractive girls. In some jurisdictions, girls are still being incarcerated for status offenses because their behavior does not measure up to concepts of proper female behavior.[130] Even though girls are still less likely to be arrested than boys, those who fail to measure up to stereotypes of "proper" female behavior are more likely to be sanctioned than male offenders.[131]

Once in the system, females receive fewer benefits than their male counterparts. Institutionalized girls report receiving fewer privileges, less space, fewer programs, and less treatment than institutionalized boys.[132] Why do these differences persist? Because correctional authorities continue to subscribe to stereotyped beliefs about the needs of young girls. Writing in 1998 with Randall Shelden, Meda Chesney-Lind found that court officials and policy makers still show a lack of concern about girls' victimization and instead are more concerned with controlling their behavior than addressing the factors which brought them to the attention of the juvenile justice system in the first place.[133]

Although these arguments are persuasive, recent data gathered by the National Center for Juvenile Justice show that there is little gender-based difference in processing of status offenders. Both girls and boys seem to have an equal chance of proceeding to formal adjudication and being sent to out-of-the-home placements for status offenses.[134] This suggests that the gender bias in some areas of the juvenile justice process may be in decline.

SUMMARY

The relationship between gender and delinquency has become a topic of considerable interest to criminologists. At one time, attention was directed solely at male offenders and the rare female delinquent was considered an oddity. The nature and extent of female delinquent activities have changed, and girls are now engaging in more frequent and serious illegal activity. Consequently, interest in gender issues in delinquency has increased.

Sociologists and psychologists recognize that there are differences in attitudes, values, and behavior between boys and girls. Females process information differently than males and have different cognitive and physical strengths. These differences may, in part, explain gender differences in delinquency.

Theories that seek to explain these differences fit into several categories. Trait views are concerned with biological and psychological differences between the sexes. Early efforts by Cesare Lombroso and his followers placed the blame for delinquency on physical differences between males and females. Girls who were delinquent had inherent masculine characteristics. Later, biosocial theorists viewed girls' psychological makeup, hormonal, and physical characteristics as key to their delinquent behavior.

Socialization has also been identified as a cause of delinquency. Males are socialized to be tough and aggressive, females to be passive and obedient. The adolescent female offender was portrayed as a troubled girl who lacked love at home and supportive peer relations. These theories treated female delinquents as sexual offenders whose criminal activities were linked to destructive relationships with men.

More recent views of gender and delinquency incorporate the changes brought about by the women's movement. It is argued that, as the roles of women change, so will their crime patterns. Although a number of studies support this view, some theorists question its validity. The female crime rate has increased, and female delinquency patterns now resemble those of males, but the gender gap has not narrowed after more than two decades. Hagan's power-control theory helps us understand why these differences exist and whether change may be coming.

The treatment girls receive by the juvenile justice system has also been the subject of debate. Originally, it was thought that police protected girls from the stigma of a delinquency label. Contemporary criminologists charge, however, that girls are discriminated against by agents of the justice system.

KEY TERMS

gender-schema theory
gender identity
masculinity hypothesis

chivalry hypothesis
precocious sexuality
liberal feminism

radical feminists, Marxist feminists
power-control theory

egalitarian families

1. Are girls delinquent for different reasons than boys? Do girls have a unique set of problems?

2. As sex roles become more homogenous, do you believe female delinquency will become identical to male delinquency in rate and type?

3. Does the sexual double standard still exist?

4. Are lower-class girls more strictly supervised than upper- and middle-class girls? Is control stratified across class lines?

5. Are girls the victims of unfairness at the hands of the justice system, or do they benefit from "chivalry"?

VIEWPOINT

In general, the girls did not feel respected. The lack of respect they felt was expressed predominantly in terms of their relationships with the staff in their agencies and institutions. They shared a number of examples in which they felt "put down" by staff. The girls' concept of respect was best articulated when they described what an ideal person and/or mentor would be like. The girls reported wanting to be listened to and loved unconditionally by caring adults who are able to set healthy limits. They wanted more one-on-one relationships to discuss their true feelings.

 For an interesting and informative account of the lives of incarcerated girls, on InfoTrac® College Edition read Joanne Belknap, Kristi Holsinger, and Melissa Dunn, "Understanding incarcerated girls: the results of a focus group study," *Prison Journal* 77:381 (1997).

The Family and Delinquency

© Sadin/Liaison/Rapho

ou are an investigator with the county bureau of social services. A case has been referred to you by a middle school's head guidance counselor. It seems that a young girl, Emily M., has been showing up to school in a dazed and listless condition. She has had a hard time concentrating in class and seems withdrawn and uncommunicative. The 13-year-old has missed more than a normal share of school days and has often been late to class. Last week, she seemed so lethargic that her homeroom teacher sent her to the school nurse. A physical examination revealed that she was malnourished and in poor physical health. She also had evidence of bruising that could only come from a severe beating. Emily told the nurse that she had been punished by her parents for doing poorly at school and for failing to do her chores at home.

When her parents were called to school to meet with the principal and guidance counselor, they claimed to be members of a religious order that believes children should be punished severely for their misdeeds. Emily had been placed on a restricted diet as well as beaten with a belt to correct her misbehavior. When the guidance counselor asked them if they would be willing to go into family therapy, they were furious and told her to "mind her own business." It's a sad day, they said, when "God-fearing American citizens cannot bring up their children according to their religious beliefs." The girl is in no immediate danger insofar as her punishment has not been life-threatening.

The case is then referred to your office. When you go to see the parents at home, they refuse to make any change in their behavior and claim they are in the right and you represent all that is wrong with society. The "lax" discipline you suggest leads to drugs, sex, and other teenage problems.

- Would you get a court order removing Emily from her house and requiring the parents to go into counseling?

- Would you report the case to the district attorney's office so it could take criminal action against her parents under the state's Child Protection Act?

- Would you take no further action, reasoning that Emily's parents have the right to discipline their child as they see fit?

- Would you talk with Emily and see what she wants to happen?

Cases like Emily's illustrate the often-volatile family relationships that many experts believe are the key ingredients in the development of the emotional deficits that eventually lead to long-term social problems.[1] Interactions between parents and children, and between siblings, provide opportunities for children to acquire or inhibit antisocial behavior patterns.[2] Children living in high-crime areas are able to resist the temptation of the streets if they receive fair discipline and support from parents who provide them with positive role models.[3] However, children in affluent families who are being raised in a household characterized by abuse and conflict, or whose parents are absent or separated, will still be at risk for delinquency.[4] Nor is the relationship between family life and delinquency unique to U.S. culture; cross-national data support a significant association between family variables and delinquency.[5]

The assumed relationship between delinquency and family life is critical today because the American family is changing. Extended families, once common, are now for the most part anachronisms. In their place is the **nuclear family**, described as a "dangerous hot-house of emotions" because of the close contact between parents and children; in these families problems are unrelieved by contact with other kin living nearby.[6]

nuclear family A family unit composed of parents and their children; this smaller family structure is subject to great stress due to the intense, close contact between parents and children.

The nuclear family is showing signs of breakdown. Much of the responsibility for childrearing is delegated to television and daycare providers. Despite these changes, some families are able to continue functioning as healthy units, producing well-adjusted children. Others have crumbled under the stress, severely damaging their children.[7] This is particularly true when child abuse and neglect become part of family life.

Because these issues are critical for understanding delinquency, this chapter is devoted to an analysis of the family's role in producing or inhibiting delinquency. We first cover the changing face of the American family. We then review the way family structure and function influence delinquent behavior. The relationship between child abuse, neglect, and delinquency is covered in some depth. Finally, programs designed to improve family functioning are briefly reviewed.

THE CHANGING AMERICAN FAMILY

The so-called traditional family, with a male breadwinner and a female who cares for the home, is a thing of the past. No longer can this family structure be considered the norm. Changing sex roles have created a family where women play a much greater role in the economic process; this has created a more egalitarian family structure. About three-quarters of all mothers of school-age children are employed, up from 50 percent in 1970 and 40 percent in 1960. The changing economic structure may be reflected in shifting sex roles. Fathers are now spending more time with their children on workdays than they did 20 years ago (2.3 hours versus 1.8), and women are spending somewhat less time (3.3 hours versus 3.0).[8] On their days off, both working men and women spend about an hour more with their children than they did 20 years ago, with women devoting about 8 hours, and men 6. So, although the time spent with children may be less than would be desirable, it has increased over the past 20 years.

Family Makeup

The proportion of American households that have children who live with both parents has declined substantially. Since the number of children in African American families that lived with two parents has declined from 64 percent to 35 percent; during the same period, the percentage of white children living with two parents has declined from 90 percent to 74 percent. As many as 40 percent of white children and 75 percent of African American children will experience parental separation or divorce before they reach age 16, and many of these children will experience multiple family disruptions over time.[9]

More single women than ever are deciding to keep and raise their children; about 30 percent of all births are to unmarried women. Although the teen birthrate has been declining, more than 500,000 babies are born to teenage mothers every year, about 200,000 to girls under age 18 (Figure 7.1).

Childcare

Charged with caring for children is a daycare system whose workers are often paid minimum wage. Of special concern are "family daycare homes," in which a single provider takes care of 3 to 9 children. Several states neither license nor monitor these private providers. Even in states that mandate registration and inspection of daycare providers, it is estimated that 90 percent or more of the facilities operate "underground." It is not uncommon for one adult to care for eight infants, an impossible task regardless of training or concern.

Children from working poor families are most likely to suffer from inadequate childcare; these children often spend time in makeshift arrangements that allow their

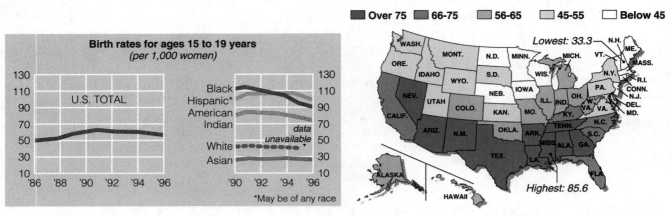

Figure 7.1
Teen Birth Trends

Source: Stephanie Ventura, Sally Curten, and T. J. Matthews, *Teenage Birth in the U.S.: National & State Trends, 1990–1996* (Washington, DC: National Center for Health Statistics, 1998).

parents to work but lack the stimulating environment children need to thrive.[10] About 3.5 million children under age 13 spend some time at home alone each week while their parents are at work.

Economic Stress

The family is also undergoing economic stress. The majority of indigent families live in substandard housing without adequate health care, nutrition, or childcare. Those whose incomes place them above the poverty line are deprived of government assistance. Recent political trends suggest that the social "safety net" is under attack, and poor families can expect less government aid in the coming years.

Will this economic pressure be reduced in the future? The number of senior citizens is on the rise. As people retire, there will be fewer workers to cover the costs of Social Security, medical care, and nursing home care. These costs will put greater economic stress on families. Voter sentiment has an impact on the allocation of public funds, and there is concern that an older generation, worried about healthcare costs, may be reluctant to spend tax dollars on at-risk kids.

THE FAMILY'S INFLUENCE ON DELINQUENCY

Most experts believe a disturbed home environment can have a significant impact on delinquency. The family is the primary unit in which children learn the values and attitudes that guide their actions throughout their lives. Family disruption or change can have a long-lasting impact on children.

Four categories of family dysfunction seem to promote delinquent behavior: families disrupted by spousal conflict or breakup, families involved in interpersonal conflict, negligent parents who are not attuned to their children's behavior and emotional problems, and families that contain deviant parents who may transmit their behavior to their children (Figure 7.2).[11] These factors may interact; for example, drug-abusing parents may be more likely to engage in family conflict, child neglect, and marital breakup. We now turn to the specific types of family problems that have been linked to delinquent behavior.

Children who are without proper care and support are at risk for abuse. Here the Rev. Joseph Combs (left) and his wife, Evangeline, await sentencing in Sullivan County Criminal Court in Blountville, Tenn., April 25, 2000. Joseph Combs was sentenced to 114 years in prison for aggravated kidnapping, aggravated assault, perjury, and multiple rape counts. Mrs. Combs was sentenced to 65 years in prison for kidnapping and aggravated child abuse. The couple was convicted of abusing a girl they took from an orphanage but never adopted. Mrs. Combs' attorney, Joe Harrison, is in background. (AP/Wide World Photos)

Family Breakup

broken home Home in which one or both parents is absent due to divorce or separation; children in such an environment may be prone to antisocial behavior.

blended families Nuclear families that are the product of divorce and remarriage; blending one parent from each of two families and their combined children into one family unit.

Figure 7.2
Family Influences on Behavior
Each of these four factors has been linked to antisocial behavior and delinquency. Interaction between these factors may escalate delinquent activity.

Family Breakup

Family Conflict

Delinquency

Family Neglect

Family Deviance

One of the most enduring controversies in the study of delinquency is the relationship between a parent absent from the home and the onset of delinquent behavior. Research indicates that parents whose marriage is secure produce children who are secure and independent.[12] In contrast, children growing up in homes with one or both parents absent may be prone to antisocial behavior.

A number of experts contend that a **broken home** is a strong determinant of a child's law-violating behavior. The connection seems self-evident because a child is first socialized at home. Any disjunction in an orderly family structure could be expected to have a negative impact on the child.

The suspected broken home–delinquency relationship is important because, if current trends continue, less than half of all children born today will live continuously with their own mother and father throughout childhood. And because stepfamilies, or so-called **blended families,** are less stable than families consisting of two biological parents, an increasing number of children will experience family breakup two or even three times during childhood.[13]

A number of studies indicate that children who have experienced family breakup are more likely to demonstrate behavior problems and hyperactivity than children in intact families.[14] Family breakup is often associated with conflict, hostility, and aggression; children of divorce are suspected of having lax supervision, weakened attachment, and greater susceptibility to peer pressure.[15] And, as a recent study of more than 4000 youth in Denver, Pittsburgh, and

Rochester found, the more often children are forced to go through family transitions the more likely they are to engage in delinquent activity.[16]

The Effects of Divorce The relationship between broken homes and delinquency was established in early research, which suggested that a significant association existed between parental absence and youthful misconduct.[17] Other efforts showed that parental absence seemed to affect girls, white youths, and the affluent more than it did males, minorities, and the indigent.[18] But the link was clear: children growing up in broken homes were much more likely to fall prey to delinquency than those who lived in two-parent households.

The studies that established the link between broken homes and delinquency used the records of police, courts, and correctional institutions.[19] This research may be tainted by sampling bias. Youths from broken homes may get arrested more often than youths from intact families, but this does not necessarily mean they engage in more frequent and serious delinquent behavior. Official statistics may reflect the fact that agents of the justice system treat children from disrupted households more severely because they cannot call on parents for support. The *parens patriae* philosophy of the juvenile courts calls for official intervention when parental supervision is considered inadequate.[20] It is not surprising then that numerous subsequent studies, using self-report data, have failed to establish any clear-cut relationship between broken homes and delinquent behavior.[21] Boys and girls from intact families seem as likely to self-report delinquency as those whose parents are divorced or separated. Children from broken homes are still more likely to show up in the official statistics. Researchers concluded that the absence of parents has a greater effect on agents of the justice system than it does on the behavior of children.[22]

Divorce Reconsidered Though some researchers still question the divorce–delinquency link, there is growing sentiment that family breakup is traumatic and most likely has a direct influence on factors related to adolescent misbehavior.[23] In her study of the effects of parental absence on children, sociologist Sara McLanahan finds that children who grow up apart from their biological fathers typically do less well than children who grow up with both biological parents. They are less likely to finish high school and attend college, less likely to find and keep a steady job, and more likely to become teen mothers. Although most children who grow up with a single parent do quite well, differences between children in one- and two-parent families are significant, and there is fairly good evidence that father absence per se is responsible for some social problems.[24] The traumas resulting from divorce were the subject of a widely read book, *The Unexpected Legacy of Divorce,* which is profiled in the accompanying Focus on Delinquency.

Family Conflict

intrafamily conflict An environment of discord and conflict within the family; children who grow up in dysfunctional homes often exhibit delinquent behaviors, having learned at a young age that aggression pays off.

Not all unhappy marriages end in divorce; some continue in an atmosphere of conflict. **Intrafamily conflict** is a common experience in many American families.[25] The link between parental conflict and delinquency was established almost 40 years ago when F. Ivan Nye found that a child's perception of his or her parents' marital happiness was a significant predictor of delinquency.[26] Contemporary studies also found that children who grow up in maladapted homes and witness discord or violence later exhibit emotional disturbance and behavior problems.[27] There seems to be little difference between the behavior of children who merely *witness* intrafamily violence and those who are its *victims.*[28] In fact, some research efforts show that observing the abuse of a parent (mother) is a more significant determinant of delinquency than being the target of child abuse.[29]

Research efforts have consistently supported the relationship between family conflict, hostility, and delinquency.[30] Adolescents who are incarcerated report growing

THE UNEXPECTED LEGACY OF DIVORCE

In their well-received 2000 book, *The Unexpected Legacy of Divorce,* Judith Wallerstein, Julia M. Lewis, and Sandra Blakeslee report on the findings of a longitudinal study, begun in the early 1970s, with 131 children whose parents divorced during their adolescence. In this book, Wallerstein and her associates check in with 93 of the original 131 children and extensively profile five children who most embody the common life experiences of the larger group. They follow their lives in detail through adolescence, delving into their love affairs, their marital successes and failures, and the parenting of their own children.

Wallerstein finds that the effects of divorce on children are not short-term and transient but long-lasting and cumulative. Children of divorce develop lingering fears about their *own* ability to develop long-term relationships; these fears often impede their ability to marry and raise families. While most spouses are able to reduce their emotional pain and get on with their lives a few years after they divorce, this is not true of their children, whose emotional turmoil may last for decades. The children often find it emotionally draining to spend time with their noncustodial parents and resent the disruption for years afterward. Some felt they had been an "inconvenience" and that their parents fit them in around their schedules. Considering their emotional turmoil, it is not surprising that these kids exhibit high levels of drug and alcohol abuse and, for girls, precocious sexuality. Consequently, only 40 percent of the kids they follow, many in their late twenties to early thirties, have ever married (compared to 81 percent of men and 87 percent of women in the general population). Some subjects told the researchers that marriage seemed impossible because their traumatic home life gave them no clue what a loving relationship was actually like!

In some cases the intense love/hate relationship developed during marriage never ends and parents continue to battle for years after separating; some collapse emotionally and physically. The authors document how some kids cope with long-term psychological turmoil by taking on the job of family caregiver. They become nurse, analyst, mentor, and confidant to their parents. One told them how, at 10 years old, she would spend time with her insomniac mother watching television and drinking beer at midnight! She frequently stayed home from school to make sure that her mother would not become depressed and suicidal or take the car out when she was drinking. Such personal burdens compromise the child's ability to develop friendships and personal interests. Such children may feel both trapped and guilty when they put their own needs ahead of the needy parent.

Wallerstein and her associates find that adolescents who grew up in homes where they experienced divorce are now struggling with the fear that their relationships will fail like those of their parents. Lacking guidance and experience, they must invent their own codes of behavior in a culture that offers few guidelines on how to become successful, protective parents themselves. This development has serious consequences, considering the theoretical importance placed on the development of positive family relationships as an inhibitor of delinquency and adult criminality.

Source: Judith S. Wallerstein, Julia M. Lewis, and Sandra Blakeslee, *The Unexpected Legacy of Divorce* (New York: Hyperion, 2000).

up in dysfunctional homes.[31] Parents of beyond-control youngsters have been found to be inconsistent rule-setters, to be less likely to show interest in their children, and to display high levels of hostile detachment.[32]

Although damaged parent–child relationships are associated with delinquency, it is difficult to assess the relationship. It is often assumed that preexisting family problems cause delinquency, but it may also be true that children who act out put enormous stress on a family. Kids who are conflict-prone may actually help to destabilize households. To avoid escalation of a child's aggression, these parents may give in to their children's demands. The children learn that aggression pays off.[33]

Parents may feel overwhelmed and shut their child out of their lives. Adolescent misbehavior may be a precursor of family conflict; strife leads to more adolescent misconduct, producing an endless cycle of family stress and delinquency.[34]

Family Conflict vs. Broken Homes Which is worse, growing up in a home marked by conflict or growing up in a broken home? Research shows that children in both broken homes and high-conflict intact homes were worse off than children in low-conflict, intact families.[35] However, children in high-conflict intact families appear to

The effects of a supportive family life can be very beneficial to children in any social environment or group. Even those children living in so-called high-crime areas are better able to resist the temptation of the streets if they receive fair discipline, care, and support from parents who provide them with strong, positive role models. (© Joel Gordon)

exhibit lower levels of adjustment than children in families where the parents had divorced. See Table 7.1 for other key findings on divorce.

Family Neglect

Many experts believe children need a warm, supportive relationship with their parents.[36] Close relations with family are important until late adolescence, when the influence of peer-group relations is heightened.

A number of studies support the link between the quality of family life and delinquency. Children who feel inhibited with their parents and refuse to discuss important issues with them are more likely to engage in deviant activities. Poor child–parent communications have been related to dysfunctional activities such as running away, and in all too many instances these children enter the ranks of homeless street youths who get involved in theft and prostitution to survive.[37] In contrast, even children who appear to be at risk are better able to resist involvement in delinquent activity when they report a strong attachment to their parents.[38] The importance of close relations with the family may diminish as children reach late adolescence and develop stronger peer-group relations, but most experts believe family influence remains considerable throughout life.[39]

Inconsistent Discipline Studies show that the parents of delinquent youths tend to be inconsistent disciplinarians, either overly harsh or extremely lenient.[40] But what conclusions can we draw from this observation?

TABLE 7.1   The Family Structure–Delinquency Link

- Children growing up in families disrupted by parental death are better adjusted than children of divorce. Parental absence is not a per se cause of antisocial behavior.
- Remarriage did not mitigate the effects of divorce on youth: children living with a stepparent exhibit (a) as many problems as youths in divorce situations and (b) considerably more problems than do children living with both biological parents.
- Continued contact with the noncustodial parent has little effect on a child's well-being.
- Evidence that the behavior of children of divorce improves over time is inconclusive.
- Postdivorce conflict between parents is related to child maladjustment.

Source: Paul Amato and Bruce Keith, "Parental Divorce and the Well-Being of Children: A Meta-Analysis," *Psychological Bulletin 110*:26–46 (1991).

The link between discipline and deviant behavior is uncertain. Most Americans still support the use of corporal punishment to discipline children. The use of physical punishment cuts across racial, ethnic, and religious groups.[41] There is growing evidence of a "violence begetting violence" cycle. Children who are subject to even minimal amounts of physical punishment may be more likely to use violence themselves. Murray Straus reviewed the concept of discipline in a series of surveys and found a powerful relationship between exposure to physical punishment and later aggression.[42]

Nonviolent societies are also ones in which parents rarely punish their children physically; there is a link between corporal punishment, delinquency, spousal abuse, and adult crime.[43] Research conducted in ten European countries shows that the degree to which parents and teachers approve of corporal punishment is related to the homicide rate.[44]

Physical punishment weakens the bond between parents and children, lowers the children's self-esteem, and undermines their faith in justice. It is not surprising, then, that Straus finds a high correlation between physical discipline and street crime. It is possible that physical punishment encourages children to become more secretive and dishonest.[45] Overly strict discipline may have an even more insidious link to antisocial behaviors: abused children have a higher risk of neurological dysfunction than the nonabused, and brain abnormalities have been linked to violent crime.[46]

Supervision   Evidence also exists that inconsistent supervision can promote delinquency. F. Ivan Nye found that mothers who threatened discipline but failed to carry it out were more likely to have delinquent children than those who were consistent in their discipline.[47] Contemporary research supports this finding with evidence that assaultive boys tend to grow up in homes in which there is inconsistent discipline.[48] There is ample evidence that effective supervision can reduce children's involvement in delinquency. Youths who believe their parents care little about their activities are more likely to engage in criminal acts than those who believe their actions will be closely monitored.[49] But simply having parents present in the household is not enough. Effective supervision is not a function of the number of parents in the home but reflects the style and quality of parenting.[50] Parents who closely supervise their children also have closer ties with them, helping to reduce their delinquent behavior.[51]

Family Size Parents may find it hard to control their children because they have such large families that resources, such as time, are spread too thin (resource dilution). Larger families are more likely to produce delinquents than smaller ones, and middle children are more likely to engage in delinquent acts than first- or last-born children.

Some sociologists assume that large family size has a direct effect on delinquency, attributing this phenomenon to stretched resources and the relatively limited supervision parents can provide for each child.[52] It is also possible that the relationship is indirect, caused by the connection of family size to some external factor; for example, resource dilution has been linked to educational underachievement, long considered a correlate of delinquency.[53] Middle children may suffer because they are most likely to be home when large numbers of siblings are also at home and economic resources are most stretched.[54]

The current trend is that affluent, two-wage-earner families are having fewer children, whereas indigent, single-parent households are growing larger. Children are at a greater risk of being both poor and delinquent because indigent families are the ones most likely to have more children.[55]

Family Deviance

A number of studies have found that parental deviance has a powerful influence on delinquent behavior.[56] Parental deviance disrupts the family's role as an agent of social control.[57] Some of the most important data on parental deviance was gathered by Donald J. West and David P. Farrington as part of the Cambridge Youth Survey. Their data (see Chapters 2 and 5) indicate that a significant number of delinquent youths have criminal fathers.[58] About 8 percent of the sons of noncriminal fathers became chronic offenders, compared to 37 percent of youths with criminal fathers.[59] In another analysis, Farrington found that one type of parental deviance, bullying, may be both inter- and intragenerational. Bullies have children who bully others, and these "second-generation bullies" grow up to become the fathers of children who are also bullies (see Chapter 10 for more on bullying).[60]

The cause of intergenerational deviance is uncertain. Genetic, environmental, psychological, and childrearing factors may all play a role. One finding that supports a genetic basis is that fathers of youths who suffer attention deficit hyperactivity disorder (ADHD), a condition linked to delinquency, are five times more likely to suffer antisocial personality disorder (APD) than fathers of non-ADHD youths.[61] This linkage may be evidence that aggressive tendencies are inherited. Similarly, research on the sons of alcoholics show that they suffer from neurological impairments related to delinquency.[62] It is possible that parental alcoholism causes genetic problems related to developmental impairment or that the children of substance-abusing parents are more prone to neurological impairment.

The quality of family life may also be key. Criminal parents may be least likely to have close relationships with their offspring, and research confirms that substance-abusing or criminal parents are more likely to use harsh and inconsistent discipline, a factor linked to delinquent behavior.[63] This association may be reinforced by stigmatization of children of known deviants. Social control agents may be quick to fix a "delinquent" label on the children of known law violators.[64] In sum, though there is some agreement that criminal parents produce delinquent offspring, the specific nature of the relationship is unknown.[65]

Sibling Influences Some evidence exists that siblings may also influence behavior. Siblings who report warm relationships and share friends are the most likely to behave in a similar fashion; those who maintain a close relationship also report similar rates of drug abuse and delinquency.[66]

DO FAMILIES MATTER?

The prevailing widsom is that the family is the key determinant of a child's attitudes, values, and behavior. However, in a controversial book, *The Nature Assumption*, psychologist Judith Rich Harris questions the cherished belief that parents play an important, if not the most important, role in a child's upbringing. Instead of family influence, Harris claims that genetics and environment determine, to a large extent, how a child turns out. Children's own temperament and peer relations shape their behavior and modify the characteristics they were born with; their interpersonal relations determine the kind of people they will be when they mature.

Harris reasons that parenting skills may be irrelevant to children's future success. Most parents don't have a single childrearing style, and they may treat each child in the family independently. They are more permissive with their mild-mannered kids and more strict and punitive with those who are temperamental or defiant. Even if every child were treated the same in a family, this would not explain why siblings raised in the same family under relatively similar conditions turn out so differently. Those sent to daycare are quite similar to those who remain at home; having working parents seems to have little long-term effect. Family structure also does not seem to matter: adults who grew up in one-parent homes are as likely to be successful as those who were raised in two-parent households.

If parenting has little direct influence on children's long-term development, what does? While Harris concedes that genetics plays the most important role in behavior, she asserts that the child's total social environment is the other key influence that shapes behavior. Kids who act one way at home may be totally different at school or with their peers. Some who are mild-mannered

around the house are hell-raisers in the schoolyard, whereas others who bully their siblings are docile with friends. Children may conform to parental expectations at home but leave them behind in their own social environment. Children develop their own culture with unique traditions, words, rules, and activities, which often conflict with parental and adult values. What parents encourage their children to pierce their bodies or get tattoos? If we are to accept Harris's vision, parents should become close to their children because they want to have them as companions and friends and not because it will improve their life chances.

Even those who disagree vehemently with Harris's research findings—and there are many—have been influenced by her book, which forced them to develop valid counterarguments. Some, such as the distinguished psychologist Eleanor Maccoby, now see parenting less in terms of one-parent-to-child influence, and more as a set of interactive processes during which parents and children react to each other and influence each other from the moment a child is born. It is foolish, she claims, to distinguish between genetics and environment because in reality they are intertwined from the moment of birth.

Some studies now show that a given parenting style can have different effects on children with different temperaments. The result is that parenting can function to make children in the same family different rather than alike.

Sources: Judith Rich Harris, *The Nature Assumption, Why Children Turn Out the Way They Do* (New York: Free Press, 1998); also Beth Azar, "A Forthcoming Book Details Evidence of How, When and in What Context Parents Influence Child Development—and Where They Might Not," *APA Monitor on Psychology* 31 (2000).

A number of interpretations of this data are possible. Siblings who live in the same environment are influenced by similar social and economic factors. Another possibility is that deviant siblings grow closer because of shared interests. It is possible that the relationship is due to personal interactions: older siblings are imitated by younger siblings. What seems to be a genetic effect may actually be the result of sibling interaction.

In summary, the research on delinquency and family relationships offers ample evidence that family life can be a potent force on a child's development. The delinquent child is likely to grow up in a large family with parents who may drink, participate in criminal acts, be harsh and inconsistent disciplinarians, be cold and unaffectionate, have marital conflicts, and be poor role models. Overall, the quality of a child's family life seems to be more important than its structure.

A provocative new book by psychologist Judith Rich Harris challenges the prevailing wisdom that family life is a critical determinant of a child's behavior. Harris's concepts are discussed in the Focus on Delinquency, "Do Families Matter?"

Checkpoints

✔ The family is undergoing change, and an increasing number of children will not live with their birth parents during their entire childhood.

✔ Families are undergoing social and economic stress.

✔ A number of factors shape the family's influence on delinquency.

✔ Most experts believe that children whose parents have divorced are at risk for delinquency.

✔ Kids who grow up in conflict-ridden households are more likely to become delinquent.

✔ Poor parent–child relations, including inconsistent discipline, have been linked to delinquency.

✔ Parents who commit crimes and use drugs are likely to have children who do so.

CHILD ABUSE AND NEGLECT

Family violence is a critical priority for criminal justice officials, political leaders, and the public.[67] Concern about the quality of family life has increased because of reports that many children are physically abused or neglected by their parents and that this treatment has serious consequences for their behavior. Because of this topic's importance, the remainder of this chapter is devoted to the issue of child abuse and neglect and its relationship to delinquent behavior.

Historical Foundation

Parental abuse and neglect is not a modern phenomenon. Maltreatment of children has occurred throughout history. Some concern for the negative effects of such maltreatment was voiced in the eighteenth century in the United States, but concerted efforts to deal with the problem did not begin until 1874.

In that year, residents of a New York City apartment building reported to a public health nurse Etta Wheeler that a child in one of the apartments was being abused by her stepmother. The nurse found a young child named Mary Ellen Wilson who had been repeatedly beaten and was malnourished from a diet of bread and water. Even though the child was seriously ill, the police agreed that the law entitled the parents to raise Mary Ellen as they saw fit. The New York City Department of Charities claimed it had no custody rights over Mary Ellen.

According to legend, Mary Ellen's removal from her parents had to be arranged through the Society for the Prevention of Cruelty to Animals (SPCA) on the ground that she was a member of the animal kingdom. The truth, however, is less sensational: Mary Ellen's case was heard by a judge. Because the child needed protection, she was placed in an orphanage.[68] The SPCA was actually founded the following year.[69]

Little research into the problems of maltreated children occurred before that of C. Henry Kempe, University of Colorado. In 1962, Kempe reported the results of a survey of medical and law-enforcement agencies that indicated the child abuse rate was much higher than had been thought. He coined a term, **battered child syndrome**, which he applied to cases of nonaccidental injury of children by their parents or guardians.[70]

battered child syndrome Nonaccidental physical injury of children by their parents or guardians.

Defining Abuse and Neglect

child abuse Any physical, emotional, or sexual trauma to a child, including neglecting to give proper care and attention, for which no reasonable explanation can be found.

Kempe's pioneering work has been expanded in a more generic expression of **child abuse** that includes neglect as well as physical abuse. Specifically, it describes any physical or emotional trauma to a child for which no reasonable explanation, such as an accident, can be found. Child abuse is generally seen as a pattern of behavior rather than a single act. The effects of a pattern of behavior are cumulative. That is, the longer the abuse continues, the more severe the effect will be.[71]

In 1874 Henry Bugh and Etta Angell Wheeler persuaded a New York court to take a child, Mary Ellen, away from her mother on the grounds of child abuse. This is the first recorded case in which a court was used to protect a child. Mary Ellen is shown at age 9 when she appeared in court showing bruises from a whipping and several gashes from a pair of scissors. The other photograph shows her a year later. (American Humane Society)

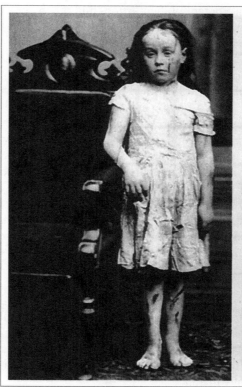 

neglect Passive neglect by a parent or guardian, depriving children of food, shelter, health care, and love.

Although the terms *child abuse* and **neglect** are sometimes used interchangeably, they represent different forms of maltreatment. Neglect refers to deprivations children suffer at the hands of their parents (lack of food, shelter, health care, love). *Abuse* is a more overt form of aggression against the child, one that often requires medical attention. The distinction between the terms is often unclear because, in many cases, both abuse and neglect occur simultaneously.

Physical abuse includes throwing, shooting, stabbing, burning, drowning, suffocating, biting, or deliberately disfiguring a child. The greatest number of injuries result from beatings. *Physical neglect* results from parents' failure to provide adequate food, shelter, or medical care for their children, as well as failure to protect them from physical danger.

Emotional abuse or neglect is manifested by constant criticism and rejection of the child.[72] Those who suffer emotional abuse have significantly lower self-esteem as adults.[73] *Emotional neglect* includes inadequate nurturing, inattention to a child's emotional development, and lack of concern about maladaptive behavior.

Sexual abuse refers to the exploitation of children through rape, incest, and molestation by parents, family members, friends, or legal guardians. Finally, **abandonment** refers to the situation in which parents leave their children with the intention of severing the parent–child relationship.[74]

abandonment Parents physically leave their children with the intention of completely severing the parent–child relationship.

There are a variety of legal definitions of abuse, but almost all contain concepts such as nonaccidental physical injury, physical neglect, emotional abuse or neglect, sexual abuse, and abandonment.[75]

Sexual Abuse

Sexual abuse can vary in content and style. It may range from rewarding children for sexual behavior that is inappropriate for their level of development to using force or the threat of force for the purposes of sex. It can involve children who are aware of the sexual content of their actions and others too young to have any idea what their actions mean. It can involve a variety of acts, from inappropriate touching to forcible sexual penetration.

The effects of sexual abuse can be devastating. Abused children suffer disrupted ego and personality development.[76] Guilt and shame are common. The ego of the victim may be overwhelmed by rage and horror over the incident, and the experience can have long-lasting repercussions.

Research indicates a correlation between the severity of abuse and its long-term effects: the less serious the abuse, the more quickly the child can recover.[77] Children who are frequently abused over long periods and suffer actual sexual penetration are most likely to experience long-term trauma, including post-traumatic stress syndrome (PTSD), precocious sexuality, and poor self-esteem.[78] Some victims find themselves sexualizing their own children in ways that lead them to sexual or physical abuse. Several studies have found a close association between sexual abuse and adolescent prostitution.[79] Finally, girls who were sexually and physically abused as children are more often suicidal as adults than the nonabused.[80]

The Extent of Child Abuse

It is almost impossible to estimate the extent of child abuse. Many victims are so young that they have not learned to communicate. Some are too embarrassed or afraid. Many incidents occur behind closed doors and, even when another adult witnesses inappropriate or criminal behavior, the adult may not want to get involved in a "family matter."

Some indications of the severity of the problem came from a 1980 survey conducted by sociologists Richard Gelles and Murray Straus.[81] Gelles and Straus estimated that between 1.4 and 1.9 million children in the United States were subject to physical abuse from their parents. This abuse was rarely a one-time act. The average number of assaults per year was 10.5, and the median was 4.5. Gelles and Straus also found that 16 percent of the couples in their sample reported spousal abuse; 50 percent of the multi-child families reported attacks between siblings; 20 percent of the families reported incidents in which children attacked parents.[82]

The Gelles and Straus survey was a milestone in identifying child abuse as a national phenomenon. Surveys conducted in 1985 and 1992 indicated that the incidence of severe violence toward children had declined.[83] One reason was that parental approval of corporal punishment, which stood at 94 percent in 1968, decreased to 68 percent by 1994.[84] Recognition of the problem may have helped moderate cultural values and awakened parents to the dangers of physically disciplining children. Nonetheless, more than 1 million children were still being subjected to severe violence annually. If the definition of "severe abuse" used in the survey had included hitting with objects such as a stick or a belt, the number of child victims would have been closer to 7 million per year.

Not all child abuse and neglect cases are reported to authorities, but those that are become the focus of state action. A number of organizations have been collecting data on reported child abuse. One source of such information is Prevent Child Abuse America (PCAA), a nonprofit organization that conducts an annual survey of child protection service (CPS) agencies to determine the number of reported child-abuse victims. In 1998 (the last data available), an estimated 3.1 million children were reported to CPS agencies as alleged victims of maltreatment. Overall, the total number of reports nationwide has increased more than 40 percent since 1988.[85] A little more than 1 million cases, or about one-third of those reported, are later substantiated by authorities—a number that corresponds with the results of the surveys conducted by Gelles, Straus, and their associates.

Highlights of a similar survey conducted by the federal government–sponsored National Child Abuse and Neglect Data System (NCANDS) is set out in Table 7.2.

Preventing child abuse before it occurs is the aim of Prevent Child Abuse America. Visit their site at http://www.preventchildabuse.org/ For an up-to-date list of Web links, go to www.wadsworth.com/ product/0534573053s

TABLE 7.2 Child Abuse and Neglect: National Statistics

- Of the estimated 2,806,000 referrals received by child protective services (CPS) agencies, approximately one-third (34%) were screened out and two-thirds (66%) were transferred for investigation or assessment.

- Slightly fewer than one-third of investigations (29.2%) resulted in a disposition of either substantiated or indicated child maltreatment. More than half (57.2%) resulted in a finding that child maltreatment was not substantiated. More than a tenth (13.6%) received another disposition.

- There were an estimated 903,000 victims of maltreatment nationwide. The 1998 rate of victimization was 12.9 per 1,000 children, a decrease from the 1997 rate of 13.9 per 1,000.

- More than half of all victims (53.5%) suffered neglect, while almost a quarter (22.7%) suffered physical abuse. Nearly 12 percent of the victims (11.5%) were sexually abused. Victims of psychological abuse and medical neglect accounted for 6 percent or fewer each. In addition, a quarter of victims (25.3%) were reported to be victims of more than one type of maltreatment.

- An estimated 1,100 children died of abuse and neglect, a rate of approximately 1.6 deaths per 100,000 children in the general population. Children not yet 1 year old accounted for 37.9 percent of the fatalities, and 77.5 percent were not yet 5 years of age.

- Nationally, an estimated 409,000 child victims received post-investigative services and an estimated additional 211,000 children who were subjects of unsubstantiated reports also received post-investigative services.

- Nationally, an estimated 144,000 child victims were placed in foster care. An estimated additional 33,000 children who were not victims were placed in the care and supervision of child welfare agencies, either in protective supervision or for a time during the investigation.

Source: U.S. Department of Health and Human Services. *Child Maltreatment 1998: Reports from the States to the National Child Abuse and Neglect Data System* (Washington, DC: U.S. Government Printing Office, 2000).

Sexual Abuse Attempts to determine the extent of sexual abuse indicate that perhaps 1 in 10 boys and 1 in 3 girls have been the victims of some form of sexual exploitation. An oft-cited survey by Diana Russell found that 16 percent of women reported sexual abuse by a relative, and 4.5 percent reported abuse by a father or stepfather.[86] It has been estimated that 30 to 75 percent of women in treatment for substance-abuse disorders experienced childhood sexual abuse.[87]

While sexual abuse is still quite prevalent, the number of reported cases has been in a significant decline. Research by Lisa Jones and David Finkelhor of the University of New Hampshire's Crimes Against Children Research Center shows that after a 15-year increase, substantiated child sexual-abuse cases in the United States dropped 31 percent between 1992 to 1998. Most states (36 out of the 47 they reviewed) showed declines of at least 30 percent.[88] This data could either mean that the actual number of cases is truly in decline or that the social service professionals are failing to recognize abuse cases because of overwork and understaffing.

Causes of Child Abuse and Neglect

Maltreatment of children is a complex problem with neither a single cause nor a single solution. It cuts across racial, ethnic, religious, and socioeconomic lines. Abusive parents cannot be categorized by sex, age, or educational level.

Of all factors associated with child abuse, three are discussed most often: (1) parents who themselves suffered abuse tend to abuse their own children; (2) the presence of an unrelated adult increases the risk of abuse; and (3) isolated and alienated families tend to become abusive. A cyclical pattern of violence seems to be perpetuated from one generation to another. Evidence indicates that a large number of abused and neglected children grow into adulthood with a tendency to engage in violent behavior. The behavior of abusive parents can often be traced to negative experiences in their own childhood—physical abuse, emotional neglect, and incest. These parents become unable to separate their own childhood traumas from their relationships with their children. Abusive parents often have unrealistic perceptions of normal development. When their children are unable to act appropriately—when they cry or strike their parents—the parents may react in an abusive manner.[89] Parents may also become abusive if they are isolated from friends, neighbors, or relatives.

Many abusive parents describe themselves as alienated from their extended families, and they lack close relationships with persons who could provide help in stressful situations.[90] The relationship between alienation and abuse may be particularly acute in homes where there has been divorce or separation, or in which parents have never actually married; abusive punishment in single-parent homes has been found to be twice that of two-parent families.[91] Parents who are unable to cope with stressful events—divorce, financial stress, recurring mental illness, drug addiction—are most at risk.[92]

Substance Abuse and Child Abuse Abusive families suffer from severe stress, and it is therefore not surprising that they frequently harbor members who turn to drugs and alcohol. Studies have found a strong association between child abuse and parental alcoholism.[93]

In addition, evidence exists of a significant relationship between cocaine and heroin abuse and neglect and abuse of children. Because this relationship is so important it is explored further in the Focus on Delinquency, "Relationship between Substance Abuse and Child Maltreatment."

Stepparents and Abuse Research indicates that stepchildren share a greater risk for abuse than do biological offspring.[94] Stepparents may have less emotional attachment to the children of another. Often the biological parent has to choose between the new mate and the child, sometimes even becoming an accomplice in the abuse.[95]

Stepchildren are over-represented in cases of **familicide,** mass murders in which a spouse and one or more children are slain. It is also more common for fathers who kill their biological children to commit suicide than those who kill stepchildren, an indication that their act was motivated by hostility and not despair.[96]

familicide Mass murders in which a spouse and one or more children are slain.

Social Class and Abuse Surveys indicate a high rate of reported abuse and neglect among people in lower economic classes. Children from families earning less than $15,000 per year experience more abuse than children living in more affluent homes.[97] More than 40 percent of CPS workers indicate that most of their clients either live in poverty or face increased financial stress due to unemployment and economic recession.[98] These findings suggest that parental maltreatment of children is predominantly a lower-class problem. Is this conclusion valid?

One view is that the statistics are generally accurate. Low-income families, especially those headed by a single parent, are often subject to greater environmental stress and have fewer resources to deal with such stress than families with higher incomes.[99] A relationship seems to exist between the burdens of raising a child without adequate resources and the use of excessive force. Self-report surveys do show that indigent parents are more likely than affluent parents to hold attitudes that condone physical chastisement of children.[100]

RELATIONSHIP BETWEEN SUBSTANCE ABUSE AND CHILD MALTREATMENT

The relationship between parental alcohol or other drug problems and child maltreatment is becoming increasingly evident. It is a serious problem because substance abuse is so widespread: An estimated 14 million adult Americans abuse alcohol, and there may be more than 12 million illicit drug users. With more than 6 million children under the age of 18 living in alcoholic households, and an additional number living in households where parents have problems with illicit drugs, it is evident that a significant number of children in this country are being raised by addicted parents.

Do parental alcohol or other drug problems cause child maltreatment?

Recent research on the connection between these problems and child maltreatment clearly indicates a connection between the two behaviors. Among confirmed cases of child maltreatment, 40 percent involve the use of alcohol or other drugs. This suggests that, of the 1.2 million confirmed victims of child maltreatment each year, an estimated 480,000 children are mistreated by a caretaker with alcohol or other drug problems. Additionally, research suggests that alcohol and other drug problems are factors in a majority of cases of emotional abuse and neglect. In fact, neglect is the major reason that children are removed from a home in which parents have alcohol or other drug problems. Children in these homes suffer from a variety of physical, mental, and emotional health problems at a greater rate than do children in the general population. Children of alcoholics suffer more injuries and poisonings than do children in the general population. Alcohol and other substances may act as disinhibitors, lessening impulse control and allowing parents to behave abusively. Children in this environment often demonstrate behavioral problems and are diagnosed as having conduct disorders. This may result in provocative behavior. Increased stress resulting from preoccupation with drugs on the part of the parent combined with behavioral problems exhibited by the child increases the likelihood of maltreatment. Frequently, these parents suffer from depression, anxiety, and low self-esteem. They live in an atmosphere of stress and family conflict. Children raised in both households are themselves more likely to have problems with alcohol and other drugs.

How does a parent's alcohol or other drug problem affect children?

Children of alcoholics are more likely than children in the general population to suffer a variety of physical, mental, and emotional health problems. They often have feelings of low self-esteem and failure and suffer from depression and anxiety. It is thought that exposure to violence in both alcohol-abusing and child-maltreating households increases the likelihood that the children will commit, and be recipients of, acts of violence. The effects don't end when these children reach adulthood; they may have difficulty with coping and with establishing healthy relationships as adults. In addition to suffering from all the effects of living in a household where alcohol or child-maltreatment problems exist, children whose parents abuse illicit drugs live with the knowledge that their parents' actions are illegal. While research is in its infancy, clinical evidence shows that children of parents who have problems with illicit drug use may suffer from an inability to trust legitimate authority because of fear of discovery of a parent's illegal habits.

As they mature, many fall victim to the same patterns exhibited by their parents. Those who have been severely physically abused often have symptoms of post-traumatic disorder and dissociation. Individuals suffering from mental health disorders may use alcohol and illicit drugs to decrease or mitigate their psychological distress. Research suggests that adults who were abused as children may be more likely to abuse their own children than adults who were not abused as children.

Can child maltreatment, when alcohol or other drugs are a problem, be successfully treated? Research has shown that when families exhibit both of these behaviors, the problems must be treated simultaneously in order to ensure a child's safety. Although ending the drug dependency does not automatically end child maltreatment, very little can be done to improve parenting skills until this step is taken. The withdrawal experienced by parents who cease using alcohol or other drugs presents specific risks. The effects of withdrawal often cause a parent to experience intense emotions, which may increase the likelihood of child maltreatment. During this time, lasting as long as two years, it is especially important that resources be available to the family.

Source: *The Relationship Between Parental Alcohol or Other Drug Problems and Child Maltreatment* (Chicago, IL: Prevent Child Abuse America, 2000).

Higher rates of maltreatment in low-income families reflect the stress caused by the limited resources lower-class parents have to help them in raising their children; in contrast, middle-class parents devote a smaller percentage of their total resources to raising a family.[101]

This burden becomes especially onerous in families with emotionally and physically handicapped children. Stressed-out parents may consider special-needs children a drain on the families' finances with little potential for future success; research finds that children with disabilities are maltreated at a rate almost double that of other children.[102]

The Child Protection System: Philosophy and Practice

For most of the nation's history, courts have assumed that parents have the right to bring up their children as they see fit. In the 2000 case *Troxel v. Granville,* the Supreme Court ruled that the due process clause of the Constitution protects against government interference with certain fundamental rights and liberty interests, including parents' fundamental right to make decisions concerning the care, custody, and control of their children.[103] If the care a child receives falls below reasonable standards, the state may take action to remove a child from the home and place her or him in a less threatening environment. In these extreme circumstances, the rights of both parents and children are constitutionally protected. In the cases of *Lassiter v. Department of Social Services* and *Santosky v. Kramer,* the U.S. Supreme Court recognized the child's right to be free from parental abuse and set down guidelines for a termination-of-custody hearing, including the right to legal representation.[104] States provide a guardian *ad litem* (a lawyer appointed by the court to look after the interests of those who do not have the capacity to assert their own rights). States also ensure confidentiality of reporting.[105]

Though child-protection agencies have been dealing with abuse and neglect since the late nineteenth century, recent awareness of the problem has prompted judicial authorities to take increasingly bold steps to ensure the safety of children.[106] The assumption that the parent–child relationship is inviolate has been challenged. In 1974 Congress passed the Child Abuse Prevention and Treatment Act (CAPTA), which provides funds to states to bolster their services for maltreated children and their parents.[107] The act provides federal funding to states in support of prevention, investigation, and treatment. It also provides grants to public agencies and nonprofit organizations for demonstration programs.

The Child Abuse Prevention and Treatment Act has been the impetus for the states to improve the legal frameworks of their child-protection systems. Abusive parents are subject to prosecution under statutes against assault, battery, and homicide. Many states have child-abuse statutes that make it a felony to injure and abuse children.

To access the Child Abuse Prevention and Treatment Act (CAPTA), go to

http://www.acf.dhhs.gov/ programs/cb/policy/capta.htm

For an up-to-date list of Web links, go to www.wadsworth.com/ product/0534573053s

Investigating and Reporting Abuse Maltreatment of children can easily be hidden from public view. Although state laws require doctors, teachers, and others who work with children to report suspected cases to child-protection agencies, many maltreated children are out of the law's reach because they are too young for school or because their parents do not take them to a doctor or a hospital. Parents abuse their children in private and, even when confronted, often accuse their children of lying or blame the children's medical problems on accidents. Social service agencies must find more effective ways to locate abused children and to handle such cases once found.

All states have statutes requiring that persons suspected of abuse and neglect be reported. Many have made failure to report child abuse a criminal offense. Though such statutes are rarely enforced, teachers have been criminally charged for failing to report abuse or neglect cases.[108]

Once reported to a child-protection agency, the case is screened by an intake worker and then turned over to an investigative caseworker. Protective service workers often work with law-enforcement officers. If the caseworker determines that the child is in imminent danger of severe harm, the caseworker may immediately remove the child from the home. A court hearing must be held shortly after to approve the

Research on sexual abuse indicates that perhaps one in ten boys and one in three girls have been victims of some form of sexual exploitation. Children who are frequently abused over long periods of time experience long-term trauma, including post-traumatic stress syndrome, precocious sexuality, and poor self-esteem. (© Denis LaCuyer/Liaison Agency)

custody. Stories abound of children erroneously taken from their homes, but it is much more likely that these "gatekeepers" will consider cases unfounded and take no action. More than 50 percent of all reported cases are so classified.[109] Among the most common reasons for screening out cases is that the reporting party is involved in a child custody case.[110]

Even when there is compelling evidence of abuse, most social service agencies will try to involve the family in voluntary treatment. Case managers will do periodic follow-ups to determine if treatment plans are being followed. If parents are uncooperative or if the danger to the children is so great that they must be removed from the home, a complaint will be filed in the criminal, family, or juvenile court system.

The Process of State Intervention Although procedures vary from state to state, most follow a similar legal process once a social service agency files a court petition alleging abuse or neglect.[111] This process is diagrammed in Figure 7.3.

If the allegation of abuse is confirmed, the child may be placed in protective custody. Most state statutes require that the court be notified "promptly" or "immediately" if the child is removed; some states, including Arkansas, North Carolina, and Pennsylvania have gone as far as requiring that no more than 12 hours elapse before official action is taken. If the child has not been removed from the home, state authorities are given more time to notify the court of suspected abuse. For example, Louisiana and

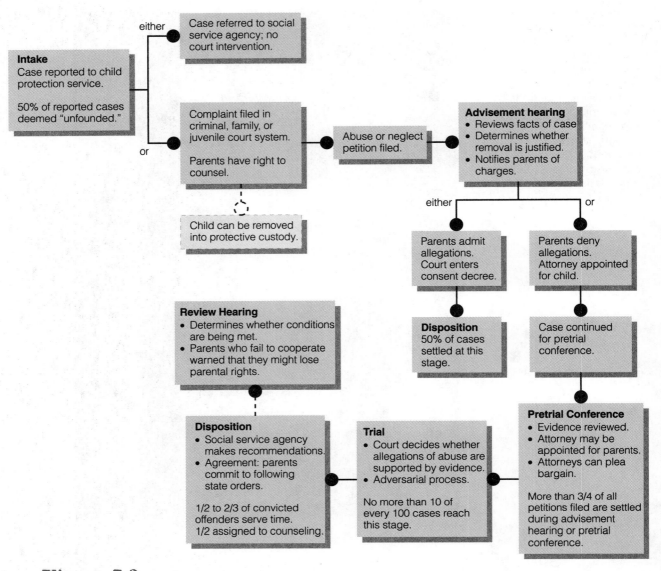

Figure 7.3
The Process of State Intervention in Cases of Abuse and Neglect

advisement hearing A preliminary protective or temporary custody hearing in which the court will review the facts and determine whether removal of the child is justified and notify parents of the charges against them.

pretrial conference The attorney for the social services agency presents an overview of the case and a plea bargain or negotiated settlement can be agreed to in a consent decree.

Maryland set a limit of 30 days to take action, whereas Wisconsin mandates that state action take no more than 20 days once the case has been investigated.

When an abuse or neglect petition is prosecuted, an **advisement hearing** (also called a *preliminary protective hearing* or *temporary custody hearing*) is held. The court will review the facts of the case, determine whether removal is justified, and notify the parents of the charges against them. Parents have the right to counsel in all cases of abuse and neglect, and many states require the court to appoint an attorney for the child as well. If the parents admit the allegations, the court enters a consent decree, and the case is continued for disposition. Approximately one-half of all cases are settled by admission at the advisement hearing. If the parents deny the petition, an attorney is appointed for the child and the case is continued for a pretrial conference.

At the **pretrial conference**, the attorney for the social service agency presents an overview of the case and the evidence. Such matters as admissibility of photos and written reports are settled. At this point the attorneys can negotiate a settlement of the case. About three-fourths of the cases that go to pretrial conference are settled by a consent decree. About 85 out of every 100 petitions filed will be settled at either the advisement hearing or the pretrial conference.

Of the fifteen remaining cases, five will generally be settled before trial. Usually no more than ten cases out of every one hundred actually reach the trial stage of the process. This is an adversarial hearing designed to prove the state's allegations.

disposition hearing The social service agency presents its case plan and recommendations for care of the child and treatment of the parents, including incarceration and counseling or other treatments.

Disposition The most crucial part of an abuse or neglect proceeding is the **disposition hearing.** The social service agency presents its case plan, which includes recommendations such as conditions for returning the child to the parents or a visitation plan if the child is to be taken from the parents. An agreement is reached by which the parents commit themselves to following the state orders. Between one-half and two-thirds of all convicted parents will be required to serve time in incarceration; almost half will be assigned to a form of treatment. As far as the children are concerned, some may be placed in temporary care; in other cases, parental rights are terminated and the child is placed in the custody of the child protective service. Legal custody can then be assigned to a relative or some other person.

balancing-of-the-interest approach Efforts of the courts to balance the parents' natural right to raise a child with the child's right to grow into adulthood free from physical abuse or emotional harm.

In making their decisions, courts are guided by three interests: the role of the parents, protection for the child, and the responsibility of the state. Frequently, these interests conflict. In fact, at times even the interests of the two parents are not in harmony. The state attempts to balance the parents' natural right to control their child's upbringing with the child's right to grow into adulthood free from harm. This is referred to as the **balancing-of-the-interest approach.**

review hearings Periodic meetings to determine whether the conditions of the case plan for an abused child are being met by the parents or guardians of the child.

Periodically, **review hearings** are held to determine if the conditions of the case plan are being met. Parents who fail to cooperate are warned that they may lose their parental rights. Most abuse and neglect cases are concluded within a year. Either the parents lose their rights and the child is given a permanent placement, or the child is returned to the parents and the court's jurisdiction ends.

The Abused Child in Court

One of the most significant problems associated with abuse cases is the trauma a child must go through in a court hearing. Children get confused and frightened and may change their testimony. Much controversy has arisen over the accuracy of children's reports of family violence and sexual abuse, resulting in hung juries in some well-known cases, including the McMartin Day Care case in California.[112]

State jurisdictions have instituted procedures to minimize the trauma to the child. Most have enacted legislation allowing videotaped statements, or interviews with child witnesses, taken at a preliminary hearing or at a formal deposition, to be admissible in court. Videotaped testimony spares child witnesses the trauma of testifying in open court. States that allow videotaped testimony usually put some restrictions on its use: some prohibit the government from calling the child to testify at trial if the videotape is used; some states require a finding that the child is "medically unavailable" because of the trauma of the case before videotaping can be used; some require that the defendant be present during the videotaping; a few specify that the child not be able to see or hear the defendant.[113]

More than two-thirds of the states now allow a child's testimony to be given on closed-circuit television (CCTV). The child is able to view the judge and attorneys, and the courtroom participants are able to observe the child. The standards for CCTV testimony vary widely. Some states, such as New Hampshire, assume that any child witness under age 12 would benefit from not having to appear in court. Others require an independent examination by a mental health professional to determine whether there is a "compelling need" for CCTV testimony.

In addition to innovative methods of testimony, children in sexual abuse cases have been allowed to use anatomically correct dolls to demonstrate happenings that they cannot describe verbally. The Victims of Child Abuse Act of 1990 allows children to use hearsay Out-of-court statements made by one person and recounted in court by another; such statements are generally not allowed as evidence except in child abuse cases wherein a child's statements to social workers, teachers, or police may be admissible.

these dolls when testifying in federal courts; at least eight states have passed similar legislation.[114] Similarly, states have relaxed their laws of evidence to allow out-of-court statements by the child to a social worker, teacher, or police officer to be used as evidence (such statements would otherwise be considered **hearsay**). Typically, corroboration is required to support these statements if the child does not also testify.

The prevalence of sexual abuse cases has created new problems for the justice system. Often accusations are made in conjunction with marital disputes. The fear is growing that children may become pawns in custody battles; the mere suggestion of sexual abuse is enough to affect the outcome of a divorce action. The justice system must develop techniques that can get at the truth without creating a lifelong scar on the child's psyche.

Legal Issues A number of cases have been brought before the Supreme Court, testing the right of children to present evidence at trial using nontraditional methods. Two issues stand out. One is the ability of physicians and mental health professionals to testify about statements made to them by children, especially when the children are incapable of testifying. The second concerns the way children testify in court.

In a 1992 case, *White v. Illinois,* the Court ruled that the state's attorney is required neither to produce young victims at trial nor to demonstrate the reason they were unavailable to serve as witnesses.[115] *White* involved statements given by the child to the child's babysitter and mother, a doctor, a nurse, and a police officer concerning the alleged assailant in a sexual assault case. The prosecutor twice tried to call the child to testify, but both times the four-year-old experienced emotional difficulty and could not appear in court. The outcome hinged solely on the testimony of the five witnesses.

By allowing others to testify as to what the child said, *White* removed the requirement that prosecutors produce child victims in court. This facilitates the prosecution of child abusers in cases where a court appearance by a victim would prove too disturbing or where the victim is too young to understand the court process.[116] The Court noted that statements made to doctors during medical exams or those made when a victim is upset carry more weight than ones made after careful reflection. The Court ruled that such statements can be repeated during trial because the circumstances in which they were made could not be duplicated simply by having the child testify to them in court.

In-Court Statements Children who are victims of sexual or physical abuse often make poor witnesses. Yet their testimony may be crucial. In a 1988 case, *Coy v. Iowa,* the Court placed limitations on efforts to protect child witnesses in court. During a sexual assault case, a "one-way" glass screen was set up so that the child victims would not be able to view the defendant (the defendant, however, could view the witnesses).[117] The Iowa statute that allowed the protective screen assumed that children would be traumatized by their courtroom experience. The Court ruled that unless there was a finding that the child witness needs special protection, the Sixth Amendment of the Constitution grants defendants "face-to-face" confrontation with their accusers. In her dissenting opinion, Justice Sandra Day O'Connor suggested that if courts found it necessary, it would be appropriate to allow children to testify via CCTV or videotape.

Justice O'Connor's views became law in *Craig v. Maryland.*[118] In this case a daycare operator was convicted of sexually abusing a six-year-old child; one-way CCTV testimony was used during the trial. The decision was overturned in the Maryland Court of Appeals on the ground that the procedures used were insufficient to show that the child could only testify in this manner because a trial appearance would be too traumatic. On appeal, the Court ruled that the Maryland statute that allows CCTV testimony is sufficient because it requires a determination that the child will suffer distress if forced to testify. The Court noted that CCTV could serve as the

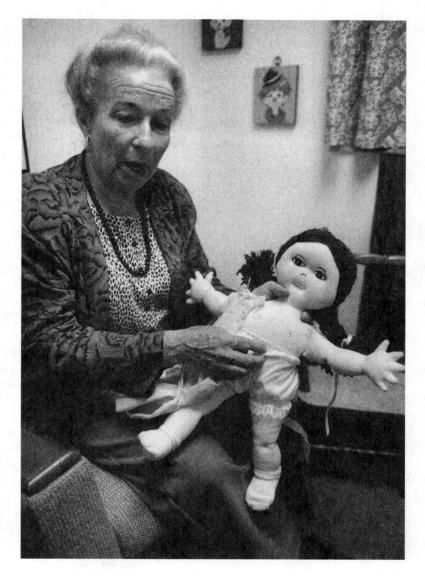

A counselor shows a doll to a victim of child abuse. Children in sexual abuse cases may use anatomically correct dolls to demonstrate happenings that they cannot describe verbally. The Victims of Child Abuse Act of 1990 allows children to use dolls when testifying in federal courts; at least eight states have passed similar legislation. (© Joel Gordon)

equivalent of in-court testimony and would not interfere with the defendant's right to confront witnesses.

Since *Coy v. Iowa*, the Supreme Court has increased the legal tools prosecutors can employ in child abuse cases. This opens the door for prosecutions in cases that would have been impossible to pursue before.

Disposition of Abuse and Neglect Cases

There is considerable controversy over what forms of intervention are helpful in abuse and neglect cases. Today, social service agents avoid removing children from the home whenever possible and instead try to employ techniques to control abusive relationships. In serious cases, the state may remove children from their parents and place them in shelter care or foster homes. Placement of children in foster care is intended to be temporary, but it is not uncommon for children to remain in foster care for 3 years or more.

Ultimately, the court has the power to terminate the rights of parents over their children, but because the effects of destroying the family unit are far-reaching, the court does so only in the most severe cases. Judicial hesitancy is illustrated in a

Virginia appellate case in which grandparents contested a father's being awarded custody of his children. Even though he had a history of alcohol abuse, had already been found to be an unfit parent, and was awaiting appeal of his conviction for killing the children's mother, the trial court claimed that he had turned his life around and granted him custody.[119]

Despite such occurrences, efforts have been ongoing to improve the child protection system. Jurisdictions have expedited case processing, instituted procedures designed not to frighten child witnesses, coordinated investigations between social service and law-enforcement agencies, and assigned an advocate or guardian *ad litem* to children in need of protection.

✔ Checkpoints

✔ While the maltreatment of juveniles has occurred throughout history, the concept of child abuse is relatively recent.

✔ C. Henry Kempe first recognized the "battered child syndrome."

✔ We now recognize sexual, physical, and emotional abuse, as well as neglect.

✔ More than 1 million confirmed cases of abuse occur each year.

✔ The number of sexual abuse cases has declined.

✔ There are a number of suspected causes of child abuse, including parental substance abuse, isolation, and a history of physical and emotional abuse.

✔ There is a child protection system which has been created to identify and try abuse cases.

✔ The courts have made it easier for children to testify in abuse cases, for example, by using closed-circuit TV.

Abuse, Neglect, and Delinquency

Because the effects of child abuse are long-term, delinquency experts fear that abused kids will experience mental and social problems across their life span. For example, victims of abuse are prone to suffer mental illness such as dissociative identity disorder (DID), formerly known as multiple personality disorder (MPD); research shows that child abuse is present in the histories of the vast majority of DID subjects. [120]

One particular area of concern is the child's own personal involvement with violence. Psychologists suggest that maltreatment encourages children to use aggression as a means of solving problems and prevents them from feeling empathy for others. It diminishes their ability to cope with stress and makes them vulnerable to the violence in the culture. Abused children have fewer positive interactions with peers, are less well liked, and are more likely to have disturbed social interactions.[121]

The link between maltreatment and delinquency is also supported by a number of criminological theories. For example:

■ *Social Control Theory.* By disrupting normal relationships and impeding socialization, maltreatment reduces the social bond and frees individuals to become involved in deviance.

■ *Social Learning Theory.* Maltreatment leads to delinquency because it teaches children that aggression and violence are justifiable forms of behavior.

■ *General Strain Theory.* Maltreatment creates the "negative affective states" that are related to strain, anger, and aggression.

A significant amount of literature suggests that abuse may have a profound effect on behavior in later years. Exposure to abuse in early life provides a foundation for violent and antisocial behavior.[122] Delinquent behavior is the means by which many abused children act out their hostility toward their parents. Some join gangs, which furnish a sense of belonging and allow pent-up anger to be expressed in group-approved delinquent acts.

Clinical Histories Studies of juvenile offenders have confirmed that between 70 and 80 percent may have had abusive backgrounds. Many of these juveniles reported serious injury, including bruises, lacerations, fractures, and being knocked unconscious by a parent or guardian.[123] Likewise, several studies reveal an association between homicide and maltreatment in early childhood.[124] Among children who kill or who attempt murder, the most common factor is a child's tendency to identify with aggressive parents and imitate their behavior.[125] One study of murder and murderous assault by juveniles indicated that in all cases "one or both parents had fostered and condoned murderous assault."[126]

Cohort Studies These findings do not necessarily prove that maltreatment causes delinquency. It is possible that child abuse is a reaction to misbehavior and not vice versa. In other words, it is possible that angry parents attack their delinquent and drug-abusing children and that child abuse is a *result* of delinquency, not its cause.

One way of solving this dilemma is to follow a cohort of youths who had been reported as victims of abuse and compare them with a similar cohort of nonabused youths. A classic study conducted by Jose Alfaro in New York found that about half of all children reported to area hospitals as abused children later acquired arrest records. Conversely, a significant number of boys (21 percent) and girls (29 percent) petitioned to juvenile court had prior histories as abuse cases. Children treated for abuse were disproportionately involved in violent offenses.[127]

Cathy Spatz Widom followed the offending careers of 908 youths reported as abused from 1967 to 1971 and compared them with a control group of 667 nonabused youths. Widom found that the abuse involved a variety of perpetrators, including parents, relatives, strangers, and even grandparents. Twenty-six percent of the abused sample had juvenile arrests, compared to 17 percent of the comparison group; 29 percent of those who were abused had adult criminal records, compared to 21 percent of the control group. Race, gender, and age also affected the probability that abuse would lead to delinquency. The highest risk group was comprised of older black males who had suffered abuse; about 67 percent of this group went on to become adult criminals. In contrast, only 4 percent of young, white, nonabused females became adult offenders.[128] Her conclusion: Being abused increased the likelihood of arrest both as a juvenile and as an adult.[129]

Widom also tested the hypothesis that victims of childhood violence resort to violence themselves as they mature. The children in her sample who suffered from physical abuse were the most likely to get arrested for violent crimes; their violent crime arrest rate was double that of the control group. More surprising was the discovery that neglected children maintained higher rates of violence than children in the comparison group. Clearly, family trauma of all kinds may influence violence.

Child Victims and Persistent Offending Widom also interviewed 500 subjects, 20 years after their childhood victimization. Preliminary analysis of this sample indicates that the long-term consequences of childhood victimization continue throughout life. Potential problems include mental health concerns, educational problems, health problems, and occupational difficulties. In a more recent analysis, Widom and Michael Maxfield found that by the time they reached age 32, abused children had a higher frequency of adult offending than the nonabused. People who began their offending careers as adults were also more likely to have been abused as children. Widom and Maxfield conclude that early intervention may be necessary to stop this cycle of violence.[130]

Sexual Abuse Cohort research shows that sexually abused youths are much more likely to suffer an arrest than nonabused children. The risk is greatest if the abuse took place when the child was less than 7 years of age and the offense was committed by a male.[131] Sexually abused girls share a significant risk of becoming violent over the life course. There is also evidence that sexual abuse victims are more likely to

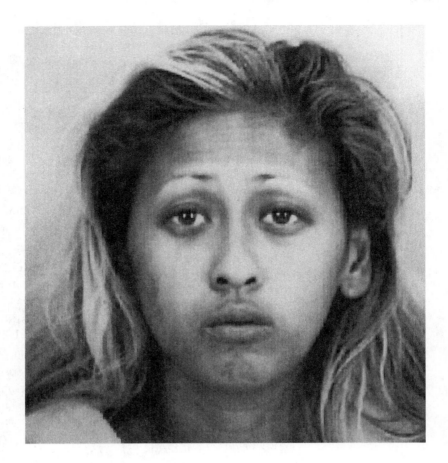

This is a Santa Clara County Sheriff booking photo of Rosemarie Randovan taken Nov. 6, 2000, in San Jose, Calif. Randovan was arraigned in a San Jose court-room Nov. 8, 2000, on two felony counts of child abuse. Over a period of four months, Randovan allegedly locked her sons in the trunk of her car while she worked. Police say Randovan was having trouble finding day care for her two sons, ages 5 and 7. One of Randovan's coworkers called police after hearing moaning coming from the back of Randovan's car. What can be done to help women such as Randovan so that they do not have to resort to such desperate measures? (AP/Wide World Photos)

abuse others, especially if they were exposed to other forms of family violence.[132] Self-report studies also confirm that child maltreatment increases the likelihood of delinquency. The most severely abused youths are at the greatest risk for long-term serious delinquency.[133]

The Abuse-Delinquency Link

These findings do not necessarily mean that most abused children become delinquent. Many do not, and many delinquent youths come from what appear to be model homes. Though Widom found that more abused than nonabused children in her cohort became involved in delinquency, the majority of *both* groups did not.[134]

Although these studies suggest an abuse–delinquency link, others find that the association is either nonsignificant or inconsistent (for example, having a greater influence on girls than boys).[135] Abused adolescents seem to get involved in more status offenses than delinquent acts—perhaps indicating that abused children are more likely to "flee than fight."[136]

THE FAMILY AND DELINQUENCY PREVENTION

Since the family is believed to play such an important role in the production of youth crime, it follows that improving family functioning can help prevent delinquency. Counselors commonly work with the families of antisocial youths as part of a court-ordered treatment strategy. Family counseling and therapy are almost mandatory when the child's acting-out behavior is suspected to be the result of family-related problems such as child abuse or neglect.[137] Some jurisdictions have integrated family counseling services into the juvenile court.[138]

Early Childhood Intervention

Another approach to involving the family in delinquency prevention is to attack the problem before it occurs. Early childhood prevention programs that target at-risk youths can relieve some of the symptoms associated with delinquency.[139] Frequent home visits by trained nurses reduce child abuse and other injuries to infants. Weekly home visits by preschool teachers to children under age 5 reduce arrests at least through age 15. Family therapy and parent training reduce risk factors for delinquency such as aggression and hyperactivity.[140]

Among the best-known of these programs is the Syracuse University Family Development Research Program. This program identifies high-risk women during the later stages of their pregnancies. After the women give birth, paraprofessionals are assigned to work with them, encouraging sound parent–child relationships, providing nutrition information, and helping them establish relationships with social service agencies. In addition, the program provides childcare at Syracuse University Children's Center. A 10-year follow-up compared children involved in the program with a control group and found that those receiving intervention were less likely to be involved in criminal activity, more likely to express positive feelings about themselves, and able to take a more active role in dealing with personal problems. Girls seemed especially to benefit, doing better in school; parents were more likely to express pro-social attitudes.[141]

The Perry Preschool in Michigan has provided disadvantaged students with a 2-year program of educational enrichment supplemented with weekly home visits; children in the program accumulated half the arrests of a comparison group and appeared to be better motivated. A long-term longitudinal study on the program's success found that participants had significantly lower rates of crime and delinquency and lower incidence of teenage pregnancy and welfare dependency. By the age of 27, program participants were nearly three times as likely to own their own homes than the control group and less than half as likely to be receiving public assistance.[142]

Improving Parenting Skills

The most widely cited parenting skills program is the one created at the Oregon Social Learning Center (OSLC) by Gerald R. Patterson and his associates.[143] Patterson's research convinced him that poor parenting skills were associated with antisocial behavior in the home and at school. Family disruption and coercive exchanges between parents and children led to increased family tension, poor academic performance, and negative peer relations. The primary cause of the problem seemed to be that parents did not know how to deal effectively with their children. Parents sometimes ignored their children's behavior, but at other times the same actions would trigger explosive rage. Some parents would discipline their children for reasons that had little to do with the children's behavior, instead reflecting their own frustrations.

The children reacted in a regular progression, from learning to be noncompliant to learning to be assaultive. Their "coercive behavior," which included whining, yelling, and temper tantrums, would sometimes be acquired by other family members. Eventually family conflict would flow out of the home and into the school and social environment.

The OSLC program uses behavior modification techniques to help parents acquire proper disciplinary methods. Parents are asked to select several behaviors for change and to count the frequency of their occurrence. OSLC personnel teach social skills to reinforce positive behaviors, and constructive disciplinary methods to discourage negative ones. Incentive programs are initiated in which a child can earn points for desirable behaviors. Points can be exchanged for allowance, prizes, or privileges. Parents are also taught disciplinary techniques that stress firmness and consistency rather than "nattering" (low-intensity behaviors, such as scowling or scolding) or explosive discipline, such as hitting or screaming. One important technique is the "time out," in

Improved parenting skills may be key to reducing the incidence of child abuse. Here, Nicholas, 9 (left), and his brother, Jared, 7, get help with homework from their mom, Wendy Hastie, at their home in Nashville, Tenn., Dec. 24, 2000. Wendy Hastie and her husband recently completed a Youth Village treatment program so they could learn to cope better with behavioral and health problems experienced by Jared. The program stresses early intervention in an attempt to head off problems before a juvenile breaks the law. (AP/Wide World Photos)

which the child is removed for brief isolation in a quiet room. Parents are taught the importance of setting rules and sticking to them.

Evidence suggests that early intervention may be the most effective method and that, the later the intervention, the more difficult the change process. Psychologist Edward Zigler and his associates found that early interventions in family functioning can result in significant improvement in parent–child relations and a concomitant reduction in antisocial activities.[144]

The parent training method used by the OSLC may be the most cost-effective method of early intervention.[145] A Rand survey found that parent training costs about one-twentieth what a home visit program costs and is more effective in preventing serious crimes. The study estimates that 501 serious crimes could be prevented for every million dollars spent on parent training, a far cheaper solution than long-term incarceration, which would cost about $16,000 to prevent a single crime![146]

SUMMARY

Poor family relationships have been linked to juvenile delinquency. Early theories viewed the broken home as a cause of youthful misconduct, but subsequent research indicates that divorce, separation, or parental death plays a smaller role than was previously thought. More recently, experts have suggested that broken homes may have a greater effect than once believed. They argue that it is more difficult for one parent to provide the same degree of discipline and support as two. The quality of family life also has a great influence on a child's behavior. Studies have explored the effect of discipline, parental misconduct, and family harmony on youth crime.

Concern over the relationship between family life and delinquency has been heightened by reports of widespread child abuse. Cases of abuse and neglect have been found in every social class. It has been estimated that there are 3 million reported cases of child abuse each year, of which 1 million are confirmed by child welfare investigators. Two factors are seen as causing child abuse. First, parents who themselves suffered abuse as children tend to abuse their own children. Second, isolated and alienated families tend to become abusive.

Local, state, and federal governments have attempted to alleviate the problem of child abuse. The major issue has been state interference in the family structure. All fifty states have statutes requiring that suspected cases of abuse be reported.

A number of studies have linked abuse to delinquency. They show that a disproportionate number of court-adjudicated youths had been abused or neglected. Although the evidence is not conclusive, it suggests that a strong relationship exists between child abuse and delinquent behavior. To make it easier to prosecute abusers, the Supreme Court has legalized the use of closed-circuit TV in some cases. Most states allow children to use anatomically correct dolls when testifying in court.

The role of the family in delinquency formation has been addressed in various prevention efforts. Family counseling and therapy are often used in cases involving antisocial youths. Parenting skills programs such as the Oregon Social Learning Center aim to prevent delinquency before it occurs.

KEY TERMS

nuclear family
broken home
blended families
intrafamily conflict

battered child syndrome
child abuse
neglect
abandonment

familicide
advisement hearing
pretrial conference
disposition hearing

balancing-of-the-interest
  approach
review hearings
hearsay

QUESTIONS FOR DISCUSSION

1. What is the meaning of the terms *child abuse* and *child neglect*?

2. Social agencies, police departments, and health groups all indicate that child abuse and neglect are increasing. What is the incidence of such action by parents against children? Are the definitions of child abuse and child neglect the key elements in determining the volume of child abuse cases in various jurisdictions?

3. What causes parents to abuse their children?

4. What is meant by the child protection system? Do courts act in the best interest of the child when they allow an abused child to remain with the family?

5. Should children be allowed to testify in court via closed-circuit TV? Does this approach prevent defendants in child abuse cases from confronting their accusers?

6. Is corporal punishment ever permissible as a disciplinary method?

VIEWPOINT

Pedophiles and child molesters share some characteristics. Most are male, and they can be heterosexual, homosexual, or bisexual. Some prefer adult sex partners but choose children because they are available and vulnerable. The sexual abuse perpetrated may be a one-time incident and may consist only of fondling. Penetration is unlikely with young children. Perpetrators' ages range from teens to midlife. Most victims are girls, and the perpetrator usually is a relative, friend, or neighbor. The home of the victim is often the setting for the incident. When boys are victims, sexual abuse may take place outside the home, and perpetrators may be strangers. Perpetrators of sexual abuse of children often claim that they themselves were victims of childhood sexual abuse.

 Who commits child sexual abuse and what are their personal characteristics? To find out, go to the following on Infotrac® College Edition: John B. Murray, "Psychological Profile of Pedophiles and Child Molesters," *The Journal of Psychology* 134:211 (2000). For further information, use *child abuse* as a subject.

Chapter 8

Peers and Delinquency: Juvenile Gangs and Groups

© Bob Daemmrich/
The Image Works

ou are a professor at a local state university who teaches courses on delinquent behavior. One day you are approached by the director of the president's National Task Force on Gangs (NTFG). This group has been formed to pool resources from a variety of federal agencies, ranging from the FBI to Health and Human services, in order to provide local jurisdictions with a comprehensive plan to fight gangs. The director claims that the gang problem is big and becoming bigger. Thousands of gangs are operating around the country, with hundreds of thousands of members. Government sources, he claims, indicate that there has been a significant growth in gang membership over the past 20 years. So far, the government has not been able to do anything at either a state or national level to stem this growing tide of organized criminal activity. They would like you to be part of the team that provides state and local jurisdictions with a gang control activity model, which, if implemented, would provide a cost-effective means of reducing both gang membership and gang activity.

- Would you recommend that police employ anti-gang units that use tactics developed in the fight against organized crime families?

- Would you recommend the redevelopment of deteriorated neighborhoods in which gangs flourish?

- Would you try to educate kids about the dangers of gang membership?

- Would you tell the director that gangs have always existed and there is probably not much the government can do to reduce their numbers?

For a general overview of gangs in America, see

http://www.ncjrs.org/pdffiles/167249.pdf

For an up-to-date list of Web links, go to www.wadsworth.com/product/0534573053s

Few issues in the study of delinquency are more important today than the problems presented by law-violating gangs and groups.[1] Although some gangs are made up of only a few loosely organized neighborhood youths, others have thousands of members who cooperate in complex illegal enterprises. A significant portion of all drug distribution in the nation's inner cities is believed to be gang controlled; gang violence accounts for more than a thousand homicides each year. There has been an outcry from politicians to increase punishment for the "little monsters" and to save the "fallen angels," or the victimized youths who are innocent.[2]

The problem of gang control is a difficult one; gangs flourish in inner-city areas that offer lower-class youths few conventional opportunities. Gang members are resistant to offers of help that cannot deliver legitimate economic hope. Although gang members may be subject to arrest, prosecution, and incarceration, a new crop of young recruits is always ready to take the place of their fallen comrades. Those sent to prison find that, upon release, their former gangs are only too willing to have them return to action.

We begin this chapter with a discussion of peer relations, showing how they influence delinquent behavior. Then we explore the definition, nature, and structure of delinquent gangs. Finally, the chapter presents theories of gang formation, the extent of gang activity, and gang-control efforts.

ADOLESCENT PEER RELATIONS

lthough parents are the primary source of influence and attention in children's early years, between ages 8 and 14 children seek out a stable peer group, and both the number and the variety of friendships increase as children go through adolescence. Friends soon begin to have a greater influence over decision making than parents.[3] By their early teens, children report that their friends give them emotional support

Gangs can be found in all parts of the country and among all ethnic groups. Barrio gangs are made up of Hispanic boys and girls whose ethnic ancestry can be traced to one of several Spanish-speaking cultures, from regions such as Puerto Rico and Mexico. They are known for their fierce loyalty to their original or "home" gang; this affiliation is maintained even if they move to a new neighborhood that contains a rival gang. Here members of the Los Angeles Crazy Rider gang gather around a fellow member crippled by gunfire. (© Robert Yager/Sipa Press)

cliques Small groups of friends who share intimate knowledge and confidences.

crowds Loosely organized groups who share interests and activities.

when they are feeling bad and that they can confide intimate feelings to peers without worrying about their confidences being betrayed.[4]

As they go through adolescence, children form **cliques**, small groups of friends who share activities and confidences.[5] They also belong to **crowds**, loosely organized groups of children who share interests and activities such as sports, religion, or hobbies. Intimate friends play an important role in social development, but adolescents are also deeply influenced by this wider circle of friends. Adolescent self-image is in part formed by perceptions of one's place in the social world.[6]

In later adolescence, acceptance by their peers has a major impact on socialization. Popular youths do well in school and are socially astute. In contrast, children who are rejected by their peers are more likely to display aggressive behavior and to disrupt group activities by bickering or behaving antisocially.[7] Lower-class youths, lacking in educational and vocational opportunities, may place even greater emphasis on friendship than middle-class youths.[8]

Peer relations, then, are a significant aspect of maturation. Some experts, such as Judith Rich Harris, suggest that peer influence may be more important than parental nurturance in the development of long-term behavior.[9] Peers guide each other and help each other learn to share and cooperate, to cope with aggressive impulses, and to discuss feelings they would not dare bring up at home. Youths can compare their own experiences with peers and learn that others have similar concerns and problems.[10]

Peer Relations and Delinquency

Research shows that peer group relationships are closely tied to delinquent behaviors: Youths who report inadequate or strained peer relations are the ones most likely to become delinquent.[11] Adolescents who maintain delinquent friends are more likely to engage in antisocial behavior and drug abuse.[12] Reviews of the research show that delinquent acts tend to be committed in small groups rather than alone, a process called co-offending.[13]

Delinquent groups tend to be small and transitory.[14] Youths often belong to more than a single deviant group or clique and develop an extensive network of delinquent associates. Multiple memberships are desirable because delinquent groups tend to "specialize" in different types of delinquent activity. Group roles can vary, and an adolescent who assumes a leadership role in one group may be a follower in another.[15]

Impact of Peer Relations

Does having antisocial peers cause delinquency, or are delinquents antisocial youths who seek out like-minded companions? Three opposing viewpoints exist on this question.

Control theorists argue that delinquents are as detached from their peers as they are from other elements of society. In an oft-cited work, James Short and Fred Strodtbeck describe the importance delinquent youths attach to their peer groups, while at the same time observing that delinquents lack the social skills to make their peer relations rewarding or fulfilling.[16] According to this view, antisocial adolescents seek out like-minded peers for criminal associations. If delinquency is committed in groups, it is because "birds of a feather flock together."

Structural and learning theorists, in contrast, link delinquency to the rewards gained by associating with like-minded youths, learning deviant values and behaviors from peers, and being influenced by "peer pressure." Youths who maintain friendships with antisocial peers are more likely to become delinquent regardless of their own personality or the type of supervision they receive at home.[17] Even previously law-abiding youths are more likely to get involved in delinquency if they become associated with friends who initiate them into delinquent careers.[18]

A third view is that peers and delinquency are mutually supporting. Antisocial youths join up with like-minded friends; deviant peers sustain and amplify delinquent careers.[19] Nondelinquent friends help to moderate delinquency.[20] As children move through the life course, antisocial friends help youths maintain delinquent careers and stop the aging-out process.[21] If adulthood brings close and sustaining ties to marriage and family and the time spent with peers declines, so too will the level of deviant behavior.[22]

Delinquent Peers

The weight of the empirical evidence indicates that youths who are loyal to delinquent friends, belong to gangs, and have "bad companions" are the ones most likely to commit crimes and engage in violence.[23] Nonetheless, having deviant peers does not necessarily mean the relationships are close, intimate, and influential.

Research shows that both delinquents and nondelinquents have similar types of friendship patterns.[24] Delinquent youths reported that their peer relations contained elements of caring and trust and that they could be open and intimate with their friends. Delinquent youths also reported getting more intrinsic rewards from their peers than did nondelinquents. However, delinquents reported more conflict with their friends, more feelings of jealousy and competition, and, not unexpectedly, more pronounced feelings of loyalty in the face of trouble. These findings support the view that delinquent peer group relations play an important part in their lifestyle.

These findings seem to contradict the control theory model, which holds that delinquents are loners, and support the cultural deviance view that delinquents form close-knit groups that sustain their behavior. Adolescents are influenced by social relationships, and these relationships can influence their behavior patterns.

YOUTH GANGS

As youths move through adolescence, they gravitate toward cliques that provide them with support, assurance, protection, and direction. In some instances the peer group provides the social and emotional basis for antisocial activity. When this happens, the clique is transformed into a **gang.**

gang Groups of youths who collectively engage in delinquent behaviors.

Today, such a powerful mystique has grown up around gangs that mere mention of the word "gang" evokes images of black-jacketed youths roaming the streets in groups bearing such names as the Latin Kings, Mafia Crips, Bounty Hunters, and Savage Skulls. Films, television shows, novels, and even Broadway musicals have popularized the youth gang.[25]

Considering the suspected role gangs play in violent crime and drug activity, it is not surprising that gangs have recently become the target of a great deal of research interest.[26] Important attempts have been made to gauge their size, location, makeup, and activities.

What Are Gangs?

Gangs are groups of youths who engage in delinquent behaviors. Yet gang delinquency differs from group delinquency. Whereas group delinquency consists of a short-lived alliance created to commit a particular crime or violent act, gang delinquency involves long-lived institutions that have a distinct structure and organization, including identifiable leadership, division of labor, rules, rituals, and possessions.

Delinquency experts are often at odds over the precise definition of a gang. The term is sometimes used broadly to describe any congregation of youths who have joined together to engage in delinquent acts. However, police departments often use it only to refer to cohesive groups that hold and defend territory, or turf.[27]

Academic experts have also created a variety of definitions. The core elements in the concept of the gang are that it is an **interstitial group** and that it maintains standard group processes such as recruiting new members, setting goals, assigning roles, and developing status.[28] Table 8.1 provides several definitions of teen gangs.

Malcolm Klein argues that two factors stand out in all of these definitions:

- *Members have self-recognition of their gang status and use special vocabulary, clothing, signs, colors, graffiti, and names. Members set themselves apart from the community and are viewed as a separate entity by others. Once they get the label of gang, members eventually accept and take pride in their status.*

- *There is a commitment to criminal activity, though even the most criminal gang members spend the bulk of their time in noncriminal activities.*[29]

interstitial group Delinquent group that fills a crack in the social fabric and maintains standard group practices.

To view current examples of gang graffiti, go to http://law.about.com/newsissues/law/gi/dynamic/offsite.htm?site=http%3A%2F%2Fwww.graffiti.org%2Findex%2Fcity.html

For an up-to-date list of Web links, go to www.wadsworth.com/product/0534573053s

How Did Gangs Develop?

The youth gang is sometimes viewed as uniquely American, but youth gangs have also been reported in several other nations.[30] Nor are gangs a recent phenomenon. In the 1600s, London was terrorized by organized gangs who called themselves "Hectors," "Bugles," "Dead Boys," and other colorful names. In the seventeenth and eighteenth centuries, English gangs wore distinctive belts and pins marked with serpents, animals, stars, and the like.[31]

In the 1920s, Frederick Thrasher initiated the study of the modern gang in his analysis of more than 1300 youth groups in Chicago.[32] He found that the social, economic, and ecological processes that affect the structure of cities create cracks in the normal fabric of society—weak family controls, poverty, and social disorganization—and referred to this as an *interstitial area*. According to Thrasher, groups of youths develop to meet such needs as play, fun, and adventure, activities that sometimes lead to delinquent acts. Impoverished areas present many opportunities for conflict between groups of youths and between youth groups and adult authority. If this conflict continues, the groups become more solidified and their activities become primarily illegal, and the groups develop into gangs.

According to Thrasher, adult society does not meet the needs of lower-class youths, and the gang solves the problem by offering excitement, fun, and opportunity. The gang is not a haven for disturbed youths but an alternative lifestyle for normal boys. Thrasher's work has had an important influence. Recent studies of delinquent gang behavior also view the gang as a means for lower-class boys to achieve advancement and opportunity as well as to defend themselves and to attack rivals.

TABLE 8.1 — Definitions of Teen Gangs

Frederick Thrasher

An interstitial group originally formed spontaneously and then integrated through conflict. It is characterized by the following types of behavior: meeting face to face, milling, movement through space as a unit, conflict, and planning. The result of this collective behavior is the development of tradition, unreflective internal structure, esprit de corps, solidarity, morale, group awareness, and attachment to local territory.

Malcolm Klein

Any denotable adolescent group of youngsters who (a) are generally perceived as a distinct aggregation by others in their neighborhood; (b) recognize themselves as a denotable group (almost invariably with a group name); and (c) have been involved in a sufficient number of delinquent incidents to call forth a consistent negative response from neighborhood residents and/or law enforcement agencies.

Desmond Cartwright

An interstitial and integrated group of persons who meet face to face more or less regularly and whose existence and activities are considered an actual or potential threat to the prevailing social order.

Walter Miller

A self-formed association of peers, bound together by mutual interests, with identifiable leadership, well-developed lines of authority, and other organizational features, who act in concert to achieve a specific purpose or purposes, which generally include the conduct of illegal activity and control over a particular territory, facility, or type of enterprise.

G. David Curry and Irving Spergel

Groups containing law-violating juveniles and adults that are complexly organized, although sometimes diffuse, and sometimes cohesive, with established leadership and membership rules. The gang also engages in a range of crime (but with significantly more violence) within a framework of norms and values in respect to mutual support, conflict relations with other gangs, and a tradition of turf, colors, signs, and symbols. Subgroups of the gang may be deferentially committed to various delinquent or criminal patterns, such as drug trafficking, gang fighting, or burglary.

James Short

Gangs are groups of young people whose members meet together with some regularity, over time, on the basis of group-defined criteria of membership and group-defined organizational characteristics. In the simplest terms, gangs are unsupervised (by adults), self-determining groups that demonstrate continuity over time.

Sources: Frederick Thrasher, *The Gang* (Chicago: University of Chicago Press, 1927), p. 57; Malcolm Klein, *Street Gangs and Street Workers* (Englewood Cliffs, NJ: Prentice Hall, 1971), p. 13; Desmond Cartwright, Barbara Tomson, and Hersey Schwarts, eds., *Gang Delinquency* (Pacific Grove, CA: Brooks/Cole, 1975), pp. 149–50; Walter Miller, "Gangs, Groups, and Serious Youth Crime," in David Schicor and Delos Kelly, eds., *Critical Issues in Juvenile Delinquency* (Lexington, MA: Lexington Books, 1980); G. David Curry and Irving Spergel, "Gang Homicide, Delinquency, and Community," *Criminology* 26:382 (1988); James Short, "The Level of Explanation Problem Revisited—The American Society of Criminology 1997 Presidential Address," *Criminology* 36:3–36 (1998), p. 16.

Gangs in the 1950s and 1960s In the 1950s and early 1960s, the threat of gangs and gang violence swept the public consciousness. Newspapers featured stories on the violent behavior of fighting gangs like the Egyptian Kings, the Vice Lords, and the Blackstone Rangers. Movies such as *The Wild Ones* and *Blackboard Jungle* were made about gangs, and the Broadway musical *West Side Story* romanticized violent gangs.

Gang activity by such groups as the Savage Skulls (pictured) reemerged in the 1970s in major cities, including New York, Detroit, El Paso, Los Angeles, and Chicago. In addition, such cities as Cleveland and Columbus, Ohio, and Milwaukee, Wisconsin, which had not experienced serious gang problems before, saw the development of local gangs. (© Michael Abramson/Black Star)

In his classic 1967 work, *Juvenile Gangs in Context*,[33] Malcolm Klein concluded that gang membership was a way to satisfy the needs of youths caught up in the emotional turmoil typical of the period between adolescence and adulthood. The inclination to form gangs is reinforced by the perception that the gang represents a substitute for unattainable rewards. The experience of being a member of a gang will dominate a youngster's values and behavior. Finally, the gang is self-reinforcing. It is within the gang more than anywhere else that a youngster may find forms of acceptance for delinquent behavior—rewards instead of negative sanctions. And, as the gang strives for internal cohesion, the negative sanctions of the "outside world" become interpreted as threats to cohesion, thus providing secondary reinforcement for the values central to the legitimization of gang behavior.[34]

By the mid-1960s, the gang menace seemed to have disappeared. Some experts attribute the decline of gang activity to successful community-based programs.[35] Others believe gangs were eliminated because police gang-control units infiltrated gangs, arrested leaders, and constantly harassed members.[36] Another explanation is the increase in political awareness that developed during the 1960s. Many gang leaders became involved in social or political activities. In addition, many gang members were drafted. Still another explanation is that many gang members became active users of heroin and other drugs, which curtailed their group-related criminal activity.[37]

Gangs Reemerge Interest in gang activity began anew in the early 1970s. Bearing such names as Savage Skulls and Black Assassins, gangs began to form in the South Bronx in the spring of 1971, quickly spread to other parts of the city, and by 1975 comprised 275 police-verified gangs with 11,000 members.[38]

Gang activity also reemerged in other major cities. Today, the number of gang youths in these major cities is at an all-time high.[39] In addition, large urban gangs have sent representatives to organize chapters in distant areas or to take over existing gangs. For example, Chicago gangs moved into Dade County, Florida and demanded cooperation and obedience from local gangs. Two major Chicago gangs established branches in Milwaukee.[40] Members of the two largest gangs in Los Angeles, the Crips and the Bloods, began operations in midwestern cities. Even medium-sized cities, such as Columbus, Ohio, saw gangs emerge from local dance and "rap" groups and neighborhood street-corner groups.[41]

The explosion of gang activities in the 1980s was reflected in the renewed media interest in gang activity. The *Los Angeles Times* printed 36 gang-related stories in 1977, and 15 in 1978. By 1988, 69 articles appeared, and in 1989 the number of stories concerning police sweeps, revenge shootings, and murder trials had risen to 267.[42] Clearly, gangs had captured the national attention.

Why Did Gangs Reemerge? One reason for the increase in gang activity may be involvement in the sale of illegal drugs.[43] Early gangs relied on group loyalty to encourage membership, but modern gang members are lured by the quest for drug profits. In some areas, gangs have replaced organized crime families as the dominant suppliers of cocaine and crack. The traditional weapons of gangs—chains, knives, and homemade guns—have been replaced by automatic weapons. Felix Padilla studied a Latino gang in Chicago and found that the gang represents a "viable and persistent business enterprise within the U.S. economy, with its own culture, logic, and systematic means of transmitting and reinforcing its fundamental business virtues."[44]

Ironically, the crackdown on organized crime in the 1980s opened the door to gangs that control the drug trade on a local level and will not hesitate to use violence to maintain and expand their authority. The division between organized crime and gang crime is narrowing.

Drug trafficking is by no means the only reason for gang activity. Gang activity may also be on the rise because of economic and social dislocation. Gang formation is the natural consequence of the evolution from a relatively high-paying manufacturing economy to a low-wage service economy.[45] U.S. cities, which required a large population base for their manufacturing plants, now face economic stress as these plants shut down. In this uneasy economic climate, gangs flourish while the influence of successful adult role models and stable families declines. The presence of gangs in areas unaccustomed to delinquent group activity can have a devastating effect on community life.

In his famous study of Milwaukee gangs, John Hagedorn uncovered some of the social foundations for gang formation.[46] Milwaukee's gangs were formed solely to profit from illegal gain and criminal activity at a time of economic downturn. They formed at the same time minority students were being bused to implement desegregation. Gang recruitment took place on the buses and in schools. Gang membership, therefore, cut across neighborhoods, rendering local social control ineffectual. Finally, the neighborhoods most likely to be plagued by gang violence were strained economically. Residential segregation and a lack of affordable housing prevented many working-class residents from leaving. The result was mixed neighborhoods of struggling working-class and poor families coexisting with drug houses, gangs, and routine violence.

Family Crisis and Gangs Many commentators link gang membership to the disorganization of the family. Gang members come from families that are torn by parental absence, substance abuse, poverty, and criminality; the gang contributes the same kind of support, security, and caring that the traditional family is supposed to provide.[47] Although this argument is compelling, a sizable portion of gang members come from stable families, and a significant number of youths from dysfunctional families avoid gang involvement. In some families, one brother or sister is "ganged up" whereas another evades gang membership. The gang may be a substitute family for some members, but it clearly does not have that appeal for all.

To access a thorough bibliography that includes books and government documents dealing with juvenile gangs dating from 1985 to the present, go to http://www.lib.usc.edu/ ~anthonya/gang.htm

For an up-to-date list of Web links, go to www.wadsworth.com/ product/0534573053s

CONTEMPORARY GANGS

The gang cannot be viewed as a uniform or homogenous social concept. Gangs vary by activity, makeup, location, leadership style, and age. The next sections describe some of the most salient features of contemporary gangs.

Extent

Estimating the extent of the gang problem today is exceedingly difficult. Youths who would be considered gang members in one jurisdiction may be ignored in another. For example, some cities have no "gang" problems but do have drug "crews" and "posses"—groups that resemble gangs. Youths who say they are gang members might belong to an informal group that falls outside the generally accepted definition of gangs. In addition, gang membership is constantly changing, making population estimates extremely problematic.

Despite these difficulties, attempts to inventory gang populations indicate that there has been a major increase in gang membership. Walter Miller conducted two national surveys of gang membership, the first in 1975 and a second in 1982. The 1972 survey indicated gang membership at 55,000; by 1980 that number that had increased to about 98,000 youths.[48]

The most recent national gang survey sponsored by the federal government illustrates that rise in gang activity over the past 20 years.[49] This survey asked representatives of more than 3000 law-enforcement agencies to assess the gang problem in their jurisdictions. As of 1999, it was estimated that nearly 4,000 U.S. cities and counties experienced gang activity. The gang problem may be stabilizing. While more than 26,000 gangs are believed to be active in the United States, the number represents a decline of about 9 percent from 1998. However, in 1998 there were an estimated 780,000 gang members; more than 840,500 gang members were estimated to be active in the United States in 1999. So, while the number of gangs is in decline, gang membership is increasing, possibly because kids are staying in gangs longer and swelling their membership roles.

Location

disorganized neighborhood
Inner-city areas of extreme poverty where the critical social control mechanisms have broken down.

While some people think of gangs as a purely urban, an estimated 15,000 gangs with 300,000 members are located in small cities, suburban counties and even in rural areas. Traditionally, gangs operated in large urban areas that were experiencing rapid population change. In these transitional neighborhoods, diverse ethnic and racial groups found themselves in competition.[50] Intergang conflict and homicide rates are high in these areas, which house the urban "underclass."[51] These eventually evolved into permanently **disorganized neighborhoods**, where population shifts had slowed down, permitting patterns of behavior and traditions to develop over a number of years. Most typical are the poverty-stricken areas of New York and Chicago and the Mexican American barrios of the southwestern states and California.[52] These areas contain large, structured gang clusters that are resistant to most attempts to modify or disband them.

The growth of gangs in suburban and rural areas has been attributed to a restructuring of the population. There has been a massive movement of people out of the central city to outlying communities and suburbs. In some cities, once-fashionable neighborhoods have declined, and downtown areas have undergone extensive urban renewal. Inner-city districts of major cities such as New York and Chicago are now devoted to finance, retail stores, restaurants, and entertainment.[53] Two aspects of this development inhibit urban gang formation: (1) there are few residential areas and thus few adolescent recruits, and (2) there is intensive police patrol.

In some areas, such as Miami and Boston, the poor inner-city populations have shifted from the downtown to formerly middle-class areas now in decay. Suburban housing projects are also gang-prone. Thus, although gangs are still located in areas of urban blight today, these neighborhoods are often at some distance from their traditional inner-city locations.[54]

Migration

Some of the gangs in smaller cities and towns appear to be home grown, but because these groups copy clothing, insignia, and hand signs of big-city gangs, authorities sometimes leap to the conclusion that they are recent arrivals.[55] Gang migration does, however, help to account for the national growth in gang activity.

The 1999 National Gang Survey estimates that 18 percent of gang members were migrants from another jurisdiction. In rural areas, 34 percent of members had come from elsewhere; in small cities, 27 percent, and in suburban counties, 20 percent were outsiders. Larger cities had the smallest percentage of migrants (17 percent), indicating that the flow of gang members was from more to less populated areas, and not vice versa. Not surprisingly, law-enforcement agents report that the appearance of gang members outside of large cities in the 1990s was caused by the migration of young people from central cities.[56]

About 700 U.S. cities have experienced some form of gang migration during the past decade. Most of the new arrivals are from Los Angeles gangs. The most common reason for migrating is social—that is, their family relocated or they came to stay with relatives. Others have a specific criminal purpose, such as expanding drug sales and markets. Most of the migrators are African American or Hispanic males who maintain close ties with members of their original gangs "back home,"[57] but some migrants join local gangs, shedding old ties and gaining new affiliations. The number of migrants is relatively small in proportion to the overall gang population, supporting the contention that most gangs actually are "home grown."

✔ Checkpoints

✔ Group relations are an essential part of childhood.

✔ Most delinquent acts are committed in small groups.

✔ Delinquent peers seem to sustain antisocial behaviors.

✔ Sometimes antisocial cliques and friendship groups are transformed into organized gangs that have names, garb, signs, and permanence.

✔ Gangs submerged during the 1960s but have once again proliferated in urban areas.

✔ It is now estimated that 26,000 gangs exist and they have more than 800,000 members.

✔ Gangs are located in both urban and suburban areas.

✔ Urban gangs have been involved in migration to other locales.

✔ Most gangs are male only, but the number of female gang members seems to be increasing.

✔ Most gangs are racially and ethnically homogenous.

Types

retreatists Gangs whose members actively engage in substance abuse.

Gangs have been categorized by activity: some are devoted to violence and to protecting neighborhood boundaries, or turf; others are devoted to theft; some specialize in drug trafficking; others are concerned with recreation rather than crime.[58]

In their early work, Richard Cloward and Lloyd Ohlin recognized that some gangs specialized in violent behavior, others were **retreatists** whose members actively engaged in substance abuse, and a third type were criminal.[59]

It has become increasingly difficult to make these distinctions because so many gang members are now involved in all three behaviors, but experts continue to find that gangs can be characterized according to their dominant activities. For example, Jeffrey Fagan found that most gangs fall into one of these four categories:

1. *Social gang:* Involved in few delinquent activities and little drug use other than alcohol and marijuana. Members more interested in social activities.

2. *Party gang:* Concentrates on drug use and sales but forgoes most delinquent behavior. Drug sales are designed to finance members' personal drug use.

3. *Serious delinquent gang:* Engages in serious delinquent behavior while eschewing most drug use. Drugs are used only on social occasions.

4. *Organized gang:* Heavily involved in criminality. Drug use and sales are related to other criminal acts. For example, violent acts are used to establish control over

drug sale territories. This gang is on the verge of becoming a formal criminal organization.[60]

Fagan's findings have been duplicated by others. C. Ronald Huff found that gangs in Columbus, Ohio could be organized into "hedonistic gangs" (similar to party gangs), "instrumental gangs" (similar to serious delinquent gangs) and "predatory gangs," whose heavy crime and crack use make them similar to the organized gang found by Fagan.[61] Carl Taylor adds to this list the *scavenger gang,* a group of impulsive youths who have no common bond beyond surviving in a tough urban environment. These youths are typically low achievers who prey on any target they encounter. Taylor contrasts the scavenger gang with the *organized/corporate gang,* which relentlessly pursues profit and market share.[62]

Cheryl Maxson finds that gangs can be categorized by their size, age range, duration of existence, territory, and criminal acts.[63] By far the most common is the compressed gang; the collective gang is the least common, followed by specialty gangs. These observations seem to validate Cloward and Ohlin's findings, which suggested that many gangs specialize in their activities. However, this does not mean that most gangs are generalists, whose members engage in a variety of criminal activities ranging from violent turf battles to drug dealing as well as social activities.[64]

Cohesion

barrio A Latino term meaning neighborhood.

The standard definition of a gang implies that it is a cohesive group. However, some experts refer to gangs as **near-groups,** which have limited cohesion, impermanence, minimal consensus of norms, shifting membership, disturbed leadership, and limited definitions of membership expectations.[65] Gangs maintain a small core of committed members, who work constantly to keep the gang going, and a much larger group of affiliated youths, who participate in gang activity only when the mood suits them. James Diego Vigil found that boys in Latino **barrio** gangs (Hispanic neighborhood gangs) could be separated into regular members and those he describes as "peripheral," "temporary," and "situational."[66]

Current research indicates that, although some gangs remain near-groups, others have become quite organized and stable. These gangs resemble traditional organized crime families more than temporary youth groups. Some, such as Chicago's Latin Kings and Gangster Disciples, have members who pay regular dues, are expected to attend gang meetings regularly, and carry out political activities to further gang ambitions.[67]

Age

The ages of gang members range widely, perhaps from as young as 8 to as old as 55.[68] However, members of offending groups are usually no more than a few years apart in age, with a leader who may be a few years older.[69]

Research indicates that youths first hear about gangs at around 9 years of age, get involved in violence at 10 or 11, and join their first gang at 12. Half of the gang members interviewed had, by age 13, (a) fired a pistol, (b) seen someone killed or seriously injured, (c) gotten a gang tattoo, and (d) been arrested.[70]

Gang experts believe the average age of gang members has been increasing yearly, a phenomenon explained in part by the changing structure of the U.S. economy.[71] Fifty percent of gang members in 1999 were ages 18 to 24, an increase from 46 percent in 1998 and 37 percent in 1996. In contrast, the proportion of gang members ages 15 to 17 decreased to 26 percent from a high of 34 percent in 1996.[72]

Why Are Gang Members Aging? Gang members are getting older. Relatively high-paid, low-skilled factory jobs that would entice older gang members to leave the gang have been lost to overseas competition. Replacing them are low-level drug dealing opportunities that require a gang affiliation. William Julius Wilson found that the inability of inner-city males to obtain adequate jobs means that they cannot afford to marry and raise families. Criminal records acquired at an early age quickly lock these youths out of the job market; remaining in a gang has become an economic necessity.[73]

John Hagedorn also found that economic change has had an impact on the age structure of gang membership. Whereas in the past older members could easily slip into the economic mainstream, less than 1 in 5 founding members of the youth gangs Hagedorn studied were able to find full-time employment by their mid-twenties. "Old heads"—older members with powerful street reputations—were held in high esteem by young gang members. In the past, ex-members helped steer gang members into conventional roles and jobs. Today, young adults continue their relationships with their old gangs and promote hustling, drug use, and sexual promiscuity. As a result, gang affiliations can last indefinitely, and it is not unusual for the children and even grandchildren of gang members to affiliate with the same gang.[74]

Hagedorn and his associates found that there are actually four types of adult gang members:

- *Legits* have left the gang and "hood" behind.
- *Dope fiends* are addicted to cocaine and need drug treatment.
- *New Jacks* have given up on the legitimate economy and see nothing wrong in selling cocaine to anyone.
- *Homeboys* are adult gang members who work regular jobs, but when they cannot make enough money they sell cocaine. They wish to have a "normal" life but believe ganging is the only way to make ends meet.[75]

Gender

Of the more than a thousand groups included in Thrasher's original survey, only half a dozen were female gangs. Females were involved in gangs in three ways: as auxiliaries (or branches) of male gangs, as part of sexually mixed gangs, or as autonomous gangs. Auxiliaries are a feminized version of the male gang name, such as the Lady Disciples of the Devil's Disciples. Today gangs continue to be male dominated. The most recent national data indicates that less than 2 percent of all gangs in the United States were female dominated (more than half the members female). Currently, about 8 percent of all gang members are females.[76] However, some local surveys that rely on interview and self-report data indicate that the number of female gang members may be on the rise in some areas.[77] Carl Taylor's analysis of Detroit gangs found that girls were very much involved in gang activity.[78] An analysis of Denver youths found that approximately 25 percent of the gang members were female.[79] A recent survey of almost 6000 youths in forty-two schools in eleven cities found that almost 40 percent of the gang members were female.[80] It is possible that law-enforcement agencies undercount female gang membership and that more young girls are gang-affiliated than previously believed.[81]

Girls in the Gang What benefits does gang membership offer to females? According to the "liberation" view, ganging can provide girls with a sense of "sisterhood," independence, and solidarity, as well as a chance to earn profit through illegal activities. Although initial female gang participation may be forged by links to male gang members, once in gangs girls form close ties with other female members and engage in group criminal activity.[82]

In contrast, the "social injury" view suggests that female members are still sexually exploited by males and are sometimes forced to exploit other females. Girls who are members of male gang auxiliaries report that males control them by determining the arenas within which they can operate (for example, the extent to which they may become involved in intergang violence). Males also play a divisive role in the girls' relationships with each other; this manipulation is absent for girls in independent gangs.[83]

The number and extent of girl gangs is increasing. In the Grape Street area of Los Angeles, a female gang member is about to kick another young woman. This is not a random or spontaneous attack but part of the "court in" ceremony in which new members are initiated into the gang. (© Nancy Siesel/Saba)

Females join gangs in an effort to cope with a harsh life.[84] Girls in gangs are more likely to engage in theft offenses than violent crimes.[85] This may indicate a desire to use their status to improve their lifestyle.

Formation

Gang formation involves a sense of territoriality. Most gang members live in close proximity to one another, and their sense of belonging extends only to their small area of the city. At first, a gang may form when members of an ethnic minority join together for self-preservation. As the group gains domination over an area, it may view the area as its own territory, or turf, which needs to be defended from outsiders.

Once formed, gangs grow when youths who admire the older gang members "apply" and are accepted for membership. Sometimes the new members will be given a special identity that reflects their apprenticeship status. Joan Moore and her associates found that *klikas,* or youth cliques, in Hispanic gangs remain together as unique groups with separate names, identities, and experiences; they also have more intimate relationships among themselves than among the general gang membership.[86] She likens *klikas* to a particular class in a university, such as the class of '03.

Moore also found that gangs can expand by including members' kin, even if they do not live in the neighborhood, and rival gang members who wish to join because they admire the gang's way of doing things. Adding outsiders gives the gang the ability to take over new territory. However, it also brings with it new problems because it usually results in greater conflicts with rival gangs.

klikas Subgroups of same-aged youths in Hispanic gangs that remain together and have separate names and a unique identity within the gang.

Leadership

Most experts describe gang leaders as cool characters who have earned their position by demonstrating fighting prowess, verbal quickness, or athletic distinction.[87] They emphasize that leadership is held by one person and varies with particular activities, such as fighting, sex, and negotiations. In fact, in some gangs each age level has its own leaders. Older members are not necessarily considered leaders by younger members. In his analysis of Los Angeles gangs, Malcolm Klein observed that many gang leaders deny leadership. He overheard one gang boy claim, "We got no leaders, man. Everybody's a leader, and nobody can talk for nobody else."[88] The most plausible explanation of this ambivalence is the boy's fear that his decisions will conflict with those of other leaders.

There appear, then, to be diverse concepts of leadership, depending on the structure of the gang. Less-organized gangs are marked by diffuse and shifting leadership. More-organized gangs have a clear chain of command and leaders who are supposed to plan activities and control members' behavior.[89]

Communications

To access a site that has a good selection of West Coast gang graffiti, go to http://www.streetgangs.com/

For an up-to-date list of Web links, go to www.wadsworth.com/product/0534573053s

graffiti Inscriptions or drawings made on a wall or structure and used by delinquents for gang messages and turf definition.

representing Tossing or flashing gang signs in the presence of rivals, often escalating into a verbal or physical confrontation.

Gangs seek recognition, both from their rivals and from the community. Image and reputation depend on the ability to communicate to the rest of the world.

One major source of communication is **graffiti** (Figure 8.1). These wall writings are especially elaborate among Latino gangs, who call them *placasos* or *placa*, meaning sign or plaque.[90] Latino graffiti usually contain the writer's street name and the name of the gang. Strength or power is asserted through the terms *rifa*, which means to rule, and *controllo*, indicating that the gang controls the area. Another common inscription is "p/v," for *por vida*; this refers to the fact that the gang expects to control the area "for life." The numeral 13 signifies that the gang is *loco*, or "wild." Crossed-out graffiti indicate that a territory is contested by a rival gang.

Gangs also communicate by means of a secret vocabulary. Members may refer to their "crew," "posse," "troop," or "tribe." Within larger gangs are "sets," who hang in particular neighborhoods, and "tips," small groups formed for particular purposes. (See Table 8.2.)

Flashing or tossing gang signs in the presence of rivals often escalates into a verbal or physical confrontation. Chicago gangs call this **representing**. Gang members will proclaim their affiliation and ask victims "Who do you ride?" or "What do you be about?" An incorrect response will provoke an attack.[91] False representing can be used to misinform witnesses and victims.

In some areas, gang members communicate their membership by wearing jackets with the name of their gang on the back. In Boston neighborhoods, certain articles of clothing (for example, sneakers) are worn to identify gang membership.[92] In Los Angeles, the Crips are identified with the color blue and will wear some article of blue clothing to communicate their allegiance; their rivals, the Bloods, identify with the color red.[93]

Criminality and Violence

Regardless of their type, gang members typically commit more crimes than any other youths in the social environment.[94] The 1999 National Youth Gang Survey found that offense types reported to be most prevalent among gang members are larceny/theft, aggravated assault, and burglary/breaking and entering, and estimated that 46 percent of youth gang members are involved in street drug sales to generate profits for the gang.[95]

Data from the Rochester Youth Development Study (RYDS), a longitudinal cohort study of 1000 youths in upstate New York, supports the gang–crime association theory. Although only 30 percent of the youths in the sample report being gang members, they account for 65 percent of all reported delinquent acts. The RYDS data show that gang members account for 86 percent of all serious crimes, 63 percent of the alcohol use, and 61 percent of the drug abuse.[96]

Gang criminality has numerous patterns.[97] Some gangs specialize. The 1999 National Youth Gang Survey found that the percentage of youth gangs that are considered

Figure 8.1
Gang Symbols Used in Graffiti
Source: Austin, Texas, Police Department Gang Control Unit, 1996.

For an analysis of youth gang drug dealing, go to
http://www.ncjrs.org/pdffiles1/ojjdp/178282.pdf

For an up-to-date list of Web links, go to www.wadsworth.com/product/0534573053s

drug gangs (that is, organized specifically for the purpose of trafficking in drugs) increased from 34 percent in 1998 to 40 percent in 1999. Drug-oriented gangs concentrate on the sale of marijuana, PCP, cocaine (crack), and amphetamines ("crystal"); organized gangs use violence to control a drug territory. But not all gangs are major players in drug trafficking, and those that are tend to distribute small amounts of drugs at the street level. The world of major dealing belongs to adults, not to gang youths.[98] Other gangs engage in a wide variety of criminal activity, ranging from felony assaults to drug dealing.[99]

Gang Violence Gang members are heavily armed, dangerous, and more violent than nonmembers. A nationwide survey of arrestees found that half of those who owned or carried guns claimed to be gang members.[100]

TABLE 8.2 Gang Slang

Busted/popped a cap: Shot at someone

Buster: Youngster trying to be a gang member/ Fake gang member

Camarada: Friend

Cap: A retort or to shoot at

Carnal: Brother

Carnala: Sister

Chale: No

Chavala: Little girl

Check it out: Listen to what I have to say

Chill out: Stop it/ Don't do that/Calm down

Chingasos: Fighting

Chiva: Heroin

Chivero: Heroin addict

Chota: Police

C.K.: Crip killer

Click up: To get along well with a homeboy

Cluck: Cocaine smoker

Colors: Gang colors (on shoes, rag, shoelaces, etc.)

O.G.: Original gangster, which you are considered to be when you have killed someone; true; original; someone who is true to the game, who never sold out

Peace out: Bye

Peace-N: Not looking for trouble

Pedo: Fight

Phat, that's: Incredible; great

Piedra: Rock cocaine, crack

Popo: Police

Por vida (P/V): Forever

Put in some work: Do a shooting

Quette: Gun

Rock star: Cocaine prostitute or user

Rooster: Piru blood street gang

Ruka: Gang chick

Salty, you: Think you know everything

Source: Austin, Texas, Police Department Gang Control Unit, 1998.

Research indicates that gang violence is impulsive and therefore comes in spurts. It typically involves defense of the gang and gang members' reputations.[101] Once a spurt ends, the level of violence may recede, but it remains at a level higher than it was previously. Spurts usually occur in specific neighborhoods during periods of intense competition over territory. Peaks in gang homicides tend to correspond to a series of escalating confrontations, usually over control of gang turf or a drug market.[102] The most dangerous areas are along disputed boundaries where a drug hot spot intersects with a turf hot spot. There are also "marauder" patterns in which members of rival gangs travel to their enemy's territory in search of victims.[103]

Violence is a core fact of gang formation and life.[104] Gang members feel threatened by other gangs and are wary of encroachments on their turf. It is not surprising that gangs try to recruit youths who are already gun owners; new members are likely to increase gun ownership and possession.[105] Gang members face a far greater chance of death at an early age than do nonmembers.[106]

Honor, Courage, and Prestige Scott Decker has found that violence is essential to the transformation of a peer group into a gang. When asked why he calls the group he belongs to a gang, one member replied: "There is more violence than a family. With a gang it's like fighting all the time, killing, shooting."[107]

When joining the gang, members may be forced to partake in violent rituals to prove their reliability. Gang members are ready to fight when others attack them or when they believe their territory or turf is being encroached upon. Violence may be directed against rival gang members accused of insults or against those involved in personal disputes. Gang members also expect to fight when they go to certain locations that are "off limits" or attend events where violence is routine.

Gang members are sensitive to any rivals who question their honor. Once an insult is perceived, the gang's honor cannot be restored until the "debt" is repaid. Police efforts to cool down gang disputes only delay the revenge, which can be a

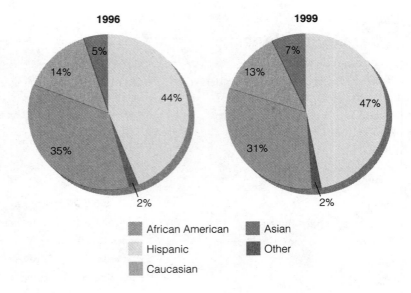

Figure 8.2
Race/Ethnicity of Youth Gang Members, 1996 and 1999

Source: National Youth Gang Survey, 1999.

1996

44%
2%
35%
14%
5%

1999

47%
2%
31%
13%
7%

African American   Asian
Hispanic   Other
Caucasian

beating or a drive-by shooting. Random acts of revenge have become so common that physicians now consider them a significant health problem—a major contributor to early morbidity and mortality among adolescents and children in major gang cities.[108]

Violence is used to maintain the gang's internal discipline. If subordinates disobey orders, perhaps by using rather than selling drugs, they may be subject to disciplinary action by other gang members.

Another common gang crime is extortion, called "turf tax," which involves forcing people to pay the gang to be protected from dangerous neighborhood youths. **Prestige crimes** occur when a gang member steals or assaults someone to gain prestige in the gang. These crimes may be part of an initiation rite or an effort to establish a special reputation, a position of responsibility, or a leadership role; to prevail in an internal power struggle; or to respond to a challenge from a rival.

prestige crimes Stealing or assaulting someone to gain prestige in the neighborhood; often part of gang initiation rites.

Ethnic and Racial Composition

The most recent National Youth Gang Survey (Figure 8.2) found that the race/ethnicity composition of gangs is as follows: Hispanic (47 percent), African American (31 percent), Caucasian (13 percent), Asian (7 percent), and other (2 percent). Although Lewis Yablonsky found racially mixed gangs, the majority of observers view gangs as racially homogeneous: all white, all black, all Hispanic/Latino, or all Asian.[109] Most intergang conflict appears to be among groups of the same ethnic and racial background.[110]

The ethnic distribution of gangs corresponds to their geographic location. For example, in Philadelphia and Detroit the overwhelming number of gang members are African American. In New York and Los Angeles, Latino gangs predominate.[111] Newly emerging immigrant groups are making their presence felt in gangs. Authorities in Buffalo, New York estimate that 10 percent of their gang population is Jamaican. A significant portion of Honolulu's gangs are Filipinos (46 percent).[112]

African American Gangs The first black youth gangs were organized in the early 1920s.[113] Since they had few rival organizations, they were able to concentrate on criminal activity rather than defending their turf. By the 1930s, the expanding number of rival gangs spawned inner-city gang warfare.

In Los Angeles, the first black youth gang formed in the 1920s was the Boozies. This gang virtually ran the inner city until the 1930s. In the next 20 years, a number of black gangs, including the Businessmen, Home Street, Slauson, and Neighborhood, emerged and met with varying degrees of criminal success. In the 1970s, the dominant Crips gang was formed. Other gangs merged into the Crips or affiliated

Gangs pose a serious problem in inner-city areas. Here Ishan Garrett watches as marchers pass through his neighborhood during a rally to take back the neighborhood in Las Vegas, March 24, 2001. More than 200 residents joined together in support of the Coalition for Community Peace to voice their opposition to the recent series of gang slayings. Garrett's neighborhood is one of eight places where gang-related slayings have occurred in the past 30 days. (AP/Wide World Photos)

with it by adding "Crips" to their name, so that the Main Street gang became the Main Street Crips. The dominance of the Crips has since been challenged by its arch rivals, the Bloods. Both of these groups, whose total membership exceeds 25,000 youths, are heavily involved in drug trafficking.

In Chicago, the Blackstone Rangers dominated illicit activities for almost 25 years, beginning in the 1960s and lasting into the early 1990s, when its leader, Jeff Fort, and many of his associates were indicted and imprisoned.[114] The Rangers, who later evolved into the El Rukn gang, worked with "legitimate" businessmen to import and sell heroin. Earning millions in profits, they established businesses that helped them launder drug money. Though many of the convictions were later overturned, the power of El Rukn was ended.

The Rangers' chief rivals, the Black Gangster Disciples, are now the dominant gang in Chicago. They have a structure, activities, and relationships similar to traditional organized gangs like the Mafia. Members are actively involved in politics. They meet regularly, commit crimes as a group, and maintain ongoing relationships with other street gangs and with prison-based gangs. The Gangster Disciples have extensive ownership of "legitimate" private businesses. They offer "protection" against rival gangs and supply stolen merchandise to customers and employees.[115]

African American gang members have some unique characteristics. They frequently use nicknames. "Little 45" might be used by someone whose favorite weapon is a large handgun. Although TV shows portray gangs as wearing distinctive attire, members usually favor nondescript attire to reduce police scrutiny. However, gang members frequently have distinctive hairstyles, such as shaving or braids, that are designed to look like their leaders'. Tattooing is popular, and members often wear colored scarves or "rags" to identify their gang affiliation. It is also common for black gang members to mark their territory with distinctive graffiti: drawings of guns, dollar signs, proclamations of individual power, and profanity.

Hispanic Gangs Hispanic gangs are made up of youths whose ethnic ancestry can be traced to one of several Spanish-speaking cultures. They are known for their fierce loyalty to their "home" gang. Admission to the gang usually involves an initiation ritual in which boys are required to prove their *machismo*. The most common test requires novices to fight several established members or to commit some crime, such as a robbery. The code of conduct associated with membership means never ratting on a brother, or even a rival.

In some areas, Hispanic gangs have a fixed leadership hierarchy. However, in Southern California, which has the largest concentration of Hispanic youth gangs, leadership is fluid. During times of crisis, those with particular skills will assume command.[116] For example, one boy will lead in combat while another negotiates drug deals.

Hispanic gang members are known for their dress codes. Some wear dark-colored caps pulled down over the ears with a small roll at the bottom. Others wear a folded bandana over the forehead and tied in back. Another popular headpiece is the "stingy brim" fedora or a baseball cap with the wearer's nickname and gang affiliation written on the bill. Members favor tank-style T-shirts that give them quick access to weapons.

Members also mark off territory with colorful and intricate graffiti. Hispanic gang graffiti has very stylized lettering and frequently uses three-dimensional designs.

Hispanic gangs have a strong sense of turf, and a great deal of gang violence is directed at warding off any threat to their control. Slights by rivals, including putdowns, stare downs ("mad-dogging"), defacing gang insignia, and territorial intrusions, can set off a violent confrontation, often with high-powered automatic weapons.

Asian Gangs Asian gangs are prominent in New York, Los Angeles, San Francisco, Seattle, and Houston. The earliest gangs, Wah Ching, were formed in the nineteenth century by Chinese youths affiliated with adult crime groups (*tongs*). In the 1960s, two other gangs formed in San Francisco, the Joe Boys and Yu Li, and they now operate, along with the Wah Ching, in many major U.S. cities. National attention focused on the activities of these Chinese gangs in 1977 when a shootout in the Golden Dragon restaurant in San Francisco left five dead and eleven wounded.

Ko-Lin Chin has described the inner workings of Chinese youth gangs.[117] Chin finds that these gangs have unique properties, such as their reliance on raising capital from the Chinese community through extortion and then investing this money in legitimate business enterprises. Chinese gangs recruit new members from the pool of disaffected youths who have problems at school.

In addition to Chinese gangs, Samoan gangs have operated on the West Coast, as have Vietnamese gangs. James Diego Vigil and Steve Chong Yun found that the formation of Vietnamese gangs can be tied to external factors, including racism and economic problems, and to internal problems, including family stress and failure to achieve the success enjoyed by other Asians. Vietnamese gangs are formed when youths feel they need their *ahns,* or brothers, for protection.[118] Asian gangs tend to victimize members of their own ethnic group. Because of group solidarity and distrust of outside authorities, little is known about their activities.

Anglo Gangs The first American youth gangs were made up of white ethnic youths of European ancestry. During the 1950s, they competed with African American and Hispanic gangs in the nation's largest cities.

Today, Anglo gang activity is not uncommon, especially in smaller towns.[119] Many are derivatives of the English punk and **skinhead** movement of the 1970s. These youths, generally children of lower-class parents, sported wildly dyed hair often shaved into "mohawks," military clothes, and iron-cross earrings. Their creed was antiestablishment, and their anger was directed toward foreigners, who they believed were taking their jobs.

American white gang members are often alienated middle-class youths rather than poor lower-class youths. They include "punkers" or "stoners," who dress in heavy-metal fashions and engage in drug- and violence-related activities. Some espouse religious beliefs involving the occult and satanic worship.[120] Some skinhead groups are devoted to white supremacist activities and are being actively recruited by adult hate groups (see Chapter 2).

Another variety of white youth gang is obsessed with occult themes, suicide, ritual killings, and animal mutilations. They get involved in devil worship, tattoo

skinhead Member of white supremacist gang, identified by a shaved skull and Nazi or Ku Klux Klan markings.

themselves with occult symbols, and gouge their bodies to draw blood for satanic rituals.

A recent survey of almost 6000 youths found that about 25 percent of youths who claimed to be gang members were white, a far higher number than that found in the national surveys.[121]

WHY DO YOUTHS JOIN GANGS?

Though gangs flourish in inner-city areas, gang membership cannot be assumed to be solely a function of lower-class identity. Many lower-class youths do not join gangs, and middle-class youths are found in suburban skinhead groups. Let's look at some of the suspected causes of gang delinquency.

The Anthropological View

In the 1950s, Herbert Block and Arthur Niederhoffer suggested that gangs appeal to adolescents' longing for the tribal process that sustained their ancestors.[122] They found that gang processes do seem similar to the puberty rites of some tribal cultures; gang rituals help the child bridge the gap between childhood and adulthood. For example, tattoos and other identifying marks are an integral part of gang culture. Gang initiation ceremonies are similar to the activities of young men in Pacific Island cultures. Many gangs put new members through a hazing to make sure they have "heart," a feature similar to tribal rites. In tribal societies, initiation into a cult is viewed as the death of childhood. By analogy, boys in lower-class urban areas yearn to join the gang and "really start to live." Membership in the gang "means the youth gives up his life as a child and assumes a new way of life."[123] Gang names are suggestive of "totemic ancestors" because they usually are symbolic (Cobras, Jaguars, and Kings, for example).

The Gang Prevention and Intervention Survey found that fully two-thirds of gang members reported having members in their gang whose parents are also active members. These data indicate that ganging is passed on as a rite of passage from one generation to the next.[124] James Diego Vigil has described the rituals of gang initiation, which include pummeling to show that the boy is ready to leave his matricentric (mother-dominated) household; this is reminiscent of tribal initiation rites.[125] These rituals become an important part of gang activities. Hand signs and graffiti have a tribal flavor. Gang members adopt nicknames that reflect personality or physical traits: the more volatile are called "Crazy," "Loco," or "Psycho," and those who wear glasses are dubbed "Professor."[126]

The Social Disorganization/Sociocultural View

Sociologists have commonly viewed the destructive sociocultural forces in poor inner-city areas as the major cause of gang formation. Thrasher introduced this concept, and it is found in the classic studies of Richard Cloward and Lloyd Ohlin and of Albert K. Cohen.[127] Irving Spergel's study, *Racketville, Slumtown, and Haulburg,* found that Slumtown—the area with the lowest income and the largest population—had the highest number of violent gangs.[128] According to Spergel, the gang gives lower-class youths a means of attaining status. Malcolm Klein's research of the late 1960s and 1970s also found that typical gang members came from dysfunctional and destitute families and lacked adequate role models.[129]

The social disorganization/sociocultural view retains its prominent position today. In *Barrio Gangs,*[130] Vigil shows that gang members are pushed into membership because of poverty and minority status. Those who join gangs are the most marginal youths in their neighborhoods and families. Vigil finds that barrio dwellers experience psychological, economic, or social "stressors." Gang members usually have more than one of these problems, causing them to suffer from "multiple marginality." Barrio youths join gangs seeking a sense of belonging.[131]

Overall, the sociocultural view assumes that gangs are a natural response to lower-class life and a status-generating medium for boys whose aspirations cannot be realized by legitimate means. Youths who join gangs may hold conventional goals, but are either unwilling or unable to accomplish them through conventional means.[132] Gangs are not solely made up of youths who seek deviant peers to compensate for parental brutality or incompetence. They recruit youths from many different kinds of families. The gang thus is a coalition of troubled youths who are socialized mainly by the streets rather than by conventional institutions.[133]

Anomie Irving Spergel suggests that youths are encouraged to join gangs during periods of social, economic, and cultural turmoil, conditions thought to produce anomie.[134] For example, gangs were present during the Russian Revolution of 1917 and after the crumbling of the Soviet Union in the early 1990s. The rise of right-wing youth gangs in Germany is associated with the unification of East and West Germany. Skinhead groups have formed in Germany in response to immigration from Turkey and North Africa. In the United States, gangs have formed in areas where rapid change has unsettled communities.

Immigration or emigration, rapidly expanding or contracting populations, and/or the incursion of different racial/ethnic groups, or even different segments or generations of the same racial/ethnic population, can create fragmented communities and gang problems.[135]

The Psychological View

Some believe that gangs serve as an outlet for psychologically disturbed youths. For example, Lewis Yablonsky's theory holds that violent gangs recruit their members from among the more sociopathic youths living in poverty-stricken communities.[136] Yablonsky views the sociopathic youth as one who "has not been trained to have human feelings or compassion or responsibility for another."[137] He supports this contention by pointing to the sexual attitudes and behavior of gang youths, who are often violent and sadistic. He sums up the sociopathic traits of gang boys as (1) a defective social conscience marked by limited feelings of guilt, (2) limited compassion or empathy for others, (3) behavior dominated by self-seeking goals, and (4) the manipulation of others for immediate self-gratification. Yablonsky's view is substantiated by cross-cultural studies that have found that gang members suffer from psychological deficits such as impulsivity.[138]

Malcolm Klein's analysis of Los Angeles gang members finds that many suffer from psychological deficits, including low self-concept, social deficits, poor impulse control, and limited life skills. Adolescents who display conduct disorders, early onset of antisocial behavior, and violent temperaments are at the greatest risk for gang membership.[139] Yet Klein does not consider most gang youths abnormal or pathological. He believes they do not need therapy so much as vocational training, educational skills, and legitimate opportunities.[140]

The Rational Choice View

Some youths may make a rational choice to join a gang. Members of the underclass turn to gangs as a method of obtaining desired goods and services, either directly, through theft and extortion, or indirectly, through drug dealing and weapons sales. In this case, joining a gang can be viewed as an "employment decision." Mercer Sullivan's study of Brooklyn gangs found that members call success at crime "getting paid." Gang boys also refer to the rewards of crime as "getting over," which refers to their pride at "beating the system" even though they are far from the economic mainstream.[141] According to this view, the gang boy has long been involved in criminal

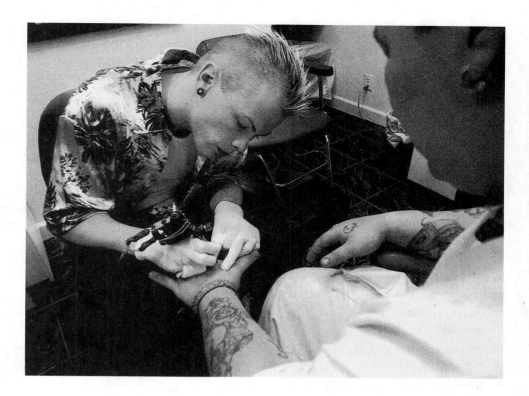

According to the anthropological view, gang membership with its signs, writings, and tattoos is similar to joining a tribal cult. Matthew Ricci (left), manager of Skyline Tattoo in Arlington, Va., works on covering up a tattoo—a gang symbol—on Chris Perry's left hand, June 15, 2000. Perry has many other tattoos on his arms and legs. A large koi fish stretches nearly the length of his right forearm. He also has a half dozen piercings on his head alone: between his eyes, in his nose, tongue, bottom lip, and a couple in each ear. (AP/Wide World Photos)

activity *prior* to his gang membership, and he joins the gang as a means of improving his illegal "productivity."[142]

Gang membership is *not* a necessary precondition for delinquency. Felix Padilla found this when he studied the Diamonds, a Latino gang in Chicago.[143] The decision to join the gang was made after an assessment of legitimate opportunities. The Diamonds made collective business decisions, and individuals who made their own deals were penalized. The gang maintained a distinct structure and carried out other functions similar to those of legitimate enterprises, including personnel recruitment and financing business ventures.

The rational choice view is endorsed by Martin Sanchez-Jankowski in *Islands in the Street.*[144] Sanchez-Jankowski found that gang mermbers maintain a "defiant individualist character." They have distinct traits: wariness or mistrust of the outside world, self-reliance, isolation from society, good survival instincts, defiance against authority, and a firm belief that only the strong survive. Youths with these traits decide to join a gang because the gang presents an opportunity to improve their lives. It offers otherwise unobtainable economic and social opportunities, including support for crime and access to social events and sexual outlets. The most successful gangs offer incentives to these ambitious youths and can control their behavior. Sanchez-Jankowski's views on membership have been supported by independent research data.[145]

Some recent research by Terence Thornberry and his colleagues at the Rochester Youth Development Study supports the rational choice model. They found that, before youths join gangs, their substance abuse and delinquency rates are no higher than nongang members'. When they are in the gang, their crime and drug abuse rates increase, only to decrease when they leave the gang. Thornberry concludes that gangs facilitate criminality rather than providing a haven for youths who are disturbed or already highly delinquent. This research is important because it lends support to the life course model: events that take place during the life cycle, such as joining a gang, have a significant impact on criminal behavior and drug abuse.[146]

Personal Safety According to Spergel, some adolescents choose to join gangs from a "rational calculation" to achieve safety.[147] Youths who are new to a community may believe they will be harassed or attacked if they remain "unaffiliated." Motivation may have its roots in interrace or interethnic rivalry; youths who reside in an area dominated by a different racial or ethnic group may be persuaded that gang membership is a means of protection. Ironically, gang members are more likely to be attacked than nonmembers.

Fun and Support Some youths join gangs simply to have fun.[148] They enjoy hanging out with others like themselves and want to get involved in exciting experiences. There is evidence that youths learn pro-gang attitudes from their peers and that these attitudes direct them to join gangs.[149]

Some experts suggest that youths join gangs in an effort to obtain a family-like atmosphere. Many gang members reported that they have limited contact with their parents, many of whom are unemployed and have substance abuse problems.[150]

Checkpoints

✔ There are different types of gangs—some are social, others criminal.

✔ Gang membership seems to be aging; kids are staying longer in gangs.

✔ Gangs communicate through wall writings (graffiti) and have their own slang terms and hand signs.

✔ Many gangs are involved in drug dealing, while others specialize in violence.

✔ Most gangs are Hispanic and African American.

✔ There are a number of reasons kids join gangs: anthropological, social, psychological, and rational choice views have been offered.

CONTROLLING GANG ACTIVITY

Two methods are used to control gang activity. One involves targeting by criminal justice agencies, and the other involves social service efforts. These methods will be discussed in the next sections.

Law-Enforcement Efforts

In recent years gang control has often been left to local police departments. Gang control takes three basic forms:

1. *Youth services programs,* in which traditional police personnel, usually from the youth unit, are given responsibility for gang control.
2. *Gang details,* in which one or more police officers, usually from youth or detective units, are assigned exclusively to gang-control work.
3. *Gang units,* established solely to deal with gang problems, to which one or more officers are assigned exclusively to gang-control work.[151]

The national assessment found that three-quarters of the departments surveyed maintained separate gang-control units. They are involved in processing information on gangs and gang leaders, prevention efforts, efforts to suppress criminal activity and apprehend those believed to have committed crimes, and follow-up investigations. About 85 percent of these units have special training in gang control for their personnel, 73 percent have specific policies directed at dealing with gang boys, and 62 percent enforce special laws designed to control gang activity.

The Chicago Police Department's gang crime section maintains intelligence on gang problems and trains its more than 400 officers to deal with gang problems. Officers identify street gang members and enter their names in a computer bank that is programmed to alert the unit if the youths are picked up or arrested. Some departments also sponsor prevention programs such as school-based lectures, police–school

Police departments around the nation now maintain specialized units, such as this one in Los Angeles, that focus on gang problems. They maintain intelligence on gang members and train officers to deal with gang problems. Some identify street gang members and enter their names in a computer bank that is programmed to alert the unit if the youths are picked up or arrested. Some departments also sponsor general prevention programs that can help control gang activities. (© Joe Rodriguez/Black Star)

liaisons, recreation programs, and street worker programs that offer counseling, assistance to parents, and other services.

Some police departments engage in "gang-breaking" activities. They attempt to arrest, prosecute, convict, and incarcerate gang leaders. For example, Los Angeles police conduct sweeps, in which more than a thousand officers are put on the street to round up gang members. Police say the sweeps let the gangs know "who the streets belong to" and show neighborhood residents that someone cares.[152] Despite such efforts, gang membership and violence remain at all-time highs. Few departments have written policies or procedures on how to deal with youths, and many do not provide gang-control training.

Traditional police tactics may not work on today's drug gangs, which may best be dealt with as organized crime families. In these cases, it might be useful to (1) develop informants through prosecutions, payments, and witness protection programs; (2) rely on electronic surveillance and undercover investigations; and (3) use statutes that create criminal liabilities for conspiracy, extortion, or engaging in criminal enterprises.[153] Of course, these policies are expensive and may be needed only against the most sophisticated gangs. In addition, as new community policing strategies are implemented (see Chapter 11), it may be possible to garner sufficient local support and information to counteract gang influences.

Community Control Efforts

detached street worker
Social workers who go out into the community and establish close relationships with juvenile gangs with the goal of modifying gang behavior to conform to conventional behaviors and to help gang members get jobs and educational opportunities.

During the late nineteenth century, social workers of the YMCA worked with youths in Chicago gangs.[154] During the 1950s, the **detached street worker** program was developed in major centers of gang activity.[155] Social workers went into the community to work with gangs on their own turf. They participated in gang activities and tried to get to know their members. The purpose was to act as an advocate of the youths, to provide them with positive role models, and to treat individual problems.

Detached street worker programs are sometimes credited with curbing gang activities in the 1950s and 1960s, although some critics claimed that they turned delinquent groups into legitimate neighborhood organizations.[156] Others believe they helped maintain group solidarity and, as a result, new members were drawn to gangs.

Today there are numerous community-level programs designed to limit gang activity. Some employ recreation areas open in the evening hours that provide supervised

TABLE 8.3	The Elements of Spergel's Community Gang Control Program

1. Community mobilization, including citizens, youth, community groups, and agencies.

2. Provision of academic, economic, and social opportunities. Special school training and job programs are especially critical for older gang members who are not in school but may be ready to leave the gang or decrease participation in criminal gang activity for many reasons, including maturation and the need to provide for family.

3. Social intervention, using street outreach workers to engage gang-involved youth.

4. Gang suppression, including formal and informal social control procedures of the juvenile and criminal justice systems and community agencies and groups. Community-based agencies and local groups must collaborate with juvenile and criminal justice agencies in the surveillance and sharing of information under conditions that protect the community and the civil liberties of youth.

5. Organizational change and development, that is, the appropriate organization and integration of the above strategies and potential reallocation of resources.

Sources: Irving Spergel and Candice Kane, *Community-Based Youth Agency Model* (Washington, DC: Office of Juvenile Justice and Delinquency Prevention, 1990); Jim Burch and Candice Kane, *Implementing the OJJDP Comprehensive Gang Model* (Washington, DC: Office of Juvenile Justice and Delinquency Prevention, 1999).

activities.[157] In some areas, citywide coordinating groups help orient gang-control efforts. For example, the Chicago Intervention Network operates field offices around the city in low-income, high-crime areas that provide neighborhood watches, parent patrols, alternative youth programming, and family support efforts. Some community efforts are partnerships with juvenile justice agencies. In Los Angeles County, the Gang Alternative Prevention Program (GAPP) provides prevention services to juveniles before they become entrenched in gangs, including (1) individual and group counseling, (2) bicultural and bilingual services to adolescents and their parents, and (3) special programs such as tutoring, parent training, job development, and recreational and educational experiences.[158]

Still another approach has been to involve schools in gang-control programs. Some invite law-enforcement agents to lecture students on the dangers of gang involvement and to teach them gang-resistance techniques. Others provide resources that can help parents prevent their children from joining gangs or, if they already are members, get them out.

Sociologist Irving Spergel, a leading expert on gangs, has developed a model for helping communities deal with gang-involved youth that has become the basis for gang-control efforts around the nation. His model includes the five distinct strategies contained in Table 8.3.

The Spergel model is now being tested in a number of communities around the country. The Policy and Practice box, "Community-Based Anti-Gang Programs," describes a number of these demonstration programs.

Why Gang Control Is Difficult

Experts have charged that, to reduce the gang problem, hundreds of thousands of high-paying jobs are needed. Economic opportunities might prove to be particularly

COMMUNITY-BASED ANTI-GANG PROGRAMS

Mesa Gang Intervention Project (Mesa, AZ)

The Mesa Gang Intervention Project (MGIP) has targeted 125 youth who are involved in gangs or at high risk for gang involvement and who either reside in or are known to be active within the target area. Key collaborators in the project, which is overseen by a steering committee made up of agency and grassroots executives, are the city of Mesa, the Mesa Police Department, the Maricopa County Adult and Juvenile Probation Departments, Prehab of Arizona, the Mesa Boys and Girls Club, Arizona State University, the United Way, and others.

A team of two gang detectives, one adult and two juvenile probation officers, a youth intervention specialist, and two full-time and two part-time street outreach workers works with and monitors the youth on a daily basis. The team is located in a storefront office within the target community. The MGIP gang detectives and probation officers provide monitoring and surveillance of youth in the program while supporting street outreach workers and staff from other community-based agencies. The MGIP team uses a team problem-solving approach to ensure that progress is made with each youth in the program. The team also provides community assistance, including educating residents about local gang problems and hearing their concerns regarding the neighborhood. Gang education is provided to community members through various professional, neighborhood, and civic groups within the target area.

A computer literacy lab was recently added to the MGIP office, through the support of the Arizona Superior Court. The state of Arizona recently provided additional support to the city of Mesa and MGIP for a mentoring component, and MGIP is supporting a Gang Prevention through Targeted Outreach program at the Mesa Boys and Girls Club.

Other services provided include a cognitive restructuring class for gang-involved youth; parenting classes; services for gang-involved girls; an arts program; a summer camp program focusing on cultural diversity; and tattoo removal services following community service, an educational session, and an agreement not to get any new tattoos for 2 years. Looking toward the prospect of sustaining local support for project activities, the Mesa Police Department has shifted administrative oversight of the project to the police department's gang unit.

Tucson Gang Project (OUR Town Family Center, Tucson, AZ)

The Tucson Gang Project focused on the Vistas neighborhoods on the south side of Tucson, which have approximately four main gangs with an estimated 350 gang members. The project served more than 100 youth. Its outreach component operated out of the local Boys & Girls Club in the target area. The primary partners in the project included the Tucson Police Department, Pima County juvenile probation and parole, the Tucson Unified School District, the Tucson Boys and Girls Club, Quail Enterprises (a research and evaluation firm), and a treatment agency known as La Fontera. The project collaborated with, received referrals from, and made referrals to a number of other local agencies. Street outreach workers, probation officers, a police gang unit officer, and others worked to provide services and opportunities on a daily basis to youth targeted by the project and held them accountable for their negative behavior using a range of graduated sanctions. Weekly staff meetings with other agency representatives were supplemented by weekly meetings among project team members to review client and community progress and needs. A community mobilizer on the project staff worked with community agencies and residents of the target neighborhood to keep attention focused on gang issues and completed a community member survey on the gang problem. The Gang Prevention through Targeted Outreach program was integrated into the project's overall strategy and focused on younger at-risk youth. Where possible, staff from other programs joined gang project staff meetings to share information and coordinate efforts. Project staffing was supplemented by the use of AmeriCorps volunteers.

Source: Office of Juvenile Justice and Delinquency Prevention, Washington, DC, August 2000.

effective, as surveys reveal that many gang members might leave gangs if such opportunities existed.[159]

This solution does not, however, seem practical. Recall from Chapter 4 that the more embedded youths become in criminal enterprise, the less likely they are to find meaningful adult work. It is unlikely that gang members can suddenly be transformed into highly paid professionals. A more effective alternative would be to devote more resources to the most deteriorated urban areas, even if it requires pulling funds from other groups that receive government aid, such as the elderly.[160]

TABLE 8.4 The Essential Ingredients of Effective Gang Control Efforts

- Community leaders must recognize the presence of gangs and seek to understand the nature and extent of the local gang problem through a comprehensive and systematic assessment.
- The combined leadership of the justice system and the community must focus on the mobilization of institutional and community resources to address gang problems.
- Those in principal roles must develop a consensus on definitions (e.g., gang, gang incident), specific targets of agency and interagency efforts, and interrelated strategies—based on problem assessment, not assumptions. Coordinated strategies should include the following:
  - Community mobilization (including citizens, youth, community groups, and agencies).
  - Social and economic opportunities, including special school, training, and job programs. These are especially critical for older gang members who are not in school but may be ready to leave the gang or decrease participation in criminal gang activity for many reasons, including maturation and the need to provide for family.
  - Social intervention (especially youth outreach and work with street gangs directed toward mainstreaming youth).
  - Gang suppression (formal and informal social control procedures of the justice systems and community agencies and groups). Community-based agencies and local groups must collaborate with juvenile and criminal justice agencies in surveillance and sharing of information under conditions that protect the community and the civil liberties of youth.
  - Organizational change and development (the appropriate organization and integration of the above strategies and potential reallocation of resources among involved agencies).
- Any approach must be guided by concern not only for safeguarding the community against youth gang activities but for providing support and supervision to present and potential gang members in a way that contributes to their prosocial development.

For more on gang prevention efforts, see

http://www.ncjrs.org/pdffiles1/ojjdp/182210.pdf

For an up-to-date list of Web links, go to www.wadsworth.com/product/0534573053s

Although social solutions to the gang problem seem elusive, the evidence shows that gang involvement is a socio-ecological phenomenon and must be treated as such. Youths who live in areas where their needs cannot be met by existing institutions join gangs when gang members are there to recruit them.[161] Social causes demand social solutions. Programs that enhance the lives of adolescents are the key to reducing gang delinquency. Table 8.4 illustrates some of the key elements of a successful gang control strategy.

SUMMARY

Gangs are a serious problem in many cities. Most gang members are males, ages 14 to 21, who live in urban ghetto areas. Gangs can be classified by their structure, behavior, or status. Some are believed to be social groups, others are criminally oriented, and still others are violent.

Gangs reached their heyday in the 1950s and early 1960s. After a lull of 10 years, gang operations began to increase again in the late 1970s. Today, an estimated 500,000 youths belong to gangs. Hundreds of thousands of crimes are believed to be committed annually by gangs.

Although most gang members are male, the number of females in gangs is growing at a faster pace. African American and Hispanic gangs predominate, but Anglo and Asian gangs are also quite common.

We are still not sure what causes gangs. One view is that they serve as a bridge between adolescence and adulthood when adult control is lacking. Another view suggests that gangs serve as an alternative means of advancement for disadvantaged youths. Still another view is that some gangs are havens for disturbed youths.

Police departments' gang-control efforts have not been well organized. A recent national survey found relatively few training efforts designed to help police officers deal with the gang problem.

KEY TERMS

cliques	disorganized neighborhood	graffiti	detached street worker
crowds	retreatists	representing	
gang	barrio	prestige crimes	
interstitial group	*klikas*	skinhead	

QUESTIONS FOR DISCUSSION

1. Do gangs serve a purpose? Differentiate between a gang and a fraternity.

2. Discuss the differences between violent, criminal, and drug-oriented gangs.

3. How do gangs in suburban areas differ from inner-city gangs?

4. Do delinquents have cold and distant relationships with their peers?

5. Can gangs be controlled without changing the economic opportunity structure of society? Are there any truly meaningful alternatives to gangs today for lower-class youths?

6. Can you think of other rituals in society that reflect an affinity or longing for more tribal times? (*Hint:* Have you ever pledged a fraternity or sorority, gone to a wedding, or attended a football game?)

VIEWPOINT

Community program directors, educators, and other knowledgeable persons need to recognize the attraction that gangs have for children who fit the criteria of high-risk factors of gang involvement. If we address these issues with children who fit the profile of someone likely to be attracted to gangs before they join one, we will make great steps toward eliminating gangs altogether.

There is a tremendous need for prevention programs. To make them available, we need the cooperation of corrections professionals, educators, families, and the community. Children considered or identified as at-risk for gang involvement need mentors, tutors, after-school programs, and counseling. Their families often need counseling and help from social workers as well. As a community, we need to provide hope and show children that success and fulfillment are within their grasp.

 To read more about gang prevention efforts, go to InfoTrac® College Edition and check out Lonnie Jackson, "Understanding and Responding to Youth Gangs: a Juvenile Corrections Approach," *Corrections Today* 16:62 (August 1999). To do more research on gangs, use *gangs* as a key word.

Schools and Delinquency

© Joel Gordon

ou are the principal of a suburban high school. It seems that one of your students, Steve Jones, has had a long running feud with Mr. Metcalf, an English teacher whom he blames for giving him a low grade unfairly and for being too strict with other students. Steve set up a home-based Web site that posted insulting images of Metcalf and contained messages describing him in unflattering terms (a slob who doesn't bathe often enough, for example). He posted a photo of the teacher with the caption "Public Enemy Number One." Word of the Web site has gotten out around school. And, while students think it's funny and "cool," the faculty is outraged. You bring Steve into your office and ask him to take down the site, explaining that its existence has had a negative effect on school discipline and morale. He refuses, arguing that the site is home-based and you have no right to ask for its removal. Besides which, he claims, it is just in fun and not really hurting anyone.

- Would you suspend Steve if he refuses your request to take down the site?

- Would you allow him to leave it posted and try to placate Mr. Metcalf?

- What would you do if Mr. Metcalf had posted a site ridiculing students and making fun of their academic abilities?

truancy Staying out of school without permission.

academic achievement Being successful in a school environment.

The U.S. Department of Education seeks to ensure equal access to education and to promote educational excellence for all Americans. View their Web site at http://www.ed.gov/

For an up-to-date list of Web links, go to www.wadsworth.com/product/0534573053s

School administrators are asked to make these kinds of decisions every day, and the wrong choice can prove costly. A case very similar to the one described above resulted in a $30,000 settlement in a damage claim against a school system wherein the principal did suspend a student for posting an insulting Web site and the student later sued for violating his right to free speech.[1] School officials must make daily decisions on discipline and crime prevention, something they may not have thought much about when they decided upon a career in academe!

Because so much of an adolescent's time is spent in school, it would seem logical that some relationship exists between delinquent behavior and what is happening—or not happening—in classrooms. This was pointed out as early as 1939, when the New Jersey Delinquency Commission found that, of 2,021 inmates of prisons and correctional institutions in that state, 2 out of every 5 had first been committed for **truancy.**[2]

Numerous studies have confirmed that delinquency is related to **academic achievement,** and experts have concluded that many of the underlying problems of delinquency are related to the nature of the school experience.[3] Some find that school-related variables are more important contributing factors to delinquent behavior than the influence of either family or friends.[4] Most theorists agree that the education system bears some responsibility for the high rate of juvenile crime.

In this chapter we first explore how educational achievement and delinquency are related and what factors in the school experience appear to contribute to delinquent behavior. Next, we turn to delinquency within the school setting—vandalism, theft, violence, and so on. Finally, we look at the attempts made by schools to prevent delinquency.

THE SCHOOL IN MODERN AMERICAN SOCIETY

The school plays a significant role in shaping the values of children.[5] In contrast to earlier periods, when formal education was a privilege of the upper classes, the U.S. system of compulsory public education has made schooling a legal obligation. Today, more than 90 percent of school-age children attend school, compared with only 7 percent in 1890.[6] In contrast to the earlier agrarian days of U.S. history, when most

Some schools are really cracking down in order to maintain school discipline. Here Leonard Lopez and his son, Vincent, sit at home surrounded by folders of newspaper clippings and legal papers on Feb. 15, 2000, in Arlington, Texas. Vincent was removed from his junior high school and placed into an alternative school for five days after one of his drawings was considered to show gang affiliation. (AP/Wide World Photos)

adolescents shared in the work of the family, today's young people spend most of their time in school. The school has become the primary instrument of socialization, the "basic conduit through which the community and adult influences enter into the lives of adolescents."[7]

Because young people spend a longer time in school, their adolescence is prolonged. As long as students are still dependent on their families and have not entered the work world, they are not considered adults. The responsibilities of adulthood come later to modern-day youths than to those in earlier generations, and some experts see this prolonged childhood as one factor that contributes to the irresponsible and often irrational behavior of many juveniles who commit delinquent acts.

Socialization and Status

Another significant aspect of the educational experience is that children spend their school hours with their peers, and most of their activities after school take place with school friends. Young people rely increasingly on school friends and become less interested in adult role models. The norms of the peer culture are often at odds with those of adult society, and a pseudoculture with a distinct social system develops. Law-abiding behavior may not be among the values promoted in such an atmosphere. Youth culture may admire bravery, defiance, and having fun much more.

In addition to its role in socialization, the school has become a primary determinant of economic and social status. In this technological age, education is the key to a job that will mark its holder as "successful." No longer can parents ensure the status of their children through social class alone. Educational achievement has become of equal, if not greater, importance as a determinant of economic success.

This emphasis on the value of education is fostered by parents, the media, and the schools themselves. Regardless of their social or economic background, most children grow up believing education is the key to success. However, many youths do not meet acceptable standards of school achievement. Whether failure is measured by test scores, not being promoted, or dropping out, the incidence of school failure continues to be a major problem for U.S. society. A single school failure often leads to a pattern of chronic failure. The links between school failure and delinquency will be explored more fully in the next sections.

Education in Crisis

The role schools play in adolescent development is underscored by the problems faced by the U.S. education system. Budget cutting has reduced educational resources in many communities and curtailed state support for local school systems. Spending on elementary and secondary education (as a percentage of the U.S. gross national product) trails that of other nations.

Cross-national surveys that compare academic achievement show that the United States actually trails in critical academic areas.[8] There has been some improvement in reading, math, and science achievement during the past decade, but the United States still lags many nations in key achievement measures. For example, as Figure 9.1 shows, eighth-graders in the United States lag behind students in some less-affluent nations (Hungary, Slovak Republic, and Bulgaria) in science and math achievement. One reason for the lack of achievement may be that many secondary school math and science teachers did not major in the subjects they teach.[9] This low national level of academic performance seems critical when considering delinquent behavior in schools.

To learn more about math and science education, go to The Eisenhower National Clearinghouse for Mathematics and Science Education (ENC) at

http://www.enc.org/

For an up-to-date list of Web links, go to www.wadsworth.com/product/0534573053s

ACADEMIC PERFORMANCE AND DELINQUENCY

underachievers Those who do not achieve success in school at the level of their expectations.

Poor academic performance has been directly linked to delinquent behavior; students who are chronic **underachievers** in school are among the most likely to be delinquent.[10] In fact, researchers find that school failure is a stronger predictor of delinquency than variables such as economic class membership, racial or ethnic background, or peer-group relations. Studies that compare the academic records of delinquents and non-delinquents—including their scores on standardized tests, failure rate, and other academic measures—have found that delinquents are often academically deficient, a condition that may lead to their leaving school and becoming involved in antisocial activities.[11] Children who report that they do not like school and do not do well in school are most likely to self-report delinquent acts.[12] In contrast, at-risk youths who do well in school are often able to avoid delinquent involvement.[13]

An association between academic failure and delinquency is commonly found among chronic offenders. Those leaving school without a diploma were more likely to become involved in chronic delinquency than high school graduates.[14] Only 9 percent of the chronic offenders in Wolfgang's Philadelphia cohort graduated from high school, compared with 74 percent of nonoffenders.[15] Chronic offenders also had more disciplinary actions than nonoffenders.[16]

The relationship between school achievement and persistent offending is supported by surveys that indicate that only 40 percent of incarcerated felons had twelve or more years of education, compared with about 80 percent of the general population.[17]

School Failure and Delinquency

school failure Failing to achieve success in school can result in frustration, anger, and reduced self-esteem, which may contribute to delinquent behavior.

Although there is general agreement that **school failure** and delinquency are related, some question remains concerning the nature of this relationship. One view is that the school experience is a direct cause of delinquent behavior. Children who fail at school soon feel frustrated and rejected. Believing they will never achieve success through conventional means, they seek out like-minded companions and together engage in antisocial behaviors. Educational failure evokes negative responses from important people in the child's life, including teachers, parents, and prospective employers. These reactions help solidify feelings of inadequacy and, in some cases, lead to a pattern of chronic delinquency.

A second view is that school failure leads to psychological dysfunction, which is the actual cause of antisocial behavior. For example, academic failure reduces self-esteem;

Figure 9.1
Average Mathematics and Science Achievement of Eigth-grade Students, by Nation: 1999

Source: Martin et al., *TIMSS 1999 International Science Report: Findings from IEA's Repeat of the Third International Mathematics and Science Study at the Eigth Grade.* Exhibit 1.1 (Chestnut Hill, MA: Boston College, 2000); Mullis et al. *TIMSS 1999 International Mathematics Report: Findings from IEA's Repeat of the Third International Mathematics and Science Study at the Eigth Grade.* Exhibit 1.1 (Chestnut Hill, MA: Boston College, 2000).

Mathematics		Science	
Nation	**Average**	**Nation**	**Average**
Singapore	604	Chinese Taipei	569
Korea, Republic of	587	Singapore	568
Chinese Taipei	585	Hungary	552
Hong Kong SAR	582	Japan	550
Japan	579	Korea, Republic of	549
Belgium-Flemish	558	Netherlands	545
Netherlands	540	Australia	540
Slovak Republic	534	Czech Republic	539
Hungary	532	England	538
Canada	531	Finland	535
Slovenia	530	Slovak Republic	535
Russian Federation	526	Belgium-Flemish	535
Australia	525	Slovenia	533
Finland[1]	520	Canada	533
Czech Republic	520	Hong Kong SAR	530
Malaysia	519	Russian Federation	529
Bulgaria	511	Bulgaria	518
Latvia-LSS[2]	505	United States	515
United States	502	New Zealand	510
England	496	Latvia-LSS[2]	503
New Zealand	491	Italy	493
Lithuania[3]	482	Malaysia	492
Italy	479	Lithuania[3]	488
Cyprus	476	Thailand	482
Romania	472	Romania	472
Moldova	469	(Israel)	468
Thailand	467	Cyprus	460
(Israel)	466	Moldova	459
Tunisia	448	Macedonia, Republic of	458
Macedonia, Republic of	447	Jordan	450
Turkey	429	Iran, Islamic Republic of	448
Jordan	428	Indonesia	435
Iran, Islamic Republic of	422	Turkey	433
Indonesia	403	Tunisia	430
Chile	392	Chile	420
Philippines	345	Philippines	345
Morocco	337	Morocco	323
South Africa	275	South Africa	243
International average of 38 nations	**487**	**International average of 38 nations**	**488**

Average is significantly higher than the U.S. average

Average is significantly lower than the U.S. average

Average does not differ significantly from the U.S. average

[1] The shading of Finland may appear incorrect; however, statistically, its placement is correct.

[2] Designated LSS because only Latvian-speaking schools were tested, which represents 61 percent of the population.

[3] Lithuania tested the same cohort of students as other nations, but later in 1999, at the beginning of the next school year.

NOTE: Eighth grade in most nations.
Parentheses indicate nations not meeting international sampling and/or other guidelines.
The international average is the average of the national averages of the 38 nations.

studies using a variety of measures of academic competence and self-esteem demonstrate that good students have a better attitude about themselves than do poor students; low self-esteem has been found to contribute to delinquent behavior.[18] The association then runs from school failure to low self-concept to delinquency. Schools may mediate these effects by taking steps to improve the self-image of academically challenged children.

A third view is that school failure and delinquency share a common cause. For example, they both may be part of a generalized problem behavior syndrome (PBS).

Therefore, it would be erroneous to conclude that school failure *precedes* antisocial behavior. In this view, the correlates of school failure and delinquency are these:

- Delinquents may have lower IQs than nondelinquents, a factor that might also explain their poor academic achievement.

- Delinquent behavior has been associated with a turbulent family life, a condition that most likely leads to academic underachievement.

- Delinquency has been associated with low self-control and impulsivity, traits that also may produce school failure.

- The adolescent who both fails at school and engages in delinquency may be experiencing drug use, depression, abuse, and disease, all symptoms of a troubled lifestyle.[19]

Causes of School Failure

Despite disagreement over the direction the relationship takes, there is little argument that delinquent behavior is influenced by educational experiences. A number of factors have been linked to school failure; the most prominent are discussed in the next sections.

Social Class and School Failure During the 1950s, research by Albert Cohen indicated that delinquency was a phenomenon of working-class students who were poorly equipped to function in middle-class schools. Cohen referred to this phenomenon as a failure to live up to "middle-class measuring rods."[20] Jackson Toby reinforced this concept, contending that the disadvantages lower-class children have in school (for example, lack of verbal skills) are a result of their position in the social structure and that they foster delinquency.[21] These views have been supported by the greater-than-average dropout rates among lower-class children.

One reason lower-class children may do poorly in school is that economic problems require them to take part-time jobs. Working while in school seems to lower commitment to educational achievement and is associated with higher levels of delinquent behavior.[22]

Not all experts agree with the social class–school failure–delinquency hypothesis. Early studies found that boys who do poorly in school, regardless of their socioeconomic background, are more likely to be delinquent than those who perform well.[23] There is evidence that affluent students are equally affected by school failure as lower-class youths, and that middle-class youths who do poorly in school are more likely to become delinquent than their lower-class peers.[24]

tracking Dividing students into groups according to their ability and achievement levels.

Tracking Most researchers have looked at academic **tracking**—dividing students into groups according to ability and achievement level—as a contributor to student delinquency. Placement in noncollege tracks means consignment to an educational oblivion without apparent purpose. Studies indicate that non–college track students experience greater academic failure and progressive deterioration of achievement, participate less in extracurricular activities, have an increased tendency to drop out, and commit more delinquent acts. These differences are at least partly caused by assignment to a low academic track, whereby the student is effectively locked out of a chance to achieve educational success.

Some school officials begin tracking students in the lowest grade levels. Educators separate youths into groups that have innocuous names ("special enrichment program"), but may carry the taint of academic incompetence. High school students may be tracked within individual subjects based on ability. Classes may be labeled in descending order: advanced placement, academically enriched, average, basic, and remedial. It is common for students to have all their courses in only one or two tracks.[25]

The effects of school labels accumulate over time. If students fail academically, they are often destined to fail again. Repeated instances of failure can help produce

Some experts believe that social class is related to school failure and that the educational system must make a special effort to reach out to underprivileged youth. Two teenage girls attending Ramona High School, an all-girl public school, walk past a mural recognizing students in a parenting class May 12, 2000, in Los Angeles. Ramona High, located in a working class area of East Los Angeles, is the last stop for girls expelled from other schools, in trouble with the law, involved with gangs, or otherwise headed down the wrong path. (AP/Wide World Photos)

the career of the "misfit" or "dropout." Using a tracking system keeps certain students from having any hope of achieving academic success, thereby causing lack of motivation, which may foster delinquent behavior.[26]

Alienation Alienation has also been identified as a link between school failure and delinquency. Students who report they neither like school nor care about their teachers' opinions are more likely to exhibit delinquent behaviors.[27] Youths who like school and report involvement in school activities are less likely to engage in delinquent behaviors.[28] Commitment to school, coupled with the belief that school rules are being consistently applied, helps youths resist criminality.[29] Attachment to teachers also helps insulate high-risk adolescents from delinquency.[30]

Alienation may be a function of students' inability to see the relevance of what they are taught. The gap between their education and the real world leads some students to feel that the school experience is a waste of time.[31]

Many students, particularly those from low-income families, believe schooling has no payoff. Because this legitimate channel appears to be meaningless, delinquent acts become increasingly more attractive. This middle- and upper-class bias is evident in the preeminent role of the college preparatory curriculum in many school systems. Furthermore, methods of instruction as well as curriculum materials reflect middle-class language and customs that have little meaning for the disadvantaged child.[32]

When kids are alienated from school they may want to **drop out,** a step that may make them even more prone to antisocial behaviors, as can be seen in the Focus on Delinquency, "Dropping Out."

dropouts Youths who leave school before completing their required program of education.

School shootings have become an all too familiar occurrence in the nation's schools. And while many experts have speculated on why they occur, there is still little hard evidence that would be useful to identify potentially dangerous students. Here students from Santana High School in Santee, California, watch the arraignment of classmate Charles Andy Williams in San Diego Superior Court, Wednesday, March 7, 2001, in El Cajon, California. Williams is accused of killing two students and wounding 13 other people at the school. (AP/Wide World Photos)

✔ Checkpoints

✔ The school is one of the key institutions of socialization in contemporary society.

✔ Despite its great wealth, the U.S. lags behind many nations in academic achievement.

✔ Academic performance has been linked to delinquency.

✔ School failure is linked to delinquency.

✔ The causes of school failure include class conflict, alienation, and tracking.

✔ Many kids drop out of school before they graduate, and dropping out has been linked to delinquent behavior.

DELINQUENCY WITHIN THE SCHOOL

In its pioneering study of school crime, *Violent Schools—Safe Schools* (1977),[33] the federal government found that, although teenagers spend only 25 percent of their time in school, 40 percent of the robberies and 36 percent of the physical attacks involving this age group occur there. A number of recent surveys highlight the problem of school-based crime in the new millennium. Let's take a closer look at each of them.

The School Crime Victimization Survey

Released in 2000, the most recent School Crime Victimization Survey is a joint effort by the Justice Department and the Education Department.[34] During the period surveyed (1992 to 1998), violent victimization rates at schools actually dropped from 48 crimes per 1,000 to 43 per 1,000 students. The percentage of students who said they were victims of crimes (including either theft or violent crimes) at school also decreased from 10 percent to 8 percent (Figure 9.2). Not surprisingly the percentage of students who reported carrying a gun, knife or other weapon on school property during the previous 30 days dropped from 12 percent to 9 percent, a 25 percent reduction.

While this pattern reflects the general decline in juvenile crime, there is still a significant amount of delinquent acts now occurring in the nation's schools. During 1998, students aged 12 through 18 were victims of more than 2.7 million crimes at school, including about 253,000 serious violent crimes (rape, sexual assault, robbery, and aggravated assault). There were 60 violent deaths at school between July 1, 1997 and June 30, 1998, including 47 homicides, 12 suicides and 1 teenager killed by a police officer in the line of duty.

DROPPING OUT

Though dropout rates are in decline, more than 10 percent of Americans ages 16 to 24 have left school permanently without a diploma; of these more than 1 million withdrew before completing tenth grade (Figure A).

Dropping out is a serious issue, because once kids leave school they are more likely to engage in drug abuse and antisocial behavior and to persist in criminal behavior throughout adulthood. For example, national surveys of substance-abuse levels among people who had been arrested by police find that juvenile arrestees who no longer attended school were more likely to abuse drugs than those who did attend school. Data from Phoenix , Arizona show that 70 percent of male arrestees who had dropped out tested positively for drugs as compared to 57 percent who were still in school; among females, 70 percent of arrestees who had dropped out tested positive as compared to 36 percent who were still in school.

Why Do Kids Drop Out?

When surveyed, most dropouts say they left either because they did not like school or because they wanted to get a job. Others could not get along with teachers, had been expelled, or were under suspension. Almost half of all female dropouts left school because they were pregnant or had already given birth.

Poverty and family dysfunction increase the chances of dropping out among all racial and ethnic groups.

Proportion of 15- to 24-year-olds in grades 10 to 12 who dropped out in the past year (event dropout rate)

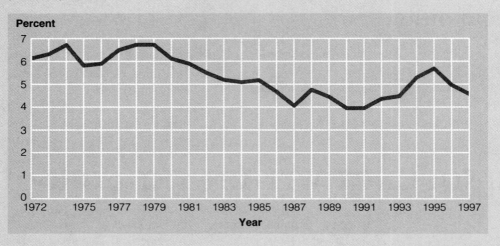

Proportion of 16- to 24-year-olds who were dropouts (status dropout rate)

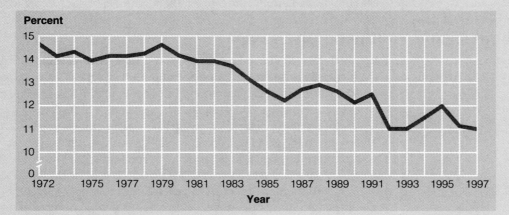

Figure A

Source: National Center for Education Statistics, U.S. Department of Education, *Digest of Education Statistics*, 1999, p. 127.

Dropouts are more likely than graduates to have lived in single-parent families headed by parents who were educational underachievers.

Some youths have no choice but to drop out. They are pushed out of school because they lack attention or have poor attendance records. Teachers label them troublemakers, and school administrators use suspensions, transfers, and other means to "convince" them that leaving school is their only option. Because minority students often come from circumstances that interfere with their attendance, they are more likely to be labeled "disobedient."

Race and Dropping Out

Race-based disciplinary practices may help sustain high minority dropout rates. Although the African American dropout rate has declined faster than the white dropout rate over the past two decades, minority students still drop out at a high rate. About 14 percent of African Americans of ages 16 to 24 are dropouts; the Hispanic dropout rate for this age group is 29 percent.

In his thoughtful book *Creating the Dropout*, Sherman Dorn shows that graduation rates have slowly but steadily risen during the twentieth century and that regional, racial, and ethnic differences in graduation rates declined. Nonetheless, Dorn argues that the relatively high dropout rate among minorities is the legacy of disciplinary policies instituted more than 40 years ago when educational administrators opposed to school desegregation employed a policy of race-based suspension and expulsion directed at convincing minority students to leave previously all-white high school districts. The legacy of these policies still infects contemporary school districts. Dorn believes that the dropout problem is a function of inequality of educational opportunity rather than the failure of individual students.. The proportion of blacks who fail to graduate from high school remains high compared to the proportion of whites failing to graduate because the educational system still fails to provide minority group members with the services and support they need.

Not All Dropouts Are Equal

The reasons students choose to drop out may have a significant impact on their future law violations. Research by Roger Jarjoura shows that youths who left school because of problems at home, for financial reasons, or because of poor grades were unlikely to increase their delinquent activity after leaving school. In contrast, those who dropped out to get married or because of pregnancy were more likely to increase their violent activities; this pattern may be linked to abuse. Those who were expelled did not increase their violent activity but were more likely to engage in theft and drug abuse.

Leaving school, then, is not a cause of misconduct per se, but youths with a history of misconduct in school often continue their antisocial behavior after dropping out. Dropouts engaged in more antisocial activity than graduates, but the reason youths dropped out influenced their offending patterns.

Dropping Out and School Policy

This debate has serious implications for educational policy. Evidence that delinquency rates decline after students leave school has caused some educators to question the wisdom of compulsory education. Some experts, such as Jackson Toby, argue that the effort to force teenagers to stay in school is counterproductive and that delinquency might be lessened by allowing them to assume a productive position in the workforce. For many youths, leaving school can have the effect of escape from a stressful situation. Toby proposes a radical solution: Make high schools voluntary, and require students to justify the expenses allocated for their education.

However, if recent findings prove to be accurate, dropping out may offer few benefits and is to be avoided. Efforts to keep children in school, provide tutoring, and create programs conducive to continued educational achievement may lower delinquency rates.

Sources: National Center for Education Statistics, *Drop Out Rates in the United States*, Washington, DC, 2000; Terence Thornberry, Melanie Moore, and R.L. Christenson, "The Effect of Dropping Out of High School on Subsequent Criminal Behavior," *Criminology 23*:3-18 (1985); Marvin Krohn, Terence Thornberry, Lori Collins-Hall, and Alan Lizotte, "School Dropout, Delinquent Behavior, and Drug Use," in Howard Kaplan, ed., *Drugs, Crime, and other Deviant Adaptations: Longitudinal Studies* (New York: Plenum Press, 1995), pp. 163–83; ADAM, *1999 Annual Report on Drug Use Among Adult and Juvenile Arrestees* (Washington, DC: United States Government Printing Office, 2000); Howard Snyder and Melissa Sickmund, *Juvenile Offenders and Victims: A National Report* (Washington, DC: Office of Juvenile Justice and Delinquency Prevention, 1995), p. 15; Jay Teachman, Kathleen Paasch, and Karen Carver, "Social Capital and the Generation of Human Capital," *Social Forces 75*:1343–60 (1997); Michel Janosz, Marc Le Blanc, Bernard Boulerice, and Richard Tremblay, *What Information Is Really Needed to Predict School Dropout? A Replication on Two Longitudinal Samples* (University of Montreal, School of Psychoeducation, 1995); Christine Bowditch, "Getting Rid of Troublemakers: High School Disciplinary Procedures and the Production of Dropouts," *Social Problems 40*:493–508 (1993); Sherman Dorn, *Creating the Dropout* (New York: Praeger, 1996); G. Roger Jarjoura, "Does Dropping Out of School Enhance Delinquent Involvement? Results from a Large-Scale National Probability Sample," *Criminology 31*:149–72 (1993); Jackson Toby, "Getting Serious about School Discipline," *The Public Interest 133*:68–74 (1998).

Figure 9.2
Total Crimes Against
Students At and
Away from School

Source: U.S. Department of Education, *National School Crime Victimization Survey* (Washington, DC: U.S. Government Printing Office, 2000), p. 4.

Number of total crimes against students ages 12 through 18 per 1,000 students: 1992–1998

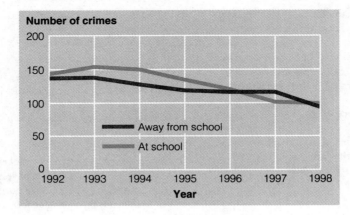

Teachers were also at risk for being victimized on school grounds. During the 1994–1998 period, teachers were the victims of 1,755,000 crimes at school, including 1,087,000 thefts and 668,000 serious violent crimes. This amounts to 83 crimes per 1,000 teachers annually.

The survey found that students ages 12 through 18 are victims of about 250,000 incidents of nonfatal serious violent crime at school. The percentages of twelfth-graders who have been injured at school has not changed notably over the past 20 years, although slightly more are now threatened with injury. Five percent of all twelfth-graders reported that they had been injured with a weapon during the past 12 months while they were at school—that is, inside or outside the school building or on a school bus—and 12 percent reported that they had been injured on purpose without a weapon while at school. Between 1992 and 1994 (the latest data available) 63 students were murdered at school and 13 committed suicide.[35]

Considering these findings, it is not surprising that the number of students who felt unsafe at school rose from 6 percent in 1989 to 9 percent in 1995. The percentage of students fearing they would be attacked while traveling to and from school rose from 4 to 7 percent.[36] Another reason for the increase in fear may be that more students are reporting the presence of gangs in school, from 15 percent of students in 1989 to 28 percent by 1995.

School Shootings

Though incidents of school-based crime and violence are common, it is the highly publicized incidents of fatal school shootings that have helped focus attention on school crime. (Table 9.1 lists some recent incidents of school-based shootings.) Though they have been the focus of much attention, there is as yet no single cause that links these incidents, nor is it possible to predict which student will become a school shooter. The United States Secret Service has developed a profile of school shootings and shooters after evaluating 41 school shooters who participated in 37 incidents.[37] They found that most attacks were neither spontaneous nor impulsive. Shooters typically developed a plan of attack well in advance; more than half had considered the attack for at least 2 weeks and had a plan for at least 2 days.

The attackers' mental anguish was well known and they had come to the attention of someone (school officials, police, fellow students) because of their bizarre and disturbing behavior prior to the attack's having taken place. One student told more than twenty friends beforehand about his plans, which included killing students and planting bombs. Threats were communicated in more than three-fourths of the cases, and in more than half the incidents the attacker told more than one person. Some people knew detailed information, while others knew "something spectacular" was

TABLE 9.1 Recent School Shootings

- March 5, 2001. A student in Santee, California, an alleged victim of schoolyard bullies, killed two students.
- February 29, 2000. A first-grader in Michigan shot and killed a fellow student, a 6-year-old girl with whom he had quarreled.
- May 20, 1999. A 15-year-old, upset over a broken romance, opened fire at Heritage High School in Conyers, Georgia, injuring six students
- April 20, 1999. Two young men killed 13 students and injured 20 others before committing suicide at Columbine High School in Colorado.
- April 16, 1999. A high-school sophomore fired two shotgun blasts in a school hallway in Notus, Idaho.
- May 21, 1998. Two teenagers were fatally shot and more than 20 people hurt when a 15-year-old boy allegedly opened fire at a high school in Springfield, Oregon. His parents were found slain at their home.
- May 19, 1998. Three days before his graduation, an 18-year-old honor student allegedly opened fire in a parking lot at a high school in Fayetteville, Tennessee, killing a classmate who was dating his ex-girlfriend.
- April 24, 1998. A science teacher was shot to death in front of students at the eighth-grade graduation dance in Edinboro, Pennsylvania.
- March 24, 1998. Four girls and a teacher were shot to death and 10 people wounded during a false fire alarm at a middle school in Jonesboro, Arkansas, when two boys, 11 and 13, opened fire from the woods.
- December 1, 1997. Three students were killed and five others wounded in a hallway at Heath High School in West Paducah, Kentucky.
- October 1, 1997. A 16-year-old boy in Pearl, Mississippi, was accused of killing his mother, then going to his high school and killing two students and wounding seven others.

going to happen on a particular date. In less than one-fourth of the cases did the attacker make a direct threat to the target.

The Secret Service found that shooters came from such a wide variety of backgrounds that no accurate or useful profile of at-risk kids could be developed. They range in age from 11 to 21 and come from a wide variety of ethnic and racial backgrounds; about 25 percent of the shooters were minority-group members. Some lived in intact families with strong ties to the community, while others were reared in foster homes with histories of neglect. Some were excellent students, while others were poor academic performers. Shooters could not be characterized as isolated and alienated; some had many friends and were considered popular. There was no evidence that shootings were a result of the onset of mental disorder. Drugs and alcohol seemed to have little involvement in school violence.

What the Secret Service found was that many of the shooters had a history of feeling extremely depressed or desperate because they had been picked on or bullied. About three-fourths either threatened to kill themselves, made suicidal gestures, or tried to kill themselves before the attack; six of the students studied killed themselves during the incident. The most frequent motivation was revenge. More than three-fourths were known to hold a grievance, real or imagined, against the target and/or others. In most cases, this was the first violent act against the target. Two-thirds of the attackers described feeling persecuted, and in more than three-fourths of the incidents the attackers had difficulty coping with a major change in a significant relationship or a loss of status, such as a lost love or a humiliating failure. Not surprisingly, most shooters had experience with guns and weapons and had access to them at home.

TABLE 9.2 Factors Linked to Children Who Engage in Serious School Violence

- *Social withdrawal.* In some situations, gradual and eventually complete withdrawal from social contacts. The withdrawal often stems from feelings of depression, rejection, persecution, unworthiness, and lack of confidence.

- *Excessive feelings of isolation* and being alone. Research indicates that in some cases feelings of isolation and not having friends are associated with children who behave aggressively and violently.

- *Excessive feelings of rejection.* Children who are troubled often are isolated from their mentally healthy peers. Some aggressive children who are rejected by nonaggressive peers seek out aggressive friends who, in turn, reinforce their violent tendencies.

- *Being a victim of violence.* Children who are victims of violence-including physical or sexual abuse in the community, at school, or at home are sometimes at risk themselves of becoming violent toward themselves or others.

- *Feelings of being picked on and persecuted.* The youth who feels constantly picked on, teased, bullied, singled out for ridicule, and humiliated at home or at school may initially withdraw socially.

- *Low school interest and poor academic performance.* In some situations—such as when the low achiever feels frustrated, unworthy, chastised, and denigrated—acting out and aggressive behaviors may occur.

- *Expression of violence in writings and drawings.* An overrepresentation of violence in writings and drawings that is consistently directed at specific individuals (family members, peers, other adults) over time, may signal emotional problems and the potential for violence.

- *Uncontrolled anger.* Patterns of impulsive and chronic hitting, intimidating, and bullying behaviors, if left unattended, may later escalate into more serious behaviors.

- *History of discipline problems.* Chronic behavior and disciplinary problems, both in school and at home, may suggest that underlying emotional needs are not being met.

- *History of violent and aggressive behavior.* Unless provided with support and counseling, a youth who has a history of aggressive or violent behavior is likely to repeat those behaviors. Similarly, youth who engage in overt behaviors such as bullying, generalized aggression and defiance, and covert behaviors such as stealing, vandalism, lying, cheating, and fire setting also are at risk for more serious aggressive behavior.

- *Membership in hate groups or the willingness to victimize* individuals with disabilities or health problems is a precursor to violence.

- *Drug use and alcohol use.* Apart from being unhealthy behaviors, drug use and alcohol use reduces self-control and exposes children and youth to violence, either as perpetrators or as victims, or both.

- *Inappropriate access to, possession of, and use of firearms.* Children and youth who inappropriately possess or have access to firearms can have an increased risk for violence or other emotional problems and should not have access to firearms and other weapons.

- *Serious threats of violence.* Recent incidents across the country clearly indicate that threats to commit violence against oneself or others should be taken very seriously. Steps must be taken to understand the nature of these threats and to prevent them from being carried out.

Source: Kevin Dwyer, *Early Warning, Timely Response: A Guide to Safe Schools* (Washington, DC: U.S. Department of Education, 1998), Section 3.

Some of the most important factors linked to extreme incidents of school violence are contained in Table 9.2.

One factor that stands out in the profile of the school shooter is that they were typically young boys who had been bullied or picked on in school. Because this issue of bullying is so important it is the topic of the Focus on Delinquency, "Bullying in School."

The School Substance Abuse Survey

The national Center for Addiction and Substance Abuse (CASA) at Columbia University in New York conducts periodic surveys with students, parents, teachers, and principals about their attitude toward cigarettes, alcohol, and illegal drugs

BULLYING IN SCHOOL

Experts define bullying among children as repeated, negative acts committed by one or more children against another. These negative acts may be physical or verbal in nature—for example, hitting or kicking, teasing or taunting—or they may involve indirect actions such as manipulating friendships or purposely excluding other children from activities. Implicit in this definition is an imbalance in real or perceived power between the bully and victim.

The most recent school safety survey (2000) indicates that in 1999 about 5 percent of students ages 12 through 18 reported that they had been bullied at school in the last 6 months. In general, females were as likely as males to report being bullied. While there are few racial differences in bullying, students in lower grades were more likely to be bullied than students in higher grades: about 10 percent of students in grades 6 and 7 reported being bullied, compared with about 5 percent of students in grades 8 and 9 and about 2 percent in grades 10 through 12.

Studies of bullying suggest that there are short- and long-term consequences for both the perpetrators and the victims of bullying. Students who are chronic victims of bullying experience more physical and psychological problems than their peers who are not harassed by other children and they tend not to grow out of the role of victim. Longitudinal studies have found that victims of bullying in early grades also reported being bullied several years later. Studies also suggest that chronically victimized students may, as adults, be at increased risk for depression, poor self-esteem, and other mental health problems, including schizophrenia.

It is not only victims who are at risk for short- and long-term problems; bullies also are at increased risk for negative outcomes. One researcher found that those elementary students who were bullies attended school less frequently and were more likely to drop out than other students. Several studies suggest that bullying in early childhood may be a critical risk factor for the development of future problems with violence and delinquency. For example, research conducted in Scandinavia found that, in addition to threatening other children, bullies were several times more likely than their nonbullying peers to commit antisocial acts, including vandalism, fighting, theft, drunkenness, and truancy, and to have an arrest by young adulthood. Another study of more than 500 children found that aggressive behavior at the age of 8 was a powerful predictor of criminality and violent behavior at the age of 30.

Can Bullying Be Prevented?

The first and best-known intervention to reduce bullying among school children was launched by Dan Olweus in Norway and Sweden in the early 1980s. Prompted by the suicides of several severely victimized children, Norway supported the development and implementation of a comprehensive program to address bullying among children in school. The program involved interventions at multiple levels:

- *Schoolwide interventions.* A survey of bullying problems at each school, increased supervision, schoolwide assemblies, and teacher inservice training to raise the awareness of children and school staff regarding bullying.

- *Classroom-level interventions.* The establishment of classroom rules against bullying, regular class meetings to discuss bullying at school, and meetings with all parents.

- *Individual-level interventions.* Discussions with students identified as bullies and victims.

The program was found to be highly effective in reducing bullying and other antisocial behavior among students in primary and junior high schools. Within two years of implementation, both boys' and girls' self-reports indicated that bullying had decreased by half. These changes in behavior were more pronounced the longer the program was in effect. Moreover, students reported significant decreases in rates of truancy, vandalism, and theft, and indicated that their school's climate was significantly more positive as a result of the program. Not surprisingly, those schools that had implemented more of the program's components experienced the most marked changes in behavior. The core components of the Olweus anti-bullying program have been adapted for use in several other cultures, including Canada, England, and the United States. Results of the anti-bullying efforts in these countries have been similar to the results experienced in the Scandinavian countries, with the efforts in Toronto schools showing somewhat more modest results. Again, as in the Scandinavian study, schools that were more active in implementing the program observed the most marked changes in reported behaviors.

Only one U.S. program has been based explicitly on the comprehensive model developed by Olweus. Gary B. Melton, Susan P. Limber, and colleagues at the Institute for Families in Society of the University of South Carolina in Columbia have adapted Olweus' model for use in rural middle schools in that state. Interventions are focused at the levels of the individual, classroom, school, and community at large. A comprehensive evaluation involving 6,500 children currently is under way to measure the effects of the program.

Sources: Phillip Kaufman et al., *Indicators of School Crime and Safety, 2000* (Washington, DC: National Center for Education Statistics, 2001); Susan P. Limber and Maury M. Nation, "Bullying among Children and Youth," in June Arnette and Marjorie Walsleben, *Combating Fear and Restoring Safety in Schools* (Washington, DC: Office of Juvenile Justice and Delinquency Prevention, 1998); Dan Olweus, "Victimization by Peers: Antecedents and Long-Term Outcomes," in K.H. Rubin and J.B. Asendorf, eds., *Social Withdrawal, Inhibitions, and Shyness* (Hillsdale, NJ: Erlbaum, 1993), pp. 315–41.

A national survey conducted by the national Center for Addiction and Substance Abuse (CASA) at Columbia University in New York found that school-based substance abuse levels were shockingly high. Teens say they are more likely to encounter drugs on school grounds or in their schools than on their neighborhood streets. (© Joel Gordon)

(marijuana, heroin, cocaine, and acid) and their presence in schools.[38] The most recent survey finds that a majority (51%) of high school students say the drug problem is getting worse and both middle and high school students say that drugs are their single biggest concern. The number of high school teens who report that drugs are used, sold, and kept at their schools is rising: from 72 percent in 1996 to 78 percent in 1998. By age 17, only 23 percent say their school is drug-free, 54 percent say that alcohol was available at most parties they attended in the past 6 months, and 35 percent say pot was available.

The Center for Addiction and Substance Abuse lists seven signs of trouble in school: smoking, drinking, drugs, weapons, expulsion for drugs, student death in drug- or alcohol-related incidents, and students showing up in class drunk or stoned.[39] Considering these problems, it is not surprising that teens, parents, teachers, and principals support firm steps to keep drugs out of schools, including random locker searches, zero tolerance policies, and drug testing of student athletes. More than half of the students (52%) and principals (53%) support drug testing of all students, compared with 42 percent of parents and 38 percent of teachers.

Who Commits School Crime?

Schools experiencing crime and drug abuse are most likely to be found in socially disorganized neighborhoods. Schools with a high proportion of students behind grade level in reading, with many students from families on welfare, and located in a community with high unemployment, crime, and poverty rates, are also at risk for delinquency.[40] In contrast, schools with high-achieving students, drug-free environments, strong discipline, and involved parents have fewer behavioral problems within the student body.[41]

A number of researchers have observed that school crime is a function of the community in which the school is located. In other words, crime in schools does not occur in isolation from crime in the community.[42] Research shows that the perpetrators and victims of school crime cannot be neatly divided into separate groups and that many offenders have been victims of delinquency themselves.[43] It is possible that school-based crimes have "survival value"—striking back against a weaker victim is a method of regaining lost possessions or self-respect.[44] There is also evidence that

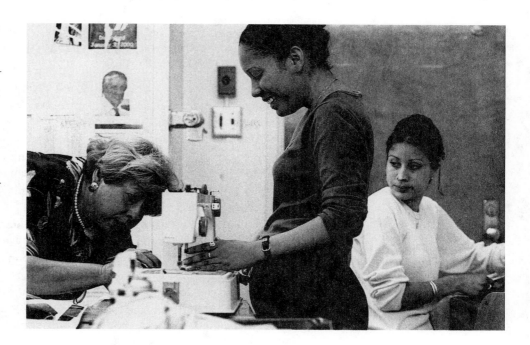

Schools have adopted a number of different delinquency prevention programs. This school is reaching out to troubled young women and helping them develop life skills that will shield them from delinquency and substance abuse. Ramona High School home economics teacher, Diane Sequine, helps student Lorena Herrera (center) repair a sewing machine as classmate Yulma Chavez watches. (AP/Wide World Photos)

crime in schools reflects the patterns of antisocial behavior that exist in the surrounding neighborhood. Schools in high-crime areas experience more crime than schools in safer areas; there is less fear in schools in safer neighborhoods than in high-crime ones. Students who report being afraid in school are actually *more afraid* of being in city parks, streets, or subways.[45]

Other research efforts confirm the community influences on school crime. Communities with a high percentage of two-parent families experience fewer school problems; neighborhoods with high population density and transient populations also have problem-prone schools.[46] One study of violent crimes in the schools of Stockholm, Sweden found that, although only one-fifth of schools were located in areas of social instability and disorganization, almost a third of school crime happened in these schools.[47] This analysis suggests that it may be futile to attempt to eliminate school crime without considering the impact prevention efforts will have on the community.

Reducing School Crime

Schools around the country have mounted a campaign to reduce the incidence of delinquency on campus. Nearly all states have developed some sort of crime-free, weapon-free, or safe-school zone statute.[48] Most have defined these zones to include school transportation and school-sponsored functions. Schools are also cooperating with court officials and probation officers to share information and monitor students who have criminal records. School districts are formulating crisis prevention and intervention policies and are directing individual schools to develop safe-school plans.

Some schools have instituted strict controls over student activity—for example, making locker searches, preventing students from having lunch off campus, and using patrols to monitor drug use. According to one national survey, a majority of schools have adopted a **zero tolerance policy** that mandates predetermined punishments for specific offenses, most typically possession of drugs, weapons, and/or tobacco, and also for engaging in violent behaviors.[49]

zero tolerance policy Mandating specific consequences or punishments for delinquent acts and not allowing anyone to avoid these consequences.

School Security Efforts Almost every school attempts to restrict entry of dangerous persons by having visitors sign in before entering, and most close the campus for lunch.[50] Schools have attempted to ensure the physical safety of students and staff by using mechanical security devices such as surveillance cameras, electronic barriers to

TABLE 9.3	School-Based Delinquency Control Efforts

- School bus drivers are tested for drug and alcohol use.
- Criminal background checks are completed on teachers and school staff members before a work assignment is made.
- Neighborhood Watch programs are established in areas near schools.
- Parents are recruited to provide safe houses along school routes and to monitor "safe corridors" or walkways to and from school.
- Parent volunteers monitor hallways, cafeterias, playgrounds, and school walkways to increase visibility of responsible adults.
- Block safety watch programs are carried out by area residents at school bus stops as a crime deterrent for schoolchildren and area residents.
- School grounds are fenced to secure campus perimeters.
- Bathroom doors are replaced with zigzag entrances to make it easier to monitor sounds, and roll-down doors are installed to secure bathrooms after hours.
- One main door is designated for entry to school; exits are equipped with push bars, and all other doors are locked to outside entry.
- Bulletproof windows are installed.
- Schools are equipped with closed-circuit video surveillance systems to reduce property crimes such as break-ins, theft, vandalism, and assaults.
- Landscaping is designed to create an inviting appearance without offering a hiding place for trespassers or criminals.
- Motion-sensitive lights illuminate dark corners in hallways or on campus.
- Convex mirrors monitor blind spots in school hallways.
- Classrooms are equipped with intercom systems connected to the central school office.
- Two-way radios are issued to security patrols or campus staff members.
- Cellular phones are available for use in crises or emergency situations.
- Photo identification badges are required for students, teachers, and staff, and identification cards are provided for visitors on campus.

Source: June L. Arnette and Marjorie C. Walsleben, *Combating Fear and Restoring Safety in Schools* (Washington, DC: Office of Juvenile Justice and Delinquency Prevention, 1998).

keep out intruders, and roving security guards. About 4 percent of schools use random metal detectors; metal detectors are much more common in large schools, especially where serious crime has taken place (15 percent).[51] One program in New York City uses random searches with hand-held detectors at the start of the school day. Students report a greater sense of security, and attendance has increased.[52] Some districts have gone so far as to infiltrate undercover detectives on school grounds. These detectives attend classes, mingle with students, contact drug dealers, make buys, and arrest campus dealers.[53]

Some schools have independent security divisions, others hire private guards, and still others cooperate with law-enforcement agencies. For example, in Houston, Texas it is routine to employ armed guards during the day. Nor does security end in the evening. In San Diego, infrared beams and silent alarms are used to protect school grounds from vandals and unwelcome visitors.[54] Rather than suspending violators, some school districts send them to a separate center for evaluation and counseling.[55] In New York City the school board maintains a force of 3,200 officers in its Division of School Safety; they patrol the more than 1,000 public schools armed only with handcuffs.[56] Table 9.3 summarizes some school-based efforts to combat delinquency within the schools.

Critics claim that, even though these methods are effective, they reduce staff and student morale. Tighter security may reduce acts of crime and violence in school, only to displace them to the community. Similarly, expelling or suspending trouble-makers puts them on the street with nothing to do. Lowering the level of crime in schools may not reduce the total amount of crime committed by young people. In fact, schools that employ strict controls are most likely to suffer increases in school-based victimization (most likely because security is aimed at a preexisting and expanding crime problem).[57]

Social Programs Another approach consists of improving the school climate and increasing educational standards. Programs have been designed to improve the standards of the teaching staff and administrators and the educational climate in the school, increase the relevance of the curriculum, and provide law-related education classes.[58]

Controlling school crime is linked to the community and to family conditions. When communities undergo changes, such as increases in unemployment and in the number of single-parent households, both school disruption and community crime rates may rise.[59] The school environment can be made safer only if community issues are addressed—for example, by taking steps to keep intruders out of school buildings, putting pressure on local police to develop community safety programs, strengthening laws on school safety, and making parents more responsible for their children's behavior.[60]

Schools must also use the resources of the community. About 70 percent of public schools provide outside referrals for students with substance-abuse problems, and 90 percent offer drug education within the school.[61]

THE ROLE OF THE SCHOOL IN DELINQUENCY PREVENTION

Numerous organizations and groups have called for reforming the educational system to make it more responsive to the needs of students. Educational leaders now recognize that children undergo enormous pressures while in school that can lead to emotional and social problems. At one extreme are the pressures to succeed academically; at the other are the crime and substance abuse students face on school grounds. It is difficult to talk of achieving academic excellence in a deteriorated school dominated by gang members.

A report by the Carnegie Corporation found that the United States is facing an educational crisis. Student dissatisfaction, which begins to increase after elementary school, is accompanied by aversion for teachers and many academic subjects. The rate of student alienation and the social problems that accompany it—absenteeism, dropping out, and substance abuse—all increase as students enter junior high.

Educators have attempted to create programs that will benefit youths and provide them with opportunities for conventional success, but change has been slow in coming. Not until the mid-1980s did concern about the educational system, prompted by the findings of the National Commission on Excellence in Education in *A Nation at Risk,* focus efforts on change.[62]

Skepticism exists over whether the U.S. school system, viewed by critics as overly conservative, can play a significant role in delinquency prevention. Some contend that no significant change in the lives of youths is possible by merely changing the schools; the entire structure of society must be altered.[63] Others suggest that alternative schools, which create a positive learning environment with low student–teacher ratios and individualized learning, may be the answer. Although in theory such programs may promote academic performance and reduce delinquency, evaluations suggest that they have little effect on delinquency rates.[64]

A danger also exists that the pressure to improve the educational experience of students can produce unforeseen problems for staff members. For example, teachers have been prosecuted for encouraging students to cheat on tests. The pressure to improve student performance on standardized tests was the motive for the faculty cheating.[65]

School-Based Prevention Programs

Education officials have instituted numerous programs to make schools more effective instruments of delinquency prevention.[66] The most prevalent strategies include:

- *Cognitive.* Increase students' awareness about the dangers of drug abuse and delinquency.
- *Affective.* Improve students' psychological assets and self-image, to give them the resources to resist antisocial behavior.
- *Behavioral.* Train students in techniques to resist peer pressure.
- *Environmental.* Establish school management and disciplinary programs that deter crime, such as locker searches.
- *Therapeutic.* Treat youths who have already manifested problems.

More specific suggestions include creating special classes or schools with individualized programs that foster success for nonadjusting students. Efforts can be made to help students deal constructively with academic failure when it does occur.

More personalized student–teacher relationships have been recommended. This effort to provide young persons with a caring, accepting adult role model will, it is hoped, strengthen the controls against delinquency. Counselors acting as liaisons between the family and the school might also be effective in preventing delinquency. These counselors try to ensure cooperation between the parents and the school and to secure needed services for troubled students.

Experiments have been proposed that integrate job training and experience with classroom instruction, allowing students to see education as a relevant prelude to their careers. Job training programs could emphasize public service, encouraging students to gain a sense of attachment to their communities.

Because 3 of 4 mothers with school-age children are employed, and two-thirds of them work full time, there is a growing need for after-school programs. Today, after-school options include childcare centers, tutoring programs at school, dance groups, basketball leagues, and drop-in clubs. State and federal budgets for education, public safety, crime prevention, and child care provide some funding for after-school programs; in 1999 $200 million in federal grants were made to enable schools to establish after-school programs called Twenty-First Century Community Learning Centers. Research shows that younger children (ages 5 to 9) and those in low-income neighborhoods gain the most from after-school programs, showing improved work habits, behavior with peers and adults, and performance in school. Young teens who attend after-school activities achieve higher grades in school and engage in less-risky behavior. These findings must be interpreted with caution. Because after-school programs are voluntary, participants may be the more-motivated youngsters in a given population and the least likely to engage in antisocial behavior.[67]

Schools may not be able to reduce delinquency single-handedly, but a number of alternatives to their present operations could aid a community-wide effort to lessen juvenile crime. A review of successful, unsuccessful, and promising school-based programs was conducted by Denise Gottfredson as part of a study to determine the best methods of delinquency prevention. Some of her findings are contained in Table 9.4.

LEGAL RIGHTS WITHIN THE SCHOOL

The actions of education officials often run into opposition from the courts, which are concerned with maintaining the legal rights of minors. The U.S. Supreme Court has sought to balance the civil liberties of students with the school's mandate to provide a

SCHOOL-BASED DELINQUENCY PREVENTION PROGRAMS

A number of programs have attempted to reduce delinquency by manipulating the learning environment. Three of the more successful ones are described below.

Project PATHE (Positive Action through Holistic Education)

Project PATHE is a comprehensive program used in secondary schools that reduces school disorder and aims to improve the school environment. The goal is to enhance students' experiences and attitudes about school by increasing students' bonds to the school, increasing their self-concept, and improving educational and occupational attainment. These improvements will help reduce juvenile delinquency.

PATHE was operated in four middle schools and three high schools in South Carolina. It focused on four elements: strengthening students' commitment to school, providing successful school experiences, encouraging attachment to the educational community, and increasing participation in school activities. By increasing students' sense of belonging and usefulness, the project sought to promote a positive school experience. The PATHE program has undergone extensive evaluation by sociologist Denise Gottfredson, who found that the schools in which it was used experienced a moderate reduction in delinquency. Replications of the project are currently under development.

Seattle Social Development Project

The Seattle Social Development Project uses a method in which teachers learn techniques that reward appropriate student behavior and minimize disruption. Students are taught in small groups given the goal of helping each other master the curriculum. Students were also singled out for training to help them master problem-solving, communication, and conflict-resolution skills. Family training classes were offered, teaching parents how to reward and encourage desirable behavior and provide negative consequences for undesirable behavior in a consistent fashion. Other parent training focused on improving their children's academic performance while reducing at-risk behaviors such as drug abuse. Evaluations of the Seattle program show that children in the intervention group enhanced their school commitment and participation. Substance-abuse rates were lowered for the girls, and the boys increased their social and schoolwork skills.

See Forever Program

Located in the Maya Angelou Public Charter School in Washington, D.C., the See Forever Program, which opened in 1997, is designed to produce positive change and a productive future for young people who have been involved in the juvenile justice system or who are at risk for persistent offending. The program provides an education combining academic and job opportunities. The students are in school year round, with a school day lasting from 9:30 A.M. until 8 P.M. From 6:45 until 8 P.M. on Mondays through Thursdays, the kids have tutors help them with homework or other schoolwork. On Wednesdays, students stay late so they can keep whatever other appointments they might have, such as drug tests or meetings with probation officers. In addition to the regular schoolwork, students are employed in a nonprofit restaurant, Untouchable Taste Catering. They are also involved in a Student Tech shop where kids can sharpen their skills in technology and graphic design and use them to teach their parents and siblings computer skills. The comprehensive program gives the students job skills as well as high school diplomas. Part of their paycheck goes into their accounts at Merrill Lynch to teach them the value of saving. The school also has a few residences where the kids can live if their home environments are not conducive to success. In late July 1999, the school had its first graduating class, and all these graduates have gone on to college.

Sources: Denise Gottfredson, "An Empirical Test of School-Based Environmental and Individual Interventions to Reduce the Risk of Delinquent Behavior," *Criminology* 24:705–31 (1986); Denise Gottfredson, "Changing School Structures to Benefit High-Risk Youth," in Peter Leone, ed., *Understanding Troubled and Troubling Youth* (Newbury Park, CA: Sage, 1990), pp. 246–71; Julie O'Donnell, J. David Hawkins, Richard Catalano, Robert Abbott, and L. Edward Day, "Preventing School Failure, Drug Use, and Delinquency among Low-Income Children: Long-Term Intervention in Elementary Schools," *Journal of Orthopsychiatry* 65:87–100 (1995); information provided by the See Forever Program, 1851 Ninth Street NW, Washington, DC, 2001 Project.

safe environment. The main issues include compulsory attendance, free speech in school, and school discipline.

The Right to Personal Privacy

One major issue is the right of school officials to search students and their possessions on school grounds. Drug abuse, theft, assault and battery, and racial conflicts in

TABLE 9.4	School-Based Delinquency Prevention Programs that Work

What Works for Delinquency?

1. Programs aimed at building school capacity to initiate and sustain innovation.

2. Programs aimed at clarifying and communicating norms about behaviors—by establishing school rules, improving the consistency of their enforcement (particularly when they emphasize positive reinforcement of appropriate behavior), or communicating norms through school-wide campaigns (e.g., anti-bullying campaigns) or ceremonies.

3. Comprehensive instructional programs that focus on a range of social competency skills (e.g., developing self-control, stress-management, responsible decision-making, social problem-solving, and communication skills) and that are delivered over a long period of time to continually reinforce skills.

What Works for Substance Abuse?

1. Programs aimed at clarifying and communicating norms about behaviors.

2. Comprehensive instructional programs that focus on a range of social competency skills (e.g., developing self-control, stress-management, responsible decision-making, social problem-solving, and communication skills) and that are delivered over a long period of time to continually reinforce skills.

3. Behavior modification programs and programs that teach "thinking skills" to high-risk youths.

What Is Promising for Crime and Delinquency?

1. Programs that group youths into smaller "schools-within-schools" to create smaller units, more supportive interactions, or greater flexibility in instruction.

2. Behavior modification programs and programs that teach "thinking skills" to high-risk youths.

What Is Promising for Substance Abuse?

1. Programs aimed at building school capacity to initiate and sustain innovation; programs that group youths into smaller "schools-within-schools" to create smaller units, more supportive interactions, or greater flexibility in instruction.

2. Programs that improve classroom management and that use effective instructional techniques.

Source: Denise C. Gottfredson, "School-Based Crime Prevention," in Lawrence W. Sherman, Denise Gottfredson, Doris Mackenzie, John Eck, Peter Reuter, and Shawn Bushway, "Preventing Crime: What Works, What Doesn't, What's Promising: A Report to the United States Congress," prepared for the National Institute of Justice (Washington, DC: National Institute of Justice, 1998.

✔ Checkpoints

✔ A significant number of crimes occur in schools each year.

✔ There has been a recent decline in school-based crime that reflects the general crime-rate decline.

✔ Almost 2 million children were victimized between 1994–1998.

✔ About 5 percent of students are bullied in school.

✔ About three-quarters of all students report drugs in their school.

✔ There are a number of efforts being made to reduce school crime, including enforcing strict security measures through use of armed guards.

✔ Schools have been active in delinquency prevention.

✔ After-school programs are becoming popular.

✔ The programs that seem most effective focus on a range of social issues, including problem-solving skills, self-control, and stress management.

Students in Rochester, New York, are shown protesting a school ruling over the presence of metal detectors. The Supreme Court allows school officials to control student speech while on school premises if it interferes with the school's mission to implant "the shared values of a civilized social order." Student protest off-campus is still an open question. In the future, the courts may be asked to rule whether schools can control such forms of speech or whether they are shielded by the First Amendment. (AP/Wide World Photos)

schools have increased the need to take action against troublemakers. School administrators have questioned students about their illegal activities, conducted searches of students' persons and possessions, and reported suspicious behavior to the police.

In 1984, in *New Jersey v. T.L.O.*, the Supreme Court helped clarify a vexing problem: whether the Fourth Amendment's prohibition against unreasonable searches and seizures applies to school officials as well as to police officers.[68] In this case, the Court found that students are in fact constitutionally protected from illegal searches but that school officials are not bound by the same restrictions as law-enforcement agents. Police need "probable cause" before they can conduct a search, but educators can legally search students when there are reasonable grounds to believe the students have violated the law or broken school rules. In creating this distinction, the Court recognized the needs of school officials to preserve an environment conducive to education and to secure the safety of students.

One question left unanswered by *New Jersey v. T.L.O.* is whether teachers and other school officials can search lockers and desks. Here, the law has been controlled by state decisions, and each jurisdiction may create its own standards. Some allow teachers a free hand in opening lockers and desks.[69]

Drug Testing

Another critical issue concerning privacy is the drug testing of students. In 1995, the Supreme Court extended schools' authority to search by legalizing a random drug-testing policy for student athletes. The Supreme Court's decision in *Vernonia School District 47J v. Acton* expanded the power of educators to ensure safe learning environments.[70]

As a result of *Vernonia*, schools may employ safe-school programs such as drug testing procedures so long as the policies satisfy the reasonableness test. *Vernonia* may bring forth a spate of suspicionless searches in public schools across the country. Metal-detection procedures, the use of drug-sniffing dogs, and random locker searches will be easier to justify. In upholding random, suspicionless drug testing for student athletes, the Supreme Court extended one step further the schools' authority to search, despite court-imposed constitutional safeguards for children. Underlying this decision, like that of *New Jersey v. T.L.O.*, is a recognition that the use of drugs is a serious threat to public safety and to the rights of children to receive a decent and safe education.

Academic Privacy

Students have the right to expect that their records will be kept private. Although state laws govern the disclosure of information from juvenile court records, a 1974 federal law—the Family Educational Rights and Privacy Act (FERPA)—restricts disclosure of information from a student's education records without parental consent.[71] The act defines an education record to include all records, files, and other materials, such as photographs, containing information related to a student that an education agency maintains. In 1994, Congress passed the Improving America's Schools Act, which allowed educational systems to disclose education records under these circumstances: (1) state law authorizes the disclosure, (2) the disclosure is to a juvenile justice agency, (3) the disclosure relates to the justice system's ability to provide preadjudication services to a student, and (4) state or local officials certify in writing that the institution or individual receiving the information has agreed not to disclose it to a third party other than another juvenile justice system agency.[72]

Free Speech

passive speech A form of expression protected by the First Amendment but not associated with actually speaking words; examples include wearing symbols or protest messages on buttons or signs.

Freedom of speech is guaranteed in the First Amendment to the U.S. Constitution. This right has been divided into two categories as it affects children in schools. The first category involves **passive speech,** a form of expression not associated with actually speaking words: examples include wearing armbands or political protest buttons. The most important U.S. Supreme Court decision concerning a student's right to passive speech was in 1969 in the case of *Tinker v. Des Moines Independent Community School District*.[73] This case involved the right to wear black armbands to protest the war in Vietnam. Two high school students, ages 16 and 17, were suspended for wearing the armbands in school. According to the Court, to justify prohibiting an expression of opinion, the school must be able to show that its action was caused by something more than a desire to avoid the unpleasantness that accompanies the expression of an unpopular view. Unless it can be shown that the forbidden conduct will interfere with the discipline required to operate the school, the prohibition cannot be sustained.[74]

The concept of free speech articulated in *Tinker* was used again in 1986 in *Bethel School District No. 403 v. Fraser*.[75] This case upheld a school system's right to discipline a student who uses obscene or profane language and gestures. The Court found that a school has the right to control offensive speech that undermines the educational mission. In a 1988 case, *Hazelwood School District v. Kuhlmeier,* the Court extended the right of school officials to censor **active speech** when it ruled that the principal could censor articles in a student publication.[76] In this case, students had written about their experiences with pregnancy and parental divorce. The majority ruled that censorship was justified because school-sponsored publications were part of the curriculum and therefore designed to impart knowledge. Control over such activities could be differentiated from the action the Tinkers initiated on their own accord. In a dissent, Justice William J. Brennan accused school officials of favoring "thought control."

active speech Expressing an opinion by speaking or writing; freedom of speech is a protected right under the First Amendment to the U.S. Constitution.

The Court may now be asked to address off-campus speech issues as well. As you may recall, students have been suspended for posting messages school officials consider defamatory on Web sites.[77] In the future, the Court may be asked to rule on whether this speech is shielded by the First Amendment.

School Prayer

One of the most divisive issues involving free speech is school prayer. While some religious-minded administrators, parents, and students want to have prayer sessions in schools or have religious convocations, others view the practice both as a violation of the principle of separation of church and state and as an infringement on the First Amendment right to freedom of religion. The 2000 case of *Santa Fe Independent School District, Petitioner v. Jane Doe* helps clarify the issue. [78]

Prior to 1995, the Santa Fe High School student who occupied the school's elective office of student council chaplain delivered a prayer over the public address system before each varsity football game for the entire season. After the practice was challenged in federal district court, the school district adopted a different policy that permitted, but did not require, prayer initiated and led by a student at all home games. The district court entered an order modifying that policy to permit only nonsectarian, nonproselytizing prayer. However, a federal appellate court held that, even as modified, the football prayer policy was invalid. This decision was upheld when the case was appealed to the United States Supreme Court. They ruled that prayers led by an "elected" student undermines the protection of minority viewpoints. Such a system encourages divisiveness along religious lines and threatens the imposition of coercion upon those students not desiring to participate in a religious exercise. The Santa Fe case severely limits school-sanctioned prayer at public events.

School Discipline

in loco parentis In the place of the parent; rights given to schools that allow them to assume parental duties in disciplining students.

Most states have statutes permitting teachers to use corporal punishment in public school systems. Under the concept of **in loco parentis,** discipline is one of the parental duties given to the school system. In the 1977 case *Ingraham v. Wright,* the Court held that neither the Eighth nor the Fourteenth Amendment was violated by a teacher's use of corporal punishment to discipline students.[79] The Court established the standard that only reasonable discipline is allowed in school systems; today 24 states still use physical punishment. With regard to suspension and expulsion, the Supreme Court ruled in 1976, in the case of *Goss v. Lopez,* that any time a student is to be suspended for up to 10 days, he or she is entitled to a hearing.[80]

In summary, schools have the right to discipline students, but students are protected from unreasonable, excessive, and arbitrary discipline.

SUMMARY

For decades, criminologists have attempted to explain the relationship between schools and delinquency. Although no clear causal relationship has been established, research points to many links between delinquent behavior and experiences within the educational system.

Youths spend much of their time in school because education has become increasingly important as a determinant of social and economic success. Educational institutions are one of the primary instruments of socialization, and this role is bound to affect the amount of delinquent behavior by school-age children.

Those who claim a causal link between schools and delinquency cite two major factors: (1) academic failure, which arises from lack of aptitude, labeling, or class conflict and results in tracking; and (2) alienation from the educational experience, which is the result of the impersonal nature of schools, the passive role assigned to students, and students' perception of their education as irrelevant to their future lives.

Student misbehaviors, which may have their roots in the school experience, range from minor infractions of school rules (for example, smoking and loitering in halls) to serious crimes such as assault, arson, drug abuse, and vandalism.

Dissatisfaction with the educational experience frequently sets the stage for more serious forms of delinquency, both in and out of school. Some dissatisfied students drop out of school, and research has shown a decline in delinquency among those who do drop out.

School administrators have attempted to prevent delinquency. Among the measures taken are security squads, electronic surveillance, and teacher training. Curriculums are being revised to make the school experience more meaningful.

KEY TERMS

truancy
academic achievement
underachievers

school failure
tracking
drop out

zero tolerance policy
passive speech
active speech

in loco parentis

1. Was there a delinquency problem in your high school? If so, how was it dealt with?

2. Should disobedient youths be suspended from school? Does this solution hurt or help?

3. What can be done to improve the delinquency prevention capabilities of schools?

4. Is school failure responsible for delinquency, or are delinquents simply school failures?

VIEWPOINT

After-school programs may be implemented to ensure that students use their free time more productively. They may also allow more organized and better monitored youth development, especially when there [are] no parental guidance, ideal models, and community opportunities. The development of after-school programs becomes more crucial in poor communities, where there are high incidences of unemployment and insufficient income. These programs are important because they help in minimizing juvenile problems, such as gang involvement, alcohol and drug abuse, and school dropouts.

Can after-school programs be an effective method of delinquency prevention? To find out go to InfoTrac® College Edition and read Peter Witt and Dwayne Baker, "Developing After-School Programs for Youth in High-Risk Environments," *JOPERD, the Journal of Physical Education, Recreation & Dance* 68:18 (Nov.–Dec. 1997).

Drug Use and Delinquency

© Gale Zucker/Stock, Boston

he president has appointed you the new "drug czar." You have $10 billion under your control with which to wage a campaign against drugs. You know that drug use is unacceptably high, especially among poor, inner-city kids, that a great deal of all criminal behavior is drug-related, and that drug-dealing gangs are expanding around the United States.

At an open hearing, drug-control experts express their policy strategies. One group favors putting the money into hiring new law-enforcement agents who will patrol borders, target large dealers, and make drug raids here and abroad. They also call for such get-tough measures as the creation of strict drug laws, the mandatory waiver of young drug dealers to the adult court system, and the death penalty for drug-related gang killings.

A second group believes that the best way to deal with drugs is to spend the money on community treatment programs, expanding the number of beds in drug detoxification units, and funding research on how to reduce drug dependency clinically.

A third group argues that neither punishment nor treatment can restrict teenage drug use and that the best course is to educate at-risk kids about the dangers of substance abuse and then legalize all drugs but control their distribution. This course of action will help to reduce crime and violence among drug users and also to balance the national debt, since drugs could be heavily taxed.

■ Do you believe drugs should be legalized and if so what might be the negative consequences of legalization?

■ Can any law enforcement strategies reduce drug consumption?

■ Is treatment an effective drug-control technique?

There is little question that adolescent **substance abuse** and its association with delinquency are vexing problems. Almost every town, village, and city in the United States has confronted some type of teenage substance abuse problem. Nor is the United States alone in experiencing a problem with substance abuse. In Australia, 19 percent of youths in detention centers report having used heroin at least once, and in the Canadian province of British Columbia almost half of all youths report using drugs. South Africa reports an increase in teen cocaine and heroin abuse, and Thailand has a serious heroin and methamphetamine problem.[1]

Self-report surveys indicate that more than half of high school seniors have tried drugs and more than 90 percent use alcohol.[2] Adolescents at high risk for drug abuse often come from the most impoverished communities and experience a multitude of problems, including school failure and family conflict.[3] Equally troubling is the association between drug use and crime.[4] Research indicates that more than half of all juvenile arrestees in some cities test positive for cocaine.[5] Self-report surveys show that drug abusers are more likely to become delinquents than are nonabusers.[6] The pattern of drug use and crime makes teenage substance abuse a key national concern.

In this chapter we address some important issues involving teenage substance abuse. First we review the kinds of drugs children and adolescents are using and how often they are using them. Then we discuss who uses drugs and what causes substance abuse. After describing the association between drug abuse and delinquent behavior, we conclude with a review of efforts to control the use of drugs in the United States.

Self-report surveys show that drug abusers are more likely to become delinquents than are non-abusers. Victor Brancaccio was convicted of murdering Mollie Mae Frazier, an 81-year-old widow who scolded him for rapping as he walked down the street. Victor dragged Mollie Mae into a field, punched and kicked her repeatedly, jumped on her rib cage, and finally bashed in her skull with a toy gun. Brancaccio claimed that he was "involuntarily intoxicated" by alcohol and the antidepressant Zoloft and unable to understand the wrongfulness of his acts. (© Paul Milette/*Palm Beach Post*)

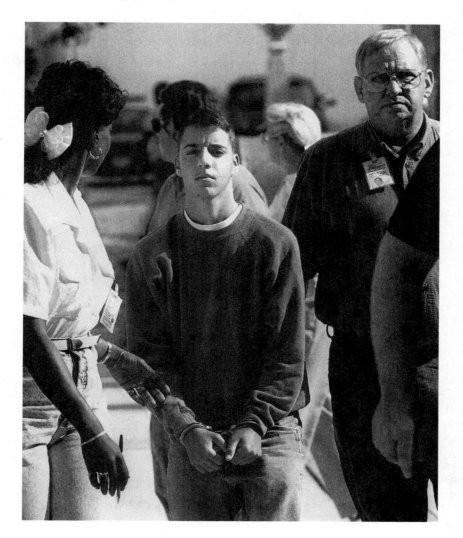

FREQUENTLY ABUSED DRUGS

substance abuse Using drugs or alcohol in such a way as to cause physical harm to yourself.

A wide variety of substances referred to as "drugs" are used by teenagers. Some are addicting, others not. Some create hallucinations, others cause a depressed stupor, and a few give an immediate uplift. In this section we will identify the most widely used substances and discuss their effects. All of these drugs can be abused and, because of the danger they present, many have been banned from private use. Others are available legally only with a physician's supervision, and a few are available to adults but prohibited for children.

Marijuana and Hashish

hashish A concentrated form of cannabis made from unadulterated resin from the female cannabis plant.

marijuana The dried leaves of the cannabis plant.

Commonly called "pot" or "grass," marijuana is produced from the leaves of *Cannabis sativa*. **Hashish** (hash) is a concentrated form of cannabis made from unadulterated resin from the female plant. The main active ingredient in both marijuana and hashish is tetrahydrocannabinol (THC), a mild hallucinogen. **Marijuana** is the drug most commonly used by teenagers.

Smoking large amounts of pot or hash can cause distortions in auditory and visual perception, even producing hallucinatory effects. Small doses produce an early excitement ("high") that gives way to drowsiness. Pot use is also related to decreased activity, overestimation of time and space, and increased food consumption. When the user is alone, marijuana produces a dreamy state. In a group, users become giddy and lose perspective.

Marijuana is not physically addicting, but its long-term effects have been the subject of much debate. During the 1970s, it was reported that smoking pot caused a variety of physical and mental problems, including brain damage and mental illness. Although the dangers of pot and hash may have been overstated, use of these drugs does present some health risks, including an increased risk of lung cancer, chronic bronchitis, and other diseases. Marijuana smoking should be avoided by prospective parents because it lowers sperm counts in male users and females experience disrupted ovulation and a greater chance of miscarriage.[7]

Cocaine

cocaine A powerful natural stimulant derived from the coca plant.

Cocaine is an alkaloid derivative of the coca plant. When first isolated in 1860, it was considered a medicinal breakthrough that could relieve fatigue, depression, and other symptoms, and it quickly became a staple of patent medicines. When its addictive qualities and dangerous side effects became apparent, its use was controlled by the Pure Food and Drug Act of 1906.

Cocaine is the most powerful natural stimulant. Its use produces euphoria, restlessness, and excitement. Overdoses can cause delirium, violent manic behavior, and possible respiratory failure. The drug can be sniffed, or "snorted," into the nostrils, or it can be injected. The immediate feeling of euphoria, or "rush," is short-lived, and heavy users may snort coke as often as every 10 minutes. Another dangerous practice is "speedballing"—injecting a mixture of cocaine and heroin.

crack A highly addictive crystalline form of cocaine containing remnants of hydrochloride and sodium bicarbonate, which emits a crackling sound when smoked.

Crack is processed street cocaine. Its manufacture involves using ammonia or baking soda (sodium bicarbonate) to remove the hydrochlorides and create a crystalline form of cocaine that can be smoked. In fact, crack gets its name from the fact that the sodium bicarbonate often emits a crackling sound when the substance is smoked. Also referred to as "rock," "gravel," and "roxanne," crack gained popularity in the mid-1980s. It is relatively inexpensive, can provide a powerful high, and is highly addictive psychologically.

heroin A narcotic made from opium and then cut with sugar or some other neutral substance until it is only 1 to 4 percent pure.

Heroin

addict A person with an overpowering physical or psychological need to continue taking a particular substance or drug.

Narcotic drugs have the ability to produce insensibility to pain and to free the mind of anxiety and emotion. Users experience relief from fear and apprehension, release of tension, and elevation of spirits. This short period of euphoria is followed by a period of apathy, during which users become drowsy and may nod off. Heroin, the most commonly used narcotic in the United States, is produced from opium, a drug derived from the opium poppy flower. Dealers cut the drug with neutral substances (sugar or lactose), and street heroin is often only 1 to 4 percent pure.

Heroin is probably the most dangerous commonly used drug. Users rapidly build up a tolerance for it, fueling the need for increased doses to obtain the desired effect. At first heroin is usually sniffed or snorted; as tolerance builds, it is "skin popped" (shot into skin, but not into a vein); and finally it is injected into a vein, or "mainlined."[8] Through this progressive use, the user becomes an **addict**—a person with an overpowering physical and psychological need to continue taking a particular substance by any means possible. If addicts cannot get enough heroin to satisfy their habit, they will suffer withdrawal symptoms, which include irritability, depression, extreme nervousness, and nausea.

What kind of people become addicts? To find out, go to http://www.druglibrary.org/schaffer/Library/studies/cu/cu4.html

For an up-to-date list of Web links, go to www.wadsworth.com/product/0534573053s

Alcohol

alcohol Fermented or distilled liquids containing ethanol, an intoxicating substance.

Alcohol remains the drug of choice for most teenagers. More than 70 percent of high school seniors reported using alcohol in the past year, and more than 80 percent say they have tried it at some time during their lifetime; by the twelfth grade about two-

Alcohol abuse remains a serious problem among teens. Police in Florida are shown here stopping an automobile containing the potentially deadly combination of teens and alcoholic beverages. (© Joel Gordon)

thirds of American youth report that they have "been drunk."[9] More than 20 million Americans are estimated to be problem drinkers, and at least half of these are alcoholics.

Alcohol may be a factor in nearly half of all murders, suicides, and accidental deaths.[10] Alcohol-related deaths number 100,000 a year, far more than all other illegal drugs combined. About 1.5 million drivers are arrested each year for driving under the influence (including 14,000 teens), and more than 1 million more are arrested for other alcohol-related violations.[11] The economic cost is staggering. An estimated $117 billion is lost each year, including $18 billion from premature deaths, $66 billion in reduced work effort, and $13 billion for treatment.[12]

Considering these problems, why do so many youths drink to excess? Youths who use alcohol report that it reduces tension, enhances pleasure, improves social skills, and transforms experiences for the better.[13] Although these reactions may follow the limited use of alcohol, alcohol in higher doses acts as a depressant. Long-term use has been linked with depression and physical ailments ranging from heart disease to cirrhosis of the liver. Many teens also think drinking stirs their romantic urges, but scientific evidence indicates that alcohol decreases sexual response.[14]

Other Drug Categories

anesthetic drugs Nervous system depressants.

Anesthetic Drugs **Anesthetic drugs** are central nervous system (CNS) depressants. Local anesthetics block nervous system transmissions; general anesthetics act on the brain to produce loss of sensation, stupor, or unconsciousness. The most widely abused anesthetic drug is *phencyclidine (PCP),* known as "angel dust." Angel dust can be sprayed on marijuana or other leaves and smoked, drunk, or injected. Originally developed as an animal tranquilizer, PCP creates hallucinations and a spaced-out feeling that causes heavy users to engage in violent acts. The effects of PCP can last up to 2 days, and the danger of overdose is high.

inhalants Volatile liquids that give off a vapor, which is inhaled, producing short-term excitement and euphoria followed by a period of disorientation.

Inhalants Some youths inhale vapors from lighter fluid, paint thinner, cleaning fluid, or model airplane glue to reach a drowsy, dizzy state that is sometimes accompanied by hallucinations. **Inhalants** produce a short-term euphoria followed by a period of disorientation, slurred speech, and drowsiness. Amyl nitrite ("poppers") is a commonly used volatile liquid packaged in capsule form, which is inhaled when the capsule is broken open.

Sedatives and Barbiturates **Sedatives,** the most commonly used drugs of the barbiturate family, depress the central nervous system into a sleep-like condition. On the illegal market, sedatives are called "goofballs" or "downers" and are often known by the color of the capsules: "reds" (Seconal), "blue devils" (Amytal), and "rainbows" (Tuinal).

Sedatives can be prescribed by doctors as sleeping pills. Illegal users employ them to create relaxed, sociable feelings; overdoses can cause irritability, repellent behavior, and unconsciousness. Barbiturates are the major cause of drug-overdose deaths.

sedatives Drugs of the barbiturate family that depress the central nervous system into a sleep-like condition.

Tranquilizers **Tranquilizers** reduce anxiety and promote relaxation. Legally prescribed tranquilizers, such as Ampazine, Thorazine, Pacatal, and Sparine, were originally designed to control the behavior of people suffering from psychoses, aggressiveness, and agitation. Less powerful tranquilizers, such as Valium, Librium, Miltown, and Equanil, are used to combat anxiety, tension, fast heart rate, and headaches. The use of illegally obtained tranquilizers can lead to addiction, and withdrawal can be painful and hazardous.

tranquilizers Drugs that reduce anxiety and promote relaxation.

Hallucinogens **Hallucinogens,** either natural or synthetic, produce vivid distortions of the senses without greatly disturbing the viewer's consciousness. Some produce hallucinations, and others cause psychotic behavior in otherwise normal people.

One common hallucinogen is mescaline, named after the Mescalero Apaches, who first discovered its potent effect. Mescaline occurs naturally in the peyote, a small cactus that grows in Mexico and the southwestern United States. After initial discomfort, mescaline produces vivid hallucinations and out-of-body sensations.

A second group of hallucinogens are synthetic alkaloid compounds, such as psilocybin. These can be transformed into lysergic acid diethylamide, commonly called LSD. This powerful substance stimulates cerebral sensory centers to produce visual hallucinations, intensify hearing, and increase sensitivity. Users often report a scrambling of sensations; they may "hear colors" and "smell music." Users also report feeling euphoric and mentally superior, although to an observer they appear disoriented. Anxiety and panic may occur, and overdoses can produce psychotic episodes, flashbacks, and even death.

hallucinogens Natural or synthetic substances that produce vivid distortions of the senses without greatly disturbing consciousness.

Stimulants **Stimulants** ("uppers," "speed," "pep pills," "crystal") are synthetic drugs that stimulate action in the central nervous system. They produce increased blood pressure, breathing rate, and bodily activity, and mood elevation. One widely used amphetamine produces psychological effects such as increased confidence, euphoria, impulsive behavior, and loss of appetite. Commonly used stimulants include Benzedrine ("bennies"), Dexedrine ("dex"), Dexamyl, Bephetamine ("whites"), and Methedrine ("meth," "speed," "crystal meth").

Methedrine is probably the most widely used and most dangerous amphetamine. Some people swallow it; heavy users inject it. Long-term heavy use can result in exhaustion, anxiety, prolonged depression, and hallucinations. A new form of methamphetamine is a crystallized substance with the street name of "ice" or "crystal." Smoking this crystal causes weight loss, kidney damage, heart and respiratory problems, and paranoia.[15]

stimulants Synthetic substances that produce an intense physical reaction by stimulating the central nervous system.

Steroids Teenagers use highly dangerous **anabolic steroids** to gain muscle bulk and strength.[16] Black-market sales of these drugs approach $1 billion annually. Although not physically addicting, steroids can become an "obsession" among teens who desire athletic success. Long-term users may spend up to $400 a week on steroids and may support their habit by dealing the drug.

anabolic steroids Drugs used by athletes and body builders to gain muscle bulk and strength.

Millions of teens still smoke cigarettes. Some jurisdictions have gone as far as creating specialized "smoking courts." Here Angie Francos (left) and her daughter, Margarita Psi-hogios (right), 17, of Pembroke Pines, Florida, appear before Judge Steven Shutter (center) in Plantation, Florida, Oct. 9, 1998. Margarita was caught smoking on school grounds and was summoned to appear in Broward County's teen smoking court. (AP/Wide World Photos)

Steroids are dangerous because of the health problems associated with their long-term use: liver ailments, tumors, kidney problems, sexual dysfunction, hypertension, and mental problems such as depression. Steroid use runs in cycles, and other drugs—Clomid, Teslac, and Halotestin, for example—that carry their own dangerous side effects are often used to curb the need for high dosages of steroids. Finally, steroid users often share needles, which puts them at high risk for contracting HIV, the virus that causes AIDS.

designer drugs Lab-made drugs designed to avoid existing drug laws.

Designer Drugs **Designer drugs** are lab-created synthetics that are designed at least temporarily to get around existing drug laws. The most widely used designer drug is "ecstasy," which is actually derived from speed and methampetamine. After being swallowed, snorted, injected, or smoked, it acts simultaneously as a stimulant and a hallucinogen, producing mood swings, disturbing sleeping and eating habits, altering thinking processes, creating aggressive behavior, interfering with sexual function, and affecting sensitivity to pain. The drug can also increase your blood pressure and heart rate. Teenage users taking ecstasy at raves have died from heat stroke because the drug can cause dehydration.

Cigarettes Approximately twenty-five countries have established laws to prohibit the sale of cigarettes to minors. The reality, however, is that in many countries children and adolescents have easy access to tobacco products.[17] In the United States, the Synar Amendment, enacted in 1992, requires states to enact and enforce laws restricting the sale of tobacco products to youths under the age of 18. States are required to reduce illegal sales rates to minors to no more than 20 percent within several years. The FDA rules require age verification for anyone under the age of 27 who is purchasing tobacco products. The FDA has also banned vending machines and self-service displays except in adults-only facilities.

DRUG USE TODAY

Surveys show that marijuana continues to be the most widely used drug and that synthetic drugs such as ecstasy have become more popular. Some Western states report that methamphetamine ("speed," "crank") use is increasing and that its low cost and high potency has encouraged manufacturers ("cookers") to increase production. Other synthetics include PCP and LSD, the use of which is focused in particular areas of the country. Synthetics are popular because labs can easily be hidden in rural areas, and traffickers do not have to worry about border searches or payoffs to foreign growers or middlemen. Users like synthetics because they are cheap and produce a powerful, long-lasting high that can be greater than that provided by more expensive natural products such as cocaine.

Crack cocaine use has been in decline in recent years. Heavy criminal penalties, tight enforcement, and social disapproval have helped to lower crack use.[18] Although it was feared that abusers would turn to heroin as a replacement, there has been little indication of a new "heroin epidemic." Heroin use has stabilized in most of the country, although there are still hundreds of thousands of regular users in large cities.[19]

Arrest data show that the most frequent users are older offenders who started their heroin abuse decades ago. There is reason to believe heroin use is in decline among adolescents, possibly because it has acquired an extremely negative street image. Most youths know that heroin is addictive and destructive to health, and that needle sharing leads to HIV. Research conducted in New York City shows that most youths avoid heroin, shun users and dealers, and wish to avoid becoming addicts.[20]

Despite concern over these "hard drugs," the most persistent teenage substance-abuse problem is alcohol. Teenage alcoholism is sometimes considered less serious than other types of substance abuse, but it actually produces far more problems. Teenage alcohol abusers suffer depression, anxiety, and other symptoms of mental distress. Also, it is well-established that alcoholism runs in families; today's teenage abusers may become the parents of the next generation of teenage alcoholics.[21]

What do national surveys tell us about the extent of drug use and what have been the recent trends in teen usage?

The Monitoring the Future (MTF) Survey

One of the most important and influential surveys of teen substance abuse is the annual Monitoring the Future survey conducted by the Institute for Social Research at the University of Michigan. In all, about 45,000 students located in 433 secondary schools participate in the study.

The most recent MTF survey indicates that, with a few exceptions, drug use among American adolescents held steady in 2000, but declined from the recent peak levels reached in 1996 and 1997. As Figure 10.1 shows, drug use peaked in the late 1970s and early 1980s and then began a decade-long decline until showing an uptick in the mid 1990s; usage for most drugs has been stable or in decline since then. Especially encouraging has been a significant drop in the use of crack cocaine among younger kids. There has also been a continuing decline in cigarette smoking and the use of smokeless tobacco products. More troubling has been the use of ecstasy, which, because of its popularity at dance clubs and raves, rose among older teens (tenth- and twelfth-graders). In 2000, 5 percent of tenth-graders reported some use of ecstasy during the previous 12 months (up from 3% in 1998); 8 percent of the twelfth-graders also reported some use (up from about 4% in 1998). Similarly, the use of anabolic steroids by males in their early- to mid-teens has also increased (about 2.5% of twelfth-grade boys now take steroids), possibly because of the reported use of similar substances by respected athletes. Heroin use has remained fairly stable (1.5% of twelfth-grade boys are users) after the rates had roughly doubled between

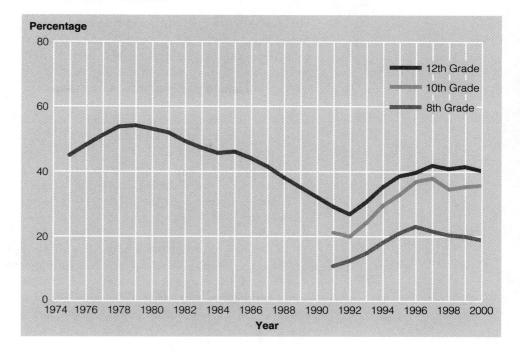

Figure 10.1
Trends in Annual
Prevalence of Illicit
Drug Use, 2000

Source: Monitoring the Future,
2000.

1991 and 1995, when non-injectable forms of heroin use became popular. It is possible that widely publicized overdose deaths of musicians and celebrities may have helped stabilize heroin abuse. Similarly, alcohol use among teens has been fairly stable over the past several years. Nonetheless, nearly one-quarter of eighth-graders, and half of twelfth-graders use alcohol regularly.

The PRIDE Survey

A second source of information on teen drug and alcohol abuse is the National Parents' Resource Institute for Drug Education (PRIDE) survey, which is also conducted annually. Typically, findings from the PRIDE survey correlate highly with the MTF drug survey. The most recent PRIDE survey (for the 1999–2000 school year) indicates decreases in drug activity in the last few years, specifically for marijuana, hallucinogens, cocaine, and inhalants. Students also reported decreasing their use of cigarettes and alcohol. About 24 percent of students in grades 6–12 claimed to have used drugs during the past year, down from 30 percent in 1995–1997 (Table 10.1). Cigarette smoking is also on a decline, from a high of 41 percent in 1996 to 32 percent today. The fact that two surveys generate the same pattern in drug abuse helps bolster their validity and give support to a decline in teenage substance abuse.

TABLE 10.1 Monthly Drug Use, 1998–99 vs. 1999–2000 Grades 6–12

	98–99	99–00	% rate of decrease
Cigarettes	23.5	18.8	20.0
Any alcohol	27.1	23.9	11.8
Any illicit drug	16.3	13.9	15.3

Source: Pride Survey, Pride Inc., 2001.

Are the Survey Results Accurate?

Student drug surveys must be interpreted with caution. First, it may be overly optimistic to expect that heavy users are going to cooperate with a drug-use survey, especially one conducted by a government agency. Even if willing, these students are likely to be absent from school during testing periods. Also, drug abusers are more likely to be forgetful and to give inaccurate accounts of their substance abuse.

Another problem is the likelihood that the most drug-dependent portion of the adolescent population is omitted from the sample. More than half of all youths arrested dropped out of school before the twelfth grade, and more than two-thirds of these arrestees are drug users (Figure 10.2).[22] Juvenile detainees (those arrested and held in a lockup) test positively for cocaine at a rate many times higher than those reporting recent use in the MTF survey.[23] The inclusion of eighth-graders in the MTF sample is one way of getting around the dropout problem. Nonetheless, high-school surveys may be excluding some of the most drug-prone young people in the population.

While these problems are serious, they are consistent over time and therefore do not hinder the *measurement of change* or trends in drug usage. That is, prior surveys also omitted dropouts and other high-risk individuals. However, since these problems are built into every wave of the survey, any change recorded in the annual substance-abuse rate is probably genuine. So, while the *validity* of these surveys may be questioned, they are probably *reliable* indicators of trends in substance abuse.

Checkpoints

✔ More than half of all high school–age kids have tried drugs.

✔ Of these drugs, the most commonly used is marijuana.

✔ Cocaine and crack use is on the decline.

✔ Alcohol remains the drug of choice for most teens.

✔ Ecstasy has become popular in recent years.

✔ Teenage drug use is measured by two national surveys, the Monitoring the Future Survey and the PRIDE survey.

✔ Both show that drug and alcohol use is on the decline.

WHY DO YOUTHS TAKE DRUGS?

Why do youths engage in an activity that is sure to bring them overwhelming problems? It is hard to imagine that even the youngest drug users are unaware of the problems associated with substance abuse. Although it is easy to understand dealers' desires for quick profits, how can we explain users' disregard for long- and short-term consequences?

Social Disorganization

One explanation ties drug abuse to poverty, social disorganization, and hopelessness. Drug use by young minority-group members has been tied to factors such as racial prejudice, low self-esteem, poor socioeconomic status, and the stress of living in a harsh urban environment.[24] The association between drug use, race, and poverty has been linked to the high level of mistrust and defiance found in lower socioeconomic areas.[25]

Despite a long association between social disorganization and drug use, the empirical data on the relationship between class and crime has been inconclusive. For example, the *National Youth Survey* (NYS), a longitudinal study of delinquent behavior conducted by Delbert Elliott and his associates, found little if any association between drug use and social class. The NYS found that drug use is higher among urban youths, but little evidence existed that minority youths or members of the lower class were more likely to abuse drugs than white youths and the more affluent.[26] Research by the

Figure 10.2
Drug Use Among
Juvenile Arrestees,
by Sex

Figure 10.2
Drug Use Among Juvenile Arrestees, by Sex

Source: Arrestee Drug Abuse Monitoring Program 1999 Annual Report, pp. 92, 95.

Denver: percent positive for drugs by sex

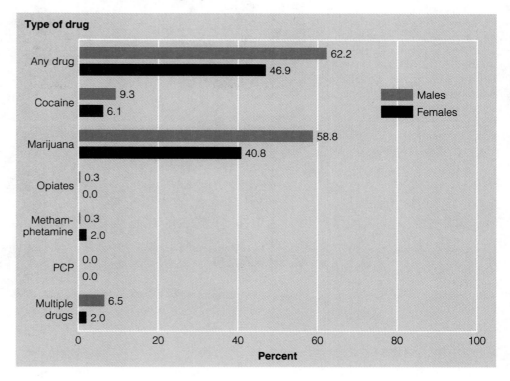

Portland: percent positive for drugs by sex

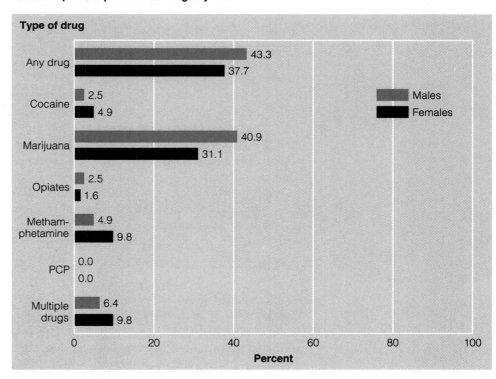

Rand Corporation indicates that many drug-dealing youths had legitimate jobs at the time they were arrested for drug trafficking.[27] Therefore, it would be difficult to describe drug abusers simply as unemployed dropouts.

The two young girls shown here are cooperating in a drug experience. Shared feelings and a sense of intimacy lead youths to become fully enmeshed in the "drug-use subculture." Drug users do in fact have intimate and warm relationships with substance-abusing peers, which help support their habits and behaviors. (© Joel Gordon)

Peer Pressure

Research shows that adolescent drug abuse is highly correlated with the behavior of best friends, especially when parental supervision is weak.[28] Youths in inner-city areas where feelings of alienation run high often come in contact with drug users who teach them that drugs provide an answer to their feelings of inadequacy and stress.[29] Perhaps they join with peers to learn the techniques of drug use; their friendships with other drug-dependent youths give them social support for their habit. Empirical research efforts show that a youth's association with friends who are substance abusers increases the probability of drug use.[30] The relationship is reciprocal: Adolescent substance abusers seek out friends who engage in these behaviors, and associating with drug abusers leads to increased levels of drug abuse.

Peer networks may be the most significant influence on long-term substance abuse. Shared feelings and a sense of intimacy lead youths to become enmeshed in what has been described as the "drug-use subculture."[31] Research indicates that drug users do in fact have warm relationships with substance-abusing peers who help support their behaviors.[32] This lifestyle provides users with a clear role, activities they enjoy, and an opportunity for attaining status among their peers.[33] One reason it is so difficult to treat hard-core users is that quitting drugs means leaving the fast life of the streets.

Family Factors

Another explanation is that drug users have a poor family life. Studies have found that the majority of drug users have had an unhappy childhood, which included harsh punishment and parental neglect.[34] The drug-abuse and family-quality association may involve both racial and gender differences: females and whites who were abused as children are more likely to have alcohol and drug arrests as adults; abuse was less likely to affect drug use in males and African Americans.[35] It is also common to find substance abusers within large families and with parents who are divorced, separated, or absent.[36]

Social psychologists suggest that drug-abuse patterns may also result from observation of parental drug use.[37] Youths who learn that drugs provide pleasurable sensations may be most likely to experiment with illegal substances; a habit may develop if the user experiences lower anxiety and fear.[38] Research shows, for example, that gang members raised in families with a history of drug use were more likely than other gang members to use cocaine and to use it seriously. Even among gang members parental abuse was a key factor in the onset of adolescent drug use.[39] Observing drug abuse may be a more important cause of drug abuse than other family-related problems.

Other family factors associated with teen drug abuse include parental conflict over childrearing practices, failure to set rules, and unrealistic demands followed by harsh punishments. Low parental attachment, rejection, and excessive family conflict have all been linked to adolescent substance abuse.[40]

Genetic Factors

To read more about the concept of addiction, go to The Psychedelic Library and read http://www.psychedelic-library. org/davies/myth4.htm

For an up-to-date list of Web links, go to www.wadsworth.com/ product/0534573053s

The association between parental drug abuse and adolescent behavior may have a genetic basis. Research has shown that biological children of alcoholics reared by nonalcoholic adoptive parents more often develop alcohol problems than the natural children of the adoptive parents.[41] A number of studies comparing alcoholism among identical and fraternal twins have found that the degree of concordance (both siblings behaving identically) is twice as high among the identical twin groups.[42]

A genetic basis for drug abuse is also supported by evidence showing that future substance-abuse problems can be predicted by behavior exhibited as early as 6 years of age. The traits predicting future abuse are independent from peer relations and environmental influences.[43]

Emotional Problems

addiction-prone personality
The view that the cause of substance abuse can be traced to a personality that has a compulsion for mood-altering drugs.

For a Web-based anti-drug education campaign, see Freevibe at http://www.freevibe.com/ index.shtml

For an up-to-date list of Web links, go to www.wadsworth.com/ product/0534573053s

Not all drug-abusing youths reside in lower-class urban areas. To explain drug abuse across social classes, some experts have linked drug use to emotional problems that can strike youths in any economic class. Psychodynamic explanations of substance abuse suggest that drugs help youths control or express unconscious needs. Some psychoanalysts believe adolescents who internalize their problems may use drugs to reduce their feelings of inadequacy. Introverted people may use drugs as an escape from real or imagined feelings of inferiority.[44] Another view is that adolescents who externalize their problems and blame others for their perceived failures are likely to engage in antisocial behaviors, including substance abuse. Research exists to support each of these positions.[45]

Drug abusers are also believed to exhibit psychopathic or sociopathic behavior characteristics, forming what is called an **addiction-prone personality**.[46] Drinking alcohol may reflect a teen's need to remain dependent on an overprotective mother or an effort to reduce the emotional turmoil of adolescence.[47]

Research on the psychological characteristics of narcotics abusers does, in fact, reveal the presence of a significant degree of pathology. Personality testing of users suggests that a significant percentage suffer from psychotic disorders. Studies have found that addicts suffer personality disorders characterized by a weak ego, a low frustration tolerance, and fantasies of omnipotence. Up to half of all drug abusers may also be diagnosed with antisocial personality disorder (ASPD), which is defined as a pervasive pattern of disregard for the rights of others.[48]

Problem Behavior Syndrome

For some adolescents, substance abuse is one of many problem behaviors that begin early in life and remain throughout the life course.[49] Longitudinal studies show that youths who abuse drugs are maladjusted, emotionally distressed, and have many

PROBLEM BEHAVIORS AND SUBSTANCE ABUSE

ccording to the *problem behavior syndrome* model, substance abuse may be one of a constellation of social problems experienced by at-risk youth. There is significant evidence to substantiate the view that kids who abuse substances are also more likely to experience an array of social problems. For example, a recent study of the relationship between adolescent illicit-drug use, physical abuse, and sexual abuse that was based on a sample of Mexican American and non-Hispanic white youths living in the southwestern United States found that youths who report physical and/or sexual abuse

are significantly more likely to report illicit drug use than those who have never been abused. As Figure A shows, 42 percent of youths who have experienced physical abuse report using marijuana in the last month, while only 28 percent of youths who have never been abused report using the drug within that time. These findings were independent of factors such as academic achievement and family structure, and they suggest that treatment directed at abused adolescents should include drug-use prevention, intervention, and education components.

Figure A
Percent of Youths Reporting Past-Month Marijuana or Past-Year Cocaine Use, by Type of Abuse (N=2,468)

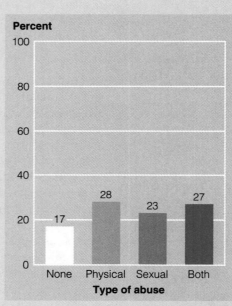

Note: These analyses were based on data collected between 1988 and 1992 for the Mexican-American Drug Use and Dropout Survey, a yearly survey of Mexican-American and non-Hispanic white school dropouts and a comparison group of enrolled students from one school district in each of three communities in the southwestern United States (see Chavez, Oetting, and Swaim, 1994).

Source: Pérez, D. M. "The Relationship Between Physical Abuse, Sexual Victimization, and Adolescent Illicit Drug Use," *Journal of Drug Issues* 30:641–62 (2000).

social problems.[50] Having a deviant lifestyle means associating with delinquent peers, living in a family in which parents and siblings abuse drugs, being alienated from the dominant values of society, and engaging in delinquent behaviors at an early age.[51] Youths who abuse drugs lack commitment to religious values, disdain educa-

Kids who abuse drugs and alcohol are also more likely to have educational problems. A recent study of substance use among Texas students in grades 7 through 12 found that those who were absent 10 or more days during the previous school year were more likely to report alcohol, tobacco, and other drug use. For example, twice as many students with high absentee rates reported using marijuana in the past month (29% vs. 14%, respectively) than students who did not miss school .

There is also a connection between substance abuse and serious behavioral and emotional problems. One national study found that behaviorally troubled youth are 7 times more likely than those with less serious problems to report that they were dependent on alcohol or illicit drugs (17.1% vs. 2.3%). In addition, youth with serious emotional problems were nearly 4 times more likely to report dependence (13.2% vs. 3.4%) (Figure B).

These studies provide dramatic evidence that drug abuse is highly associated with other social problems—abuse, school failure, and emotional disorders. They imply that getting kids off drugs may take a lot more effort than relying on some simple solution like "Just Say No."

Sources: Deanna Pérez , "The Relationship between Physical Abuse, Sexual Victimization, and Adolescent Illicit Drug Use," *Journal of Drug Issues 30*:641–62 (2000); Texas Commission on Alcohol and Drug Abuse, "Substance Use among Youths at High Risk of Dropping Out: Grades 7–12 in Texas, 1998," *Texas Commission on Alcohol and Drug Abuse Research Brief*, June 2000; Substance Abuse and Mental Health Services Administration, Office of Applied Studies, "The Relationship between Mental Health and Substance Abuse among Adolescents," Analytic Series: A-9, 1999. Data and tables supplied by the Center for Substance Abuse Research, University of Maryland, College Park (2001).

Figure B
Percent of Youth Aged 12 to 17 Reporting Dependence on Alcohol or Illicit Drugs, by Behavioral and Emotional Problem Scores,* 1994–1996

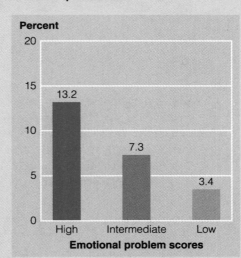

*Severity levels (high, intermediate, and low) for behavioral and emotional problem scale were determined using values set in the Youth Self-Report (YSR), an instrument extensively used in adolescent studies to assess psychological difficulties.

Source: Substance Abuse and Mental Health Services Administration, Office of Applied Studies, "The Relationship between Mental Health and Substance Abuse among Adolescents," Analytic Series A-9, 1999.

tion, and spend most of their time in peer activities.[52] Youths who take drugs do poorly in school, have high dropout rates, and maintain their drug use after they leave school.[53] This view of adolescent drug taking is discussed in the Focus on Delinquency, "Problem Behaviors and Substance Abuse."

Most experts believe that drug involvement begins with drinking alcohol at an early age, which progresses to experimentation with marijuana and finally to cocaine and then heroin. Though most recreational users do not progress to addictive drugs, few addicts begin their drug involvement with narcotics. (© Joel Gordon)

Rational Choice

Youths may choose to use drugs because they want to get high, relax, improve their creativity, escape reality, or increase their sexual responsiveness. Research indicates that adolescent alcohol abusers believe getting high will increase their sexual performance and facilitate their social behavior; they care little about negative consequences.[54] Substance abuse, then, may be a function of the rational, albeit mistaken, belief that substance abuse benefits the user.

PATHWAYS TO DRUG ABUSE

gateway drug A substance that leads to use of more serious drugs; alcohol use has long been thought to lead to more serious drug abuse.

While there is not single path to becoming a drug abuser, it is generally believed that most users start at a young age using alcohol as a **gateway drug** to harder substances. That is, drug involvement begins with drinking alcohol at an early age, which progresses to experimentation with marijuana, and finally to using cocaine and even heroin. Research on adolescent drug users in Miami found that youths who began their substance abuse careers early—by experimenting with alcohol at age 7, getting drunk at age 8, having alcohol with an adult present by age 9, and becoming regular drinkers by the time they were 11 years old—later became crack users.[55] Drinking with an adult present was a significant precursor of substance abuse and delinquency.[56]

Although the gateway concept is still being debated, there is little disagreement that serious drug users begin their involvement with alcohol.[57] Though most recreational users do not progress to "hard stuff," most addicts first experiment with recreational alcohol and recreational drugs before progressing to narcotics. By implication, if teen drinking could be reduced, the gateway to hard drugs would be narrowed.

What are the patterns of teenage drug use? Are all abusers similar, or are there different types of drug involvement? Research indicates that drug-involved youths do take on different roles, lifestyles, and behavior patterns, some of which are described in the next sections.[58]

Adolescents Who Distribute Small Amounts of Drugs

Many adolescents who use and distribute small amounts of drugs do not commit any other serious delinquent acts. They occasionally sell marijuana, "crystal," and PCP to support their own drug use. Their customers include friends, relatives, and acquaintances. Deals are arranged over the phone, in school, or at public meeting places; however, the actual distribution takes place in more private arenas, such as at home or in cars.

Petty dealers do not consider themselves "seriously" involved in drugs. One girl commented: "I don't consider it dealing, I'll sell hits of speed to my friends and joints and nickel bags [of marijuana] to my friends, but that's not dealing."

Petty dealers are insulated from the justice system because their activities rarely result in apprehension. In fact, few adults notice their activities because these adolescents are able to maintain a relatively conventional lifestyle. In several jurisdictions, however, agents of the justice system are cooperating in the development of educational programs to provide nonusers with the skills to resist the "sales pitch" of petty dealers.

Adolescents Who Frequently Sell Drugs

A small number of adolescents are high-rate dealers who bridge the gap between adult drug distributors and the adolescent user. Though many are daily users, they take part in many normal activities, including going to school and socializing with friends.

Frequent dealers often have adults who "front" for them—that is, sell them drugs for cash. The teenagers then distribute the drugs to friends and acquaintances. They return most of the proceeds to the supplier, keeping a commission for themselves. They may also keep drugs for their personal use, and, in fact, some consider their drug dealing as a way of "getting high for free." One young user, Winston, age 17, told investigators, "I sell the cracks for money and for cracks. The man, he give me this *much*. I sell most of it and I get the rest for me. I like this much. Every day I do this."[59] James Inciardi and his associates found that about 80 percent of the youths who dealt crack regularly were daily users.[60]

Frequent dealers are more likely to sell drugs in parks, schools, or other public places. Deals occur irregularly, so the chance of apprehension is not significant, nor is the payoff substantial. Robert MacCoun and Peter Reuter found that drug dealers make about $30 per hour when they are working and clear on average about $2,000 per month. These amounts are greater than most dealers could hope to have earned in legitimate jobs, but they are not enough to afford a steady stream of luxuries. Most small-time dealers also hold conventional jobs.[61]

Teenage Drug Dealers Who Commit Other Delinquent Acts

A more serious type of drug-involved youth is the one who distributes multiple substances and commits both property and violent crimes. These youngsters make up about 2 percent of the teenage population, but they may commit up to 40 percent of the robberies and assaults and about 60 percent of all teenage felony thefts and drug sales. Few gender or racial differences exist among these youths: girls are as likely as boys to become persistent drug-involved offenders, white youths as likely as black youths, middle-class adolescents raised outside cities as likely as lower-class city children.[62]

In cities, these youths frequently are hired by older dealers to act as street-level drug runners. Each member of a crew of 3 to 12 youths will handle small quantities of drugs; the supplier receives 50 to 70 percent of the drug's street value. The crew members also act as lookouts, recruiters, and guards. Although they may be recreational drug users themselves, crew members refrain from using addictive drugs such as heroin. Between drug sales, the young dealers commit robberies, burglaries, and other thefts.

Most youngsters in the street drug trade either terminate their dealing or become drug-dependent. A few, however, develop entrepreneurial skills. Those who are rarely apprehended by police advance in the drug business. They develop their own crews and may handle more than half a million dollars a year.

In many instances, these drug dealer-delinquents are members of teenage gangs. The gangs maintain "rock houses," or "stash houses," that receive drug shipments arranged by members who have the overseas connections and financial backing needed to wholesale drugs. The wholesalers pay the gang for permission to deal in their territory. Lower-echelon gang members help transport the drugs and work the houses, retailing cocaine and other drugs to neighborhood youths. Each member makes a profit for every ounce of rock sold. Police estimate that youths who work in rock houses will earn $700 and up for a 12-hour shift.[63]

Some experts question whether gangs are responsible for as much drug dealing as the media would have us believe. Some believe that the tightly organized "super" gangs are being replaced with loosely organized neighborhood groups. The turbulent environment of drug dealing is better handled by flexible organizations than by rigid, vertically organized gangs with a leader who is far removed from the action.[64]

Losers and Burnouts

Some drug-involved youths do not have the savvy to join gangs or groups and instead begin committing unplanned crimes that increase their chances of arrest. Their heavy drug use increases their risk of apprehension and decreases their value for organized drug distribution networks.

Drug-involved "losers" can earn a living by steering customers to a seller in a "copping" area, touting drug availability for a dealer, or acting as a lookout. However, they are not considered trustworthy or deft enough to handle drugs or money. Though these offenders get involved in drugs at an early age, they receive little attention from the justice system until they have developed an extensive arrest record. By then they are approaching the end of their minority and will either desist or become so entrapped in the drug–crime subculture that little can be done to deter their illegal activities.

Persistent Offenders

About two-thirds of substance-abusing youths continue to use drugs in adulthood, but about half desist from other criminal activities. Those who persist in both substance abuse and crime maintain these characteristics:

- They come from poor families.
- Other criminals are members of their families.
- They do poorly in school.
- They started using drugs and committing other delinquent acts at an early age.
- They use multiple types of drugs and commit crimes frequently.
- They have few opportunities in late adolescence to participate in legitimate and rewarding adult activities.[65]

Some evidence exists that these drug-using persisters have low nonverbal IQs and poor physical coordination. Nonetheless, there is little evidence to explain why some drug-abusing youths drop out of crime while others remain active.

Checkpoints

✔ Some kids take drugs because they live in disorganized areas that have a high degree of hopelessness, poverty and despair.

✔ There is peer pressure to take drugs and to drink.

✔ Kids whose parents take drugs are more likely to become abusers themselves.

✔ Some experts believe that drug dependency is a genetic condition.

✔ Youngsters with emotional problems may be drug-prone.

✔ Drug use may be part of a general problem behavior syndrome.

✔ Drug use may also be rational: kids take drugs and drink alcohol simply because they enjoy the experience.

✔ There are a number of pathways to drug abuse.

✔ Some users distribute small amounts of drugs, others are frequent dealers, while another group supplements drug dealing with other crimes.

✔ Some users are always in trouble and are considered burnouts.

DRUG USE AND DELINQUENCY

An association between drug use and delinquency has been established, and this connection can take a number of forms. Crime may be an instrument of the drug trade: Violence erupts when rival gangs use weapons to settle differences and establish territorial monopolies. In New York City, authorities report that crack gangs will burn down their rival's headquarters. It is estimated that between 35 and 40 percent of New York's homicides are drug-related.[66]

Drug users may also commit crimes to pay for their habits.[67] One study conducted in Miami found that 573 narcotics users *annually* committed more than 200,000 crimes to obtain cash. Similar research with a sample of 356 addicts accounted for 118,000 crimes annually.[68] If such proportions hold true, the nation's estimated 700,000 heroin addicts alone may be committing more than 100 million crimes each year.

Drug users may be more willing to take risks because their inhibitions are lowered by substance abuse. Cities with high rates of cocaine abuse are also more likely to experience higher levels of armed robbery. It is possible that crack and cocaine users are more willing to engage in a risky armed robbery to get immediate cash than a burglary, which requires more planning and effort.[69]

The relationship between alcohol and drug abuse and delinquency has been substantiated by a number of studies. Some have found that youths who abuse alcohol are most likely to engage in violence; as adults, those with long histories of drinking are more likely to report violent offending patterns.[70]

The National Institute of Justice's Arrestee Drug Abuse Monitoring (ADAM) program tracks trends in drug use among arrestees in urban areas. Some, but not all, of its 34 sites collect data on juveniles. The most recent (1999) report finds that, among juvenile detainees, more than 40 percent of juvenile males and 20 percent of juvenile females tested positive for marijuana, the most commonly used drug, and its prevalence was more than 6 times higher than cocaine use for both juvenile males and females.[71] In general, however, male detainees were more likely to test positive for the use of any drug than were female detainees. Figure 10.2 (page 247) shows the ADAM survey results for two cities, Denver, Colorado and Portland, Oregon, that collect data on juvenile detainees. Note that in Denver more than half of all juveniles, and in Portland about 40 percent, test positively for at least one drug, most commonly marijuana. While males and minority-group members have somewhat higher positive test rates than females and Caucasians, drug use is prevalent among juvenile arrestees, reaffirming the close association between substance abuse and criminality.

There is evidence that incarcerated youths are much more likely to be involved in substance abuse than adolescents in the general population. For example, research by

David Cantor on incarcerated youths in Washington, D.C. found their drug involvement more than double that of nonincarcerated area youths.[72]

Drugs and Chronic Offending

It is possible that most delinquents are not drug users but that police are more likely to apprehend muddle-headed substance abusers than clear-thinking abstainers. A second, more plausible, interpretation of the existing data is that the drug abuse–crime connection is so powerful because many criminals are in fact substance abusers. Research by Bruce Johnson and his associates confirms this suspicion. Using data from a national self-report survey, these researchers found that less than 2 percent of the youths who responded to the survey (a) report using cocaine or heroin, and (b) commit two or more index crimes each year. However, these drug-abusing adolescents accounted for 40 to 60 percent of all the index crimes reported in the sample. Less than one-quarter of these delinquents committed crimes solely to support a drug habit. These data suggest that a small core of substance-abusing adolescents commits a significant proportion of all serious crimes. It is also evident that a behavior, drug abuse, that develops late in adolescence influences the extent of delinquent activity through the life course.[73]

The relationship between drug abuse and chronic offending is illustrated by Inciardi, Horowitz, and Pottienger's interviews with crack-involved youths in Miami. The 254 kids in their sample reported committing 223,439 criminal offenses during the 12 months prior to their interviews. It is not surprising that 87 percent of the sample had been arrested. The greater the involvement in the crack business, the greater the likelihood of committing violent crime. About 74 percent of the dealers committed robbery and 17 percent engaged in assault. Only 12 percent of the nondealers committed robbery and 4 percent engaged in assault.[74]

Explaining Drug Use and Delinquency

The association between delinquency and drug use has been established in a variety of cultures.[75] It is far from certain, however, whether (a) drug use *causes* delinquency, (b) delinquency *leads* youths to engage in substance abuse, or (c) both drug abuse and delinquency are *functions* of some other factor.[76]

Some of the most sophisticated research on this topic has been conducted by Delbert Elliott and his associates at the Institute of Behavioral Science at the University of Colorado.[77] Using data from the National Youth Survey, a longitudinal study of self-reported delinquency and drug use, Elliott and his colleagues David Huizinga and Scott Menard found a strong association between delinquency and drug use.[78] However, the direction of the relationship is unclear. As a general rule, drug abuse appears to be a *type* of delinquent behavior and not a *cause* of delinquency. Most youths become involved in delinquent acts *before* they are initiated into drugs; it is difficult, therefore, to conclude that drug use causes crime.

According to the Elliott research, both drug use and delinquency seem to reflect developmental problems; they are both part of a disturbed lifestyle. This research reveals some important associations between substance abuse and delinquency:

1. Alcohol abuse seems to be a cause of marijuana and other drug abuse because (a) most drug users started with alcohol, and (b) youths who abstain from alcohol almost never take drugs.

2. Marijuana use is a cause of multiple-drug use: about 95 percent of youths who use more serious drugs started on pot; only 5 percent of serious drug users never smoked pot.

3. Youths who commit felonies started off with minor delinquent acts. Few delinquents (1 percent) report committing felonies only.

The Elliott research has been supported by other studies also indicating that delinquency and substance abuse are part of a general pattern of deviance or problem behavior syndrome, such as association with an antisocial peer group and educational failure.[79] There seems to be a pattern in which troubled youths start by committing petty crimes and drinking alcohol and proceed to harder drugs and more serious crimes. Both their drug abuse and the delinquency are part of an urban underclass lifestyle involving limited education, few job skills, unstable families, few social skills, and patterns of law violations.[80]

DRUG CONTROL STRATEGIES

Billions of dollars are being spent each year to reduce the importation of drugs, deter drug dealers, and treat users. Yet, although the overall incidence of drug use has declined, drug use has concentrated in the nation's poorest neighborhoods, with a consequent association between substance abuse and crime.

A number of drug-control strategies have been tried. Some are designed to deter drug use by stopping the flow of drugs into the country, apprehending dealers, and cracking down on street-level drug deals. Another approach is to prevent drug use by educating would-be users and convincing them to "say no" to drugs. A third approach is to treat users so that they can terminate their addictions. Some of these efforts are discussed in the following sections.

Law-Enforcement Efforts

Law enforcement strategies are aimed at reducing the supply of drugs and, at the same time, deterring would-be users from drug abuse.

Source Control One approach to drug control is to deter the sale of drugs through apprehension of large-volume drug dealers, coupled with enforcement of drug laws that carry heavy penalties. This approach is designed to punish known dealers and users and to deter those who are considering entering the drug trade.

A major effort has been made to cut off supplies of drugs by destroying overseas crops and arresting members of drug cartels; this approach is known as *source control*. The federal government has been encouraging exporting nations to step up efforts to destroy drug crops and to prosecute dealers. Three South American nations—Peru, Bolivia, and Colombia—have agreed to coordinate control efforts with the United States. However, translating words into deeds is a formidable task. Drug lords fight back through intimidation, violence, and corruption. The United States was forced to invade Panama with 20,000 troops in 1989 to stop its leader, General Manuel Noriega, from trafficking in cocaine.

Even when efforts are successful in one area, they may shift production to another. For example, between 1994 and 1999, enforcement efforts in Peru and Bolivia were so successful that they altered cocaine cultivation patterns. As a consequence, Colombia became the premier coca-cultivating country when the local drug cartels encouraged growers to cultivate coca plants. When the Colombian government mounted an effective eradication campaign in the traditional growing areas, the cartel linked up with rebel groups in remote parts of the country for their drug supply.[81] Leaders in neighboring countries expressed fear when, in August 2000, the U.S. announced $1.3 billion in military aid to fight Columbia's rural drug dealers/rebels, assuming that success would drive traffickers over the border. [82]

Border Control Law-enforcement efforts have also been directed at interdicting drug supplies as they enter the country. Border patrols and military personnel have been involved in massive interdiction efforts and many billion-dollar seizures have been made. It is estimated that between one-quarter and one-third of the annual cocaine supply

Drug Abuse Resistance Education (D.A.R.E.) is an elementary school course designed to give students the skills for resisting peer pressure to experiment with tobacco, drugs, and alcohol. It is unique because it employs uniformed police officers to carry the anti-drug message to the students before they enter junior high school. Critics question whether the program is actually as effective as advertised. (© Joel Gordon)

shipped to the United States is seized by drug-enforcement agencies. Yet U.S. borders are so vast and unprotected that meaningful interdiction is impossible; between 240 and 340 tons of cocaine and 33 tons of heroin are imported each year.[83]

If all importation were ended, homegrown marijuana and lab-made drugs such as Ecstasy could become the drugs of choice. Even now, their easy availability and relatively low cost are increasing their popularity; they are a $10 billion business in the United States today.

Targeting Dealers Law-enforcement agencies have also made a concerted effort to focus on drug trafficking. Efforts have been made to bust large-scale drug rings. The long-term consequence has been to decentralize drug dealing and to encourage teenage gangs to become major suppliers. Ironically, it has proven easier for federal agents to infiltrate traditional organized crime groups than to take on drug-dealing gangs.

Police can also intimidate and arrest street-level dealers and users in an effort to make drug use so much of a hassle that consumption is cut back. Some street-level enforcement efforts have had success, but others are considered failures. "Drug sweeps" have clogged correctional facilities with petty offenders while proving a drain on police resources. These sweeps are also suspected of creating a displacement effect: stepped-up efforts to curb drug dealing in one area or city may encourage dealers to seek out friendlier territory.[84] People arrested on drug-related charges are the fastest growing segment of both the juvenile and adult justice systems. National surveys have found that juvenile court judges are prone to use a get-tough approach on drug-involved offenders. They are more likely to be adjudicated, waived to adult court, and receive out-of-home placements than other categories of delinquent offenders, including those who commit violent crimes.[85] Despite these efforts, juvenile drug use continues to grow, indicating that a get-tough policy is not sufficient to deter drug use.

Education Strategies

To go to the official site of D.A.R.E., check out

http://www.D.A.R.E.-america.com/index_3.htm

For an up-to-date list of Web links, go to www.wadsworth.com/product/0534573053s

Another approach to reducing teenage substance abuse relies on educational programs. Drug education now begins in kindergarten and extends through the twelfth grade. More than 80 percent of public school districts include these components: teaching students about the causes and effects of alcohol, drug, and tobacco use; teaching students to resist peer pressure; and referring students for counseling and treatment.[86] Education programs such as Project ALERT, based in middle schools in California and Oregon, appear to be successful in training youths to avoid recreational drugs and to resist peer pressure to use cigarettes and alcohol.[87] The most widely used drug prevention program, D.A.R.E., is discussed in the Policy and Practice box, "Drug Abuse Resistance Education."

Checkpoints

✔ There is a strong association between drug use and delinquency.

✔ Juvenile arrestees often test positive for drugs.

✔ Chronic offenders are often drug abusers.

✔ Though drug use and delinquency are associated, it is difficult to show that abusing drugs leads kids into a delinquent way of life.

✔ There are a number of drug-control strategies, some relying on law enforcement efforts and others on treatment.

✔ There are a number of drug education initiatives.

✔ D.A.R.E. is a popular school-based prevention program that has been the target of recent criticism; it is being revamped.

Community Strategies

Another type of drug-control effort relies on local community groups. Representatives of local government agencies, churches, civic organizations, and similar institutions are being brought together to create drug-prevention programs. Their activities include drug-free school zones, which encourage police to keep drug dealers away from schools; Neighborhood Watch programs, which are geared to reporting drug dealers; citizen patrols, which frighten dealers away from public-housing projects; and community centers, which provide an alternative to the street culture.

Community-based programs reach out to high-risk youths, getting them involved in after-school programs; offering counseling; delivering clothing, food, and medical care when needed; and encouraging school achievement. Community programs also sponsor drug-free activities involving the arts, clubs, and athletics. Evaluations of community programs have shown that they may encourage anti-drug attitudes and help insulate participating youths from an environment that encourages drugs.[88]

Treatment Strategies

Several approaches are available to treat users. Some efforts stem from the perspective that users have low self-esteem and use various techniques to build up the user's

DRUG ABUSE RESISTANCE EDUCATION (D.A.R.E.)

The most widely known drug education program, **Drug Abuse Resistance Education (D.A.R.E.),** is an elementary school course designed to give students the skills for resisting peer pressure to experiment with tobacco, drugs, and alcohol. It is unique because it employs uniformed police officers to carry the anti-drug message to the students before they enter junior high school. The program focuses on five major areas:

1. Providing accurate information about tobacco, alcohol and drugs

2. Teaching students techniques to resist peer pressure

3. Teaching students respect for the law and law enforcers

4. Giving students ideas for alternative for drug use

5. Building the self-esteem of students

The D.A.R.E. program is based on the concept that the young students need specific analytical and social skills to resist peer pressure and "say no" to drugs. Instructors work with children to raise their self-esteem, provide them with decision-making tools, and help them identify positive alternatives to substance abuse.

The D.A.R.E. approach has been adopted so rapidly since its founding 18 years ago that it is now taught in 75 percent of school districts nationwide and in 54 other countries. Millions of students have already taken the D.A.R.E. program. More than 40 percent of all school districts incorporate assistance from local law-enforcement agencies in their drug-prevention programming. New community policing strategies commonly incorporate the D.A.R.E. program within their efforts to provide services to local neighborhoods at the grassroots level.

Does D.A.R.E. Work?

While D.A.R.E. is popular with both schools and police agencies, national evaluations have not found it to have a big impact on student drug usage. For example, in a highly sophisticated evaluation of the program, Dennis Rosenbaum and his associates found that D.A.R.E. had only a marginal impact on student drug use and attitudes. Though D.A.R.E. may work better in some settings and with some groups than others, Rosenbaum found that it had little overall effect on substance-abuse rates. One of the most critical reviews of D.A.R.E. was conducted by psychologist Donald Lynam and his colleagues. They followed a cohort of sixth-grade children who attended a total of 31 schools. Twenty-three of the schools were randomly assigned to receive D.A.R.E. in the sixth grade, while the other eight received whatever drug education was routinely provided in their classes.

The research team assessed the participants yearly through the tenth grade and then recontacted them when they were 20 years old. They found that D.A.R.E. had no effect on students' drug use at any time through tenth grade. The 10-year follow-up failed to find any hidden or "sleeper" effects that were delayed in developing. At age 20, there were no differences between those who received D.A.R.E. and those who did not in their use of cigarettes, alcohol, marijuana or other drugs; the only difference was that those who received D.A.R.E. reported slightly lower levels of self-esteem at age 20, an effect that proponents were not aiming for.

Changing the D.A.R.E. Curriculum

While national evaluations have questioned the validity of D.A.R.E. and a few communities have discontinued its use, it is still widely employed in school districts around the United States. To meet criticism head on, D.A.R.E. began testing a new curriculum in 2001. The new program is aimed at older students and relies more on having them question their assumptions about drug use than on listening to lectures on the subject. The new program will work largely on changing social norms, teaching students to question whether they really have to use drugs to fit in with their peers. Emphasis will shift from fifth-grade students to those in the seventh grade, and will add a booster program in ninth grade, when kids are more likely to experiment with drugs. Police officers will now serve more as coaches than as lecturers, encouraging students to challenge the social norm of drug use in discussion groups. Students also do more role-playing in an effort to learn decision-making skills. There will also be an emphasis on the role of media and advertising in shaping behavior. The new curriculum is undergoing tests in 80 high schools and 176 middle schools—half the schools will continue using the curriculum they do now, and the other half will use the new D.A.R.E. program—so that the new curriculum may be scientifically evaluated.

Sources: Kate Zernike, "Antidrug Program Says It Will Adopt a New Strategy," *New York Times,* February 15, 2001, p.1; Donald R. Lynam, Rich Milich, Rick Zimmerman, Scott Novak, T.K. Logan, Catherine Martin, Carl Leukefeld, and Richard Clayton, "Project D.A.R.E.: No Effects at 10-Year Follow-Up," *Journal of Consulting and Clinical Psychology 67*:590–93 (1999); Dennis Rosenbaum, Robert Flewelling, Susan Bailey, Chris Ringwalt, Deanna Wilkinson, "Cops in the Classroom: A Longitudinal Evaluation of Drug Abuse Resistance Education (D.A.R.E.)", *Journal of Research in Crime and Delinquency 31*:3–31(1994); David Carter, *Community Policing and D.A.R.E.: A Practitioner's Perspective* (Washington, DC: Bureau of Justice Assistance, 1995).

The juvenile drug court is one example of how the juvenile justice system is trying to focus on teen substance abuse. Here, Tyler Anter, 15, kisses his grandmother, Sonja Curtis, after teasing her by putting on her hat at their home in Las Vegas, April 5, 2000. Anter is in the fourth phase of Clark County's juvenile drug court program. The innovative juvenile drug court program was the first in the nation when it began in 1995. Now it has 91 imitators and many success stories—and failures—to its credit. Read more about these and other specialized juvenile courts in Chapter 11. (AP/Wide World Photos)

multisystemic treatment (MST) Addresses a variety of family, peer, and psychological problems by focusing on problem solving and communication skills training.

sense of self. Some use psychological counseling, and others, such as the **multisystemic treatment (MST)** technique developed by Scott Henggeler, direct attention to family, peer, and psychological problems by focusing on problem solving and communication skills.[89] Henggeler has found that adolescent abusers who have gone through MST programs are less likely to recidivate than youths in traditional counseling services.[90]

Another approach is to involve users in outdoor activities, wilderness training, and after-school community programs.[91] More intensive efforts use group therapy, in which leaders try to give users the skills and support that can help them reject the social pressure to use drugs. These programs are based on the Alcoholics Anonymous philosophy that users must find the strength to stay clean and that support from those who understand their experiences can be a successful way to achieve a drug-free life.

Residential programs are used with more heavily involved drug abusers. Some are detoxification units that use medical procedures to wean patients from the more addicting drugs. Others are therapeutic communities that attempt to deal with the psychological causes of drug use. Hypnosis, aversion therapy (getting users to associate drugs with unpleasant sensations, such as nausea), counseling, biofeedback, and other techniques are often used.

Little evidence exists that these residential programs can efficiently terminate teenage substance abuse. Many are restricted to families whose health insurance will pay for short-term residential care; when the coverage ends, the children are released. Adolescents do not often enter these programs voluntarily, and most have little motivation to change.[92] A stay can stigmatize residents as "addicts" even though they never used hard drugs; while in treatment, they may be introduced to hardcore users with whom they will associate upon release. Evaluations of residential programs show that drug abuse is sometimes curtailed during the residential phase of treatment, but once the offender is returned to the community the abuse continues. Even programs that feature intensive aftercare show little evidence that substance abuse can be reversed through treatment.[93]

WHAT DOES THE FUTURE HOLD?

The United States appears willing to go to great lengths to fight the drug war. Law-enforcement efforts, along with prevention programs and treatment projects, have been stepped up. Yet all drug-control strategies are doomed to fail as long as youths want to take drugs and dealers find that their sale is a lucrative source of income. Prevention, deterrence, and treatment strategies ignore the core reasons for the drug problem: poverty, alienation, and family disruption. As the gap between rich and poor widens and the opportunities for legitimate advancement decrease, it should come as no surprise that adolescent drug use continues.

Some commentators have called for the **legalization of drugs.** This approach can have the short-term effect of reducing the association between drug use and crime (since, presumably, the cost of drugs would decrease), but it may have grave consequences. Drug use would most certainly increase, creating an overflow of unproductive people who must be cared for by the rest of society. The problems of teenage alcoholism should serve as a warning of what can happen when controlled substances are made readily available. However, the implications of decriminalization should be further studied: What effect would a policy of partial decriminalization (for example, legalizing small amounts of marijuana) have on drug-use rates? Does a get-tough policy on drugs "widen the net"? Are there alternatives to the criminalization of drugs that could help reduce their use?[94] The Rand Corporation study of drug dealing in Washington, D.C. suggests that law-enforcement efforts can have little influence on drug-abuse rates as long as dealers can earn more than the minimal salaries they might earn in the legitimate world. Only by giving youths legitimate future alternatives can hardcore users be made to forgo drug use willingly.[95]

legalization of drugs Decriminalizing drug use to reduce the association between drug use and crime.

To find out more about the federal government's drug control strategies, go to http://206.6.118.10/CRACK/EXEC.HTM

For an up-to-date list of Web links, go to www.wadsworth.com/product/0534573053s

SUMMARY

Drug abuse has been linked to juvenile delinquency. Among the most popular drugs are marijuana; cocaine and its derivative, crack; crystal; LSD; and PCP. However, the most commonly used drug is alcohol, which contributes to almost 100,000 deaths per year.

Self-report surveys indicate that, after years of decline, more teenagers are using drugs today than earlier in the decade. Surveys of arrestees indicate that a significant proportion of teenagers are drug users and many are high-school dropouts. The number of drug users may be even higher than surveys suggest, because surveys of teen abusers may be missing the most delinquent youths.

A variety of youths use drugs. Some are occasional users who might sell to friends. Others are seriously involved in both drug abuse and delinquency; many of these are gang members. There are also "losers," who filter in and out of the justice system. A small percentage of teenage users remain involved with drugs into adulthood.

It is not certain whether drug abuse causes delinquency. Many adolescents who break the law later abuse drugs. Some experts believe there is a common cause for both delinquency and drug abuse—perhaps alienation and rage.

Many attempts have been made to control the drug trade. Some have attempted to inhibit the importation of drugs, others have been aimed at closing down major drug rings, and a few have tried to stop street-level dealing. There have also been attempts to treat users through rehabilitation programs and to reduce juvenile use by educational efforts. Communities have mounted grassroots drives to reduce drug abuse. So far, these efforts have not been totally successful, although overall use of drugs may have declined somewhat.

KEY TERMS

substance abuse	addict	hallucinogens	multisystemic treatment
hashish	alcohol	stimulants	(MST)
marijuana	anesthetic drugs	anabolic steroids	legalization of drugs
cocaine	inhalants	designer drugs	
crack	sedatives	addiction-prone personality	
heroin	tranquilizers	gateway drug	

1. Discuss the differences among the various categories and types of substances of abuse. Is the term *drugs* too broad to have real meaning?

2. Why do you think youths take drugs? Do you know anyone with an addiction-prone personality?

3. What policy might be the best strategy to reduce teenage drug use: source control? reliance on treatment? national education efforts? community-level enforcement?

4. Under what circumstances, if any, might the legalization or decriminalization of drugs be beneficial to society?

5. Do you consider alcohol a drug? Should greater control be placed on the sale of alcohol?

6. Do TV shows and films glorify drug usage and encourage youths to enter the drug trade? Should all images of drinking and smoking be banned from TV? What about advertisements that try to convince youths how much fun it is to drink beer or smoke cigarettes?

VIEWPOINT

. . . [M]en control access to illicit drugs, and this may be seen as yet another way in which men limit women's social access and options. Moreover, the ways in which men obtain illicit drugs can be described as essentially secular, based, as they are, on the exchange of cash for a commodity. By contrast, the ways in which women obtain illicit drugs are almost always shown to revolve around some form of sexual manipulation or outright prostitution.

 To read more about adolescent girls and their drug abuse on InfoTrac® College Edition, go to Jessica Warner, Timothy R. Weber, and Ricardo Albanes, "Girls Are Retarded When They're Stoned: Marijuana and the Construction of Gender Roles among Adolescent Females," *Sex Roles: A Journal of Research* 4:25 (Jan. 1999). For more information, use *teenage drug use* as a subject guide.

Chapter 11

The History and Development of Juvenile Justice

American Correctional Association

ourteen-year-old Daphne A., a product of the city's best private schools, lives with her wealthy family in a luxury condo in a fashionable neighborhood. Her father is an executive at a local financial services conglomerate and earns close to a million dollars per year. Daphne, however, has a hidden, dark side. She is always in trouble at school, and teachers report she is impulsive and has poor self-control. At times she can be kind and warm, but on other occasions she is obnoxious, unpredictable, insecure, and demanding of attention. She is overly self-conscious about her body and has a drinking problem. Daphne attends AA meetings and is on the waiting list at High Cliff Village, a residential substance-abuse treatment program. Her parents seem intimidated by her, confused by her complexities; her father filed a harassment complaint against her once, saying she slapped him.

Despite repeated promises to get her life together, Daphne likes to hang out at night in a local park, drinking with neighborhood kids. On more than one occasion she has gone to the park with her friend and confidant Christopher G., a quiet boy who has his own set of personal problems. His parents have separated and he is prone to suffer severe anxiety attacks. Chris has been suspended from school and diagnosed with depression, for which he takes two drugs—Zoloft, an antidepressant, and Lorazepam, a sedative.

One night in the park, Daphne and Chris met up with Michael M., a 44-year-old man with a long history of problems with alcohol. After a night of drinking, a fight broke out and Michael was stabbed, his throat cut, and his body dumped in a pond. Soon after the attack, Daphne called 911, telling police that a friend "jumped in the lake and didn't come out." Police searched the area and found Michael's slashed and stabbed body in the water; he had been disemboweled by Chris and Daphne in an attempt to sink the body. When the authorities traced the call, Daphne was arrested; she confessed to police that she had helped Chris murder the victim.

During an interview with court psychiatrists, Daphne admits she participated in the killing but cannot articulate what caused her to get involved. She had been drinking and remembers little of the events. She said she was flirting with Michael and Chris stabbed him in a jealous rage. She speaks in a flat, hollow voice and shows little remorse for her actions. It was a spur-of-the-moment thing, she claims, and after all it was Chris who had the knife and not she. Later, Chris claims that Daphne instigated the fight, egged him on, taunting him that he was too scared to kill someone. Chris says that Daphne, while drunk, often talked of killing an adult because she hates older people, especially her parents.

Daphne's parents claim that, while she has been a burden with her mood swings and volatile behavior, she is still a child and can be helped with proper treatment. They are willing to supplement any state intervention with privately funded psychiatrists. They believe that, given this is her first real offense and she is just 14, home confinement with intense treatment is the best course. If Daphne is tried as a juvenile she can be kept in institutions until she is 17; the sentence could be expanded to age 21, but only if, while in custody, she is a behavior problem and demonstrates conclusive need for further secure treatment.

- Should the case of Daphne A. be dealt with in the juvenile court, even though the maximum possible sentence she can receive is 2 to 6 years?

- If not, over what kind of cases should the juvenile court have jurisdiction?

- How does the concept of *parens patriae* apply to cases such as Daphne A.?

- If you believe that the juvenile court is not equipped to handle cases of extremely violent youth, then should it be abolished?

The opening scenario is based on a true story. Fifteen-year-old Daphne Abdela was a troubled product of some of New York City's best private schools. Always in trouble, she had poor self-control, was overly self-conscious about her weight, and had a drinking problem. On March 11, 1998, Daphne pleaded guilty to manslaughter in the death of a drinking companion in Central Park. As a juvenile, she received a sentence of 3⅓ to 10 years in prison. (Jim Alcorn/ *New York Post* Pool/CORBIS)

In recent years many communities have seen significant declines in serious violent crime among teenagers. But even as rates of urban juvenile delinquency are declining, hundreds of thousands of cases like Daphne's (which is based on an actual New York City case) have rekindled debate over the juvenile justice system. According to some experts, the country has a long way to go before claiming victory over juvenile delinquency.[1] What kinds of punishment can society use to fit these crimes? How can such crimes be prevented? What reforms must be made in the juvenile justice system to rehabilitate adolescents such as Daphne? Or should we even try? Formulating effective policies to meet such challenges requires a clear understanding of the history and development of juvenile justice.

This chapter begins with a discussion of the major social changes leading to creation of the first modern juvenile court in Chicago in 1899. We then cover the reform efforts of the twentieth century, including the movement to grant children the procedural rights typically given to adult offenders. This discussion includes descriptions of some of the landmark Supreme Court decisions that have influenced present-day juvenile justice procedures.

The second part of this chapter presents an overview of the contemporary juvenile justice system and the various philosophies, processes, organizations, and legal constraints that dominate its operations. The chapter describes the process that takes a youthful offender through a series of steps, beginning with arrest and concluding with reentry into society. What happens to young people who violate the law? Do they have legal rights? How are they helped? How are they punished? Should juvenile killers be released from custody prior to their eighteenth birthday? Should the goal of the system be rehabilitation or punishment?

To help address such questions, we have included a discussion of the similarities and differences between the adult and juvenile justice systems. This discussion draws attention to the principle that children are treated separately. By segregating delinquent children from adult offenders, society has placed greater importance on the delinquent being a *child* rather than being a *criminal*. Consequently, rehabilitation rather than punishment has traditionally been the goal. Today, with children committing more serious crimes, the juvenile justice system is having great difficulty handling these offenders.

In the final section, we discuss the need for a comprehensive juvenile justice strategy and the role of the federal government in juvenile justice reform—the key element in funding state juvenile justice and delinquency prevention efforts.

JUVENILE JUSTICE IN THE NINETEENTH CENTURY

At the beginning of the nineteenth century, delinquent, neglected, and runaway children in the United States were treated the same as adult criminal offenders.[2] Like children in England, when convicted of crimes they received harsh sentences similar to those imposed on adults. The adult criminal code applied to children, and no juvenile court existed.

Through the early nineteenth century, various pieces of legislation were introduced to humanize criminal procedures for children. The concept of probation, introduced in Massachusetts in 1841, was geared toward helping young people avoid imprisonment. Many books and reports written during this time heightened public interest in juvenile care.

Despite this interest, no special facilities existed for the care of youths in trouble with the law, nor were there separate laws or courts to control their behavior. Youths who committed petty crimes, such as stealing or vandalism, were viewed as wayward children or victims of neglect and were placed in community asylums or homes. Youths who were involved in more serious crimes were subject to the same punishments as adults—imprisonment, whipping, or death.

Several events led to reforms and nourished the eventual development of the juvenile justice system: (1) urbanization, (2) the child-saving movement and growing interest in the concept of *parens patriae,* and (3) development of institutions for the care of delinquent and neglected children.

Urbanization

To learn more about this era, go to the Library of Congress Web page devoted to American history at

http://www.americaslibrary.gov/cgi-bin/page.cgi

For an up-to-date list of Web links, go to www.wadsworth.com/product/0534573053s

Especially during the first half of the nineteenth century, the United States experienced rapid population growth, primarily due to an increased birthrate and expanding immigration. The rural poor and immigrant groups were attracted to urban commercial centers that promised jobs in manufacturing. In 1790, 5 percent of the population lived in cities. By 1850, the share of the urban population had increased to 15 percent; it jumped to 40 percent in 1900, and 51 percent in 1920.[3] New York had more than quadrupled its population in the 30-year stretch between 1825 and 1855—from 166,000 in 1825 to 630,000 in 1855.[4]

Urbanization gave rise to increased numbers of young people at risk, who overwhelmed the existing system of work and training. To accommodate destitute youths, local jurisdictions developed poorhouses (almshouses) and workhouses. The poor, the insane, the diseased, and vagrant and destitute children were housed there in crowded and unhealthy conditions.

By the late eighteenth century, many began to question the family's ability to exert control over children. Villages developed into urban commercial centers and work began to center around factories, not the home. Children of destitute families left home or were cast loose to make out as best they could; wealthy families could no longer absorb vagrant youth as apprentices or servants.[5] Chronic poverty became an American dilemma. The affluent began to voice concern over the increase in the number of people in what they considered the "dangerous classes"—the poor, single, criminal, mentally ill, and unemployed.

Urbanization and industrialization also generated the belief that certain segments of the population (youths in urban areas, immigrants) were susceptible to the influences of their decaying environment. The children of these classes were considered a group that might be "saved" by a combination of state and community intervention.[6] Intervention in the lives of these so-called dangerous classes became acceptable for wealthy, civic-minded citizens. Such efforts included settlement houses, a term used around the turn of the twentieth century to describe shelters, or nonsecure residential facilities for vagrant children.

Child-Saving Movement

To read more about the child savers, go to http://www.ncjrs.org/criminal_justice2000/vol_2/02b2.pdf

For an up-to-date list of Web links, go to www.wadsworth.com/product/0534573053s

House of Refuge A care facility developed by the child savers to protect potential criminal youths by taking them off the street and providing a family-like environment.

The problems generated by urban growth sparked interest in the welfare of the "new" Americans, whose arrival fueled this expansion. In 1817, prominent New Yorkers formed the Society for the Prevention of Pauperism. Although they concerned themselves with attacking taverns, brothels, and gambling parlors, they also were concerned that the moral training of children of the dangerous classes was inadequate. Soon other groups concerned with the plight of poor children began to form. Their focus was on extending government control over youthful activities (drinking, vagrancy, and delinquency) that had previously been left to private or family control.

These activists became known as *child savers*. Prominent among them were penologist Enoch Wines; Judge Richard Tuthill; Lucy Flowers, of the Chicago Women's Association; Sara Cooper, of the National Conference of Charities and Corrections; and Sophia Minton, of the New York Committee on Children.[7] Poor children could become a financial burden, and the child savers believed these children presented a threat to the moral fabric of society. Child-saving organizations influenced state legislatures to enact laws giving courts the power to commit children who were runaways or criminal offenders to specialized institutions.

The most prominent of the care facilities developed by child savers was the **House of Refuge** in New York, which opened in 1825.[8] It was founded on the concept of protecting potential criminal youths by taking them off the streets and reforming them in a family-like environment. When the House of Refuge opened, the majority of children admitted were status offenders placed there because of vagrancy or neglect. Children were placed in the institution by court order, sometimes over parents' objections. Their length of stay depended on need, age, and skill. Once there, youths were required to do piecework provided by local manufacturers or to work part of the day in the community. The institution was run like a prison, with strict discipline and absolute separation of the sexes. Such a harsh program drove many children to run away, and the House of Refuge was forced to take a more lenient approach.

Despite criticism, the concept enjoyed expanding popularity. In 1826, the Boston City Council founded the House of Reformation for juvenile offenders. Similar institutions were opened in Massachusetts and New York in 1847.[9] The courts committed children found guilty of criminal violations, or found to be beyond the control of their parents, to these schools. Because the child savers considered parents of delinquent children to be as guilty as convicted offenders, they sought to have the reform schools establish control over the children. Refuge managers believed they were preventing poverty and crime by separating destitute and delinquent children from their parents and placing them in an institution.[10]

The philosophy of *parens patriae* was extended to refuge programs, which were given parental control over a committed child. Scholar Robert Mennel summarizes this attitude: "The doctrine of *parens patriae* gave refuge managers the best of two worlds, familial and legal: it separated delinquent children from their natural parents and it circumvented the rigor of criminal law by allowing courts to commit children, under loosely worded statutes, to specially created schools instead of jails."[11]

Were They Really Child Savers?

Debate continues over the true objectives of the early child savers. Some historians conclude that they were what they seemed—concerned citizens motivated by humanitarian ideals.[12] Modern scholars, however, have reappraised the child-saving movement. In *The Child Savers*, Anthony Platt paints a picture of representatives of the ruling class who were galvanized by immigrants and the urban poor to take action to preserve their way of life.[13] He claims

> *The child savers should not be considered humanists: (1) their reforms did not herald a new system of justice but rather expedited traditional policies which had been informally developed during the nineteenth century; (2) they implicitly assumed the natural dependence of adolescents and created a special court to impose sanctions on premature independence and behavior unbecoming to youth; (3) their attitudes toward delinquent youth were largely paternalistic and romantic but their commands were backed up by force; (4) they promoted correctional programs requiring longer terms of imprisonment, longer hours of labor, and militaristic discipline, and the inculcation of middle class values and lower class skills.[14]*

Other critical thinkers followed Platt in finding that child saving was motivated more by self-interest than by benevolence. For example, Randall Shelden and Lynn Osborne traced the child-saving movement in Memphis, Tennessee and found that its leaders were a small group of upper-class citizens who desired to control the behavior and lifestyles of lower-class youth. The outcome was ominous. Most cases petitioned to the juvenile court (which opened in 1910) were for petty crimes and status offenses, yet 25 percent of the youths were committed to some form of incarceration; more than 96 percent of the actions with which females were charged were status offenses.[15]

In summary, these scholars believe that the reformers applied the concept of *parens patriae* for their own purposes, including the continuance of middle- and upper-class values and the furtherance of a child labor system consisting of marginal and lower-class skilled workers.

In the course of "saving children" by turning them over to houses of refuge, the basic legal rights of children were violated: Children were simply not granted the same constitutional protections as adults.

Development of Juvenile Institutions

State intervention in the lives of children continued well into the twentieth century. The child savers influenced state and local governments to create institutions, called *reform schools*, devoted to the care of vagrant and delinquent youths. State institutions opened in Westboro, Massachusetts in 1848 and in Rochester, New York in 1849.[16] Institutional programs began in Ohio in 1850 and in Maine, Rhode Island, and Michigan in 1906. Children spent their days working in the institution, learning a trade where possible, and receiving some basic education. They were racially and sexually segregated, discipline was harsh, and their physical care was poor. Beverly Smith found that girls admitted to the Western House of Refuge in Rochester, New York during the 1880s were often labeled as criminal, but were in reality abused and neglected. They too were subject to harsh working conditions, strict discipline, and

RESCUE.

HOMELESS.

OFF FOR THE WEST.

THE YOUNG FARMER.

ADOPTED.

To read more about the life of Charles Loring Brace, go to http://longman.awl.com/nash/ primarysource_21_4.htm

For an up-to-date list of Web links, go to www.wadsworth.com/ product/0534573053s

Children's Aid Society
Child-saving organization that took children from the streets of large cities and placed them with farm families on the prairie.

intensive labor.[17] Most of these institutions received state support, unlike the privately funded houses of refuge and settlement houses.

Although some viewed reform schools as humanitarian answers to poorhouses and prisons, many were opposed to such programs. As an alternative, New York philanthropist Charles Loring Brace helped develop the **Children's Aid Society** in 1853.[18] Brace's formula for dealing with delinquent youths was to rescue them from the harsh environment of the city and provide them with temporary shelter.

Deciding there were simply too many needy children to care for in New York City, and believing the urban environment was injurious to children, Brace devised what he called his *placing-out plan* to send these children to western farms where they could be cared for and find a home. They were placed on what became known as **orphan trains,** which made pre-announced stops in Western farming communities. Families

orphan train A practice of the Children's Aid Society in which urban youths were sent West on trains for adoption with local farm couples.

wishing to take in children would meet the train, be briefly introduced to the passengers, and leave with one of the children. Brace's plan was activated in 1854 and very soon copied by other child-care organizations. Though the majority of the children benefited from the plan and did find a new life, others were less successful and some were exploited and harmed by the experience. By 1930, political opposition to Brace's plan, coupled with the negative effects of the economic depression, spelled the end of the orphan trains, but not before 150,000 children were placed in rural homesteads.

Society for the Prevention of Cruelty to Children (SPCC) First established in 1874, these organizations protected children subjected to cruelty and neglect at home or at school.

Society for the Prevention of Cruelty to Children (SPCC) In 1874, the first **Society for the Prevention of Cruelty to Children (SPCC)** was established in New York; by 1900 there were 300 such societies in the United States.[19] Leaders of the SPCCs were concerned that abused boys would become lower-class criminals and that mistreated young girls might become sexually promiscuous women. A growing crime rate and concern about a rapidly changing population served to swell SPCC membership. In addition, these organizations protected children who had been subjected to cruelty and neglect at home and at school.

SPCC groups influenced state legislatures to pass statutes protecting children from parents who did not provide them with adequate food and clothing or made them beg or work in places where liquor was sold.[20] Criminal penalties were created for negligent parents, and provisions were established for removing children from the home. In some states, agents of the SPCC could actually arrest abusive parents; in others, they would inform the police about suspected abuse cases and accompany officers when they made an arrest.[21]

The organization and control of SPCCs varied widely. For example, the New York City SPCC was a city agency supported by municipal funds. It conducted investigations of delinquent and neglected children for the court. In contrast, the Boston SPCC emphasized delinquency prevention and worked with social welfare groups; the Philadelphia SPCC emphasized family unity and was involved with other charities.[22]

A CENTURY OF JUVENILE JUSTICE

Although reform groups continued to lobby for government control over children, the committing of children under the doctrine of *parens patriae* without due process of law began to be questioned. Could the state incarcerate children who had not violated the criminal law? Should children be held in the same facilities that housed adults? Serious problems challenged the effectiveness of the existing system: institutional deficiencies, the absence of due process for poor, ignorant, and noncriminal delinquents, and the treatment of these children by inadequate private organizations all spurred the argument that a juvenile court should be established.

Increasing delinquency rates also hastened the development of a juvenile court. Theodore Ferdinand's analysis of the Boston juvenile court found that in the 1820s and 1830s very few juveniles were charged with serious offenses. By 1850, juvenile delinquency was the fastest growing component of the local crime problem.[23] Ferdinand concluded that the flow of juvenile cases strengthened the argument that juveniles needed their own court.

Checkpoints

✔ The movement to treat children in trouble with the law as a separate category began in the nineteenth century.

✔ Urbanization created a growing number of at-risk youth in the nation's cities.

✔ The child savers sought to control children of the lower classes.

✔ The House of Refuge was developed to care for unwanted or abandoned youth.

✔ Some critics now believe that the child savers were motivated by self-interest and not benevolence.

✔ Charles Loring Brace created the Children's Aid Society to place urban kids with farm families.

The Illinois Juvenile Court Act and Its Legacy

The child-saving movement culminated in passage of the Illinois Juvenile Court Act of 1899. The principles motivating the Illinois reformers were these:

1. Children should not be held as accountable as adult transgressors;
2. The objective of the juvenile justice system is to treat and rehabilitate rather than punish;
3. Disposition should be predicated on analysis of the youth's special circumstances and needs; and
4. The system should avoid the trappings of the adult criminal process with all its confusing rules and procedures.

This was a major event in the juvenile justice movement. Its significance was such that, by 1917, juvenile courts had been established in all but three states. Just what were the ramifications of passage of the Illinois Juvenile Court Act? The traditional interpretation is that the reformers were genuinely motivated to pass legislation that would serve the best interests of the child. U.S. Supreme Court Justice Abe Fortas took this position in the landmark 1967 *In re Gault* case:

> *The early reformers were appalled by adult procedures and penalties and by the fact that children could be given long prison sentences and mixed in jails with hardened criminals. They were profoundly convinced that society's duty to the child could not be confined by the concept of justice alone. . . . The child—essentially good, as they saw it—was to be made to feel that he was the object of the state's care and solicitude, not that he was under arrest or on trial. . . . The idea of crime and punishment was to be abandoned. The child was to be treated and rehabilitated and the procedures from apprehension through institutionalization were to be clinical rather than punitive.*[24]

The child savers believed that children were influenced by their environments. Society was to be concerned with what their problems were and how these problems could be handled in the interests of the children and the state.

Interpretations of its intentions differ, but unquestionably the Illinois Juvenile Court Act established juvenile delinquency as a legal concept. For the first time the distinction was made between children who were neglected and those who were delinquent. Delinquent children were those under the age of 16 who violated the law. Most important, the act established a court and a probation program specifically for children. In addition, the legislation allowed children to be committed to institutions and reform programs under the control of the state. The key provisions of the act were these:

- A separate court was established for delinquent and neglected children.

- Special procedures were developed to govern the adjudication of juvenile matters.

- Children were to be separated from adults in courts and in institutional programs.

- Probation programs were to be developed to assist the court in making decisions in the best interests of the state and the child.

Following passage of the Illinois Juvenile Court Act, similar legislation was enacted throughout the nation. The special courts these laws created maintained jurisdiction over predelinquent (neglected and dependent) and delinquent children. Juvenile court jurisdiction was based primarily on a child's noncriminal actions and status, not strictly on a violation of criminal law. The *parens patriae* philosophy predominated, ushering in a form of personalized justice that still did not provide juvenile offenders with the full array of constitutional protections available to adult criminal offenders. The court's process was paternalistic rather than adversarial. Attorneys were not required, and hearsay evidence, inadmissible in criminal trials, was admissible in the adjudication of juvenile offenders. Verdicts were based on a *preponderance of the evidence* instead of the stricter standard used by criminal courts, *beyond a reasonable doubt*, and children were often not granted any right to appeal their convictions.

The major functions of the juvenile justice system were to prevent juvenile crime and to rehabilitate juvenile offenders. The roles of the judge and the probation staff were to diagnose the child's condition and prescribe programs to alleviate it. Until 1967, judgments about children's actions and consideration for their constitutional rights had been secondary.

By the 1920s, noncriminal behavior in the form of incorrigibility and truancy from school was added to the jurisdiction of many juvenile court systems. Of particular interest was the sexual behavior of young girls, and the juvenile court enforced a strict moral code on working-class girls, not hesitating to incarcerate those who were sexually active.[25] Programs of all kinds, including individualized counseling and institutional care, were used to *cure* juvenile criminality.

By 1925, juvenile courts existed in virtually every jurisdiction in every state. Although the juvenile court concept expanded rapidly, it cannot be said that each state implemented it thoroughly. Some jurisdictions established elaborate juvenile court systems, whereas others passed legislation but provided no services. Some courts had trained juvenile court judges; others had nonlawyers sitting in juvenile cases. Some courts had extensive probation departments; others had untrained probation personnel.

Great diversity also marked juvenile institutions. Some maintained a lenient orientation, but others relied on harsh punishments, including beatings, straitjacket restraints, immersion in cold water, and solitary confinement with a diet of bread and water.

These conditions were exacerbated by the rapid growth in the juvenile institutional population. Between 1890 and 1920, the number of institutionalized youths jumped 112 percent, a rise that far exceeded the increase in the total number of adolescents in the United States.[26] Although social workers and court personnel deplored the increased institutionalization of youth, the growth was due in part to the successful efforts by reformers to close poorhouses, thereby creating a need for institutions to house their displaced populations. In addition, the lack of a coherent national policy on needy children allowed private entrepreneurs to fill the void.[27] Although the increase in institutionalization seemed contrary to the goal of rehabilitation, such an approach was preferable to the poorhouse and the streets.

Reforming the System

Reform of this system was slow in coming. In 1912, the U.S. Children's Bureau was formed as the first federal child-welfare agency. By the 1930s, the bureau began to investigate the state of juvenile institutions and tried to expose some of their more repressive aspects.[28] After World War II, critics such as Paul Tappan and Francis Allen began to identify problems in the juvenile justice system, among which were the neglect of procedural rights and the warehousing of youth in ineffective institutions. Status offenders commonly were housed with delinquents and given sentences that were more punitive than those given to delinquents.[29]

From its origin, the juvenile court system denied children procedural rights normally available to adult offenders. Due-process rights, such as representation by counsel, a jury trial, freedom from self-incrimination, and freedom from unreasonable search and seizure were not considered essential for the juvenile court system because its primary purpose was not punishment but rehabilitation. However, the dream of trying to rehabilitate children was not achieved. Individual treatment approaches failed, and delinquency rates soared.

Reform efforts, begun in earnest in the 1960s, changed the face of the juvenile justice system. In 1962, New York passed legislation creating a family court system.[30] The new court assumed responsibility for all matters involving family life, with emphasis on delinquent and neglected children. In addition, the legislation established the PINS classification (person in need of supervision). This category included individuals involved in such actions as truancy and incorrigibility. By using labels like PINS and CHINS (children in need of supervision) to establish jurisdiction over children, juvenile courts expanded their role as social agencies. Because noncriminal children were now involved in the juvenile court system to a greater degree, many juvenile courts had to improve their social services. Efforts were made to personalize the system of justice for children. These reforms were soon followed by a due-process revolution, which ushered in an era of procedural rights for court-adjudicated youth. The next section discusses some key cases that transformed the practice of juvenile justice.

In the 1960s and 1970s, the U.S. Supreme Court radically altered the juvenile justice system when it issued a series of decisions that established the right of juveniles to receive due process of law.[31] The Court established that juveniles had the same rights as adults in important areas of trial process, including the right to confront witnesses, notice of charges, and the right to counsel. Table 11.1 illustrates some of the most important legal cases bringing procedural due process to the juvenile justice process.

Federal Commissions In addition to the legal revolution brought about by the Supreme Court, a series of national commissions sponsored by the federal government helped change the shape of juvenile justice. In 1967, the *President's Commission on Law Enforcement and the Administration of Justice*, organized by President Lyndon Johnson, suggested that the juvenile justice system must provide underprivileged youths with opportunities for success, including jobs and education. The commission also recognized the need to develop effective law-enforcement procedures to control hard-core offenders, while at the same time granting them due process. The commission's report acted as a catalyst for passage of the federal *Juvenile Delinquency Prevention and Control (JDP) Act of 1968*. This law created a Youth Development and Delinquency Prevention Administration, which concentrated on helping states develop new juvenile justice programs, particularly those involving diversion of youth, decriminalization, and decarceration. In 1968, Congress also passed the *Omnibus Safe Streets and Crime Control Act*.[32] Title I of this law established the **Law Enforcement Assistance Administration (LEAA)** to provide federal funds for improving the adult and juvenile justice systems. In 1972, Congress amended the JDP Act to allow the LEAA to focus its funding on juvenile justice and delinquency-prevention programs. State and local governments were required to develop and adopt comprehensive plans to obtain federal assistance.

Because crime continued to receive much publicity, a second effort called the *National Advisory Commission on Criminal Justice Standards and Goals* was established in 1973 by the Nixon administration.[33] Its report identified such strategies as (1) preventing delinquent behavior, (2) developing diversion activities, (3) establishing dispositional alternatives, (4) providing due process for all juveniles, and (5) controlling violent and chronic delinquents. This commission's recommendations formed the basis for the *Juvenile Justice and Delinquency Prevention Act of 1974*.[34] This act eliminated the Youth Development and Delinquency Prevention Administration and replaced it with the **Office of Juvenile Justice and Delinquency Prevention (OJJDP)** within the LEAA. In 1980, the LEAA was phased out, and the OJJDP became an independent agency in the Department of Justice. Throughout the 1970s, its two most important goals were (1) removing juveniles from detention in adult jails, and (2) eliminating the incarceration together of delinquents and status offenders. During this period, the OJJDP stressed the creation of formal diversion and restitution programs.

The latest effort was the *Violent Crime Control and Law Enforcement Act of 1994*.[35] The largest piece of crime legislation in the history of the United States, it provided 100,000 new police officers and billions of dollars for prisons and prevention programs

Law Enforcement Assistance Administration (LEAA) Unit in the U.S. Department of Justice established by the Omnibus Crime Control and Safe Streets Act of 1968 to administer grants and provide guidance for crime prevention policy and programs.

Office of Juvenile Justice and Delinquency Prevention (OJJDP) Branch of the U.S. Justice Department charged with shaping national juvenile justice policy through disbursement of federal aid and research funds.

To read about the Juvenile Justice and Delinquency Prevention Act of 1974, go to http://ojjdp.ncjrs.org/about/ojjjjact.txt

For an up-to-date list of Web links, go to www.wadsworth.com/product/0534573053s

TABLE 11.1

Leading Constitutional Cases in Juvenile Justice

***Oklahoma Publishing Co. v. District Court* (1977)** ruled that a state court could not prohibit the publication of information obtained in an open juvenile proceeding. When photographs were taken and published of an eleven-year-old boy suspected of homicide and the local court prohibited further disclosure, the publishing company claimed that the court order was a restraint in violation of the First Amendment. The Supreme Court agreed.

***Smith v. Daily Mail Publishing Co.* (1979)** involved the discovery and subsequent publication of the identity of a juvenile suspect in violation of a state statute prohibiting publication. The Supreme Court declared the statute unconstitutional because it believed the state's interest in protecting the child was not of such magnitude as to justify the use of a criminal statute. Criminal trials are open to the public, but juvenile proceedings are meant to be private and confidential, which ordinarily does not violate the First Amendment right to free press discussed in the above two cases.

***Fare v. Michael C.* (1979)** held that a child's request to see his probation officer at the time of interrogation did not operate to invoke his Fifth Amendment right to remain silent. According to the Court, the probation officer cannot be expected to offer the type of advice that an accused would expect from an attorney. The landmark *Miranda v. Arizona* case ruled that a request for a lawyer is an immediate revocation of a person's right to silence, but this rule is not applicable for a request to see the probation officer.

***Eddings v. Oklahoma* (1982)** ruled that a defendant's age should be a mitigating factor in deciding whether to apply the death penalty.

***Schall v. Martin* (1984)** upheld a statute allowing for the placement of children in preventive detention before their adjudication. The Court concluded that it was not unreasonable to detain juveniles for their own protection.

***New Jersey v. T.L.O.* (1984)** determined that the Fourth Amendment applies to school searches. The Court adopted a "reasonable suspicion" standard, as opposed to the stricter standard of "probable cause," to evaluate the legality of searches and seizures in a school setting.

***Thompson v. Oklahoma* (1988)** ruled that imposing capital punishment on a juvenile murderer who was fifteen years old at the time of the offense violated the Eighth Amendment's constitutional prohibition against cruel and unusual punishment.

***Stanford v. Kentucky* and *Wilkins v. Missouri* (1989)** concluded that the imposition of the death penalty on a juvenile who committed a crime between the ages of sixteen and eighteen was not unconstitutional and that the Eighth Amendment's cruel and unusual punishment clause did not prohibit capital punishment.

***Vernonia School District v. Acton* (1995)** held that the Fourth Amendment's guarantee against unreasonable searches is not violated by the suspicionless drug testing of all students choosing to participate in interscholastic athletics. The Supreme Court expanded power of public educators to ensure safe learning environments in schools.

***United States v. Lopez* (1995)** ruled that Congress exceeded its authority under the Commerce Clause when it passed the Gun-Free School Zone Act, which made it a federal crime to possess a firearm within one thousand feet of a school.

Sources: *Oklahoma Publishing Co. v. District Court,* 430 U.S. 308, 97 S.Ct. 1045, 51 L.Ed. 2d (1977); *Smith v. Daily Mail Publishing Co.,* 443 U.S. 97, 99 S.Ct. 2667, 61 L.Ed. 2d 399 (1979); *Fare v. Michael C.,* 442 U.S. 707, 99 S.Ct. 2560 (1979); *Eddings v. Oklahoma,* 455 U.S. 104, 102 S.Ct. 869, 71 L.Ed. 2d 1 (1982); *Schall v. Martin,* 467 U.S. 253, 104 S.Ct. 2403 (1984); *New Jersey v. T.L.O.,* 469 U.S. 325, 105 S.Ct. 733 (1985); *Thompson v. Oklahoma,* 487 U.S. 815, 108 S.Ct. 2687, 101 L.Ed. 2d 702 (1988); *Stanford v. Kentucky,* 492 U.S., 109 S.Ct. 2969 (1989); *Vernonia School District v. Acton,* 515 U.S. 646 115 S.Ct. 2386, 132 L.Ed. 2d 564 (1995); *Wilkins v. Missouri,* 492 U.S. 361, 109 S.Ct. 2969 (1989); *United States v. Lopez,* 115 S.Ct. 1624 (1995).

In the 1982 case *Eddings v. Oklahoma*, the U.S. Supreme Court ruled that a defendant's age should be a mitigating factor in deciding whether to apply the death penalty. Should very young juvenile killers be eligible for capital punishment, or are they too immature to appreciate the seriousness of their misdeeds? (Copyright © 1998 Time, Inc. Reprinted by permission of TimePix)

for both adult and juvenile offenders. A revitalized juvenile justice system would need both a comprehensive strategy to prevent and control delinquency and a consistent program of federal funding.[36]

Checkpoints

✔ The juvenile court movement spread rapidly around the nation.

✔ Separate courts and correctional systems were created for youth.

✔ However, children were not given the same legal rights as adults.

✔ Reformers helped bring due-process rights to minors and create specialized family courts.

✔ Federal commissions focused attention on juvenile justice and helped revise the system.

JUVENILE JUSTICE TODAY

Today the juvenile justice system exercises jurisdiction over two distinct categories of offenders—delinquents and status offenders.[37] *Delinquent children* are those who fall under a jurisdictional age limit, which varies from state to state, and who commit an act in violation of the penal code. *Status offenders* are commonly characterized in state statutes as persons or children in need of supervision (PINS or CHINS). Most states distinguish such behavior from delinquent conduct to lessen the effect of any stigma on children as a result of their involvement with the juvenile court. In addition, juvenile courts generally have jurisdiction over situations involving conduct directed at (rather than committed by) juveniles, such as parental neglect, deprivation, abandonment, and abuse.

The states have also set different maximum ages below which children fall under the jurisdiction of the juvenile court. Many states include all children under 18, others set the upper limit at 17, and still others include children under 16.

Some states exclude certain classes of offenders or offenses from the juvenile justice system. For example, youths who commit serious violent offenses such as rape and/or murder may be automatically excluded from the juvenile justice system and treated as adults, on the premise that they stand little chance of rehabilitation within the confines of the juvenile system. Juvenile court judges may also transfer, or *waive*, repeat offenders who they deem untreatable by the juvenile authorities.

Today's juvenile justice system exists in all states by statute. Each jurisdiction has a juvenile code and a special court structure to accommodate children in trouble. Nationwide, the juvenile justice system consists of thousands of public and private agencies, with a total budget amounting to hundreds of millions of dollars. Most of the nation's police agencies have juvenile components, and there are more than 3000 juvenile courts and about an equal number of juvenile correctional facilities.

About 2.5 million juveniles are arrested annually; Figure 11.1 depicts the numbers of juvenile offenders removed at various stages of the juvenile justice process. These figures do not take into account the large number of children who are referred to community diversion and mental health programs. There are thousands of these programs throughout the nation. This multitude of agencies and people dealing with juvenile delinquency has led to the development of what professionals view as an incredibly expansive and complex juvenile justice system.

The Juvenile Justice Process

How are children processed by the juvenile justice system?[38] Most children come into the justice system as a result of contact with a police officer. When a juvenile commits a serious crime, the police are empowered to make an arrest. Less-serious offenses may also require police action, but in these instances, instead of being arrested, the child may be warned or a referral may be made to a social-service program. Only about half of all children arrested are referred to the juvenile court. Figure 11.2 outlines the **juvenile justice process,** and a detailed analysis of this process is presented in the next sections.

juvenile justice process
Under the paternal (*parens patriae*) philosophy, juvenile justice procedures are informal and nonadversarial, invoked *for* the juvenile offender rather than *against* him or her; a petition instead of a complaint is filed; courts make findings of involvement or adjudication of delinquency instead of convictions; and juvenile offenders receive dispositions instead of sentences.

Police Investigation When youths commit a crime, police have the authority to investigate the incident and decide whether to release the youths or commit them to the juvenile court. This is often a discretionary decision, based not only on the nature of the offense but also on conditions existing at the time of the arrest. Such factors as the seriousness of the offense, the child's past contacts with the police, and whether the child denies committing the crime determine whether a petition is filed. Juveniles in custody have constitutional rights similar to those of adult offenders. Children are protected against unreasonable search and seizure under the Fourth and Fourteenth Amendments of the Constitution. The Fifth Amendment places limitations on police interrogation procedures.

Detention If the police decide to file a petition, the child is referred to juvenile court. The primary decision at this point is whether the child should remain in the

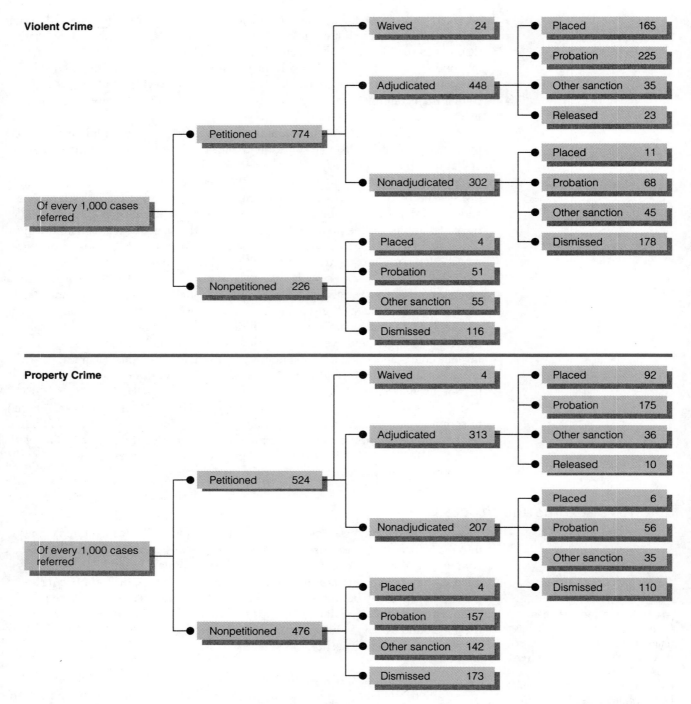

Violent Crime

Of every 1,000 cases referred

- Petitioned 774
  - Waived 24
  - Adjudicated 448
    - Placed 165
    - Probation 225
    - Other sanction 35
    - Released 23
  - Nonadjudicated 302
    - Placed 11
    - Probation 68
    - Other sanction 45
    - Dismissed 178
- Nonpetitioned 226
  - Placed 4
  - Probation 51
  - Other sanction 55
  - Dismissed 116

Property Crime

Of every 1,000 cases referred

- Petitioned 524
  - Waived 4
  - Adjudicated 313
    - Placed 92
    - Probation 175
    - Other sanction 36
    - Released 10
  - Nonadjudicated 207
    - Placed 6
    - Probation 56
    - Other sanction 35
    - Dismissed 110
- Nonpetitioned 476
  - Placed 4
  - Probation 157
  - Other sanction 142
  - Dismissed 173

Note: More than half (57%) of all formally processed cases in 1997 resulted in the youth being adjudicated delinquent. With the exception of criminal homicide, cases involving more serious offenses were more likely to be adjudicated than were other cases. The relatively low likelihood of adjudication for criminal homicide cases is because nearly one-third (31%) of these cases were judicially waived to criminal court for processing. As a result, petitioned criminal homicide cases were the most likely to receive a formal judicial response—either judicial waiver or adjudication.

The likelihood of adjudication also varied within the general offense categories. For example, within person offenses, 61% of petitioned robbery cases were adjudicated in 1997, compared with 51% of petitioned simple assault cases. In general, the more serious the charge, the more likely the case was to result in adjudication.

Figure 11.1

Case Processing of Typical Violent Crime and Property Crime in the Juvenile Justice System

Source: *Juvenile Court Statistics, 1997* (Washington, DC: Office of Juvenile Justice and Delinquency Prevention, 2000).

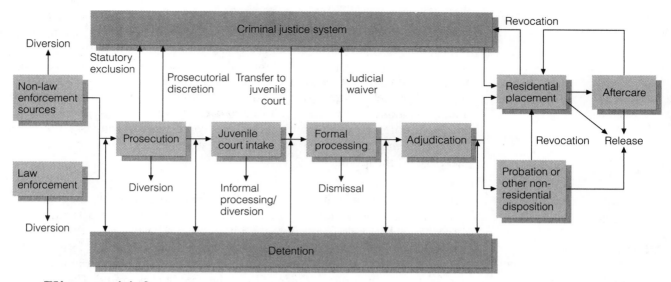

Figure 11.2
Case Flow through the Juvenile Justice Process

Source: This figure can be accessed online through the Office of Juvenile Justice and Delinquency Prevention at http://www.ojjdp.ncjrs.org/facts/casejpg.html.

detention hearing A hearing by a judicial officer of a juvenile court to determine whether a juvenile is to be detained or released while juvenile proceedings are pending in the case.

community or be placed in a detention facility or shelter home. In the past, children were routinely held in detention facilities to await court appearances. Normally, a **detention hearing** is held to determine whether to remand the child to a shelter. At this point, the child has a right to counsel and other procedural safeguards. A child who is not detained is usually released to a parent or guardian. Most state juvenile-court acts provide for a child to return home to await further court action, except when it is necessary to protect the child, when the child presents a serious danger to the public, or when it is not certain that the child will return to court. In many cases the police will refer the child to a community-service program instead of filing a formal charge.

Pretrial Procedures In most jurisdictions, the adjudication process begins with some sort of hearing. At this hearing juvenile court rules normally require that juveniles be informed of their right to a trial, that the plea or admission be voluntary, and that they understand the charges and consequences of the plea. The case will often not be further adjudicated if a child admits to the crime at the initial hearing.

In some cases, youths may be detained at this stage pending a trial. Juveniles who are detained are eligible for bail in a handful of jurisdictions. Plea bargaining may also occur at any stage of the proceedings. A plea bargain is an agreement between the prosecution and the defense by which the juvenile agrees to plead guilty for certain considerations, such as a lenient sentence. This issue is explored more thoroughly in Chapter 13, which discusses pretrial procedures.

adjudicatory hearing The fact-finding process wherein the juvenile court determines whether there is sufficient evidence to sustain the allegations in a petition.

If the child denies the allegation of delinquency, an **adjudicatory hearing** or trial is scheduled. Under extraordinary circumstances, a juvenile who commits a serious crime may be transferred or waived to an adult court. Today, most jurisdictions have laws providing for such transfers. Whether such a transfer occurs depends on the type of offense, the youth's prior record, the availability of treatment services, and the likelihood that the youth will be rehabilitated in the juvenile court system.

Adjudication Adjudication is the trial stage of the juvenile-court process. If the child does not admit guilt at the initial hearing and is not transferred to an adult court, an adjudication hearing is held to determine the facts of the case. The court hears evidence on the allegations in the delinquency petition. This is a trial on the merits (dealing with issues of law and facts), and rules of evidence similar to those of criminal proceedings generally apply. At this stage, the juvenile offender is entitled to many of the procedural guarantees given adult offenders. These include the right to counsel, freedom from self-incrimination, the right to confront and cross-examine witnesses, and, in certain instances, the right to a jury trial. In addition, many states have their own procedures concerning rules of evidence, competence of witnesses, pleadings, and pretrial motions. At the end of the adjudicatory hearing, the court enters a judgment against the juvenile.

Disposition If the adjudication process finds the child delinquent, the court must decide what should be done to treat the child. Most juvenile court acts require a dispositional hearing separate from the adjudication. This two-stage decision is often referred to as a **bifurcated process.** The dispositional hearing is less formal than adjudication. Here, the judge imposes a **disposition** on the offender in light of the offense, the youth's prior record, and his or her family background. The judge can prescribe a wide range of dispositions, ranging from a reprimand to probation to institutional commitment. In theory, the judge's decision serves the best interests of the child, the family, and the community.

Treatment After disposition in juvenile court, delinquent offenders may be placed in some form of correctional treatment. Probation is the most commonly used formal sentence for juvenile offenders, and many states require that a youth fail on probation before being sent to an institution (unless the criminal act is extremely serious). Probation involves placing the child under the supervision of the juvenile probation department for the purpose of community treatment. The most severe of the statutory dispositions available to the juvenile court involves commitment of the child to an institution. The committed child may be sent to a state training school or a private residential treatment facility. These are usually minimum-security facilities with small populations and an emphasis on treatment and education. Some states, however, maintain facilities with populations of over a thousand youths. Currently there are more than 100,000 youths in some form of correctional institution.

Some jurisdictions allow for a program of juvenile aftercare or parole. A youth can be paroled from an institution and placed under the supervision of a parole officer. This means that he or she will complete the period of confinement in the community and receive assistance from the parole officer in the form of counseling, school referral, and vocational training.

Juveniles who are committed to programs of treatment and control have a legal right to treatment. States are required to provide suitable rehabilitation programs that include counseling, education, and vocational services. Appellate courts have ruled that, if such minimum treatment is not provided, individuals must be released from confinement.

Conflicting Values in Juvenile Justice This overview of the juvenile-justice process hints at the often-conflicting values at the heart of the juvenile-justice system. Efforts to ensure that juveniles are given appropriate treatment are consistent with the doctrine of *parens patriae* that predominated in the first half of the twentieth century. (See Table 11.2 for a time line of ideologies of juvenile justice during the twentieth century.) Over the past century, the juvenile court has struggled to provide treatment for juvenile offenders while guaranteeing them constitutional due process. But the system has been so overwhelmed by the increase in violent juvenile crime and family

bifurcated process The procedure of separating adjudicatory and dispositionary hearings so different levels of evidence can be heard at each.

disposition The equivalent of sentencing for adult offenders, the juvenile disposition is aimed at rehabilitation rather than retribution.

TABLE 11.2   Time Frame of Juvenile Justice Ideology

Time Frame	Activity
Prior to 1899	Juveniles treated similarly to adult offenders. No distinction by age or capacity to commit criminal acts.
From 1899 to 1950s	Children treated differently, beginning with the Illinois Juvenile Court Act of 1899. By 1925 juvenile court acts are established in virtually every state.
1950s to 1970s	Recognition by experts that the rehabilitation model and the protective nature of *parens patriae* have failed to prevent delinquency.
1960s to 1970s	Constitutional due process is introduced into the juvenile justice system. The concept of punishing children or protecting them under *parens patriae* is under attack by the courts.
1970s to 1980s	Failure of rehabilitation and due process protections to control delinquency leads to a shift to a crime control and punishment philosophy similar to that of the adult criminal justice system.
Early 1990s	Mixed constitutional protections with some treatment. Uncertain goals and programs; the juvenile justice system relies on punishment and deterrence.
Mid-1990s to present	Attention given to strategy that focuses on reducing the threat of juvenile crime and expanding options for handling juvenile offenders. Emphasis is placed on "what works" and implementing the best intervention and control programs. Effort is made to utilize the restorative justice model, which involves balancing the needs of the victim, the community, and the juvenile.

breakdown that some judges and politicians have suggested abolishing the juvenile system. Even those experts who want to retain an independent juvenile court have called for its restructuring. Crime-control advocates want to reduce the court's jurisdiction over juveniles charged with serious crimes and liberalize the prosecutor's ability to try them in adult courts. In contrast, child advocates suggest that the court scale back its judicial role and transfer its functions to community groups and social service agencies.[39]

It is not surprising, then, that the current system reflects a multiplicity of values and viewpoints. In many instances, juveniles are now granted the same due-process rights (for example, competent legal counsel) as adult offenders. There are also efforts underway to reduce the stigma of a juvenile-delinquency label by diverting youth from the formal justice process and placing them in treatment-oriented programs. There are also conservative efforts at reform that have led both to a toughening of juvenile sentencing statutes and also to restrictions on cases which can be handled in juvenile courts; cases involving extreme violence and multiple recidivists are now routinely sent to the adult system. As a result of these conflicting practices, no single ideology or program dominates the juvenile justice system.

Elements of a comprehensive juvenile justice strategy are (1) prevention in early childhood; (2) intervention methods for at-risk teenage youths; (3) graduated sanctions to hold juvenile offenders accountable for juvenile crimes; (4) proper utilization of juvenile detention and confinement; and (5) the placement of serious juvenile offenders into adult courts. Here a youth worker lends a helping hand to a youngster, allowing him to build stronger ties to society. (© Glen Korengold/ Stock, Boston)

Despite these differences, it is likely that the juvenile court will remain a critical social institution; there are few viable alternatives. The question is not *whether* there will be a juvenile court but what form it will take. Changes in court jurisdiction might include some of the revisions listed in Table 11.3.

Checkpoints

✔ There has been a movement to toughen the juvenile justice system.

✔ There are a number of stages in the juvenile justice process, beginning with police investigation.

✔ One critical decision is whether a child should be detained prior to trail.

✔ The adjudicatory hearing is the trial stage of the process.

✔ If they are found to be delinquent, a proper sentence of disposition must be found.

TABLE 11.3	Possible Changes in the Juvenile Court System

1. Elimination of some of the courts' function by transferring more kids to the adult court and removing status offenders from court jurisdiction.
2. Expansion of the court's role over abuse and neglect cases.
3. Restructuring the juvenile court into a unified family court.
4. Utilizing alternative dispute resolution (ADR) techniques.
5. Integrating the juvenile court with the private sector and volunteer resources.
6. Creating a comprehensive juvenile justice system where there is an appropriate response for each child who comes before the court.

Source: The Center for the Future of Children, *The Juvenile Court* (Los Altos, CA: David and Lucille Packard Foundation, 1996).

TABLE 11.4	Comparison of Terms Used in Adult and Juvenile Justice Systems	
	Juvenile Terms	Adult Terms
The Person and the Act	Delinquent child	Criminal
	Delinquent act	Crime
Preadjudicatory Stage	Take into custody	Arrest
	Petition	Indictment
	Agree to a finding	Plead guilty
	Deny the petition	Plead not guilty
	Adjustment	Plea bargain
	Detention facility; child care shelter	Jail
Adjudicatory Stage	Substitution	Reduction of charges
	Adjudication or fact-finding hearing	Trial
	Adjudication	Conviction
Postadjudicatory Stage	Dispositional hearing	Sentencing hearing
	Disposition	Sentence
	Commitment	Incarceration
	Youth development center; treatment; training school	Prison
	Residential child care facility	Halfway house
	Aftercare	Parole

Criminal Justice vs. Juvenile Justice

The components of the adult and juvenile criminal processes are similar. However, the juvenile system has a separate organizational structure. In many communities, juvenile justice is administered by people who bring special skills to the task. Also, more kinds of facilities and services are available to juveniles than to adults.

One concern of the juvenile court reform movement was to make certain that the stigma attached to a convicted offender would not be affixed to young people in juvenile proceedings. Thus, even the language used in the juvenile court differs from that used in the adult criminal court (Table 11.4). Juveniles are not indicted for a crime; they have a **petition** filed against them. Secure pretrial holding facilities are called *detention centers* rather than jails. Similarly, the criminal trial is called a *hearing* in the juvenile justice system. The Focus on Delinquency, "Similarities and Differences between Juvenile and Adult Justice Systems," compares the two systems.

petition Document filed in juvenile court alleging that a juvenile is a delinquent, a status offender, or a dependent and asking that the court assume jurisdiction over the juvenile.

A COMPREHENSIVE JUVENILE JUSTICE STRATEGY

At a time when much attention is focused on serious juvenile offenders, a comprehensive strategy has been called for to deal with all aspects of juvenile crime. This strategy focuses on crime prevention and expanding options for handling juvenile offenders. It addresses the links between crime and poverty, child abuse, drugs, weapons,

SIMILARITIES AND DIFFERENCES BETWEEN JUVENILE AND ADULT JUSTICE SYSTEMS

Since its creation, the juvenile justice system has sought to maintain its independence from the adult justice system. Yet there are a number of similarities that characterize the institutions, processes, and law of the two systems.

Similarities between the Juvenile and Adult Justice Systems

Police officers, judges, and correctional personnel use discretion in decision making in both the adult and the juvenile systems.

The right to receive Miranda warnings applies to juveniles as well as to adults.

Juveniles and adults are protected from prejudicial lineups or other identification procedures.

Similar procedural safeguards protect juveniles and adults when they make an admission of guilt.

Prosecutors and defense attorneys play equally critical roles in juvenile and adult advocacy.

Juveniles and adults have the right to counsel at most key stages of the court process.

Pretrial motions are available in juvenile and criminal court proceedings.

Negotiations and plea bargaining exist for juvenile and adult offenders.

Juveniles and adults have a right to a hearing and an appeal.

The standard of evidence in juvenile delinquency adjudications, as in adult criminal trials, is proof beyond a reasonable doubt.

Juveniles and adults can be placed on probation by the court.

Both juveniles and adults can be placed in pretrial detention facilities.

Juveniles and adults can be kept in detention without bail if they are considered dangerous.

After trial, both can be placed in community treatment programs.

Juveniles and adults can be required to undergo drug testing.

Differences between the Juvenile and Adult Justice Systems

The primary purpose of juvenile procedures is protection and treatment. With adults, the aim is to punish the guilty.

Age determines the jurisdiction of the juvenile court. The nature of the offense determines jurisdiction in the adult system. Juveniles can be ordered to the criminal court for trial as adults.

Juveniles can be apprehended for acts that would not be criminal if they were committed by an adult (status offenses).

Juvenile proceedings are not considered criminal; adult proceedings are.

Juvenile court procedures are generally informal and private. Those of adult courts are more formal and are open to the public.

Courts cannot release identifying information about a juvenile to the press, but they must release information about an adult.

Parents are highly involved in the juvenile process but not in the adult process.

The standard of arrest is more stringent for adults than for juveniles.

Juveniles are released into parental custody. Adults are generally given the opportunity for bail.

Juveniles have no constitutional right to a jury trial. Adults have this right. Some state statutes provide juveniles with a jury trial.

Juveniles can be searched in school without probable cause or a warrant.

A juvenile's record is generally sealed when the age of majority is reached. The record of an adult is permanent.

A juvenile court cannot sentence juveniles to county jails or state prisons; these are reserved for adults.

The U.S. Supreme Court has declared that the Eighth Amendment does not prohibit the death penalty for crimes committed by juveniles ages 16 and 17, but it is not a sentence given to children under age 16.

and school behavior. Programs are based on a continuum of care that begins in early childhood and progresses through late adolescence. The components of this strategy include: (1) prevention in early childhood; (2) intervention for at-risk teenage youths; (3) graduated sanctions to hold juvenile offenders accountable for crimes; (4) proper utilization of detention and confinement; and (5) placement of serious juvenile offenders in adult courts.[40]

Family Court Judge Bob Gaston applauds a young man for his performance in Clark County's juvenile drug court program on May 4, 2000 in Las Vegas. The program, which began in 1995, was created to help juveniles quit drugs instead of sending them to prison. (AP/Wide World Photos)

Prevention

Research has identified certain factors that may suggest future delinquency. For young children, these include abuse and neglect, domestic violence, educational underachievement, and health problems. Early-childhood services may prevent delinquency and make a child less vulnerable to future criminality. State legislatures are increasingly investing in state-funded early-education programs like Head Start to reduce juvenile crime, and Smart Start is designed to make certain children are healthy before starting school. Home-visiting programs target families at risk because of child abuse and neglect.

Intervention

Many jurisdictions are developing new intervention programs for teenage youths. An example is the Big Brother/Big Sister program, which matches a volunteer adult with a youngster. More and more cities are finding that night curfews can reduce gang violence and vandalism. Curfews may also contribute to a feeling of safety among residents in high-crime neighborhoods. Efforts are also being made to deter young people from becoming involved with gangs, because gang members ordinarily have higher rates of serious violent behavior.

Graduated Sanctions

Graduated sanction programs for juveniles are another solution being explored by states across the country. Types of graduated sanctions include: (1) immediate sanctions for nonviolent offenders; (2) intermediate sanctions such as probation and electronic monitoring, which target repeat minor offenders and first-time serious offenders; and (3) secure institutional care, which is reserved for repeat serious offenders and violent offenders. A survey conducted on more than 3,000 intervention programs found that about 425 of these programs showed success in juvenile treatment and control.[41]

Peer courts are becoming a popular alternative to traditional juvenile courts. Here, youth peer court prosecutor Dante Ballensky, a freshman at Mazama High School, confers with David Schutt, the court's judge and a Klamath County deputy district attorney, during a session of court in Klamath Falls, Oregon, on June 26, 2000. (AP/Wide World Photos)

Institutional Programs

To read more about juvenile drug courts, go to http://www.ncjrs.org/pdffiles/173425.pdf

For an up-to-date list of Web links, go to www.wadsworth.com/product/0534573053s

Another key to a comprehensive strategy is improving institutional programs. Many experts believe juvenile incarceration is overused, particularly for nonviolent offenders. That is why the concept of deinstitutionalization—removing as many youths from secure confinement as possible—was established by the Juvenile Justice and Delinquency Act of 1974. Considerable research supports the fact that warehousing juveniles without proper treatment does little to deter criminal behavior. The most-effective secure corrections programs are those that provide individual services for a small number of participants.

Alternative Courts

drug courts Courts whose focus is providing treatment for youths accused of drug-related acts.

teen courts Courts that make use of peer juries to decide non-serious delinquency cases.

New venues of juvenile justice are being implemented around the United States which provide special services to youth while at the same time helping to alleviate the case flow problems that plague overcrowded juvenile courts. For example, there are more than 40 juvenile **drug courts,** which have jurisdiction over the burgeoning number of cases involving substance abuse and trafficking. The aim is to place nonviolent first offenders into intensive treatment programs rather than placing them in a custodial institution. The Policy and Practice box, "Teen Courts," discusses the alternative of **teen courts.**

Checkpoints

✔ There are conflicting values in juvenile justice. Some experts want to get tough with young criminals, while others want to focus on rehabilitation.

✔ There are distinct differences between the juvenile and adult justice system.

✔ The terminology used in juvenile justice is designed to shield kids from stigma.

✔ Some state jurisdictions are creating comprehensive juvenile-care mechanisms using a variety of treatment programs.

✔ Some are experimenting with peer-run teen courts.

TEEN COURTS

To relieve overcrowding and provide an alternative to traditional forms of juvenile courts, more than 300 jurisdictions are now experimenting with teen courts. These differ from other juvenile justice programs because young people rather than adults determine the disposition in a case. Cases handled in these courts typically involve young juveniles (ages 10 to 15) with no prior arrest records, who are being charged with minor law violations (shoplifting, vandalism, and disorderly conduct). Typically, young offenders are asked to volunteer to have their case heard in a teen court instead of the more formal court of the traditional juvenile justice system.

As in a regular juvenile court, teen court defendants may go through an intake process, a preliminary review of charges, a court hearing, and sentencing. In a teen court, however, other young people are responsible for much of the process. Charges may be presented to the court by a 15-year-old "prosecutor." Defendants may be represented by a 16-year-old "defense attorney." Other youth may serve as jurors, court clerks, and bailiffs. In some teen courts, a youth "judge" (or panel of youth judges) may choose the best disposition or sanction for each case. In a few teen courts, youth even determine whether the facts in a case have been proven by the prosecutor (similar to a finding of guilt). Offenders are often ordered to pay restitution or perform community service. Some teen courts require offenders to write formal apologies to their victims; others require offenders to serve on a subsequent teen court jury. Many courts use other innovative dispositions, such as requiring offenders to attend classes designed to improve their decision-making skills, enhance their awareness of victims, and deter them from future theft.

Though decisions are made by juveniles, adults are also involved in teen courts. They often administer the programs, and they are usually responsible for essential functions such as budgeting, planning, and personnel. In many programs, adults supervise the courtroom activities, and they often coordinate the community service placements, where youth work to fulfill the terms of their dispositions. In some programs, adults act as the judges while teens serve as attorneys and jurors.

Proponents of teen court argue that the process takes advantage of one of the most powerful forces in the life of an adolescent—the desire for peer approval and the reaction to peer pressure. According to this argument, youth respond better to pro-social peers than to adult authority figures. Thus, teen courts are seen as a potentially effective alternative to traditional juvenile courts that are staffed with paid professionals such as lawyers, judges, and probation officers. Teen court advocates also point out that the benefits extend beyond defendants. Teen courts may benefit the volunteer youth attorneys and judges, who probably learn more

about the legal system than they ever could in a classroom. The presence of a teen court may also encourage the entire community to take a more active role in responding to juvenile crime. In sum, teen courts offer at least four potential benefits:

1. *Accountability.* Teen courts may help to ensure that young offenders are held accountable for their illegal behavior, even when their offenses are relatively minor and would not likely result in sanctions from the traditional juvenile justice system.

2. *Timeliness.* An effective teen court can move young offenders from arrest to sanctions within a matter of days rather than the months that may pass with traditional juvenile courts. This rapid response may increase the positive impact of court sanctions, regardless of their severity.

3. *Cost savings.* Teen courts usually depend heavily on youth and adult volunteers. If managed properly, they may handle a substantial number of offenders at relatively little cost to the community.

4. *Community cohesion.* A well-structured and expansive teen court program may affect the entire community by increasing public appreciation of the legal system, enhancing community–court relationships, encouraging greater respect for the law among youth, and promoting volunteerism among both adults and youth.

The teen court movement is just beginning and its effectiveness is still a matter of debate. But currently there are over 300 of these courts in operation around the United States. Recent evaluations of teen courts have found that they did not "widen the net" of justice by handling cases that in the absence of the peer court would have been subject to a lesser level of processing. However, research by Kevin Minor and his associates of teen courts in Kentucky, and by Paige Harrison and her colleagues in New Mexico, indicate that recidivism levels range from 25 to 30 percent. Considering that these cases typically involve offenses of only moderate seriousness, the findings do not suggest that the program can play a significant role in reducing teenage crime rates.

Sources: Jeffrey A. Butts and Janeen Buck, "Teen Courts: A Focus on Research," *Juvenile Justice Bulletin October 2000* (Washington, DC: Office of Juvenile Justice and Delinquency Prevention, 2000); Kevin Minor, James Wells, Irinia Soderstrom, Rachel Bingham, and Deborah Williamson, "Sentence Completion and Recidivism among Juveniles Referred to Teen Courts," *Crime and Delinquency* 45:467–80 (1999); Paige Harrison, James Maupin, and G. Larry Mays, "Are Teen Courts an Answer to Our Delinquency Problems?" *Juvenile and Family Court Journal* 51:27–33 (2000).

TABLE 11.5

Recent Changes in the Arizona Juvenile Justice System

In November 1996, voters approved an amendment to the Arizona Constitution known as Proposition 102, the *Stop Juvenile Crime Initiative*. The amendment authorized the legislature or the people to enact by initiative or referendum substantive and procedural laws regarding all proceedings and matters affecting juveniles. The amendment was required so that new transfer laws would not be challenged for being unconstitutional. As a result, Senate Bill 1446, the Juvenile Justice Reform Act, became law effective July 21, 1997, and implemented many provisions of the initiative. Senate Bill 1446 created the following:

- Statutory exclusion for 15-, 16-, or 17-year-olds charged with violent crime (murder, sexual assault, armed robbery, drive-by shooting, discharging a firearm at a structure, and aggravated assault with serious injury or use of a deadly weapon) or if the juvenile had two prior felony adjudications and was charged with any third felony.

- Direct file for 14-year-olds charged with a violent crime or if arrested for any third felony. Chronic offender classification with procedures for notice of possible consequences, dispositions, and determination of whether prior offenses occurred.

- Reverse waiver, where, at a pretrial hearing, a juvenile does not qualify as a chronic felony offender.

- Once an adult, always an adult, where, if a juvenile was previously tried and convicted in criminal court, any future offenses involving that juvenile will be tried in adult court.

- Proceedings and records open to the public.

- Mandatory sentencing, where a juvenile age 14 and older adjudicated for any second felony in juvenile court must either serve mandated juvenile detention time, be incarcerated in the Arizona Department of Juvenile Corrections, or be placed under juvenile intensive supervision. The juvenile also may be tried as an adult.

- The appropriation of funds for the purpose of providing short-term detention for juveniles on intensive probation, for expanding the juvenile intensive supervision and progressively increasing sanction programs, and for investigating and prosecuting juvenile gang offenses.

Source: Patricia Torbet and Linda Szymanski, *State Legislative Responses to Violent Crime: 1996–97 Update* (Washington, DC: Office of Juvenile Justice and Delinquency Prevention, 1998).

FUTURE OF JUVENILE JUSTICE

The future of the juvenile court is now being debated. Some experts, including Barry Feld, believe that over the years the juvenile justice system has taken on more of the characteristics of the adult courts; he refers to this as the "criminalizing" of the juvenile court.[42] Robert Dawson suggests that, because the legal differences between the juvenile and criminal systems are narrower than they ever have been, it may be time to abolish the juvenile court.[43]

There concerns reflect the change that has been ongoing in the juvenile justice system. There has been a nationwide effort to modify the system in response to the public's perceived fear of predatory juvenile offenders and the reaction to high-profile cases such as the Columbine tragedy. As a result, states have begun to institute policies that critics believe undermine the true purpose of the juvenile court movement.[44] Some have made it easier to transfer children to the adult courts. During the past five years, at least four states lowered the age limit for transfer to adult court, seven have added crimes, and four added or modified prior-record provisions. As a result, more juvenile offenders are being sentenced as adults and incarcerated in adult prisons.[45] Getting tough on juvenile crime is the primary motivation for moving cases to the adult criminal-justice system. Some commentators argue that transferring juveniles is a statement that juvenile crime is taken seriously by society; others believe the fear of being transferred serves as a deterrent.[46] Some states, such as Arizona, have initiated legislation that significantly restricts eligibility for juvenile justice processing and criminalizing acts that heretofore would have fallen under the jurisdiction of the juvenile court (Table 11.5).[47] There is other evidence of this get-tough movement. More states are now permitting juvenile court judges to commit a juvenile to the corrections department for a longer period of time than the court's original jurisdiction, typically to age 21. During the past 5 years, at least five states (Florida, Kansas, Kentucky, Montana, Tennessee) increased the age for extended juvenile court jurisdiction for serious and violent juvenile offenders.[48]

These changes concern juvenile justice advocates such as Hunter Hurst, director of the National Center for Juvenile Justice, who warns:

> How could the wholesale criminalization of children possibly be a wise thing? If their vulnerability to predation in jails and prisons does not destroy them, won't the so-called taint of criminality that they carry with them for the rest of their lives be an impossible social burden for them and us? . . . Have our standards of decency devolved to the point where protection of children is no longer a compelling state interest? In may ways the answer is yes.[49]

Those who support the juvenile justice concept believe that it is too soon to write off the rehabilitative ideal that has always underpinned the separate treatment of juvenile offenders. They note that fears of a juvenile crime wave are misplaced and that the actions of a few violent children should not mask the needs of millions who can benefit from solicitous treatment rather than harsh punishments. Alida Merlo, Peter Benekos, and William Cook note that a child is more likely to be hit by lightning than shot in a school.[50]

SUMMARY

The juvenile justice system was established at the turn of the twentieth century after decades of effort by child-saving groups. These reformers sought to create an independent category of delinquent offender and keep their treatment separate from adults.

The juvenile justice process consists of a series of steps: the police investigation, the intake procedure in the juvenile court, the pretrial procedures used for juvenile offenders, and the adjudication, disposition, and postdispositional procedures.

Over the past four decades, the U.S. Supreme Court and lower courts have granted juveniles procedural safeguards and the protection of due process in juvenile courts. Major court decisions have laid down the constitutional requirements for juvenile court proceedings. It is important to recognize that in years past the protections currently afforded to both adults and children were not available to children.

How the juvenile justice system deals with the adolescent is also determined by ever-changing theoretical perspectives and models. Elements of a comprehensive strategy for juvenile justice include: (1) delinquency prevention, (2) intervention programs, (3) graduated sanctions, (4) improvement of institutional programs, and (5) treating juveniles like adults. New courts, such as drug courts and teen courts, are now in place.

It is doubtful any real progress in improving the juvenile justice system could be made without significant support from the federal government. By reauthorizing the Juvenile Justice and Delinquency Prevention Act of 1974 and by passing the Violent Crime Control and Law Enforcement Act of 1994, Congress has made a historic financial effort to address juvenile justice reform.

The future of the juvenile justice system is in doubt. A number of state jurisdictions are now revising their juvenile codes to restrict eligibility in the juvenile justice system and eliminate the most serious offenders.

KEY TERMS

House of Refuge
Children's Aid Society
orphan trains
Society for the Prevention
 of Cruelty to Children

Law Enforcement Assistance
 Administration (LEAA)
Office of Juvenile Justice
 and Delinquency
 Prevention (OJJDP)

juvenile justice process
detention hearing
adjudicatory hearing
bifurcated process
disposition

petition
drug courts
teen courts

1. What factors precipitated the development of the Illinois Juvenile Court Act of 1899?

2. One of the most significant reforms in dealing with the juvenile offender was the opening of the New York House of Refuge in 1825. What were the social and judicial consequences of this reform on the juvenile justice system?

3. What are the basic elements of each model of juvenile justice?

4. Should there be a juvenile justice system, or should juveniles who commit serious crimes be treated as adults, while the others are handled by social welfare agencies?

5. The Supreme Court has made a number of major decisions in the area of juvenile justice. What are these decisions? What is their impact on the juvenile justice system?

6. What is the meaning of the term *procedural due process of law*? Explain why and how procedural due process has had an impact on juvenile justice.

7. The formal components of the criminal justice system are often considered to be the police, the court, and the correctional agency. How do these components relate to the major areas of the juvenile justice system? Is the operation of justice similar in the juvenile and adult systems?

8. How would each model of juvenile justice consider the use of capital punishment as a criminal sanction for first-degree murder by a juvenile offender?

9. What role has the federal government played in the juvenile justice system over the last 25 years?

"The great majority of our little emigrants," claimed Charles Loring Brace, *"are the 'waifs and strays' of the streets in a large city."* When the Children's Aid Society opened its doors in March 1853, according to Brace, a *"crowd of wandering little ones"* immediately found their way to the small office on Amity Street. *"Ragged young girls who had nowhere to lay their heads; children driven from drunkards' homes; orphans who slept where they could find a box or a stairway; boys cast out by step-mothers or step-fathers; newsboys, whose incessant answer to our question 'Where do you live?' rung in our ears, 'Don't live nowhere!'"*

For a detailed review of Charles Loring Brace and the Children's Aid Society on InfoTrac® College Edition, read Clay Gish, "Rescuing the 'Waifs and Strays' of the City: The Western Emigration Program of the Children's Aid Society," *Journal of Social History* 33:121 (1999).

Police Work with Juveniles

Chapter 12

© Joel Gordon

ou are a newly appointed police officer assigned to a juvenile unit of a medium-sized urban police department. Wayne G. is an 18-year-old white male who was caught shoplifting with two friends of the same age and sex. Wayne attempted to leave a large department store with a $25 shirt and was apprehended by a police officer in front of the store.

Wayne seemed quite remorseful about the offense. He said several times that he didn't know why he did it and that he had not planned to do it. He seemed upset and scared and, while admitting the offense, did not want to go to court. Wayne had three previous contacts with the police as a juvenile: one for malicious mischief when he destroyed some property, another involving a minor assault of a boy, and a third involving another shoplifting charge. In all three cases, Wayne promised to refrain from ever committing such acts again, and as a result, he was not required to go to court. The other shoplifting involved a small baseball worth only $3.

Wayne appeared at the police department with his mother. His parents are divorced. The mother did not seem overly concerned about the case and felt that her son was not really to blame. She argued that he was always getting in trouble and she was not sure how to control him. She blamed most of his troubles with the law on his being in the wrong crowd. Besides, a $25 shirt was "no big deal" and she offered to pay back the store. The store had left matters in the hands of the police and would support any decision you make.

- Would you submit Wayne's case for prosecution, release him with a warning or use some other tactic?

- Should police officers be forced to act as counselors for troubled youth?

Deciding what to do in a case like Wayne's is a routine activity for most police officers. When dealing with juveniles, they must consider not only the nature of the offense but also the needs of the juvenile. Police officers realize that the action they take can have a long-term effect on an adolescent's future. This chapter focuses on police work in juvenile justice. It covers the role and responsibilities of the police; the history of policing juveniles; the organization and management of police-juvenile operations; legal aspects of police work, including custodial interrogation; the concept of police discretion; and the relationship between police and community efforts to prevent crime.

HISTORY OF JUVENILE POLICING

pecialized police services for juveniles is a relatively recent phenomenon. At one time citizens were responsible for protecting themselves and maintaining order.

The origin of police agencies can be traced to early English society.[1] Before the Norman conquest of England, the **pledge system** assumed that neighbors would protect each other from thieves and warring groups. Individuals were entrusted with policing themselves and resolving minor problems. By the thirteenth century, however, the **watch system** was created to police larger communities. Men were organized in church parishes to patrol areas at night and guard against disturbances and breaches of the peace. This was followed by establishment of the constable, who was responsible for dealing with more serious crimes. By the seventeenth century, the constable, the justice of the peace, and the night watchman formed the nucleus of the police system.

pledge system Early English system in which neighbors protected each other from thieves and warring groups.

watch system Replaced the pledge system in England; watchmen patrolled urban areas at night to provide protection from harm.

www
To gain a comprehensive history of the
London Metropolitan Police from 1829 to 1999, go to

http://www.met.police.uk/police/mps/history/index.htm

For an up-to-date list of Web links, go to
www.wadsworth.com/product/0534573053s

When the Industrial Revolution brought thousands of people from the country-side to work in factories, the need for police protection increased. As a result, the first organized police force was established in London in 1829. The British "bobbies" (so-called after their founder, Sir Robert Peel) were not successful at stopping crime and were influenced by the wealthy for personal and political gain.[2]

In the American colonies, the local sheriff became the most important police official. By the mid-1800s, city police departments had formed in Boston, New York, and Philadelphia. Officers patrolled on foot, and conflicts often arose between un-trained officers and the public.

By this time, children began to be treated as a distinguishable group (Chapter 1). When children violated the law they were often treated the same as adult offenders. But even at this stage a belief existed that the enforcement of criminal law should be applied differently to children.

During the late nineteenth century and into the twentieth, the problems of how to deal with growing numbers of unemployed and homeless youths increased. Groups such as the Wickersham Commission of 1931 and the International Associa-tion of Chiefs of Police became the leading voices for police reform.[3] Their efforts resulted in creation of specialized police units, known as delinquency control squads.

The most famous police reformer of the 1930s was August Vollmer. As the police chief of Berkeley, California, Vollmer instituted numerous reforms, including univer-sity training, modern management techniques, prevention programs, and juvenile aid bureaus.[4] These bureaus were the first organized police services for juvenile offenders.

In the 1960s, policing entered a turbulent period.[5] The U.S. Supreme Court handed down decisions designed to restrict police operations and discretion. Civil unrest produced growing tensions between police and the public. Urban police de-partments were unable to handle the growing crime rate. Federal funding from the Law Enforcement Assistance Administration (LEAA), an agency set up to fund justice-related programs, was a catalyst for developing hundreds of new police programs and enhancement of police services for children. By the 1980s, most urban police depart-ments recognized that the problem of juvenile delinquency required special attention.

The role of the juvenile police officer (officer assigned to juvenile work) has taken on added importance, particularly with the increase in violent juvenile crime. Today the majority of the nation's urban law-enforcement agencies have specialized juvenile police programs. Typically, such programs involve (1) prevention (police athletic leagues, Project D.A.R.E., community outreach), and (2) law enforcement work (ju-venile court, school policing, gang control). Other concerns of the programs include child abuse, domestic violence, and missing children.

POLICE AND JUVENILE OFFENDERS

In the minds of most citizens, the primary responsibility of the police is to protect the public. From films, books, and TV shows that depict the derring-do of police officers, the public has obtained an image of crime fighters who always get their man. Since the 1960s, however, the public has become increasingly aware that the reality of police work is substantially different from its fictional glorification. When police departments failed to bring the crime rate down despite massive government subsidies, when citi-zens complained of civil rights violations, and when tales of police corruption became widespread, it was evident that a crisis was imminent in American policing.

Recently, a new view of policing has emerged. Rather than being seen as a crime fighter who tracks down serious criminals or stops armed robberies in progress, many police departments adopted the concept that the police role should be to main-tain order and be a visible and accessible component of the community. The argu-ment is that police efforts can be successful only when conducted in partnership with concerned citizens. This movement is referred to as **community policing**.[6]

community policing Police strategy that emphasizes fear reduction, community organiza-tion, and order maintenance rather than crime fighting.

juvenile officers Police officers who specialize in dealing with juvenile offenders; they may operate alone or as part of a juvenile police unit within the department.

Police Roles

role conflicts Conflicts police officers face that revolve around the requirement to perform their primary duty of law enforcement and a desire to aid in rehabilitating youthful offenders.

Interest in community policing does not mean that the crime-control model of law enforcement is history. An ongoing effort is being made to improve the crime-fighting capability of police agencies and there are some indications that the effort is paying off. Research indicates that aggressive action by police can help reduce the incidence of repeat offending, and innovations such as computerized fingerprinting systems may bring about greater efficiency.[7] Nonetheless, little evidence exists that adding police or improving their skills has had a major impact on crime-fighting success.

Working with juvenile offenders may be especially challenging for police officers because the desire to help young people and to steer them away from crime seems to conflict with the traditional police duties of crime prevention and order maintenance. In addition, the police are faced with a nationwide adolescent drug problem and renewed gang activity. While the need to help troubled youths may conflict with traditional police roles, it fits nicely with the newly emerging community policing models. Improving these relationships is critical because many juveniles do not have a high regard for the police; minority teens are especially critical of police performance.[8]

Juvenile officers operate either as specialists within a police department or as part of the juvenile unit of a police department. Their role is similar to that of officers working with adult offenders: to intervene if the actions of a citizen produce public danger or disorder. Most officers regard the violations of juveniles as nonserious unless they are committed by chronic troublemakers or involve significant damage to persons or property. Police encounters with juveniles are generally the result of reports made by citizens, and the bulk of such encounters pertain to matters of minor legal consequence.[9]

Of course, police must also deal with serious juvenile offenders whose criminal acts are similar to those of adults, but these are a small minority of the offender population. Thus, police who deal with delinquency must concentrate on being peacekeepers and crime preventers.[10]

Handling juvenile offenders can produce major **role conflicts** for police. They may experience a tension between their desire to perform what they consider their primary duty, law enforcement, and the need to aid in the rehabilitation of youthful offenders. Police officers' actions in cases involving adults are usually controlled by the law and their own judgment or discretion. (The concept of *discretion* is discussed later in this chapter.) In contrast, a case involving a juvenile often demands that the officer consider the "best interests of the child" and how the officer's actions will influence the child's future well-being. Consequently, police are much less likely to refer juvenile offenders to courts. It is estimated that between 30 and 40 percent of all juvenile arrests are handled informally within the police department or are referred to a community-service agency (Figure 12.1). These informal dispositions are the result of the police officer's discretionary authority.[11]

500
Juvenile arrests

320
Referred to juvenile court

140
Informally handled and released

25
Referred to criminal court

10
Referred to welfare

5
Referred to other police departments

Figure 12.1
The Police Response to Juvenile Crime

To understand how police deal with juvenile crime, picture a funnel, with the result shown here. For every five hundred juveniles taken into custody, a little more than 60 percent are sent to juvenile court, and almost 33 percent are released.

Source: Melissa Sickmund, Howard Snyder, and Eileen Poe-Yamagata, *Juvenile Offenders and Victims: 1997* (Washington, DC: OJJDP, 1997).

Police officers must deal with serious offenders whose violent acts are similar to those of adults, but these are a small minority of the offender population. Here, San Diego Sheriff's deputies lead three of the seven teenage defendants from Juvenile Court Department 8 after an arraignment hearing July 19, 2000 in San Diego. The seven San Diego area youths are charged with attacks against several migrant workers. The victims, all men in their 60s, told police that a group of eight to ten young men fired at them with a BB gun, beat them with pipes, and stole money from them at a migrant workers' camp in northern San Diego. (AP/Wide World Photos)

Police intervention in situations involving juveniles can be difficult and emotional. The officer often encounters hostile behavior from the juvenile offender, as well as agitated witnesses. Overreaction by the officer can result in a violent incident. Even if the officer succeeds in quieting or dispersing the witnesses, they will probably reappear the next day, often in the same place.[12]

Role conflicts are common, because most police-juvenile encounters are brought about by loitering and rowdiness rather than by serious law violations. Public concern has risen about out-of-control youth. Yet, because of legal constraints and family interference, the police are often limited as to the ways in which they can respond to such offenders.[13]

What role should the police play in mediating problems with youths—law enforcer, or delinquency-prevention worker? The answer may lay somewhere in between. Most police departments operate juvenile programs that combine law enforcement and delinquency-prevention roles, and the police work with the juvenile court to determine a role most suitable for their community.[14] Actually, police officers may also act as prosecutors in some rural courts when attorneys are not available. Thus, the police–juvenile role extends from the on-the-street encounter to the station house to the court. For juvenile matters involving minor criminal conduct or incorrigible behavior, the police ordinarily select the least-restrictive alternative, which includes such measures as temporary assistance or referral to community agencies. In contrast, violent juvenile crime requires that the police arrest youths while providing constitutional safeguards similar to those available to adult offenders.

Violent juvenile offenders are defined as those adjudicated delinquent for crimes of homicide, rape, robbery, aggravated assault, and kidnapping. Juveniles typically account for nearly 20 percent of all violent crime arrests. Though the juvenile violence rate has recently declined, the future is still uncertain. Some experts believe that a surge of violence will occur as the children of baby boomers enter their "prime crime" years. Some experts predict that juvenile arrests for violent crime will double by the year 2010 (Chapter 2).[15]

As a result of these predictions, police and other justice agencies are experimenting with different methods of controlling violent youth. Some of these methods, such as placing more officers on the beat, have existed for decades; others rely on state-of-the-art technology to pinpoint the locations of violent crimes and develop immediate countermeasures. Research shows that the following practices have been used with some success: (1) intensified motorized patrol; (2) field interrogation (ordering persons to stay briefly and answer questions in regard to suspicious behavior); (3) foot patrol and storefront police stations; (4) citizen contact patrols (citizen volunteer groups patrolling high-crime neighborhoods); and (5) community mobilization, including neighborhood block-watch programs. These strategies address problems of community disorganization and, when combined with other laws and policies, such as restricting the possession of firearms, can be effective deterrents. Although many of these policing strategies are not new, implementing them as one element of an overall police plan may have an impact on preventing juvenile violence.

One of the most promising programs involves intensified motorized patrols in marked cars at night in high-crime locations coupled with field interrogations.[16] These tactics indicate that an increased police presence directed at high-risk times, areas, and persons can deter juvenile violence. More research is needed, however, to ensure the long-term effectiveness of this or any other police strategy.

Finally, one key component of any innovative police program dealing with violent juvenile crime is improved communications between the police and the community. Community policing is discussed in more detail at the conclusion of this chapter.

ORGANIZATION OF POLICE SERVICES FOR JUVENILES

The alarming increase in serious juvenile crime in the past few years has made it obvious that the police can no longer neglect youthful antisocial behavior. Departments need to assign resources to the problem and have the proper organization for coping with it. The theory and practice of police organization have undergone many changes and, as a result, police departments are giving greater emphasis to the juvenile function. The organization of juvenile work depends on the size of the police department, the kind of community in which the department is located, and the amount and quality of resources available in the community.

Police who work with juvenile offenders usually have skills and talents that go beyond those generally associated with regular police work. In large urban police departments, juvenile services are often established through a special unit. Ordinarily this unit is the responsibility of a command-level police officer, who assigns officers to deal with juvenile problems throughout the police department's jurisdiction. Police departments with very few officers have little need for an internal division with special functions. Most small departments make one officer responsible for handling juvenile matters for the entire community.

The number of police officers assigned to juvenile work has increased in recent years. The International Association of Chiefs of Police found that approximately 500 departments, of the 1,400 surveyed in 1960, had juvenile units. By 1970, the number of police departments with a juvenile specialist had doubled.[17]

In neither large nor small departments can it be assumed that only officers assigned to work with juveniles will be involved in handling juvenile offenses. When officers on patrol encounter a youngster committing a crime, they are responsible for dealing with the problem initially. However, they generally refer the case to the juvenile unit or to a juvenile police officer for follow-up. Most juvenile officers are appointed after having had some general patrol experience. A desire to work with juveniles, along with an aptitude for working with young people, are considered essential for the job. Officers must also have a thorough knowledge of the law, especially the constitutional protections available to juveniles.

Checkpoints

✔ Modern policing developed in England at the beginning of the nineteenth century.

✔ Most modern police agencies have specialized units that interface with teens.

✔ Many juvenile cases are handled informally.

✔ Police are using intensive, aggressive patrol to control high-risk juveniles.

✔ Police who work with juvenile offenders usually have skills and talents that go beyond those generally associated with regular police work.

✔ The number of police officers assigned to juvenile work has increased in recent years.

✔ Most juvenile officers are appointed after they have had some general patrol experience.

POLICE AND THE RULE OF LAW

When police are involved with criminal activity of juvenile offenders, their actions are controlled by statute, constitutional case law, and judicial review. Police methods of investigation and control include (1) the arrest procedure, (2) search and seizure, and (3) custodial interrogation.

The Arrest Procedure

arrest Taking a person into the custody of the law to restrain the accused until he or she can be held accountable for the offense in court proceedings.

probable cause Reasonable ground to believe that an offense was committed and that the accused committed that offense.

When a juvenile is apprehended, the police must decide whether to release him or her or make a referral to the juvenile court. Cases involving serious crimes against property or persons are often referred to court. Less serious cases, such as disputes between juveniles, petty shoplifting, runaways, and assaults of minors, are often diverted from court action.

Most states require that the law of **arrest** be the same for both adults and juveniles. To make a legal arrest, an officer must have probable cause to believe that an offense took place and that the suspect is the guilty party. **Probable cause** is usually defined as falling somewhere between a mere suspicion and absolute certainty. In misdemeanor cases the police officer must personally observe the crime to place a suspect in custody. For a felony, the police officer may make the arrest without having observed the crime if the officer has probable cause to believe the crime occurred and the person being arrested committed it.

The main difference between arrests of adult and juvenile offenders is the broader latitude police have to control youthful behavior. Most juvenile codes, for instance, provide broad authority for the police to take juveniles into custody.[18] Such statutes are designed to give the police the authority to act in loco parentis (Latin for "in place of the parent"). Accordingly, the broad power granted to police is consistent with the notion that a juvenile is not arrested but taken into custody, which implies a protective rather than a punitive form of detention.[19] Once a juvenile is arrested, however, the constitutional safeguards of the Fourth and Fifth Amendments available to adults are applicable to the juvenile as well.

Section 13 of the Uniform Juvenile Court Act is an example of the provisions used in state codes regarding juvenile arrest procedures (Table 12.1). There is currently a

TABLE 12.1

Uniform Juvenile Court Act, Section 13. (Taking into Custody)

a. A child may be taken into custody:

1. pursuant to an order of the court under this Act;

2. pursuant to the laws of arrest;

3. by a law enforcement officer (or duly authorized officer of the court) if there are reasonable grounds to believe that the child is suffering from illness or injury or is in immediate danger from his surroundings, and that his removal is necessary; or

4. by a law enforcement officer (or duly authorized officer of the court) if there are reasonable grounds to believe that the child has run away from his parents, guardian, or other custodian.

b. The taking of a child into custody is not an arrest, except for the purpose of determining its validity under the constitution of this State or of the United States.

Source: National Conference of Commissioners on Uniform State Laws, *Uniform Court Act* (Chicago: National Conference on Uniform State Laws, 1968), Sect. 13.

trend toward treating juvenile offenders more like adults. Related to this trend are efforts by the police to provide a more legalistic and less informal approach to the arrest process, and a more balanced approach to case disposition.[20]

Search and Seizure

search and seizure The U.S. Constitution protects citizens from any search and seizure by police without a lawfully obtained search warrant; such warrants are issued when there is probable cause to believe that an offense has been committed.

Do juveniles have the same right to be free from unreasonable **search and seizure** as adults? In general, a citizen's privacy is protected by the Fourth Amendment of the Constitution, which states:

The right of the people to be secure in their persons, houses, papers, and effects, against unreasonable searches and seizures, shall not be violated, and no warrants shall issue, but upon probable cause, supported by oaths or affirmation, and particularly describing the place to be searched, and the persons or things to be seized.[21]

Most courts have held that the Fourth Amendment ban against unreasonable search and seizure applies to juveniles and that illegally seized evidence is inadmissible in a juvenile trial. To exclude incriminating evidence, a juvenile's attorney makes a pretrial motion to suppress the evidence, the same procedure that is used in the adult criminal process.

A full discussion of search and seizure is beyond the scope of this text, but it is important to note that the Supreme Court has ruled that police may stop a suspect and search for evidence without a warrant under certain circumstances. A person may be searched after a legal arrest, but then only in the immediate area of the suspect's control. For example, after an arrest for possession of drugs, the pockets of a suspect's jacket may be searched;[22] an automobile may be searched if there is probable cause to believe a crime has taken place;[23] a suspect's outer garments may be frisked if police are suspicious of his or her activities;[24] and a search may be conducted if a person volunteers for the search.[25] These rules are usually applied to juveniles as well as to adults.

Custodial Interrogation

custodial interrogation Questions posed by the police to a suspect held in custody in the prejudicial stage of the juvenile justice process; juveniles have the same rights against self-incrimination as adults do when being questioned.

In years past, police often questioned juveniles without their parents or even an attorney present. Any incriminatory statements arising from such **custodial interroga-**

Officers search students at a high school. The Supreme Court allows police officers and security agents greater latitude in searching students than they would have with other citizens, on the grounds that the campus must be a safe and crime-free environment. (© Kelly Wilkinson/*Indianapolis Star*/Sipa)

Miranda **warning** Supreme Court decisions require police officers to inform individuals under arrest of their constitutional rights; warning must also be given when suspicion begins to focus on an individual in the accusatory stage.

To read more about the *Miranda* decision, go to
http://www.rh.cc.ca.us/departments/academic/pubserv/leo/miranda.htm

For an up-to-date list of Web links, go to www.wadsworth.com/product/0534573053s

tion could be used at trial. However, in the 1966 *Miranda* case, the Supreme Court placed constitutional limitations on police interrogation procedures with adult offenders. *Miranda* held that persons in police custody must be told the following:

- They have the right to remain silent.
- Any statements they make can be used against them.
- They have the right to counsel.
- If they cannot afford counsel, it will be furnished at public expense.[26]

These **Miranda warnings** have been made applicable to children taken into custody. The Supreme Court case of *in re Gault* stated that constitutional privileges against self-incrimination are applicable in juvenile as well as adult cases. Because *in re Gault* implies that *Miranda* applies to custodial interrogation in criminal procedure, state court jurisdictions apply the requirements of *Miranda* to juvenile proceedings as well. Since the *Gault* decision in 1967, virtually all courts that have ruled on the question of the *Miranda* warning have concluded that the warning does apply to the juvenile process.

One problem associated with custodial interrogation of juveniles has to do with waiver of *Miranda* rights: Under what circumstances can juveniles knowingly and willingly waive the rights given them by *Miranda v. Arizona*? Does a youngster, acting alone, have sufficient maturity to appreciate the right to remain silent?

Most courts have concluded that parents or attorneys need not be present for children effectively to waive their rights.[27] In a frequently cited California case, *People v. Lara*, the court said that the question of a child's waiver is to be determined by the totality of the circumstances doctrine.[28] This means that the validity of a waiver rests not only on the age of the child but also on a combination of other factors, including the education of the accused, the accused's knowledge of the charge, whether the youth was allowed to consult with family or friends, and the method of interrogation.[29] The general rule is that juveniles can waive their rights to protection from self-incrimination, but that the validity of this waiver is determined by the circumstances of each case.

The waiver of *Miranda* rights by a juvenile is one of the most controversial legal issues addressed in the state courts. It has also been the subject of federal constitutional review. In two cases, *Fare v. Michael C.* and *California v. Prysock*, the Supreme Court has attempted to clarify children's rights when they are interrogated by the police. In *Fare v. Michael C.*, the Court ruled that a child's asking to speak to his probation officer was not the equivalent of asking for an attorney; consequently, statements he made to the police absent legal counsel were admissible in court.[30] In *California v. Prysock*, the Court was asked to rule on the adequacy of a *Miranda* warning given Randall Prysock, a youthful murder suspect.[31] After reviewing the taped exchange between the police interrogator and the boy, the Court upheld Prysock's conviction when it ruled that even though the *Miranda* warning was given in slightly different language and out of exact context, its meaning was easily understandable, even to a juvenile.

Taken together, *Fare* and *Prysock* make it seem indisputable that juveniles are at least entitled to receive the same *Miranda* rights as adults. *Miranda v. Arizona* is a historic decision that continues to protect the rights of all suspects placed in custody.[32]

DISCRETIONARY JUSTICE

Today juvenile offenders receive nearly as much procedural protection as adult offenders. However, the police have broader authority in dealing with juveniles than with adults. Granting such **discretion** to juvenile officers raises some important questions: Under what circumstances should an officer arrest status offenders? Should a summons be used in lieu of arrest? Under what conditions should a juvenile be taken into protective custody?

When police confront a case involving a juvenile offender, they rely on their discretion to choose an appropriate course of action. *Police discretion* is selective enforcement of the law by authorized police agents. Discretion gives officers a choice among possible courses of action within the limits on their power.[33] It is a prime example of low-visibility decision making, or decisions by public officials that the public is not in a position to regulate or criticize.[34]

Discretion exists not only in the police function but also in prosecutorial decision making, judicial judgments, and corrections. Discretion results in the law being applied differently in similar situations. For example, two teenagers are caught in a stolen automobile; one is arrested, the other released. Two youths are drunk and disorderly; one is sent home, the other to juvenile court. A group of youngsters is involved in a gang fight; only a few are arrested, the others are released.

Much discretion is exercised in juvenile work because of the informality that has been built into the system in an attempt to individualize justice.[35] Furthermore, officials in the juvenile justice system make decisions about children that often are without oversight or review. The daily procedures of juvenile personnel are rarely subject to judicial review, except when they clearly violate a youth's constitutional rights. As a result, discretion sometimes deteriorates into discrimination and other abuses on the part of the police. The real danger in discretion is that it allows the law to discriminate against precisely those elements in the population—the poor, the ignorant, the unpopular—who are least able to draw attention to their plight.[36]

The problem of discretion in juvenile justice is one of extremes. Too little discretion provides insufficient flexibility to treat juvenile offenders as individuals. Too much discretion can lead to injustice. Guidelines and controls are needed to structure the use of discretion.

Generally, the first contact a youth has with the juvenile justice system is with the police. Research indicates that most police decisions arising from this initial contact involve discretion.[37] These studies show that many juvenile offenders are never referred to the juvenile court.

In a classic study, Nathan Goldman examined the arrest records for more than 1,000 juveniles from four communities in Pennsylvania.[38] He concluded that more than 64 percent of police contacts with juveniles were handled informally. Subse-

---

To read about trends in juvenile arrests, go to

http://www.ncjrs.org/pdffiles1/ojjdp/185236.pdf

For an up-to-date list of Web links, go to www.wadsworth.com/product/0534573053s

discretion Use of personal decision making and choice in carrying out operations in the criminal justice system, such as deciding whether to make an arrest or when to accept a plea bargain.

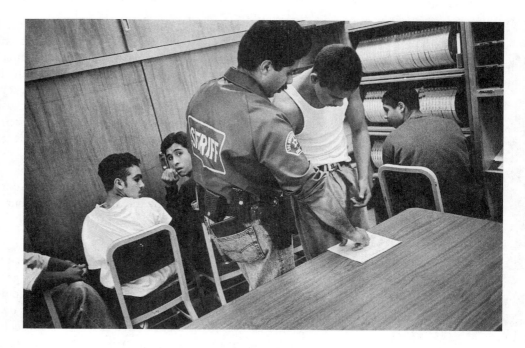

A teen in Los Angeles in police custody hopes that the officers will release him with a warning. His friends are also concerned about their futures. Police have discretion to take formal action against youthful offenders or to release them with a warning or take some other informal action. (© Joe Rodriguez/Black Star)

quent research offered additional evidence of informal disposition of juvenile cases.[39] Only about 50 percent of all children who come in contact with the police get past the initial stage of the juvenile justice process.[40] More current data show an increase in the number of cases referred to the juvenile court. The FBI estimates that about two-thirds of all juvenile arrests are referred to juvenile court.[41] Despite the variations between the estimates, these studies indicate that the police use significant discretion in their decisions regarding juvenile offenders. Research shows that differential decision making goes on without clear guidance.

If all police officers acted in a fair and just manner, the seriousness of the crime, the situation in which it occurred, and the legal record of the juvenile would be the factors that affect decision making. Research does show that police are much more likely to take formal action if the crime is serious and has been reported by a victim who is a respected member of the community, and if the offender is well known to them.[42] However, these factors are not the only ones that influence discretion. There are others that are believed to shape police discretion.

Environmental Factors

How does a police officer decide what to do with a juvenile offender? The norms of the community also affect the decision. Some officers work in communities that tolerate a fair amount of personal freedom. In liberal environments, the police may be inclined to release juveniles rather than arrest them. Other officers work in conservative communities that expect a no-nonsense approach to police enforcement. Here, police may be more inclined to arrest a juvenile.

Police officers may be influenced by their perception of community alternatives to police intervention. Some officers may use arrest because they believe nothing else can be done.[43] Others may favor referring juveniles to social-service agencies, particularly if they believe a community has a variety of good resources. These referrals save time and effort; records do not have to be filled out, and court appearances can be avoided. The availability of such options allows for greater latitude in police decision making.[44]

Police Policy

The policies and customs of the local police department also influence decisions. Juvenile officers may be pressured to make more arrests or to refrain from making arrests under certain circumstances. Directives instruct officers to be alert to certain types of juvenile violations. The chief of police might initiate policies governing the arrest practices of the juvenile department. For example, if local merchants complain that youths congregating in a shopping-center parking lot are inhibiting business, police may be called on to make arrests. Under other circumstances, an informal warning might be given. Similarly, a rash of deaths caused by teenage drunk driving may galvanize the local media to demand police action. The mayor and the police chief, sensitive to possible voter dissatisfaction, may then demand that formal police action be taken in cases of drunk driving.

Another source of influence is pressure from supervisors. Some supervising officers may believe it is important to curtail disorderly conduct or drug use. In addition, officers may be influenced by the discretionary decisions made by their peers.

Situational Factors

In addition to the environment, a variety of situational factors affect a police officer's decisions. Situational factors are those attached to a particular crime, such as specific traits of offenders. Traditionally, it was believed that police officers rely heavily on the demeanor and appearance of the juvenile in making decisions. Some research shows that the decision to arrest is often based on factors such as dress, attitude, speech, and level of hostility toward the police.[45] Kids who display "attitude" were believed to be the ones more likely to be arrested than those who are respectful and contrite.[46] However, more recent research has challenged the influence of demeanor on police decision making, suggesting that it is delinquent behavior and actions that occur during police detention that influence the police decision to take formal action.[47] For example, a person who struggles or touches police during a confrontation is a likely candidate for arrest, but those who merely sport a bad attitude or negative demeanor are as likely to suffer an arrest than the polite and contrite.[48] It is possible that the earlier research reflected a time when police officers demanded absolute respect and were quick to take action when their authority was challenged. The more recent research may indicate that police, through training or experience, are now less sensitive to slights and confrontational behavior and view them as just part of the job. Most studies conclude that these variables are important in the police discretionary process:[49]

- The attitude of the complainant
- The type and seriousness of the offense
- The race, sex, and age of the offender
- The attitude of the offender
- The offender's prior contacts with the police
- The perceived willingness of the parents to assist in solving the problem (in the case of a child)
- The setting or location in which the incident occurs
- Whether the offender denies the actions or insists on a court hearing (in the case of a child)
- The likelihood that a child can be served by an agency in the community

Bias and Police Discretion

Do police allow bias to affect their decisions on whether to arrest youths? Do they routinely use "racial profiling" when they decide to make an arrest? A great deal of debate has been generated over this issue. Some experts believe that police decision making is deeply influenced by the offender's personal characteristics, whereas others maintain that crime-related variables are more significant.

When a juvenile commits a crime, police have the authority to investigate the incident and decide whether to release the child or place him under arrest. This is often a discretionary decision based not only on the nature of the offense but also on such factors as the seriousness of the crime, the child's past record, and whether the victim wishes to press charges. (© Michael A. Dwyer/Stock, Boston)

Racial Bias It has long been charged that police are more likely to act formally with African American suspects and use their discretion to benefit whites.[50] As Table 12.2 shows, minority youth are arrested at a rate disproportionate to their representation in the population. Research on this issue has yielded mixed conclusions. One view is that, while discrimination may have existed in the past, there is no longer a need to worry about racial discrimination because minorities now possess sufficient political status to protect them within the justice system.[51] As Harvard University law professor Randall Kennedy forcefully argues, even if a law-enforcement policy exists that disproportionately affects African American suspects, it might be justified

TABLE 12.2	Minority Representation in Arrest Statistics
Most serious offense	**Black proportion of juvenile arrests in 1999**
Murder	49%
Forcible rape	35
Robbery	54
Aggravated assault	35
Burglary	24
Larceny-theft	26
Motor vehicle theft	39
Weapons	30
Drug abuse violations	29
Curfew and loitering	25
Runaways	18

Source: *FBI Crime in the United States 1999,* (Washington, DC: U.S. Government Printing Office, 2000).

as a "public good" because law-abiding African Americans are statistically more often victims of crimes committed by other African Americans.[52]

In contrast to these views, several research efforts do show evidence of police discrimination against African American youths.[53] Donna Bishop and Charles Frazier found that race can have a direct effect on decisions made at several junctures of the juvenile justice process.[54] According to Bishop and Frazier, African Americans are more likely than whites to be recommended for formal processing, referred to court, adjudicated delinquent, and given harsher dispositions for comparable offenses. In the arrest category, specifically, being African American increases the probability of formal police action.[55]

Similarly, a study by the National Council on Crime and Delinquency revealed significant overrepresentation by black youths at every point in the California juvenile justice system. Although they make up less than 9 percent of the state youth population, black youths accounted for 19 percent of juvenile arrests. According to the study, the causes for the disparity included (1) institutional racism, (2) environmental factors, (3) family dysfunction, (4) cultural barriers, and (5) school failure.[56]

In summary, studies of bias in police decision making have revealed the following:

1. Some researchers have concluded that the police discriminate against minority youths.

2. Other researchers do not find evidence of discrimination.

3. Racial disparity is most often seen at the arrest stage but probably exists at other stages.

4. The higher arrest rates of minorities are related to interpersonal, family, community, and organizational differences. Other influences may include police discretion, street crime visibility, and high crime rates within a particular group. Such factors, however, may also be linked to general societal discrimination.

Gender Bias Is there a difference between police treatment of male and female offenders? Some experts favor the chivalry or paternalism hypothesis, which holds that police are likely to act paternally toward young girls and not arrest them. Others believe that police may be more likely to arrest female offenders because their actions violate officers' stereotypes of the female.

There is some research support for various forms of gender bias. The nature of this bias may vary according to the seriousness of the offense and the age of the offender. Some of the conclusions reached in these studies are:

- Police tend to be more lenient toward females than males with regard to acts of delinquency. Merry Morash found that boys who engage in "typical male" delinquent activities are much more likely to develop police records than females.[57]

- Females who have committed minor or status offenses seem to be referred to juvenile court more often than males. Meda Chesney-Lind has found that adolescent female status offenders are arrested for less-serious offenses than boys.[58]

- Younger female offenders are treated by police in a harsher manner than older ones—an apparent confirmation of the paternalism theory. Research by Christy Visher showed that police officers took a more paternalistic (stricter) position toward young females to "deter any further violation of appropriate sex-role behavior." Age and race were more important factors in arrest decisions for females as compared to males.[59]

- Recent evidence has confirmed earlier studies showing that the police, and most likely the courts, apply a double standard in dealing with male and female juvenile offenders. Bishop and Frazier found that both female status offenders and male delinquents are differently disadvantaged in the juvenile justice system.[60]

There appears to be general agreement that police are less likely to process females for delinquent acts and that they discriminate against them by arresting them for status offenses.

Organizational Bias The policies of some police departments may result in biased practices. Research has found that police departments can be characterized by their professionalism (skills and knowledge) and bureaucratization.[61] Departments that are highly bureaucratized (high emphasis on rules and regulations) and at the same time unprofessional are most likely to be insulated from the communities they serve. Organizational policy may be influenced by the perceptions of police decision makers. A number of experts have found that law-enforcement administrators have a stereotyped view of the urban poor as troublemakers who must be kept under control.[62] Consequently, lower-class neighborhoods experience much greater police scrutiny than middle-class areas, and their residents face a proportionately greater chance of arrest. For example, there is a significant body of literature that shows that police are more likely to "hassle" or arrest African American males in poor neighborhoods.[63] It is therefore not surprising, as criminologist Robert Sampson has found, that teenage residents of neighborhoods with low socioeconomic status have a significantly greater chance of acquiring police records than youths living in higher socioeconomic areas, regardless of the actual crime rates in these areas.[64] Sampson's research indicates that, although police officers may not discriminate on an individual level, departmental policy that focuses on lower-class areas may result in class and racial bias in the police processing of delinquent youth.

Not all experts believe there is rampant police organizational bias. For example, when Ronald Weitzer surveyed people in three Washington, D.C. neighborhoods, he found that residents in primarily African American neighborhoods value racially integrated police services.[65] Similarly, Thomas Priest and Deborah Brown Carter have found that the African American community is supportive of the local police, especially when they respond quickly to calls for service. It is unlikely that African Americans would appreciate rapid service, or the presence of white officers, if police routinely practiced racial discrimination.[66]

One reason for these contrasting views is that racial influences on police decision making are often quite subtle and hard to detect. For example, research consistently shows that the victim's race, and not the criminal's, is the key to racial bias; police officers are more likely to take formal action when the victim of crime is white than when the victim is a minority-group member. This data suggests that any study of police discretion must take into account both victim and offender characteristics if it is to be truly valid.

In summary, the policies, practices, and customs of the local police department influence discretion. Conditions vary from department to department and depend on the judgment of the chief and others in the organizational hierarchy. Because the police retain a large degree of discretionary power, the ideal of nondiscrimination is often difficult to achieve in practice. However, policies to limit police discretion can help eliminate bias.

To read about what is being done to reduce racial profiling, go to

http://www.ncjrs.org/txtfiles1/bja/184768.txt

For an up-to-date list of Web links, go to www.wadsworth.com/product/0534573053s

✔ Checkpoints

✔ Most states require that the law of arrest be the same for both adults and juveniles.

✔ The main difference between arrests of adult and juvenile offenders is the broader latitude police have to control youthful behavior.

✔ Most courts have held that the Fourth Amendment ban against unreasonable search and seizure applies to juveniles.

✔ Most courts have concluded that parents or attorneys need not be present for children effectively to waive their right to remain silent.

✔ The police have broader authority in dealing with juveniles than in dealing with adults.

✔ A great deal of discretion is exercised in juvenile work because of the informality that has been built into the system.

✔ It has long been charged that police are more likely to act formally with African American youth and use their discretion to benefit white adolescents.

✔ Police tend to be more lenient toward females than males with regard to acts of delinquency but more restrictive with status offenders.

POLICE WORK AND DELINQUENCY PREVENTION

ne method of contemporary delinquency prevention relies on aggressive patrolling targeted on specific patterns of delinquency. Police departments in Chicago and Los Angeles have at one time used saturation patrol, targeting gang areas and arresting members for any law violations. These tactics have not proven to be effective against gangs. For example, in 1996 the Dallas Police Department initiated a successful gang-control effort that employed such tactics as saturating known gang areas with anti-gang units, as well as aggressive enforcement of curfew and truancy laws. Targeting truancy and curfew laws led to a significant reduction in gang activity, whereas the saturation patrols proved ineffective.[67]

Some police departments are now replacing these more-aggressive measures with cooperative community-based efforts. Because police officers are responsible for the care of juveniles taken into custody, it is essential that they work closely with social-service groups day by day. In addition, the police are now assuming a leadership role in identifying the needs of children in the community and helping the community meet those needs. In helping to develop delinquency prevention programs, the police are working closely with youth service bureaus, schools, recreational facilities, welfare agencies, schools, and employment programs.[68]

Using community services for juveniles has many advantages. Such services allow young people to avoid the stigma of being processed by a police agency. They also improve the community's awareness of the needs of young people and make it possible to restrict court referral to cases involving serious crime.

One of the most important institutions playing a role in delinquency prevention is the school. Liaison prevention programs between the police and the schools have been implemented in many communities. Liaison officers from schools and police departments have played a leadership role in developing recreational programs for juveniles. In some instances, they have actually operated such programs. In others, they have encouraged community support for recreational activities, including Little League baseball, athletic clubs, camping outings, and police athletic and scouting programs. For example, the Gang Resistance Education and Training (G.R.E.A.T.) program was developed among a number of Arizona police departments in an effort to reduce adolescent involvement in criminal behavior; today more than 2400 officers from 47 states and the District of Columbia have completed G.R.E.A.T. training.[69] The program has nine main goals, which are listed in Table 12.3. Evaluations of the

---

TABLE 12.3 ## The Nine Stages of the G.R.E.A.T. Program

1. *Introduction.* Students get acquainted with the G.R.E.A.T. program and the presenting officer.

2. *Crime, Victims, and Your Rights.* Students learn about crimes, their victims, and their impact on school and neighborhood.

3. *Cultural Sensitivity and Prejudice.* Students explore how cultural differences affect their school and neighborhood.

4.–5. *Conflict Resolution* (two lessons). Students are taught how to create an atmosphere of understanding that enables all parties to better address problems and work on solutions together.

6. *Meeting Basic Needs.* Students learn how to meet their basic needs without joining a gang.

7. *Drugs and Neighborhoods.* Students are educated about how drugs affect their school and neighborhood.

8. *Responsibility.* Students examine the diverse responsibilities of people in their school and neighborhood.

9. *Goal Setting.* Students learn the need for goal setting and how to establish short- and long-term goals.

Source: Finn-Aage Esbensen and D. Wayne Osgood, *National Evaluation of G.R.E.A.T.* (Washington, DC: National Institute of Justice, 1997).

The SHIELD program of the Westminster, California police department is designed to accomplish two primary goals. First, it uses the contacts that police officers make in the course of their normal duties to identify youth who they think are likely to become involved in violent behavior, substance abuse, and gang activities. At-risk youth are identified as those who are exposed to family risk factors such as domestic violence and other criminal activities in the home. Second, SHIELD provides youth with services that are tailored to meet their individual needs by using a multidisciplinary team of representatives from the community, schools, and service agencies.

The SHIELD youth-referral process gives officers a procedure for providing assistance to youth who are exposed to family risk factors. All patrol officers in Westminster are given the following orders as part of the youth referral protocol:

> Police personnel are required to obtain the name, age, and school attended of any minor youth living in a home where a report is filed involving the following police activity: family violence of any type, neglect or abandonment, gang activity, drug sales or usage, arrests made associated with alcohol abuse, or any other call for service where the welfare of minor youth is at risk due to the behavior of older siblings or adults living in, or frequenting, the home.

Whenever the SHIELD Resource Officer (SRO) receives a report from the officer on the scene, they screen the case to determine whether the circumstances make the youth appropriate for SHIELD intervention. If appropriate, a student referral report is created that contains a short synopsis of the incident as it pertains to the youth as well as demographic and personal information, including assessments of both risk and protective factors. The SRO then sends the student referral report to the Youth and Family Resource Team. This multidisciplinary team includes officials from the local school district, such as the pupil personnel administrator, the district nurse, a specialist in drug abuse prevention, and school principals; counseling staff from a community service provider; a county social worker; the Westminster Community Services Recreation Supervi-

sor; the SRO; and a second officer formerly assigned to Drug Abuse Resistance Education (D.A.R.E.).

When they receive the student referral report, the members of the Youth and Family Resource Team consider a range of school- and community-based treatment options and make recommendations for treatment. The Youth and Family Resource Team reassesses the treatment recommendations and progress of each youth 3 weeks after the initial recommendation. While a youth is involved in treatment, the service providers send monthly progress reports to the SHIELD staff at the Westminster Police Department. These reports allow for ongoing tracking and reassessment of the services provided to program youth.

The treatment delivery systems that SHIELD relies on are already in the community. The program works closely with all of the local schools and the local Boys and Girls Club. Individual and group counseling are commonly used in both school and community settings. Issues covered in counseling vary according to the circumstances of the individual case, but common themes include anger management, goal setting, pregnancy prevention, conflict resolution, and other coping skills. Informal school-based monitoring is also frequently included in treatment plans. When teachers and administrators are aware of the risk factors that a student faces outside the classroom and they are actively monitoring that student, they are more likely to detect and respond to early signs of problem behavior, abuse, or neglect.

To date, there has been no definitive evaluation of the SHIELD program. Nevertheless, the identification and referral activities stand as the central program elements of SHIELD, and these show great promise as a model for the mobilization of community resources to prevent delinquency.

Sources: Adapted from Phelan A. Wyrick, "Law Enforcement Referral of At-Risk Youth: The SHIELD Program," *Juvenile Justice Bulletin, November 2000* (Washington, DC: Office of Juvenile Justice and Delinquency Prevention, 2000); personal communication with SHIELD program officers, 2001.

You can visit
G.R.E.A.T.'s Web site at
http://www.atf.treas.gov/great/
For an up-to-date list of
Web links, go to
www.wadsworth.com/
product/0534573053s

program indicate that students who complete the curriculum develop more pro-social attitudes and have lower rates of delinquent behaviors than those in a comparison group who were not exposed to G.R.E.A.T.[70]

Today, many experts consider delinquency-prevention efforts to be crucial to the development of a comprehensive approach to youth crime. Although such efforts cut across the entire juvenile justice system, police programs have become increasingly popular. See the Policy and Practice box, "The SHIELD Program," for more on this topic.

To be successful, community policing requires that citizens play a dynamic role in law enforcement. Sometimes this means taking an active role in delinquency prevention. Here, Lyn Jones (left), a member of the Mighty Moms, reminds a group of teenagers about the Mall of America's policy that children under 16 must be accompanied by an adult on weekend evenings. Jones is part of a team of 30 paid parents called Mighty Moms and Dedicated Dads who walk among the thousands of visitors at the mall looking for unsupervised teens and helping to keep the peace. (AP/Wide World Photos)

Checkpoints

✔ Police departments have used aggressive saturation patrol, targeting gang areas and arresting members for any law violations.

✔ Police are now identifying the needs of children in the community and helping the community meet those needs.

✔ Prevention programs between the police and the schools have been implemented in many communities.

✔ Many experts consider police-based delinquency prevention efforts to be crucial to the development of a comprehensive approach to youth crime.

COMMUNITY POLICING IN THE NEW MILLENNIUM

One of the most important changes in U.S. law enforcement is the emergence of the community policing model of crime prevention. This concept is based on the premise that the police can carry out their duties more effectively if they gain the trust and assistance of concerned citizens. Under this model, the main police role should be to increase feelings of community safety and encourage area residents to cooperate with their local police agencies.[71] Advocates of community policing regard the approach as useful in juvenile justice for a number of reasons:

1. Direct engagement with a community gives police more immediate information about problems unique to a neighborhood and insights into their solutions.

2. Freeing officers from the emergency response system permits them to engage more directly in proactive crime prevention.

3. Making police operations more visible increases police accountability to the public.

4. Decentralizing operations allows officers to develop greater familiarity with the needs of various constituencies in the community and to adapt procedures to accommodate those needs.

5. Encouraging officers to view citizens as partners improves relations between police and the public.

6. Moving decision making to patrol officers places more authority in the hands of the people who best know the community's problems and expectations.[72]

The community policing model has been translated into a number of policy initiatives. It has encouraged police departments to get officers out of patrol cars, where they were insulated from the community, and into the streets via foot patrol.[73] In addition, the police have encouraged citizens to create neighborhood watches and crime prevention groups. The Police Foundation has reviewed such efforts and found them to be effective methods of increasing citizen cooperation. One of the best-known programs is the Philadelphia Block Watch, which cooperates with the police in delinquency control and victim-aid projects. Another is the Innovative Neighborhood-Oriented Policing (INOP) program.[74] The main objectives of the INOP program are to foster community policing initiatives and to implement drug-reduction efforts aimed at juveniles and adults.[75]

In summary, important efforts have been made by police departments to involve citizens in delinquency control. Community policing is a philosophy that promotes community, government, and police partnerships that address both adult and juvenile crime.[76]

Although little clear evidence exists that these efforts can lower crime rates, they seem to be effective methods of improving perceptions of community safety and the quality of community life while involving citizens in the juvenile justice network. Under the community policing philosophy, prevention programs may become more effective crime control measures. Programs that combine reintegration of youth into the community after institutionalization with police surveillance and increased communication are vital for improving police effectiveness with juveniles.[77]

SUMMARY

As rates of delinquency have soared, the police have become more important to the juvenile justice system. It is almost always the police officer who has the initial contact with young people committing antisocial acts. This contact can have a significant impact on an offender's future.

Numerous factors influence the decisions police make about juvenile offenders. They include the seriousness of the offense, the harm inflicted on the victim, and the likelihood that the juvenile will break the law again.

Police officers must be familiar with procedural law because their contact with young people includes the legal aspects of arrest, custodial interrogation, and lineups. Through the *Miranda v. Arizona* decision, the U.S. Supreme Court established a clearly defined procedure for custodial interrogation. Such practices are applicable to juvenile suspects. Search and seizure actions, lineups, and other police procedures are also subject to court review.

Another important issue is police discretion in dealing with juvenile offenders. Discretion is a low-visibility decision made in the administration of adult and juvenile justice. Discretionary decisions are made without guidelines from the police administrator. Discretion is essential in providing individualized justice, but problems such as discrimination, unfairness, and bias toward particular groups of juveniles must be controlled.

New initiatives in law enforcement to reduce the incidence of youth crime include (1) crime prevention and education programs, (2) mentoring programs, (3) curfew laws, and (4) gang control and drug and firearm interventions. The community policing philosophy, which emphasizes partnerships between police and citizens, has been applied to both adult and juvenile crime.

KEY TERMS

pledge system
watch system
community policing

juvenile officers
role conflicts
arrest

probable cause
search and seizure
custodial interrogation

Miranda warning
discretion

1. The term *discretion* is often defined as selective decision making by police and others in the juvenile justice system who are faced with alternative modes of action. Discuss some of the factors affecting the discretion of the police when dealing with juvenile offenders.

2. What role should police organizations play in delinquency prevention and control? Is it feasible to expect police departments to provide social services to children and families? How should police departments be better organized to provide for the control of juvenile delinquency?

3. What qualities should a police juvenile officer have? Should a college education be a requirement?

4. For the first time in a decade, arrests of juveniles for violent crime have declined. What do you believe caused this decline?

5. In light of the traditional and protective roles assumed by law-enforcement personnel in juvenile justice, is there any reason to have a *Miranda* warning for youths taken into custody?

6. Can the police and community be truly effective in forming a partnership to reduce juvenile delinquency? Discuss the role of the juvenile police officer in preventing and investigating juvenile crime.

VIEWPOINT

The Boston Police Department, together with concerned clergy members, youth outreach workers, social workers, alternative incarceration-provider service workers, and school police officers, developed a crime-control strategy called Operation Night Life. This program aims to prevent and intervene in possible youth and gang violence of probationers by regularly visiting their homes. Operation Night Life's main task enforcer is the forty-member Youth Violence Strike Force.

 To read more about Operation Night Life on InfoTrac® College Edition, go to James T. Jordan, "Boston's Operation Night Life: New Roles, New Rules," *FBI Law Enforcement Bulletin* 67:1 (Aug. 1998). To find further information, use *police* and *juveniles* as key terms.

Chapter 13

Juvenile Court Process: Pretrial, Trial, and Sentencing

AP/Wide World Photos

s an experienced family court judge, you are often faced with difficult decisions, but few are more difficult than the case of John M., who was arrested at age 14 for robbery and rape. His victim, a young neighborhood girl, was seriously injured in the attack and needed extensive hospitalization; she is now in counseling. Even though the charges are serious, because of his age John can still be subject to the jurisdiction of the juvenile division of the state family court. However, the prosecutor has filed a petition to waive jurisdiction to the adult court. Under existing state law, a hearing must be held to determine whether there is sufficient evidence that John cannot be successfully treated in the juvenile justice system and therefore warrants transfer to the adult system; the final decision on the matter is yours alone.

At the waiver hearing, you discover that John is the oldest of three siblings living in a single-parent home. He has had no contact with his father for more than 10 years. His psychological evaluation showed hostility, anger toward females, and great feelings of frustration. His intelligence is below average, and his behavioral and academic records are poor. In addition, John seems to be involved with a local youth gang, although he denies any formal association with the group. This is John's first formal involvement with the juvenile court. Previous contact was limited to an informal complaint for disorderly conduct at age 13, which was dismissed by the court's intake department. During the hearing, John verbalizes what you interpret to be superficial remorse for his offenses.

To the prosecutor, John seems to be a youth with poor controls who is likely to commit future crimes. The defense attorney argues that there are effective treatment opportunities within the juvenile justice system that can meet John's needs. Her views are supported by an evaluation of the case conducted by the court's probation staff, which concludes that the case can be dealt with in the confines of juvenile corrections.

If the case remains in the juvenile court, John can be kept in custody in a juvenile facility until age 18; if the case is transferred to felony court, he could be sentenced to up to 20 years in a maximum-security prison. As the judge, you recognize the seriousness of the crimes committed by John and realize that it is very difficult to predict or assess John's future behavior and potential dangerousness.

- Would you authorize a waiver to adult court or keep the case in the juvenile justice system?

- Can 14-year-olds truly understand the seriousness of their behavior?

- Should a juvenile court judge consider the victim in making a disposition decision?

Cases such as that of John M. are still all too common in the juvenile justice system. They require juvenile court judges to make decisions that will shape the rest of a child's life. Because the judicial process is one of the most critical points in the juvenile justice process, it is covered here in some detail. We begin with a discussion of the juvenile court and its jurisdiction. We then turn to issues involving the pre-adjudicatory stage of juvenile justice: detention, intake, diversion, pretrial release, plea bargaining, and waiver. We then turn to the trial stage, looking at the rights of the child at trial—particularly those rights dealing with counsel and trial by jury—through a detailed analysis of U.S. Supreme Court decisions. Procedural rules that govern the adjudicatory and dispositional hearings are also reviewed. We conclude with a discussion of dispositional alternatives and trends in sentencing.

THE JUVENILE COURT AND ITS JURISDICTION

Today's juvenile-delinquency cases are sometimes handled as part of a criminal trial court jurisdiction, or even within the probate court. However, in most jurisdictions they are treated within the structure of a family court or an independent juvenile court (14 states use more than one method to process juvenile cases).[1] The independent juvenile court is a specialized court for children, designed to promote rehabilitation of youth within a framework of procedural due process. It is concerned with acting both in the best interest of the child and in the best interest of public protection, two often-incompatible goals. Family courts, in contrast, have broad jurisdiction over a wide range of personal and household problems, including delinquency, paternity, child support, and custody issues. The major advantages of such a system are that it can serve sparsely populated areas, it permits judicial personnel and others to deal exclusively with children's matters, and it can obtain legislative funding more readily than other court systems.

Court Case Flow

Today, more than 1.7 million delinquency cases are adjudicated annually. Between 1988 and 1997 (the last data available) case flow increased 48 percent. The increasing numbers of cases were the product of a significant rise in the number of drug law violation cases, which increased 125 percent, and cases involving personal offenses (up 97%); property offense cases increased a more modest 19 percent.[2]

There were distinct gender- and race-based differences in the juvenile court population. Seventy-seven percent of delinquency cases in 1997 involved a male and 23 percent a female. However, the number of females processed by juvenile courts has increased from 1988, when less than 20 percent of the cases involved female offenders. Similarly, about 31 percent of the juvenile court population was comprised of African American youth, although they make up only about 15 percent of the general population.

The Actors in the Juvenile Courtroom

The key players in the juvenile court are prosecutors, judges, and defense attorneys.

The Defense Attorney As the result of a series of Supreme Court decisions, the right of a delinquent youth to have counsel at state trials has become a fundamental part of the juvenile justice system.[3] Today, courts must provide counsel to indigent defendants who face the possibility of incarceration. Over the past three decades, the rules of juvenile justice administration have become extremely complex. Preparation of a case for juvenile court often involves detailed investigation of a crime, knowledge of court procedures, use of rules of evidence, and skills in trial advocacy. The right to counsel is essential if children are to have a fair chance of presenting their cases in court.

juvenile defense attorneys
Represent children in juvenile court and play an active role at all stages of the proceedings.

In many respects, the role of **juvenile defense attorney** is similar to that in the criminal and civil areas. Defense attorneys representing children in the juvenile court play an active and important part in virtually all stages of the proceedings. For example, the defense attorney helps to clarify jurisdictional problems and to decide whether there is sufficient evidence to warrant filing a formal petition. The defense attorney helps outline the child's position regarding detention hearings and bail, and explores the opportunities for informal adjustment of the case. If no adjustment or diversion occurs, the defense attorney represents the child at adjudication, presenting evidence and cross-examining witnesses to see that the child's position is made clear to the court. Defense attorneys also play a critical role in the dispositional hearing. They present evidence bearing on the treatment decision and help the court formulate alternative

Juvenile defense attorneys play an active and important part in virtually all stages of the juvenile court proceedings, ranging from representing youths in police custody to filing their final appeals. (© Shelley Gazin/CORBIS)

guardian *ad litem* A court-appointed attorney who protects the interests of the child in cases involving the child's welfare.

Volunteer Court Appointed Special Advocates (CASA) are people who are appointed by judges to advocate for the best interests of abused and neglected children. To read more about the CASA program, go to

http://www.nationalcasa.org/

For an up-to-date list of Web links, go to www.wadsworth.com/ product/0534573053s

public defender An attorney who works in a public agency or under private contractual agreement as defense counsel to indigent defendants.

plans for the child's care. Finally, defense attorneys pursue any appeals from the trial, represent the child in probation revocation proceedings, and generally protect the child's right to treatment.

In some cases, a **guardian *ad litem*** may be appointed by the court.[4] The guardian *ad litem*—ordinarily seen in abuse, neglect, and dependency cases—may be appointed in delinquency cases where there is a question of a need for a particular treatment (for example, placement in a mental health center) and offenders and their attorneys resist placement. The guardian *ad litem* may advocate for the commitment on the ground that it is in the child's best interests. The guardian *ad litem* fulfills many roles, ranging from legal advocate to concerned individual who works with parents and human service professionals in developing a proper treatment plan that best serves the interests of the minor child.[5]

Court Appointed Special Advocates (CASA) Court Appointed Special Advocates (CASA) employ volunteers who advise the juvenile court about child placement. The CASA programs (*casa* is Spanish for "home") have demonstrated that volunteers can investigate the needs of children and provide a vital link between the judge, the attorneys, and the child in protecting the juvenile's right to a safe placement.[6]

Public Defender Services for Children To satisfy the requirement that indigent children be provided with counsel, the federal government and the states have expanded **public defender** services. Three alternatives exist for providing children with legal counsel: (1) an all-public defender program, (2) an appointed private-counsel system, and (3) a combination system of public defenders and appointed private attorneys.

The public-defender program is a statewide program established by legislation and funded by the state government to provide counsel to children at public expense. This program allows access to the expertise of lawyers, who spend a considerable amount of time representing juvenile offenders every day. Defender programs generally provide separate office space for juvenile-court personnel, as well as support staff, and training programs for new lawyers.

In many rural areas, where individual public-defender programs are not available, defense services are offered through appointed private counsel. Private lawyers are assigned to individual juvenile court cases and receive compensation for the time and services they provide. When private attorneys are used in large urban areas, they are generally selected from a list established by the court, and they often operate in conjunction with a public-defender program. The weaknesses of a system of assigned private counsel include assignment to cases for which the lawyers are unqualified, inadequate compensation, and lack of supportive or supervisory services.

Though efforts have been made to supply juveniles with adequate legal representation, many juveniles still go to court unrepresented, or with an overworked lawyer who provides inadequate representation. Many juvenile-court defense lawyers work on more than 500 cases per year, and more than half leave their jobs in under two years.[7] Other problems facing public defenders include: (1) lack of resources for independent evaluations, expert witnesses, and investigatory support; (2) lack of computers, telephones, files, and adequate office space; (3) juvenile public defenders' inexperience, lack of training, low morale, and salaries lower than those of their counterparts who defend adults or serve as prosecutors; and (4) inability to keep up with rapidly changing juvenile codes.[8] With juvenile offenders facing the prospect of much-longer sentences, mandatory minimum sentences, and time in adult prisons, the need for quality defense attorneys for juveniles has never been greater.

The Prosecutor in the Juvenile Court The **juvenile prosecutor** is the attorney responsible for bringing the state's case against the accused juvenile. Depending on the level of government and the jurisdiction, the prosecutor can be called a district attorney, a county attorney, a state attorney, or a United States attorney. Prosecutors are members of the bar selected for their positions by political appointment or popular election.

Ordinarily, the juvenile prosecutor is a staff member of the prosecuting attorney's office. If the office of the district attorney is of sufficient size, the juvenile prosecutor may work exclusively on juvenile and other family law matters. If the caseload of juvenile offenders is small, the juvenile prosecutor may also have criminal prosecution responsibilities.

For the first 60 years of its existence, the juvenile court did not include a prosecutor, because the concept of an adversary process was seen as inconsistent with the philosophy of treatment. The court followed a social-service helping model, and informal proceedings were believed to be in the best interests of the child. Today, in a more legalistic juvenile court, almost all jurisdictions require by law that a prosecutor be present in the juvenile court.

A number of states have passed legislation giving prosecutors control over intake and waiver decisions. Some have passed concurrent-jurisdiction laws that allow prosecutors to decide in which court to bring serious juvenile cases. In some jurisdictions, it is the prosecutor and not the juvenile-court judge who is entrusted with the decision of whether to transfer a case to adult court. Consequently, the role of juvenile-court prosecutor is now critical in the juvenile justice process. Including a prosecutor in juvenile court balances the interests of the state, the defense attorney, the child, and the judge, preserving the independence of each party's functions and responsibilities.

The prosecutor has the power either to initiate or to discontinue delinquency or status-offense allegations. Like police officers, prosecutors have broad discretion in the exercise of their duties. Because due-process rights have been extended to juveniles, the prosecutor's role in the juvenile court has in some ways become similar to the prosecutor's role in the adult court.

Because children are committing more serious crimes today and because the courts have granted juveniles constitutional safeguards, the prosecutor is likely to play an increasingly significant role in the juvenile court system. According to Shine and Price, the prosecutor's involvement will promote a due-process model that should result in a fairer, more just system for all parties. But they also point out that, to meet current and future challenges, prosecutors need more information on such issues as (1) how

juvenile prosecutor Government attorney responsible for representing the interests of the state and bringing the case against the accused juvenile.

TABLE 13.1	Duties of the Juvenile Court Judge

- Rule on pretrial motions involving such legal issues as arrest, search and seizure, interrogation, and lineup identification
- Make decisions about the continued detention of children prior to trial
- Make decisions about plea-bargaining agreements and the informal adjustment of juvenile cases
- Handle trials, rule on the appropriateness of conduct, settle questions of evidence and procedure, and guide the questioning of witnesses
- Assume responsibility for holding dispositional hearings and deciding on the treatment accorded the child
- Handle waiver proceedings
- Handle appeals where allowed by statute

to identify repeat offenders, (2) how to determine which programs are most effective, (3) how early-childhood experiences relate to delinquency, and (4) what measures can be used in place of secure placements without reducing public safety.[9]

Today, prosecutors are addressing the problems associated with juvenile crime. A balanced approach has been recommended—one that emphasizes enforcement, prosecution, and detention of serious offenders and the use of proven prevention and intervention programs.[10]

juvenile court judge A judge elected or appointed to preside over juvenile cases and whose decisions can only be reviewed by a judge of a higher court.

The Juvenile Court Judge Even with the elevation of the prosecutor's role, the **juvenile court judge** is still the central character in a court of juvenile or family law. Her or his responsibilities have become far more extensive and complex in recent years. Juvenile or family court judges perform the functions listed in Table 13.1.

In addition, judges often have extensive influence over other agencies of the court: probation, the court clerk, the law-enforcement officer, and the office of the juvenile prosecutor. Juvenile court judges exercise considerable leadership in developing solutions to juvenile justice problems. In this role they must respond to the pressures the community places on juvenile court resources. According to the *parens patriae* philosophy, the juvenile judge must ensure that the necessary community resources are available so that the children and families who come before the court can receive the proper care and help.[11] This may be the most untraditional role for the juvenile court judge, but it may also be the most important.

In some jurisdictions juvenile court judges handle family-related cases exclusively. In others they preside over criminal and civil cases as well. Traditionally, juvenile court judges have been relegated to a lower status than other judges. Judges assigned to juvenile courts have not ordinarily been chosen from the highest levels of the legal profession. Such groups as the American Judicature Society have noted that the field of juvenile justice has often been shortchanged by the appointment of unqualified judges. In some jurisdictions, particularly major urban areas, juvenile court judges may be of the highest caliber, but many courts continue to function with mediocre judges.

Inducing the best-trained individuals to accept juvenile court judgeships is a very important goal. Where the juvenile court is part of the highest general court of trial jurisdiction, the problem of securing qualified personnel is not as great. However, if the juvenile court is of limited or specialized jurisdiction and has the authority to try only minor cases, it may attract only poorly trained personnel. Lawyers and judges who practice in juvenile court receive little respect. The juvenile court has a negative image, because even though what it does is of great importance to parents, children, and society in general, it has been placed at the lowest level of the judicial hierarchy.

Many critical decisions are made before the juvenile trial begins. At this stage of the juvenile justice system: whether to detain youths or release them to the community; whether to waive them to the adult court or retain them in the juvenile justice system; whether to treat them in the community or send them to a secure treatment center. These teens are waiting during the intake process in the juvenile court in Orlando, Florida. The intake process refers to the screening of cases by the juvenile court system. Intake officers, who are often probation staff members, determine whether the services of the juvenile court are needed. (© Joel Gordon)

Checkpoints

✔ In most jurisdictions, kids are adjudicated within the structure of either a family court or an independent juvenile court.

✔ More than 1.7 million delinquency cases are adjudicated annually.

✔ All juveniles must be provided with legal counsel if they face the possibility of incarceration.

✔ A guardian *ad litem* is an attorney who represents the child during legal proceedings.

✔ Court Appointed Special Advocates (CASA) are volunteers who advise the juvenile court about child placement.

✔ The juvenile prosecutor is the attorney responsible for bringing the state's case against the accused juvenile.

✔ The juvenile judge must ensure that the children and families that come before the court can receive the proper care and help.

JUVENILE COURT PROCESS

Now that we have briefly described the setting of the juvenile court and the major players who control its operations, we turn to a discussion of the procedures that shape the contours of juvenile justice—the pretrial process and the juvenile trial and disposition. Many critical decisions are made at this stage of juvenile justice system: whether to detain a youth or release the youth to the community; whether to waive youths to the adult court or retain them in the juvenile justice system; whether to treat them in the community or send them to a secure treatment center. Each of these can have a profound influence on the child, with effects lasting throughout the life course. What are these critical stages, and how are decisions made within them?

Release or Detain?

After a child has been taken into custody and a decision is made to treat the case formally (that is, with a juvenile court hearing), a decision must be made to either release the child into the custody of parents or to detain the child in the temporary care of the state, in physically restrictive facilities pending court disposition or transfer to another agency.[12] Nationally, about 70 percent of all states had detention centers administered at the county level, about 34 percent had state-level facilities,

16 percent had court-administered facilities, and 11 percent contracted with private vendors to operate facilities.[13]

Detention can be a traumatic experience because many facilities are prison-like, with locked doors and barred windows. Consequently, most experts in juvenile justice advocate that detention be limited to alleged offenders who require secure custody for the protection of themselves and others. However, children who are neglected and dependent, runaways, and those who are homeless may under some circumstances be placed in secure detention facilities along with violent and dangerous youth until more suitable placements can be found.[14] Others have had a trial but have not been sentenced, or are awaiting the imposition of their sentence. Some may have violated probation and are awaiting a hearing while being kept alongside a severely mentally ill adolescent for whom no appropriate placement can be found. Another group are adjudicated delinquents awaiting admittance to a correctional training school.[15] Consequently, it is possible for nonviolent status offenders to be housed in the same facility with delinquents who have committed felony-type offenses.

To remedy this situation, an ongoing effort has been made to remove status offenders and neglected or abused children from detention facilities that also house juvenile delinquents. In addition, alternatives to detention centers—temporary foster homes, detention boarding homes, and programs of neighborhood supervision—have been developed. These alternatives, referred to as **shelter care,** enable youths to live in a more home-like setting while the courts dispose of their cases.

National Detention Trends Despite the efforts to reduce the number of juveniles held in short-term detention facilities, their numbers increased by 31 percent between 1986 and 1997, rising from 244,000 to 327,000 youths. Juveniles were securely detained in 19 percent of the delinquency cases processed in 1997.[16]

The typical delinquent detainee was male, over 15 years of age, and charged with a property crime, whereas the typical status offender was female, under 16 years of age, and a runaway.[17] Racial minorities are overrepresented in detention, especially those who are indigent and whose families may be receiving public assistance. Minority overrepresentation is particularly vexing, considering that detention may increase the risk of a youth's being adjudicated and eventually confined.[18]

This rise in the juvenile detention rate is occurring at a time when the overall population of juvenile offenders is decreasing. Experts believe the steady increase in detention use may result from (1) a steady rise in the rate of serious juvenile offenses, (2) an increasing number of drug-related crimes, and (3) the involvement of younger children in the juvenile justice system.[19] However, some things about juvenile detention have not changed: there remains a serious problem of overrepresentation of minorities in secure detention.[20]

The Decision to Detain The majority of children taken into custody by the police are released to their parents or guardians. Some are held overnight until their parents can be notified of the arrest. Police officers normally take a child to a place of detention only after other alternatives have been exhausted. Many juvenile courts in urban areas have staff members, such as intake probation officers, on duty 24 hours a day to screen detention admissions.

Ordinarily, delinquent children are detained if the police believe they are inclined to run away while awaiting trial, or if they are likely to commit an offense dangerous to the parent. There is evidence that some decision makers are more likely to detain minority youth, especially if they dwell in dangerous lower-class areas.[21]

Typically, children should not be held in a detention facility or shelter-care unit for more than 24 hours without a formal petition (a written request to the court) being filed to extend the detention period. To detain a juvenile, there must be clear evidence of probable cause that the child has committed the offense and that he or she will flee if not detained. Although the requirements for detention hearings vary,

shelter care A place for temporary care of children in physically unrestricting facilities.

To find out more about the needs of detention, go to the *Juvenile Detention Training Needs Assessment Research Report* by David W. Roush. You can find it at

http://www.ncjrs.org/txtfiles/jdtna.txt

For an up-to-date list of Web links, go to www.wadsworth.com/product/0534573053s

THE DETENTION DIVERSION ADVOCACY PROGRAM

he concept behind the **Detention Diversion Advocacy Program (DDAP)** approach is case advocacy employing the efforts of a staff of laypersons or nonlegal experts acting on behalf of youthful offenders at disposition hearings. It relies on a case-management strategy that involves coordination of human services, opportunities, or benefits. Case-management efforts are designed to integrate services across a cluster of organizations, to ensure continuity of care, and to facilitate development of client skills (for example, job interviewing, or reading and writing skills) by involving a variety of social networks and service providers (social agencies that provide specific services to youth, like drug counseling and crisis intervention).

Detention advocacy involves identifying youth likely to be detained pending their adjudication. Detention Diversion Advocacy Program clients are identified primarily through referrals from the public defender's office, the probation department, community agencies, and parents. Admission to DDAP is restricted to youth currently held, or likely to be held, in secure detention. Once a potential client is identified, DDAP case managers present a release plan to the judge that includes a list of appropriate community services (tutoring, drug counseling, family counseling) that will be made available on the youth's behalf. Additionally, the plan includes specified objectives (improved grades, victim restitution, drug-free status) as a means of evaluating the youth's progress in the program. Emphasis is placed on allowing the youth to live at home while going through the program. If home placement is not a viable option, program staff will identify and secure a suitable alternative. If the judge deems the release plan acceptable, the youth is released to DDAP supervision.

The DDAP case-management model provides frequent and consistent support and supervision to youth and their families. Case managers link youth to community-based services and closely monitor their progress. The DDAP program requires the case manager to have daily contact with the youth, the family, and significant others, including a minimum of three in-person meetings a week with the youth. The youth's family members, particularly parents and guardians, are provided with additional services that typically include assistance in securing employment, daycare, drug treatment services, and income support (for example, food stamps).

Evaluations of the DDAP program indicated that it is very successful:

- The overall recidivism rate of the DDAP group was 34 percent, compared with 60 percent for the comparison group.

- Only 14 percent of the DDAP group had two or more subsequent referrals, compared with 50 percent of the comparison group.

- Only 9 percent of the DDAP group returned to court on a violent crime charge, compared with 25 percent of the comparison group.

- Only 5 percent of the DDAP group had two or more subsequent petitions, compared with 22 percent of the comparison group.

Source: Randall G. Shelden, "Detention Diversion Advocacy: An Evaluation," *Juvenile Justice Bulletin* (Washington, DC: Office of Juvenile Justice and Delinquency Prevention, 1999).

---

most jurisdictions require that they occur almost immediately after the child's admission to a detention facility and provide the youth with notice and counsel.

New Approaches to Detention Efforts have been ongoing to improve the process and conditions of detention. Experts maintain that detention facilities should provide youth with education, visitation, private communications, counseling, continuous supervision, medical and health care, nutrition, recreation, and reading. Detention should also include, or provide, a system for clinical observation and diagnosis that complements the wide range of helpful services.[22]

The consensus today is that juvenile detention centers should be reserved for youths who present a clear threat to the community. In some states, nonsecure facilities are being used to service juveniles for a limited period. Alternatives to secure detention include (1) in-home monitoring, (2) home detention, (3) day-center electronic monitoring, (4) high-intensity community supervision, and (5) comprehensive case management programs. (See the Policy and Practice box, "The Detention Diversion Advocacy Program.")

Undoubtedly, juveniles pose special detention problems, but some efforts are being made to improve programs and to reduce pretrial detention use, especially in secure settings. Of all the problems associated with detention, however, none is as critical as the issue of placing youths in adult jails.

Restricting Detention in Adult Jails A significant problem in juvenile justice is placing youths in adult jails. This is usually done in rural areas where no other facility exists. Almost all experts agree that placing children under the age of 18 in any type of jail facility should be prohibited because youngsters can easily be victimized by other inmates and staff, be forced to live in squalid conditions, and be subject to physical and sexual abuse.

Until a few years ago, placing juveniles in adult facilities was common, but efforts have been made to change this situation. In 1989, the Juvenile Justice and Delinquency Prevention Act (JJDPA) of 1974 was amended to require that the states remove all juveniles from adult jails and lockups. According to federal guidelines, all juveniles in state custody must be separated from adult offenders or the state could lose federal juvenile justice funds. The OJJDP defines separation as the condition in which juvenile detainees have either totally independent facilities or shared facilities that are designed so that juveniles and adults neither have contact nor share programs or staff.[23]

Much debate has arisen over whether the initiative to remove juveniles from adult jails has succeeded. Most indications are that the number of youths being held in adult facilities has declined significantly from the almost 500,000 a year recorded in 1979.[24] Today, less than 100,000 juveniles are detained annually in adult jails. These figures may be misleading, however, because they do not include youths held in urban jails for under 6 hours, or in rural ones for under 24 hours; youths transferred to adult courts; or youths in states that consider anyone over 16 or 17 to be an adult.

With federal help, some progress appears to have been made in removing juveniles from adult facilities, but thousands each year continue to be held in close contact with adults, and thousands more are held in facilities that, although physically separate, put them in close proximity to adults. To the youths held within their walls, there may appear to be little difference between the juvenile detention facilities and the adult jail.

Removing Status Offenders Along with removing all juveniles from adult jails, the OJJDP has made deinstitutionalization of status offenders a cornerstone of its policy. The Juvenile Justice and Delinquency Prevention Act of 1974 prohibits the placement of status offenders in secure detention facilities.

Removing status offenders from secure facilities serves two purposes: (1) it reduces interaction with serious offenders, and (2) it insulates status offenders from the stigma associated with being a detainee in a locked facility. Efforts appear to be working, and the number of status offenders being held in some sort of secure confinement has been on a two-decade decline. Nonetheless, the debate over the most effective way to handle juvenile status offenders continues, and some critics have argued that if the juvenile court is unable to take effective action in status-offender cases it should be stripped of jurisdiction over these youths. Most judges would prefer to retain jurisdiction so they can help children and families resolve problems that cause runaways, truancy, and other status offense behaviors.[25]

Bail for Children One critical detention issue is whether juveniles can be released on **bail.** Adults retain the right, via the Eighth Amendment to the Constitution, to reasonable bail in noncapital cases. Most states, however, refuse juveniles the right to bail. They argue that juvenile proceedings are civil, not criminal, and that detention is rehabilitative, not punitive. In addition, they argue that juveniles do not need a constitutional right to bail because statutory provisions allow children to be released into parental custody.

State juvenile bail statutes fall into three categories: (1) those guaranteeing the right to bail, (2) those that grant the court discretion to give bail, and (3) those that deny a

bail Amount of money that must be paid as a condition of pretrial release to ensure that the accused will return for subsequent proceedings; bail is normally set by the judge at the initial appearance, and if unable to make bail, the accused is detained in jail.

JUVENILE LAW IN REVIEW

SCHALL V. MARTIN

Facts

Gregory Martin was arrested in New York City on December 13, 1977, on charges of robbery, assault, and criminal possession of a weapon. Because he was arrested at 11:30 P.M. and lied about his residence, Martin was kept overnight in detention and brought to juvenile court the next day for an "initial appearance" accompanied by his grandmother. The family court judge, citing possession of a loaded weapon, the false address given to police, and the fact that Martin was left unsupervised late in the evening, ordered him detained before trial under section 320.5(3)(6) of the New York State code, which authorizes pretrial detention of an accused juvenile delinquent if "there is a substantial probability that he will not appear in court on the return date or there is a serious risk that he may before the return date commit an act which if committed by an adult would constitute a crime." Later, at trial, Martin was found to be a delinquent and sentenced to two years' probation.

While he was in pretrial detention, Martin's attorneys filed a class action on behalf of all youths subject to preventive detention in New York, charging that this form of detention was a denial of due-process rights under the Fifth and Fourteenth Amendments. The New York appellate courts upheld Martin's claim on the ground that because, at adjudication, most delinquents are released or placed on probation it was unfair to incarcerate them before trial. The prosecution brought the case to the U.S. Supreme Court for final judgment.

Decision

The U.S. Supreme Court upheld the state's right to place juveniles in preventive detention, holding that the practice serves the legitimate objective of protecting both the juvenile and society from pretrial crime. Pretrial detention need not be considered punishment merely because the juvenile is eventually released or put on probation. In addition, there are procedural safeguards, such as notice and a hearing, and a statement of facts that must be given to juveniles before they are placed in detention. The Court also found that detention based on prediction of future behavior was not a violation of due process. Many decisions are made in the justice system, such as the decision to sentence or grant parole, that are based in part on a prediction of future behavior, and these have all been accepted by the courts as legitimate exercises of state power.

Significance of the Case

Schall v. Martin established the right of juvenile court judges to deny youths pretrial release if they perceive them to be dangerous. However, the case also established a due-process standard for detention hearings that includes notice and a statement of substantial reasons for the detention. Despite these measures, opponents hold that preventive detention deprives offenders of their freedom because guilt has not been proven. It is also unfair, they claim, to punish people for what judicial authorities believe they may do in the future, as it is impossible to predict who will be a danger to the community. Moreover, because judges are able to use discretion in their detention decisions, an offender could unfairly be deprived of freedom without legal recourse.

Source: *Schall v. Martin,* 104 S.Ct. 2403 (1984).

---

juvenile the right to bail.[26] This disparity may be a function of the lack of legal guidance on the matter. The U.S. Supreme Court has never decided the issue of juvenile bail. Some courts have stated that bail provisions do not apply to juveniles. Others rely on the Eighth Amendment against cruel and unusual punishment, or on state constitutional provisions or statutes, and conclude that juveniles do have a right to bail.

preventive detention Keeping the accused in custody prior to trial because the accused is suspected of being a danger to the community.

Preventive Detention Even if the U.S. Supreme Court has not yet decided whether juveniles have a right to traditional money bail, they have concluded that the state has a right to detain dangerous youth until their trial, a practice called **preventive detention.** On June 4, 1984, the U.S. Supreme Court dealt with this issue in *Schall v. Martin,* when it upheld the State of New York's preventive-detention statute.[27] Because this is a key case in juvenile justice, it is the subject of the accompanying Juvenile Law in Review. Today, most states allow "dangerous" youths to be held indefinitely before trial. Because preventive detention may attach a stigma of guilt to a child presumed innocent, the practice remains a highly controversial one, and the efficacy of such laws remains unknown.[28]

The Intake Process

The term **intake** refers to the screening of cases by the juvenile court system. The child and his or her family are screened by intake officers to determine whether the services of the juvenile court are needed. Intake officers may (1) send the youth home with no further action, (2) divert the youth to a social agency, (3) petition the youth to the juvenile court, or (4) file a petition and hold the youth in detention. The intake process reduces demands on court resources, screens out cases that are not within the court's jurisdiction, and enables assistance to be obtained from community agencies without court intervention.

About 19 percent (335,400) of all delinquency cases in 1997 were dismissed at intake, often because they were not legally sufficient. Another 24 percent (423,700) were processed informally, with the juvenile voluntarily agreeing to the recommended disposition (for example, voluntary treatment).[29] Juvenile court intake is provided for by statute in almost all the states. Intake screening allows juvenile courts to enter into consent decrees with juveniles without filing petitions and without formal adjudication. (The consent decree is a court order authorizing disposition of the case without a formal label of delinquency. It is based on an agreement between the intake department of the court and the juvenile who is the subject of the complaint.)

Intake also has some problems. Although almost all state juvenile court systems provide intake and diversion programs, there are few formal criteria for selecting children for such alternatives. There are also legal problems associated with the intake process. Among them are whether the child has a right to counsel, whether the child is protected against self-incrimination, and to what degree the child needs to consent to nonjudicial disposition as recommended by the intake officer. Finally, intake dispositions are often determined by the prior record rather than by the seriousness of the offense or the social background of the child. This practice departs from the philosophy of *parens patriae*.[30]

The shift from rehabilitation has led to changes in the intake process. One trend has been the increased influence of prosecutors. Traditionally, the intake process has been controlled by probation personnel whose decisions influenced the judge's view of which cases to handle formally and which should be settled without court action. This approach to intake, in which probation personnel seek to dispense the least disruptive amount of rehabilitative justice, is being replaced in some jurisdictions by a model in which a prosecutor is the central figure. Some states now require that intake officers get approval from the prosecutor before either accepting or rejecting a delinquency petition. Other states allow the complaining party to appeal petitions rejected by intake officers to the prosecutor.[31]

Diversion

One of the most important alternatives chosen at intake is nonjudicial disposition or, as it is variously called, nonjudicial adjustment, handling or processing, informal disposition, adjustment, or (most commonly) **diversion.** Juvenile diversion is the process of placing youths suspected of law-violating behavior into treatment-oriented programs prior to formal trial and disposition to minimize their penetration into the justice system and thereby avoid stigma and labeling.

Diversion implies more than simply screening out cases for which no additional treatment is needed. Screening involves abandoning efforts to apply coercive measures to a defendant. In contrast, diversion encourages an individual to participate in some specific program or activity to avoid further prosecution.

Most court-based diversion programs employ a particular formula for choosing youths for diversion. Criteria such as being a first offender, a nonviolent offender, or a status offender, or being drug- or alcohol-dependent, are used to select clients. In some programs, youths will be asked to partake of services voluntarily in lieu of a court appearance. In other programs, prosecutors will agree to defer, and then dis-

The majority of children taken into custody by the police are released to their parents or guardians. Some are held overnight until their parents can be notified of the arrest. Police officers normally take a child to a place of detention only after other alternatives have been exhausted. Many juvenile courts in urban areas have staff members, such as intake probation officers, on duty twenty-four hours a day to screen detention admissions. (Rich Graulieh/*Palm Beach Post*)

miss, a case once a youth has completed a treatment program. Finally, some programs can be initiated by the juvenile court judge after an initial hearing.

In summary, diversion programs have been created to remove nonserious offenders from the justice system, provide them with nonpunitive treatment services, and help them avoid the stigma of a delinquent label.

Issues in Diversion: Widening the Net Diversion has been viewed as a promising alternative to official procedures, but over the years its basic premises have been questioned.[32] The most damaging criticism has been that diversion programs are involving children in the juvenile justice system who previously would have been released without official notice. This is referred to as **widening the net.** Various studies indicate that police and court personnel are likely to use diversion programs for youths who ordinarily would have been turned loose at the intake or arrest stage.[33] Why does net-widening occur? One explanation is that police and prosecutors find diversion a more attractive alternative than both official processing and outright release—diversion helps them resolve the conflict between doing too much and doing too little.

Diversion has also been criticized as ineffective; that is, youths being diverted make no better adjustment in the community than those who go through official channels. However, not all experts are critical of diversion. Some challenge the net-widening concept as naive: How do we know that diverted youths would have had less interface with the justice system if diversion didn't exist?[34] Even if juveniles escaped official labels for their current offense, might they not eventually fall into the hands of the police? The rehabilitative potential of diversion should not be overlooked.[35] Juvenile diversion programs represent one alternative to the traditional process.

widening the net Phenomenon that occurs when programs created to divert youths from the justice system actually involve them more deeply in the official process.

The Petition

complaint Report made by the police or some other agency to the court that initiates the intake process.

A **complaint** is the report made by the police or some other agency to the court to initiate the intake process. Once the agency makes a decision that judicial disposition is required, a petition is filed. The petition is the formal complaint that initiates judicial action against a juvenile charged with delinquency or a status offense. The petition includes basic information such as the name, age, and residence of the child; the parents' names; and the facts alleging the child's delinquency. The police officer, a family member, or a social-service agency can file a petition.

If, after being given the right to counsel, the child admits the allegation in the petition, an initial hearing is scheduled for the child to make the admission before the court and information is gathered to develop a treatment plan. If the child does not admit to any of the facts in the petition, a date is set for a hearing on the petition. This hearing, whose purpose is to determine the merits of the petition, is similar to the adult trial. Once a hearing date has been set, the probation department is normally asked to prepare a social study report. This predisposition report contains relevant information about the child, along with recommendations for treatment and service.

When a date has been set for the hearing on the petition, parents or guardians and other persons associated with the petition (witnesses, the arresting police officer, and victims) are notified. On occasion, the court may issue a summons—a court order requiring the juvenile or others involved in the case to appear for the hearing. The statutes in a given jurisdiction govern the contents of the petition. Some jurisdictions, for instance, allow for a petition to be filed based on the information of the complainant alone. Others require that the petition be filed under oath or that an affidavit accompany the petition. Some jurisdictions authorize only one official, such as a probation officer or prosecutor, to file the petition. Others allow numerous officials, including family and social-service agencies, to set forth facts in the petition.

Checkpoints

✔ Detention is the temporary care of children by the state in physically restrictive facilities pending court disposition or transfer to another agency.

✔ The federal government has encouraged the removal of status offenders from detention facilities that also house juvenile delinquents; it has encouraged the removal of delinquents from adult jails.

✔ Racial minorities are overrepresented in detention.

✔ Experts maintain that detention facilities should provide youth with treatment such as education, counseling, and health care.

✔ Intake refers to the screening of cases by the juvenile court system to determine whether the services of the juvenile court are needed.

✔ One of the most important alternatives chosen at intake is nonjudicial disposition or, as it is variously called, nonjudicial adjustment, handling or processing, informal disposition, adjustment, or (most commonly) diversion.

✔ The petition is the formal complaint that initiates judicial action against a juvenile charged with delinquency or a status offense.

The Plea and Plea Bargaining

plea bargaining The exchange of prosecutorial and judicial concessions for a guilty plea by the accused; plea bargaining usually results in a reduced charge or a more lenient sentence.

In the adult criminal justice system, the defendant normally enters a plea of guilty or not guilty. More than 90 percent of all adult defendants plead guilty. A large proportion of those pleas involve **plea bargaining**, the exchange of prosecutorial and judicial concessions for guilty pleas.[36] Plea bargaining permits a defendant to plead guilty to a less-serious charge in exchange for an agreement by the prosecutor to recommend a reduced sentence to the court. It involves a discussion between the child's attorney and the prosecutor by which the child agrees to plead guilty to obtain a reduced charge or a lenient sentence.

Few juvenile codes require a guilty or not-guilty plea when a petition is filed against a child. In most jurisdictions an initial hearing is held at which the child either submits to a finding of the facts or denies the petition.[37] If the child admits to the facts, the court determines an appropriate disposition. If the child denies the allegations, the case normally proceeds to trial. When a child enters no plea, the court ordinarily imposes a denial of the charges. This may occur where a juvenile doesn't understand the nature of the complaint or isn't represented by an attorney.

A high percentage of juvenile offenders enter guilty pleas; that is, they admit to the facts of the petition. How many of these pleas involve plea bargaining is unknown. In the past it was believed that plea bargaining was unnecessary in the juvenile justice system because there was little incentive to bargain in a system that does not have jury trials or long sentences. In addition, because the court must dispose of cases in the best interests of the child, plea negotiation seemed unnecessary. Consequently, there has long been a debate over the appropriateness of plea bargaining in juvenile justice. The arguments in favor of plea bargaining include lower court costs and efficiency. Counterarguments hold that plea bargaining with juveniles is an unregulated and unethical process. When used, experts believe the process requires the highest standards of good faith by the prosecutor.[38]

Growing concern about violent juvenile crime has spurred attorneys increasingly to seek to negotiate a plea rather than accept the so-called good interests of the court judgment—a judgment that might result in harsher sanctions. The extension of the adversary process to children has led to an increase in plea bargaining, creating an informal trial process that parallels the adult system. Other factors in the trend toward juvenile plea bargaining include the use of prosecutors rather than probation personnel and police officers in juvenile courts, and the ever-increasing caseloads in such courts.

Plea bargaining negotiations generally involve one or more of the following: (1) reduction of a charge, (2) change in the proceedings from that of delinquency to a status offense, (3) elimination of possible waiver to the criminal court, and (4) agreements regarding dispositional programs for the child. In states where youths are subject to long mandatory sentences, reduction of the charges may have a significant impact on the outcome of the case. In states where youths may be waived to the adult court for committing certain serious crimes, a plea reduction may result in the juvenile court's maintaining jurisdiction.

Little clear evidence exists of how much plea bargaining there is in the juvenile justice system, but it is apparent that such negotiations do take place and seem to be increasing. Joseph Sanborn found that about 20 percent of the cases processed in Philadelphia resulted in a negotiated plea. Most were for reduced sentences, typically probation in lieu of incarceration. Sanborn found that plea bargaining was a complex process, depending in large measure on the philosophy of the judge and the court staff. In general, he found it to have greater benefit for the defendants than for the court.[39]

In summary, the majority of juvenile cases that are not adjudicated seem to be the result of admissions to the facts rather than actual plea bargaining. Plea bargaining is less common in juvenile courts than in adult courts because incentives such as dropping multiple charges or substituting a misdemeanor for a felony are unlikely. Nonetheless, plea bargaining is firmly entrenched in the juvenile process. Any plea bargain, however, must be entered into voluntarily and knowingly; otherwise, the conviction may be overturned on appeal.

transfer process Transferring a juvenile offender from the jurisdiction of juvenile court to adult criminal court.

TRANSFER TO THE ADULT COURT

One of the most significant actions that can occur in the early court processing of a juvenile offender is the **transfer process.** Otherwise known as waiver, bindover, or removal, this process involves transferring a juvenile from the juvenile court to the criminal court. Virtually all state statutes allow for this kind of transfer.

Figure 13.1

Figure 13.1
Delinquency Cases Waived to Juvenile Court, 1988–1997

Source: Charles Puzzanchera, *Delinquency Cases Waived to Juvenile Court 1988–1997,* OJJDP Fact Sheet (Washington, DC: U.S. Department of Justice, Office of Juvenile Justice and Delinquency Prevention 2000) p. 1.

Delinquency cases judicially waived to criminal court

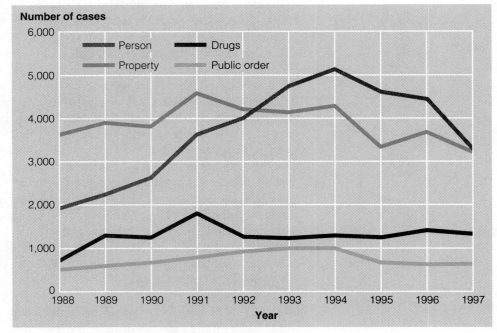

Note: The number of delinquency cases judicially waived to criminal court grew 73% between 1988 and 1994 and then declined 28% through 1997. However, trends varied across offense categories.

The number of delinquency cases judicially waived to criminal court reached a peak in 1994 with 11,700 cases and then began to decline. In 1997, U.S. courts waived approximately 8,400 cases to the adult court. This number represents less than 1 percent of the formally processed delinquency caseload.[40] As Figure 13.1 shows, the proportion of youths waived for personal offenses involving violence is now equal to the waived cases involving property crimes.

Waiver Procedures

Today, all states allow juveniles to be tried as adults in criminal courts in one of three ways:

1. *Concurrent jurisdiction.* In about 15 states, the prosecutor has the discretion of filing charges for certain offenses in either juvenile or criminal court.

2. *Excluded offenses.* In about 28 states, certain offenses are automatically excluded from juvenile court. These offenses can be minor, such as traffic violations, or serious, such as murder or rape. Statutory exclusion accounts for the largest number of juveniles tried as adults.

3. *Judicial waiver.* In a procedure known as *binding over,* or *certifying,* juvenile cases to criminal court, a hearing is held before a juvenile court judge, who then decides whether jurisdiction should be waived and the case transferred to criminal court. Nearly all states offer provisions for juvenile waivers.[41]

Due Process in Transfer Proceedings

The standards for transfer procedures are set by state statute. Some jurisdictions allow for transfer between the ages of 14 and 17. Others restrict waiver proceedings to mature juveniles and specify particular offenses. In a few jurisdictions, any child can be sentenced to the criminal court system, regardless of age.

Opponents of waiver suggest that the transfer process is often applied unfairly and is at odds with the treatment philosophy of the juvenile court. Furthermore, some children tried in the adult criminal court may be incarcerated under conditions so extreme that they will be permanently damaged. Another serious disadvantage of transfering a child is the stigma that may be attached to a conviction in the criminal court. Labeling children as adult offenders early in life may seriously impair their future educational and employment opportunities. (© Joel Gordon)

Those states that have amended their waiver policies now exclude certain serious offenses from juvenile court jurisdiction. For example, Indiana excludes cases involving 16- and 17-year-olds charged with kidnapping, rape, and robbery. In Illinois, youths ages 15 and 16 who are charged with murder, assault, or robbery with a firearm are automatically sent to criminal court; in Pennsylvania, any child accused of murder, regardless of age, is tried before the criminal court.[42] Other jurisdictions use exclusion to remove traffic offenses and public-ordinance violations.

The trend toward excluding serious violent offenses from juvenile court jurisdictions is growing in response to the demand to "get tough on crime." In addition, large numbers of youth under age 18 are tried as adults in states where the upper age of juvenile court jurisdiction is 15 or 16.

In a minority of states, statutes allow prosecutors to file particularly serious cases in either the juvenile court or the adult court.[43] Prosecutor discretion may occasionally be a more effective transfer mechanism than the waiver process, because the prosecutor can file a petition in criminal or juvenile court without judicial approval.

Since 1966, the U.S. Supreme Court and other federal and state courts have attempted to ensure fairness in the waiver process by handing down decisions that spell out the need for due process. Two Supreme Court decisions, *Kent v. United States* (1966) and *Breed v. Jones* (1975), are relevant.[44] (See Juvenile Law in Review on the following page.) The *Kent* case declared a District of Columbia transfer statute unconstitutional and attacked the subsequent conviction of the child by granting him the specific due-process rights of having a attorney present at the hearing and access to the evidence that would be used in the case. In *Breed v. Jones*, the U.S. Supreme Court declared that the child was to be granted the protection of the double-jeopardy clause

KENT V. UNITED STATES AND BREED V. JONES

Kent v. United States: Facts

Morris Kent was arrested at the age of 16 in connection with charges of housebreaking, robbery, and rape. As a juvenile, he was subject to the exclusive jurisdiction of the District of Columbia Juvenile Court. The District of Columbia statute declared that the court could transfer the petitioner "after full investigation" and remit him to trial in the U.S. District Court. Kent admitted his involvement in the offenses and was placed in a receiving home for children. Subsequently, his mother obtained counsel, and they discussed with the social-service director the possibility that the juvenile court might waive its jurisdiction.

Kent was detained at the receiving home for almost a week. There was no arraignment, no hearing, and no hearing for petitioner's apprehension. Kent's counsel arranged for a psychiatric examination, and a motion requesting a hearing on the waiver was filed. The juvenile court judge did not rule on the motion and entered an order stating "After full investigation, the court waives its jurisdiction and directs that a trial be held under the regular proceedings of the criminal court." The judge made no finding and gave no reasons for his waiver decision. It appeared that the judge denied motions for a hearing, recommendations for hospitalization for psychiatric observation, requests for access to the social-service file, and offers to prove that the petitioner was a fit subject for rehabilitation under the juvenile court.

After the juvenile court waived its jurisdiction, Kent was indicted by the grand jury and was subsequently found guilty of housebreaking and robbery and not guilty by reason of insanity on the charge of rape. Kent was sentenced to serve a period of 30 to 90 years on his conviction.

Decision

The petitioner's lawyer appealed the decision on the basis of the infirmity of the proceedings by which the juvenile court waived its jurisdiction. He further attacked the waiver on statutory and constitutional grounds, stating:

"(1) no hearing occurred, (2) no findings were made, (3) no reasons were stated before the waiver, and (4) counsel was denied access to the social service file." The U.S. Supreme Court found that the juvenile court order waiving jurisdiction and remitting the child to trial in the district court was invalid. Its arguments were based on the following criteria:

- The theory of the juvenile court act is rooted in social welfare procedures and treatments.

- The philosophy of the juvenile court, namely *parens patriae*, is not supposed to allow procedural unfairness.

- Waiver proceedings are critically important actions in the juvenile court.

- The juvenile court act requiring full investigation in the District of Columbia should be read in the context of constitutional principles relating to due process of law. These principles require at a minimum that the petitioner be entitled to a hearing, access to counsel, access by counsel to social service records, and a statement of the reason for the juvenile court decision.

Significance of the Case

This examined for the first time the substantial degree of discretion associated with a transfer proceeding in the District of Columbia. Thus, the Supreme Court significantly limited its holding to the statute involved but

of the Fifth Amendment after he was tried as a delinquent in the juvenile court: Once found to be a delinquent, the youth can no longer be tried as an adult.

Today, as a result of *Kent* and *Breed*, states that have transfer hearings provide (1) a legitimate transfer hearing, (2) sufficient notice to the child's family and defense attorney, (3) the right to counsel, and (4) a statement of the reason for the court order regarding transfer. These rights recognize that the transfer proceeding is critical in determining the statutory rights of the juvenile offender.

Should Youths Be Transferred to Adult Court?

Most juvenile justice experts oppose waiver because it clashes with the rehabilitative ideal. Basing waiver decisions on type and seriousness of offense rather than on the rehabilitative needs of the child has advanced the *criminalization* of the juvenile court and interfered with its traditional mission of treatment and rehabilitation.[45] And despite this sacrifice, there is little evidence that strict waiver policies can lower crime rates.[46]

justified its reference to constitutional principles relating to due process and the assistance of counsel. In addition, it said that the juvenile court waiver hearings need to measure up to the essentials of due process and fair treatment. Furthermore, in an appendix to its opinion, the Court set up criteria concerning waiver of the jurisdictions. These are:

- The seriousness of the alleged offense to the community
- Whether the alleged offense was committed in an aggressive, violent, or willful manner
- Whether the alleged offense was committed against persons or against property
- The prosecutive merit of the complaint
- The sophistication and maturity of the juvenile
- The record and previous history of the juvenile
- Prospects for adequate protection of the public and the likelihood of reasonable rehabilitation

Breed v. Jones: Facts

In 1971, a petition in the juvenile court of California was filed against Jones, who was then 17, alleging that he had committed an offense that, if committed by an adult, would constitute robbery. The petitioner was detained pending a hearing. At the hearing the juvenile court took testimony, found that the allegations were true, and sustained the petition. The proceedings were continued for a disposition hearing, at which point Jones was found unfit for treatment in the juvenile court. It was ordered that he be prosecuted as an adult offender. At a subsequent preliminary hearing, the petitioner was held for criminal trial, an information was filed against him for robbery, and he was tried and found guilty. He was committed to the California Youth Authority over objections that he was being subjected to double jeopardy.

Petitioner Jones sought an appeal in the federal district court on the basis of the double-jeopardy argument that jeopardy attaches at the juvenile-delinquency proceedings. The writ of habeas corpus was denied.

Decision

The U.S. Supreme Court held that the prosecution of Jones as an adult in the California Superior Court, after an adjudicatory finding in the juvenile court that he had violated a criminal statute and a subsequent finding that he was unfit for treatment as a juvenile, violated the double-jeopardy clause of the Fifth Amendment to the U.S. Constitution as applied to the states through the Fourteenth Amendment. Thus, Jones's trial in the California Superior Court for the same offense as that for which he was tried in the juvenile court violated the policy of the double-jeopardy clause, even if he never faced the risk of more than one punishment. Double jeopardy refers to the risk or potential risk of trial and conviction, not punishment.

Significance of the Case

The *Breed* case provided answers on several important transfer issues: (1) *Breed* prohibits trying a child in an adult court when there has been a prior adjudicatory juvenile proceeding; (2) probable cause may exist at a **transfer hearing,** and this does not violate subsequent jeopardy if the child is transferred to the adult court; (3) because the same evidence is often used in both the transfer hearing and subsequent trial in either the juvenile or adult court, a different judge is often required for each hearing.

Sources: *Kent v. United States*, 383 U.S. 541, 86 S.Ct. 1045, 16 L.Ed.2d 84 (1966); *Breed v. Jones*, 421 U.S. 519, 95 S.Ct. 1779 (1975).

Waiver can also create long-term harm. Waived children may be stigmatized by a conviction in the criminal court. Labeling children as adult offenders early in life may seriously impair their future educational, employment, and other opportunities. Youthful offenders convicted in adult courts are more likely to be incarcerated and to receive longer sentences than had they remained in the juvenile court. And these children may be incarcerated under conditions so extreme, and in institutions where they may be physically and sexually exploited, that they will become permanently damaged.[47]

Waivers don't always support the goal of increased public protection. Because juveniles may only serve a fraction of the prison sentence imposed by the criminal court, the actual treatment of delinquents in adult court is similar to what they might have received had they remained in the custody of juvenile authorities.[48] In the majority of cases involving transferred juveniles sentenced to incarceration, the length of sentence does not exceed 3 years, a length of time typically within the range of options available to juvenile courts.[49] Once they are released, waived juveniles have a higher recidivism rate than those kept in juvenile court. This has prompted some critics to ask: Why bother transferring these children?

Sometimes waiver can add an undue burden to youthful offenders. Studies have found that, although transfer to criminal court was intended for the most serious juvenile offenders, many transferred juveniles were not violent offenders but repeat property offenders.[50] Cases involving waiver take significantly longer than a comparable juvenile court case, during which time the waived youth is more likely to be held in a **detention** center. This finding is vexing, considering that some research shows that many waived youths were no more dangerous than youths who remain in juvenile courts.[51]

Transfer decisions are not always carried out fairly or equitably and there is evidence that minorities are waived at a rate that is greater than their representation in the population.[52] From 1988 through 1997 (the latest data available), the number of judicially waived cases involving black youth increased 35 percent, compared with a 14 percent increase for white youth. Almost half (46%) of all waived youth are African Americans, even though they represent less than a third (31%) of the juvenile court population.[53]

In Support of Waiver Not all experts challenge the waiver concept. Waiver is attractive to conservatives because it jibes with the get-tough policy currently popular. Some have argued that the increased use of waiver can help get violent offenders off the streets and should be mandatory for juveniles committing serious violent crimes.[54] Others point to studies that show that, for the most part, transfer is reserved for the most serious cases and the most serious juvenile offenders. Kids are most likely to be transferred to criminal court if they have injured someone with a weapon or if they have a long juvenile court record.[55] Frank Zimring argues that, despite its faults, waiver is superior to alternative methods for handling the most serious juvenile offenders.[56] Some cases involving serious offenses, he argues, require a minimum criminal penalty greater than that available to the juvenile court. It is also possible that some juveniles take advantage of decisions to transfer them to the adult court. Although the charge against a child may be considered serious in the juvenile court, the adult criminal court will not find it so; consequently, a child may have a better chance for dismissal of the charges, or acquittal after a jury trial.

In sum, though the use of waiver has leveled off somewhat, it is still being used today as an important strategy for attacking serious youth crime.[57] Its continued use can be attributed to the get-tough attitude toward the serious juvenile offender.

JUVENILE COURT TRIAL

If the case cannot be decided during the pretrial stage, it will be brought forth for a trial in the juvenile court. An adjudication hearing is held to determine the merits of the petition claiming that a child is either a delinquent youth or in need of court supervision. The judge is required to make a finding based on the evidence and arrive at a judgment. Adjudication is comparable to an adult trial. Rules of evidence in adult criminal proceedings are generally applicable in juvenile court, and the standard of proof used—*beyond a reasonable doubt*—similar to that used in adult trials.

State juvenile codes vary with regard to the basic requirements of due process and fairness. Most juvenile courts have bifurcated hearings—that is, separate hearings for adjudication and disposition (sentencing). At disposition hearings, evidence can be submitted that reflects nonlegal factors such as the child's home life.

Most state juvenile codes provide specific rules of procedure. These rules require that a written petition be submitted to the court, ensure the right of a child to have an attorney, provide that the adjudication proceedings be recorded, allow the petition to be amended, and provide that a child's plea be accepted. Where the child admits

When making waiver decisions judges will consider the child's age, his need for treatment, the seriousness of the act, his home life, and other personal factors. It is a very difficult decision that can have far-reaching consequences. Here, James R. Lopez, 16, is escorted from a Kansas courthouse, March 15, 2001, after pleading guilty to the criminal use of explosives in a Columbine-style plot against his school. The judge dismissed the state's request to have Lopez tried as an adult, keeping the matter in the juvenile justice system. (AP/Wide World Photos)

to the facts of the petition, the court generally seeks assurance that the plea is voluntary. If plea bargaining is used, prosecutors, defense counsel, and trial judges take steps to ensure the fairness of such negotiations.

At the end of the adjudication hearing, most juvenile court statutes require the judge to make a factual finding on the legal issues and evidence. In the criminal court, this finding is normally a prelude to reaching a verdict. In the juvenile court, however, the finding itself is the verdict—the case is resolved in one of three ways:

1. The juvenile court judge makes a finding of fact that the child or juvenile is not delinquent or in need of supervision.

2. The juvenile court judge makes a finding of fact that the juvenile is delinquent or in need of supervision.

3. The juvenile court judge dismisses the case because of insufficient or faulty evidence.

In some jurisdictions, informal alternatives are used, such as filing the case with no further consequences or continuing the case without a finding for a period of time such as 6 months. If the juvenile does not get into further difficulty during that time, the case is dismissed. These alternatives involve no determination of delinquency or noncriminal behavior. Because of the philosophy of the juvenile court that emphasizes rehabilitation over punishment, a delinquency finding is not the same thing as a criminal conviction. The disabilities associated with conviction,

To get information on juvenile courts, go to the Web site of the National Center for State Courts at

http://www.ncsc.dni.us/

For an up-to-date list of Web links, go to www.wadsworth.com/product/0534573053s

such as disqualifications for employment or being barred from military service, do not apply in an adjudication of delinquency.

There are other differences between adult and juvenile proceedings. For instance, while adults are entitled to public trials by a jury of their peers, these rights are not extended to juveniles.[58] Because juvenile courts are treating some defendants similar to adult criminals, an argument can be made that the courts should extend to these youths the Sixth Amendment right to a public jury trial.[59] For the most part, however, state juvenile courts operate without recognizing a juvenile's constitutional right to a jury trial.

Constitutional Rights at Trial

due process Basic constitutional principle based on the concept of the primacy of the individual and the complementary concept of limitation on governmental power; safeguards the individual from unfair state procedures in judicial or administrative proceedings; due process rights have been extended to juvenile trials.

In addition to mandating state juvenile-code requirements, the U.S. Supreme Court has mandated the application of constitutional due-process standards to the juvenile trial. **Due process** is addressed in the Fifth and Fourteenth Amendments to the U.S. Constitution. It refers to the need for rules and procedures that protect individual rights. Having the right to due process means that no person can be deprived of life, liberty, or property without such protections as legal counsel, an open and fair hearing, and an opportunity to confront those making accusations against the person.

For many years, children were deprived of their due-process rights because the *parens patriae* philosophy governed their relationship to the juvenile justice system. Such rights as having counsel and confronting one's accusers were deemed unnecessary. After all, why should children need protection from the state when the state was seen as acting in their interest? As we have seen, this view changed in the 1960s, when the U.S. Supreme Court began to grant due-process rights and procedures to minors. The key case was that of Gerald Gault; it articulated the basic requirements of due process that must be satisfied in juvenile court proceedings. Because *Gault* remains the key constitutional case in the juvenile justice system, it is set forth in the accompanying Juvenile Law In Review.

For a review of due process issues in juvenile justice, go to:

http://www.ncjrs.org/txtfiles/fs9749.txt

For an up-to-date list of Web links, go to www.wadsworth.com/product/0534573053s

The *Gault* decision reshaped the constitutional and philosophical nature of the juvenile court system and, with the addition of legal representation, made it more similar to the adult system.[60] Following the *Gault* case, the U.S. Supreme Court decided *in re Winship* that the amount of proof required in juvenile delinquency adjudications is "beyond a reasonable doubt," a level equal to the requirements in the adult system.[61]

Although the ways in which the juvenile court operates were altered by *Gault* and *Winship*, the trend toward increased rights for juveniles was somewhat curtailed by the U.S. Supreme Court's decision in *McKeiver v. Pennsylvania* (1971), which held that trial by jury in a juvenile court's adjudicative stage is not a constitutional requirement.[62] This decision does not prevent states from giving the juvenile a trial by jury, but in the majority of states a child has no such right.

Once an adjudicatory hearing has been completed, the court is normally required to enter a judgment or finding against the child. This may take the form of declaring the child delinquent, adjudging the child to be a ward of the court, or possibly even suspending judgment so as to avoid the stigma of a juvenile record. After a judgment has been entered, the court can begin its determination of possible dispositions.

To read more about *Gault* or get the actual case transcript, go to

http://lawbooksusa.com/cconlaw/gaultinre.htm

For an up-to-date list of Web links, go to www.wadsworth.com/product/0534573053s

Disposition

The sentencing step of the juvenile justice process is called disposition. At this point the court orders treatment for the juvenile.[63] According to prevailing juvenile justice philosophy, dispositions should be in the *best interest of the child*, which in this context means providing the help necessary to resolve or meet the adolescent's personal needs, while at the same time meeting society's needs for protection.

In most jurisdictions, adjudication and disposition hearings are separated, or bifurcated, so that evidence that could not be entered during the juvenile trial can be considered at the dispositional hearing. At the hearing, the defense counsel represents the child, helps the parents understand the court's decision, and influences the direction of

Facts

Gerald Gault, 15 years of age, was taken into custody by the sheriff of Gila County, Arizona because a woman complained that he and another boy had made an obscene telephone call to her. At the time, Gerald was under a 6-month probation after being found delinquent for stealing a wallet. As a result of the woman's complaint, Gerald was taken to a children's home. His parents were not informed that he was being taken into custody. His mother appeared in the evening and was told by the superintendent of detention that a hearing would be held in the juvenile court the following day. On the day in question, the police officer who had taken Gerald into custody filed a petition alleging his delinquency. Gerald, his mother, and the police officer appeared before the judge in his chambers. Mrs. Cook, the complainant, was not at the hearing. Gerald was questioned about the telephone calls and was sent back to the detention home and subsequently released a few days later.

On the day of Gerald's release, Mrs. Gault received a letter indicating that a hearing would be held on Gerald's delinquency a few days later. A hearing was held, and the complainant again was not present. There was no transcript or recording of the proceedings, and the juvenile officer stated that Gerald had admitted making the lewd telephone calls. Neither the boy nor his parents were advised of any right to remain silent, right to be represented by counsel, or any other constitutional rights. At the conclusion of the hearing, the juvenile court committed Gerald as a juvenile delinquent to the state industrial school for the period of his minority.

This meant that, at the age of 15, Gerald Gault was sentenced to remain in the state school until he reached the age of 21, unless he was discharged sooner. An adult charged with the same crime would have received a maximum punishment of no more than a $50 fine or 2 months in prison.

Decision

Gerald's attorneys filed a writ of habeas corpus, which was denied by the Superior Court of the State of Arizona. That decision was subsequently affirmed by the Arizona Supreme Court. On appeal to the U.S. Supreme Court, Gerald's counsel argued that the juvenile code of Arizona under which Gerald was found delinquent was invalid because it was contrary to the due-process clause of the Fourteenth Amendment. In addition, Gerald was denied the following basic due-process rights: (1) notice of the charges with respect to their timeliness and specificity, (2) right to counsel, (3) right to confrontation and cross-examination, (4) privilege against self-incrimination, (5) right to a transcript of the trial record, and (6) right to appellate review. In deciding the case, the U.S. Supreme Court had to determine whether procedural due process of law within the context of fundamental fairness under the Fourteenth Amendment applied to juvenile delinquency proceedings in which a child is committed to a state industrial school.

The Court, in a far-reaching opinion, agreed that Gerald's constitutional rights had been violated. Notice of charges was an essential ingredient of due process of law, as was the right to counsel, the right to cross-examine and to confront witnesses, and the privilege against self-incrimination. The questions of appellate review and a right to a transcript were not answered by the Court in this case.

Significance of the Case

The *Gault* case established that a child has the due-process constitutional rights listed here in delinquency adjudication proceedings, where the consequences were that the child could be committed to a state institution. It was confined to rulings at the adjudication state of the juvenile process.

This decision was significant not only because of the procedural reforms it initiated but also because of its far-reaching impact throughout the entire juvenile justice system. *Gault* instilled in juvenile proceedings the development of due-process standards at the pretrial, trial, and posttrial stages of the juvenile process. While recognizing the history and development of the juvenile court, it sought to accommodate the motives of rehabilitation and treatment with children's rights. It recognized the principle of fundamental fairness of the law for children as well as for adults. Judged in the context of today's juvenile justice system, *Gault* redefined the relationships between juveniles, their parents, and the state. It remains the single most significant constitutional case in the area of juvenile justice.

Source: *In re Gault*, 387 U.S. 1; 87 S.Ct. 1248 (1967).

the disposition. Others involved at the dispositional stage include representatives of social-service agencies, psychologists, social workers, and probation personnel.

The Predisposition Report After the child has admitted to the allegations, or the allegations have been proved in a trial, the judge normally orders the probation

The appeal of Gerald Gault (center) heralded in the due process revolution in juvenile justice. (AP/Wide World Photos)

department to complete a predisposition report. The predisposition report, which is similar to the pre-sentence report of the adult justice system, has a number of purposes:

- It helps the judge decide which disposition is best for the child.
- It aids the juvenile probation officer in developing treatment programs where the child is in need of counseling or community supervision.
- It helps the court develop a body of knowledge about the child that can aid others in treating the child.[64]

Sources of dispositional data include family members, school officials, and statements from the juvenile offenders themselves. The results of psychological testing, psychiatric evaluations, and intelligence testing may be relevant. Furthermore, the probation officer might include information about the juvenile's feelings concerning his or her case.

Some state statutes make the predisposition report mandatory. Other jurisdictions require the report only when there is a probability that the child will be institutionalized. Some appellate courts have reversed orders institutionalizing children where the juvenile court did not use a predisposition report in reaching its decision. Access to predisposition reports is an important legal issue.

In the final section of the predisposition report, the probation department recommends a disposition to the presiding judge. This is a critical aspect of the report because it has been estimated that the court follows more than 90 percent of all probation-department recommendations.

Juvenile Court Dispositions Historically, the juvenile court has had broad discretionary power to make dispositional decisions. The major categories of dispositional choices are: (1) community release, (2) out-of-home placements, (3) fines or restitution, (4) community service, and (5) institutionalization. A more detailed list of the dispositions open to the juvenile court judge appears in Table 13.2.[65]

TABLE 13.2 Common Juvenile Dispositions

Disposition	Action Taken
Informal consent decree	In minor or first offenses, an informal hearing is held, and the judge will ask the youth and his or her guardian to agree to a treatment program, such as counseling. No formal trial or disposition hearing is held.
Probation	A youth is placed under the control of the county probation department and required to obey a set of probation rules and participate in a treatment program.
Home detention	A child is restricted to his or her home in lieu of a secure placement. Rules include regular school attendance, curfew observance, avoidance of alcohol and drugs, and notification of parents and the youth worker of the child's whereabouts.
Court-ordered school attendance	If truancy was the problem that brought the youth to court, a judge may order mandatory school attendance. Some courts have established court-operated day schools and court-based tutorial programs staffed by community volunteers.
Financial restitution	A judge can order the juvenile offender to make financial restitution to the victim. In most jurisdictions, restitution is part of probation (see Chapter 16), but in a few states, such as Maryland, restitution can be a sole order.
Fines	Some states allow fines to be levied against juveniles age 16 and over.
Community service	Courts in many jurisdictions require juveniles to spend time in the community working off their debt to society. Community service orders are usually reserved for victimless crimes, such as possession of drugs, or crimes against public order, such as vandalism of school property. Community service orders are usually carried out in schools, hospitals, or nursing homes.
Outpatient psychotherapy	Youths who are diagnosed with psychological disorders may be required to undergo therapy at a local mental health clinic.
Drug and alcohol treatment	Youths with drug- or alcohol-related problems may be allowed to remain in the community if they agree to undergo drug or alcohol therapy.
Commitment to secure treatment	In the most serious cases a judge may order an offender admitted to a long-term treatment center, such as a training school, camp, ranch, or group home. These may be either state- or privately run institutions, usually located in remote regions. Training schools provide educational, vocational, and rehabilitation programs in a secure environment (see Chapter 17).
Commitment to a residential community program	Youths who commit crimes of a less serious nature but who still need to be removed from their homes can be placed in community-based group homes or halfway houses. They attend school or work during the day and live in a controlled, therapeutic environment at night.
Foster home placement	Foster homes are usually used for dependent or neglected children and status offenders. Today judges are placing delinquents with insurmountable problems at home in state-licensed foster care homes.

Most state statutes allow the juvenile court judge to select whatever disposition seems best suited to the child's needs, including institutionalization. In some states the court determines commitment to a specific institution; in other states the youth corrections agency determines where the child will be placed. In addition to the dispositions in Table 13.2, some states grant the court the power to order parents into treatment or to suspend a youth's driver's license.

Today it is common for juvenile court judges to employ a graduated sanction program for juveniles : (1) immediate sanctions for nonviolent offenders, which consist of community-based diversion and day treatment imposed on first-time nonviolent offenders; (2) intermediate sanctions, which target repeat minor offenders and first-time serious offenders; and (3) secure care, which is reserved for repeat serious offenders and violent offenders.[66]

Juvenile Sentencing Structures

For most of the juvenile court's history, disposition was based on the presumed needs of the child. Although critics have challenged the motivations of early reformers in championing rehabilitation, there is little question that the rhetoric of the juvenile court has promoted that ideal.[67] For example, in their classic work *Beyond the Best Interest of the Child*, Joseph Goldstein, Anna Freud, and Albert Solnit say that placement of children should be based on the **least detrimental alternative** available in order to foster the child's development.[68] Most states have adopted this ideal in their sentencing efforts and state courts usually insist that the purpose of disposition must be rehabilitation and not punishment.[69] Consequently, it is common for state courts to require judges to justify their sentencing decisions if it means that juveniles are to be incarcerated in a residential treatment center: They must set forth in writing the reasons for the placement, address the danger the child poses to society, and explain why a less-restrictive alternative has not been used.[70]

least detrimental alternative Choosing a program for the child that will best foster a child's growth and development.

Traditionally, states have used the **indeterminate sentence** in juvenile court. In about half of the states, this means having the judge place the offender with the state department of juvenile corrections until correctional authorities consider the youth ready to return to society or until the youth reaches legal majority. A preponderance of states consider 18 to be the age of release; others peg the termination age at 19; a few can retain minority status until their twenty-first birthday. In practice, few youths remain in custody for the entire statutory period, but juveniles are usually released if their rehabilitation has been judged to have progressed satisfactorily. This practice is referred to as the **individualized treatment model.**

indeterminate sentence Does not specify the length of time the juvenile must be held; rather, correctional authorities decide when the juvenile is ready to return to society.

Another form of the indeterminate sentence allows judges to specify a maximum term. Under this form of sentencing, youths may be released if the corrections department considers them to be rehabilitated or they reach the automatic age of termination (usually 18 or 21). In states that stipulate a maximum sentence, the court may extend the sentence, depending on the youth's progress in the institutional facility.

A number of states have changed from an indeterminate to a **determinate sentence.** This means sentencing juvenile offenders to a fixed term of incarceration that must be served in its entirety. Other states have passed laws creating **mandatory sentences** for serious juvenile offenders. Juveniles receiving mandatory sentences are usually institutionalized for the full sentence and are not eligible for early parole. The difference between mandatory and determinate sentences is that the mandatory sentence carries a statutory requirement that a certain penalty be set in all cases on conviction for a specified offense.

determinate sentence Sentence that specifies a fixed term of detention that must be served.

mandatory sentence Sentence is defined by a statutory requirement that states the penalty to be set for all cases of a specific offense.

Sentencing Reform

During the past decade there have been a number of attempts to create rational sentencing within juvenile justice. In some instances the goal has been to reduce judicial discretion, in others to toughen sentencing practices and create mandatory periods of incarceration for juveniles who commit serious crimes. However, not all statutory changes have had the desired effect. For instance, New York State has implemented a juvenile offender law requiring that juveniles accused of violent offenses be tried in criminal court as a get-tough-on-crime measure; evaluations found many youths ended up receiving lighter sentences than they would have in the family court.[71]

Probably the best-known effort to reform sentencing in the juvenile court is the state of Washington's Juvenile Justice Reform Act of 1977. This act created a mandatory sentencing policy requiring juveniles ages 8 to 17 who are adjudicated delin-

When making disposition decisions, juvenile court judges may select programs that will enhance life skills and help youths form a positive bond with society. Here, juvenile offenders work with severely disabled kids at El Camino School as part of their jail time and rehabilitation. (© Tony Savino/The Image Works)

quent to be confined in an institution for a minimum time.[72] The intent of the act was to make juveniles accountable for criminal behavior and to provide for punishment commensurate with the (1) age, (2) crime, and (3) prior history of the offender. Washington's approach is based on the principle of *proportionality*. How much time a youth must spend in confinement is established by the Juvenile Dispositions Standards Commission, based on the three stated criteria. The introduction of such mandatory-sentencing procedures reduces disparity in the length of sentences, according to advocates of a get-tough juvenile justice system.

The growing realization that the juvenile crime rate has stabilized may slow the tide of legislative change in juvenile justice. What is more likely is that states will continue to pass legislation making it easier to transfer youths to the adult court or giving the adult court original jurisdiction over serious cases. Thus, rather than toughening juvenile law for everyone, the system may reserve the harshest measures for the few more serious cases.

Blended Sentences State sentencing trends indicate that punishment and accountability, in addition to rehabilitation, have become equally important in juvenile justice policy. As a result, many states have created blended sentencing structures for cases involving serious offenders. Blended sentencing allows the imposition of juvenile and adult sanctions for juvenile offenders adjudicated in juvenile court or convicted in criminal court. In other words, this expanded sentencing authority allows criminal and juvenile courts to impose either a juvenile or an adult sentence, or both, in cases involving juvenile offenders. When both sentences are imposed simultaneously, the court suspends the adult sanction. If the youth follows the conditions of the juvenile sentence and commits no further violation, the adult sentence is revoked. This type of statute has become popular in recent years, with Connecticut, Kentucky, and Minnesota among the states adopting it since 1994.[73]

The Death Penalty for Juveniles

Juveniles who have been waived to adult court can receive the death penalty. The execution of minor children has not been uncommon in our nation's history; about 350 juvenile offenders have been executed since 1642. This represents about 2 percent of the total of more than 18,000 executions carried out since colonial times.

During the past 20 years, 196 juvenile death sentences have been imposed (about 3 percent of the almost 6,900 total U.S. death sentences). Approximately two-thirds of these have been imposed on 17-year-olds and nearly one-third on 15- and 16-year-olds.[74] As of 2000, l 74 offenders were on death row in 16 different states. All were male; 73 percent committed their crimes at age 17; 63 percent are minorities. Texas, with 24 juvenile offenders on death row, held 34 percent of the national total of such offenders.[75]

Legal Issues In *Thompson v. Oklahoma* (1988), the U.S. Supreme Court prohibited the execution of persons *under age sixteen* but left open the age at which execution would be legally appropriate.[76] They then answered this question in two 1989 cases, *Wilkins v. Missouri* and *Stanford v. Kentucky,* in which they ruled that states were free to impose the death penalty for murderers who committed their crimes after they reached age 16 or 17.[77] According to the majority opinion, society has not formed a consensus that the execution of such minors constitutes a cruel and unusual punishment.

Those who oppose the death penalty for children find that it has little deterrent effect on youngsters who are impulsive and do not have a realistic view of the destructiveness of their misdeeds or their consequences. Victor Streib, the leading critic of the death penalty for children, argues that such a practice is cruel and unusual punishment because: (1) the condemnation of children makes no measurable contribution to the legitimate goals of punishment, (2) condemning any minor to death violates contemporary standards of decency, (3) the capacity of the young for change, growth, and rehabilitation makes the death penalty particularly harsh and inappropriate, and (4) both legislative attitudes and public opinion reject juvenile executions.[78] Supporters of the death penalty hold that people, regardless of their age, can form criminal intent and therefore should be responsible for their actions. If the death penalty is legal for adults, they argue, then it can also be used for children who commit serious crimes.

The fact that the United States is not alone in executing criminals appears to support retention of the death penalty. However, the fact that many countries have abolished capital punishment encourages those who want capital punishment to be abandoned .

Checkpoints

✔ A high percentage of juvenile offenders enter guilty pleas; that is, they admit to the facts of the petition before a trial takes place.

✔ The transfer involves transferring a juvenile from the juvenile court to the criminal court, where they are tried as an adult.

✔ Most juvenile courts have bifurcated hearings—that is, separate hearings for adjudication and disposition (sentencing).

✔ While adults are entitled to public trials by a jury of their peers, these rights are not extended to juveniles.

✔ *In re Gault* is the key legal case that set out the basic requirements of due process that must be satisfied in juvenile court proceedings.

✔ The major categories of dispositional choice in juvenile cases are (1) community release, (2) out-of-home placements, (3) fines or restitution, (4) community service, and (5) institutionalization.

✔ Most states use the indeterminate sentence in juvenile court.

✔ States have passed laws creating mandatory sentences for serious juvenile offenders.

✔ The Supreme Court has ruled that states were free to impose the death penalty for murderers who committed their crimes after they reached age 16 or 17.

The Child's Right to Appeal

final order Order that ends litigation between two parties by determining all their rights and disposing of all the issues.

appellate process Allows the juvenile an opportunity to have the case brought before a reviewing court after it has been heard in juvenile or family court.

Regardless of the sentence imposed, juveniles may want to appeal the decision made by the juvenile court judge. Juvenile court statutes normally restrict appeals to cases where the juvenile seeks review of a **final order,** one that ends the litigation between two parties by determining all their rights and disposing of all the issues.[79] The **appellate process** gives the juvenile the opportunity to have the case brought before a reviewing court after it has been heard in the juvenile or family court. Today, the law does not recognize a federal constitutional right of appeal. In other words, the U.S. Constitution does not require any state to furnish an appeal to a juvenile charged and found to be delinquent in a juvenile or family court. Consequently, appellate review of a juvenile case is a matter of statutory right in each jurisdiction. However, the majority of states do provide juveniles with some method of statutory appeal.

The appeal process was not always part of the juvenile law system. In 1965, few states extended the right of appeal to juveniles.[80] Even in the *Gault* case in 1967, the U.S. Supreme Court refused to review the Arizona juvenile code, which provided no appellate review in juvenile matters. It further rejected the right of a juvenile to a transcript of the original trial record.[81] Today, however, most jurisdictions that provide a child with some form of appeal also provide for counsel and for securing a record and transcript, which are crucial to the success of any appeal.

Because juvenile appellate review is defined by individual statutes, each jurisdiction determines for itself what method of review will be used. There are two basic methods of appeal: the direct appeal and the collateral attack.

The *direct appeal* normally involves an appellate court review to determine whether, based on the evidence presented at the trial, the rulings of law and the judgment of the court were correct. The second major area of review involves the collateral attack of a case. The term *collateral* implies a secondary or indirect method of attacking a final judgment. Instead of appealing the juvenile trial because of errors, prejudice, or lack of evidence, *collateral review* uses extraordinary legal writs to challenge the lower-court position. One such procedural device is the writ of habeas corpus. Known as the *Great Writ,* the **writ of habeas corpus** refers to a procedure for determining the validity of a person's custody. In the context of the juvenile court, it is used to challenge the custody of a child in detention or in an institution. This writ is often the method by which the Supreme Court exercises its discretionary authority to hear cases regarding constitutional issues. Even though there is no constitutional right to appeal a juvenile case and each jurisdiction provides for appeals differently, juveniles have a far greater opportunity for appellate review today than in years past.

writ of habeas corpus Judicial order requesting that a person detaining another produce the body of the prisoner and give reasons for his or her capture and detention.

Confidentiality in Juvenile Proceedings

confidentiality Restricting information in juvenile court proceedings in the interest of protecting the privacy of the juvenile.

Along with the rights of juveniles at adjudication and disposition, the issue of **confidentiality** in juvenile proceedings has also received attention in recent years. The debate on confidentiality in the juvenile court deals with two areas: (1) open versus closed hearings, and (2) privacy of juvenile records. Confidentiality has become moot in some respects, as many legislatures have broadened access to juvenile records.

Open vs. Closed Hearings Generally, juvenile trials are closed to the public and the press, and the names of the offenders are kept secret. The U.S. Supreme Court has ruled on the issue of privacy in three important decisions. In *Davis v. Alaska,* the Court concluded that any injury resulting from the disclosure of a juvenile's record is outweighed by the right to completely cross-examine an adverse witness.[82] The *Davis* case involved an effort to obtain testimony from a juvenile probationer who was a witness in a criminal trial. After the prosecutor was granted a court order preventing the defense from making any reference to the juvenile's record, the Supreme Court reversed the state court, claiming that a juvenile's interest in confidentiality was secondary to the constitutional right to confront adverse witnesses.

The decisions in two subsequent cases, *Oklahoma Publishing Co. v. District Court* and *Smith v. Daily Mail Publishing Co.*, sought to balance juvenile privacy with freedom of the press. In the *Oklahoma* case, the Supreme Court ruled that a state court was not allowed to prohibit the publication of information obtained in an open juvenile proceeding.[83] The case involved an 11-year-old boy suspected of homicide, who appeared at a detention hearing where photographs were taken and published in local newspapers. When the local district court prohibited further disclosure, the publishing company claimed that the court order was a restraint in violation of the First Amendment, and the Supreme Court agreed.

The *Smith* case involved the discovery and publication of the identity of a juvenile suspect in violation of a state statute prohibiting publication. The Supreme Court, however, declared the statute unconstitutional because it believed the state's interest in protecting the child's identity was not of such a magnitude as to justify the use of such a statute.[84] Therefore, if newspapers lawfully obtain pictures or names of juveniles, they may publish them. Based on these decisions, it appears that the Supreme Court favors the constitutional rights of the press over the right to privacy of the juvenile offender.

None of the decisions, however, give the press complete access to juvenile trials. Some jurisdictions still bar the press from juvenile proceedings unless they show at a hearing that their presence will not harm the youth. In other words, when states follow a *parens patriae* philosophy, ordinarily the public and press are excluded. However, the court has discretion to permit interested parties to observe the hearings.

Privacy of Juvenile Records For most of the twentieth century, juvenile records were kept confidential.[85] Today, however, the record itself, or information contained in it, can be opened by court order in many jurisdictions on the basis of statutory exception. The following groups can ordinarily gain access to juvenile records: (1) law-enforcement personnel, (2) the child's attorney, (3) the parents or guardians, (4) military personnel, and (5) public agencies such as schools, court-related organizations, and correctional institutions.

Many states have enacted laws authorizing a central repository for juvenile arrest records. Some states allow a juvenile adjudication for a criminal act to be used as evidence in an adult criminal proceeding for the same act, to show predisposition or criminal nature. In addition, a juvenile's records may be used during the disposition or sentencing stage of an adult criminal trial in some states. Knowledge of a defendant's juvenile record may help prosecutors and judges determine appropriate sentencing for offenders ages 18 to 24, the age group most likely to be involved in violent crime.

Today, most states recognize the importance of juvenile records in sentencing. Many first-time adult offenders committed numerous crimes as juveniles, and evidence of these crimes may not be available to sentencing for the adult offenses unless states pass statutes allowing access. According to experts such as Ira Schwartz, the need for confidentiality to protect juveniles is far less than the need to open up the courts to public scrutiny.[86] The problem of maintaining confidentiality of juvenile records will become more acute in the future as electronic information storage makes these records both more durable and more accessible.

In conclusion, virtually every state provides prosecutors and judges access to the juvenile records of adult offenders. There is great diversity, however, regarding provisions for the collection and retention of juvenile records.[87]

SUMMARY

Many decisions about what happens to a child may occur prior to adjudication. Detention in secure facilities for those charged with juvenile delinquency and involuntary placement in shelter care for those involved in noncriminal behavior place severe limitations on the rights of the child and the parents. There has been a major effort to remove juveniles from detention in adult jails and to make sure status offenders are not placed in secure detention facilities.

Most statutes require a hearing if the initial decision is to keep the child in custody. The child has a right to counsel and is generally given other procedural due-process safeguards, notably the privilege against self-incrimination and the right to confront and cross-examine witnesses.

In addition, most juvenile court procedures provide criteria to be used in deciding whether to detain a child. These include (1) the need to protect the child, (2) the likelihood that the child presents a serious danger to the public, and (3) the likelihood that the child will return to court for adjudication.

The intake stage is a screening process. The law-enforcement officer is required to make decisions about court action or referral to social agencies. In addition, it is important for law-enforcement agencies and the juvenile courts to have sound working relationships. Their objective is the same: to protect the child and the community.

In the last decade, juvenile justice practitioners have made efforts to divert as many children as possible from the juvenile courts and place them in nonsecure treatment programs. Critics charge that diversion programs actually involve more youths in the justice system than would be the case had the programs not been in operation, a concept referred to as widening the net. Moreover, the effectiveness of diversion as a crime-reducing policy has been questioned.

Those who are held for trial are generally released to their parents, on bail or through other means. Because the juvenile justice system is not able to try every child accused of a crime or a status offense due to personnel limitations, diversion programs seem to hold greater hope for the control of delinquency. As a result, such subsystems as diversion, statutory intake proceedings, plea bargaining, and other informal adjustments are essential ingredients in the administration of the juvenile justice system.

An issue related to bail is preventive detention, which refers to the right of a judge to deny persons release before trial on the grounds that they may be dangerous to themselves or others. Advocates of preventive detention argue that dangerous juvenile offenders should not be granted bail and pretrial release because they would then have an opportunity to intimidate witnesses and commit further crimes. Opponents retaliate that defendants are *innocent until proven guilty* and therefore should be allowed freedom before trial.

Prior to the creation of the first juvenile court in 1899, juveniles were tried in adult courts. However, even with the development of the juvenile court system, it is recognized that certain crimes require that children be tried as adults.

Each year, thousands of youths are transferred to adult courts because of the serious nature of their crimes. This process, known as waiver, is an effort to remove serious offenders from the juvenile process and into the more punitive adult system. Despite controversy surrounding this practice, most states have modified their laws, making it easier to prosecute juveniles in criminal court. Today, virtually all jurisdictions provide for waiver of juvenile offenders to the criminal courts. The number of juveniles transferred to criminal court has grown substantially, although a slight decline occurred in 1995. More research is needed on the impact of transferring juveniles to the adult justice system.

Most jurisdictions have a bifurcated juvenile code system that separates the adjudication hearing from the dispositional hearing. Juveniles alleged to be delinquent have virtually all the rights given a criminal defendant at trial—except possibly the right to a trial by jury. In addition, juvenile proceedings are generally closed to the public.

Types of dispositional orders include dismissal, fine, probation, and institutionalization. The use of such dispositions has not curtailed the rising rate of juvenile crime, however. As a result, legislatures and national commissions have begun to take a tougher position with regard to the sentencing of some juvenile offenders. The traditional notion of rehabilitation and treatment as the proper goals for disposition is being questioned, and some jurisdictions have replaced it with proportionality and determinacy in sentencing procedures. However, many juvenile codes do require that the court consider the *least-restrictive* alternative.

The predisposition report is the primary informational source for assisting the court in making a judgment. Once a juvenile is found delinquent, or in need of supervision, the juvenile court is empowered to make fundamental changes in the child's life. In recent years a number of states have made drastic changes in juvenile sentencing law, moving away from the indeterminate sentence and embracing more determinate forms of disposition. States have passed laws allowing judges to hand down blended sentences to children found guilty of serious crimes: a juvenile sentence that remains in effect until the defendant turns 21 and a suspended adult sentence that can be reinstated if the juvenile has any further brushes with the law.

The most extreme form of punishment is the death penalty, which in some states can be administered to children as young as 16. The use of capital punishment has been the subject of much debate, but at present 67 persons remain on death row for crimes committed as juveniles.

Finally, many state statutes require that juvenile hearings be closed and that the privacy of juvenile records be maintained to protect the child from public scrutiny and to provide a greater opportunity for rehabilitation. This approach may be inconsistent with the public's interest in taking a closer look at the juvenile justice system.

juvenile defense attorneys
guardian *ad litem*
public defender
juvenile prosecutor
juvenile court judge
shelter care

bail
preventive detention
intake
diversion
widening the net
complaint

plea bargaining
transfer process
due process
least detrimental alternative
indeterminate sentence
determinate sentence

mandatory sentence
final order
appellate process
writ of habeus corpus
confidentiality

QUESTIONS FOR DISCUSSION

1. Discuss and identify the major participants in the juvenile adjudication process. What are each person's role and responsibilities in the course of a juvenile trial?

2. The criminal justice system in the United States is based on the adversarial process. Does the same adversary principle apply in the juvenile justice system?

3. Children have certain constitutional rights at adjudication, such as the right to an attorney and the right to confront and cross-examine witnesses. But they do not have the right to a trial by jury. Should juvenile offenders have a constitutional right to a jury trial? Should each state make that determination? Discuss the legal decision that addresses this issue.

4. What is the point of obtaining a predisposition report in the juvenile court? Is it of any value in cases where the child is released to the community? Does it have a significant value in serious juvenile crime cases?

5. The standard of proof in juvenile adjudication is to show that the child is guilty beyond a reasonable doubt. Explain the meaning of this standard of proof in the U.S. judicial system.

6. Should states adopt get-tough sentences in juvenile justice or adhere to the individualized treatment model?

7. Do you agree with the principle of imposing the death penalty on juveniles found to have committed certain capital crimes?

8. What are blended sentences?

9. Should individuals who committed murder while under age 16 be legally executed?

VIEWPOINT

Three teenagers are arraigned on hate-crime charges in a U.S. district court. The judge refuses to let reporters attend any hearings in the case and orders that any information that could identify the juveniles be deleted from case records before they are released to the press. A newspaper appeals the judge's order, but a federal appeals court affirms the decision and declares that juvenile proceedings in federal court are presumptively closed. Believing that important rights are at stake, the newspaper petitions for U.S. Supreme Court review, arguing that the First Amendment creates a right of public access to juvenile court proceedings.

This is precisely what happened in United States v. Three Juveniles, *a case involving The Boston Globe.* The Globe Newspaper Co. *filed a petition for writ of certiorari in November 1995, and the U.S. Supreme Court denied review on April 29, 1996.*

 To read more about the issue of open access to juvenile trials, go to the following article on InfoTrac® College Edition: Thomas A. Hughes, "Opening the doors to juvenile court: Is there an emerging right of public access?" Communications and the Law *19:1–50 (1997).*

Chapter 14

Juvenile Corrections: Probation, Community Treatment, and Institutionalization

© Gale Zucker/Stock, Boston

s a local juvenile court judge you have been assigned the case of Jim Butler, a 13-year-old juvenile so short he can barely see over the bench. On trial for armed robbery, Jim has been accused of threatening a woman with a knife and stealing her purse. Barely a teenager, Jim has already had a long history of involvement with the law. At age 11 he was arrested for drug possession and placed on probation; soon after, he stole a car. At age 12 he was arrested for shoplifting. Jim is accompanied by his legal guardian, his maternal grandmother. His parents are unavailable because his father abandoned the family years ago and his mother is currently undergoing inpatient treatment at a local drug clinic. After talking with his attorney, Jim decides to admit to the armed robbery. At a dispositional hearing, his court-appointed attorney tells you of the tough life Jim has been forced to endure. His grandmother states that, while she loves the boy, her advanced age makes it impossible for her to provide the care he needs to stay out of further trouble. She tells you that Jim is a good boy who has developed a set of bad companions; his current scrape was precipitated by his ill-chosen friends. A representative of the school system testifies that Jim has above-average intelligence and is actually respectful of teachers. He has potential but his life circumstances have short-circuited his academic success. Jim himself shows remorse and appears to be a sensitive youngster who is easily led astray by older youths.

You must now make a decision in the case. You can place Jim on probation and allow him to live with his grandmother while being monitored by county probation staff. You can place him in a secure incarceration facility for up to 3 years. You could also put him into an intermediate program such as a community-based facility, which would allow him to attend school during the day while residing in a halfway house and receiving group treatment in the evenings. Your decision is difficult because, while Jim appears salvageable, his crime was serious and involved the use of a weapon. If he remains in the community he may offend again; if he is sent to a correctional facility he will interact with older, tougher kids. What mode of correctional treatment would you decide?

- Would you place Jim on probation and allow him to live with his grandmother while being monitored by county probation staff?

- Would you send him to a secure incarceration facility for up to three years?

- Would you put him into an intermediate program such as a community-based facility, which would allow him to attend school during the day while residing in a halfway house and receiving group treatment in the evenings?

There is actually a wide choice of correctional treatments available for juveniles, which can be subdivided into two major categories: community treatment and institutional treatment. **Community treatment** refers to efforts to provide care, protection, and treatment for juveniles in need. These efforts include probation; treatment services (such as individual and group counseling); restitution; and other programs. The term *community treatment* also refers to the use of privately maintained residences, such as foster homes, small-group homes, and boarding schools, which are located in the community. Nonresidential programs, where youths remain in their own homes but are required to receive counseling, vocational training, and other services, also fall under the rubric of community treatment.

Institutional treatment facilities are correctional centers operated by federal, state, and county governments; these facilities restrict the movement of residents through staff monitoring, locked exits, and interior fence controls. These institutional facilities serve a number of functions within juvenile corrections, including: (1) reception cen-

community treatment Using nonsecure and noninstitutional residences, counseling services, victim restitution programs, and other community services to treat juveniles in their own communities.

Some juvenile community sentences are quite innovative! Juvenile Court Judge Paul Perachi stands in his office next to a small statue of William Shakespeare, Dec. 12, 2000, in Pittsfield, Mass. Perachi is working with the Massachusetts-based Shakespeare and Company, sending troubled youth to serve sentences in Shakespeare plays. (AP/Wide World Photos)

suppression effect A reduction of the number of arrests per year for youths who have been incarcerated or otherwise punished.

ters that screen juveniles and assign them to an appropriate facility; (2) specialized facilities that provide specific types of care, such as drug treatment; (3) training schools or reformatories for youths needing a long-term secure setting; (4) ranch or forestry camps that provide long-term residential care; and (5) boot camps, which seek to rehabilitate youth through the application of rigorous physical training.

Choosing a proper mode of juvenile corrections can be difficult. Some experts believe that any hope for rehabilitating juvenile offenders and resolving the problems of juvenile crime lies in community treatment programs. Such programs are smaller than secure facilities for juveniles, operate in a community setting, and offer creative approaches to treating the offender. In contrast, institutionalizing young offenders may do more harm than good. It exposes them to prison-like conditions and to more-experienced delinquents without giving them the benefit of constructive treatment programs.

Those who favor secure treatment are concerned about the threat that violent young offenders present to the community and believe that a stay in a juvenile institution may have a long-term deterrent effect. They point to the findings of Charles Murray and Louis B. Cox, who uncovered what they call a **suppression effect,** a reduction in the number of arrests per year following release from a secure facility, which is not achieved when juveniles are placed in less-punitive programs.[1] Murray and Cox concluded that the justice system must choose which outcome its programs are aimed at achieving: prevention of delinquency, or the care and protection of needy youths. If the former is a proper goal, institutionalization or the threat of institutionalization is desirable. Not surprisingly, secure treatment is still being used extensively, and the populations of these facilities continue to grow as state legislators pass more stringent and punitive sentencing packages aimed at repeat juvenile offenders.

We begin this chapter with a detailed discussion of community treatment, examining both traditional probation and new approaches for providing probation services to juvenile offenders. Next, we trace the development of alternatives to incarceration, including community-based, nonsecure treatment programs and graduated sanctions (programs that provide community-based options while reserving secure care for violent offenders). The current state of secure juvenile corrections is then reviewed, beginning with some historical background, followed by a discussion of life in institutions, treatment issues, legal rights, and aftercare programs.

JUVENILE PROBATION

probation Nonpunitive, legal disposition for juveniles emphasizing community treatment in which the juvenile is closely supervised by an officer of the court and must adhere to a strict set of rules to avoid incarceration.

Probation and other forms of community treatment generally refer to nonpunitive legal disposition for delinquent youths, emphasizing treatment without incarceration. Probation is the primary form of community treatment used by the juvenile justice system. A juvenile who is on probation is maintained in the community under the supervision of an officer of the court. Probation also encompasses a set of rules and conditions that must be met for the offender to remain in the community. Juveniles on probation may be placed in a wide variety of community-based treatment programs that provide services ranging from group counseling to drug treatment.

Community treatment is based on the idea that the juvenile offender is not a danger to the community and has a better chance of being rehabilitated within the community. It provides offenders with the opportunity to be supervised by trained personnel who can help them reestablish forms of acceptable behavior in a community setting. When applied correctly, community treatment (1) maximizes the liberty of the individual while at the same time vindicating the authority of the law and protecting the public; (2) promotes rehabilitation by maintaining normal community contacts; (3) avoids the negative effects of confinement, which often severely complicate the reintegration of the offender into the community; and (4) greatly reduces the financial cost to the public.[2]

Historical Development

Although the major developments in community treatment have occurred in the twentieth century, its roots go back much further. In England specialized procedures for dealing with youthful offenders were recorded as early as 1820, when the magistrates of the Warwickshire quarter sessions (periodic court hearings held in a county, or shire, of England) adopted the practice of sentencing youthful criminals to prison terms of one day, then releasing them conditionally under the supervision of their parents or masters.[3]

In the United States, juvenile probation developed as part of the wave of social reform characterizing the latter half of the nineteenth century. Massachusetts took the first step. Under an act passed in 1869, an agent of the state board of charities was authorized to appear in criminal trials involving juveniles, to find them suitable homes, and to visit them periodically. These services were soon broadened, so that by 1890 probation had become a mandatory part of the court structure.[4]

Probation was a cornerstone in the development of the juvenile court system. In fact, in some states, supporters of the juvenile court movement viewed probation as the first step toward achieving the benefits that the new court was intended to provide. The rapid spread of juvenile courts during the first decades of the twentieth century encouraged the further development of probation. The two were closely related and, to a large degree, both sprang from the conviction that the young could be rehabilitated and that the public was responsible for protecting them.

Expanding Community Treatment

By the mid-1960s, juvenile probation had become a complex institution that touched the lives of an enormous number of children. To many experts, institutionalization of even the most serious delinquent youths is a mistake. Reformers believed that confinement in a high-security institution could not solve the problems that brought a youth into a delinquent way of life, and that the experience could actually help amplify delinquency once the youth returns to the community.[5] Surveys indicating that 30 to 40 percent of adult prison inmates had prior experience with the juvenile court, and that many had been institutionalized as youths, gave little support to the argument that an institutional experience can be beneficial or reduce recidivism.[6]

The Massachusetts Experience The expansion of community programs was energized by correctional reform in the state of Massachusetts. Since the early 1970s, Massachusetts has led the movement to keep juvenile offenders in the community. After decades of documenting the failures of the youth correctional system, Massachusetts, led by its juvenile correctional commissioner Jerome Miller, closed most of its secure juvenile facilities.[7] Today, 30 years later, the Massachusetts Department of Youth Services still operates a community-based correctional system. The majority of youths are serviced in nonsecure community settings, and only a few dangerous or unmanageable youths are placed in some type of secure facilities.

Many of the early programs suffered from residential isolation and limited services. Over time, however, many of the group homes and unlocked structured residential settings were relocated in residential community environments and became highly successful in addressing the needs of juveniles, while presenting little or no security risk to themselves or others. For example, the Roxbury Youthworks is an inner-city program in Boston that aims to control delinquency through a comprehensive range of resources that include: (1) evaluation and counseling at a local court clinic, (2) employment and training, (3) detention diversion, and (4) outreach and tracking to help youths reenter the community. Contracting with the state, Roxbury Youthworks provides intensive community supervision for almost 90 percent of the youths under its jurisdiction.[8]

Though the efforts to turn juvenile corrections into a purely community-based system has not been adopted elsewhere, the Massachusetts model encouraged development of nonpunitive programs, which have proliferated across the nation. The concept of probation has been expanded and new programs have been created.

Contemporary Juvenile Probation

Traditional probation is still the backbone of community-based corrections. As Figure 14.1 shows, more than 300,000 juveniles are currently being placed on formal probation each year, which amounts to more than 50 percent of all juvenile dispositions. The use of probation has increased significantly since 1988, when less than 200,000 adjudicated youths were being placed on probation.[9] These figures show that, regardless of public sentiment, probation continues to be a popular dispositional alternative for judges. Here are the arguments in favor of probation:

1. For youths who can be supervised in the community, probation represents an appropriate disposition.
2. Probation allows the court to tailor a program to each juvenile offender, including those involved in person-oriented offenses.
3. The justice system continues to have confidence in rehabilitation, while accommodating demands for legal controls and public protection, even when caseloads may include many more serious offenders than in the past.
4. Probation is often the disposition of choice, particularly for status offenders.[10]

The Nature of Probation In the majority of jurisdictions, probation is a direct judicial order that allows a youth who is found to be a delinquent or status offender to remain in the community under court-ordered supervision. A probation sentence implies a contract between the court and the juvenile. The court promises to hold a period of institutionalization in abeyance; the juvenile promises to adhere to a set of rules mandated by the court. If the rules are violated—and especially if the juvenile commits another offense—the probation may be revoked. In that case, the contract is terminated and the original commitment order may be enforced. The rules of probation vary, but they typically involve conditions such as attending school or work, keeping regular hours, remaining in the jurisdiction, and staying out of trouble.

Figure 14.1
Probation and Correctional Population Trends

Source: Adapted from C. Puzzanchera, A. Stahl, T. Finnegan, H. Snyder, R. Poole, and N. Tierney, *Juvenile Court Statistics, 1997* (Washington, DC: Office of Juvenile Justice and Delinquency Prevention, 2000).

Delinquency cases judicially waived to criminal court

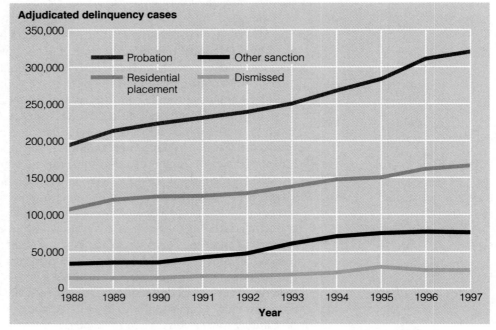

Note: There has been a substantial increase in the number of cases in which the youth was placed on probation or ordered to a residential facility between 1988 and 1997.

In the juvenile court, probation is often ordered for an indefinite period. Depending on the statutes of the jurisdiction, the seriousness of the offense, and the juvenile's adjustment on probation, youths can remain under supervision until the court no longer has jurisdiction over them (that is, when they reach the age of majority). State statutes determine if a judge can specify how long a juvenile may be placed under an order of probation. In most jurisdictions, the status of probation is reviewed regularly to ensure that a juvenile is not kept on probation needlessly. Generally, discretion lies with the probation officer to discharge youths who are adjusting to the treatment plan.

Conditions of Probation Probation conditions are rules mandating that a juvenile on probation behave in a particular way. They can include restitution or reparation, intensive supervision, intensive counseling, participation in a therapeutic program, or participation in an educational or vocational training program. In addition to these specific conditions, state statutes generally allow courts to insist that probationers lead law-abiding lives, maintain a residence in a family setting, refrain from associating with certain types of people, and remain in a particular area unless they have permission to leave.

Probation conditions vary, but they are never supposed to be capricious, cruel, or beyond the capacity of the juvenile to satisfy. Furthermore, conditions of probation should relate to the crime that was committed and to the conduct of the child.

Courts have invalidated probation conditions that were harmful or that violated the juvenile's due process rights. Restricting a child's movement, insisting on a mandatory program of treatment, ordering indefinite terms of probation, and demanding financial reparation where this is impossible are all grounds for appellate court review. For example, it would not be appropriate for a probation order to bar a youth from visiting his girlfriend (unless he had threatened or harmed her) merely because her parents objected to the relationship.[11] However, courts have ruled that it is permissible to bar juveniles from such sources of danger as a "known gang area" in order to protect them from harm.[12]

Juvenile probation officers provide supervision and treatment in the community. The treatment plan is a product of the intake, diagnostic, and investigative aspects of probation. Treatment plans vary in terms of approach and structure. Some juveniles simply report to the probation officer and follow the conditions of probation. In other cases, juvenile probation officers will supervise children more intensely, monitor their daily activities, and work with them in directed treatment programs. (© Lee Celano/ Liaison Agency)

If a youth violates the conditions of probation or breaks the law again, the court can revoke probation. The juvenile court ordinarily handles a decision to revoke probation upon recommendation of the probation officer. Today, as a result of Supreme Court decisions dealing with the rights of adult probationers, a juvenile is normally entitled to legal representation and a hearing when a violation of probation occurs.[13]

Organization and Administration

Probation services are administered by the local juvenile court, or by the state administrative office of courts, in twenty-three states and the District of Columbia. In another fourteen states, juvenile probation services are split, with the juvenile court having control in urban counties and a state executive serving in smaller counties. About ten states have a statewide office of juvenile probation located in the executive branch. In three states, county executives administer probation.[14] These agencies employ an estimated 18,000 juvenile probation officers throughout the United States.

In the typical juvenile probation department, the chief probation officer is central to its effective operation. In addition, large probation departments include one or more assistant chiefs, each of whom is responsible for one aspect of probation service. One assistant chief might oversee training, another might supervise special offender groups, and still another might act as liaison with police or community-service agencies.

Although juvenile probation services continue to be predominantly organized under the judiciary, recent legislative activity has been in the direction of transferring those services from the local juvenile court judge to a state court administrative office. Whether local juvenile courts or state agencies should administer juvenile probation services is debatable. In years past, the organization of probation services depended primarily on the size of the program and the number of juveniles under its supervision. Because of this momentum to develop unified court systems, many juvenile court services are being consolidated into state court systems.

juvenile probation officer
Officer of the court involved in all four stages of the court process—intake, predisposition, postadjudication, and postdisposition—who assists the court and supervises juveniles placed on probation.

Duties of Juvenile Probation Officers

The **juvenile probation officer** plays an important role in the justice process, beginning with intake and continuing throughout the period in which a juvenile is under court supervision. Probation officers are involved at four stages of the court process.

At *intake*, they screen complaints by deciding to adjust the matter, refer the child to an agency for service, or refer the case to the court for judicial action. During the *predisposition* stage, they participate in release or detention decisions. At the *post-adjudication* stage, they assist the court in reaching its dispositional decision. During *postdisposition*, they supervise juveniles placed on probation.

At intake, the probation staff has preliminary discussions with the child and the family to determine whether court intervention is necessary or whether the matter can be better resolved by some form of social service. If the child is placed in a detention facility, the probation officer helps the court decide whether the child should continue to be held or released pending the adjudication and disposition of the case.

The probation officer exercises tremendous influence over the child and the family by developing a **social investigation,** or **predisposition, report** and submitting it to the court. This report is a clinical diagnosis of the child's problems and of the need for court assistance based on an evaluation of social functioning, personality, and environmental issues. The report includes an analysis of the child's feelings about the violations and of capacity for change. It also examines the influence of family members, peers, and other environmental influences in producing and possibly resolving the problems. All of this information is brought together in a complex but meaningful picture of the offender's personality, problems, and environment.

Juvenile probation officers also provide the child with supervision and treatment in the community. Treatment plans vary in terms of approach and structure. Some juveniles simply report to the probation officer and follow the **conditions of probation.** In other cases, the probation officer may need to provide extensive counseling to the child and family or, more typically, refer them to other social service agencies, such as a drug treatment center. Figure 14.2 provides an overview of the juvenile probation

social investigation report, predisposition report Developed by the juvenile probation officer, this report consists of a clinical diagnosis of the juvenile and his or her need for court assistance, relevant environmental and personality factors, and any other information that would assist the court in developing a treatment plan for the juvenile.

conditions of probation The rules and regulations mandating that a juvenile on probation behave in a particular way.

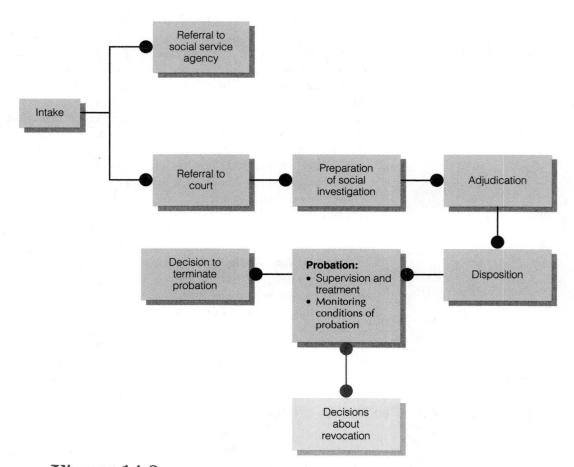

Figure 14.2
The Juvenile Probation Officer's Influence

TABLE 14.1 The Duties of the Juvenile Probation Officer

- Providing direct counseling and casework services
- Interviewing and collecting social service data
- Making diagnostic recommendations
- Maintaining working relationships with law enforcement agencies
- Using community resources and services
- Directing volunteer case aides
- Writing predisposition or social investigation reports
- Working with families of children under supervision
- Providing specialized services, such as group therapy
- Supervising specialized caseloads involving children with special problems
- Making decisions about the revocation of probation and its termination

officer's sphere of influence. Table 14.1 summarizes the probation officer's role. Performance of such a broad range of functions requires good training. Today, juvenile probation officers have legal or social-work backgrounds or special counseling skills.

Checkpoints

✔ Community treatment refers to efforts to provide care, protection, and treatment for juveniles in need.

✔ Institutional treatment facilities restrict the movement of residents through staff monitoring, locked exits, and interior fence controls.

✔ Probation is the primary form of community treatment used by the juvenile justice system

✔ First developed in Massachusetts, probation had become a cornerstone of the court structure by 1890.

✔ Massachusetts has closed most of its secure juvenile facilities and relies almost entirely on community treatment.

✔ Probation is a direct judicial order that allows a youth to remain in the community under court-ordered supervision.

✔ Probation conditions are rules mandating that a juvenile on probation behave in a particular way.

✔ The juvenile probation officer plays an important role in the justice process, beginning with intake and continuing throughout the period in which a juvenile is under court supervision.

PROBATION INNOVATIONS

Community corrections have traditionally emphasized offender rehabilitation. The probation officer has been viewed as a caseworker or counselor, whose primary job is to help the offender adjust to society. Offender surveillance and control has seemed more appropriate for law enforcement, jails, and prisons than for community corrections.[15] Since 1980, a more conservative justice system has reoriented toward social control. While the rehabilitative ideals of probation have not been abandoned, new programs have been developed that add a control dimension to community corrections. These programs can be viewed as "probation plus," since they add restrictive penalties and conditions to community-service orders. More punitive than probation, intermediate sanctions can be politically attractive to conservatives, while still appealing to liberals as alternatives to incarceration. What are some of these new alternative sanctions?

juvenile intensive probation supervision (JIPS) A true alternative to incarceration that involves almost daily supervision of the juvenile by the probation officer assigned to the case.

Intensive Supervision

Juvenile intensive probation supervision (JIPS) involves treating offenders who would normally have been sent to a secure treatment facility as part of a very small probation caseload that receives almost daily scrutiny.[16] The primary goal of JIPS is *decarceration*; without intensive supervision, youngsters would normally be sent to secure juvenile facilities that are already overcrowded. The second goal is control; high-risk juvenile offenders can be maintained in the community under much closer security than traditional probation efforts can provide. A third goal is maintaining community ties and reintegration; offenders can remain in the community and complete their education while avoiding the pains of imprisonment.

Intensive probation programs get mixed reviews. Some jurisdictions find that they are more successful than traditional probation supervision and come at a much cheaper cost than incarceration.[17] However, most research indicates that the failure rate is high and that younger offenders who commit petty crimes are the most likely to fail when placed in intensive supervision programs.[18] It is not surprising that intensive probation clients fail more often because, after all, they are more serious offenders who might otherwise have been incarcerated and are now being watched and supervised more closely than probationers.

Electronic Monitoring

house arrest An offender is required to stay at home during specific periods of time; monitoring is done by random phone calls and visits or by electronic devices.

electronic monitoring Active monitoring systems consist of a radio transmitter worn by the offender that sends a continuous signal to the probation department computer, alerting officials if the offender leaves his or her place of confinement; passive systems employ computer-generated random phone calls that must be responded to in a certain period of time from a particular phone or other device.

Another program, which has been used with adult offenders and is finding its way into the juvenile justice system, is **house arrest,** which is often coupled with **electronic monitoring.** This program allows offenders sentenced to probation to remain in the community on condition that they stay at home during specific periods (for example, after school or work, on weekends, and in the evenings). Offenders may be monitored through random phone calls, visits, or, in some jurisdictions, electronic devices.

Two types of electronic systems are used: active and passive. *Active systems* monitor the offender by continuously sending a signal back to the central office. If an offender leaves home at an unauthorized time, the signal is broken and the failure recorded. In some cases, the control officer is automatically notified through a beeper. In contrast, *passive systems* usually involve random phone calls generated by computers to which the juvenile offender must respond within a particular time (for example, 30 seconds). Some passive systems require the offender to place the monitoring device in a verifier box that sends a signal back to the control computer; another approach is to have the arrestee repeat words that are analyzed by a voice verifier and compared with tapes of the juvenile's voice.

Most systems employ radio transmitters that receive a signal from a device worn by the offender and relay it back to the computer via telephone lines. Probationers are fitted with an unremovable monitoring device that alerts the probation department's computers if they leave their place of confinement.[19]

Recent indications are that electronic monitoring can be effective. Evaluations show that recidivism rates are no higher than in traditional programs, costs are lower, and overcrowding is reduced. Also, electronic monitoring seems to work better with some individuals than others: serious felony offenders, substance abusers, repeat offenders, and people serving the longest sentences are the most likely to fail.[20]

Electronic monitoring combined with house arrest is being hailed as one of the most important developments in correctional policy. Its supporters claim that it has the benefits of relatively low cost and high security, while at the same time it helps offenders avoid imprisonment in overcrowded, dangerous state facilities. Furthermore, fewer supervisory officers are needed to handle large numbers of offenders. Despite these strengths, electronic monitoring has its drawbacks: existing systems can be affected by faulty telephone equipment, most electronic monitoring/house arrest programs do not provide rehabilitation services, and some believe electronic monitoring is contrary to a citizen's right to privacy.[21]

balanced probation Programs that integrate community protection, accountability of the juvenile offender, competency, and individualized attention to the juvenile offender; based on the principle that juvenile offenders must accept responsibility for their behavior.

Balanced Probation

In recent years some jurisdictions have turned to a **balanced probation** approach in an effort to enhance the success of probation.[22] Balanced probation systems integrate

Balanced probation systems integrate community protection, the accountability of the juvenile offender, and individualized attention to the offender. Here, one probationer, Charley Cobb (right), talks with her lawyer, Jennifer Sobel, in Grafton County Superior Court in Haverhill, N.H., May 8, 2000. Cobb, a teenager who accidentally killed her newborn baby in January 1999 and fell behind in her community service work, told the judge today that she has completed 70 hours of her 500 hours community service, attends counseling regularly, and expects to graduate from high school later this month. The judge added six months to Cobb's probation. (AP/Wide World Photos)

community protection, the accountability of the juvenile offender, and individualized attention to the offender. These programs are based on the view that juveniles are responsible for their actions and have an obligation to society whenever they commit an offense. The probation officer establishes a program tailored to the offender while helping the offender accept responsibility for his or her actions. The balanced approach is promising because it specifies a distinctive role for the juvenile probation system.[23] The balanced approach has been implemented with some success, as these examples demonstrate:

- In Pittsburgh, probationers in an intensive day-treatment program solicit suggestions from community organizations about service projects they would like to see completed. They work with community residents on projects such as home repair and gardening for the elderly, voter registration, painting homes and public buildings, and cultivating community gardens.

- In Florida, offenders, sponsored by the Florida Department of Juvenile Justice and supervised by The 100 Black Men of Palm Beach County, Inc., create shelters for abused, abandoned, and HIV-positive infants. Victims' rights advocates also train juvenile justice staff on sensitivity in their interaction with victims and help prepare victim awareness curriculums for youths in residential programs.

- In cities and towns in Pennsylvania, Montana, and Minnesota, family members and other citizens acquainted with a juvenile offender, or the victim of a juvenile crime, gather to determine the best response to the offense. Held in schools, churches, or other community facilities, these conferences ensure that offenders hear community disapproval of their behavior. Participants develop an agreement for repairing the damage to the victim and the community and define a plan for reintegrating the offender.[24]

Although balanced probation programs are still in their infancy and their effectiveness remains to be tested, they have generated great interest because of their potential for relieving overcrowded correctional facilities and reducing the pain and stigma of incarceration. There seems to be little question that the use of these innovations, and juvenile probation in general, will increase in the years ahead. Given the $40,000 cost of a year's commitment to a typical residential facility, it should not be a great burden to develop additional probation services.

Restitution

monetary restitution A requirement that juvenile offenders compensate crime victims for out-of-pocket losses caused by the crime, including property damage, lost wages, and medical expenses.

victim service restitution The juvenile offender is required to provide some service directly to the crime victim.

community service restitution The juvenile offender is required to assist some worthwhile community organization for a period of time.

Victim restitution is another widely used method of community treatment. In most jurisdictions, restitution is part of a probationary sentence and is administered by the county probation staff. In many jurisdictions, independent restitution programs have been set up by local governments; in others, restitution is administered by a private nonprofit organization.[25]

Restitution can take several forms. A juvenile can reimburse the victim of the crime or donate money to a charity or public cause; this is referred to as **monetary restitution.** In other instances, a juvenile may be required to provide some service directly to the victim (**victim service restitution**) or to assist a community organization (**community service restitution**).

Requiring youths to reimburse the victims of their crimes is the most widely used method of restitution in the United States. Less widely used, but more common in Europe, is restitution to a charity. In the past few years numerous programs have been set up to enable the juvenile offender to provide service to the victim or to participate in community programs—for example, working in schools for retarded children. In some cases, juveniles are required to contribute both money and community service. Other programs emphasize employment.[26]

Restitution programs can be employed at various stages of the juvenile justice process. They can be part of a diversion program prior to conviction, a method of informal adjustment at intake, or a condition of probation. Restitution has a number of advantages: it provides alternative sentencing options; it offers monetary compensation or service to crime victims; it allows the juvenile the opportunity to compensate the victim and take a step toward becoming a productive member of society; it helps relieve overcrowded juvenile courts, probation caseloads, and detention facilities. Finally, like other alternatives to incarceration, restitution has the potential for allowing vast savings in the operation of the juvenile justice system. Monetary restitution programs in particular may improve the public's attitude toward juvenile justice by offering equity to the victims of crime and ensuring that offenders take responsibility for their actions.

Despite its many advantages, some believe restitution supports retribution rather than rehabilitation because it emphasizes justice for the victim and criminal responsibility for illegal acts. There is some concern that restitution creates penalties for juvenile offenders where none existed before.

The use of restitution is increasing. In 1977 there were fewer than 15 formal restitution programs around the United States. By 1985, formal programs existed in 400 jurisdictions, and 35 states had statutory provisions that gave courts the authority to order juvenile restitution.[27] Today, all 50 states, as well as the District of Columbia, have statutory restitution programs.

Does Restitution Work? How successful is restitution as a treatment alternative? Most evaluations have shown that it is reasonably effective, and should be expanded.[28] In an analysis of federally sponsored restitution programs, Peter Schneider and his associates found that about 95 percent of youths who received restitution as a condi-

The juvenile shown here is being supervised while serving in a restitution program. Most evaluations have shown that these programs are reasonably effective and should be expanded. (© Joel Gordon)

tion of probation successfully completed their orders.[29] Factors related to success were family income, good school attendance, few prior offenses, minor current offense, and size of restitution order. Schneider found that the youths who received restitution as a sole sanction (without probation) were those originally viewed by juvenile court judges as the better risks, and consequently they had lower failure and recidivism rates than youths ordered to make restitution after being placed on probation.

Anne Schneider conducted a thorough analysis of restitution programs in four different states and found that participants had lower recidivism rates than youths in control groups (regular probation caseloads).[30] Although Schneider's data indicate that restitution may reduce recidivism, the number of youths who had subsequent involvement in the justice system still seemed high. In short, there is evidence that most restitution orders are successfully completed and that youths who make restitution are less likely to become recidivists; however, the number of repeat offenses committed by juveniles who made restitution suggests that, by itself, restitution is not the answer to the delinquency problem.

Restitution programs may be difficult to implement in some circumstances. Offenders may find it difficult to make monetary restitution without securing new employment, which can be difficult during periods of high unemployment. Problems also arise when offenders who need jobs suffer from drug abuse or emotional problems. Public and private agencies are likely sites for community-service restitution, but their directors are sometimes reluctant to allow delinquent youths access to their organizations. Beyond these problems, some juvenile probation officers view restitution programs as a threat to their authority and to the autonomy of their organizations.

Another criticism of restitution programs is that they foster involuntary servitude. Indigent clients may be unfairly punished when they are unable to make restitution payments or face probation violations. To avoid such bias, probation officers should first determine why payment has stopped and then suggest appropriate action, rather than simply treating nonpayment as a matter of law enforcement.

Finally, restitution orders are subject to the same abuses as traditional sentencing methods. The restitution orders one delinquent offender receives may be quite different from those given another in a comparable case. To remedy this situation, a number of jurisdictions have been using guidelines to encourage standardization of orders.

Residential Community Treatment

Many experts believe that institutionalization of even the most serious delinquent youths is a mistake. Confinement in a high-security institution usually cannot solve the problems that brought a youth into a delinquent way of life, and the experience may actually amplify delinquency once the youth returns to the community. Many agree that warehousing juveniles without attention to their treatment needs does little to prevent their return to criminal behavior. Research has shown that the most effective secure-corrections programs provided individualized services for a small number of participants. Large training schools have not proved to be effective.[31] This realization has produced a wide variety of residential community-treatment programs to service youths who need a more secure environment than can be provided by probation services but who do not require a placement in a state-run juvenile correctional facility.

How are community corrections implemented? In some cases, youths are placed under probation supervision, and the probation department maintains a residential treatment facility. Placement can also be made to the department of social services or juvenile corrections with the direction that the youth be placed in a residential facility. **Residential programs** are typically divided into four major categories: (1) group homes, including boarding schools and apartment-type settings; (2) foster homes; (3) family group homes; and (4) rural programs.

Group homes are nonsecure residences that provide counseling, education, job training, and family living. They are staffed by a small number of qualified persons, and generally house 12–15 youngsters. The institutional quality of the environment is minimized, and youths are given the opportunity to build a close relationship with the staff. Youths reside in the home, attend public schools, and participate in community activities.

Foster care programs involve one or two juveniles who live with a family— usually a husband and wife who serve as surrogate parents. The juveniles enter into a close relationship with the foster parents and receive the attention and care they did not receive at home. The quality of the foster home experience depends on the foster parents. Foster care for adjudicated juvenile offenders has not been extensive in the United States. Welfare departments generally handle foster placements, and funding of this treatment option has been a problem for the juvenile justice system. However, foster home services have expanded as a community treatment approach.

Family group homes combine elements of foster care and group home placements. Juveniles are placed in a group home that is run by a family rather than by a professional staff. Troubled youths have an opportunity to learn to get along in a family-like situation, and at the same time the state avoids the startup costs and neighborhood opposition often associated with establishing a public institution.

Rural programs include forestry camps, ranches, and farms that provide recreational activities or work for juveniles. Programs typically handle from 30 to 50 youths. Such programs have the disadvantage of isolating juveniles from the community, but reintegration can be achieved if the youth's stay is short and if family and friends are allowed to visit.

Most residential programs use group counseling as the major treatment tool. Although group facilities have been used less often than institutional placements, there is a trend toward developing community-based residential facilities.

Pros and Cons of Residential Community Treatment The public may have a negative impression of community treatment, especially when it is offered to juvenile offenders who pose a threat to society. It is not uncommon for neighborhood groups to oppose the location of corrections programs in their community. Is their fear realistic?

There are indications that young people can be treated in the community as effectively as youths placed in an institution. **Meta-analysis** studies, which review the findings of many studies, have given support to community rehabilitation.[32] Accord-

residential programs Placement of a juvenile offender in a residential, nonsecure facility such as a group home, foster home, family group home, or rural home where the juvenile can be closely monitored and develop close relationships with staff members.

group homes Nonsecured, structured residences that provide counseling, education, job training, and family living.

foster care programs Juveniles who are orphans or whose parents cannot care for them are placed with families who provide the attention, guidance, and care they did not receive at home.

family group homes A combination of foster care and a group home in which a juvenile is placed in a private group home run by a single family rather than by professional staff.

rural programs Specific recreational and work opportunities provided for juveniles in a rural setting such as a forestry camp, a farm, or a ranch.

meta-analysis An analysis technique that synthesizes results across many programs over time.

ing to Barry Krisberg and his associates, the most successful community-based programs seem to share at least some of these characteristics: (1) comprehensiveness, dealing with many aspects of youths' lives; (2) intensivity, involving multiple contacts; (3) operation outside the justice system; (4) foundation upon youths' strengths; and (5) adoption of a socially grounded approach to understanding a juvenile's situation rather than an individual-level (medical or therapeutic) approach.[33]

Community-based programs continue to present the most promising alternative to the poor results of reform schools, for these reasons:

- Some states have found that residential and nonresidential settings produce comparable or lower recidivism rates. Some researchers have found that youths in nonsecure settings are less likely to become recidivists than those placed in more secure settings.

- Community-based programs have lower costs and are especially appropriate for large numbers of nonviolent juveniles and those guilty of lesser offenses.

- Public opinion of community corrections remains positive. Many citizens prefer community-based programs for all but the most serious juvenile offenders.[34]

As jurisdictions continue to face ever-increasing costs for juvenile justice services, community-based programs will play an important role in providing rehabilitation of juvenile offenders and ensuring public safety.

Checkpoints

✔ There are new programs being developed that are "probation plus," since they add restrictive penalties and conditions to community service orders.

✔ Juvenile intensive probation supervision (JIPS) involves treatment as part of a very small probation caseload that receives almost daily scrutiny.

✔ Electronic monitoring combined with house arrest is being implemented in juvenile correction policy.

✔ Balanced probation systems integrate community protection, accountability of the juvenile offender, and individualized attention to the offender.

✔ Monetary restitution allows a juvenile to reimburse the victim of the crime or donate money to a charity or public cause.

✔ Community service restitution allows juveniles to engage in public works as part of their disposition.

✔ Residential community programs are typically divided into four major categories: (1) group homes, including boarding schools and apartment-type settings; (2) foster homes; (3) family group homes; and (4) rural programs.

SECURE CORRECTIONS

When the court determines that community treatment can't meet the special needs of a delinquent youth, a judge may refer the juvenile to a secure treatment program. Today, correctional institutions operated by federal, state, and county governments are generally classified as secure or open facilities. Secure facilities restrict the movement of residents through staff monitoring, locked exits, and interior fence controls. Open institutions generally do not restrict the movement of the residents and allow much greater freedom of access to the facility.[35] In the following sections, we analyze the state of secure juvenile corrections, beginning with some historical background. This is followed by a discussion of life in institutions, the juvenile client, treatment issues, legal rights, and aftercare programs.

History of Juvenile Institutions

Until the early 1800s, juvenile offenders, as well as neglected and dependent children, were confined in adult prisons. The inhumane conditions in these institutions were

reform schools Institutions in which educational and psychological services are used in an effort to improve the conduct of juveniles who are forcibly detained.

cottage system Housing juveniles in a compound containing a series of small cottages, each of which accommodates twenty to forty children and is run by a set of cottage parents who create a home-like atmosphere.

among the factors that led social reformers to create a separate children's court system in 1899.[36] Early juvenile institutions were industrial schools modeled after adult prisons but designed to protect children from the evil influences in adult facilities. The first was the New York House of Refuge, established in 1825. Not long after this, states began to establish **reform schools** for juveniles. Massachusetts was the first, opening the Lyman School for Boys in Westborough in 1846. New York opened the State Agricultural and Industrial School in 1849, and Maine opened the Maine Boys' Training School in 1853. By 1900, 36 states had reform schools.[37] Although it is difficult to determine exact population of these institutions, by 1880 there were approximately 11,000 youths in correctional facilities, a number that more than quadrupled by 1980.[38] Early reform schools were generally punitive in nature and were based on the concept of rehabilitation (or reform) through hard work and discipline.

In the second half of the nineteenth century, emphasis shifted to the **cottage system.** Juvenile offenders were housed in compounds of cottages, each of which could accommodate 20–40 children. A set of parents ran each cottage, creating a home-like atmosphere. This setup was believed to be more conducive to rehabilitation.

The first cottage system was established in Massachusetts in 1855, the second in Ohio in 1858.[39] The system was held to be a great improvement over training schools. The belief was that, by moving away from punishment and toward rehabilitation, not only could offenders be rehabilitated but also crime among unruly children could be prevented.[40]

Twentieth-Century Developments The early twentieth century witnessed important changes in juvenile corrections. Because of the influence of World War I, reform schools began to adopt a militaristic style. Living units became barracks; cottage groups became companies; house fathers became captains; and superintendents became majors or colonels. Military-style uniforms were standard wear.

In addition, the establishment of the first juvenile court in 1899 reflected the expanded use of confinement for delinquent children. As the number of juvenile offenders increased, the forms of juvenile institutions varied to include forestry camps, ranches, and vocational schools. Beginning in the 1930s, camps modeled after the camps run by the Civilian Conservation Corps became a part of the juvenile correctional system. These camps centered on conservation activities and work as a means of rehabilitation.

Los Angeles County was the first to use camps during this period.[41] Southern California was experiencing problems with transient youths who came to California with no money and then got into trouble with the law. Rather than filling up the jails, the county placed these offenders in conservation camps, paid them low wages, and released them when they had earned enough money to return home. The camps proved more rehabilitative than training schools, and by 1935 California had established a network of forestry camps for delinquent boys. The idea soon spread to other states.[42]

Also during the 1930s, the U.S. Children's Bureau sought to reform juvenile corrections. The bureau conducted studies to determine the effectiveness of the training school concept. Little was learned from these programs because of limited funding and bureaucratic ineptitude, and the Children's Bureau failed to achieve any significant change. But such efforts recognized the important role of positive institutional care.[43]

Another innovation came in the 1940s with passage of the American Law Institute's Model Youth Correction Authority Act. This act emphasized reception/classification centers. California was the first to try out this idea, opening the Northern Reception Center and Clinic in Sacramento in 1947. Today, there are many such centers scattered around the United States.

Since the 1970s, a major change in institutionalization has been the effort to remove status offenders from institutions housing juvenile delinquents. This includes removing status offenders from detention centers and removing all juveniles from contact with adults in jails. This *decarceration* policy mandates that courts use the

least restrictive alternative
Choosing a program with the least
restrictive or secure setting that
will best benefit the child.

least restrictive alternative in providing services for status offenders. A noncriminal youth should not be put in a secure facility if a community-based program is available. In addition, the federal government prohibits states from placing status offenders in separate facilities that are similar in form and function to those used for delinquent offenders. This is to prevent states from merely shifting their institutionalized population around so that one training school houses all delinquents and another houses all status offenders, but actual conditions remain the same.

Throughout the 1980s and into the 1990s, admissions to juvenile correctional facilities grew substantially.[44] Capacities of juvenile facilities also increased, but not enough to avoid overcrowding. Training schools became seriously overcrowded in some states, causing private facilities to play an increased role in juvenile corrections. Reliance on incarceration became costly to states: inflation-controlled juvenile corrections expenditures for public facilities grew to more than $2 billion in 1995, an increase of 20 percent from 1982.[45] A 1994 report issued by the OJJDP said that crowding, inadequate health care, lack of security, and poor control of suicidal behavior was widespread in juvenile corrections facilities. Despite new construction, crowding persisted in more than half the states.[46]

JUVENILE INSTITUTIONS TODAY: PUBLIC AND PRIVATE

Most juveniles are housed in public institutions that are administered by state agencies: child and youth services, health and social services, corrections, or child welfare.[47] In some states these institutions fall under a centralized system that covers adults as well as juveniles. Recently, a number of states have removed juvenile corrections from an existing adult corrections department or mental health agency. However, the majority of states still place responsibility for the administration of juvenile corrections within social-service departments.

Supplementing publicly funded institutions are private facilities that are maintained and operated by private agencies funded or chartered by state authorities. The majority of today's private institutions are relatively small facilities holding fewer than 30 youths. Many have a specific mission or focus (for example, treating females who display serious emotional problems). Although about 80 percent of public institutions can be characterized as secure, only 20 percent of private institutions are high-security facilities.

Population Trends

Whereas most delinquents are held in public facilities, most status offenders are held in private facilities. At last count, there were slightly more than 100,000 juveniles being held in public (75%) and private (25%) facilities in the United States.[48] There has been relatively little increase in the number of juveniles being held in custody since 1992.[49] The juvenile custody rate varies widely among states: California makes the greatest use of custodial treatment, incarcerating close to 500 delinquents in public facilities per 100,000 juveniles in the general population. In contrast, about half of the states had rates of about 200 juveniles per 100,000. Some states rely heavily on privately run facilities, while others place many youths in out-of-state facilities.

Although the number of institutionalized youths has stabilized, the data may reveal only the tip of the iceberg. The data do not include many minors who are incarcerated after they are waived to adult courts or who have been tried as adults because of exclusion statutes. Most states place under-age juveniles convicted of adult charges in youth centers until they reach the age of majority, whereupon they are transferred to an adult facility. In addition, there may be a hidden, or subterranean, correctional system that places wayward youths in private mental hospitals and substance-abuse clinics for behaviors that might otherwise have brought them a stay in a correctional facility or

The physical condition of some juvenile facilities is far less than ideal. An inmate looks out the window of his cell at the New Jersey Training School for Boys. The state budget includes a special $1 million appropriation to renovate cells for suicide prevention due to a growing problem of mentally ill inmates. The toilet and sink will be replaced with safer versions as part of the numerous changes being made during the renovation. (AP/Wide World Photos)

community-based program.[50] These data suggest that the number of institutionalized children may be far greater than reported in the official statistics.[51]

Physical Conditions

The physical plants of juvenile institutions vary in size and quality. Many of the older training schools still place all offenders in a single building, regardless of the offense. More acceptable structures include a reception unit with an infirmary, a security unit, and dormitory units or cottages. Planners have concluded that the most effective design for training schools is to have facilities located around a community square. The facilities generally include a dining hall and kitchen area, a storage warehouse, academic and vocational training rooms, a library, an auditorium, a gymnasium, an administration building, and other basic facilities.

The individual living areas also vary, depending on the type of facility and the progressiveness of its administration. Most traditional training school conditions were appalling. Today, however, most institutions provide toilet and bath facilities, beds, desks, lamps, and tables. New facilities usually provide a single room for each individual.

Most experts recommend that juvenile facilities have leisure areas, libraries, education spaces, chapels, facilities where youths can meet with their visitors, windows in all sleeping accommodations, and fire-safety equipment and procedures. Because institutions for delinquent youths vary in purpose, it is not necessary that they meet identical standards. Security measures used in some closed institutions, for instance, may not be required in a residential program.

The physical conditions of secure facilities for juveniles have come a long way from the training schools of the turn of the century. However, many administrators realize that more modernization is necessary to comply with national standards for juvenile institutions. Correctional administrators have described conditions as horrendous, and health officials have cited institutions for violations such as pollution by vermin and asbestos.[52] Although some improvements have been made, there are still enormous problems to overcome.

Two residents at the Preston Youth Correctional Facility create garments and blankets for the "Newborn in Need" program. Although correctional officers were worried at first that the juvenile offenders might take scissors and needles, none of the materials disappeared during the first six months of the program. (Dick Schmidt/*Sacramento Bee*)

THE INSTITUTIONALIZED JUVENILE

The typical resident of a juvenile facility is a 15- to 16-year-old white male incarcerated for an average stay of 5 months in a public facility or 6 months in a private facility. Private facilities tend to house younger youths, while public institutions provide custodial care for older youths, including a small percentage of youths between 18 and 21 years of age. Most incarcerated youths are person, property, or drug offenders.

Racial makeup differs widely between private and public facilities. More than half of those in private institutions are white, whereas more than two-thirds of the residents in public facilities are African American or Hispanic. Although the number of white juveniles held in public facilities has been decreasing, the number of African American and Hispanic juveniles in custody remains disproportionately high.

Research has found that minority youths are incarcerated at a rate 3 to 4 times that of white youths and that this overrepresentation is not a result of differentials in arrest rates. Minority youths accused of delinquent acts are less likely than white youths to be diverted from the court system into informal sanctions and are more likely to receive sentences involving incarceration.[53] In response, some jurisdictions have initiated studies of racial disproportion in their juvenile justice systems.[54]

More than two decades ago, shocking exposés focused public attention on the problems of juvenile corrections. Today, some critics believe public scrutiny has improved conditions within training schools. There is greater professionalism among the staff, and staff brutality seems to have diminished. Status offenders and delinquents are, for the most part, held in separate facilities. Confinement length is shorter, and rehabilitative programming has increased. However, there are significant differences in the experiences of male and female delinquents within the institution.

To read about life in a secure Canadian facility, go to the Web site maintained by the Prince George Youth Custody Center in British Columbia, a secure facility providing a range of programs to allow youths to make maximal constructive use of their time while in custody.

http://members.pgonline.com/ ~pgycc/index.html#mainmenu

For an up-to-date list of Web links, go to www.wadsworth.com/ product/0534573053s

Male Inmates

Males make up the great bulk of institutionalized youth, and most programs are directed towards their needs. In many ways their experiences mirror those of adult offenders. In an important paper, Clement Bartollas and his associates identified an inmate value system that they believed was common in juvenile institutions:

> *Exploit whomever you can.*
> *Don't play up to staff.*
> *Don't rat on your peers.*
> *Don't give in to others.*[55]

Girls in a Marlin, Texas, juvenile facility. According to the most recent surveys, minority youth outnumbered non-minority white youth in public custody facilities by more than 2 to 1. Minorities represent more than two-thirds of all residents in public long-term facilities. Because these data may represent a trend of racial discrimination in juvenile sentencing, some states have undertaken a variety of programs aimed at eliminating any racial disparities in the juvenile justice system. (© David Woo/Stock, Boston)

In addition to these general rules, the researchers found that there were separate norms for African American inmates (*exploit whites*; *no forcing sex on blacks*; *defend your brother*) and for whites (*don't trust anyone*; *everybody for himself*).

Other research efforts confirm the notion that residents do in fact form cohesive groups and adhere to an informal inmate culture.[56] The more serious the youth's record and the more secure the institution, the greater the adherence to the inmate social code. Male delinquents are more likely to form allegiances with members of their own racial group and to attempt to exploit those outside the group. They also scheme to manipulate staff and take advantage of weaker peers. However, in institutions that are treatment-oriented, and where staff-inmate relationships are more intimate, residents are less likely to adhere to a negativistic inmate code.

Female Inmates

The growing involvement of girls in criminal behavior and the influence of the feminist movement have drawn more attention to the female juvenile offender. This attention has revealed a double standard of justice. For example, girls are more likely than boys to be incarcerated for status offenses. Institutions for girls are generally more restrictive than those for boys, and they have fewer educational and vocational programs and fewer services. Institutions for girls also do a less-than-adequate job of rehabilitation. It has been suggested that this double standard operates because of a male-dominated justice system that seeks to "protect" young girls from their own sexuality.[57]

Over the years, the number of females held in public institutions has declined. This represents the continuation of a long-term trend to remove girls, many of whom are nonserious offenders, from closed institutions and place them in private or community-based facilities. So, although a majority of males are housed in public facilities today, most female delinquents reside in private facilities.

The same double standard that brings a girl into an institution continues to exist once she is in custody. Females tend to be incarcerated for longer terms than males. In addition, institutional programs for girls tend to be oriented toward reinforcing traditional roles for women. How well these programs rehabilitate girls is questionable.

Many of the characteristics of juvenile female offenders are similar to those of their male counterparts, including poor social skills and low self-esteem. Other problems are more specific to the female juvenile offender (sexual abuse issues, victimization histories, lack of placement options). In addition, there have been numerous allegations of emotional and sexual abuse by correctional workers, who either exploit vulnerable young women or callously disregard their emotional needs. A recent (1998) interview survey conducted by the National Council on Crime and Delinquency uncovered numerous incidents of abuse, and bitter resentment by the young women over the brutality of their custodial treatment.[58]

Although there are more coed institutions for juveniles than in the past, most girls remain incarcerated in single-sex institutions that are isolated in rural areas and rarely offer adequate rehabilitative services. Several factors account for the different treatment of girls. One is sexual stereotyping by administrators, who believe that teaching girls "appropriate" sex roles will help them function effectively in society. These beliefs are often held by the staff as well, many of whom hold highly sexist ideas of what is appropriate behavior for adolescent girls. Girls' institutions tend to be smaller than boys' institutions and lack the money to offer as many programs and services as do the larger male institutions.[59]

It appears that, although society is more concerned about protecting girls who act out, it is less concerned about rehabilitating them because the crimes they commit are not serious. These attitudes translate into fewer staff, older facilities, and poorer educational and recreational programs than those found in boys' institutions.[60]

Checkpoints

✔ Massachusetts opened the first juvenile correctional facility, the Lyman School for Boys in Westborough in 1846.

✔ Since the 1970s, a major change in institutionalization has been the effort to remove status offenders from institutions housing juvenile delinquents.

✔ Throughout the 1980s and into the 1990s, admissions to juvenile correctional facilities grew substantially.

✔ Today there are slightly more than 100,000 juveniles being held in public and private facilities.

✔ There may be a hidden juvenile correctional system that places wayward youths in private mental hospitals and substance abuse clinics.

✔ The typical resident of a juvenile facility is a 15- to 16-year-old white male incarcerated for an average stay of 5 months in a public facility or 6 months in a private facility.

✔ Minority youths are incarcerated at a rate 3 to 4 times that of white youths.

✔ Males make up the great bulk of institutionalized youth, and most programs are directed towards their needs.

✔ Female inmates are believed to be the target of sexual-abuse and are denied the same treatment options as males.

CORRECTIONAL TREATMENT FOR JUVENILES

Nearly all juvenile institutions implement some form of treatment program: counseling, vocational and educational training, recreational programs, and religious counseling. In addition, most institutions provide medical programs as well as occasional legal service programs. Generally, the larger the institution, the greater the number of programs and services offered.

The purpose of these programs is to rehabilitate youths to become well-adjusted individuals and send them back into the community to be productive citizens. Despite good intentions, however, the goal of rehabilitation is rarely attained. A significant number of juvenile offenders commit more crimes after release and some experts believe that correctional treatment has little effect on recidivism.[61] However, a careful evaluation of both community-based and institutional treatment services found that juveniles who receive treatment have recidivism rates about 10 percent lower than untreated juveniles, and that the best programs reduced recidivism between 20 and 30 percent.[62] The most successful programs provide training designed to improve interpersonal skills, self-control, and school achievement. These programs also tend to be the most intensive in terms of the amount and duration of attention to youths. Programs of a more psychological orientation, such as individual, family, and group counseling, showed only moderate positive effects on delinquents. Education, vocational training, and specific counseling strategies can be effective if they are intensive, relate to program goals, and meet the youth's individual needs.[63]

What are the drawbacks to correctional rehabilitation? One of the most common problems in efforts to rehabilitate juveniles is a lack of well-trained staff members. Budgetary limitations are a primary concern. It costs a substantial amount of money per year to keep a child in an institution, which explains why institutions generally do not employ large professional staffs.

The most glaring problem with treatment programs is that they are not being administered as intended. Although the official goals of many institutions may be treatment and rehabilitation, the actual programs may center around security and punishment. The next sections describe some treatment approaches that aim to rehabilitate offenders.

Individual Treatment Techniques: Past and Present

In general, effective individual treatment programs are built around combinations of psychotherapy, reality therapy, and behavior modification. **Individual counseling** is one of the most common treatment approaches, and virtually all juvenile institutions use it to some extent. This is not surprising, as psychological problems such as depression are prevalent in juvenile institutions.[64] Individual counseling does not attempt to change a youth's personality. Rather, it attempts to help individuals understand and solve their current adjustment problems. Some institutions employ counselors who are not professionally qualified, which subjects offenders to a superficial form of counseling.

Professional counseling may be based on psychotherapy. **Psychotherapy** requires extensive analysis of the individual's childhood experiences. A skilled therapist attempts to help the individual make a more positive adjustment to society by altering negative behavior patterns learned in childhood. Another frequently used treatment is **reality therapy**.[65] This approach, developed by William Glasser during the 1970s, emphasizes current, rather than past, behavior by stressing that offenders are completely responsible for their own actions. The object of reality therapy is to make individuals more responsible people. This is accomplished by giving youths confidence through developing their ability to follow a set of expectations as closely as possible. The success of reality therapy depends greatly on the warmth and concern of the counselor. Many institutions rely heavily on this type of therapy because they believe trained professionals aren't needed to administer it. Actually, a skilled therapist is essential to the success of this form of treatment.

Behavior modification is used in many institutions.[66] It is based on the theory that all behavior is learned and that current behavior can be shaped through rewards and punishments. This type of program is easily used in an institutional setting that offers privileges as rewards for behaviors such as work, study, or the development of skills. It is reasonably effective, especially when a contract is formed with the youth to modify certain behaviors. When youths are aware of what is expected of them, they plan their actions to meet these expectations and then experience the anticipated consequences. In this way, youths can be motivated to change. Behavior modification is effective in controlled settings where a counselor can manipulate the situation, but once the youth is back in the real world it becomes difficult to use.

If you want to learn more about improving the conditions of children in custody, then go to http://www.ojjdp.ncjrs.org/pubs/walls/contents.html

For an up-to-date list of Web links, go to www.wadsworth.com/product/0534573053s

To learn more about reality therapy, go to William Glasser's Web site at http://www.wglasserinst.com/

For an up-to-date list of Web links, go to www.wadsworth.com/product/0534573053s

individual counseling Counselors help juveniles understand and solve their current adjustment problems.

psychotherapy Highly structured counseling in which a skilled therapist helps a juvenile solve conflicts and make a more positive adjustment to society.

reality therapy A form of counseling that emphasizes current behavior and that requires the individual to accept responsibility for all of his or her actions.

behavior modification A technique for shaping desired behaviors through a system of rewards and punishments.

Group Treatment Techniques

group therapy Counseling several individuals together in a group session; individuals can obtain support from other group members as they work through similar problems.

Group therapy is more economical than individual therapy because one therapist can counsel more than one individual at a time. Also, the support of the group is often valuable to individuals in the group, and individuals derive hope from other members of the group who have survived similar experiences. Another advantage of group therapy is that a group can often solve a problem more effectively than an individual.

One disadvantage of group therapy is that it provides little individual attention. Everyone is different, and some group members may need more-individualized treatment. Others may be afraid to speak up in the group and thus fail to receive the benefits of the group experience. Conversely, some individuals may dominate group interaction, making it difficult for the leader to conduct an effective session. Finally, group condemnation may seriously hurt a participant.

guided group interaction (GGI) Through group interactions a delinquent can acknowledge and solve personal problems with support from other group members.

More than any other group treatment technique, group psychotherapy probes into an individual's personality and attempts to restructure it. Relationships in these groups tend to be intense. The group is used to facilitate expression of feelings, solve problems, and teach members to empathize with one another.

Unfortunately, the ingredients for an effective group session—interaction, cooperation, and tolerance—are in conflict with the antisocial and antagonistic orientation of delinquents. This technique can be effective when the members of the group are in attendance voluntarily, but such is not the case with institutionalized delinquents. Consequently, the effectiveness of these programs is questionable.

positive peer culture (PPC) Counseling program in which peer leaders encourage other group members to modify their behavior and peers help reinforce acceptable behaviors.

Guided group interaction (GGI) is a fairly common method of group treatment. It is based on the theory that, through group interactions, a delinquent can acknowledge and solve personal problems. A leader facilitates interaction, and a group culture develops. Individual members can be mutually supportive and can reinforce acceptable behavior. In the 1980s, a version of GGI called **positive peer culture (PPC)** became popular. These programs used groups in which peer leaders encourage other youths to conform to conventional behaviors. The rationale is that if negative peer influence can encourage youths to engage in delinquent behavior then positive peer influence can help them conform.[67] Though research results are inconclusive, there is evidence that PPC may facilitate communication ability for incarcerated youth.[68]

To see how positive peer culture can be used effectively, go to http://www.nida.nih.gov/MeetSum/CODA/Youth.html

For an up-to-date list of Web links, go to www.wadsworth.com/product/0534573053s

milieu therapy All aspects of the environment are part of the treatment, and meaningful change, increased growth, and satisfactory adjustment are encouraged; this is often accomplished through peer pressure to conform to the group norms.

Another common group treatment approach, **milieu therapy**, seeks to make all aspects of the inmates' environment part of their treatment and to minimize differences between custodial staff and treatment personnel. Milieu therapy, based on psychoanalytic theory, was developed during the late 1940s and early 1950s by Bruno Bettelheim.[69] This therapy attempted to create a conscience, or superego, in delinquent youths by getting them to depend on their therapists to a great extent and then threatening them with loss of the caring relationship if they failed to control their behavior. Today, milieu therapy more often makes use of peer interactions and attempts to create an environment that encourages meaningful change, growth, and satisfactory adjustment. This is often accomplished through peer pressure to conform to group norms.

Today, group counseling often focuses on drug and alcohol issues, self-esteem development, or role-model support. In addition, because more violent juveniles are entering the system than in years past, group sessions often deal with appropriate expressions of anger and methods for controlling such behavior.

Educational, Vocational, and Recreational Programs

Because educational programs are an important part of social development and have therapeutic as well as instructional value, they are an essential part of most treatment programs. What takes place through education is related to all other aspects of the institutional program—work activities, cottage life, recreation, and clinical services.

Most juvenile facilities have ongoing vocational and educational programs. Some, such as this California Youth Authority program in Ventura County, offer computer training that will help juveniles gain employment upon their release. (© A. Ramey/Stock, Boston)

Educational programs are probably the best-staffed programs in training schools, but even at their best most are inadequate. Training programs must contend with a myriad of problems. Many of the youths coming into these institutions are mentally challenged, have learning disabilities, and are far behind their grade levels in basic academics. Most have become frustrated with the educational experience, dislike school, and become bored with any type of educational program. Their sense of frustration often leads to disciplinary problems.

Ideally, institutions should allow the inmates to attend a school in the community or offer programs that lead to a high school diploma or GED certificate. Unfortunately, not all institutions offer these types of programs. Secure institutions, because of their large size, are more likely than group homes or day treatment centers to offer programs such as remedial reading, physical education, and tutoring. Some offer computer-based learning and programmed learning modules.

Vocational training has long been used as a treatment technique for juveniles. Early institutions were even referred to as "industrial schools." Today, vocational programs in institutions include auto repair, printing, woodworking, mechanical drawing, food service, cosmetology, secretarial training, and data processing. A common drawback of vocational training programs is sex-typing. The recent trend has been to allow equal access to all programs offered in institutions that house girls and boys. Sex-typing is more difficult to avoid in single-sex institutions, because funds aren't usually available for all types of training.

These programs alone are not panaceas. Youths need to acquire the kinds of skills that will give them hope for advancement. The Ventura School for Female Juvenile Offenders, established under the California Youth Authority, has been a pioneer in the work placement concept. Private industry contracts with the youth authority to establish businesses on the institution's grounds. The businesses hire, train, and pay for work. Wages are divided into a victim's restitution fund, room and board fees, and forced savings, with a portion given to the juvenile to purchase canteen items.[70]

Recreational activity is also an important way to help relieve adolescent aggressions, as evidenced by the many programs that focus on recreation as the primary treatment technique.

In summary, the treatment programs that seem to be most effective for rehabilitating juvenile offenders are those that use a combination of techniques. Programs that

TABLE 14.2 **Turn About Ranch**

Turn About Ranch is a private, short-term, high-impact therapy program that emphasizes family values and relationships. Its clientele are 27 boys and girls from 12 to 18 years of age, who spend at least 60 days (90 days is the average) at its facility in the southern Utah canyonlands country. The objective of Turn About Ranch is to provide troubled teens with a tough, hard-hitting, high-impact program that helps remold their lives The program objectives are facilitated through the environment of a historic, real-life cow-calf ranch, utilizing old-time values and morals such as honesty, respect, teamwork, and accountability. No smoking, drinking, tobacco, drugs, sex, or swearing is allowed. Turn About Ranch employs a behavior modification program that promotes positive behavioral changes; counselors are with the youth 24 hours a day. Problems are dealt with swiftly and fairly. Through this consistent correction and positive direction, day after day, in a hard-working, real-life, down-to-earth ranch environment, the seed of life being "turned-about" begins to emerge.

Source: Personal communication with Annette Ormond, administrative assistant, January 4, 2001; programs descriptions may be obtained from Turn About Ranch, 280 North 300 East, P.O. Box 345, Escalante, UT 84726.

are comprehensive, build on a juvenile's strengths, and adopt a socially grounded position have a much greater chance for success. Successful programs address issues relating to school, peers, work, and community.

Wilderness Programs

wilderness probation Programs involving outdoor expeditions that provide opportunities for juveniles to confront the difficulties of their lives while achieving positive personal satisfaction.

Wilderness probation programs involve troubled youths in outdoor activities as a mechanism to improve their social skills, self-concept, and self-control. Typically, wilderness programs maintain exposure to a wholesome environment; where the concepts of education and the work ethic are taught and embodied in adult role models, troubled youth can regain a measure of self-worth. One such program, which is privately funded and takes cases which might otherwise go to a state correctional facility, is the Turn About Ranch (Table 14.2).

Little is known about the effects of wilderness programs on recidivism. A study of the Spectrum Wilderness Program in Illinois found that successful completion of the program often resulted in arrest reductions that began immediately and lasted for about 1 year. Although results of such studies are mixed, these programs are promising alternatives to traditional juvenile justice placements.[71]

Juvenile Boot Camps

boot camps Juvenile programs that combine get-tough elements from adult programs with education, substance abuse treatment, and social skills training.

Correctional **boot camps** combine the get-tough elements of adult programs with education, substance-abuse treatment, and social-skills training. The American Correctional Association's Juvenile Project sees merit in well-run boot camp programs provided they incorporate these elements: (1) a focus on concrete feelings and increasing self-esteem, (2) discipline through physical conditioning, and (3) programming in literacy as well as academic and vocational education.[72]

In theory, a successful boot camp program should rehabilitate juvenile offenders, reduce the number of beds needed in secure institutional programs, and thus reduce the overall cost of care. The Alabama boot camp program for youthful offenders estimated savings of $1 million annually when compared with traditional institutional sentences.[73] However, no one seems convinced that participants in these programs have lower recidivism rates than those who serve normal sentences. Ronald Corbett and Joan Petersilia do note, however, that boot camp participants seem to be less antisocial upon returning to society.[74]

Juvenile boot camps apply rigorous, military-style training and discipline in an attempt to reshape the attitudes and behavior of unruly youth. (© Jacques Brund/Design Concepts)

To read more about boot camps, go to

http://www.ncjrs.org/txtfiles/164258.txt

For an up-to-date list of Web links, go to www.wadsworth.com/product/0534573053s

Some juvenile corrections agencies feature shock incarceration programs, with high-intensity military discipline and physical training for short periods. The expectation is that the offender will be "shocked" into going straight. These programs are being used with young adult offenders and juveniles who have been waived to the adult system in many jurisdictions.

Some experts point out that (1) boot camps cannot save money unless they have hundreds of beds and the stay is limited to 3 months, conditions that would make the programs pointless; (2) boot camps often keep costs down by leaving aftercare to overloaded parole officers; and (3) no documentation exists that boot camps decrease delinquency.[75]

Bootcamp Evaluation In 1992 OJJDP funded three juvenile boot camps designed to overcome these objections and meet the special needs of adolescent offenders. The programs were conducted in Cleveland, Ohio, Denver, Colorado, and Mobile, Alabama.[76] Focusing on nonviolent offenders under the age of 18, the highly structured, three-month residential programs were followed by 6 to 9 months of community-based aftercare. During the aftercare period, youths were to pursue academic and vocational training or employment while under progressively diminishing supervision.

The Office of Juvenile Justice and Delinquency Prevention undertook evaluations for all three sites, comparing recidivism rates for juveniles who participated in the programs with those of control groups. The evaluations also compared the cost-effectiveness of juvenile boot camps with other dispositional alternatives. The findings indicated these successes:

- Most participants completed the residential program and graduated to aftercare. Program completion rates were 96 percent in Cleveland, 87 percent in Mobile, and 76 percent in Denver.
- At the two sites where educational gains were measured, substantial improvements in academic skills were noted. In Mobile, approximately three-quarters of the participants improved their performance in reading, spelling, language, and math by one grade level or more. In Cleveland, the average participant improved reading, spelling, and math skills by approximately one grade level.

- Where employment records were available, a significant number of participants found jobs while in aftercare. The pilot programs, however, did not demonstrate a reduction in recidivism. In Denver and Mobile no statistically significant difference could be found between the recidivism rates of boot camp participants and those of the control groups (youths confined in state or county institutions or released on probation). In Cleveland, program participants evidenced a higher recidivism rate than offenders confined in traditional juvenile correctional facilities.

In spite of these mixed results, more than 75 boot camps now are in operation in more than 30 states. They appear to have a place among the array of sentencing options, if for no other reason than to appease the public with the promise of tougher sentences and lower costs.[77] If boot camps are to become a viable alternative for juvenile corrections they must be seen, not as a panacea that provides an easy solution to the problems of delinquency, but merely part of a comprehensive approach to juvenile care that is appropriate to a select group of adolescents.[78]

✔ Checkpoints

✔ Nearly all juvenile institutions implement some form of treatment program.

✔ Reality therapy, a commonly used individual approach, emphasizes current, rather than past, behavior by stressing that offenders are completely responsible for their own actions.

✔ Group therapy, because it is economical, is more commonly used with kids than individual therapy; one therapist can counsel more than one individual at a time.

✔ Guided group interaction (GGI) and positive peer culture (PPC) are popular group treatment techniques.

✔ Many but not all institutions allow kids to attend a school in the community or offer programs that lead to a high school diploma or GED certificate.

✔ Wilderness programs involve troubled youth using outdoor activities as a mechanism to improve their social skills, self concepts, and self-control.

✔ Correctional boot camps combine the get-tough elements of adult programs with education, substance abuse treatment, and social skills training.

THE LEGAL RIGHT TO TREATMENT

The primary goal of placing juveniles in institutions is to help them reenter the community successfully. Therefore, lawyers claim that children in state-run institutions have a legal right to treatment.

The concept of a **right to treatment** was introduced to the mental health field in 1960 by Morton Birnbaum, who argued that individuals who are deprived of their liberty because of a mental illness are entitled to treatment to correct that condition.[79] The right to treatment has expanded to include the juvenile justice system, an expansion bolstered by court rulings that mandate that rehabilitation and not punishment or retribution be the basis of juvenile court dispositions.[80] It stands to reason then that, if incarcerated, juveniles are entitled to the appropriate social services that will promote their rehabilitation.

One of the first cases to highlight this issue was *Inmates of the Boys' Training School v. Affleck* in 1972.[81] In its decision, a federal court argued that rehabilitation is the true purpose of the juvenile court and that without that goal due-process guarantees are violated. It condemned such devices as solitary confinement, strip cells, and lack of educational opportunities, and held that juveniles have a statutory right to treatment. The court also established the following minimum standards for all juveniles confined in training schools:

- A room equipped with lighting sufficient for an inmate to read until 10 P.M.
- Sufficient clothing to meet seasonal needs.

right to treatment Philosophy espoused by many courts that juvenile offenders have a statutory right to treatment while under the jurisdiction of the courts.

To learn more about the right to treatment, read "Meeting the Needs of the Mentally Ill—A Case Study of the 'Right to Treatment' as Legal Rights Discourse in the USA" by Michael McCubbin and David N. Weisstub, available on the Web at http://www.academyanalyticarts.org/mccweiss.html

For an up-to-date list of Web links, go to www.wadsworth.com/product/0534573053s

- Bedding, including blankets, sheets, pillows, pillow cases, and mattresses, to be changed once a week.
- Personal hygiene supplies, including soap, toothpaste, towels, toilet paper, and toothbrush.
- A change of undergarments and socks every day.
- Minimum writing materials: pen, pencil, paper, and envelopes.
- Prescription eyeglasses, if needed.
- Equal access to all books, periodicals, and other reading materials located in the training school.
- Daily showers.
- Daily access to medical facilities, including provision of a 24-hour nursing service.
- General correspondence privileges.[82]

In 1974, in the case of *Nelson v. Heyne,* the First Federal Appellate Court affirmed that juveniles have a right to treatment and condemned the use of corporal punishment in juvenile institutions.[83] In *Morales v. Turman,* the court held that all juveniles confined in training schools in Texas have a right to treatment, including development of education skills, delivery of vocational education, medical and psychiatric treatment, and adequate living conditions.[84] In a more recent case, *Pena v. New York State Division for Youth,* the court held that the use of isolation, hand restraints, and tranquilizing drugs at Goshen Annex Center violated the Fourteenth Amendment right to due process and the Eighth Amendment right to protection against cruel and unusual punishment.[85]

The right to treatment has also been limited. For example, in *Ralston v. Robinson,* the Supreme Court rejected a youth's claim that he should continue to be given treatment after he was sentenced to a consecutive term in an adult prison for crimes committed while in a juvenile institution.[86] In the *Ralston* case, the offender's proven dangerousness outweighed the possible effects of rehabilitation. Similarly, in *Santana v. Callazo,* the U.S. First Circuit Court of Appeals rejected a suit brought by residents at the Maricao Juvenile Camp in Puerto Rico on the ground that the administration had failed to provide them with an individualized rehabilitation plan or adequate treatment. The circuit court concluded that it was a legitimate exercise of state authority to incarcerate juveniles solely to protect society if they are dangerous.

The Struggle for Basic Civil Rights

Several court cases have led federal, state, and private groups—for example, the American Bar Association, the American Correctional Association, and the National Council on Crime and Delinquency—to develop standards for the juvenile justice system. These standards provide guidelines for conditions and practices in juvenile institutions and call on administrators to maintain a safe and healthy environment for incarcerated youths.

For the most part, state-sponsored brutality has been outlawed, although the use of restraints, solitary confinement, and even medication for unruly residents has not been eliminated. The courts have ruled that corporal punishment in any form violates standards of decency and human dignity.

There are a number of mechanisms for enforcing these standards. For example, the federal government's Civil Rights of Institutionalized Persons Act (CRIPA) gives the Civil Rights Division of the U.S. Department of Justice (DOJ) the power to bring actions against state or local governments for violating the civil rights of persons institutionalized in publicly operated facilities.[87] CRIPA does not create any new substantive rights; it simply confers power on the U.S. Attorney General to bring action to enforce previously established constitutional or statutory rights of institutionalized persons; about 25 percent of cases involve juvenile detention and correctional facilities. There are many examples in which CRIPA-based litigation has helped insure that incarcerated adolescents obtain their basic civil rights. For example, in November 1995, a federal court in Kentucky ordered state officials to remedy serious deficiencies in Kentucky's thirteen juvenile treatment facilities. The decree required the state to take a number of steps to protect juveniles from abuse, mistreatment, and injury; to ensure adequate medical and mental health care; and to provide adequate educational, vocational, and aftercare services. Another CRIPA consent decree, ordered by a federal court in Puerto Rico in October 1994, addressed life-threatening conditions at eight juvenile detention and correction facilities. These dire conditions included juveniles committing and attempting suicide without staff intervention or treatment, widespread infection-control problems caused by rats and other vermin, and defective plumbing that forced juveniles to drink from their toilet bowls.

What provisions does the juvenile justice system make to help institutionalized offenders return to society? The remainder of this chapter is devoted to this topic.

JUVENILE AFTERCARE

aftercare Transitional assistance to juveniles equivalent to adult parole to help youths adjust to community life.

Aftercare in the juvenile justice system is the equivalent of parole in the adult criminal justice system. When juveniles are released from an institution, they may be placed in an aftercare program of some kind, so that youths who have been institutionalized are not simply returned to the community without some transitional assistance. Whether individuals who are in aftercare as part of an indeterminate sentence remain in the community or return to the institution for further rehabilitation depends on their actions during the aftercare period. Aftercare is an extremely important stage in the juvenile justice process because few juveniles age out of custody. In some jurisdictions, the proportion of children released to parole or aftercare is 100 percent.[88]

In a number of jurisdictions, a paroling authority, which may be an independent body or part of the corrections department or some other branch of state services, makes the release decision. Juvenile aftercare authorities, like adult parole officers, review the youth's adjustment within the institution, whether there is chemical dependence, what the crime was, and other specifics of the case. Some juvenile authorities are even making use of **parole guidelines** first developed with adult parolees. Each youth who enters a secure facility is given a recommended length of confinement that is explained at the initial interview with parole authorities. The stay is computed on the basis of the offense record, influenced by aggravating and mitigating factors. The parole authority is not required to follow the recommended sentence but uses it as a tool in making parole decisions.[89] Whatever approach is used, several primary factors are considered by virtually all jurisdictions when recommending a juvenile for release: (1) institutional adjustment, (2) length of stay and general attitude, and (3) likelihood of success in the community.

parole guidelines Recommended length of confinement and kinds of aftercare assistance most effective for a juvenile who committed a specific offense.

Risk classifications have also been designed to help parole officers make decisions about which juveniles should receive aftercare services.[90] The risk-based system uses an empirically derived risk scale to classify youths. Juveniles are identified as most likely or least likely to commit a new offense based on factors such as prior record, type of offense, and degree of institutional adjustment.

Supervision

One purpose of aftercare is to provide support during the readjustment period following release. First, individuals whose activities have been regimented for some time may not find it easy to make independent decisions. Second, offenders may perceive themselves as scapegoats, cast out by society. Finally, the community may view the returning minor with a good deal of prejudice; adjustment problems may reinforce a preexisting need to engage in deviant behavior.

Juveniles in aftercare programs are supervised by parole caseworkers or counselors whose job is to maintain contact with the juvenile, make sure that a corrections plan is followed, and show interest and caring. The counselor also keeps the youth informed of services that may assist in reintegration and counsels the youth and his or her family. Unfortunately, aftercare caseworkers, like probation officers, often carry such large caseloads that their jobs are next to impossible to do adequately.

Recent state legislation underscores the importance of aftercare for juvenile offenders. For example, the Texas Youth Commission operates an "independent living program" that provides prerelease and transition assistance to male and female offenders ages 16 to 18 who are returning to the community; an aftercare program in Cuyahoga County, Ohio begins with education and employment training while a youth is incarcerated and continues after the youth is released; a reintegration program for youths released from the New Mexico Boys' School has been successful because clients spend less time in secure correction.[91]

Intensive Aftercare Program (IAP) A balanced, highly structured, comprehensive continuum of intervention for serious and violent juvenile offenders returning to the community.

The Intensive Aftercare Program (IAP) Model New models of aftercare have been aimed at the chronic and/or violent offender. The **Intensive Aftercare Program (IAP)** model developed by David Altschuler and Troy Armstrong offers a continuum of intervention for serious juvenile offenders returning to the community following placement. The IAP model begins by drawing attention to five basic principles, which collectively establish a set of fundamental operational goals:

1. Preparing youth for progressively increased responsibility and freedom in the community
2. Facilitating youth-community interaction and involvement
3. Working with both the offender and targeted community support systems (families, peers, schools, employers) on qualities needed for constructive interaction and the youths' successful community adjustment
4. Developing new resources and supports where needed
5. Monitoring and testing the youths and the community on their ability to deal with each other productively

These basic goals are then translated into practice, which incorporates individual case planning with a family and community perspective. The program stresses a mix of intensive surveillance and services and a balance of incentives and graduated consequences coupled with the imposition of realistic, enforceable conditions. There is also "service brokerage," in which community resources are used and linkage with social networks established.[92]

The IAP initiative was designed to help correctional agencies implement effective aftercare programs for chronic and serious juvenile offenders. After more than 12 years of testing, the program is now being aimed at determining how juveniles are prepared for reentry into their communities, how the transition is handled, and how the aftercare in the community is provided.[93] The Policy and Practice box, "Using the Intensive Aftercare Program (IAP) Model," illustrates how the model is being used in three state jurisdictions.

Aftercare Revocation Procedures

Juvenile parolees are required to meet set standards of behavior, which typically include but are not limited to the following:

- Adhere to a reasonable curfew set by youth worker or parent.
- Refrain from associating with persons whose influence would be detrimental.
- Attend school in accordance with the law.
- Abstain from drugs and alcohol.

USING THE INTENSIVE AFTERCARE PROGRAM (IAP) MODEL

How has the IAP model been used around the nation?

Colorado

While adolescents are still institutionalized, community-based providers begin weekly services (including multi-family counseling and life-skills services) that continue during aftercare. Sixty days prior to release, IAP youths begin a series of step-down measures, including supervised trips to the community and, 30 days before release, overnight or weekend home passes. Upon release to parole, most program youths go through several months of day treatment programming that, in addition to services, provides a high level of structure during the day. Trackers provide evening and weekend monitoring during this period of reentry. As a youth's progress warrants, the frequency of supervision decreases. The planned frequency of contact is once a week during the first few months of supervision, with gradual reductions to once a month in later stages of supervision.

Nevada

Once the parole plan is finalized, all IAP youth begin a 30-day prerelease phase, during which IAP staff provide a series of services that continue through the early months of parole. These consist primarily of two structured curriculums on life skills (Jettstream) and substance abuse (Rational Recovery). In addition, a money management program (The Money Program) is initiated. Youth are provided with mock checking accounts from which "bills" must be paid for rent, food, insurance, and other necessities. Youth can also use their accounts to purchase recreation and other privileges, but each youth must have a balance of at least $50 at the end of the 30 days to purchase his bus ticket home. The initial 30 days of release are considered an institutional furlough (i.e., youth are still on the institutional rolls) that involves intensive supervision and service, any time during which the youth may be returned to the institution for significant program infractions. During furlough, youth are involved in day programming and are subject to frequent drug testing and evening and weekend surveillance. Upon successful completion of the furlough, the IAP transition continues through the use of phased levels of supervision. During the first 3 months, three contacts per week with the case manager or field agent are required. This level of supervision is reduced to two contacts per week for the next 2 months, and then to once per week during the last month of parole.

Virginia

Virginia's transition differs from the other two sites in that its central feature is the use of group home placements as a bridge between the institution and the community. Immediately after release from the institution, youth enter one of two group homes for a 30- to 60-day period. The programs and services in which they will be involved in the community are initiated shortly after placement in the group home. Virginia uses a formal step-down system to ease the intensity of parole supervision gradually. In the 2 months following the youth's release from the group home, staff are required to contact him 5 to 7 times per week. This is reduced to 3 to 5 times per week during the next 2 months, and again to three times per week during the final 30 days.

Source: Richard G. Wiebush, Betsie McNulty, and Thao Le, "Implementation of the Intensive Community-Based Aftercare Program," *Juvenile Justice Bulletin* (Washington, DC: Office of Juvenile Justice and Delinquency Prevention, 2000).

- Report to the youth worker when required.
- Refrain from acts that would be crimes if committed by an adult.
- Refrain from operating an automobile without permission of the youth worker or parent.
- Refrain from being habitually disobedient and beyond the lawful control of parent or other legal authority.
- Refrain from running away from the lawful custody of parent or other lawful authority.

If these rules are violated, the juvenile may have his parole revoked and be returned to the institution. Most states have extended the same legal rights enjoyed by adults at parole revocation hearings to juveniles who are in danger of losing their aftercare privileges, as follows:

- Juveniles must be informed of the conditions of parole and receive notice of any obligations.
- Juveniles have the right to legal counsel at state expense if necessary.
- They maintain the right to confront and cross-examine witnesses against them.
- They have the right to introduce documentary evidence and witnesses.
- They have the right to a hearing before an officer who shall be an attorney but not an employee of the revoking agency.[94]

SUMMARY

Community treatment encompasses efforts to keep offenders in the community and spare them the pain and stigma of incarceration. Its primary purpose is to address the needs of juveniles in a nonrestrictive or home setting, employing educational, vocational, counseling, and employment services.

The most widely used method of community treatment is probation. Youths on probation must obey rules given to them by the court and participate in some form of treatment program. Their behavior is monitored by probation officers. If rules are violated, youths can have their probation revoked.

It is now common to enhance probation with more restrictive forms of treatment, such as intensive supervision and house arrest with electronic monitoring. Restitution programs involve having juvenile offenders either reimburse their victims or do community service. Some community programs allow youths to live at home while receiving treatment in a nonpunitive, community-based center. There are also residential programs that require that youths reside in group homes while receiving treatment.

The secure juvenile institution was developed in the mid-nineteenth century as an alternative to placing youths in adult prisons. Youth institutions evolved from large, closed institutions to cottage-based education- and rehabilitation-oriented institutions. Today most institutions for youths are low-security facilities.

The juvenile institutional population has increased in recent years despite efforts to decarcerate status offenders and petty delinquent offenders. In addition, increasing numbers of youths are "hidden" in private medical centers and drug treatment clinics. A disproportionate number of minorities are being incarcerated in more secure, state-run youth facilities.

Most institutions maintain intensive treatment programs featuring individual or group therapy. Although a variety of techniques are used, little evidence has been found that any single method is effective in reducing recidivism. Yet rehabilitation remains an important goal of juvenile practitioners. Recent studies indicate that some programs do work.

The right to treatment is an important issue in juvenile justice. Legal decisions have mandated that a juvenile cannot simply be warehoused in a correctional center but must receive proper care and treatment to aid rehabilitation. What constitutes proper care is still being debated, however, and recent court decisions have backed off from the belief that every youth can be rehabilitated.

Juveniles released from institutions are often placed on parole or aftercare. However, there is little evidence that community supervision is more beneficial than simply releasing youths. Many jurisdictions are experiencing success with halfway houses and reintegration centers.

Deciding when to use secure incarceration and providing appropriate programs for serious offenders that include aftercare are key components to a comprehensive system of juvenile justice. At a time when the amount of juvenile crime is significant, strengthening and defining the use of juvenile corrections is vital.

KEY TERMS

community treatment
suppression effect
probation
juvenile probation officer
social investigation report,
    predisposition report
conditions of probation

juvenile intensive probation
    supervision (JIPS)
house arrest
electronic monitoring
balanced probation
monetary restitution
victim service restitution

community service
    restitution
residential programs
group homes
foster care programs
family group homes
rural programs

meta-analysis
reform schools
cottage system
least restrictive alternative
individual counseling
psychotherapy
reality therapy

behavior modification
group therapy
guided group interaction
    (GGI)

positive peer culture (PPC)
milieu therapy
wilderness probation
boot camps

right to treatment
aftercare
parole guidelines

Intensive Aftercare Program
    (IAP)

QUESTIONS FOR DISCUSSION

1. Would you want a community treatment program in your neighborhood? Why or why not?

2. Is widening the net a real danger, or are treatment-oriented programs simply a method of helping troubled youths?

3. If youths violate the rules of probation, should they be placed in a secure institution?

4. Is juvenile restitution fair? Should a poor child have to pay back a wealthy victim, such as a store owner?

5. What are the most important advantages to community treatment for juvenile offenders?

6. What is the purpose of juvenile probation? Identify some conditions of probation and discuss the responsibilities of the juvenile probation officer.

7. What are graduated sanctions?

8. Has community treatment generally proven successful?

VIEWPOINT

D.H., 17, hanged himself with a bed sheet tied to the cell door at a juvenile detention facility in a southern state on Jan. 6. M.S., 14, hanged herself with a bed sheet tied to a shower brace at a public juvenile training school in a western state on Dec. 22, 1999. J.S., 16, hanged himself with a bed sheet tied to a sprinkler head on the ceiling of his room at a county juvenile boot camp in an eastern state on Nov. 2,1999. K.T., 13, hanged himself with a bed sheet tied to a ceiling grate at a private juvenile training school in a northwestern state on Oct. 15, 1999.

These deaths represent only a handful of the unknown number of suicides that occur each year in juvenile facilities across the country. Youth suicide in the general population is a major public health problem. According to the Centers for Disease Control, as of 1995 the suicide rate of adolescents (ages 15 to 19) has quadrupled from 2.7 per 100,000 in 1950 to 10.8 per 100,000 in 1992. More teenagers die from suicide than from cancer, heart disease, AIDS, birth defects, stroke, pneumonia and influenza, and chronic lung disease combined, according to the U.S. Department of Health and Human Services.

 Suicide in youth correctional institutions is of major concern to juvenile justice administrators. To learn more about this issue, go to InfoTrac® College Edition and read Lindsay M. Hayes, "Juvenile Suicide in Confinement: A National Survey," *Corrections Today* 62:26 (July 2000). For more information, use *juvenile corrections* as a key term.

Concluding Notes: American Delinquency

We have reviewed in this text the current knowledge of the nature, cause, and correlates of juvenile delinquency and society's efforts to bring about its elimination and control. We have analyzed research programs, theoretical models, governmental policies, and legal cases. Taken in sum, this information presents a rather broad and complex picture of the youth crime problem and the most critical issues confronting the juvenile justice system. Delinquents come from a broad spectrum of society; kids of every race, gender, class, region, family type, and culture are involved in delinquent behaviors. To combat youthful law violations, society has tried a garden variety of intervention and control strategies: tough law enforcement; counseling, treatment and rehabilitation; provision of legal rights; community action; educational programs; family change strategies. Yet, despite decades of intense effort and study, it is still unclear why delinquency occurs and what, if anything, can be done to control its occurrence. One thing is for certain, juvenile crime is one of the most serious domestic problems faced by Americans.

Though uncertainty prevails, it is possible to draw some inferences about youth crime and its control. After reviewing the material contained in this volume, certain conclusions seem self-evident. Some involve social facts; that is, particular empirical relationships and associations have been established that have withstood multiple testing and verification efforts. Other conclusions involve social questions; there are issues that need clarification, and the uncertainty surrounding them has hampered progress in combating delinquency and treating known delinquents.

In sum, we have reviewed some of the most important social facts concerning delinquent behavior and posed some of the critical questions that still remain to be answered.

The statutory concept of juvenile delinquency is in need of review and modification.
Today, the legal definition of a juvenile delinquent is a minor child, usually under the age of 17, who has been found to have violated the criminal law (juvenile code). The concept of juvenile delinquency still occupies a legal position falling somewhere between criminal and civil law; juveniles still enjoy more rights, protections, and privileges than adults. Nonetheless, concerns about teen violence may eventually put an end to the separate juvenile justice system. If kids are equally or even more violent as adults, why should they be given a special legal status consideration? If the teen violence rate begins to rise again, so too may calls for the abolition of a separate juvenile justice system.

The concept of the status offender (PINS, CHINS, and MINS) may be in for revision.
Special treatment for the status offender conforms with the *parens patriae* roots of the juvenile justice system. Granting the state authority to institutionalize noncriminal youth in order "to protect the best interest of the child" cannot be considered an abuse of state authority. While it is likely that the current system of control will remain in place for the near future, it is not beyond the realm of possibility to see the eventual restructuring of the definition of status offenders, with jurisdiction of "pure" noncriminal first offenders turned over to a department of social services, and chronic status offenders and those with prior records of delinquency petitioned to juvenile court as delinquency cases.

Juvenile offenders are becoming more violent.
Official delinquency data suggests that there has been a decade-long rise in the juvenile violence rate. At a time when adult violence is in decline, juvenile offenders are committing murder and other serious felony offenses at

an increasing pace. While there has been a recent stabilization in the violence rate, forecasters suggest that an increasing juvenile population portends a long-term increase in the overall violence rate.

Easy availability of guns is a significant contributor to teen violence.

Research indicates a close tie between gun use, control of drug markets, and teen violence. Unless efforts are made to control the spread of handguns or devise programs to deter handgun use, teenage murder rates will continue to rise.

The chronic violent juvenile offender is a serious social problem for society and the juvenile justice system.

Official crime data indicate that the juvenile violence rate is at an all-time high. Chronic male delinquent offenders commit a disproportionate amount of violent behavior including a significant amount of the most serious juvenile crimes, such as homicides, rapes, robberies, and aggravated assaults. Many chronic offenders become adult criminals and eventually end up in the criminal court system. How to effectively deal with chronic juvenile offenders and drug users remains a high priority for the juvenile justice system.

Chronic juvenile delinquency has unquestionably become a major concept within the field. The best approach to dealing with chronic offenders remains uncertain, but concern about such offenders has shifted juvenile justice policy toward a punishment-oriented philosophy.

There is still debate about whether the propensity to commit crime changes as people mature.

Delinquency experts are now researching such issues as the onset, escalation, termination, and continuation of a delinquent career. There is an ongoing debate concerning change in delinquent behavior patterns. One position is that people do not change—conditions and opportunities do. A second view is that real human change is conditioned by life events. If the former position holds true there is little hope of using treatment strategies to change known offenders; a more productive approach would be to limit their criminal opportunities through the use of long-term incarceration. If the latter position is accurate, effective treatment and provision of legitimate opportunities might produce real behavioral changes.

Female delinquency has been increasing at a faster pace than male delinquency.

The nature and extent of female delinquent activities changed in the late 1980s, and it now appears that girls are engaging in more frequent and serious illegal activity in the 1990s. While gender differences in the rate of the most serious crimes such as murder still persist, it is possible that further convergence will occur in the near future.

There is little question that family environment affects patterns of juvenile behavior.

Family relationships have been linked to the problem of juvenile delinquency by many experts. Broken homes, for instance, are not in and of themselves a cause of delinquency, but some evidence indicates that single-parent households are more inclined to contain children who manifest behavioral problems. Limited resource allocations limit the single parent's ability to control and supervise children. In addition, there seems to be a strong association in family relationships between child abuse and delinquency. Cases of abuse and neglect have been found in every level of the economic strata, and a number of studies have linked child abuse and neglect to juvenile delinquency. While the evidence is not conclusive, it does suggest that a strong relationship exists between child abuse and subsequent delinquent behavior. This relationship does not bode well for delinquency rates because the extent of reported child abuse is on the increase. Some experts believe a major effort is needed to reestablish parental accountability and responsibility.

Juvenile gangs have become a serious and growing problem in many major metropolitan areas throughout the United States.

Ethnic youth gangs, mostly males aged 14 to 21, appear to be increasing in such areas as Los Angeles, Chicago, Boston, and New York. National surveys of gang activity now estimate that there are about 700,000 members in the United States, up sharply over the previous twenty years. One view of gang development is that such groups serve as a bridge between adolescence and adulthood in communities where adult social control is not available. Another view suggests that gangs are a product of lower-class social disorganization and that they serve as an alternative means of economic advancement for poorly motivated and uneducated youth. Today's gangs are more often commercially than culturally oriented, and the profit motive may be behind increasing memberships. It is unlikely that gang control strategies can be successful as long as legitimate economic alternatives are lacking. Look for rapid growth in ganging when the current adolescent population matures and limited job opportunities encourage gang members to prolong their involvement in illegal activities.

Many of the underlying problems of youth crime and delinquency are directly related to education.

Numerous empirical studies have confirmed that lack of educational success is an important contributing factor in delinquency; experts generally agree chronic offenders have had a long history of school failure. Dropping out of school is now being associated with long-term antisocial behavior. About 10 percent of all victimizations occur on school grounds. School-based crime control projects have not been very successful, and a great deal more effort is needed in this critical area of school-delinquency prevention control.

Substance abuse is closely associated with juvenile crime and delinquency.
Self-reported teen substance abuse has increased during the 1990s. Surveys of arrested juveniles indicate sizable numbers of young people are substance abusers. Most efforts in the juvenile justice system to treat young offenders involved with substance abuse seem to be unsuccessful. Traditional prevention efforts and education programs have not had encouraging results.

An analysis of the history of juvenile justice over the past 100 years shows how our policy regarding delinquency has gone through cycles of reform.
Many years ago, society primarily focused on the treatment of youth who committed criminal behavior often through no fault of their own. Early in the nineteenth century, juveniles were tried in criminal courts, like everyone else. Reformers developed the idea of establishing separate institutions for juvenile offenders in which the rehabilitation idea could proceed without involvement with criminal adults. As a result, the House of Refuge Movement was born. By the late 1890s the system proved unworkable, because delinquent juveniles, minor offenders and neglected children weren't benefiting from institutional placement. The 1899 Illinois Juvenile Court Act was an effort to regulate the treatment of children and secure institutional reform. *Parens patriae* was the justification to ignore legal formalities in the juvenile courts up until the early twentieth century. In the 1960s, the *Gault* decision heralded the promise of legal rights for children and interrupted the goal of individualized rehabilitation. The 1970s yielded progress in the form of the Juvenile Justice and Delinquency Prevention Act. Throughout the 1980s and 1990s, the juvenile justice system seemed suspended between the assurance of due process and efforts to provide services for delinquent children and their families. Today, society is concerned with the control of serious juvenile offenders and the development of firm sentencing provisions in the juvenile courts. These cycles represent the shifting philosophies of the juvenile justice system.

Today no single ideology or view dominates the direction, programs, and policies of the juvenile justice system.

Throughout the past decade, numerous competing positions regarding juvenile justice have emerged. As the liberal program of the 1970s has faltered, more restrictive sanctions have been imposed. The "crime control" position seems most formidable as we enter the new millennium. However, there remains a great deal of confusion over what the juvenile justice system does, what it should do, and how it should deal with youthful antisocial behavior. The juvenile justice system operates on distinctly different yet parallel tracks. On the one hand, significant funding is available for prevention and treatment strategies. At the same time, states are responding to anxiety about youth crime by devising more punitive measures.

Today's problems in the juvenile justice system can often be traced to the uncertainty of its founders, the "child savers."
Such early twentieth-century groups formed the juvenile justice system on the misguided principle of reforming wayward youth and remodeling their behavior. The "best interest of the child" standard has long been the guiding light in juvenile proceedings, calling for the strongest available rehabilitative services. Today's juvenile justice system is often torn between playing the role of social versus crime control agent.

In recent years, the juvenile justice system has become more legalistic by virtue of U.S. Supreme Court decisions that have granted children procedural safeguards in various court proceedings.
The case of *In re Gault* of the 1960s motivated state legislators to revamp their juvenile court legal procedures. Today, the Supreme Court is continuing to struggle with making distinctions between the legal rights of adults and those of minors. Recent Court decisions that allowed children to be searched by teachers and denied their right to a jury trial showed that the Court continues to recognize a legal separation between adult and juvenile offenders.

Despite some dramatic distinctions, juveniles have gained many of the legal due process rights adults enjoy.
Among the more significant elements of due process are the right to counsel, evidence efficiency, protection from double jeopardy and self-incrimination, and the right to appeal. The public continues to favor providing juveniles with the same due process and procedural guarantees accorded to adults.

A recent report of the American Bar Association on juvenile access to counsel and the quality of legal representation in juvenile court found that the many constitutional protections that adults receive are not actually provided to juvenile offenders. High caseloads, poor pretrial preparation and trial performance, and the lack of dispositional representation are issues where juveniles are being denied due process of law. More resources are needed to implement constitutional procedures so that legal protections are not discarded.

The key area in which due process is required by *Gault* is the right to counsel. While progress has been made in improving the availability and quality of legal counsel afforded youth in delinquency proceedings in the three decades since *Gault,* much remains to be done.

States are increasingly taking legislative action to ensure that juvenile arrest and disposition records are available to prosecutors and judges.
Knowledge of defendants' juvenile records may help determine appropriate sentencing for offenders age 18 to 24, the age group most likely to be involved in violent crime. Laws that are being passed include (1) police fingerprinting of juveniles charged with crimes that are felonies if committed by an adult; (2) centralized juvenile arrest and disposition recordholding and dissemination statutes; (3) prosecutor and court access to juvenile disposition records; and (4) limitations on expungement of juvenile records when there are subsequent adult convictions.

The Juvenile Court is the focal point of the contemporary juvenile justice system.
Created at the turn of the century, it was adopted as an innovative solution to the problem of wayward youth. In the first half of the century, these courts (organized by the states) and based on the historic notion of *parens patriae,* were committed to the treatment of the child. They functioned without procedures employed in the adult criminal courts. When the system was reviewed by the U.S. Supreme Court in 1966, due process was imposed on the juvenile court system. Thirty years have since passed and numerous reform efforts have been undertaken. But the statement of Judge Abe Fortas "that the child receives the worst of both worlds—neither the protection afforded adults nor the treatment needed for children" still rings true. Reform efforts have been disappointing.

What are the remedies for the current juvenile court system?
Some suggest abolishing the delinquency-status jurisdiction of the courts. This is difficult to do because the organization of the courts is governed by state law. Others want to strengthen the legal rights of juveniles by improving the quality of services of legal counsel. The vast majority of experts believe there is an urgent need to develop meaningful dispositional programs and ex-

pand treatment services. Over the last half-century, the juvenile court system has been transformed from a rehabilitative to a quasi-criminal court. With limited resources and procedural deficiencies, there is little likelihood of much change in the near future. On the one-hundredth anniversary of the juvenile court, one important change is the rise of juvenile drug courts for youth struggling with substance abuse.

The death penalty for children has been upheld by the Supreme Court.
According to the *Wilkens v. Missouri* and *Standford v. Kentucky* cases in 1989, the Supreme Court concluded that states are free to impose the death penalty for murderers who commit their crimes while age 16 or 17. According to the majority decision written by Justice Antonin Scalia, society has not formed a consensus that such executions are a violation of the cruel and unusual punishment clause of the Eighth Amendment.

One of the most significant changes in American law enforcement has been the emergence of community policing in the field of delinquency prevention.
Community participation and cooperation, citizen crime prevention programs, and education programs such as Project D.A.R.E. (drug education) have become a mainstay of law enforcement in the 1980s and 1990s and have had a particularly significant impact on improving perceptions of community safety and the quality of community life in many areas.

The Violent Crime Control and Law Enforcement Act of 1994, described as the largest piece of criminal legislation in the history of the country and four years in the making, provides major new opportunities for the field of juvenile crime prevention and community policing. Fighting to retain this law's major focus on prevention will be a future goal.

The use of detention in the juvenile justice system continues to be a widespread problem.
After almost three decades of work, virtually all jurisdictions have passed laws requiring that status offenders be placed in shelter care programs rather than detention facilities. Another serious problem related to the use of juvenile detention is the need to remove young people from lockups in adult jails. The Office of Juvenile Justice and Delinquency Prevention continues to give millions of dollars in aid to encourage the removal of juveniles from such adult lockups. But eliminating the confinement of children in adult institutions remains an enormously difficult task in the juvenile justice system. Although most delinquency cases do not involve detention, its use is more common for cases involving males,

minorities, and older juveniles. Juvenile detention is one of the most important elements of the justice system and one of the most difficult to administer. It is experiencing a renewed emphasis on programs linked to short-term confinement.

The use of waiver, bind-over, and transfer provisions in juvenile court statutes has been growing.
This trend has led toward a criminalization of the juvenile system. Because there are major differences between the adult and juvenile court systems, transfer to an adult court exposes youths to more serious consequences of their antisocial behavior and is a strong recommendation of those favoring a crime-control model. Waiver of serious offenders is one of the most significant developments in the trend to criminalize the juvenile court. According to the National Conference of State Legislatures, every state has transfer proceedings. Many states are considering legislation that makes it easier to transfer juveniles into adult courts. States continue to modify age and offense criteria, allowing more serious offenders to be tried as criminals; some are considering new transfer laws, such as mandatory and presumptive waiver provisions.

The role of the attorney in the juvenile justice process requires further research and analysis.
Most attorneys appear to be uncertain whether they should act as adversaries or advocates in the juvenile process. In addition, the role of the juvenile prosecutor has become more significant as a result of new and more serious statutory sentencing provisions, as well as legal standards promulgated by such organizations as the American Bar Association and the National District Attorneys Association. Juvenile defendants also need and are entitled to effective legal representation. Through creative and resourceful strategies, many more states are providing comprehensive representation for delinquent youth. These programs include law internships, attorney mentoring, and neighborhood defender services.

Juvenile sentencing procedures now reflect the desire to create uniformity and limited discretion in the juvenile court, and this trend is likely to continue.
Many states have now developed programs such as mandatory sentences, sentencing guidelines, and limited-discretion sentencing to bring uniformity into the juvenile justice system. As a result of the public's fear about serious juvenile crime, legislators have amended juvenile codes to tighten up juvenile sentencing provisions. Graduated sanctions are the latest type of sentencing solution being explored by states. The most popular piece of juvenile crime legislation in the near future will be tougher sentences for violent and repeat offenders.

Perhaps the most dramatic impact on sentencing will be felt by the imposition of "blended sentences" that combine juvenile and adult sentences. Blended sentencing statutes, which allow courts to impose juvenile and/or adult correctional sanctions on certain young offenders, were in place in twenty states at the end of 1997.

In the area of community sentencing, new forms of probation supervision have become commonplace in recent years.
Intensive probation supervision, balanced probation, wilderness probation, and electronic monitoring have become important community-based alternatives over the last few years. Probation continues to be the single most significant intermediate sanction available to the juvenile court system.

Restorative Community Juvenile Justice is a new designation that refers to a preference for neighborhood-based, more accessible, and less formal juvenile services.
The restorative justice idea pioneered by Gorden Bazemore is understood by examining the relationship between the victim, the community, and the offender. For the victim, restorative justice offers the hope of restitution or other forms of reparation, information about the case, support for healing, the opportunity to be heard, and input into the case, as well as expanded opportunities for involvement and influence. For the community, there is the promise of reduced fear and safer neighborhoods, a more accessible justice process, and accountability, as well as the obligation for involvement and participation in sanctioning crime, supporting victim restoration, reintegrating offenders, and crime prevention and control. For the offender, restorative justice requires accountability in the form of obligations to repair the harm to individual victims and victimized communities, and the opportunity to develop new competencies, social skills, and the capacity to avoid future crime.

Victim restitution is another widely used and programmatic method of community treatment in today's juvenile justice system.
In what is often referred to as monetary restitution, children are required to pay the victims of their crimes or in some instances provide some community service directly to the victim. Restitution provides the court with an important alternative sentencing option and has been instituted by statute in virtually every jurisdiction in the country.

Deinstitutionalization has become an important goal of the juvenile justice system.

The Office of Juvenile Justice and Delinquency Prevention has provided funds to encourage this process. In the early 1980s, the deinstitutionalization movement seemed to be partially successful. Admissions to public juvenile correctional facilities declined in the late 1970s and early 1980s. In addition, the number of status offenders being held within the juvenile justice system was reduced. However, the number of institutionalized children in the 1990s has increased, and the deinstitutionalization movement has failed to meet all of its optimistic goals. Nonetheless, the majority of states have achieved compliance with the DSO mandate. Because juvenile crime is a high priority, the challenge to the states will be to retain a focus on prevention despite societal pressures for more punitive approaches. If that can be achieved, then deinstitutionalization will remain a central theme in the juvenile justice system.

The number of incarcerated youths continues to rise.

Today, there are over 100,000 youths in some type of correctional institution. The juvenile courts seem to be using the most severe of the statutory dispositions, that is, commitment to the juvenile institution, rather than the "least restrictive statutory alternative." In addition, there seems to be a disproportionate number of minority youths incarcerated in youth facilities. The minority incarceration rate is almost four times greater than that for whites, and minorities seem to be placed more often in public than in private treatment facilities. The OJJDP is committed to ensuring that the country address situations where there is disproportionate confinement of minority offenders in the nation's juvenile justice system. The overall organization of the juvenile justice system in the United States is changing. Early on, institutional services for children were provided by the public sector. Today, private facilities and programs service a significant proportion of juvenile admissions. In the next decade, many more juvenile justice systems will most likely adopt privatization of juvenile correctional services.

Despite the growth of alternative treatment programs such as diversion, restitution, and probation, the number of children under secure institutional care has increased, and the success of such programs remains very uncertain.

Nearly all juvenile institutions utilize some form of treatment program for the children in their care. Despite generally positive intentions, the goal of rehabilitation in an institutional setting is very difficult to achieve. Recent studies indicate some programs do work. Those secure programs that emphasize individual attention, reinte-

grate youths into their homes and communities, and provide intensive aftercare can be successful.

The future of the legal right to treatment for juveniles remains uncertain.

The appellate courts have established minimum standards of care and treatment on a case-by-case basis, but it does not appear that the courts can be persuaded today to expand this constitutional theory to mandate that incarcerated children receive adequate treatment. Eventually, this issue must be clarified by the Supreme Court. Reforms in state juvenile institutions often result from class-action lawsuits filed on behalf of incarcerated youth.

A serious crisis exists in the U.S. juvenile justice system.

How to cope with the needs of large numbers of children in trouble remains one of the most controversial and frustrating issues in our society. The magnitude of the problem is such that over 2 million youths are arrested each year; over 1.5 million delinquency dispositions and 150,000 status offense cases are heard in court; and drug abuse is a significant factor in more than 60 percent of all the cases referred to the juvenile courts. Today, the system and the process seem more concerned with crime control and more willing to ignore the rehabilitative ideal. Perhaps the answer lies outside the courtroom in the form of greater job opportunities, improved family relationships, and more effective education. Much needs to be done in delinquency prevention. One fact is also certain: According to many experts, the problem of violent juvenile crime is a national crisis. While the good news is that the juvenile crime rate declined in recent years, violence by juveniles is still too prevalent and remains an issue of great concern. Developing programs to fight juvenile violence seems to overshadow all other juvenile justice objectives.

Federal funding for juvenile delinquency is essential to improving state practices and programs.

The Juvenile Justice and Delinquency Prevention Act of 1974 has had a tremendous impact on America's juvenile justice system. Its mandates to deinstitutionalize status offenders and remove juveniles from adult jails have spurred change for over two decades. The survival of many state programs will likely depend on this federal legislation. Because the Act has contributed to a wide range of improvements, Congress will most likely approve future financial incentives. Reauthorization of JJDPA through 2002 was approved in the 106th Congress (1999).

In 1996, The Coordinating Council on Juvenile Justice and Delinquency Prevention, an independent organization in the executive branch of the federal government, presented its National Juvenile Justice Action Plan.

The Plan is a blueprint for action designed to reduce the impact of juvenile violence and delinquency. It calls upon states and communities to implement the following objectives: (1) provide immediate intervention sanctions and treatment for delinquent juveniles; (2) prosecute serious, violent, and chronic juvenile offenders in criminal court; (3) reduce youth involvement with guns, drugs, and gangs; (4) provide educational and employment opportunities for children and youth; (5) break the cycle of violence by dealing with youth victimization, abuse, and neglect; (6) strengthen and mobilize communities; (7) support the development of innovative approaches to research and evaluation; and (8) implement an aggressive outreach campaign to combat juvenile violence. This text provides numerous examples of the innovative and effective strategies that are described in the National Juvenile Justice Action Plan.

Today, the juvenile justice system and court of one-hundred years is under attack more than ever before.

Yet it has weathered criticism for failing to control and rehabilitate juveniles. It is a unique American institution duplicated in many other countries as being the best model for handling juveniles who commit crime. The major recommendations of such important organizations as the National Council of Juvenile Court Judges, the American Bar Association, and the Office of Juvenile Justice and Delinquency Prevention for the new century are (1) the court should be a leader for juvenile justice in the community; (2) people (judges, attorneys, and probation officers) are the key to the health of the juvenile justice system; (3) public safety and rehabilitation are the goals of the juvenile justice system; (4) juvenile court workloads are shaped today and in the future by the increase of substance abuse cases that must be resolved; and (5) the greatest future needs of the juvenile court in particular are resources and funding for more services, more staff, and more facilities.

Excerpts from the U.S. Constitution

Amendment I (1791)

Congress shall make no law respecting an establishment of religion, or prohibiting the free exercise thereof; or abridging the freedom of speech, or of the press; or the right of the people peaceably to assemble, and to petition the government for a redress of grievances.

Amendment II (1791)

A well regulated militia, being necessary to the security of a free state, the right of the people to keep and bear arms, shall not be infringed.

Amendment III (1791)

No soldier shall, in time of peace, be quartered in any house, without the consent of the owner, nor in time of war, but in a manner to be prescribed by law.

Amendment IV (1791)

The right of the people to be secure in their persons, houses, papers, and effects, against unreasonable searches and seizures, shall not be violated, and no warrants shall issue, but upon probable cause, supported by oath or affirmation, and particularly describing the place to be searched, and the persons or things to be seized.

Amendment V (1791)

No person shall be held to answer for a capital, or otherwise infamous, crime unless on a presentment or indictment of a grand jury, except in cases arising in the land or naval forces, or in the militia, when in actual service in time of war or public danger; nor shall any person be subject for the same offense to be twice put in jeopardy of life or limb; nor shall be compelled in any criminal case to be a witness against himself, nor be deprived of life, liberty, or property; without due process of law; nor shall private property be taken for public use without just compensation.

Amendment VI (1791)

In all criminal prosecutions, the accused shall enjoy the right to a speedy and public trial, by an impartial jury of the state and district wherein the crime shall have been committed, which district shall have been previously ascertained by law, and to be informed of the nature and cause of the accusation; to be confronted with the witnesses against him; to have compulsory process for obtaining witnesses in his favor, and to have the assistance of counsel for his defense.

Amendment VII (1791)

In suits at common law, where the value in controversy shall exceed twenty dollars, the right of trial by jury shall be preserved, and no fact tried by a jury shall be otherwise reexamined in any court of the United States, than according to the rules of common law.

Amendment VIII (1791)

Excessive bail shall not be required, nor excessive fines imposed, nor cruel and unusual punishment inflicted.

Amendment IX (1791)

The enumeration in the Constitution of certain rights shall not be construed to deny or disparage others retained by the people.

Amendment X (1791)

The powers not delegated to the United States by the Constitution, nor prohibited by it to the states, are reserved to the states respectively, or to the people.

Amendment XIV (1868)

Section I. All persons born or naturalized in the United States, and subject to the jurisdiction thereof, are citizens of the United States and of the state wherein they reside. No state shall make or enforce any laws which abridge the privilege or immunities of citizens of the United States; nor shall any state deprive any person of life, liberty, or property, without due process of law; nor deny to any person within its jurisdiction the equal protection of the laws.

Notes

Chapter 1

1. Nanette Davis, *Youth Crisis: Growing Up in the High-Risk Society* (New York: Praeger, Greenwood, 1998).

2. Susan Crimmins and Michael Foley, "The Threshold of Violence in Urban Adolescents." Paper presented at the annual meeting of the American Society of Criminology, Reno, Nevada, November 1989.

3. Ibid., p. 21.

4. Task Force on Education of Young Adolescents, *Turning Points, Preparing American Youth for the 21st Century* (New York: Carnegie Council on Adolescent Development, 1989).

5. Erik Erikson, *Childhood and Society* (New York: Norton, 1963).

6. Roger Gould, "Adult Life Stages: Growth Toward Self-Tolerance," *Psychology Today* 8:74–78 (1975).

7. Kevin Thompson, David Brownfield, and Ann Marie Sorenson, "At-Risk Behavior and Gang Involvement: A Latent Structure Analysis," *Journal of Gang Research* 5:1–15(1998).

8. Task Force on Education of Young Adolescents, *Turning Points*, p. 27.

9. "Booming Economy Leaves Millions of Children Behind: 12.1 Million Children Still Living in Poverty." Children's Defense Fund Press Release, Washington, DC, September 26, 2000.

10. David Eggebeen and Daniel Lichter, "Race, Family Structure, and Changing Poverty among American Children," *American Sociological Review* 56:801–817 (1991).

11. W. Rees Davis and Michael Clatts, "High Risk Youth and the NYC Street Economy: Policy Implications." Paper presented at the American Society of Criminology Meeting, Boston, November 1995.

12. Stephanie Venture, Sally Curtin, and T. J. Matthews, *Teen Age Births in the United States: National and State Trends, 1990–1996* (Washington, DC: National Center for Health Statistics, 1998).

13. Ibid.

14. National Education Goals Panel, *The National Education Goals Report, Building a Nation of Learners* (Washington, DC: U.S. Government Printing Office, 1997), pp. iii–iv.

15. News release: "Kids Count Survey, 1998" (Annie E. Casey Foundation, Baltimore, Maryland, May 5, 1998).

16. National Education Goals Panel, *The National Education Goals Report.*

17. Bruce Johnson, George Thomas, and Andrew Golub, "Trends in Heroin Use among Manhattan Arrestees from the Heroin and Crack Era," in James Inciardi and Lana Harrison, eds., *Heroin in the Age of Crack-Cocaine* (Thousand Oaks, CA: Sage, 1998), pp. 108–30.

18. Federal Bureau of Investigation, *Crimes in the United States, 1999* (Washington, DC: U.S. Government Printing Office, 2000), p. 220.

19. John Whitehead and Steven Lab, "A Meta-Analysis of Juvenile Correctional Treatment," *Journal of Research in Crime and Delinquency* 26:276–95 (1989).

20. Francis Cullen, Sandra Evans Skovron, Joseph Scott, and Velmer Burton, "Public Support for Correctional Treatment: The Tenacity of Rehabilitative Ideology," *Criminal Justice and Behavior* 17:6–18 (1990).

21. Rhena Izzo and Robert Ross, "Meta-Analysis of Rehabilitation Programs for Juvenile Delinquents," *Criminal Justice and Behavior* 17:134–42 (1990).

22. Gordon Bazemore and Lynette Feder, "Judges in the Punitive Juvenile Court: Organizational, Career and Ideological Influences on Sanctioning Orientation," *Justice Quarterly* 14:87–114 (1997).

23. *Stanford v. Kentucky,* and *Wilkins v. Missouri,* 109 S.Ct. 2969 (1989).

24. See Lawrence Stone, *The Family, Sex, and Marriage in England: 1500–1800* (New York: Harper & Row, 1977).

25. This section relies on Jackson Spielvogel, *Western Civilization* (St. Paul: West, 1991), pp. 279–86.

26. Ibid.

27. See Philipe Aries, *Century of Childhood: A Social History of Family Life* (New York: Vintage, 1962).

28. See Douglas R. Rendleman, "*Parens Patriae:* From Chancery to the Juvenile Court," *South Carolina Law Review* 23:205 (1971).

29. See Stone, *The Family, Sex, and Marriage in England;* and Lawrence Stone, ed., *Schooling and Society: Studies in the History of Education* (Baltimore: Johns Hopkins University Press, 1970).

30. Ibid.

31. See Wiley B. Sanders, *Some Early Beginnings of the Children's Court Movement in England,* National Probation Association Yearbook (New York: National Council on Crime and Delinquency, 1945).

32. Rendleman, "*Parens Patriae,*" p. 205.

33. Douglas Besharov, *Juvenile Justice Advocacy—Practice in a Unique Court* (New York: Practicing Law Institute, 1974), p. 2.

34. *Wellesley v. Wellesley,* 4 Eng. Rep. 1078 (1827).

35. Rendleman, "*Parens Patriae,*" p. 209.

36. Anthony Platt, "The Rise of the Child Saving Movement: A Study in Social Policy and Correctional Reform," *Annals of the American Academy of Political and Social Science* 381:21–38 (1969).

37. Robert Bremmer, ed., and John Barnard, Hareven Tamara, and Robert Mennel, asst. eds., *Children and Youth in America* (Cambridge: Harvard University Press, 1970), p. 64.

38. Elizabeth Pleck, "Criminal Approaches to Family Violence, 1640–1980," in Lloyd Ohlin and Michael Tonry, eds., *Family Violence* (Chicago: University of Chicago Press, 1989), pp. 19–58.

39. Ibid.

40. John R. Sutton, *Stubborn Children: Controlling Delinquency in the United States, 1640–1981* (Berkeley: University of California Press, 1988).

41. Pleck, "Criminal Approaches to Family Violence," p. 29.

42. John Demos, *Past, Present and Personal* (New York: Oxford University Press, 1986), pp. 80–88.

43. Elizabeth Pleck, *Domestic Tyranny: The Making of Social Policy against Family Violence from Colonial Times to the Present* (New York: Oxford University Press, 1987), pp. 28–30.

44. Graeme Newman, *The Punishment Response* (Philadelphia: Lippincott, 1978), pp. 53–79; Philippe Aries, *Centuries of Childhood: A Social History of Family Life* (New York: Knopf, 1962). The history of childhood juvenile justice is discussed in detail in Chapter 12.

45. Stephen J. Morse, "Immaturity and Irresponsibility," *Journal of Criminal Law and Criminology* 88:15–67 (1997).

46. Ibid.

47. John L. Hutzler, *Juvenile Court Jurisdiction over Children's Conduct: 1982 Comparative Analysis of Juvenile and Family Codes and National Standards* (Pittsburgh: National Center for Juvenile Justice, 1982), p. 2.

48. See, generally, David Rothman, *The Discovery of the Asylum* (Boston: Little, Brown, 1971).

49. Reports of the Chicago Bar Association Committee, 1899, cited in Anthony Platt, *The Child Savers* (Chicago: University of Chicago Press, 1969) p. 119.

50. Susan Datesman and Mikel Aickin, "Offense Specialization and Escalation among Status Offenders," *Journal of Criminal Law and Criminology* 75:1246–75 (1985).

51. Ibid.

52. 42 U.S.C.A. 5601B5751 (1983 & Supp. 1987).

53. Claudia Wright, "Contempt No Excuse for Locking Up Status Offenders, Says Florida Supreme Court," *Youth Law News* 13:1–3 (1992).

54. *A.A. v. Rolle,* 604 So. 2d 813 (1992).

55. National Council on Crime and Delinquency, "Juvenile Curfews—A Policy Statement," *Crime and Delinquency* 18:132–33 (1972).

56. National Advisory Commission on Criminal Justice Standards and Goals, *Juvenile Justice and Delinquency Prevention* (Washington, DC: U.S. Government Printing Office, 1977), p. 311.

57. Martin Rouse, "The Diversion of Status Offenders, Criminalization, and the New York Family Court," rev. version. Paper presented at the American Society of Criminology, Reno, NV, November 1989, p. 12.

58. Barry Feld, "Criminalizing the American Juvenile Court," in Michael Tonry, ed., *Crime and Justice, A Review of Research* (Chicago: University of Chicago Press, 1993), p. 232.

59. Marc Miller, "Changing Legal Paradigms in Juvenile Justice," in Peter Greenwood, ed., *The Juvenile Rehabilitation Reader* (Santa Monica, CA: Rand, 1985) p. V.44.

60. Thomas Kelley, "Status Offenders Can Be Different: A Comparative Study of Delinquent Careers," *Crime and Delinquency* 29:365–80 (1983).

61. Ira Schwartz, *Justice for Juveniles: Rethinking the Best Interests of the Child* (Lexington, MA: Lexington Books, 1989), p. 171.

62. Ibid.

63. Carolyn Smith, "Factors Associated with Early Sexual Activity among Urban Adolescents," *Social Work* 42:334–46 (1997).

Chapter 2

1. Jim Yardley, "A Violent Life: Gangs and Guns Shaped a Suspect in the Death of an Officer," *New York Times,* 10 August 1998, p. A16; Mayor Rudolph W. Giuliani, "Early Release from Prison Causes Another Preventable Tragedy," Mayor's WINS radio address, 2 August 1998.

2. Howard Snyder and Melissa Sickmund, *Juvenile Offenders and Victims: A National Report* (Washington, DC: National Center for Juvenile Justice, 1995).

3. Federal Bureau of Investigation, *Crime in the United States, 1999* (Washington, DC: United State Government Printing Office, 2000). Herein Cited as FBI, UCR, 1999.

4. FBI, UCR, 1999.

5. All population statistics used in the chapter are from U.S. Bureau of the Census, unpublished data, 1994 (Washington, DC: U.S. Department of Census, 1995).

6. Thomas Bernard, "Juvenile Crime and the Transformation of Juvenile Justice: Is There a Juvenile Crime Wave?", *Justice Quarterly* 16: 336–56 (1999).

7. James A. Fox, *Trends in Juvenile Violence: A Report to the United States Attorney General on Current and Future Rates of Juvenile Offending* (Boston: Northeastern University, 1996).

8. Steven Levitt, "The Limited Role of Changing Age Structure in Explaining Aggregate Crime Rates," *Criminology* 37: 581-599 (1999).

9. "Fox Butterfield Possible Manipulation of Crime Data Worries Top Police," *New York Times,* 3 August 1998, p.1.

10. A pioneering effort of self-report research is A. L. Porterfield's *Youth in Trouble* (Fort Worth, TX: Leo Potishman Foundation, 1946); for a review, see Robert Hardt and George Bodine, *Development of Self-Report Instruments in Delinquency Research: A Conference Report* (Syracuse, NY: Syracuse University Youth Development Center, 1965); see also Fred Murphy, Mary Shirley, and Helen Witmer, "The Incidence of Hidden Delinquency," *American Journal of Orthopsychiatry* 16:686–96 (1946).

11. For example, the following studies have noted the great discrepancy between official statistics and self-report studies: Maynard Erickson and LaMar Empey, "Court Records, Undetected Delinquency, and Decision-Making," *Journal of Criminal Law, Criminology, and Police Science* 54:456–69 (1963); Martin Gold, "Undetected Delinquent Behavior," *Journal of Research in Crime and Delinquency* 3:27–46 (1966); James Short and F. Ivan Nye, "Extent of Unrecorded Delinquency, Tentative Conclusions," *Journal of Criminal Law, Criminology, and Police Science* 49:296–302 (1958).

12. Jerald Bachman, Lloyd Johnston, and Patrick O'Malley, *Monitoring the Future: Questionnaire Responses from the Nation's High School Seniors, 1999* (Ann Arbor, MI: Institute for Social Research, 2000), p. 102.

13. Rosemary Sarri, "Gender Issues in Juvenile Justice," *Crime and Delinquency* 29:381–97 (1983).

14. For a discussion of sex bias, see Meda Chesney-Lind, "Guilty by Reason of Sex: Young Women and the Criminal Justice System." Paper presented at the American Society of Criminology Meeting, Toronto, Canada, 1980.

15. Cited in David Farrington, "Juvenile Delinquency," in John Coleman, *The School Years* (London: Routledge, 1992), p. 132.

16. Hindelang, Hirschi, and Weis, *Measuring Delinquency;* Gary Jensen and Raymond Eve, "Sex Differences in Delinquency: An Examination of Popular Sociological Explanation," *Criminology* 13:427–48 (1976); Michael Hindelang, "Age, Sex, and the Versatility of Delinquent Involvements," *Social Problems* 18:522–35 (1979); James Short and F. Ivan Nye, "Extent of Unrecorded Juvenile Delinquency, Tentative Conclusions," *Journal of Criminal Law, Criminology, and Police Science* 49:296–302 (1958).

17. For a review, see Meda Chesney-Lind and Randall Shelden, *Girls, Delinquency and Juvenile Justice* (Pacific Grove, CA: Brooks/Cole, 1992), pp. 7–14.

18. Leroy Gould, "Who Defines Delinquency? A Comparison of Self-Report and Officially Reported Indices of Delinquency for Three Racial Groups," *Social Problems* 16:325–36 (1969); Harwin Voss, "Ethnic Differentials in Delinquency in Honolulu," *Journal of Criminal Law, Criminology, and Police Science* 54:322–27 (1963);

Ronald Akers, Marvin Krohn, Marcia Radosevich, and Lonn Lanza-Kaduce, "Social Characteristics and Self-Reported Delinquency," in Gary Jensen, ed., *Sociology of Delinquency* (Beverly Hills, CA: Sage, 1981), pp. 48–62.

19. David Huizinga and Delbert Elliott, "Juvenile Offenders: Prevalence, Offender Incidence, and Arrest Rates by Race," *Crime and Delinquency* 33:206–223 (1987); see also Dale Dannefer and Russell Schutt, "Race and Juvenile Justice Processing in Court and Police Agencies," *American Journal of Sociology* 87:1113–32 (1982).

20. Paul Tracy, "Race and Class Differences in Official and Self-Reported Delinquency," in Marvin Wolfgang, Terrence Thornberry, and Robert Figlio, eds., *From Boy to Man, from Delinquency to Crime* (Chicago: University of Chicago Press, 1987), p. 120.

21. Bachman, Johnston, and O'Malley, *Monitoring the Future,* pp. 102–104.

22. Samuel Walker, Cassia Spohn, and Miriam DeLone, *The Color of Justice: Race, Ethnicity and Crime in America* (Belmont, CA: Brooks/Cole, 1992), pp. 46–47.

23. Miriam Sealock and Sally Simpson, "Unraveling Bias in Arrest Decisions: The Role of Juvenile Offender Typescripts," *Justice Quarterly* 15:427–57 (1998).

24. Christina Polsenberg and Kenneth Jackson, "Putting Race into Context: Race, Juvenile Justice Processing and Urbanization." Paper presented at the American Society of Criminology Meeting, Boston, November 1995 (updated version, 1996); for a general review, see Carl Pope and William Feyerherm, "Minority Status and Juvenile Justice Processing (Part I)," *Criminal Justice Abstracts* 22:327–35 (1990); see also Douglas Smith and Jody Klein, "Police Control of Interpersonal Disputes," *Social Problems* 31:468–81 (1984).

25. Christina DeJong and Kenneth Jackson, "Putting Race into Context: Race, Juvenile Justice Processing, and Urbanization," *Justice Quarterly* 15:487–504 (1998).

26. Donna Bishop and Charles Frazier, "The Influence of Race in Juvenile Justice Processing," *Journal of Research in Crime and Delinquency* 25:242–63 (1989).

27. For a general review, see William Wilbanks, *The Myth of a Racist Criminal Justice System* (Pacific Grove, CA: Brooks/Cole, 1987).

28. Walker, Spohn, and DeLone, *The Color of Justice,* pp. 47–48.

29. Fox Butterfield, *All God's Children: The Bosket Family and the American Tradition of Violence* (New York: Avon, 1996).

30. Michael Leiber and Jayne Stairs, "Race, Contexts and the Use of Intake diversion," *Journal of Research in Crime and Delinquency* 36 (1999), 56–86; Darrell Steffensmeier, Jeffery Ulmer, and John Kramer, "The Interaction of Race, Gender, and Age in Criminal Sentencing: The Punishment Cost of Being Young, Black, and Male," *Criminology* 36: 763–98 (1998).

31. Tracy Nobiling, Cassia Spohn, and Miriam DeLone, "A Tale of Two Counties: Unemployment and Sentence Severity," *Justice Quarterly* 15:459–86(1998).

32. Alexander Weiss and Steven Chermak, "The News Value of African-American Victims: An Examination of the Media's Presentation of Homicide," *Journal of Crime and Justice* 21:71–84 (1998).

33. Melvin Thomas, "Race, Class and Personal Income: An Empirical Test of the Declining Significance of Race Thesis, 1968–1988," *Social Problems* 40:328–39 (1993).

34. Mallie Paschall, Robert Flewelling, and Susan Ennett, "Racial Differences in Violent Behavior among Young Adults: Moderating and Confounding Effects," *Journal of Research in Crime and Delinquency* 35:148–65 (1998).

35. Julie Phillips, "Variation in African-American Homicide Rates: An Assessment of Potential Explanations," *Criminology* 35:527–59 (1997).

36. Carl Pope and William Feyerherm, "Minority Status and Juvenile Processing: An Assessment of the Research Literature." Paper presented at the American Society of Criminology Meeting, Reno, Nevada, November 1989.

37. Jefferey Fagan, Elizabeth Piper, and Melinda Moore, "Violent Delinquents and Urban Youths," *Criminology* 24:439–71 (1986).

38. Robert Agnew, "A General Strain Theory of Community Differences in Crime Rates," *Journal of Research in Crime and Delinquency* 36:123–55 (1999).

39. Bonita Veysey and Steven Messner, "Further Testing of Social Disorganization Theory: An Elaboration of Sampson and Groves's 'Community Structure and Crime'," *Journal of Research in Crime and Delinquency* 36:156–74 (1999).

40. James Short and Ivan Nye, "Reported Behavior as a Criterion of Deviant Behavior," *Social Problems* 5:207–13 (1958).

41. Classic studies include Ivan Nye, James Short, and Virgil Olsen, "Socio-economic Status and Delinquent Behavior," *American Journal of Sociology* 63:381–89 (1958); Robert Dentler and Lawrence Monroe, "Social Correlates of Early Adolescent Theft," *American Sociological Review* 26:733–43 (1961); Charles Tittle, Wayne Villemez, and Douglas Smith, "The Myth of Social Class and Criminality: An Empirical Assessment of the Empirical Evidence," *American Sociological Review* 43:643–56 (1978).

42. R. Gregory Dunaway, Francis Cullen, Velmer Burton, and T. David Evans, "The Myth of Social Class and Crime Revisited: An Examination of Class and Adult Criminality," *Criminology* 38:589–632 (2000).

43. Delbert Eliott and Suzanne Ageton, "Reconciling Race and Class Differences in Self-Reported and Official Estimates of Delinquency," *American Sociological Review* 45:95–110 (1980); for a similar view, see John Braithwaite, "The Myth of Social Class and Criminality Reconsidered," *American Sociological Review* 46:35–58 (1981); Margaret Farnworth, Terence Thornberry, Marvin Krohn, and Alan Lizotte, *Measurement in the Study of Class and Delinquency: Integrating Theory and Research,* working paper no. 4, rev. (Albany, NY: Rochester Youth Development Survey, 1992), p. 19.

44. G. Roger Jarjoura and Ruth Triplett, "Delinquency and Class: A Test of the Proximity Principle," *Justice Quarterly* 14:765–92 (1997).

45. See, generally, David Farrington, "Age and Crime," in Michael Tonry and Norval Morris, eds., *Crime and Justice, An Annual Review,* vol. 7 (Chicago: University of Chicago Press, 1986), pp. 189–250.

46. Patrick O'Malley, Jerald Bachman, and Lloyd Johnston, "Period, Age and Cohort Effects on Substance Abuse among Young Americans: A Decade of Change, 1976–1986," *American Journal of Public Health* 78:1315–21 (1989); Darrell Steffensmeier, Emilie Allan, Miles Harer, and Cathy Streifel, "Age and the Distribution of Crime," *American Journal of Sociology* 94:803–31 (1989); Alfred Blumstein and Jacqueline Cohen, "A Characterizing Criminal Careers," *Science* 237:985–91 (1987).

47. Ibid.

48. Travis Hirschi and Michael Gottfredson, "Age and the Explanation of Crime," *American Journal of Sociology* 89:552–84 (1983).

49. Michael Gottfredson and Travis Hirschi, "The True Value of Lambda Would Appear to Be Zero: An Essay on Career Criminals, Criminal Careers, Selective Incapacitation, Cohort Studies, and Related Topics," *Criminology* 24:213–34 (1986); further support for their position can be found in Lawrence Cohen and Kenneth Land, "Age Structure and Crime," *American Sociological Review* 52:170–83 (1987).

50. David Greenberg, "Age, Crime and Social Explanation," *American Journal of Sociology* 91:1–21 (1985).

51. Robert Sampson and John Laub, *Crime in the Making: Pathways and Turning Points Through Life* (Cambridge: Harvard University Press, 1993).

52. Marvin Wolfgang, Robert Figlio, and Thorsten Sellin, *Delinquency in a Birth Cohort* (Chicago: University of Chicago Press, 1972); Lyle Shannon, *Assessing the Relationship of Adult Criminal Careers to Juvenile Careers: A Summary* (Washington, DC: U.S. Department of Justice, 1982); D. J. West and David P. Farrington, *The Delinquent Way of Life* (London: Heinemann, 1977); Donna Hamparian, Richard Schuster, Simon Dinitz, and John Conrad, *The Violent Few* (Lexington, MA: Lexington Books, 1978).

53. Rolf Loeber and Howard Snyder, "Rate of Offending in Juvenile Careers: Findings of Constancy and Change in Lambda," *Criminology* 28:97–109 (1990).

54. Margo Wilson and Martin Daly, "Life Expectancy, Economic Inequality, Homicide, and Reproductive Timing in Chicago Neighbourhoods," *British Journal of Medicine* 31:1271–74 (1997).

55. Edward Mulvey and John LaRosa, "Delinquency Cessation and Adolescent Development: Preliminary Data," *American Journal of Orthopsychiatry* 56:212–24 (1986).

56. Timothy Brezina, "Delinquent Problem-Solving: An Interpretive Framework for Criminological Theory and Research," *Journal of Research in Crime and Delinquency* 37:3–30 (2000).

57. Gordon Trasler, "Cautions for a Biological Approach to Crime," in Sarnoff Mednick, Terrie Moffitt, and Susan Stack, eds., *The Causes of Crime, New Biological Approaches* (Cambridge: Cambridge University Press, 1987), pp. 7–25.

58. Alicia Rand, "Transitional Life Events and Desistance from Delinquency and Crime," in Marvin Wolfgang, Terence Thornberry, and Robert Figlio, eds., *From Boy to Man, from Delinquency to Crime* (Chicago: University of Chicago Press, 1987), pp. 134–63.

59. Marc Le Blanc, "Late Adolescence Deceleration of Criminal Activity and Development of Self- and Social-Control," *Studies on Crime and Crime Prevention* 2:51–68 (1993).

60. Barry Glassner, Margaret Ksander, Bruce Berg, and Bruce Johnson, "Note on the Deterrent Effect of Juvenile vs. Adult Jurisdiction," *Social Problems* 31:219–21 (1983).

61. Neal Shover and Carol Thompson, "Age, Differential Expectations, and Crime Desistance," *Criminology* 30:89–104 (1992).

62. D. Wayne Osgood, "The Covariation among Adolescent Problem Behaviors." Paper presented at the American Society of Criminology Meeting, Baltimore, MD, November 1990.

63. Stephen Tibbetts, "Low Birth Weight, Disadvantaged Environment and Early Onset: A Test of Moffitt's Interactional Hypothesis." Paper presented at the American Society of Criminology Meeting, Boston, November 1995.

64. Arnold Barnett, Alfred Blumstein, and David Farrington, "A Prospective Test of a Criminal Career Model," *Criminology* 27:373–88 (1989).

65. Wolfgang, Figlio, and Sellin, *Delinquency in a Birth Cohort*.

66. Paul Tracy, Marvin Wolfgang, and Robert Figlio, *Delinquency in Two Birth Cohorts, Executive Summary* (Washington, DC: U.S. Department of Justice, 1985).

67. Shannon, *Assessing the Relationship of Adult Criminal Careers to Juvenile Careers;* Howard Snyder, *Court Careers of Juvenile Offenders* (Washington, DC: Office of Juvenile Justice and Delinquency Prevention, 1988); D.J. West and David P. Farrington, *The Delinquent Way of Life* (London: Heinemann, 1977); Donna Hamparian, Richard Schuster, Simon Dinitz, and John Conrad, *The Violent Few* (Lexington, MA: Lexington Books, 1978).

68. See, generally, Marvin Wolfgang, Terence Thornberry, and Robert Figlio, eds., *From Boy to Man, from Delinquency to Crime* (Chicago: University of Chicago Press, 1987).

69. Paul Tracy and Kimberly Kempf-Leonard, *Continuity and Discontinuity in Criminal Careers* (New York: Plenum Press, 1996).

70. R. Tremblay, R. Loeber, C. Gagnon, P. Charlebois, S. Larivee, and M. Le Blanc, "Disruptive Boys with Stable and Unstable High Fighting Behavior Patterns during Junior Elementary School," *Journal of Abnormal Child Psychology* 19:285–300 (1991).

71. Jennifer White, Terrie Moffitt, Felton Earls, Lee Robins, and Phil Silva, "How Early Can We Tell? Predictors of Childhood Conduct Disorder and Adolescent Delinquency," *Criminology* 28:507–535 (1990).

72. Kimberly Kempf, "Crime Severity and Criminal Career Progression," *Journal of Criminal Law and Criminology* 79:524–40 (1988).

73. Jeffrey Fagan, "Social and Legal Policy Dimensions of Violent Juvenile Crime," *Criminal Justice and Behavior* 17:93–133 (1990).

74. Peter Greenwood, *Selective Incapacitation* (Santa Monica, CA: Rand, 1982).

75. Terence Thornberry, David Huizinga, and Rolf Loeber, "The Prevention of Serious Delinquency and Violence," in James Howell, Barry Krisberg, J. David Hawkins, and John Wilson, eds., *Sourcebook on Serious, Violent, and Chronic Juvenile Offenders* (Thousand Oaks, CA: Sage, 1995).

76. Ted Miller, Mark Cohen, and Brian Wiersema, *The Extent and Costs of Crime Victimization: A New Look* (Washington, DC: National Institute of Justice, 1995).

77. Callie Marie Rennison, *Criminal Victimization 1999, Changes 1998–99, with Trends 1993–99* (Washington, DC: Bureau of Justice Statistics, 2000).

78. Craig A. Perkins, *Age Patterns of Victims of Serious Violent Crime* (Washington, DC: Bureau of Justice Statistics, 1997).

79. L. Edward Wells and Joseph Rankin, "Juvenile Victimization: Convergent Validation of Alternative Measurements," *Journal of Research in Crime and Delinquency* 32:301–304 (1995).

80. Gerald Hotaling and David Finkelhor, "Estimating the Number of Stranger Abduction Homicides of Children: A Review of Available Evidence," *Journal of Criminal Justice* 18:385–99 (1990).

Chapter 3

1. Marvin Wolfgang, Robert Figlio, and Thorsten Sellin, *Delinquency in a Birth Cohort* (Chicago: University of Chicago Press, 1972).

2. Alan Lizotte, Terence Thornberry, Marvin Krohn, Deborah Chard-Wierschem, and David McDowall, "Neighborhood Context and Delinquency: A Longitudinal Analysis," in H. J. Kerner and E. Weitekamp, eds., *Cross-National Longitudinal Research on Human Development and Criminal Behavior* (Dordrecht, The Netherlands: Kluwer Academic Publishers, 1993), pp. 11–15.

3. Jeremy Bentham, in Wilfred Harrison, ed., *A Fragment on Government and an Introduction to the Principles of Morals and Legislation* (Oxford: Basic Blackwell, 1967).

4. See, generally, Ernest Van den Haag, *Punishing Criminals* (New York: Basic Books, 1975).

5. Pierre Tremblay and Carlo Morselli, "Patterns in Criminal Achievement: Wilson and Abrahamsen Revisited," *Criminology* 38:633–60 (2000).

6. See, generally, James Q. Wilson, *Thinking about Crime* (New York: Basic Books, 1975).

7. Cesare Beccaria, *On Crimes and Punishments,* 6th ed., trans. Henry Paolucci (Indianapolis: Bobbs-Merrill, 1977), p. 43.

8. F. E. Devine, "Cesare Beccaria and the Theoretical Foundations of Modern Penal Jurisprudence," *New England Journal on Prison Law* 7:8–21 (1982).

9. John Petraitis, Brian Flay, and Todd Miller, "Reviewing Theories of Adolescent Substance Use: Organizing Pieces in the Puzzle," *Psychological Bulletin* 117:67–86 (1995).

10. Mary Tuck and David Riley, "The Theory of Reasoned Action: A Decision Theory of Crime," in D. Cornish and R. Clarke, eds., *The Reasoning Criminal* (New York: Springer-Verlag, 1986), pp. 156–69.

11. Felix Padilla, *The Gang as an American Enterprise* (New Brunswick, NJ: Rutgers University Press, 1992); see also Martin Sanchez-Jankowski, *Islands in the Street: Gangs and American Urban Society* (Berkeley: University of California Press, 1991).

12. Bruce Jacobs, "Crack Dealers' Apprehension Avoidance Techniques: A Case of Restrictive Deterrence," *Justice Quarterly* 13:359–81 (1996).

13. Ibid., p. 367.

14. Travis Hirschi, "Rational Choice and Social Control Theories of Crime," in D. Cornish and R. Clarke, eds., *The Reasoning Criminal* (New York: Springer-Verlag, 1986), p. 114.

15. See, generally, Derek Cornish and Ronald Clarke, eds., *The Reasoning Criminal* (New York: Springer-Verlag, 1986); see also Philip Cook, "The Demand and Supply of Criminal Opportunities," in Michael Tonry and Norval Morris, eds., *Crime and Justice,* vol. 7 (Chicago: University of Chicago Press, 1986), pp. 1–28; Ronald Clarke and Derek Cornish, "Modeling Offenders' Decisions: A Framework for Research and Policy," in Michael Tonry and Norval Morris, eds., *Crime and Justice,* vol. 6 (Chicago: University of Chicago Press, 1985), pp. 147–87; Morgan Reynolds, *Crime by Choice: An Economic Analysis* (Dallas: Fisher Institute, 1985).

16. Michael Hindelang, Michael Gottfredson, and James Garofalo, *Victims of Personal Crime: An Empirical Foundation for a Theory of Personal Victimization* (Cambridge, MA: Ballinger, 1978).

17. James Massey, Marvin Krohn, and Lisa Bonati, "Property Crime and the Routine Activities of Individuals," *Journal of Research in Crime and Delinquency* 26:378–400 (1989).

18. Lawrence Cohen and Marcus Felson, "Social Change and Crime Rate Trends: A Routine Activities Approach," *American Sociological Review* 44:588–608 (1979).

19. David Maume, "Inequality and Metropolitan Rape Rates: A Routine Activity Approach," *Justice Quarterly* 6:513–27 (1989).

20. Gordon Knowles, "Deception, Detection, and Evasion: A Trade Craft Analysis of Honolulu, Hawaii's Street Crack Cocaine Traffickers," *Journal of Criminal Justice* 27:443–55 (1999).

21. Paul Bellair, "Informal Surveillance and Street Crime: A Complex Relationship," *Criminology* 38:137–67 (2000).

22. Denise Osborn, Alan Trickett, and Rob Elder, "Area Characteristics and Regional Variates as Determinants of Area Property Crime Levels," *Journal of Quantitative Criminology* 8:265–82 (1992).

23. Matthew Robinson, "Lifestyles, Routine Activities, and Residential Burglary Victimization," *Journal of Criminal Justice* 22:37–52 (1999).

24. Massey, Krohn, and Bonati, "Property Crime and Routine Activities of Individuals," p. 397.

25. Lawrence Cohen, Marcus Felson, and Kenneth Land, "Property Crime Rates in the United States: A Macrodynamic Analysis, 1947–1977, with Ex-Ante Forecasts for the Mid-1980s," *American Journal of Sociology* 86:90–118 (1980).

26. William Smith, Sharon Glave Frazee, and Elizabeth Davison, "Furthering the Integration of Routine Activity and Social Disorganization Theories: Small Units of Analysis and the Study of Street Robbery as a Diffusion Process," *Criminology* 38:489–521 (2000).

27. Steven Messner and Kenneth Tardiff, "The Social Ecology of Urban Homicide: An Application of the 'Routine Activities' Approach," *Criminology* 23:241–67 (1985).

28. Leslie Kennedy and David Forde, "Routine Activities and Crime: An Analysis of Victimization in Canada," *Criminology* 28:137–52 (1990).

29. Robert O'Brien, "Relative Cohort Sex and Age-Specific Crime Rates: An Age-Period-Relative-Cohort-Size Model," *Criminology* 27:57–78 (1989).

30. D. Wayne Osgood, Janet Wilson, Patrick O'Malley, Jerald Bachman, and Lloyd Johnston, "Routine Activities and Individual Deviant Behavior," *American Sociological Review* 61:635–55 (1996).

31. Matthew Ploeger, "Youth Employment and Delinquency: Reconsidering a Problematic Relationship," *Criminology* 35:659–75 (1997).

32. Ernest Van den Haag, "The Criminal Law as a Threat System," *Journal of Criminal Law and Criminology* 73:709–85 (1982).

33. Beccaria, *On Crimes and Punishments.*

34. For the classic analysis on the subject, see Johannes Andenaes, *Punishment and Deterrence* (Ann Arbor: University of Michigan Press, 1974).

35. Gordon Bazemore and Mark Umbreit, "Rethinking the Sanctioning Function in Juvenile Court: Retributive or Restorative Responses to Youth Crime," *Crime and Delinquency* 41:296–316 (1995).

36. Bruce Jacobs, "Anticipatory Undercover Targeting in High Schools," *Journal of Criminal Justice* 22:445–57 (1994).

37. Leona Lee, "Factors Determining Waiver in a Juvenile Court," *Journal of Criminal Justice* 22:329–39 (1994).

38. *Wilkins v. Missouri, Stanford v. Kentucky,* 109 S.Ct. 2969 (1989).

39. Carol Kohfeld and John Sprague, "Demography, Police Behavior, and Deterrence," *Criminology* 28:111–36 (1990).

40. Steven Klepper and Daniel Nagin, "The Deterrent Effect of Perceived Certainty and Severity of Punishment Revisited," *Criminology* 27:721–46 (1989).

41. See, generally, Raymond Paternoster, "The Deterrent Effect of Perceived Certainty and Severity of Punishment: A Review of the Evidence and Issues," *Justice Quarterly* 42:173–217 (1987); idem, "Absolute and Restrictive Deterrence in a Panel of Youth: Explaining the Onset, Persistence/Desistance, and Frequency of Delinquent Offending," *Social Problems* 36:289–307 (1989).

42. Eric Jensen and Linda Metsger, "A Test of the Deterrent Effect of Legislative Waiver on Violent Juvenile Crime," *Crime and Delinquency* 40:96–104 (1994).

43. Wanda Foglia, "Perceptual Deterrence and the Mediating Effect of Internalized Norms among Inner-City Teenagers," *Journal of Research in Crime and Delinquency* 34:414–42 (1997); Donald Green, "Measures of Illegal Behavior in Individual-Level Deterrence Research," *Journal of Research in Crime and Delinquency* 26:253–75 (1989); Charles Tittle, *Sanctions and Social Deviance: The Question of Deterrence* (New York: Praeger, 1980).

44. Bureau of Justice Statistics, *Prisoners and Drugs* (Washington, DC: U.S. Government Printing Office, 1983); idem, *Prisoners and Alcohol* (Washington, DC: U.S. Government Printing Office, 1983).

45. Maynard Erickson and Jack Gibbs, "Punishment, Deterrence, and Juvenile Justice," in D. Shichor and D. Kelly, eds., *Critical Issues in Juvenile Justice* (Lexington, MA: Lexington Books, 1980), pp. 183–202.

46. Christina Dejong, "Survival Analysis and Specific Deterrence: Integrating Theoretical and Empirical Models of Recidivism," *Criminology* 35:561–76 (1997).

47. Paul Tracy and Kimberly Kempf-Leonard, *Continuity and Discontinuity in Criminal Careers* (New York: Plenum, 1996).

48. Pamela Lattimore, Christy Visher, and Richard Linster, "Predicting Rearrest for Violence among Serious Youthful Offenders," *Journal of Research in Crime and Delinquency* 32:54–83 (1995).

49. David Altschuler, "Juveniles and Violence: Is There an Epidemic and What Can Be Done?" Paper presented at the American Society of Criminology Meeting, Boston, November 1995; Charles Murray and Louis B. Cox, *Beyond Probation* (Beverly Hills, CA: Sage, 1979).

50. Marcus Felson, "Routine Activities and Crime Prevention, in National Council for Crime Prevention," *Studies on Crime and Crime Prevention, Annual Review,* vol. 1 (Stockholm: Scandinavian University Press, 1992), pp. 30–34.

51. Barry Webb, "Steering Column Locks and Motor Vehicle Theft: Evaluations for Three Countries," in Ronald Clarke, ed., *Crime Prevention Studies* (Monsey, NY: Criminal Justice Press, 1994), pp. 71–89.

52. Kenneth Novak, Jennifer Hartman, Alexander Holsinger, and Michael Turner, "The Effects of Aggressive Policing of Disorder on Serious Crime," *Policing* 22:171–90 (1999).

53. Lawrence Sherman, "Police Crackdowns: Initial and Residual Deterrence," in Michael Tonry and Norval Morris, eds., *Crime and Justice: A Review of Research,* vol. 12 (Chicago: University of Chicago Press, 1990), pp. 1–48.

54. Anthony Braga, David Weisburd, Elin Waring, Lorraine Green Mazerolle, William Spelman, Francis Gajewski, "Problem-Oriented Policing in Violent Crime Places: A Randomized Controlled Experiment," *Criminology* 39 (1999): 541–8055.

55. Eric Fritsch, Tory Caeti, and Robert Taylor, "Gang Suppression through Saturation Patrol, Aggressive Curfew, and Truancy Enforcement: A Quasi-Experimental Test of the Dallas Anti-Gang Initiative," *Crime and Delinquency* 45 (1999): 122–39.

56. Taken from the famous title of an article by Walter Reckless, Simon Dinitz, and Ellen Murray, "The Good Boy in a High Delinquency Area," *Journal of Criminal Law, Criminology, and Police Science* 48 (1957) pp. 18–26.

57. Massey, Krohn, and Bonati, "Property Crime and the Routine Activities of Individuals."

58. David Shantz, "Conflict, Aggression, and Peer Status: An Observational Study," *Child Development* 57:1322–32 (1986).

59. For an excellent review of Lombroso's work, as well as that of other well-known theorists, see Randy Martin, Robert Mutchnick, and W. Timothy Austin, *Criminological Thought, Pioneers Past and Present* (New York: Macmillan, 1990).

60. Marvin Wolfgang, "Cesare Lombroso," in Herman Mannheim, ed., *Pioneers in Criminology* (Montclair, NJ: Patterson Smith, 1970), pp. 232–71.

61. Gina Lombroso-Ferrero, *Criminal Man According to the Classification of Cesare Lombroso* (1911; reprint, Montclair, NJ: Patterson Smith, 1972), p. 7.

62. Edwin Driver, "Charles Buckman Goring," in Herman Mannheim, ed., *Pioneers in Criminology* (Montclair, NJ: Patterson Smith, 1970), pp. 429–42.

63. See, generally, Thorsten Sellin, "Enrico Ferri," in Herman Mannheim, ed., *Pioneers in Criminology* (Montclair, NJ: Patterson Smith, 1970), pp. 361–84.

64. Driver, "Charles Buckman Goring," pp. 434–35.

65. Ibid., p. 440.

66. See Richard Dugdale, *The Jukes* (New York: Putnam, 1910); Arthur Estabrook, *The Jukes in 1915* (Washington, DC: Carnegie Institute of Washington, 1916).

67. Ernst Kretschmer, *Physique and Character,* trans. W. J. H. Spratt (London: Kegan Paul, 1925).

68. William Sheldon, *Varieties of Delinquent Youth* (New York: Harper, 1949).

69. For a review of Sheldon's legacy, see C. Peter Herman, "The Shape of Man," *Contemporary Psychology* 37:525–30 (1992).

70. Nicole Hahn Rafter, "Criminal Anthropology in the United States," *Criminology* 30:525–47 (1992).

71. B.R. McCandless, W. S. Persons, and A. Roberts, "Perceived Opportunity, Delinquency, Race, and Body Build among Delinquent Youth," *Journal of Consulting and Clinical Psychology* 38:281–83 (1972).

72. Edmond O. Wilson, *Sociobiology: The New Synthesis* (Cambridge: Harvard University Press, 1975).

73. For a general review, see John Archer, "Human Sociobiology: Basic Concepts and Limitations," *Journal of Social Issues* 47:11–26 (1991).

74. Arthur Caplan, *The Sociobiology Debate: Readings on Ethical and Scientific Issues* (New York: Harper & Row, 1978).

75. See C. Ray Jeffrey, "Criminology as an Interdisciplinary Behavioral Science," *Criminology* 16:149–67 (1978).

76. Dalton Conley and Neil Bennett, "Is Biology Destiny? Birth Weight and Life Chances," *American Sociological Review* 654:458–67 (2000).

77. Diana Fishbein, "Selected Studies on the Biology of Crime," in John Conklin, ed., *New Perspectives in Criminology* (Needham Heights, MA: Allyn & Bacon, 1996), pp. 26–38.

78. Anthony Walsh and Lee Ellis, "Shoring Up the Big Three: Improving Criminological Theories with Biosocial Concepts." Paper presented at the Annual Society of Criminology Meeting, San Diego, November 1997, p. 15.

79. Terrie Moffitt, "Adolescence-Limited and Life Course–Persistent Antisocial Behavior: A Developmental Taxonomy," *Psychological Review* 100:674–701 (1993).

80. For a thorough review of the biosocial perspective, see Diana Fishbein, "Biological Perspectives in Criminology," *Criminology* 28:27–72 (1990).

81. See, generally, Adrian Raine, *The Psychopathology of Crime* (San Diego: Academic Press, 1993); see also Leonard Hippchen, *The Ecologic-Biochemical Approaches to Treatment of Delinquents and Criminals* (New York: Van Nostrand Reinhold, 1978).

82. Paul Marshall, "Allergy and Depression: A Neurochemical Threshold Model of the Relation between the Illnesses," *Psychological Bulletin* 113:23–43 (1993); Elizabeth McNeal and Peter Cimbolic, "Antidepressants and Biochemical Theories of Depression," *Psychological Bulletin* 99:361–74 (1986); for an opposing view, see "Adverse Reactions to Food in Young Children," *Nutrition Reviews* 46:120–21 (1988).

83. Ibid.

84. Raine, *The Psychopathology of Crime,* p. 212.

85. Deborah Denno, "Human Biology and Criminal Responsibility: Free Will or Free Ride?" *University of Pennsylvania Law Review* 137:615–71 (1988).

86. Leonard Hippchen, "Some Possible Biochemical Aspects of Criminal Behavior," *Journal of Behavioral Ecology* 2:1–6 (1981); Sarnoff Mednick and Jan Volavka, "Biology and Crime," in N. Morris and M. Tonry, eds., *Crime and Justice,* vol. 2 (Chicago: University of Chicago Press, 1980), pp. 85–159.

87. Stephen Schoenthaler, "Malnutrition and Maladaptive Behavior: Two Correlational Analyses and a Double-Blind Placebo-Controlled Challenge in Five States," in W. B. Essman, ed., *Nutrients and Brain Function* (New York: Karger, 1987); Alexander Schauss and C. Simonsen, "A Critical Analysis of the Diets of Chronic Juvenile Offenders, Part I," *Journal of Orthomolecular Psychiatry* 8:149–57 (1979).

88. Diana Fishbein, "Neuropsychological Function, Drug Abuse, and Violence, a Conceptual Framework," *Criminal Justice and Behavior* 27:139–59 (2000).

89. Stephen Schoenthaler, *Intelligence, Academic Performance, and Brain Function* (California State University Stanislaus, 2000); see also S. Schoenthaler and I. Bier, "The Effect of Vitamin-Mineral Supplementation on Juvenile Delinquency among American Schoolchildren: A Randomized Double-Blind Placebo-Controlled Trial," *The Journal of Alternative and Complementary Medicine: Research on Paradigm, Practice, and Policy* 6:7–18 (2000).

90. Marcel Kinsbourne, "Sugar and the Hyperactive Child," *The New England Journal of Medicine* 330:355–56 (1994); Richard Milich and William Pelham, "Effects of Sugar Ingestion on the Classroom and Playgroup Behavior of Attention Deficit Disordered Boys," *Journal of Counseling and Clinical Psychology* 54:714–18 (1986).

91. Mark Wolraich, Scott Lindgren, Phyllis Stumbo, Lewis Stegink, Mark Appelbaum, and Mary Kiritsy, "Effects of Diets High in Sucrose or Aspartame on the Behavior and Cognitive Performance of Children," *The New England Journal of Medicine* 330:303–306 (1994).

92. Christy Miller Buchanan, Jacquelynne Eccles, and Jill Becker, "Are Adolescents the Victims of Raging Hormones? Evidence for Activational Effects of Hormones on Moods and Behavior at Adolescence," *Psychological Bulletin* 111:62–107 (1992).

93. Diana Fishbein, "Selected Studies on the Biology of Antisocial Behavior."

94. Diana Fishbein, David Lozovsky, and Jerome Jaffe, "Impulsivity, Aggression, and Neuroendocrine Responses to Serotonergic Stimulation in Substance Abusers." Paper presented at the American Society of Criminology Meeting, Reno, Nevada, November 1989.

95. Kytja Voeller, "Right-Hemisphere Deficit Syndrome in Children," *American Journal of Psychiatry* 143:1004–9 (1986).

96. Terrie Moffitt, "Adolescence-Limited and Life Course–Persistent Antisocial Behavior: A Developmental Taxonomy," *Psychological Review* 100:674–701 (1993).

97. Leila Beckwith and Arthur Parmelee, "EEG Patterns of Preterm Infants, Home Environment, and Later IQ," *Child Development* 57:777–89 (1986).

98. Adrian Raine, Patricia Brennan, Brigitte Mednick, and Sarnoff Mednick, "High Rates of Violence, Crime, Academic Problems, and Behavioral Problems in Males with Both Early Neuromotor Deficits and Unstable Family Environments," *Archives of General Psychiatry* 53:544–49 (1966).

99. Stephen Tibbetts, "Low Birth Weight, Disadvantaged Environment and Early Onset: A Test of Moffitt's Interactional Hypothesis." Paper presented at the American Society of Criminology Meeting, Boston, November 1995.

100. Dorothy Otnow Lewis, Jonathan Pincus, Marilyn Feldman, Lori Jackson, and Barbara Bard, "Psychiatric, Neurological, and Psychoeducational Characteristics of 15 Death Row Inmates in the United States," *American Journal of Psychiatry* 143:838–45 (1986).

101. See, generally, R. R. Monroe, *Brain Dysfunction in Aggressive Criminals* (Lexington, MA: D.C. Heath, 1978).

102. Adrian Raine et al., "Interhemispheric Transfer in Schizophrenics, Depressives, and Normals with Schizoid Tendencies," *Journal of Abnormal Psychology* 98:35–41 (1989).

103. D. Williams, "Neural Factors Related to Habitual Aggression—Consideration of Differences between Habitual Aggressives and Others Who Have Committed Crimes of Violence," *Brain* 92:503–20 (1969).

104. Charlotte Johnson and William Pelham, "Teacher Ratings Predict Peer Ratings of Aggression at Three-Year Follow-Up in Boys with Attention Deficit Disorder with Hyperactivity," *Journal of Consulting and Clinical Psychology* 54:571–72 (1987).

105. Cited in Charles Post, "The Link between Learning Disabilities and Juvenile Delinquency: Cause, Effect, and 'Present Solutions'," *Juvenile and Family Court Journal* 31:59 (1981).

106. For a general review, see Concetta Culliver, "Juvenile Delinquency and Learning Disability: Any Link?" Paper presented at the Academy of Criminal Justice Sciences, San Francisco, April 1988.

107. Joel Zimmerman, William Rich, Ingo Keilitz, and Paul Broder, "Some Observations on the Link between Learning Disabilities and Juvenile Delinquency," *Journal of Criminal Justice* 9:9–17 (1981); J. W. Podboy and W. A. Mallory, "The Diagnosis of Specific Learning Disabilities in a Juvenile Delinquent Population," *Juvenile and Family Court Journal* 30:11–13 (1978).

108. Charles Murray, *The Link between Learning Disabilities and Juvenile Delinquency: A Current Theory and Knowledge* (Washington, DC: U.S. Government Printing Office, 1976).

109. Terrie Moffitt, "The Neuropsychology of Conduct Disorder," mimeo (University of Wisconsin-Madison, 1992).

110. Ibid.

111. National Center for Addiction and Substance Abuse (CASA) at Columbia University, *Substance Abuse and Learning Disabilities: Peas in a Pod or Apples and Oranges?* (New York: author, 2000).

112. Elizabeth Kandel and Sarnoff Mednick, "Perinatal Complications Predict Violent Offending," *Criminology* 29:519–30 (1991).

113. Jack Katz, *Seduction of Crime: Moral and Sensual Attractions of Doing Evil* (New York: Basic Books, 1988), pp. 12–15.

114. Lee Ellis, "Arousal Theory and the Religiosity-Criminality Relationship," in Peter Cordella and Larry Siegel, eds., *Contemporary Criminological Theory* (Boston: Northeastern University, 1996), pp. 65–84.

115. Adrian Raine, Peter Venables, and Sarnoff Mednick, "Low Resting Heart Rate at Age 3 Years Predisposes to Aggression at Age 11 Years: Evidence from the Mauritius Child Health Project," *Journal of the American Academy of Adolescent Psychiatry* 36:1457–64 (1997).

116. For a review, see Lisabeth Fisher DiLalla and Irving Gottesman, "Biological and Genetic Contributors to Violence—Widom's Untold Tale," *Psychological Bulletin* 109:125–29 (1991).

117. L. Erlenmeyer-Kimling, Robert Golden, and Barbara Cornblatt, "A Taxometric Analysis of Cognitive and Neuromotor Variables in Children at Risk for Schizophrenia," *Journal of Abnormal Psychology* 98:203–8 (1989).

118. A. A. Sandberg, G. F. Koeph, T. Ishiara, and T. S. Hauschka, "An XYY Human Male," *Lancet* 262:448–49 (1961); T. R. Sarbin and L. E. Miller, "Demonism Revisited: The XYY Chromosome Anomaly," *Issues in Criminology* 5:195–207 (1970).

119. David Rowe, Joseph Rogers, and Sylvia Meseck-Bushey, "Sibling Delinquency and the Family Environment: Shared and Unshared Influences," *Child Development* 63:59–67 (1992).

120. David Rowe, "Sibling Interaction and Self-Reported Delinquent Behavior: A Study of 265 Twin Pairs," *Criminology* 23:223–40 (1985); Nancy Segal, "Monozygotic and Dizygotic

Twins: A Comparative Analysis of Mental Ability Profiles," *Child Development* 56:1051–1058 (1985).

121. Mednick and Volavka, "Biology and Crime," in Norval Morris and Michael Tonry, eds., *Crime and Justice*, vol. 1 (Chicago; University of Chicago Press, 1980), pp. 85–159; Lee Ellis, "Genetics and Criminal Behavior," *Criminology* 10:43–66 (1982); Karl O. Christiansen, "A Preliminary Study of Criminality among Twins," in S. A. Mednick and Karl O. Christiansen, eds., *The Biosocial Bases of Criminal Behavior* (New York: Gardner, 1977).

122. T. J. Bouchard, D. T. Lykken, D. T. McGue, N. L. Segal, and A. Tellegen, "Sources of Human Psychological Differences: The Minnesota Study of Twins Reared Apart," *Science* 250:223–28 (1990).

123. D. T. Lykken, M. McGue, A. Tellegen, and T. J. Bouchard Jr., "Emergenesis, Genetic Traits that May Not Run in Families," *American Psychologist* 47:1565–77 (1992).

124. Remi Cadoret, Colleen Cain, and Raymond Crowe, "Evidence for a Gene–Environment Interaction in the Development of Adolescent Antisocial Behavior," *Behavior Genetics* 13:301–10 (1983).

125. David Rowe, *The Limits of Family Influence: Genes, Experiences, and Behavior* (New York: Guilford, 1995); Remi Cadoret, Colleen Cain, and Raymond Crowe, "Evidence for a Gene–Environment Interaction in the Development of Adolescent Antisocial Behavior," *Behavior Genetics* 13:301–10 (1983).

126. Bernard Hutchings and Sarnoff Mednick, "Criminality in Adoptees and Their Adoptive and Biological Parents: A Pilot Study," in S. A. Mednick and Karl O. Christiansen, eds., *Biosocial Bases of Criminal Behavior* (New York: Gardner, 1977).

127. For similar findings, see William Gabrielli and Sarnoff Mednick, "Urban Environment, Genetics, and Crime," *Criminology* 22:645–53 (1984).

128. Jody Alberts-Corush, Philip Firestone, and John Goodman, "Attention and Impulsivity Characteristics of the Biological and Adoptive Parents of Hyperactive and Normal Control Children," *American Journal of Orthopsychiatry* 56:413–23 (1986).

129. Wilson and Hernstein, *Crime and Human Nature*, p. 131.

130. Walters, "A Meta-Analysis of the Gene–Crime Relationship."

131. Ibid., p. 108.

132. For a thorough review of this issue, see David Brandt and S. Jack Zlotnick, *The Psychology and Treatment of the Youthful Offender* (Springfield, IL: Charles C Thomas, 1988).

133. Spencer Rathus, *Psychology* (New York: Holt, Rinehart & Winston, 1996), pp. 11–21.

134. See, generally, Sigmund Freud, *An Outline of Psychoanalysis*, trans. James Strachey (New York: Norton, 1963).

135. Seymour Halleck, *Psychiatry and the Dilemmas of Crime* (Berkeley: University of California Press, 1971).

136. See, generally, Erik Erikson, *Identity, Youth, and Crisis* (New York: Norton, 1968).

137. David Abrahamsen, *Crime and the Human Mind* (New York: Columbia University Press, 1944), p. 137.

138. See, generally, Fritz Redl and Hans Toch, "The Psychoanalytic Perspective," in Hans Toch, ed., *Psychology of Crime and Criminal Justice* (New York: Holt, Rinehart & Winston, 1979), pp. 193–95.

139. August Aichorn, *Wayward Youth* (New York: Viking Press, 1935).

140. Halleck, *Psychiatry and the Dilemmas of Crime*.

141. James Sorrells, "Kids Who Kill," *Crime and Delinquency* 23:312–20 (1977).

142. Richard Rosner et al., "Adolescents Accused of Murder and Manslaughter: A Five-Year Descriptive Study," *Bulletin of the American Academy of Psychiatry and the Law* 7:342–51 (1979).

143. Brandt and Zlotnick, *The Psychology and Treatment of the Youthful Offender*, pp. 72–73.

144. See Albert Bandura and Frances Menlove, "Factors Determining Vicarious Extinction of Avoidance Behavior through Symbolic Modeling," *Journal of Personality and Social Psychology* 8:99–108 (1965); and Albert Bandura and Richard Walters, *Social Learning and Personality Development* (New York: Holt, Rinehart & Winston, 1963).

145. David Perry, Louise Perry, and Paul Rasmussen, "Cognitive Social Learning Mediators of Aggression," *Child Development* 57:700–11 (1986).

146. Bonnie Carlson, "Children's Beliefs about Punishment," *American Journal of Orthopsychiatry* 56:308–312 (1986).

147. Albert Bandura and Richard Walters, *Adolescent Aggression* (New York: Ronald Press, 1959), p. 32.

148. Joyce Sprafkin, Kenneth Gadow, and Monique Dussault, "Reality Perceptions of Television: A Preliminary Comparison of Emotionally Disturbed and Nonhandicapped Children," *American Journal of Orthopsychiatry* 56:147–52 (1986).

149. Steven Messner, "Television Violence and Violent Crime: An Aggregate Analysis," *Social Problems* 33:218–35 (1986).

150. See, generally, Jean Piaget, *The Moral Judgement of the Child* (London: Kegan Paul, 1932).

151. Lawrence Kohlberg, *Stages in the Development of Moral Thought and Action* (New York: Holt, Rinehart & Winston, 1969).

152. L. Kohlberg, K. Kauffman, P. Scharf, and J. Hickey, *The Just Community Approach in Corrections: A Manual* (Niantic, CN: Connecticut Department of Corrections, 1973).

153. Scott Henggeler, *Delinquency in Adolescence* (Newbury Park, CA: Sage, 1989), p. 26.

154. K. A. Dodge, "A Social Information Processing Model of Social Competence in Children," in M. Perlmutter, ed., *Minnesota Symposium in Child Psychology*, vol. 18 (Hillsdale, NJ: Erlbaum, 1986), pp. 77–125.

155. Adrian Raine, Peter Venables, and Mark Williams, "Better Autonomic Conditioning and Faster Electrodermal Half-Recovery Time at Age 15 Years as Possible Protective Factors against Crime at Age 29 Years," *Developmental Psychology* 32:624–30 (1996).

156. L. Huesman and L. Eron, "Individual Differences and the Trait of Aggression," *European Journal of Personality* 3:95–106 (1989).

157. J. E. Lochman, "Self and Peer Perceptions and Attributional Biases of Aggressive and Nonaggressive Boys in Dyadic Interactions," *Journal of Consulting and Clinical Psychology* 55:404–410 (1987).

158. Kathleen Cirillo, B. E. Pruitt, Brian Colwell, Paul M. Kingery, Robert S. Hurley, and Danny Ballard, "School Violence: Prevalence and Intervention Strategies for At-Risk Adolescents," *Adolescence* 33:319–31 (1998).

159. Leilani Greening, "Adolescent Stealers' and Nonstealers' Social Problem-Solving Skills," *Adolescence* 32:51–56 (1997).

160. Graeme Newman, *Understanding Violence* (New York: Lippincott, 1979) pp. 145–46.

161. Cirillo et al., "School Violence: Prevalence and Intervention Strategies for At-Risk Adolescents," *Adolescence* 33:319–31 (1998).

162. See, generally, G. Patterson, J. Reid, and T. Dishion, *Antisocial Boys* (Eugene, OR: Castalia, 1992).

163. See, generally, Walter Mischel, *Introduction to Personality*, 4th ed. (New York: Holt, Rinehart & Winston, 1986).

164. D.A. Andrews and J. Stephen Wormith, "Personality and Crime: Knowledge and Construction in Criminology," *Justice Quarterly* 6:289–310 (1989); Donald Gibbons, "Comment—Personality and Crime: Non-Issues, Real Issues, and a Theory and Research Agenda," *Justice Quarterly* 6:311–24 (1989).

165. Sheldon Glueck and Eleanor Glueck, *Unraveling Juvenile Delinquency* (Cambridge: Harvard University Press, 1950).

166. See, generally, Hans Eysenck, *Personality and Crime* (London: Routledge and Kegan Paul, 1977).

167. David Farrington, "Psychobiological Factors in the Explanation and Reduction of Delinquency," *Today's Delinquent* 7:37–51 (1988).

168. Edelyn Verona and Joyce Carbonell, "Female Violence and Personality," *Criminal Justice and Behavior* 27 (2000): 176–195.

169. Laurie Frost, Terrie Moffitt, and Rob McGee, "Neuropsychological Correlates of Psychopathology in an Unselected Cohort of Young Adolescents," *Journal of Abnormal Psychology* 98:307–313 (1989).

170. Hans Eysenck and M. W. Eysenck, *Personality and Individual Differences* (New York: Plenum, 1985).

171. Linda Mealey, "The Sociobiology of Sociopathy: An Integrated Evolutionary Model," *Behavioral and Brain Sciences* 18:523–40 (1995).

172. Lewis Yablonsky, *The Violent Gang* (Baltimore: Penguin, 1971), pp. 195–205.

173. Helene Raskin White, Erich Labouvie, and Marsha Bates, "The Relationship between Sensation Seeking and Delinquency: A Longitudinal Analysis," *Journal of Research in Crime and Delinquency* 22:197–211 (1985).

174. Rathus, *Psychology*, p. 452.

175. See, for example, R. Starke Hathaway and Elio Monachesi, "The M.M.P.I. in the Study of Juvenile Delinquents," in A. M. Rose, ed., *Mental Health and Mental Disorder* (London: Routledge, 1956).

176. R. Starke Hathaway and Elio Monachesi, *Analyzing and Predicting Juvenile Delinquency with the M.M.P.I.* (Minneapolis: University of Minnesota Press, 1953).

177. Karl Schuessler and Donald Cressey, "Personality Characteristics of Criminals," *American Journal of Sociology* 55:476–84 (1950); Gordon Waldo and Simon Dinitz, "Personality Attributes of the Criminal: An Analysis of Research Studies, 1950–1965," *Journal of Research in Crime and Delinquency* 4:185–201 (1967); David Tennenbaum, "Research Studies of Personality and Criminality," *Journal of Criminal Justice* 5:1–19 (1977).

178. Donald Calsyn, Douglass Roszell, and Edmund Chaney, "Validation of MMPI Profile Subtypes among Opioid Addicts Who Are Beginning Methadone Maintenance Treatment," *Journal of Clinical Psychology* 45:991–99 (1989).

179. L. M. Terman, "Research on the Diagnosis of Predelinquent Tendencies," *Journal of Delinquency* 9:124–30 (1925); L. M. Terman, *Measurement of Intelligence* (Boston: Houghton-Mifflin, 1916); for example, see M. G. Caldwell, "The Intelligence of Delinquent Boys Committed to Wisconsin Industrial School," *Journal of Criminal Law and Criminology* 20:421–28 (1929); and C. Murcheson, *Criminal Intelligence* (Worcester, MA: Clark University, 1926), pp. 41–44.

180. Henry Goddard, *Efficiency and Levels of Intelligence* (Princeton, NJ: Princeton University Press, 1920).

181. William Healy and Augusta Bronner, *Delinquency and Criminals: Their Making and Unmaking* (New York: Macmillan, 1926).

182. Joseph Lee Rogers, H. Harrington Cleveland, Edwin van den Oord, and David Rowe, "Resolving the Debate Over Birth Order, Family Size, and Intelligence," *American Psychologist* 55:599–612 (2000).

183. Kenneth Eels, *Intelligence and Cultural Differences* (Chicago: University of Chicago Press, 1951), p. 181.

184. Sorel Cahahn and Nora Cohen, "Age versus Schooling Effects on Intelligence Development," *Child Development* 60:1239–49 (1989).

185. Robert McCall and Michael Carriger, "A Meta-Analysis of Infant Habituation and Recognition Memory Performance as Predictors of Later IQ," *Child Development* 64:57–79 (1993).

186. Edwin Sutherland, "Mental Deficiency and Crime," in Kimball Young, ed., *Social Attitudes* (New York: Henry Holt, 1973), Ch. 15.

187. H. D. Day, J. M. Franklin, and D. D. Marshall, "Predictors of Aggression in Hospitalized Adolescents," *Journal of Psychology* 132:427–35 (1998); Scott Menard and Barbara Morse, "A Structuralist Critique of the IQ–Delinquency Hypothesis: Theory and Evidence," *American Journal of Sociology* 89:1347–78 (1984).

188. Travis Hirschi and Michael Hindelang, "Intelligence and Delinquency: A Revisionist Review," *American Sociological Review* 42:471–586 (1977).

189. Terrie Moffitt and Phil Silva, "IQ and Delinquency: A Direct Test of the Differential Detection Hypothesis," *Journal of Abnormal Psychology* 97:1–4 (1988); E. Kandel, S. Mednick, L. Sorenson-Kirkegaard, B. Hutchings, J. Knop, R. Rosenberg, and F. Schulsinger, "IQ as a Protective Factor for Subjects at a High Risk for Antisocial Behavior," *Journal of Consulting and Clinical Psychology* 56:224–26 (1988); Christine Ward and Richard McFall, "Further Validation of the Problem Inventory for Adolescent Girls: Comparing Caucasian and Black Delinquents and Nondelinquents," *Journal of Consulting and Clinical Psychology* 54:732–33 (1986).

190. Terri Moffitt, William Gabrielli, Sarnoff Mednick, and Fini Schulsinger, "Socioeconomic Status, IQ, and Delinquency," *Journal of Abnormal Psychology* 90:152–56 (1981); for a similar finding, see L. Hubble and M. Groff, "Magnitude and Direction of WISC-R Verbal Performance IQ Discrepancies among Adjudicated Male Delinquents," *Journal of Youth and Adolescence* 10:179–83 (1981).

191. Jennifer White, Terrie Moffitt, and Phil Silva, "A Prospective Replication of the Protective Effects of IQ in Subjects at High Risk for Juvenile Delinquency," *Journal of Consulting and Clinical Psychology* 37:719–24 (1989).

192. Donald Lynam, Terrie Moffitt, and Magda Stouthamer-Loeber, "Explaining the Relations between IQ and Delinquency: Class, Race, Test Motivation, School Failure or Self-Control," *Journal of Abnormal Psychology* 102:187–96 (1993).

193. David Farrington, "Juvenile Delinquency," in John C. Coleman, ed., *The School Years* (London: Routledge, 1992), p. 137.

194. Glenn Walters and Thomas White, "Heredity and Crime: Bad Genes or Bad Research," *Justice Quarterly* 27:455–85 (1989), p. 478.

195. Ellis, "Genetics and Criminal Behavior," *Criminology* 10:43–66 (1982), p. 58.

196. Sheryl Ellis, "It Does Take a Village: A Youth Violence Program in Kincheloe, Michigan Galvanizes the Community," *Corrections Today* 60:100–103 (1998).

197. Joan McCord and William McCord, "A Follow-Up Report on the Cambridge-Somerville Youth Study," *Annals* 322:89–98 (1959).

198. Edwin Schur, *Radical Nonintervention: Rethinking the Delinquency Problem* (Englewood Cliffs, NJ: Prentice-Hall, 1973).

Chapter 4

1. Steven Messner and Richard Rosenfeld, *Crime and the American Dream* (Belmont, CA: Wadsworth, 1994), p. 11.

2. See, generally, Stephen Cernkovich and Peggy Giordano, "Family Relationships and Delinquency," *Criminology* 25:295–321 (1987); Paul Howes and Howard Markman, "Marital Quality and Child Functioning: A Longitudinal Investigation," *Child Development* 60:1044–1051 (1989).

3. Gary LaFree, *Losing Legitimacy: Street Crime and the Decline of Social Institutions in America* (Boulder, CO: Westview, 1998).

4. Emilie Andersen Allan and Darrell Steffensmeier, "Youth, Underemployment, and Property Crime: Differential Effects of Job Availability and Job Quality on Juvenile and Young Adult Arrest Rates," *American Sociological Review* 54: 107–23 (1989).

5. Edwin Lemert, *Human Deviance, Social Problems and Social Control* (Englewood Cliffs, NJ: Prentice-Hall, 1967).

6. Julian Chow and Claudia Coulton, "Was There a Social Transformation of Urban Neighborhoods in the 1980s?" *Urban Studies* 35:135–75 (1998).

7. Oscar Lewis, "The Culture of Poverty," *Scientific American* 215:19–25 (1966).

8. Laura G. De Haan and Shelley MacDermid, "The Relationship of Individual and Family Factors to the Psychological Well-Being of Junior High School Students Living in Urban Poverty," *Adolescence* 33:73–90 (1998).

9. Rodrick Wallace, "Expanding Coupled Shock Fronts of Urban Decay and Criminal Behavior: How U.S. Cities Are Becoming 'Hollowed Out'," *Journal of Quantitative Criminology* 7:333–55 (1991).

10. Ken Auletta, *The Under Class* (New York: Random House, 1982).

11. William Julius Wilson, *The Truly Disadvantaged* (Chicago: University of Chicago Press, 1987).

12. Richard McGahey, "Economic Conditions, Organization, and Urban Crime," in Albert Reiss and Michael Tonry, eds., *Communities and Crime* (Chicago: University of Chicago Press, 1986), pp. 231–70.

13. Jeanne Brooks-Gunn and Greg J. Duncan, "The Effects of Poverty on Children," *The Future of Children* 7:34–39 (1997).

14. Greg Duncan, W. Jean Yeung, Jeanne Brooks-Gunn, and Judith Smith, "How Much Does Childhood Poverty Affect the Life Chances of Children?" *American Sociological Review* 63:406–423 (1998).

15. Ibid., p. 29.

16. Brooks-Gunn and Duncan, "The Effects of Poverty on Children."

17. G.R. Patterson, L. Crosby, and S. Vuchnich, "Predicting Risk for Early Police Arrest," *Journal of Quantitative Criminology* 8:335–53 (1992).

18. Ibid., p. 52.

19. Frederick Thrasher, *The Gang* (Chicago: University of Chicago Press, 1927).

20. Robert Bursik and Harold Grasmick, "The Multiple Layers of Social Disorganization." Paper presented at the annual meeting of the American Society of Criminology, New Orleans, November 1992; Robert Bursik and Harold Grasmick, "Longitudinal Neighborhood Profiles in Delinquency: The Decomposition of Change," *Journal of Quantitative Criminology* 8:247–56 (1992).

21. Clifford R. Shaw and Henry D. McKay, *Juvenile Delinquency and Urban Areas,* rev. ed. (Chicago: University of Chicago Press, 1972).

22. Elliott et al., "The Effects of Neighborhood Disadvantage on Adolescent Development," p. 414.

23. Robert Bursik and Harold Grasmick, "Economic Deprivation and Neighborhood Crime Rates, 1960–1980," *Law and Society Review* 27:263–78 (1993).

24. Robert Sampson and W. Byron Groves, "Community Structure and Crime: Testing Social Disorganization Theory," *American Journal of Sociology* 94:774–802 (1989); Denise Gottfredson, Richard McNeill, and Gary Gottfredson, "Social Area Influences on Delinquency: A Multilevel Analysis," *Journal of Research in Crime and Delinquency* 28: 197–206 (1991).

25. Ruth Peterson, Lauren Krivo, and Mark Harris, "Disadvantage and Neighborhood Violent Crime: Do Local Institutions Matter?" *Journal of Research in Crime and Delinquency* 37:31–63 (2000).

26. D. Wayne Osgood and Jeff Chambers, "Social Disorganization Outside the Metropolis: An Analysis of Rural Youth Violence," *Criminology* 38:81–117 (2000).

27. Beverly Stiles, Xiaoru Liu, and Howard Kaplan, "Relative Deprivation and Deviant Adaptations: The Mediating Effects of Negative Self-Feelings," *Journal of Research in Crime and Delinquency* 37:64–90 (2000).

28. Judith Blau and Peter Blau, "The Cost of Inequality: Metropolitan Structure and Violent Crime," *American Sociological Review* 147:114–29 (1982).

29. Karen Parker and Matthew Pruitt, "Poverty, Poverty Concentration, and Homicide," *Social Science Quarterly* 81:555–82 (2000).

30. Margo Wilson and Martin Daly, "Life Expectancy, Economic Inequality, Homicide, and Reproductive Timing in Chicago Neighbourhoods," *British Journal of Medicine* 314:1271–74 (1997).

31. Ora Simcha-Fagan and Joseph Schwartz, "Neighborhood and Delinquency: An Assessment of Contextual Effects," *Criminology* 24:667–703 (1986).

32. Leo Scheurman and Solomon Kobrin, "Community Careers in Crime," in Albert Reiss and Michael Tonry, eds., *Communities and Crime* (Chicago: University of Chicago Press, 1986), pp. 67–100.

33. Ibid., p. 96.

34. Ellen Kurtz, Barbara Koons, and Ralph Taylor, "Land Use, Physical Deterioration, Resident-Based Control, and Calls for Service on Urban Streetblocks," *Justice Quarterly* 15:121–49 (1998).

35. Janet Heitgerd and Robert Bursik Jr., "Extracommunity Dynamics and the Ecology of Delinquency," *American Journal of Sociology* 92:775–87 (1987).

36. Pamela Wilcox Rountree and Kenneth Land, "Burglary Victimization, Perceptions of Crime Risk, and Routine Activities: A Multilevel Analysis across Seattle Neighborhoods and Census Tracts," *Journal of Research in Crime and Delinquency* 33:147–80 (1996).

37. Randy LaGrange, Kenneth Ferraro, and Michael Supancic, "Perceived Risk and Fear of Crime: Role of Social and Physical Incivilities," *Journal of Research in Crime and Delinquency* 29:311–34 (1992).

38. See, generally, Wesley Skogan, "Fear of Crime and Neighborhood Change," in Albert Reiss and Michael Tonry, eds., *Communities and Crime* (Chicago: University of Chicago Press, 1986), pp. 191–232; Stephanie Greenberg, "Fear and Its Relationship to Crime, Neighborhood Deterioration, and Informal Social Control," in James Byrne and Robert Sampson, eds., *The Social Ecology of Crime* (New York: Springer-Verlag, 1985), pp. 47–62.

39. Jeffery Will and John McGrath, "Crime, Neighborhood Perceptions, and the Underclass: The Relationship between Fear of Crime and Class Position," *Journal of Criminal Justice* 23:163–76 (1995).

40. Wilson and Daly, "Life Expectancy, Economic Inequality, Homicide, and Reproductive Timing in Chicago Neighborhoods."

41. Catherine Ross, "Fear of Victimization and Health," *Journal of Quantitative Criminology* 9:159–65 (1993).

42. Donald Black, "Social Control as a Dependent Variable," in D. Black, ed., *Toward a General Theory of Social Control* (Orlando: Academic, 1990).

43. Bursik and Grasmick, "The Multiple Layers of Social Disorganization," pp. 8–10.

44. Robert Sampson and W. Byron Groves, "Community Structure and Crime: Testing Social Disorganization Theory," *American Journal of Sociology* 94:774–802 (1989).

45. Denise Gottfredson, Richard McNeill, and Gary Gottfredson, "Social Area Influences on Delinquency: A Multilevel Analysis," *Journal of Research in Crime and Delinquency* 28:197–206 (1991).

46. Elijah Anderson, *Streetwise: Race, Class and Change in an Urban Community* (Chicago: University of Chicago Press, 1990), pp. 243–44.

47. Michael Greene, "Chronic Exposure to Violence and Poverty: Interventions that Work for Youth," *Crime and Delinquency* 39:106–124 (1993).

48. Ibid., p. 110–111.

49. See, for example, Robert Merton, *Social Theory and Social Structure* (Glencoe, IL: Free Press, 1957).

50. Agnew, "Foundation for a General Strain Theory of Crime and Delinquency."

51. Ibid., p. 57.

52. Timothy Brezina, "Adolescent Maltreatment and Delinquency: The Question of Intervening Processes," *Journal of Research in Crime and Delinquency* 35:71–99 (1998).

53. Paul Mazerolle, Velmer Burton, Francis Cullen, T. David Evans, and Gary Payne, "Strain, Anger, and Delinquent Adaptations Specifying General Strain Theory," *Journal of Criminal Justice* 28:89–101 (2000).

54. Stephen Cernkovich, Peggy Giordano, and Jennifer Rudolph, "Race, Crime and the American Dream," *Journal of Research in Crime and Delinquency* 37: 131–70 (2000).

55. Albert Cohen, *Delinquent Boys* (New York: Free Press, 1955).

56. Richard Cloward and Lloyd Ohlin, *Delinquency and Opportunity* (New York: Free Press, 1960).

57. See, for example, Irving Spergel, *Racketville, Slumtown, and Haulburg* (Chicago: University of Chicago Press, 1964).

58. James Short, "Gangs, Neighborhoods, and Youth Crime," *Criminal Justice Research Bulletin* 5:1–11 (1990).

59. Michael Leiber, Mahesh Nalla, and Margaret Farnworth, "Explaining Juveniles' Attitudes toward the Police," *Justice Quarterly* 15:151–73 (1998).

60. A. Leigh Ingram, "Type of Place, Urbanism, and Delinquency: Further Testing of the Determinist Theory," *Journal of Research in Crime and Delinquency* 30:192–212 (1993).

61. Alan Lizotte, Terence Thornberry, Marvin Krohn, Deborah Chard-Wierschem, and David McDowall, "Neighborhood Context and Delinquency: A Longitudinal Analysis," in H. J. Kerner and E. Weitekamp, eds., *Cross-National Longitudinal Research on Human Development and Criminal Behavior* (Dordrecht, The Netherlands: Kluwer Academic Publishers, 1993), pp. 1–11.

62. Lawrence Rosen, "Family and Delinquency: Structure or Function," *Criminology* 23:553–73 (1985).

63. Ronald Simons, Chyi-In Wu, Kuei-Hsiu Lin, Leslie Gordon, and Rand Conger, "A Cross-Cultural Examination of the Link Between Corporal Punishment and Adolescent Antisocial Behavior," *Criminology* 38:47–79 (2000).

64. Kenneth Polk and Walter Schafer, eds., *Schools and Delinquency* (Englewood Cliffs, NJ: Prentice-Hall, 1972).

65. Thomas Berndt, "The Features and Effects of Friendship in Early Adolescence," *Child Development* 53:1447–60 (1982).

66. David Fergusson, L. John Horwood, and Daniel Nagin, "Offending Trajectories in a New Zealand Birth Cohort," *Criminology* 38:525–51 (2000).

67. Edwin Sutherland, *Principles of Criminology* (Philadelphia: Lippincott, 1939).

68. Gresham Sykes and David Matza, "Techniques of Neutralization: A Theory of Delinquency," *American Sociological Review* 22:664–70 (1957); David Matza, *Delinquency and Drift* (New York: Wiley, 1964).

69. Ibid.

70. For a review of existing research, see Kimberly Kempf, "The Empirical Status of Hirschi's Control Theory," in Bill Laufer and Freda Adler, eds., *Advances in Criminological Theory* (New Brunswick, NJ: Transaction, 1992).

71. Bobbi Jo Anderson, Malcolm Holmes, and Erik Ostresh, "Male and Female Delinquent's Attachments and Effects of Attachments on Severity of Self-Reported Delinquency," *Criminal Justice and Behavior* 26:425–52 (1999).

72. Patricia Jenkins, "School Delinquency and the School Social Bond," *Journal of Research in Crime and Delinquency* 34:337–67 (1997).

73. Stephen Cernkovich, Peggy Giordano, and Jennifer Rudolph, "Race, Crime and the American Dream," *Journal of Research in Crime and Delinquency* 37:131–70 (2000).

74. Richard Lawrence, "Parents, Peers, School and Delinquency." Paper presented at the American Society of Criminology meeting, Boston, November 1995.

75. Peggy Giordano, Stephen Cernkovich, and M. D. Pugh, "Friendships and Delinquency," *American Journal of Sociology* 91:1170–1202 (1986).

76. Denise Kandel and Mark Davies, "Friendship Networks, Intimacy, and Illicit Drug Use in Young Adulthood: A Comparison of Two Competing Theories," *Criminology* 29:441–67 (1991).

77. Leslie Samuelson, Timothy Hartnagel, and Harvey Krahn, "Crime and Social Control among High School Dropouts," *Journal of Crime and Justice* 18:129–61 (1990).

78. For a review of this position, see Anne R. Mahoney, "The Effect of Labeling upon Youths in the Juvenile Justice System: A Review of the Evidence," *Law and Society Review* 8:583–614 (1974); see also David Matza, *Becoming Deviant* (Englewood Cliffs, NJ: Prentice-Hall, 1974).

79. The self-labeling concept originated in Edwin Lemert, *Social Pathology* (New York: McGraw-Hill, 1951); see also Frank Tannenbaum, *Crime and the Community* (Boston: Ginn, 1936).

80. Nalini Ambady and Robert Rosenthal, "Half a Minute: Predicting Teacher Evaluations from Thin Slices of Nonverbal Behavior and Physical Attractiveness," *Journal of Personality and Social Psychology* 64:431–41 (1993).

81. Monica Harris, Richard Milich, Elizabeth Corbitt, Daniel Hoover, and Marianne Brady, "Self-Fulfilling Effects of Stigmatizing Information on Children's Social Interactions," *Journal of Personality and Social Psychology* 33:41–50 (1992).

82. Harold Garfinkel, *Conditions of Successful Degradation Ceremonies* (Irvington Pub, 1993).

83. M. A. Bortner, *Inside a Juvenile Court: The Tarnished Ideal of Individualized Justice* (New York: NYU Press, 1982).

84. Edwin Lemert, *Human Deviance, Social Problems, and Social Control* (Englewood Cliffs, NJ: Prentice-Hall, 1967), p. 15.

85. Charles H. Cooley, *Human Nature and the Social Order* (New York: Scribner's, 1902).

86. Ross Matsueda, "Reflected Appraisals, Parental Labeling, and Delinquency: Specifying a Symbolic Interactionist Theory," *American Journal of Sociology* 97:1577–1611 (1992).

87. Howard Kaplan and Hiroshi Fukurai, "Negative Social Sanctions, Self-Rejection, and Drug Use," *Youth and Society* 23:275–98 (1992).

88. Howard Kaplan, *Toward a General Theory of Deviance: Contributions from Perspectives on Deviance and Criminality* (College Station, TX: Texas A & M University, n.d.).

89. Harris et al., "Self-Fulfilling Effects of Stigmatizing Information on Children's Social Interactions," pp. 48–50.

90. Kaplan, *Toward a General Theory of Deviance*.

91. Howard Kaplan, Robert Johnson, and Carol Bailey, "Deviant Peers and Deviant Behavior: Further Elaboration of a Model," *Social Psychology Quarterly* 30:277–84 (1987).

92. Tannenbaum, *Crime and the Community*.

93. Aaron Cicourel, *The Social Organization of Juvenile Justice* (New York: Wiley, 1968).

94. Matza, *Becoming Deviant*.

95. Ibid., p. 78.

96. Stanton Wheeler and Leonard Cottrell, "Juvenile Delinquency: Its Prevention and Control," in Donald Cressey and David Ward, eds., *Delinquency, Crime, and Social Processes* (New York: Harper & Row, 1969), p. 609.

97. Garfinkel, *Conditions of Successful Degradation Ceremonies*, p. 424.

98. Charles Murray and Lewis Cox, *Beyond Probation* (Beverly Hills: Sage, 1979).

99. Raymond Paternoster and Leeann Iovanni, "The Labeling Perspective and Delinquency: An Elaboration of the Theory and an Assessment of the Evidence," *Justice Quarterly* 6:358–94 (1989).

100. Meier, "The New Criminology," p. 463.

101. Sykes, "The Rise of Critical Criminology," pp. 211–13.

102. Ibid.

103. David Jacobs and David Britt, "Inequality and Police Use of Deadly Force: An Empirical Assessment of a Conflict Hypothesis," *Social Problems* 26:403–412 (1979).

104. Malcolm Homes, "Minority Threat and Police Brutality: Determinants of Civil Rights Criminal Complaints in U.S. Municipalities," *Criminology* 38:343–68 (2000).

105. Ibid.

106. Robert Gordon, "Capitalism, Class, and Crime in America," *Crime and Delinquency* 19:174 (1973).

107. Richard Quinney, *Class, State, and Crime* (New York: Longman, 1977), p. 52.

108. Anthony Platt, "The Triumph of Benevolence: The Origins of the Juvenile Justice System in the United States," in Richard Quinney, ed., *Criminal Justice in America: A Critical Understanding* (Boston: Little, Brown, 1974), p. 367; see also Anthony Platt, *The Child Savers* (Chicago: University of Chicago Press, 1969).

109. Barry Krisberg and James Austin, *Children of Ishmael* (Palo Alto, CA.: Mayfield, 1978), p. 2.

110. Herman Schwendinger and Julia Schwendinger, "Delinquency and Social Reform: A Radical Perspective," in Lamar Empey, ed., *Juvenile Justice* (Charlottesville: University of Virginia Press, 1979), p. 250.

111. Ibid., p. 252.

112. Operation Weed and Seed Executive Offices, U.S. Department of Justice, Washington, DC, 1998; Executive Office for Weed and Seed, Weed and Seed In-sites, Series: Volume VI, Number 5, August/September 1998.

113. Terence Thornberry, David Huizinga, and Rolf Loeber, "The Prevention of Serious Delinquency and Violence," in James Howell, Barry Krisberg, J. David Hawkins, and John Wilson, eds., *Sourcebook on Serious, Violent, and Chronic Juvenile Offenders* (Thousand Oaks, CA: Sage, 1995).

114. Adapted from Daniel McGillis, *Beacons of Hope: New York City's School-Based Community Centers* (Washington, DC: National Institute of Justice, 1996; updated 2000).

115. Malcolm Klein, "Deinstitutionalization and Diversion of Juvenile Offenders: A Litany of Impediments," in Norval Morris and Michael Tonry, eds., *Crime and Justice,* vol. 1 (Chicago: University of Chicago Press, 1979).

116. James Austin and Barry Krisberg, "The Unmet Promise of Alternatives to Incarceration," *Crime and Delinquency* 28:3–19 (1982).

117. William Selke, "Diversion and Crime Prevention," *Criminology* 20:395–406 (1982).

118. Kathleen Daly and Russ Immarigeon, "The Past, Present, and Future of Restorative Justice: Some Critical Reflections," *Contemporary Justice Review* 1:21–45 (1998).

119. Gene Stephens, "The Future of Policing: From a War Model to a Peace Model," in Brendan Maguire and Polly Radosh, eds., *The Past, Present and Future of American Criminal Justice* (Dix Hills, NY: General Hall, 1996), pp. 77–93.

120. Peter Cordella, "Justice." Unpublished paper, St. Anselm College, Manchester, NH, 1997; see also Herbert Bianchi, *Justice as Sanctuary* (Bloomington: Indiana University Press, 1994); Nils Christie, "Conflicts as Property," *The British Journal of Criminology* 17:1–15 (1977); L. Hulsman, "Critical Criminology and the Concept of Crime," *Contemporary Crises* 10:63–80 (1986).

121. Pranis, "Peacemaking Circles," p. 74.

122. Carol LaPrairie, "The 'New' Justice: Some Implications for Aboriginal Communities," *Canadian Journal of Criminology* 40:61–79 (1998).

123. Gordon Bazemore, "What's New about the Balanced Approach?" *Juvenile and Family Court Journal* 48:1–23 (1997); Gordon Bazemore and Mara Schiff, "Community Justice/Restorative Justice: Prospects for a New Social Ecology for Community Corrections," *International Journal of Comparative and Applied Criminal Justice* 20:311–35 (1996).

124. Jay Zaslaw and George Ballance, "The Socio-Legal Response: A New Approach to Juvenile Justice in the 90s," *Corrections Today* 58:72–75 (1996).

125. Gordon Bazemore, "Restorative Justice and Earned Redemption: Communities, Victims, and Offender Reintegration," *American Behavioral Scientist* 41:768–814 (1998).

Chapter 5

1. Gerald Patterson and Karen Yoeger, "Developmental Models for Delinquent Behavior," in *Mental Disorder and Crime*, ed. Sheilagh Hodgins (Newbury Park, CA: Sage, 1993), pp. 150–59.

2. See, generally, Sheldon Glueck and Eleanor Glueck, *Unraveling Juvenile Delinquency* (Cambridge: Harvard University Press, 1950); Sheldon Glueck and Eleanor Glueck, *500 Criminal Careers* (New York: Knopf, 1930); Sheldon Glueck and Eleanor Glueck, *One Thousand Juvenile Delinquents* (Cambridge: Harvard University Press, 1934); Sheldon Glueck and Eleanor Glueck, *Predicting Delinquency and Crime* (Cambridge: Harvard University Press, 1967), pp. 82–83.

3. Glueck and Glueck, *Unraveling Juvenile Delinquency*, p. 48.

4. John Laub and Robert Sampson, "Unraveling Families and Delinquency: A Reanalysis of the Gluecks' Data." *Criminology* 26:355–80 (1988).

5. Rolf Loeber and Marc LeBlanc, "Toward a Developmental Criminology," in *Crime and Justice*, vol. 12, ed. Norval Morris and Michael Tonry (Chicago: University of Chicago Press, 1990), pp. 375–473; Rolf Loeber and Marc Leblanc, "Developmental Criminology Updated," in *Crime and Justice*, vol. 23, ed. Michael Tonry (Chicago: University of Chicago Press, 1998), pp. 115–98.

6. G.R. Patterson, L. Crosby, and S. Vuchinich, "Predicting Risk for Early Police Arrest," *Journal of Quantitative Criminology* 8:335–55 (1992); Rolf Loeber, Magda Stouthamer-Loeber, Welmoet Van Kammen, and David Farrington, "Initiation, Escalation, and Desistance in Juvenile Offending and Their Correlates," *Journal of Criminal Law and Criminology* 82:36–82 (1991).

7. Raymond Paternoster, Charles Dean, Alex Piquero, Paul Mazerolle, and Robert Brame, "Generality, Continuity, and Change in Offending," *Journal of Quantitative Criminology* 13:231–66 (1997).

8. Marvin Krohn, Alan Lizotte, and Cynthia Perez, "The Interrelationship Between Substance Use and Precocious Transitions to Adult Sexuality," *Journal of Health and Social Behavior* 38:87–103 at 88 (1997).

9. G.R. Patterson, Barbara DeBaryshe, and Elizabeth Ramsey, "A Developmental Perspective on Antisocial Behavior," *American Psychologist* 44:329–35 (1989).

10. Paul Mazerolle, "Delinquent Definitions and Participation Age: Assessing the Invariance Hypothesis," *Studies on Crime and Crime Prevention* 6:151–68 (1997).

11. Magda Stouthamer-Loeber and Evelyn Wei, "The Precursors of Young Fatherhood and Its Effect on Delinquency of Teenage Males," *Journal of Adolescent Health* 22:56–65 (1998); Richard Jessor, John Donovan, and Francis Costa, *Beyond Adolescence: Problem Behavior and Young Adult Development* (New York: Cambridge University Press, 1991).

12. Marvin Krohn, Alan Lizotte, and Cynthia Perez, "The Interrelationship Between Substance Use and Precocious Transitions to Adult Sexuality," *Journal of Health and Social Behavior* 38:87–103 at 88 (1997); Richard Jessor, "Risk Behavior in Adolescence: A Psychosocial Framework for Understanding and Action," in *Adolescents at Risk: Medical and Social Perspectives*, ed. D.E. Rogers and E. Ginzburg (Boulder, CO: Westview, 1992).

13. Deborah Capaldi and Gerald Patterson, "Can Violent Offenders Be Distinguished from Frequent Offenders: Prediction from Childhood to Adolescence," *Journal of Research in Crime and Delinquency* 33:206–231 (1996); D. Wayne Osgood, "The Covariation among Adolescent Problem Behaviors" (paper presented at the annual meeting of the American Society of Criminology, Baltimore, November 1990).

14. Terence Thornberry, Carolyn Smith, and Gregory Howard, "Risk Factors for Teenage Fatherhood," *Journal of Marriage and the Family* 59:502–522 (1997); Todd Miller, Timothy Smith, Charles Turner, Margarita Guijarro, and Amanda Hallet, "A Meta-Analytic Review of Research on Hostility and Physical Health," *Psychological Bulletin* 119:322–48 (1996); Marianne Junger, "Accidents and Crime," in *The Generality of Deviance*, ed. T. Hirschi and M. Gottfredson (New Brunswick, NJ: Transaction Press, 1993).

15. Robert Johnson, S. Susan Su, Dean Gerstein, Hee-Choon Shin, and John Hoffman, "Parental Influences on Deviant Behavior in Early Adolescence: A Logistic Response Analysis of Age- and Gender-Differentiated Effects," *Journal of Quantitative Criminology* 11:167–92 (1995); Judith Brooks, Martin Whiteman, and Patricia Cohen, "Stage of Drug Use, Aggression, and Theft/Vandalism," in *Drugs, Crime and Other Deviant Adaptations: Longitudinal Studies*, ed. Howard Kaplan (New York: Plenum Press, 1995), pp. 83–96; Robert Hoge, D.A. Andrews, and Alan Leschied, "Tests of Three Hypotheses Regarding the Predictors of Delinquency," *Journal of Abnormal Child Psychology* 22:547–59 (1994).

16. David Huizinga, Rolf Loeber, and Terence Thornberry, "Longitudinal Study of Delinquency, Drug Use, Sexual Activity, and Pregnancy among Children and Youth in Three Cities," *Public Health Reports* 108:90–96 (1993).

17. Terence Thornberry, Evelyn Wei, Magda Stouthamer-Loeber, and Joyce Van Dyke, *Teenage Fatherhood and Delinquent Behavior* (Washington, DC: Office of Juvenile Justice and Delinquency Prevention, 2000)

18. David Huizinga, Rolf Loeber, Terence Thornberry, and Lynn Cothern, "Co-Occurrence of Delinquency and Other Problem Behaviors," *Juvenile Justice Bulletin*, November 2000 (Washington, DC: Office of Juvenile Justice and Delinquency Prevention, 2000).

19. Rolf Loeber, Phen Wung, Kate Keenan, Bruce Giroux, Magda Stouthamer-Loeber, Wemoet Van Kammen, and Barbara Maughan, "Developmental Pathways in Disruptive Behavior," *Development and Psychopathology* 23:12–48 (1993).

20. Amy D'Unger, Kenneth Land, Patricia McCall, and Daniel Nagin, "How Many Latent Classes of Delinquent/Criminal Careers? Results from Mixed Poisson Regression Analyses," *American Journal of Sociology* 103:1593–1630 (1998).

21. Terrie Moffitt, "Natural Histories of Delinquency," in *Cross-National Longitudinal Research on Human Development and Criminal Behavior*, ed. Elmar Weitekamp and Hans-Jurgen Kerner (Dordrecht, Netherlands: Kluwer, 1994), pp. 3–65.

22. Michael Newcomb, "Pseudomaturity among Adolescents: Construct Validation, Sex Differences, and Associations in Adulthood," *Journal of Drug Issues* 26:477–504 (1996).

23. Rolf Loeber and Magda Stouthamer-Loeber, "Development of Juvenile Aggression and Violence," *American Psychologist* 53:242–59 (1998).

24. Terrie Moffitt, "Adolescence-Limited and Life-Course Persistent Antisocial Behavior: A Developmental Taxonomy," *Psychological Review* 100:674–701 (1993).

25. David Fergusson, L. John Horwood, and Daniel Nagin, "Offending Trajectories in a New Zealand Birth Cohort," *Criminology* 38:525–51 (2000).

26. Paul Mazerolle, Robert Brame, Ray Paternoster, Alex Piquero, and Charles Dean, "Onset Age, Persistence, and Offending Versatility: Comparisons across Gender," *Criminology* 38:1143–72 (2000).

27. Ronald Simons, Chyi-In Wu, Rand Conger, and Frederick Lorenz, "Two Routes to Delinquency: Differences between Early and Later Starters in the Impact of Parenting and Deviant Careers," *Criminology* 32:247–75 (1994).

28. Mark Lipsey and James Derzon, "Predictors of Violent or Serious Delinquency in Adolescence and Early Adulthood: A Synthesis of Longitudinal Research," in *Serious and Violent Juvenile Offenders: Risk Factors and Successful Interventions*, ed. Rolf Loeber and David Farrington (Thousand Oaks, CA: Sage, 1998).

29. G.R. Patterson and Karen Yoerger, "Differentiating Outcomes and Histories for Early and Late Onset Arrests." Paper presented at the annual meeting of the American Society of Criminology, Phoenix, November 1993.

30. Marshall Jones and Donald Jones, "The Contagious Nature of Antisocial Behavior," *Criminology* 38:25–46 (2000).

31. See, for example, the Rochester Youth Development Study, Hindelang Criminal Justice Research Center, 135 Western Avenue, Albany, New York 12222.

32. David Farrington, "The Development of Offending and Antisocial Behavior from Childhood to Adulthood." Paper presented at

the Congress on Rethinking Delinquency, University of Minho, Braga, Portugal, July 1992.

33. Joseph Weis and J. David Hawkins, *Reports of the National Juvenile Assessment Centers, Preventing Delinquency* (Washington, DC: U.S. Department of Justice, 1981); Joseph Weis and John Sederstrom, *Reports of the National Juvenile Justice Assessment Centers, The Prevention of Serious Delinquency: What to Do* (Washington, DC: U.S. Department of Justice, 1981).

34. Julie O'Donnell, J. David Hawkins, and Robert Abbott, "Predicting Serious Delinquency and Substance Use among Aggressive Boys," *Journal of Consulting and Clinical Psychology* 63:529–37 (1995).

35. Terence Thornberry, "Toward an Interactional Theory of Delinquency," *Criminology* 25:863–91 (1987).

36. Ross Matsueda and Kathleen Anderson, "The Dynamics of Delinquent Peers and Delinquent Behavior," *Criminology* 36:269–308 (1998).

37. Thornberry, "Toward an Interactional Theory of Delinquency."

38. Thornberry, "Toward an Interactional Theory of Delinquency," p. 863.

39. Thornberry et al., *Delinquent Peers, Beliefs, and Delinquent Behavior*, pp. 628–29.

40. Robert Sampson and John Laub, *Crime in the Making: Pathways and Turning Points through Life* (Cambridge: Harvard University Press, 1993); John Laub and Robert Sampson, "Turning Points in the Life Course: Why Change Matters to the Study of Crime" (paper presented at the annual meeting of the American Society of Criminology, New Orleans, November 1992).

41. Terri Orbuch, James House, Richard Mero, and Pamela Webster, "Marital Quality over the Life Course," *Social Psychology Quarterly* 59:162–71 (1996); Lee Lillard and Linda Waite, "'Til Death Do Us Part: Marital Disruption and Mortality," *American Journal of Sociology* 100:1131–56 (1995).

42. Mark Warr, "Life-Course Transitions and Desistance from Crime," *Criminology* 36:183–216 (1998).

43. Pamela Webster, Terri Orbuch, and James House, "Effects of Childhood Family Background on Adult Marital Quality and Perceived Stability," *American Journal of Sociology* 101:404–432 (1995).

44. John Hagan, Ross MacMillan, and Blair Wheaton, "New Kid in Town: Social Capital and the Life Course Effects of Family Migration on Children," *American Sociological Review* 61:368–85 (1996).

45. Sampson and Laub, *Crime in the Making*, p. 249.

46. Raymond Paternoster and Robert Brame, "Multiple Routes to Delinquency? A Test of Developmental and General Theories of Crime," *Criminology* 35:49–84 (1997).

47. Robert Hoge, D.A. Andrews, and Alan Leschied, "An Investigation of Risk and Protective Factors in a Sample of Youthful Offenders," *Journal of Child Psychology and Psychiatry* 37:419–24 (1996).

48. Candace Kruttschnitt, Christopher Uggen, and Kelly Shelton, "Individual Variability in Sex Offending and Its Relationship to Informal and Formal Social Controls" (paper presented at the American Society of Criminology meeting, San Diego, 1997); Mark Collins and Don Weatherburn, "Unemployment and the Dynamics of Offender Populations," *Journal of Quantitative Criminology* 11:231–45 (1995).

49. Avshalom Caspi, Terrie Moffitt, Bradley Entner Wright, and Phil Silva, "Early Failure in the Labor Market: Childhood and Adolescent Predictors of Unemployment in the Transition to Adulthood," *American Sociological Review* 63:424–51 (1998).

50. Erich Labouvie, "Maturing Out of Substance Use: Selection and Self-Correction," *Journal of Drug Issues* 26:457–74 (1996).

51. Mark Warr, "Life-Course Transitions and Desistance from Crime," *Criminology* 36:502–535 (1998).

52. Robert Sampson and John Laub, "Socioeconomic Achievement in the Life Course of Disadvantaged Men: Military Service as a Turning Point, circa 1940–1965," *American Sociological Review* 61:347–67 (1996).

53. Daniel Nagin and Raymond Paternoster, "Personal Capital and Social Control: The Deterrence Implications of a Theory of Criminal Offending," *Criminology* 32:581–606 (1994).

54. David Rowe, D. Wayne Osgood, and W. Alan Nicewander, "A Latent Trait Approach to Unifying Criminal Careers," *Criminology* 28:237–70 (1990).

55. Lee Ellis, "Neurohormonal Bases of Varying Tendencies to Learn Delinquent and Criminal Behavior," in *Behavioral Approaches to Crime and Delinquency*, ed. E. Morris and C. Braukmann (New York: Plenum, 1988), pp. 499–518.

56. David Rowe, Alexander Vazsonyi, and Daniel Flannery, "Sex Differences in Crime: Do Means and Within-Sex Variation Have Similar Causes?" *Journal of Research in Crime and Delinquency* 32:84–100 (1995).

57. Michael Gottfredson and Travis Hirschi, *A General Theory of Crime* (Stanford, CA: Stanford University Press, 1990).

58. Ibid., p. 27.

59. Ibid., p. 90.

60. Ibid., p. 89.

61. Alex Piquero and Stephen Tibbetts, "Specifying the Direct and Indirect Effects of Low Self-Control and Situational Factors in Offenders' Decision Making: Toward a More Complete Model of Rational Offending," *Justice Quarterly* 13:481–508 (1996).

62. David Forde and Leslie Kennedy, "Risky Lifestyles, Routine Activities, and the General Theory of Crime," *Justice Quarterly* 14:265–94 (1997).

63. Marianne Junger and Richard Tremblay, "Self-Control, Accidents, and Crime," *Criminal Justice and Behavior* 26:485–501 (1999).

64. Gottfredson and Hirschi, *A General Theory of Crime*, p. 112.

65. Ibid.

66. Dennis Giever, "An Empirical Assessment of the Core Elements of Gottfredson and Hirschi's General Theory of Crime." Paper presented to the American Society of Criminology, Boston, November 1995.

67. Robert Agnew, "The Contribution of Social-Psychological Strain Theory to the Explanation of Crime and Delinquency," *Advances in Criminological Theory* 6 (1994).

68. David Brownfield and Ann Marie Sorenson, "Self-Control and Juvenile Delinquency: Theoretical Issues and an Empirical Assessment of Selected Elements of a General Theory of Crime," *Deviant Behavior* 14:243–64 (1993); Harold Grasmick, Charles Tittle, Robert Bursik, and Bruce Arneklev, "Testing the Core Empirical Implications of Gottfredson and Hirschi's General Theory of Crime," *Journal of Research in Crime and Delinquency* 30:5–29 (1993); John Cochran, Peter Wood, and Bruce Arneklev, "Is the Religiosity–Delinquency Relationship Spurious? A Test of Arousal and Social Control Theories," *Journal of Research in Crime and Delinquency* 31:92–123 (1994); Marc LeBlanc, Marc Ouimet, and Richard Tremblay, "An Integrative Control Theory of Delinquent Behavior: A Validation 1976–1985," *Psychiatry* 51:164–76 (1988).

69. Xiaogang Deng and Lening Zhang, "Correlates of Self-Control: An Empirical Test of Self-Control Theory," *Journal of Crime and Justice* 21:89–103 (1998).

70. Linda Pagani, Richard Tremblay, Frank Vitaro, and Sophie Parent, "Does Preschool Help Prevent Delinquency in Boys with a

History of Perinatal Complications?" *Criminology* 36:245–68 (1998).

71. John Gibbs, Dennis Giever, and Jamie Martin, "Parental Management and Self-Control: An Empirical Test of Gottfredson and Hirschi's General Theory," *Journal of Research in Crime and Delinquency* 35:40–70 (1998).

72. Vic Bumphus and James Anderson, "Family Structure and Race in a Sample of Offenders," *Journal of Criminal Justice* 27:309–320 (1999).

73. Ronald Akers, "Self-Control as a General Theory of Crime," *Journal of Quantitative Criminology* 7:201–211 (1991).

74. Alan Feingold, "Gender Differences in Personality: A Meta Analysis," *Psychological Bulletin* 116:429–56 (1994).

75. Gottfredson and Hirschi, *A General Theory of Crime*, p. 153.

76. Charles R. Tittle and Harold G. Grasmick, "Criminal Behavior and Age: A Test of Three Provocative Hypotheses," *Journal of Criminal Law and Criminology* 88:309–342 (1997).

77. Scott Menard, Delbert Elliott, and Sharon Wofford, "Social Control Theories in Developmental Perspective," *Studies on Crime and Crime Prevention* 2:69–87 (1993).

78. Kevin Thompson, "Sexual Harassment and Low Self-Control: An Application of Gottfredson and Hirschi's General Theory of Crime." Paper presented at the annual meeting of the American Society of Criminology, Phoenix, November 1993.

Chapter 6

1. Cesare Lombroso, *The Female Offender* (New York: Appleton, 1920); W. I. Thomas, *The Unadjusted Girl* (New York: Harper & Row, 1923).

2. Cesare Lombroso and William Ferrero, *The Female Offender* (New York: Philosophical Library, 1895).

3. James Messerschmidt, *Masculinities and Crime: Critique and Reconceptualization of Theory* (Lanham, MD: Rowman and Littlefield, 1993).

4. Paul Mazerolle, Robert Brame, Ray Paternoster, Alex Piquero, and Charles Dean, "Onset Age, Persistence, and Offending Versatility: Comparisons across Sex." Paper presented at the annual Society of Criminology meeting, San Diego, November 1997.

5. Kathleen Daly, "From Gender Ratios to Gendered Lives: Women's Gender in Crime and Criminological Theory," in Michael Tonry, ed., *The Handbook of Crime and Punishment* (New York: Oxford University Press, 1998).

6. Rita James Simon, *The Contemporary Woman and Crime* (Washington, DC: U.S. Government Printing Office, 1975).

7. Rolf Loeber and Dale Hay, "Key Issues in the Development of Aggression and Violence from Childhood to Early Adulthood," *Annual Review of Psychology* 48:371–410 (1997).

8. This section relies on Spencer Rathus, *Psychology in the New Millennium* (Fort Worth, TX: Harcourt, Brace, 1996); see also Darcy Miller, Catherine Trapani, Kathy Fejes-Mendoza, Carolyn Eggleston, and Donna Dwiggins, "Adolescent Female Offenders: Unique Considerations," *Adolescence* 30:429–35 (1995).

9. Allison Morris, *Women, Crime and Criminal Justice* (Oxford: Basil Blackwell, 1987).

10. Dennis Giever, "An Empirical Assessment of the Core Elements of Gottfredson and Hirschi's General Theory of Crime." Paper presented at the American Society of Criminology meeting, Boston, November 1995.

11. Loeber and Hay, "Key Issues in the Development of Aggression and Violence from Childhood to Early Adulthood," p. 378.

12. John Mirowsky and Catherine Ross, "Sex Differences in Distress: Real or Artifact?" *American Sociological Review* 60:449–68 (1995).

13. Ibid., pp. 460–65.

14. For a review of this issue, see Anne Campbell, *Men, Women and Aggression* (New York: Basic Books, 1993).

15. Ann Beutel and Margaret Mooney Marini, "Gender and Values," *American Sociological Review* 60:436–48 (1995).

16. American Association of University Women, *Shortchanging Girls, Shortchanging America: Executive Summary* (Washington, DC: author, 1991).

17. John Gibbs, Dennis Giever, and Jamie Martin, "Parental Management and Self-Control: An Empirical Test of Gottfredson and Hirschi's General Theory," *Journal of Research in Crime and Delinquency* 35:40–70 (1998); Velmer Burton, Francis Cullen, T. David Evans, Leanne Fiftal Alarid, and R. Gregory Dunaway, "Gender, Self-Control, and Crime," *Journal of Research in Crime and Delinquency* 35:123–47 (1998).

18. David Rowe, Alexander Vazsonyi, and Daniel Flannery, "Sex Differences in Crime: Do Means and Within-Sex Variation Have Similar Causes?" *Journal of Research in Crime and Delinquency* 32:84–100 (1995).

19. Sandra Bem, *The Lenses of Gender* (New Haven: Yale University Press, 1993).

20. Walter DeKeseredy and Martin Schwartz, "Male Peer Support and Woman Abuse," *Sociological Spectrum* 13:393–413 (1993).

21. Eleanor Maccoby, *The Two Sexes : Growing Up Apart, Coming Together* (Cambridge, MA: Belknap Press, 1999).

22. Daniel Mears, Matthew Ploeger, and Mark Warr, "Explaining the Gender Gap in Delinquency: Peer Influence and Moral Evaluations of Behavior," *Journal of Research in Crime and Delinquency* 35:251–66 (1998).

23. Messerschmidt, *Masculinities and Crime: Critique and Reconceptualization of Theory*.

24. D.J. Pepler and W.M. Craig, "A Peek Behind the Fence: Naturalistic Observations of Aggressive Children with Remote Audiovisual Recording," *Developmental Psychology* 31:548–53 (1995).

25. Stacey Nofziger, "Sex and Gender Identity: A Gendered Look at Delinquency." Paper presented at the American Society of Criminology meeting, Boston, November 1995 (rev. version, January 1996).

26. Federal Bureau of Investigation, *Crime in the United States, 1999* (Washington, DC: U.S. Government Printing Office, 2000) pp. 22–23.

27. Ibid., p. 22.

28. Lombroso and Ferrero, *The Female Offender*.

29. Ibid., p. 122.

30. Ibid., pp. 51–52.

31. For a review, see Anne Campbell, *Girl Delinquents* (Oxford: Basic Blackwell, 1981), pp. 41–48.

32. Ibid., p. 151.

33. Ibid., pp. 150–52.

34. Cyril Burt, *The Young Delinquent* (New York: Appleton, 1925); see also Warren Middleton, "Is There a Relation between Kleptomania and Female Periodicity in Neurotic Individuals?" *Psychology Clinic* (December 1933), pp. 232–47.

35. William Healy and Augusta Bronner, *Delinquents and Criminals, Their Making and Unmaking* (New York: Macmillan, 1926).

36. Otto Pollak, *The Criminality of Women* (Philadelphia: University of Pennsylvania Press, 1950).

37. Ibid., p. 158.

38. Ibid., p. 10.

39. Miriam Sealock and Sally Simpson, "Unraveling Bias in Arrest Decisions: The Role of Juvenile Offender Typescripts," *Justice Quarterly* 15:427–57 (1998); Christina Polsenberg and Kenneth Jackson, "Putting Race into Context: Race, Juvenile Justice Processing and Urbanization." Paper presented at the American Society of Criminology meeting, Boston, November 1995 (rev. version, January 1996); for a general review, see Carl Pope and William Feyerherm, "Minority Status and Juvenile Justice Processing (Part I)," *Criminal Justice Abstracts* 22:327–35 (1990); see also Douglas Smith and Jody Klein, "Police Control of Interpersonal Disputes," *Social Problems* 31:468–81 (1984).

40. Sigmund Freud, *An Outline of Psychoanalysis,* trans. James Strachey (New York: Norton, 1949), p. 278.

41. Dorie Klein, "The Etiology of Female Crime: A Review of the Literature," in Freda Adler and Rita Simon, eds., *The Criminology of Deviant Women* (Boston: Houghton Mifflin, 1979), pp. 69–71.

42. Phyliss Chesler, *Women and Madness* (Garden City, NY: Doubleday, 1972); Karen Horney, *Feminine Psychology* (New York: Norton, 1967).

43. Peter Blos, "Preoedipal Factors in the Etiology of Female Delinquency," *Psychoanalytic Studies of the Child* 12:229–42 (1957).

44. Sheldon Glueck and Eleanor Glueck, *Five Hundred Delinquent Women* (New York: Knopf, 1934).

45. J. Cowie, V. Cowie, and E. Slater, *Delinquency in Girls* (London: Heinemann, 1968).

46. Anne Campbell, "On the Invisibility of the Female Delinquent Peer Group," *Women and Criminal Justice* 2:41–62 (1990).

47. Carolyn Smith, "Factors Associated with Early Sexual Activity among Urban Adolescents," *Social Work* 42:334–46 (1997).

48. For a review, see Christy Miller Buchanan, Jacquelynne Eccles, and Jill Becker, "Are Adolescents the Victims of Raging Hormones? Evidence for Activational Effects of Hormones on Moods and Behavior at Adolescence," *Psychological Bulletin* 111:63–107 (1992).

49. Avshalom Caspi, Donald Lyman, Terrie Moffitt, and Phil Silva, "Unraveling Girls' Delinquency: Biological, Dispositional, and Contextual Contributions to Adolescent Misbehavior," *Developmental Psychology* 29:283–89 (1993).

50. Eleanor Maccoby and Carol Jacklin, *The Psychology of Sex Differences* (Stanford, CA: Stanford University Press, 1974).

51. Alan Booth and D. Wayne Osgood, "The Influence of Testosterone on Deviance in Adulthood: Assessing and Explaining the Relationship," *Criminology* 31:93–118 (1993).

52. Walter Gove, "The Effect of Age and Gender on Deviant Behavior: A Biopsychosocial Perspective," in A. S. Rossi, ed., *Gender and the Life Course* (New York: Aldine, 1985), pp. 115–44.

53. Lee Ellis, "Evolutionary and Neurochemical Causes of Sex Differences in Victimizing Behavior: Toward a Unified Theory of Criminal Behavior and Social Stratification," *Social Science Information* 28:625–26 (1989).

54. D.H. Baucom, P.K. Besch, and S. Callahan, "Relationship between Testosterone Concentration, Sex Role Identity, and Personality among Females," *Journal of Personality and Social Psychology* 48:1218–26 (1985).

55. Lee Ellis, "Evidence of Neuroandrogenic Etiology of Sex Roles from a Combined Analysis of Human, Nonhuman Primate and Nonprimate Mammalian Studies," *Personality and Individual Differences* 7:519–52 (1986).

56. Diana Fishbein, "Selected Studies on the Biology of Antisocial Behavior," in John Conklin, ed., *New Perspectives in Criminology* (Needham Heights, MA: Allyn & Bacon, 1996), pp. 26–38.

57. Diana Fishbein, "The Psychobiology of Female Aggression," *Criminal Justice and Behavior* 19:99–126 (1992).

58. Spencer Rathus, *Psychology,* 3rd ed. (New York: Holt, Rinehart & Winston, 1987), p. 88.

59. See, generally, Katharina Dalton, *The Premenstrual Syndrome* (Springfield, IL: Charles C Thomas, 1971).

60. Fishbein, "Selected Studies on the Biology of Antisocial Behavior."

61. Fishbein, "Selected Studies on the Biology of Antisocial Behavior"; Karen Paige, "Effects of Oral Contraceptives on Affective Fluctuations Associated with the Menstrual Cycle," *Psychosomatic Medicine* 33:515–37 (1971).

62. B. Harry and C. Balcer, "Menstruation and Crime: A Critical Review of the Literature from the Clinical Criminology Perspective," *Behavioral Sciences and the Law* 5:307–322 (1987).

63. Julie Horney, "Menstrual Cycles and Criminal Responsibility," *Law and Human Nature* 2:25–36 (1978).

64. Lee Ellis, "The Victimful-Victimless Crime Distinction and Seven Universal Demographic Correlates of Victimful Criminal Behavior," *Personality and Individual Differences* 9:525–48 (1988).

65. Eleanor Maccoby and Carol Jacklin, *The Psychology of Sex Differences* (Stanford, CA: Stanford University Press, 1974).

66. Ellis, "Evolutionary and Neurochemical Causes of Sex Differences in Victimizing Behavior," pp. 605–636.

67. Buchanan, Eccles, and Becker, "Are Adolescents the Victims of Raging Hormones?" p. 94.

68. Ann Frodi, J. Maccauley, and P. R. Thome, "Are Women Always Less Aggressive than Men? A Review of the Experimental Literature," *Psychological Bulletin* 84:634–60 (1977).

69. Thomas, *The Unadjusted Girl.*

70. Ibid., p. 109.

71. David Farrington, "Juvenile Delinquency," in John Coleman, ed., *The School Years* (London: Routledge, 1992), p. 133.

72. Ibid.

73. Ruth Morris, "Female Delinquents and Relational Problems," *Social Forces* 43:82–89 (1964).

74. Cowie, Cowie, and Slater, *Delinquency in Girls,* p. 27.

75. Gisela Konopka, *The Adolescent Girl in Conflict* (Englewood Cliffs, NJ: Prentice-Hall, 1966).

76. Ibid., p. 40.

77. Konopka, *The Adolescent Girl in Conflict,* p. 50.

78. Morris, "Female Delinquency and Relational Problems."

79. Clyde Vedder and Dora Somerville, *The Delinquent Girl* (Springfield, IL: Charles C Thomas, 1970).

80. Sheldon Glueck and Eleanor Glueck, *Unraveling Juvenile Delinquency* (Cambridge, MA: Harvard University Press, 1950).

81. Ibid., pp. 281–82.

82. Glueck and Glueck, *Five Hundred Delinquent Women.*

83. Ibid., p. 90.

84. Ames Robey, Richard Rosenwal, John Small, and Ruth Lee, "The Runaway Girl: A Reaction to Family Stress," *American Journal of Orthopsychiatry* 34:763–67 (1964).

85. William Wattenberg and Frank Saunders, "Sex Differences among Juvenile Court Offenders," *Sociology and Social Research* 39:24–31 (1954).

86. Don Gibbons and Manzer Griswold, "Sex Differences among Juvenile Court Referrals," *Sociology and Social Research* 42:106–110 (1957).

87. Gordon Barker and William Adams, "Comparison of the Delinquencies of Boys and Girls," *Journal of Criminal Law, Criminology, and Police Science* 53:470–75 (1962).

88. George Calhoun, Janelle Jurgens, and Fengling Chen, "The Neophyte Female Delinquent: A Review of the Literature," *Adolescence* 28:461–71 (1993).

89. Joanne Belknap, Kristi Holsinger, and Melissa Dunn, "Understanding Incarcerated Girls: The Results of a Focus Group Study," *Prison Journal* 77:381–405 (1997).

90. Kimberly Barletto, "Who's at Risk: Delinquent Trajectories of Children with Attention and Conduct Problems." Paper presented at the American Society of Criminology meeting, San Diego, 1997; Veronica Herrera, "Equals in Risk? The Differential Impact of Family Violence on Male and Female Delinquency." Paper presented at the annual Society of Criminology meeting, San Diego, November 1997.

91. Meda Chesney-Lind, "Girls' Crime and Women's Place: Toward a Feminist Model of Female Delinquency." Paper presented at the American Society of Criminology meeting, Montreal, November 1987.

92. Ibid., p. 20.

93. Joan Moore, *Going Down to the Barrio: Homeboys and Homegirls in Change* (Philadelphia: Temple University Press, 1991), p. 93.

94. Ibid., p. 101.

95. D. Wayne Osgood, Janet Wilson, Patrick O'Malley, Jerald Bachman, and Lloyd Johnston, "Routine Activities and Individual Deviant Behaviors," *American Sociological Review* 61:635–55 (1996).

96. Simon, *The Contemporary Woman and Crime;* Freda Adler, *Sisters in Crime* (New York: McGraw-Hill, 1975).

97. Adler, *Sisters in Crime.*

98. Ibid., pp. 10–11.

99. Rita James Simon, "Women and Crime Revisited," *Social Science Quarterly* 56:658–63 (1976).

100. Ibid., pp. 660–61.

101. Roy Austin, "Women's Liberation and Increase in Minor, Major, and Occupational Offenses," *Criminology* 20:407–30 (1982).

102. Delinquency Involvements," *Social Forces* 14:525–34 (1971).

103. Martin Gold, *Delinquent Behavior in an American City* (Pacific Grove, CA: Brooks/Cole, 1970), p. 118; John Clark and Edward Haurek, "Age and Sex Roles of Adolescents and Their Involvement in Misconduct: A Reappraisal," *Sociology and Social Research* 50:495–508 (1966); Nancy Wise, "Juvenile Delinquency in Middle-Class Girls," in E. Vaz, ed., *Middle Class Delinquency* (New York: Harper & Row, 1967), pp. 179–88; Gary Jensen and Raymond Eve, "Sex Differences in Delinquency: An Examination of Popular Sociological Explanations," *Criminology* 13:427–48 (1976).

104. Beth Bjerregaard and Carolyn Smith, "Gender Differences in Gang Participation and Delinquency," *Journal of Quantitative Criminology* 9:329–50 (1993).

105. Darrell Steffensmeier and Dana Haynie, "Gender, Structural Disadvantage, and Urban Crime: Do Macrosocial Variables Also Explain Female Offending Rates?" *Criminology* 38:403–438 (2000).

106. Henry Brownstein, Barry Spunt, Susan Crimmins, and Sandra Langley, "Women Who Kill in Drug Market Situations," *Justice Quarterly* 12:472–98 (1995).

107. Darrell Steffensmeier and Renee Hoffman Steffensmeier, "Trends in Female Delinquency," *Criminology* 18:62–85 (1980); see also, idem, "Crime and the Contemporary Woman: An Analysis of Changing Levels of Female Property Crime, 1960–1975," *Social Forces* 57:566–84 (1978); Darrell Steffensmeier and Michael Cobb, "Sex Differences in Urban Arrest Patterns, 1934–1979," *Social Problems* 29:37–49 (1981).

108. Darrell Steffensmeier, "National Trends in Female Arrests, 1960–1990: Assessment and Recommendations for Research," *Journal of Quantitative Criminology* 9:411–37 (1993).

109. Carol Smart, "The New Female Offender: Reality or Myth?" *British Journal of Criminology* 19:50–59 (1979).

110. Roy Austin, "Recent Trends in Official Male and Female Crime Rates: The Convergence Controversy," *Journal of Criminal Justice* 21:447–66 (1993).

111. Beth Bjerregaard and Carolyn Smith, "Gender Differences in Gang Participation, Delinquency, and Substance Abuse," *Journal of Quantitative Criminology* 9:329–55 (1993).

112. Austin, "Recent Trends in Official Male and Female Crime Rates," p. 464.

113. Julia Schwendinger and Herman Schwendinger, *Rape and Inequality* (Beverly Hills: Sage, 1983).

114. For a review of feminist theory, see Sally Simpson, "Feminist Theory, Crime and Justice," *Criminology* 27:605–32 (1989).

115. Ibid., p. 611.

116. Messerschmidt, *Masculinities and Crime: Critique and Reconceptualization of Theory.*

117. Center for Research on Women, *Secrets in Public: Sexual Harassment in Our Schools* (Wellesley, MA: Wellesley College, 1993).

118. Belknap, Holsinger, and Dunn, "Understanding Incarcerated Girls: The Results of a Focus Group Study."

119. Kathleen Daly and Meda Chesney-Lind, "Feminism and Criminology," *Justice Quarterly* 5:497–538 (1988).

120. Jane Siegel and Linda Meyer Williams, "Aggressive Behavior among Women Sexually Abused as Children." Paper presented at the American Society of Criminology meeting, Phoenix, 1993 (rev. version).

121. James Messerschmidt, *Capitalism, Patriarchy and Crime* (Totowa, NJ: Rowman and Littlefield, 1986); for a critique of this work, see Herman Schwendinger and Julia Schwendinger, "The World According to James Messerschmidt," *Social Justice* 15:123–45 (1988).

122. John Hagan, A.R. Gillis, and John Simpson, "The Class Structure and Delinquency: Toward a Power-Control Theory of Common Delinquent Behavior," *American Journal of Sociology* 90:1151–78 (1985); John Hagan, John Simpson, and A.R. Gillis, "Class in the Household: A Power-Control Theory of Gender and Delinquency," *American Journal of Sociology* 92:788–816 (1987).

123. John Hagan, A.R. Gillis, and John Simpson, "Clarifying and Extending Power-Control Theory," *American Journal of Sociology* 95:1024–37 (1990).

124. Gary Jensen and Kevin Thompson, "What's Class Got to Do with It? A Further Examination of Power-Control Theory," *American Journal of Sociology* 95:1009–1023 (1990); Kevin Thompson, "Gender and Adolescent Drinking Problems: The Effects of Occupational Structure," *Social Problems* 36:30–44 (1989); for some critical research, see Simon Singer and Murray Levine, "Power-Control Theory, Gender and Delinquency: A Partial Replication with Additional Evidence on the Effects of Peers," *Criminology* 26:627–48 (1988).

125. Meda Chesney-Lind, "Judicial Enforcement of the Female Sex Role: The Family Court and the Female Delinquent," *Issues in Criminology* 8:51–59 (1973).

126. Donna Bishop and Charles Frazier, "Gender Bias in Juvenile Justice Processing: Implications of the JJDP Act," *Journal of Criminal Law and Criminology* 82:1162–86 (1992).

127. Meda Chesney-Lind and Randall Shelden, *Girls, Delinquency and Juvenile Justice* (Belmont, CA: West/Wadsworth, 1998).

128. Bishop and Frazier, "Gender Bias in Juvenile Justice Processing," p. 1186.

129. Jean Rhodes and Karla Fischer, "Spanning the Gender Gap: Gender Differences in Delinquency among Inner City Adolescents," *Adolescence* 28:880–89 (1993).

130. Jill Leslie Rosenbaum and Meda Chesney-Lind, "Appearance and Delinquency: A Research Note," *Crime and Delinquency* 40:250–61 (1994).

131. Sealock and Simpson, "Unraveling Bias in Arrest Decisions: The Role of Juvenile Offender Typescripts."

132. Belknap, Holsinger, and Dunn, "Understanding Incarcerated Girls: The Results of a Focus Group Study."

133. Chesney-Lind and Shelden, *Girls, Delinquency and Juvenile Justice*, p. 243.

134. General Accounting Office, *Juvenile Justice: Minimal Gender Bias Occurred in Processing Noncriminal Juveniles* (Gaithersburg, MD: author, 1995).

Chapter 7

1. Paul Amato and Bruce Keith, "Parental Divorce and the Well-Being of Children: A Meta-Analysis," *Psychological Bulletin* 110:26–46 (1991).

2. Rolf Loeber and Magda Stouthamer-Loeber "Development of Juvenile Aggression and Violence," *American Psychologist* 53:242–59 (1998), at 250.

3. Joan McCord, "Family Relationships, Juvenile Delinquency, and Adult Criminality," *Criminology* 29:397–417 (1991); Scott Henggeler, ed., *Delinquency and Adolescent Psychopathology: A Family Ecological Systems Approach* (Littleton, MA: Wright–PSG, 1982).

4. For a general review of the relationship between families and delinquency, see Alan Jay Lincoln and Murray Straus, *Crime and the Family* (Springfield, IL: Charles C Thomas, 1985); Rolf Loeber and Magda Stouthamer-Loeber, "Family Factors as Correlates and Predictors of Juvenile Conduct Problems and Delinquency," in Michael Tonry and Norval Morris, eds., *Crime and Justice*, vol. 7 (Chicago: University of Chicago Press, 1986), pp. 29–151.

5. David Farrington, "Juvenile Delinquency," in John Coleman, ed., *The School Years* (London: Routledge, 1992), pp. 139–40.

6. Ruth Inglis, *Sins of the Fathers: A Study of the Physical and Emotional Abuse of Children* (New York: St. Martin's Press, 1978), p. 131.

7. See Joseph J. Costa and Gordon K. Nelson, *Child Abuse and Neglect: Legislation, Reporting, and Prevention* (Lexington, MA: D.C. Heath, 1978), p. xiii.

8. Tamar Lewin, "Men Assuming Bigger Role at Home, New Survey Shows," *New York Times*, 15 April 1998, p. A18.

9. Terence P. Thornberry, Carolyn A. Smith, Craig Rivera, David Huizinga, and Magda Stouthamer-Loeber, *Family Disruption and Delinquency, Juvenile Justice Bulletin*, Sept. 1999 (Washington, DC: Office of Juvenile Justice and Delinquency Prevention, 1999)

10. News Release, "Kids Count Survey 1998," Annie E. Casey Foundation, Baltimore, May 5, 1998.

11. Loeber and Stouthamer-Loeber, "Family Factors," pp. 39–41.

12. Paul Howes and Howard Markman, "Marital Quality and Child Functioning: A Longitudinal Investigation," *Child Development* 60:1044–51 (1989).

13. Barbara Dafoe Whitehead, "Dan Quayle Was Right," *Atlantic Monthly* 271:47–84 (1993).

14. C. Patrick Brady, James Bray, and Linda Zeeb, "Behavior Problems of Clinic Children: Relation to Parental Marital Status, Age, and Sex of Child," *American Journal of Orthopsychiatry* 56:399–412 (1986).

15. Scott Henggeler, *Delinquency in Adolescence* (Newbury Park, CA: Sage, 1989), p. 48.

16. Thornberry, Smith, Rivera, Huizinga, and Stouthamer-Loeber, *Family Disruption and Delinquency*.

17. Sheldon Glueck and Eleanor Glueck, *Unraveling Juvenile Delinquency* (Cambridge: Harvard University Press, 1950); Ashley Weeks, "Predicting Juvenile Delinquency," *American Sociological Review* 8:40–46 (1943).

18. Jackson Toby, "The Differential Impact of Family Disorganization," *American Sociological Review* 22:505–512 (1957); Ruth Morris, "Female Delinquency and Relation Problems," *Social Forces* 43:82-89 (1964); Roland Chilton and Gerald Markle, "Family Disruption, Delinquent Conduct, and the Effects of Sub-Classification," *American Sociological Review* 37:93–99 (1972).

19. For a review of these early studies, see Thomas Monahan, "Family Status and the Delinquent Child: A Reappraisal and Some New Findings," *Social Forces* 35:250–58 (1957).

20. Clifford Shaw and Henry McKay, *Report on the Causes of Crime, Social Factors in Juvenile Delinquency*, vol. 2 (Washington, DC: U.S. Government Printing Office, 1931), p. 392.

21. John Laub and Robert Sampson, "Unraveling Families and Delinquency: A Reanalysis of the Gluecks' Data," *Criminology* 26:355–80 (1988); Lawrence Rosen, "The Broken Home and Male Delinquency," in M. Wolfgang, L. Savitz, and N. Johnston, eds., *The Sociology of Crime and Delinquency* (New York: Wiley, 1970), pp. 489–95.

22. Christina DeJong and Kenneth Jackson, "Putting Race into Context: Race, Juvenile Justice Processing, and Urbanization," *Justice Quarterly* 15:487–504 (1998).

23. Robert Johnson, John Hoffman, and Dean Gerstein, *The Relationship between Family Structure and Adolescent Substance Abuse* (Washington, DC: Office of Applied Studies, Substance Abuse and Mental Health Services Administration, 1996).

24. Sara McLanahan, "Father Absence and the Welfare of Children." Working paper prepared for the John D. and Catherine MacArthur Research Foundation, Chicago, 1998.

25. Judith Smetena, "Adolescents' and Parents' Reasoning about Actual Family Conflict," *Child Development* 60:1052–67 (1989).

26. F. Ivan Nye, "Child Adjustment in Broken and Unhappy Unbroken Homes," *Marriage and Family* 19:356–61 (1957); idem, *Family Relationships and Delinquent Behavior* (New York: Wiley, 1958).

27. Michael Hershorn and Alan Rosenbaum, "Children of Marital Violence: A Closer Look at the Unintended Victims," *American Journal of Orthopsychiatry* 55:260–66 (1985).

28. Peter Jaffe, David Wolfe, Susan Wilson, and Lydia Zak, "Similarities in Behavior and Social Maladjustment among Child Victims and Witnesses to Family Violence," *American Journal of Orthopsychiatry* 56:142–46 (1986).

29. Veronica Herrera, "Equals in Risk? The Differential Impact of Family Violence on Male and Female Delinquency." Paper presented at the Annual Society of Criminology meeting, San Diego, November 1997.

30. Henggeler, *Delinquency in Adolescence*, p. 39.

31. Jill Leslie Rosenbaum, "Family Dysfunction and Female Delinquency," *Crime and Delinquency* 35:31–44 (1989), at 41.

32. Paul Robinson, "Parents of 'Beyond Control' Adolescents," *Adolescence* 13:116–19 (1978).

33. Loeber and Stouthamer-Loeber, "Development of Juvenile Aggression and Violence," p. 251.

34. Carolyn Smith, Sung Joon Jang, and Susan Stern, "The Effect of Delinquency on Families," *Family and Corrections Network Report* 13:1–11 (1997).

35. Amato and Keith, "Parental Divorce and the Well-Being of Children."

36. Adrian Raine, Patricia Brennan, and Sarnoff Mednick, "Interaction between Birth Complications and Early Maternal Rejection in Predisposing Individuals to Adult Violence: Specificity to Serious, Early-Onset Violence," *American Journal of Psychiatry* 154:1265–71 (1997).

37. Bill McCarthy and John Hagan, "Mean Streets: The Theoretical Significance of Situational Delinquency among Homeless Youth," *American Journal of Sociology* 98:597–627 (1992).

38. Carolyn Smith, Alan Lizotte, Terence Thornberry, and Marvin Krohn, "Resilience to Delinquency," *The Prevention Researcher* 4:4–7 (1997).

39. Sung Joon Jang and Carolyn Smith, "A Test of Reciprocal Causal Relationships among Parental Supervision, Affective Ties, and Delinquency," *Journal of Research in Crime and Delinquency* 34:307–36 (1997).

40. Gerald Patterson and Magda Stouthamer-Loeber, "The Correlation of Family Management Practices and Delinquency," *Child Development* 55:1299–1307 (1984); Gerald R. Patterson, *A Social Learning Approach: Coercive Family Process,* vol. 3 (Eugene, OR: Castalia, 1982).

41. Christopher Ellison and Darren Sherkat, "Conservative Protestantism and Support for Corporal Punishment," *American Sociological Review* 58:131–44 (1993).

42. Murray Straus, "Discipline and Deviance: Physical Punishment of Children and Violence and Other Crime in Adulthood," *Social Problems* 38:101–23 (1991).

43. Murray A. Straus, "Spanking and the Making of a Violent Society: The Short- and Long-Term Consequences of Corporal Punishment," *Pediatrics* 98:837–43 (1996).

44. Ibid.

45. Loeber and Stouthamer-Loeber, "Development of Juvenile Aggression and Violence," p. 251.

46. Nathaniel Pallone and James Hennessy, "Brain Dysfunction and Criminal Violence," *Society* 35:21–27 (1998).

47. Nye, *Family Relationships and Delinquent Behavior.*

48. Rolf Loeber and Thomas Dishion, "Boys Who Fight at Home and School: Family Conditions Influencing Cross-Setting Consistency," *Journal of Consulting and Clinical Psychology* 52:759–68 (1984).

49. Lisa Broidy, "Direct Supervision and Delinquency: Assessing the Adequacy of Structural Proxies," *Journal of Criminal Justice* 23:541–54 (1995).

50. Stephen Cernkovich and Peggy Giordano, "Family Relationships and Delinquency," *Criminology* 25:295–321 (1987).

51. Jang and Smith, "A Test of Reciprocal Causal Relationships among Parental Supervision, Affective Ties, and Delinquency."

52. Linda Waite and Lee Lillard, "Children and Marital Disruption," *American Journal of Sociology* 96:930–53 (1991).

53. Douglas Downey, "When Bigger Is Not Better: Family Size, Parental Resources, and Children's Educational Performance," *American Sociological Review* 60:746–61 (1995).

54. G. Rahav, "Birth Order and Delinquency," *British Journal of Criminology* 20:385–95 (1980); D. Viles and D. Challinger, "Family Size and Birth Order of Young Offenders," *International Journal of Offender Therapy and Comparative Criminology* 25:60–66 (1981).

55. David Eggebeen and Daniel Lichter, "Race, Family Structure, and Changing Poverty among American Children," *American Sociological Review* 56:801–817 (1991).

56. For an early review, see Barbara Wooton, *Social Science and Social Pathology* (London: Allen and Unwin, 1959).

57. Laub and Sampson, "Unraveling Families and Delinquency," p. 375.

58. D J. West and D.P. Farrington, eds., "Who Becomes Delinquent?" in *The Delinquent Way of Life* (London: Heinemann, 1977); D.J. West, *Delinquency, Its Roots, Careers, and Prospects* (Cambridge: Harvard University Press, 1982).

59. West, *Delinquency,* p. 114.

60. David Farrington, "Understanding and Preventing Bullying," in Michael Tonry, ed., *Crime and Justice,* vol. 17 (Chicago: University of Chicago Press, 1993), pp. 381–457.

61. Leonore Simon, "Does Criminal Offender Treatment Work?" *Applied and Preventive Psychology,* Summer:1–22 (1998).

62. Philip Harden and Robert Pihl, "Cognitive Function, Cardiovascular Reactivity, and Behavior in Boys at High Risk for Alcoholism," *Journal of Abnormal Psychology* 104:94–103 (1995).

63. Laub and Sampson, "Unraveling Families and Delinquency," p. 370.

64. D.P. Farrington, Gwen Gundry, and D.J. West, "The Familial Transmission of Criminality," in Alan Lincoln and Murray Straus, eds., *Crime and the Family* (Springfield, IL: Charles C Thomas, 1985), pp. 193–206.

65. See, generally, Wooton, *Social Science and Social Pathology;* H. Wilson, "Juvenile Delinquency, Parental Criminality, and Social Handicaps," *British Journal of Criminology* 15:241–50 (1975).

66. David Rowe and Bill Gulley, "Sibling Effects on Substance Use and Delinquency," *Criminology* 30:217–32 (1992); see also David Rowe, Joseph Rogers, and Sylvia Meseck-Bushey, "Sibling Delinquency and the Family Environment: Shared and Unshared Influences," *Child Development* 63:59–67 (1992).

67. Charles De Witt, director of the National Institute of Justice, quoted in National Institute of Justice, Research in Brief, *The Cycle of Violence* (Washington, DC: National Institute of Justice, 1992), p. 1.

68. Richard Gelles and Claire Pedrick Cornell, *Intimate Violence in Families,* 2nd ed. (Newbury Park, CA: Sage, 1990), p. 33.

69. Lois Hochhauser, "Child Abuse and the Law: A Mandate for Change," *Harvard Law Journal* 18:200 (1973); see also Douglas J. Besharov, "The Legal Aspects of Reporting Known and Suspected Child Abuse and Neglect," *Villanova Law Review* 23:458 (1978).

70. C. Henry Kempe, F.N. Silverman, B.F. Steele, W. Droegemueller, and H.K. Silver, "The Battered-Child Syndrome," *Journal of the American Medical Association* 181:17–24 (1962).

71. Brian G. Fraser, "A Glance at the Past, a Gaze at the Present, a Glimpse at the Future: A Critical Analysis of the Development of Child Abuse Reporting Statutes," *Chicago-Kent Law Review* 54:643 (1977–78).

72. See, especially, Inglis, *Sins of the Fathers,* ch. 8.

73. William Downs and Brenda Miller, "Relationships between Experiences of Parental Violence during Childhood and Women's Self-Esteem," *Violence and Victims* 13:63–78 (1998).

74. Ruth S. Kempe and C. Henry Kempe, *Child Abuse* (Cambridge: Harvard University Press, 1978), pp. 6–7.

75. Ibid.

76. Herman Daldin, "The Fate of the Sexually Abused Child," *Clinical Social Work Journal* 16:20–26 (1988).

77. Judith Herman, Diana Russell, and Karen Trocki, "Long-Term Effects of Incestuous Abuse in Childhood," *American Journal of Psychiatry* 143:1293–96 (1986).

78. Kathleen Kendall-Tackett, Linda Meyer Williams, and David Finkelhor, "Impact of Sexual Abuse on Children: A Review and Synthesis of Recent Empirical Studies," *Psychological Bulletin* 113:164–80 (1993).

79. Magnus Seng, "Child Sexual Abuse and Adolescent Prostitution: A Comparative Analysis," *Adolescence* 24:665–75 (1989); Dorothy Bracey, *Baby Pros: Preliminary Profiles of Juvenile Prostitutes* (New York: John Jay Press, 1979).

80. Kendall-Tackett, Williams, and Finkelhor, "Impact of Sexual Abuse on Children," p. 171.

81. Murray Straus, Richard Gelles, and Suzanne Steinmentz, *Behind Closed Doors: Violence in the American Family* (Garden City, NY: Anchor Books, 1980); Richard Gelles and Murray Straus, "Violence in the American Family," *Journal of Social Issues* 35:15–39 (1979).

82. Gelles and Straus, "Violence in the American Family," p. 24.

83. Gelles and Straus, *Intimate Violence,* pp. 108–109; Murray A. Straus and Glenda Kaufman Kantor, "Trends in Physical Abuse by Parents from 1975 to 1992: A Comparison of Three National Surveys." Paper presented at the Annual Meeting of the American Society of Criminology, Boston, 1995.

84. Murray A. Straus and Anita K. Mathur, "Social Change and Trends in Approval of Corporal Punishment by Parents from 1968 to 1994," in D. Frehsee, W. Horn, and K. Bussman, eds., *Violence against Children* (New York: de Gruyter, 1996), pp. 91–105.

85. Ching-Tung Wang and Deborah Daro, *Current Trends in Child Abuse Reporting and Fatalities: The Results of the 1997 Annual Fifty State Survey* (Chicago: The Center on Child Abuse Prevention Research, National Committee to Prevent Child Abuse, 1998).

86. Diana Russell, *Sexual Exploitation: Rape, Child Sexual Abuse, and Workplace Harassment* (Beverly Hills: Sage, 1984).

87. Maria Root, "Treatment Failures: The Role of Sexual Victimization in Women's Addictive Behavior," *American Journal of Orthopsychiatry* 59:543–49 (1989).

88. Lisa Jones and David Finkelhor, *The Decline in Child Sexual Abuse Cases* (Washington, DC: Office of Juvenile Justice and Delinquency Prevention, 2001).

89. Carolyn Webster-Stratton, "Comparison of Abusive and Nonabusive Families with Conduct-Disordered Children," *American Journal of Orthopsychiatry* 55:59–69 (1985); Fontana, "To Prevent the Abuse of the Future," p. 16; Fontana, "The Maltreated Children of Our Times," p. 451; Brandt F. Steele and Carl B. Pollock, "A Psychiatric Study of Parents Who Abuse Infants and Small Children," in Ray Helfer and C. Henry Kempe, eds., *The Battered Child* (Chicago: University of Chicago Press, 1968), pp. 103–145.

90. Brandt F. Steele, "Violence within the Family," in Ray E. Helfer and C. Henry Kempe, eds., *Child Abuse and Neglect: The Family and the Community* (Cambridge, MA: Ballinger, 1976), p. 13.

91. William Sack, Robert Mason, and James Higgins, "The Single-Parent Family and Abusive Punishment," *American Journal of Orthopsychiatry* 55:252–59 (1985).

92. Fontana, "The Maltreated Children of Our Times," pp. 450–51; see also Blair Justice and Rita Justice, *The Abusing Family* (New York: Human Sciences Press, 1976); Steele, "Violence within the Family," p. 12; Nanette Dembitz, "Preventing Youth Crime by Preventing Child Neglect," *American Bar Association Journal* 65:920–23 (1979).

93 Douglas Ruben, *Treating Adult Children of Alcoholics: A Behavioral Approach* (New York: Academic, 2000).

94. Martin Daly and Margo Wilson, "Violence against Stepchildren," *Current Directions in Psychological Science* 5:77–81 (1996).

95. Ibid.

96. Margo Wilson, Martin Daly, and Atonietta Daniele, "Familicide: The Killing of Spouse and Children," *Aggressive Behavior* 21:275–91 (1995).

97. Wang and Daro, *Current Trends in Child Abuse,* p. 10.

98. Ibid., p. 12.

99. Richard Gelles, "Child Abuse and Violence in Single-Parent Families: Parent Absence and Economic Deprivation," *American Journal of Orthopsychiatry* 59:492–501 (1989).

100. Susan Napier and Mitchell Silverman, "Family Violence as a Function of Occupation Status, Socioeconomic Class, and Other Variables." Paper presented at the American Society of Criminology meeting, Boston, November 1995.

101. Robert Burgess and Patricia Draper, "The Explanation of Family Violence," in Ohlin and Tonry, eds., *Family Violence* (Chicago: University of Chicago Press, 1989), pp. 59–117.

102. Ibid., pp. 103–104.

103 *Troxel et vir. v. Granville* No. 99–138 (June 5, 2000).

104. 452 U.S. 18, 101 S.Ct. 2153 (1981); 455 U.S. 745, 102 S.Ct. 1388 (1982).

105. For a survey of each state's reporting requirements, abuse and neglect legislation, and available programs and agencies, see Costa and Nelson, *Child Abuse and Neglect.*

106. Linda Gordon, "Incest and Resistance: Patterns of Father–Daughter Incest, 1880–1930," *Social Problems* 33:253–67 (1986).

107. P.L. 93B247 (1974); P.L. 104B235 (1996).

108. Martha Brannigan, "Arrests Spark Furor over the Reporting of Suspected Abuse," *Wall Street Journal,* 7 June 1989, p. B8.

109. Debra Whitcomb, *When the Victim Is a Child* (Washington, DC: National Institute of Justice, 1992), p. 5.

110. "False Accusations of Abuse Devastating to Families," *Crime Victims Digest* 6(2):4–5 (1989).

111. This section relies heavily on Shirley Dobbin, Sophia Gatowski, and Margaret Springate, "Child Abuse and Neglect," *Juvenile and Family Court Journal* 48:43–54 (1997).

112. For an analysis of the accuracy of children's recollections of abuse, see Candace Kruttschnitt and Maude Dornfeld, "Will They Tell? Assessing Preadolescents' Reports of Family Violence," *Journal of Research in Crime and Delinquency* 29:136–47 (1992).

113. Ibid.

114. Whitcomb, *When the Victim Is a Child,* p. 33.

115. *White v. Illinois,* 502 U.S. 346; 112 S.Ct. 736 (1992).

116. Myrna Raeder, "*White's* Effect on the Right to Confront One's Accuser," *Criminal Justice,* Winter 1993, pp. 2–7.

117. *Coy v. Iowa,* 487 U.S. 1012 (1988).

118. *Maryland v. Craig,* 110 S.Ct. 3157 (1990).

119. *Walker v. Fagg,* 400 S.E. 2d 708 (Va. App. 1991).

120. Wendy Fisk, "Childhood Trauma and Dissociative Identity Disorder," *Child and Adolescent Psychiatric Clinics of North America* 5:431–47 (1996).

121. Mary Haskett and Janet Kistner, "Social Interactions and Peer Perceptions of Young Physically Abused Children," *Child Development* 62:679–90 (1991).

122. Gelles and Straus, "Violence in the American Family."

123. National Center on Child Abuse and Neglect, Department of Health, Education, and Welfare, *1977 Analysis of Child Abuse and Neglect Research* (Washington, DC: U.S. Government Printing Office, 1978), p. 29.

124. Steele, "Violence within the Family," p. 22.

125. L. Bender and F. J. Curran, "Children and Adolescents Who Kill," *Journal of Criminal Psychopathology* 1:297 (1940), cited in Steele, "Violence within the Family," p. 21.

126. W.M. Easson and R.M. Steinhilber, "Murderous Aggression by Children and Adolescents," *Archives of General Psychiatry* 4:1–11 (1961), cited in Steele, "Violence within the Family," p. 22; see also J. Duncan and G. Duncan, "Murder in the Family: A

Study of Some Homicidal Adolescents," *American Journal of Psychiatry* 127:1498–1502 (1971); C. King, "The Ego and Integration of Violence in Homicidal Youth," *American Journal of Orthopsychiatry* 45:134–45 (1975); James Sorrells, "Kids Who Kill," *Crime and Delinquency* 23:312–26 (1977).

127. Jose Alfaro, "Report of the Relationship between Child Abuse and Neglect and Later Socially Deviant Behavior." Unpublished paper (Albany, NY: n.d.), pp. 175–219.

128. Cathy Spatz Widom, "Child Abuse, Neglect, and Violent Criminal Behavior," *Criminology* 27:251–71 (1989).

129. Widom, *The Cycle of Violence,* p. 1.

130. Michael Maxfield and Cathy Spatz Widom, "Childhood Victimization and Patterns of Offending through the Life Cycle: Early Onset and Continuation." Paper presented at the American Society of Criminology meeting, Boston, November 1995.

131. Jane Siegel and Linda Meyer Williams, "Violent Behavior among Men Abused as Children." Paper presented at the American Society of Criminology meeting, Boston, November 1995; Jane Siegel and Linda Meyer Williams, "Aggressive Behavior among Women Sexually Abused as Children." Paper presented at the American Society of Criminology meeting, Phoenix, 1993 (rev. version).

132. David Skuse, Arnon Bentovim, Jill Hodges, Jim Stevenson, Chriso Andreou, Monica Lanyado, Michelle New, Bryn Williams, and Dean McMillan, "Risk Factors for Development of Sexually Abusive Behaviour in Sexually Victimised Adolescent Boys: Cross Sectional Study," *British Medical Journal* 317:175–80 (1998).

133. Carolyn Smith and Terence Thornberry, "The Relationship between Childhood Maltreatment and Adolescent Involvement in Delinquency," *Criminology* 33:451–77 (1995).

134. Widom, "Child Abuse, Neglect, and Violent Criminal Behavior," p. 267.

135. Bruce Rind, Philip Tromovitch, and Robert Bauserman, "A Meta-Analytic Examination of Assumed Properties of Child Sexual Abuse Using College Samples," *Psychological Bulletin* 124:22–53 (1998); Kimberly Barletto, "Who's at Risk: Delinquent Trajectories of Children with Attention and Conduct Problems." Paper presented at the American Society of Criminology meeting, San Diego, 1997; Veronica Herrera, "Equals in Risk? The Differential Impact of Family Violence on Male and Female Delinquency." Paper presented at the Annual Society of Criminology meeting, San Diego, November, 1997.

136. Matthew Zingraff, "Child Maltreatment and Youthful Problem Behavior," *Criminology* 31:173–202 (1993).

137. Leonard Edwards and Inger Sagatun, "Dealing with Parent and Child in Serious Abuse Cases," *Juvenile and Family Court Journal* 34:9–14 (1983).

138. Susan McPherson, Lance McDonald, and Charles Ryer, "Intensive Counseling with Families of Juvenile Offenders," *Juvenile and Family Court Journal* 34:27–34 (1983).

139. The programs in this section are described in Edward Zigler, Cara Taussig, and Kathryn Black, "Early Childhood Intervention, a Promising Preventative for Juvenile Delinquency," *American Psychologist* 47:997–1006 (1992).

140. Lawrence W. Sherman, Denise C. Gottfredson, Doris L. MacKenzie, John Eck, Peter Reuter, and Shawn D. Bushway, *Preventing Crime: What Works, What Doesn't, What's Promising* (Washington, DC: National Institute of Justice, 1998).

141. Peter Greenwood, Karyn Model, and C. Peter Rydell, *The Cost-Effectiveness of Early Intervention as a Strategy for Reducing Violent Crime* (Santa Monica, CA: Rand, 1995).

142. Greg Parks, "The High/Scope Perry Preschool Project," *Juvenile Justice Bulletin*, October 2000 (Washington, DC: Office of Juvenile Justice and Delinquency Prevention, 2000), p. 1.

143. See, generally, Gerald Patterson, "Performance Models for Antisocial Boys," *American Psychologist* 41:432–44 (1986); idem, *Coercive Family Process* (Eugene, OR: Castalia, 1982).

144. Zigler, Taussig, and Black, "Early Childhood Intervention: A Promising Preventative for Juvenile Delinquency," pp. 1000–1004.

145. N. A. Wiltz and G. R. Patterson, "An Evaluation of Parent Training Procedures Designed to Alter Inappropriate Aggressive Behavior in Boys," *Behavior Therapy* 5:215–21 (1974).

146. Peter Greenwood, Karyn Model, and C. Peter Rydell, *The Cost-Effectiveness of Early Intervention as a Strategy for Reducing Violent Crime* (Santa Monica, CA: Rand, 1995).

Chapter 8

1. For a general review, see Scott Cummings and Daniel Monti, *Gangs: The Origin and Impact of Contemporary Youth Gangs in the United States* (Albany: SUNY Press, 1993); this chapter also makes extensive use of George Knox et al., *Gang Prevention and Intervention: Preliminary Results from the 1995 Gang Research Task Force* (National Gang Crime Research Center, 9501 S. King Drive, Chicago, IL, 1995).

2. Paul Perrone and Meda Chesney-Lind, "Representations of Gangs and Delinquency: Wild in the Streets?" *Social Justice* 24:96–117 (1997).

3. Thomas Berndt, "The Features and Effects of Friendships in Early Adolescence," *Child Development* 53:1447–69 (1982).

4. Thomas Berndt and T. B. Perry, "Children's Perceptions of Friendships as Supportive Relationships," *Developmental Psychology* 22:640–48 (1986).

5. Spencer Rathus, *Understanding Child Development* (New York: Holt, Rinehart & Winston, 1988), p. 462.

6. Peggy Giordano, "The Wider Circle of Friends in Adolescence," *American Journal of Sociology* 101:661–97 (1995).

7. Ibid., p. 463.

8. See, generally, Penelope Eckert, *Jocks and Burnouts: Social Categories and Identity in the High School* (New York: Teachers College Press, 1989).

9. Judith Rich Harris, *The Nurture Assumption: Why Children Turn Out the Way They Do* (New York: The Free Press, 1998).

10. Ibid., p. 463.

11. Robert Agnew and Timothy Brezina, "Relational Problems with Peers, Gender, and Delinquency," *Youth and Society* 29:84–111 (1997).

12. David Cantor, "Drug Involvement and Offending among Incarcerated Juveniles." Paper presented at the American Society of Criminology meeting, Boston, November 1995.

13. Albert Reiss, "Co-Offending and Criminal Careers," in Michael Tonry and Norval Morris, eds., *Crime and Justice,* vol. 10 (Chicago: University of Chicago Press, 1988).

14. Mark Warr, "Organization and Instigation in Delinquent Groups," *Criminology* 34:11–37 (1996).

15. Ibid., pp. 31–33.

16. James Short and Fred Strodtbeck, *Group Process and Gang Delinquency* (Chicago: Aldine, 1965).

17. Kate Keenan, Rolf Loeber, Quanwu Zhang, Magda Stouthamer-Loeber, and Welmoet Van Kammen, "The Influence of Deviant Peers on the Development of Boys' Disruptive and Delinquent Behavior: A Temporal Analysis," *Development and Psychopathology* 7:715–26 (1995).

18. John Cole, Robert Terry, Shari-Miller Johnson, and John Lochman, "Longitudinal Effects of Deviant Peer Groups on Criminal Offending in Late Adolescence." Paper presented at the American Society of Criminology meeting, Boston, November 1995.

19. Terence Thornberry, and Marvin Krohn, "Peers, Drug Use and Delinquency," in David Stoff, James Breiling, and Jack Maser, eds., *Handbook of Antisocial Behavior* (New York: Wiley, 1997), pp. 218–33; Thomas Dishion, Deborah Capaldi, Kathleen Spracklen, and Fuzhong Li, "Peer Ecology of Male Adolescent Drug Use," *Development and Psychopathology* 7:803–824 (1995).

20. Sara Battin, Karl Hill, Robert Abbott, Richard Catalano, and J. David Hawkins, "The Contribution of Gang Membership to Delinquency Beyond Delinquent Friends," *Criminology* 36:93–116 (1998).

21. Mark Warr, "Age, Peers and Delinquency," *Criminology* 31: 17–40 (1993).

22. Mark Warr, "Life-Course Transitions and Desistance from Crime," *Criminology* 36:502–536 (1998).

23. David Farrington and Rolf Loeber, "Epidemiology of Juvenile Violence," *Child and Adolescent Psychiatric Clinics of North America* 9:733–48 (2000); Cindy Hanson, Scott Henggeler, William Haefele, and J. Douglas Rodick, "Demographic, Individual, and Family Relationship Correlates of Serious Repeated Crime among Adolescents and Their Siblings," *Journal of Consulting and Clinical Psychology* 52:528–38 (1984).

24. Peggy Giordano, Stephen Cernkovich, and M. D. Pugh, "Friendships and Delinquency," *American Journal of Sociology* 91:1170–1202 (1986).

25. Other well-known movie representations of gangs include *The Wild Ones* and *Hell's Angels on Wheels,* which depict motorcycle gangs, and *Saturday Night Fever,* which focused on neighborhood street toughs; see also David Dawley, *A Nation of Lords* (Garden City, NY: Anchor, 1973).

26. For a recent review of gang research, see James Howell, "Recent Gang Research: Program and Policy Implications," *Crime and Delinquency* 40:495–515 (1994).

27. Walter Miller, *Violence by Youth Gangs and Youth Groups as a Crime Problem in Major American Cities* (Washington, DC: U.S. Government Printing Office, 1975).

28. Ibid., p. 20.

29. Malcolm Klein, *The American Street Gang, Its Nature, Prevalence and Control* (New York: Oxford University Press, 1995), p. 30.

30. Irving Spergel, *The Youth Gang Problem: A Community Approach* (New York: Oxford University Press, 1995).

31. Ibid., p. 3.

32. Frederick Thrasher, *The Gang* (Chicago: University of Chicago Press, 1927).

33. Malcolm Klein, ed., *Juvenile Gangs in Context* (Englewood Cliffs, NJ: Prentice-Hall, 1967), pp. 1–12.

34. Ibid., p. 6.

35. Irving Spergel, *Street Gang Work: Theory and Practice* (Reading, MA: Addison-Wesley, 1966).

36. Miller, *Violence by Youth Gangs,* p. 2.

37. Miller, *Violence by Youth Gangs,* pp. 1–2.

38. Ibid.

39. "LA Gang Warfare Called Bloodiest in 5 Years," *Boston Globe,* 18 December 1986, p. A4.

40. National School Safety Center, *Gangs in Schools, Breaking Up Is Hard to Do* (Malibu, CA: Pepperdine University, 1988), p. 8.

41. C. Ronald Huff, "Youth Gangs and Public Policy," *Crime and Delinquency* 35:524–37 (1989).

42. Joan Moore, *Going Down to the Barrio: Homeboys and Homegirls in Change* (Philadelphia: Temple University Press, 1991), p. 3.

43. Felix Padilla, *The Gang as an American Enterprise* (New Brunswick, NJ: Rutgers University Press, 1992), p. 3.

44. Pamela Irving Jackson, "Crime, Youth Gangs, and Urban Transition: The Social Dislocations of Postindustrial Economic Development," *Justice Quarterly* 8:379–97 (1991).

45. Moore, *Going Down to the Barrio,* pp. 89–101.

46. National School Safety Center, *Gangs in Schools,* p. 7.

47. Miller, *Violence by Youth Gangs;* idem., *Crime by Youth Gangs and Groups in the United States* (Washington, DC: Office of Juvenile Justice Delinquency Prevention, 1982).

48. Curry, Fox, Ball, and Stone, *National Assessment.*

49. Arlen Egley, Jr., *1999 Youth Gang Survey, Executive Summary* (Washington, DC: Office of Juvenile Justice and Delinquency Prevention, 2000). Herein cited as 1999 National Youth Gang Survey.

50. William Julius Wilson, *The Truly Disadvantaged* (Chicago: University of Chicago Press, 1987).

51. Vigil, *Barrio Gangs.*

52. Miller, *Violence by Youth Gangs,* pp. 17–20.

53. Jerome Needle and W. Vaughan Stapleton, *Reports of the National Juvenile Justice Assessment Centers, Police Handling of Youth Gangs* (Washington, DC: Office of Juvenile Justice and Delinquency Prevention, 1983), p. 12.

54. Richard Zevitz and Susan Takata, "Metropolitan Gang Influence and the Emergence of Group Delinquency in a Regional Community," *Journal of Criminal Justice* 20:93–106 (1992).

55. Cheryl Maxson, Kristi Woods, and Malcolm Klein, "Street Migration in the United States: Executive Summary" (Los Angeles: Center for the Study of Crime and Social Control, University of Southern California, 1995).

56. 1999 National Youth Gang Survey.

57. John Hagedorn, "Gangs, Neighborhoods and Public Policy," *Social Problems* 20:529–41 (1991).

58. Richard Cloward and Lloyd Ohlin, *Delinquency and Opportunity* (New York: Free Press, 1960), pp. 1–12.

59. Fagan, "The Social Organization of Drug Use and Drug Dealing among Urban Gangs."

60. Huff, "Youth Gangs and Public Policy," pp. 528–29.

61. Carl Taylor, *Dangerous Society* (East Lansing: Michigan State University Press, 1990).

62. Cheryl Maxson, "Investigating Gang Structures," *Journal of Gang Research* 3:33–40 (1995).

63. Scott Decker, Tim Bynum, and Deborah Weisel, "A Tale of Two Cities: Gangs and Organized Crime Groups," *Justice Quarterly* 15:395–425 (1998), at 410.

64. Saul Bernstein, *Youth in the Streets: Work with Alienated Youth Gangs* (New York: Associated Press, 1964).

65. Lewis Yablonsky, *The Violent Gang* (Baltimore: Penguin, 1966), p. 109.

66. James Diego Vigil, *Barrio Gangs* (Austin: Texas University Press, 1988), pp. 11–19.

67. Scott Decker, Tim Bynum, and Deborah Weisel, "A Tale of Two Cities: Gangs and Organized Crime Groups," *Justice Quarterly* 15:395–425 (1998).

68. Mark Warr, "Organization and Instigation in Delinquent Groups," *Criminology* 34:11–37 (1996).

69. Knox et al., *Gang Prevention and Intervention,* p. vii.

70. Spergel, *Youth Gangs,* p. 7.

71. Wilson, *The Truly Disadvantaged.*

72. 1999 Youth Gang Survey.

73. National School Safety Center, *Gangs in Schools,* p. 7.

74. John Hagedorn, Jerome Wonders, Angelo Vega, and Joan Moore, "The Milwaukee Drug Posse Study," unpublished leaflet, n.d.

75. Mary Glazier, "Small Town Delinquent Gangs: Origins, Characteristics and Activities." Paper presented at the American Society of Criminology meeting, Boston, November 1995.

76. 1998 Youth Gang Survey, p. 17.

77. Taylor, *Dangerous Society,* p. 109.

78. Finn-Aage Esbensen and David Huizinga, "Gangs, Drugs and Delinquency in a Survey of Urban Youth," *Criminology* 31:565–87 (1993).

79. Finn-Aage Esbensen, "Race and Gender Differences between Gang and Nongang Youths: Results from a Multisite Survey," *Justice Quarterly* 15:504–525 (1998).

80. Curry, "Female Gang Involvement."

81. Joan Moore, James Diego Vigil, and Robert Garcia, "Residence and Territoriality in Chicano Gangs," *Social Problems* 31:182–94 (1983).

82. Karen Joe Laidler and Geoffrey Hunt, "Violence and Social Organization in Female Gangs," *Social Justice* 24:148–87 (1997); Moore, *Going Down to the Barrio;* Anne Campbell, *The Girls in the Gang* (Cambridge, MA: Basil Blackwood, 1984).

83. Karen Joe and Meda Chesney-Lind, "'Just Every Mother's Angel': An Analysis of Gender and Ethnic Variations in Youth Gang Membership," *Gender and Society* 9:408–430 (1995).

84. Curry, "Female Gang Involvement."

85. Moore and Terrett, *Highlights of the 1996 National Youth Gang Survey;* Irving Spergel, "Youth Gangs: Continuity and Change," in Michael Tonry and Norval Morris, eds., *Crime and Justice,* vol. 12 (Chicago: University of Chicago Press, 1990), pp. 171–275.

86. William F. Whyte, *Street Corner Society* (Chicago: University of Chicago Press, 1955).

87. Malcolm Klein, "Impressions of Juvenile Gang Members," *Adolescence* 3:59 (1968).

88. Decker, Bynum, and Weisel, "A Tale of Two Cities."

89. Los Angeles County Sheriff's Department, *Street Gangs of Los Angeles County, White Paper* (Los Angeles: LACSD, n.d.), p. 14.

90. LeRoy Martin, *Collecting, Organizing and Reporting Street Gang Crime* (Chicago: Chicago Police Department, 1988).

91. Patricia Wen, "Boston Gangs: A Hard World," *Boston Globe,* 10 May 1988, p. 1.

92. Rick Graves and Ed Allen, *Black Gangs and Narcotics* (Los Angeles: Los Angeles County Sheriff's Department, n.d.).

93. Joseph Sheley, Joshua Zhang, Charles Brody, and James Wright, "Gang Organization, Gang Criminal Activity, and Individual Gang Members' Criminal Behavior," *Social Science Quarterly* 76:53-68 (1995).

94. Terence Thornberry and James Burch, *Gang Members and Delinquent Behavior* (Washington, D.C.: Office of Juvenile Justice and Delinquency Prevention, 1997).

95. 1999 National Youth Gang Survey.

96. Terence P. Thornberry and James H. Burch II, *Gang Members and Delinquent Behavior* (Washington, DC: Office of Juvenile Justice and Delinquency Prevention, 1997); James C. Howell, "Youth Gang Drug Trafficking and Homicide: Policy and Program Implications," *Juvenile Justice Journal* 4:3–5 (1997).

97. Malcolm Klein, Cheryl Maxson, and Lea Cunningham, "Crack, Street Gangs and Violence," *Criminology* 4:623–50 (1991); Mel Wallace, "The Gang-Drug Debate Revisited." Paper presented at the annual meeting of the American Society of Criminology, New Orleans, November 1992.

98. Kevin Thompson, David Brownfield, and Ann Marie Sorenson, "Specialization Patterns of Gang and Nongang Offending: A Latent Structure Analysis," *Journal of Gang Research* 3:25–35 (1996).

99. Sara Battin, Karl Hill, Robert Abbott, Richard Catalano, and J. David Hawkins, "The Contribution of Gang Membership to Delinquency Beyond Delinquent Friends," *Criminology* 36:93–116 (1998).

100. Scott Decker, "Collective and Normative Features of Gang Violence," *Justice Quarterly* 13:243–64 (1996).

101. Ibid.

102. Ibid.

103. Scott Decker, Susan Pennell, and Ami Caldwell, *Arrestees and Guns: Monitoring the Illegal Firearms Market* (Washington, DC: National Institute of Justice, 1996).

104. Beth Bjerregaard and Alan Lizotte, "Gun Ownership and Gang Membership," *Journal of Criminal Law and Criminology* 86:37–53 (1995).

105. Pamela Lattimore, Richard Linster, and John MacDonald, "Risk of Death among Serious Young Offenders," *Journal of Research in Crime and Delinquency* 34:187–209 (1997).

106. Decker, "Collective and Normative Features of Gang Violence," p. 253.

107. H. Range Hutson, Deirdre Anglin, and Michael Pratts Jr., "Adolescents and Children Injured or Killed in Drive-By Shootings in Los Angeles," *New England Journal of Medicine* 330:324–27 (1994).

108. Miller, *Violence by Youth Gangs,* pp. 2–26.

109. Kevin Cullen, "Gangs Are Seen as Carefully Organized," *Boston Globe,* 7 January 1987, p. 17.

110. Curry, Fox, Ball, and Stone, *National Assessment,* pp. 60–61.

111. The following description of ethnic gangs leans heavily on the material developed in National School Safety Center, *Gangs in Schools,* pp. 11–23.

112. Curry, Fox, Ball, and Stone, *National Assessment,* pp. 60–61.

113. The following description of ethnic gangs leans heavily on the material developed in National School Safety Center, *Gangs in Schools,* pp. 11–23.

114. Spergel, *The Youth Gang Problem,* pp. 136–37.

115. Decker, Bynum, and Weisel, "A Tale of Two Cities."

116. Los Angeles County Sheriff's Department, *Street Gangs of Los Angeles County.*

117. Ko-Lin Chin, *Chinese Subculture and Criminality: Nontraditional Crime Groups in America* (Westport, CN: Greenwood Press, 1990).

118. James Diego Vigil and Steve Chong Yun, "Vietnamese Youth Gangs in Southern California," in C. Ronald Huff, ed., *Gangs in America* (Newbury Park, CA: Sage, 1990), pp. 146–63.

119. See Glazier, "Small Town Delinquent Gangs."

120. For a review, see Lawrence Trostle, *The Stoners, Drugs, Demons and Delinquency* (New York: Garland, 1992).

121. Esbensen, "Race and Gender Differences between Gang and Nongang Youths."

122. Herbert Block and Arthur Niederhoffer, *The Gang: A Study in Adolescent Behavior* (New York: Philosophical Library, 1958).

123. Ibid., p. 113.

124. Knox et al., *Gang Prevention and Intervention,* p. 44.

125. James Diego Vigil, "Group Processes and Street Identity: Adolescent Chicano Gang Members," *Ethos* 16:421–45 (1988).

126. James Diego Vigil and John Long, "Emic and Etic Perspectives on Gang Culture: The Chicano Case," in C. Ronald Huff, ed., *Gangs in America* (Newbury Park, CA: Sage, 1990), p. 66.

127. Albert Cohen, *Delinquent Boys* (New York: Free Press, 1955), pp. 1–19.

128. Irving Spergel, *Racketville, Slumtown, and Haulburg: An Exploratory Study of Delinquent Subcultures* (Chicago: University of Chicago Press, 1964).

129. Malcolm Klein, *Street Gangs and Street Workers* (Englewood Cliffs, NJ: Prentice-Hall, 1971), pp. 12–15.

130. Vigil, *Barrio Gangs.*

131. Vigil and Long, "Emic and Etic Perspectives on Gang Culture," p. 61.

132. David Brownfield, Kevin Thompson, and Ann Marie Sorenson, "Correlates of Gang Membership: A Test of Strain, Social Learning, and Social Control," *Journal of Gang Research* 4:11–22 (1997).

133. John Hagedorn, Jose Torres, and Greg Giglio, "Cocaine, Kicks, and Strain: Patterns of Substance Use in Milwaukee Gangs," *Contemporary Drug Problems* 25:113–45 (1998).

134. Spergel, *The Youth Gang Problem,* pp. 4–5.

135. Ibid.

136. Yablonsky, *The Violent Gang,* p. 237.

137. Ibid., pp. 239–41.

138. Marc Le Blanc and Nadine Lanctot, "Social and Psychological Characteristics of Gang Members according to the Gang Structure and Its Subcultural and Ethnic Making," paper presented at the American Society of Criminology meeting, Miami, 1994.

139. Klein, *The American Street Gang.*

140. Ibid., p. 163.

141. Mercer Sullivan, *Getting Paid: Youth Crime and Work in the Inner City* (Ithaca, NY: Cornell University Press, 1989), pp. 244–45.

142. Esbensen and Huizinga, "Gangs, Drugs and Delinquency in a Survey of Urban Youth," p. 583; G. David Curry and Irving Spergel, "Gang Involvement and Delinquency among Hispanic and African-American Adolescent Males," *Journal of Research in Crime and Delinquency* 29:273–91 (1992).

143. Padilla, *The Gang as an American Enterprise,* p. 103.

144. Martin Sanchez-Jankowski, *Islands in the Street: Gangs and American Urban Society* (Berkeley: University of California Press, 1991).

145. Gary Jensen, "Defiance and Gang Identity: Quantitative Tests of Qualitative Hypothesis." Paper presented at the American Society of Criminology meeting, Boston, November 1995.

146. Terence Thornberry, Marvin Krohn, Alan Lizotte, and Deborah Chard-Wierschem, "The Role of Juvenile Gangs in Facilitating Delinquent Behavior," *Journal of Research in Crime and Delinquency* 30:55–87 (1993).

147. Spergel, *The Youth Gang Problem,* pp. 93–94.

148. Ibid., p. 93.

149. L. Thomas Winfree Jr., Teresa Vigil Backstrom, and G. Larry Mays, "Social Learning Theory, Self-Reported Delinquency and Youth Gangs, A New Twist on a General Theory of Crime and Delinquency," *Youth and Society* 26:147–77 (1994).

150. Karen Joe Laidler and Geoffrey Hunt, "Violence and Social Organization in Female Gangs," *Social Justice* 24:148–87 (1997).

151. Needle and Stapleton, *Police Handling of Youth Gangs,* p. 19.

152. Scott Armstrong, "Los Angeles Seeks New Ways to Handle Gangs," *Christian Science Monitor,* 23 April 1988, p. 3.

153. Mark Moore and Mark A. R. Kleiman, *The Police and Drugs* (Washington, DC: National Institute of Justice, 1989), p. 8.

154. Barry Krisberg, "Preventing and Controlling Violent Youth Crime: The State of the Art," in Ira Schwartz, ed., *Violent Juvenile Crime* (Minneapolis: University of Minnesota, Hubert Humphrey Institute of Public Affairs, n.d.).

155. See, generally, Spergel, *Street Gang Work.*

156. For a revisionist view of gang delinquency, see Hedy Bookin-Weiner and Ruth Horowitz, "The End of the Youth Gang," *Criminology* 21:585–602 (1983).

157. Quint Thurman, Andrew Giacomazzi, Michael Reisig, and David Mueller, "Community-Based Gang Prevention and Intervention: An Evaluation of The Neutral Zone," *Crime and Delinquency* 42:279–96 (1996).

158. Michael Agopian, "Evaluation of the Gang Alternative Prevention Program." Paper presented at the American Society of Criminology meeting, Boston, November 1995.

159. James Houston, "What Works: The Search for Excellence in Gang Intervention Programs." Paper presented at the American Society of Criminology meeting, Boston, November 1995.

160. Hagedorn, "Gangs, Neighborhoods and Public Policy."

161. Curry and Spergel, "Gang Involvement and Delinquency among Hispanic and African-American Adolescent Males."

Chapter 9

1. Terry Mcmanus, "Home Web Sites Thrust Students into Censorship Disputes," *New York Times,* 13 August 1998, p. E9.

2. *Justice and the Child in New Jersey,* report of the New Jersey Juvenile Delinquency Commission (1939), cited in Paul H. Hahn, *The Juvenile Offender and the Law* (Cincinnati: Anderson, 1978), p. 110.

3. U.S. Senate Subcommittee on Delinquency, *Challenge for the Third Century: Education in a Safe Environment* (Washington, DC: U.S. Government Printing Office, 1977), p. 1.

4. Delbert S. Eliott and Harwin L. Voss, *Delinquency and the Dropout* (Lexington, MA: Lexington Books, 1974), p. 204.

5. See, generally, Richard Lawrence, *School Crime and Juveniles* (New York: Oxford University Press, 1998).

6. U.S. Office of Education, *Digest of Educational Statistics* (Washington, DC: U.S. Government Printing Office, 1969), p. 25.

7. Kenneth Polk and Walter E. Schafer, eds., *Schools and Delinquency* (Englewood Cliffs, NJ: Prentice-Hall, 1972), p. 13.

8. Patrick Gonzales, et al., National Center for Education Statistics, *Pursuing Excellence: Comparisons of Eighth-Grade Science and Mathematics Achievement from a U.S. Perspective, 1995–1999* (Washington, DC: U.S. Government Printing Office, 2000).

9. National Education Goals Report, *Goals Report, 1997* (Washington, DC: U.S. Government Printing Office, 1997).

10. For reviews see Bruce Wolford and LaDonna Koebel, "Kentucky Model for Youths at Risk," *Criminal Justice* 9:5–55 (1995); J. David Hawkins, Richard Catalano, Diane Morrison, Julie O'Donnell, Robert Abbott, and L. Edward Day, "The Seattle Social Development Project," in Joan McCord and Richard Tremblay, eds., *The Prevention of Antisocial Behavior in Children* (New York: Guilford, 1992), pp. 139–60.

11. Eugene Maguin and Rolf Loeber, "Academic Performance and Delinquency," in *Crime and Justice: A Review of Research,* vol. 20, ed. Michael Tonry (Chicago: University of Chicago Press, 1995), pp. 145–264.

12. Terence Thornberry, Alan Lizotte, Marvin Krohn, Margaret Farnworth, and Sung Joon Jang, "Testing Interactional Theory: An Examination of Reciprocal Causal Relationships among Family, School, and Delinquency," *Journal of Criminal Law and Criminology* 82:3–35 (1991).

13. Carolyn Smith, Alan Lizotte, Terence Thornberry, and Marvin Krohn, "Resilience to Delinquency," *The Prevention Researcher* 4:4–7 (1997); Matthew Zingraff, Jeffrey Leiter, Matthew Johnsen,

and Kristen Myers, "The Mediating Effect of Good School Performance on the Maltreatment–Delinquency Relationship," *Journal of Research in Crime and Delinquency* 31:62–91 (1994).

14. Lyle Shannon, *Assessing the Relationship of Adult Criminal Careers to Juvenile Careers: A Summary* (Washington, DC: U.S. Government Printing Office, 1982).

15. Marvin Wolfgang, Robert Figlio, and Thorsten Sellin, *Delinquency in a Birth Cohort* (Chicago: University of Chicago Press, 1972).

16. Ibid., p. 94.

17. Bureau of Justice Statistics, *Prisons and Prisoners* (Washington, DC: U.S. Government Printing Office, 1982), p. 2.

18. Martin Gold, "School Experiences, Self-Esteem, and Delinquent Behavior: A Theory for Alternative Schools," *Crime and Delinquency* 24:294–95 (1978).

19. Michael Gottfredson and Travis Hirschi, *A General Theory of Crime* (Stanford, CA: Stanford University Press, 1990); J.D. McKinney, "Longitudinal Research on the Behavioral Characteristics of Children with Learning Disabilities," *Journal of Learning Disabilities* 22:141–50 (1990).

20. Albert K. Cohen, *Delinquent Boys* (New York: Free Press, 1955); see also Kenneth Polk, Dean Frease, and F. Lynn Richmond, "Social Class, School Experience, and Delinquency," *Criminology* 12:84–95 (1974).

21. Jackson Toby, "Orientation to Education as a Factor in the School Maladjustment of Lower-Class Children," *Social Forces* 35:259–66 (1957).

22. John Paul Wright, Francis Cullen, and Nicolas Williams, "Working while in School and Delinquent Involvement: Implications for Social Policy," *Crime and Delinquency* 43:203–221 (1997).

23. Polk, Frease, and Richmond, "Social Class, School Experience, and Delinquency," p. 92.

24. Delos Kelly and Robert Balch, "Social Origins and School Failure," *Pacific Sociological Review* 14:413–30 (1971).

25. Jeannie Oakes, *Keeping Track, How Schools Structure Inequality* (New Haven: Yale University Press, 1985), p. 48.

26. Delos Kelly, *Creating School Failure, Youth Crime, and Deviance* (Los Angeles: Trident Shop, 1982), p. 11.

27. Travis Hirschi, *Causes of Delinquency* (Berkeley: University of California Press, 1969), pp. 113–24, 132.

28. Richard Lawrence, "Parents, Peers, School and Delinquency." Paper presented at the American Society of Criminology meeting, Boston, November 1995.

29. Patricia Jenkins, "School Delinquency and the School Social Bond," *Journal of Research in Crime and Delinquency* 34:337–67 (1997).

30. Smith, Lizotte, Thornberry, and Krohn, "Resilience to Delinquency"; Zingraff, Leiter, Johnsen, and Myers, "The Mediating Effect of Good School Performance on the Maltreatment–Delinquency Relationship."

31. *Learning into the 21st Century, Report of Forum 5* (Washington, DC: White House Conference on Children, 1970).

32. Polk and Schafer, *Schools and Delinquency*, p. 23.

33. National Institute of Education, U.S. Department of Health, Education and Welfare, *Violent Schools—Safe Schools: The Safe Schools Study Report to the Congress*, vol. 1 (Washington, DC: U.S. Government Printing Office, 1977).

34. Phillip Kaufman, Xianglei Chen, Susan P. Choy, Sally Ruddy, Amanda Millere, Jill Fleury, Kathryn Chandler, Michael Rand, Patsy Klaus, Michael Planty, *Indicators of School Crime and Safety, 2000* (Washington, DC: U.S. Department of Education and Bureau of Justice Statistics, 2000). See also *2000 Annual Report on School Safety.*

35. Ibid., p. 20.

36. Ibid., p. 30.

37. Bryan Vossekuil, Marisa Reddy, Robert Fein, Randy Borum, William Modzeleski, *Safe School Initiative, An Interim Report On the Prevention of Targeted Violence in Schools* (Washington, DC: United States Secret Service, 2000).

38. Joseph A. Califano, Jr. and Alyse Booth, *1998 CASA National Survey of Teens, Teachers, and Principals* (The National Center for Addiction and Substance Abuse at Columbia University, 1998).

39. Luntz Research Companies and QEV Analytics, *Back to School 1997—The CASA National Survey of American Attitudes on Substance Abuse III: Teens and Their Parents, Teachers, and Principals* (New York: National Center for Addiction and Substance Abuse, Columbia University, 1998).

40. Gary Gottfredson and Denise Gottfredson, *Victimization in Schools* (New York: Plenum Press, 1985), p. 18.

41. Nancy Weishew and Samuel Peng, "Variables Predicting Students' Problem Behaviors," *Journal of Educational Research* 87:5–17 (1993).

42. James Q. Wilson, "Crime in Society and Schools," in J.M. McPartland and E.L. McDill, eds., *Violence in Schools: Perspective, Programs and Positions* (Lexington, MA: D.C. Heath, 1977), p. 48.

43. Joan McDermott, "Crime in the School and in the Community: Offenders, Victims, and Fearful Youth," *Crime and Delinquency* 29:270–83 (1983).

44. Ibid.

45. Ibid.

46. Daryl Hellman and Susan Beaton, "The Pattern of Violence in Urban Public Schools: The Influence of School and Community," *Journal of Research in Crime and Delinquency* 23:102–127 (1986).

47. Peter Lindstrom, "Patterns of School Crime: A Replication and Empirical Extension," *British Journal of Criminology* 37:121–31 (1997).

48. June L. Arnette and Marjorie C. Walsleben, *Combating Fear and Restoring Safety in Schools* (Washington, DC: Office of Juvenile Justice and Delinquency Prevention, 1998).

49. Heaviside and Burns, *Violence and Discipline Problems in U.S. Public Schools.*

50. Ibid., p. 20.

51. Ibid.

52. American Academy of Pediatrics Committee on School Health, "Violence in Schools: Current Status and Prevention," *School Health: Policy and Practice* (Elk Grove Village, IL: American Academy of Pediatrics Committee on School Health), pp. 363–80, at 369.

53. Bruce Jacobs, "Anticipatory Undercover Targeting in High Schools," *Journal of Criminal Justice* 22:445–57 (1994).

54. Kevin Bushweller, "Guards with Guns," *The American School Board Journal* 180:34–36 (1993).

55. Bella English, "Hub Program to Counsel Violent Pupils," *Boston Globe,* 24 February 1987, p. 1.

56. Randal C. Archibold, "City Schools Tentatively Agree to Let the Police Run Security," *New York Times,* 29 August 1998.

57. Steven Lab and John Whitehead, *The School Environment and School Crime: Causes and Consequences* (Washington, DC: National Institute of Justice, 1992), p. 5.

58. Jackie Kimbrough, "School-Based Strategies for Delinquency Prevention," in Peter Greenwood, ed., *The Juvenile Rehabilitation Reader* (Santa Monica, CA: Rand, 1985), pp. ix, 1–22.

59. Hellman and Beaton, "The Pattern of Violence in Urban Public Schools," pp. 122–23.

60. Julius Menacker, Ward Weldon, and Emanuel Hurwitz, "Community Influences on School Crime and Violence," *Urban Education* 25:68–80 (1990).

61. Wendy Mansfield and Elizabeth Farris, *Public School Principal Survey on Safe, Disciplined and Drug-Free Schools* (Washington, DC: U.S. Government Printing Office, 1992), p. iii.

62. National Commission on Excellence in Education, *A Nation at Risk* (Washington, DC: U.S. Government Printing Office, 1983).

63. Alexander Liazos, "Schools, Alienation, and Delinquency," *Crime and Delinquency* 24:355–61 (1978).

64. Stephen Cox, William Davidson, and Timothy Bynum, "A Meta-Analytic Assessment of Delinquency-Related Outcomes of Alternative Education Programs," *Crime and Delinquency* 41:219–34 (1995).

65. Gary Putka, "Cheaters in Schools May Not Be Students But Their Teachers," *Wall Street Journal,* 2 November 1989, p. 1.

66. U.S. Senate Subcommittee on Delinquency, *Challenge for the Third Century,* p. 95.

67. Executive Summary, "When School Is Out," *The Future of Children* 9: Fall 1999, a publication of the David and Lucile Packard Foundation, Los Altos, CA.

68. *New Jersey v. T.L.O.,* 469 U.S. 325, 105 S.Ct. 733 (1985).

69. *People v. Overton,* 24 N.Y.2d 522, 301 N.Y.S.2d 479, 249 N.E.2d 366 (1969); Brenda Walts, "*New Jersey v. T.L.O.*: Questions the Court Did Not Answer about School Searches," *Law and Education Journal* 14:421 (1985).

70. *Vernonia School District 47J v. Acton,* 115 S.Ct. 2394 (1995); Bernard James and Jonathan Pyatt, "Supreme Court Extends School's Authority to Search," *National School Safety Center News Journal* 26:29 (1995).

71. Michael Medaris, *A Guide to the Family Educational Rights and Privacy Act* (Washington, DC: Office of Juvenile Justice and Delinquency Prevention, 1998).

72. Ibid.

73. 393 U.S. 503, 89 S.Ct. 733 (1969).

74. Ibid.

75. *Bethel School District No. 403 v. Fraser,* 478 U.S. 675, 106 S.Ct. 3159, 92 L.Ed.2d 549 (1986).

76. *Hazelwood School District v. Kuhlmeier,* 484 U.S. 260, 108 S.Ct. 562, 98 L.Ed.2d 592 (1988).

77. Terry McManus, "Home Web Sites Thrust Students into Censorship Disputes," *New York Times,* 13 August 1998, p. E9.

78. Santa Fe Independent School District, Petitioner v. Jane Doe, individually and as next friend for her minor children, Jane and John Doe, et al., No. 99—62 [June 19, 2000].

79. *Ingraham v. Wright,* 430 U.S. 651, 97 S.Ct. 1401 (1977).

80. *Goss v. Lopez,* 419 U.S. 565, 95 S.Ct. 729 (1976).

Chapter 10

1. National Institute on Drug Abuse, Community Epidemiology Work Group, *Epidemiological Trends in Drug Abuse* (Washington, DC: National Institute on Drug Abuse, 1997).

2. University of Michigan, Institute for Social Research, News Release, 11 December 2000.

3. Peter Greenwood, "Substance Abuse Problems among High-Risk Youth and Potential Interventions," *Crime and Delinquency* 38:444–58 (1992).

4. U.S. Department of Justice, *Drugs and Crime Facts, 1988* (Washington, DC: Bureau of Justice Statistics, 1989), pp. 3–4.

5. Thomas Feucht, Richard Stephens, and Michael Walker, "Drug Use among Juvenile Arrestees: A Comparison of Self-Report, Urinalysis, and Hair Assay," *Journal of Drug Issues* 24:99–116 (1994).

6. Mary Ellen Macksey-Amiti and Michael Fendrich, "Delinquent Behavior and Inhalant Use among High School Students." Paper presented at the American Society of Criminology meeting, Boston, November 1995.

7. Dennis Coon, *Introduction to Psychology* (St. Paul: West, 1992), p. 178.

8. Alan Neaigus, Aylin Atillasoy, Samuel Friedman, Xavier Andrade, Maureen Miller, Gilbert Ildefonso, and Don Des Jarlais, "Trends in the Noninjected Use of Heroin and Factors Associated with the Transition to Injecting," in James Inciardi and Lana Harrison, eds., *Heroin in the Age of Crack-Cocaine* (Thousand Oaks, CA: Sage, 1998), pp. 108–30.

9. University of Michigan, News Release, pp. 1–3.

10. Special Issue, "Drugs—The American Family in Crisis," *Juvenile and Family Court* 39:45–46 (1988).

11. Federal Bureau of Investigation, *Crime in the United States, 1999* (Washington, DC: U.S. Government Printing Office, 2000), Table 29.

12. Robyn Cohen, *Drunk Driving* (Washington, DC: Bureau of Justice Statistics, 1992), p. 2.

13. D.J. Rohsenow, "Drinking Habits and Expectancies about Alcohol's Effects for Self versus Others," *Journal of Consulting and Clinical Psychology* 51:75–56 (1983).

14. Spencer Rathus, *Psychology,* 4th ed. (New York: Holt, Rinehart & Winston, 1990), p. 161.

15. Mary Tabor, "'Ice' in an Island Paradise," *Boston Globe,* 8 December 1989, p. 3.

16. Paul Goldstein, "Anabolic Steroids: An Ethnographic Approach." Unpublished paper (Narcotics and Drug Research, Inc., March 1989).

17. Centers for Disease Control, *Center Facts about Access to Tobacco by Minors* (Atlanta: Centers for Disease Control, 23 May 1997).

18. Andrew Lang Golub and Bruce Johnson, "Crack's Decline: Some Surprises across U.S. Cities," *National Institute of Justice Research in Brief* (Washington, DC: National Institute of Justice, 1997); Bruce Johnson, Andrew Lang Golub, and Jeffrey Fagan, "Careers in Crack, Drug Use, Drug Distribution, and Nondrug Criminality," *Crime and Delinquency* 41:275–95 (1995).

19. Ibid., p. 10.

20. Bruce Johnson, George Thomas, and Andrew Golub, "Trends in Heroin Use among Manhattan Arrestees from the Heroin and Crack Era," in James Inciardi and Lana Harrison, eds., *Heroin in the Age of Crack-Cocaine* (Thousand Oaks, CA: Sage, 1998), pp. 108–30.

21. Robert Brooner, Donald Templer, Dace Svikis, Chester Schmidt, and Spyros Monopolis, "Dimensions of Alcoholism: A Multivariate Analysis," *Journal of Studies on Alcohol* 51:77–81 (1990).

22. Joyce Ann O'Neil and Eric Wish, *Drug Use Forecasting, Cocaine Use* (Washington, DC: U.S. Government Printing Office, 1989), p. 7.

23. Eric Wish, "U.S. Drug Policy in the 1990s: Insights from New Data from Arrestees," *International Journal of the Addictions* 25:1–15 (1990).

24. G.E. Vallant, "Parent–Child Disparity and Drug Addiction," *Journal of Nervous and Mental Disease* 142:534–39 (1966).

25. Charles Winick, "Epidemiology of Narcotics Use," in D. Wilner and G. Kassenbaum, eds., *Narcotics* (New York: McGraw-Hill, 1965), pp. 3–18.

26. Delbert Elliott, David Huizinga, and Scott Menard, *Multiple Problem Youth: Delinquency, Substance Abuse and Mental Health Problems* (New York: Springer-Verlag, 1989).

27. Peter Reuter, Robert MacCoun, and Patrick Murphy, *Money from Crime: A Study of the Economics of Drug Dealing in Washington, D.C.* (Santa Monica, CA: Rand, 1990).

28. Thomas Dishion, Deborah Capaldi, Kathleen Spracklen, and Fuzhong Li, "Peer Ecology of Male Adolescent Drug Use," *Development and Psychopathology* 7:803–824 (1995).

29. C. Bowden, "Determinants of Initial Use of Opioids," *Comprehensive Psychiatry* 12:136–40 (1971).

30. Terence Thornberry and Marvin Krohn, "Peers, Drug Use and Delinquency," in David Stoff, James Breiling, and Jack Maser, eds., *Handbook of Antisocial Behavior* (New York: Wiley, 1997), pp. 218–33.

31. R. Cloward and L. Ohlin, *Delinquency and Opportunity: A Theory of Delinquent Gangs* (Glencoe, IL: Free Press, 1960).

32. Denise Kandel and Mark Davies, "Friendship Networks, Intimacy and Illicit Drug Use in Young Adulthood: A Comparison of Two Competing Theories," *Criminology* 29:441–71 (1991).

33. James Inciardi, Ruth Horowitz, and Anne Pottieger, *Street Kids, Street Drugs, Street Crime: An Examination of Drug Use and Serious Delinquency in Miami* (Belmont, CA: Wadsworth, 1993), p. 43.

34. D. Baer and J. Corrado, "Heroin Addict Relationships with Parents during Childhood and Early Adolescent Years," *Journal of Genetic Psychology* 124:99–103 (1974).

35. Timothy Ireland and Cathy Spatz Widom, *Childhood Victimization and Risk for Alcohol and Drug Arrests* (Washington, DC: National Institute of Justice, 1995).

36. See S. F. Bucky, "The Relationship between Background and Extent of Heroin Use," *American Journal of Psychiatry* 130:709–710 (1973); I. Chien, D. L. Gerard, R. Lee, and E. Rosenfield, *The Road to H: Narcotics Delinquency and Social Policy* (New York: Basic Books, 1964).

37. J. S. Mio, G. Nanjundappa, D. E. Verlur, and M. D. DeRios, "Drug Abuse and the Adolescent Sex Offender: A Preliminary Analysis," *Journal of Psychoactive Drugs* 18:65–72 (1986).

38. G.T. Wilson, "Cognitive Studies in Alcoholism," *Journal of Consulting and Clinical Psychology* 55:325–31 (1987).

39. John Hagedorn, Jose Torres, and Greg Giglio, "Cocaine, Kicks, and Strain: Patterns of Substance Use in Milwaukee Gangs," *Contemporary Drug Problems* 25:113–45 (1998).

40. For a thorough review, see Karol Kumpfer, "Impact of Maternal Characteristics and Parenting Processes on Children of Drug Abusers." Paper presented at the American Society of Criminology meeting, Boston, November 1995.

41. D.W. Goodwin, "Alcoholism and Genetics," *Archives of General Psychiatry* 42:171–74 (1985).

42. Ibid.

43. Patricia Dobkin, Richard Tremblay, Louise Masse, and Frank Vitaro, "Individual and Peer Characteristics in Predicting Boys' Early Onset of Substance Abuse: A Seven-Year Longitudinal Study," *Child Development* 66:1198–1214 (1995).

44. Ric Steele, Rex Forehand, Lisa Armistead, and Gene Brody, "Predicting Alcohol and Drug Use in Early Adulthood: The Role of Internalizing and Externalizing Behavior Problems in Early Adolescence," *American Journal of Orthopsychiatry* 65:380–87 (1995).

45. Ibid., pp. 380–81.

46. Jerome Platt and Christina Platt, *Heroin Addiction* (New York: Wiley, 1976), p. 127.

47. Rathus, *Psychology*, p. 158.

48. Eric Strain, "Antisocial Personality Disorder, Misbehavior and Drug Abuse," *Journal of Nervous and Mental Disease* 163:162–65 (1995).

49. Patricia Dobkin, Richard Tremblay, Louise Masse, and Frank Vitaro, "Individual and Peer Characteristics in Predicting Boys' Early Onset of Substance Abuse: A Seven-Year Longitudinal Study," *Child Development* 66:1198–1214 (1995).

50. J. Shedler and J. Block, "Adolescent Drug Use and Psychological Health: A Longitudinal Inquiry," *American Psychologist* 45:612–30 (1990).

51. Greenwood, "Substance Abuse Problems among High-Risk Youth and Potential Interventions," p. 448.

52. John Wallace and Jerald Bachman, "Explaining Racial/Ethnic Differences in Adolescent Drug Use: The Impact of Background and Lifestyle," *Social Problems* 38:333–57 (1991).

53. Marvin Krohn, Terence Thornberry, Lori Collins-Hall, and Alan Lizotte, "School Dropout, Delinquent Behavior, and Drug Use," in Howard Kaplan, ed., *Drugs, Crime and Other Deviant Adaptations: Longitudinal Studies* (New York: Plenum Press, 1995), pp. 163–83.

54. B.A. Christiansen, G.T. Smith, P.V. Roehling, and M.S. Goldman, "Using Alcohol Expectancies to Predict Adolescent Drinking Behavior after One Year," *Journal of Counseling and Clinical Psychology* 57:93–99 (1989).

55. Inciardi, Horowitz, and Pottieger, *Street Kids, Street Drugs, Street Crime*, p. 135.

56. Ibid., p. 136.

57. Mary Ellen Mackesy-Amiti, Michael Fendrich, and Paul Goldstein, "Sequence of Drug Use among Serious Drug Users: Typical vs. Atypical Progression," *Drug and Alcohol Dependence* 45:185–96 (1997).

58. The following sections lean heavily on Marcia Chaiken and Bruce Johnson, *Characteristics of Different Types of Drug-Involved Youth* (Washington, DC: National Institute of Justice, 1988).

59. Ibid., p. 100.

60. Ibid., p. 101.

61. Robert MacCoun and Peter Reuter, "Are the Wages of Sin $30 an Hour? Economic Aspects of Street-Level Drug Dealing," *Crime and Delinquency* 38:477–91 (1992).

62. Chaiken and Johnson, *Characteristics of Different Types of Drug-Involved Youth*, p. 12.

63. Rick Graves and Ed Allen, *Narcotics and Black Gangs* (Los Angeles: Los Angeles County Sheriff's Department, n.d.).

64. John Hagedorn, "Neighborhoods, Markets, and Gang Drug Organization," *Journal of Research in Crime and Delinquency* 31:264–94 (1994).

65. Chaiken and Johnson, *Characteristics of Different Types of Drug-Involved Youth*, p. 14.

66. Eric Baumer, Janet Lauritsen, Richard Rosenfeld, and Richard Wright, "The Influence of Crack Cocaine on Robbery, Burglary, and Homicide Rates: A Cross-City, Longitudinal Analysis," *Journal of Research in Crime and Delinquency* 35:316–40 (1998).

67. Ibid.

68. James Inciardi, "Heroin Use and Street Crime," *Crime and Delinquency* 25:335–46 (1979); idem, *The War on Drugs* (Palo Alto, CA: Mayfield, 1986); see also W. McGlothlin, M. Anglin, and B. Wilson, "Narcotic Addiction and Crime," *Criminology* 16:293–311 (1978); George Speckart and M. Douglas Anglin, "Narcotics Use and Crime: An Overview of Recent Research Advances," *Contemporary Drug Problems* 13:741–69 (1986); Charles Faupel and Carl Klockars, "Drugs-Crime Connections: Elaborations from the Life Histories of Hard-Core Heroin Addicts," *Social Problems* 34:54–68 (1987).

69. Eric Baumer, "Poverty, Crack and Crime: A Cross-City Analysis," *Journal of Research in Crime and Delinquency* 31:311–27 (1994).

70. Marvin Dawkins, "Drug Use and Violent Crime among Adolescents," *Adolescence* 32:395–406 (1997); Robert Peralta, "The

Relationship between Alcohol and Violence in an Adolescent Population: An Analysis of the Monitoring the Future Survey." Paper presented at the annual Society of Criminology meeting, San Diego, November 1997; Helene Raskin White and Stephen Hansell, "The Moderating Effects of Gender and Hostility on the Alcohol–Aggression Relationship," *Journal of Research in Crime and Delinquency* 33:450–70 (1996); D. Wayne Osgood, "Drugs, Alcohol, and Adolescent Violence." Paper presented at the annual meeting of the American Society of Criminology, Miami, 1994.

71. National Institute Of Justice, Press Release, "Study Shows Substantial Levels of Drug Use Among Arrestees across the Nation," July 20, 2000.

72. David Cantor, "Drug Involvement and Offending of Incarcerated Youth." Paper presented at the American Society of Criminology meeting, Boston, November 1995.

73. B.D. Hohnson, E.Wish, J. Schmeidler, and D. Huizinga, "Concentration of Delinquent Offending: Serious Drug Involvement and High Delinquency Rates," *Journal of Drug Issues* 21:205–229 (1991).

74. Inciardi, Horowitz, and Pottienger.

75. W. David Watts and Lloyd Wright, "The Relationship of Alcohol, Tobacco, Marijuana, and Other Illegal Drug Use to Delinquency among Mexican-American, Black, and White Adolescent Males," *Adolescence* 25:38–54 (1990).

76. For a general review of this issue, see Helene Raskin White, "The Drug Use–Delinquency Connection in Adolescence," in Ralph Weisheit, ed., *Drugs, Crime and Criminal Justice* (Cincinnati: Anderson, 1990), pp. 215–56; Speckart and Anglin, "Narcotics Use and Crime"; Faupel and Klockars, "Drugs–Crime Connections."

77. Delbert Elliott, David Huizinga, and Susan Ageton, *Explaining Delinquency and Drug Abuse* (Beverly Hills: Sage, 1985).

78. David Huizinga, Scott Menard, and Delbert Elliott, "Delinquency and Drug Use: Temporal and Developmental Patterns," *Justice Quarterly* 6:419–55 (1989).

79. Helene Raskin White, Robert Padina, and Randy LaGrange, "Longitudinal Predictors of Serious Substance Use and Delinquency," *Criminology* 25:715–40 (1987).

80. Wish, "U.S. Drug Policy in the 1990s."

81. U.S. Department of State, 1998 International Narcotics Control Strategy Report, February 1999.

82. Clifford Krauss, "Neighbors Worry about Colombian Aid," *New York Times*, August 25, 2000, A3.

83. William Rhodes et al., *What America's Users Spend on Illegal Drugs, 1988–1993* (Cambridge, MA: ABT Associates, 1995).

84. Mark Moore, *Drug Trafficking* (Washington, DC: National Institute of Justice, 1988).

85. Jeffrey Butts and Melissa Sickmund, *Offenders in Juvenile Court, 1989* (Washington, DC: Office of Juvenile Justice and Delinquency Prevention, 1992), p. 1.

86. Ibid.

87. Phyllis Ellickson and Robert Bell, *Prospects for Preventing Drug Use among Young Adolescents* (Santa Monica, CA: Rand, 1990).

88. Wayne Lucan and Steven Gilham, "Impact of a Drug Use Prevention Program: An Empirical Assessment." Paper presented at the annual meeting of the American Society of Criminology, New Orleans, November 1992.

89. Scott Henggeler, *Delinquency and Adolescent Psychopathology: A Family–Ecological Systems Approach* (Littleton, MA: Wright-PSG, 1982).

90. Scott Henggeler, "Effects of Multisystemic Therapy on Drug Use and Abuse in Serious Juvenile Offenders: A Progress Report from Two Outcome Studies," *Family Dynamics of Addiction Quarterly* 1:40–51 (1991).

91. Eli Ginzberg, Howard Berliner, and Miriam Ostrow, *Young People at Risk: Is Prevention Possible?* (Boulder: Westview Press, 1988), p. 99.

92. Ibid.

93. Miriam Sealock, Denise Gottfredson, and Catherine Gallagher, "Addressing Drug Use and Recidivism in Delinquent Youth: An Examination of Residential and Aftercare Treatment Programs." Paper presented at the American Society of Criminology meeting, Boston, November 1995.

94. Kathryn Ann Farr, "Revitalizing the Drug Decriminalization Debate," *Crime and Delinquency* 36:223–37 (1990).

95. Reuter, MacCoun, and Murphy, *Money from Crime*, pp. 165–68.

Chapter 11

1. Timothy Egan, "From Adolescent Angst to Shooting Up Schools," *New York Times,* 14 June 1998, p. 1; James Alan Fox, "Again School Attacks Show Need for New Strategies," *Boston Sunday Globe,* 24 May 1998, pp. D1–2; Patricia King and Andrew Murr, "A Son Out of Control," *Newsweek,* 1 June 1998, pp. 32–33; Jerome Shestack, "What about Juvenile Justice?" *American Bar Association Journal* 84:8 (1998).

2. Robert M. Mennel, "Origins of the Juvenile Court: Changing Perspectives on the Legal Rights of Juvenile Delinquents," *Crime and Delinquency* 18:68–78 (1972).

3. Anthony Salerno, "The Child Saving Movement: Altruism or Conspiracy," *Juvenile and Family Court Journal* 42:37 (1991).

4. Frank J. Coppa and Philip C. Dolce, *Cities in Transition: From the Ancient World to Urban America* (Chicago: Nelson Hall, 1974), p. 220.

5. Robert Mennel, "Attitudes and Policies toward Juvenile Delinquency," *Crime and Justice,* vol. 5 (Chicago: University of Chicago Press, 1983), p. 198.

6. Anthony M. Platt, *The Child Savers: The Invention of Delinquency* (Chicago: University of Chicago Press, 1969).

7. Ibid.

8. Sanford J. Fox, "Juvenile Justice Reform: A Historical Perspective," *Stanford Law Review* 22:1187 (1970).

9. Robert S. Pickett, *House of Refuge—Origins of Juvenile Reform in New York State, 1815–1857* (Syracuse, NY: Syracuse University Press, 1969).

10. Mennel, "Origins of the Juvenile Court," pp. 69–70.

11. Ibid., pp. 70–71.

12. Salerno, "The Child Saving Movement," p. 37.

13. Platt, *The Child Savers: The Invention of Delinquency.*

14. Ibid., p. 116.

15. Randall Shelden and Lynn Osborne, "'For Their Own Good': Class Interests and the Child Saving Movement in Memphis, Tennessee, 1900–1917," *Criminology* 27:747–67 (1989).

16. U.S. Department of Justice, Juvenile Justice and Delinquency Prevention, *Two Hundred Years of American Criminal Justice: An LEAA Bicentennial Study* (Washington, DC: LEAA, 1976).

17. Beverly Smith, "Female Admissions and Paroles of the Western House of Refuge in the 1880s, An Historical Example of Community Corrections," *Journal of Research in Crime and Delinquency* 26:36–66 (1989).

18. Fox, "Juvenile Justice Reform," p. 1229.

19. Elizabeth Pleck, "Criminal Approaches to Family Violence, 1640–1980," in Lloyd Ohlin and Michael Tonry, eds., *Family Violence* (Chicago: University of Chicago Press, 1989), pp. 19–58.

20. Elizabeth Pleck, *Domestic Tyranny: The Making of Social Policy against Family Violence from Colonial Times to the Present* (New York: Oxford University Press, 1987), pp. 28–30.

21. Linda Gordon, *Family Violence and Social Control* (New York: Viking, 1988).

22. Kathleen Block and Donna Hale, "Turf Wars in the Progressive Era of Juvenile Justice: The Relationship of Private and Public Child Care Agencies," *Crime and Delinquency* 37:225–41 (1991).

23. Theodore Ferdinand, "Juvenile Delinquency or Juvenile Justice: Which Came First?" *Criminology* 27:79–106 (1989).

24. *In re Gault,* 387 U.S. 1, 87 S.Ct. 1428, 18 L.Ed. 2d 527 (1967).

25. Mary Odem and Steven Schlossman, "Guardians of Virtue: The Juvenile Court and Female Delinquency in Early 20th-Century Los Angeles," *Crime and Delinquency* 37:186–203 (1991).

26. John Sutton, "Bureaucrats and Entrepreneurs: Institutional Responses to Deviant Children in the United States, 1890–1920," *American Journal of Sociology* 95:1367–1400 (1990).

27. Ibid., p. 1383.

28. Margueritte Rosenthal, "Reforming the Juvenile Correctional Institution: Efforts of the U.S. Children's Bureau in the 1930s," *Journal of Sociology and Social Welfare* 14:47–74 (1987); see also David Steinhart, "Status Offenses," The Center for the Future of Children, The Juvenile Court (Los Altos, Calif.: David and Lucille Packard Foundation, 1996).

29. For an overview of these developments, see Theodore Ferdinand, "History Overtakes the Juvenile Justice System," *Crime and Delinquency* 37:204–224 (1991).

30. N.Y. Fam. Ct. Act, Art. 7, Sec. 712 (Consol. 1962).

31. *Kent v. United States,* 383 U.S. 541, 86 S.Ct. 1045, 16 L.Ed.2d 84 (1966); *In re Gault,* 387 U.S. 1, 87 S.Ct. 1428, 18 L.Ed.2d 527 (1967): Juveniles have the right to notice, counsel, confrontation, and cross-examination, and to the privileges against self-incrimination in juvenile court proceedings. *In re Winship,* 397 U.S. 358, 90 S.Ct. 1068, 25 L.Ed.2d 368 (1970): Proof beyond a reasonable doubt is necessary for conviction in juvenile proceedings. *Breed v. Jones,* 421 U.S. 519, 95 S.Ct. 1779, 44 L.Ed.2d 346 (1975): Jeopardy attaches in a juvenile court adjudicatory hearing, thus barring subsequent prosecution for the same offense as an adult.

32. Public Law 90–351, Title I—Omnibus Safe Streets and Crime Control Act of 1968, 90th Congress, June 1968.

33. National Advisory Commission on Criminal Justice Standards and Goals, *A National Strategy to Reduce Crime* (Washington, DC: U.S. Government Printing Office, 1973).

34. Juvenile Justice and Delinquency Prevention Act of 1974, Public Law 93–415 (1974). For a critique of this legislation, see Ira Schwartz, *Justice for Juveniles—Rethinking the Best Interests of the Child* (Lexington, MA: D.C. Heath, 1989), p. 175.

35. For an extensive summary of the Violent Crime Control and Law Enforcement Act of 1994, see *Criminal Law Reporter* 55:2305–2430 (1994).

36. Shay Bilchik, "A Juvenile Justice System for the 21st Century," *Crime and Delinquency* 44:89 (1998).

37. For a comprehensive view of juvenile law see, generally, Joseph J. Senna and Larry J. Siegel, *Juvenile Law: Cases and Comments* (St. Paul: West, 2d ed., 1992).

38. For an excellent review of the juvenile process, see Adrienne Volenik, *Checklists for Use in Juvenile Delinquency Proceedings* (Washington, DC: American Bar Association, 1985); see also Jeffrey Butts and Gregory Halemba, *Waiting for Justice—Moving Young Offenders through the Juvenile Court Process* (Pittsburgh: National Center for Juvenile Justice, 1996).

39. Fox Butterfield, "Justice Besieged," *New York Times,* 21 July 1997, A16.

40. National Conference of State Legislatures, *A Legislator's Guide to Comprehensive Juvenile Justice, Juvenile Detention, and Corrections* (Denver: National Conference of State Legislators, 1996).

41. James Howell, ed., *Guide for Implementing the Comprehensive Strategy for Serious, Violent, and Chronic Juvenile Offenders* (Washington, DC: OJJDP, 1995).

42. Barry Feld, "Criminology and the Juvenile Court: A Research Agenda for the 1990s," in Ira M. Schwartz, *Juvenile Justice and Public Policy—Toward a National Agenda* (New York: Lexington Books, 1992), p. 59.

43. Robert O. Dawson, "The Future of Juvenile Justice: Is It Time to Abolish the System?" *Journal of Criminal Law and Criminology* 81:136–55 (1990); see also Leonard P. Edwards, "The Future of the Juvenile Court: Promising New Directions in the Center for the Future of Children," The Juvenile Court (Los Altos, CA: David and Lucille Packard Foundation, 1996).

44. Hunter Hurst, "Juvenile Court: As We Enter the Millennium," *Juvenile and Family Court Journal* 50:21–27 (1999).

45. Carol J. DeFrances and Kevin Strom, *Juveniles Prosecuted in the State Criminal Courts* (Washington, DC: Bureau of Justice Statistics, 1997).

46. Shay Bilchik, "A Juvenile Justice System for the 21st Century," *Crime and Delinquency* 44:89 (1998).

47. Patricia Torbet and Linda Szymanski, *State Legislative Responses to Violent Crime: 1996–97 Update* (Washington, DC: Office of Juvenile Justice and Delinquency Prevention,1998).

48. Ibid.

49. Hunter Hurst, "Juvenile Court: As We Enter the Millennium," p. 25.

50. Alida Merlo, Peter Benekos, and William Cook, "The Juvenile Court at 100 Years: Celebration or Wake?" *Juvenile and Family Court Journal* 50:1–9 at 7 (1999).

Chapter 12

1. This section relies on sources such as Malcolm Sparrow, Mark Moore, and David Kennedy, *Beyond 911, A New Era for Policing* (New York: Basic Books, 1990); Daniel Devlin, *Police Procedure, Administration, and Organization* (London: Butterworth, 1966); Robert Fogelson, *Big City Police* (Cambridge, MA: Harvard University Press, 1977); Roger Lane, *Policing the City, Boston 1822–1885* (Cambridge, MA: Harvard University Press, 1967); Roger Lane, "Urban Police and Crime in Nineteenth-Century America," in Norval Morris and Michael Tonry, eds., *Crime and Justice,* vol. 2 (Chicago: University of Chicago Press, 1980), pp. 1–45; J.J. Tobias, *Crime and Industrial Society in the Nineteenth Century* (New York: Schocken, 1967); Samuel Walker, *A Critical History of Police Reform: The Emergence of Professionalism* (Lexington, MA: Lexington Books, 1977); idem, *Popular Justice* (New York: Oxford University Press, 1980); President's Commission on Law Enforcement and the Administration of Justice, *Task Force Report: The Police* (Washington, DC: U.S. Government Printing Office, 1967), pp. 1–9.

2. See, generally, Walker, *Popular Justice,* p. 61.

3. Law Enforcement Assistance Administration, *Two Hundred Years of American Criminal Justice* (Washington, DC: U.S. Government Printing Office, 1976).

4. August Vollmer, *The Police and Modern Society* (Berkeley: University of California Press, 1936).

5. O.W. Wilson, *Police Administration,* 2nd ed. (New York: McGraw-Hill, 1963).

6. Herman Goldstein, "Toward Community-Oriented Policing: Potential Basic Requirements and Threshold Questions," *Crime and Delinquency* 33:630 (1987); see also Janet Reno, "Taking

America Back for Our Children," *Crime and Delinquency* 44:75 (1998).

7. Lawrence Sherman and Richard Berk, "The Specific Deterrent Effects of Arrest for Domestic Assault," *American Sociological Review* 49:261–72 (1984).

8. Yolander Hurst, James Frank, and Sandra Lee Browning, "The Attitudes of Juvenile Toward the Police, A Comparison of Black and White Youth," *Policing* 23:37–53 (2000).

9. Donald Black and Albert J. Reiss Jr., "Police Control of Juveniles," *American Sociological Review* 35:63 (1970); Richard Lundman, Richard Sykes, and John Clark, "Police Control of Juveniles: A Replication," *Journal of Research on Crime and Delinquency* 15:74 (1978).

10. American Bar Association, *Standards Relating to Police Handling of Juvenile Problems* (Cambridge, MA: Ballinger, 1977), p. 1.

11. FBI, *Uniform Crime Reports 1991* (Washington, DC: U.S. Government Printing Office, 1990). More than 40 percent of police–juvenile contacts are referred to juvenile court; see also David Huizinga and Finn Esbensen, "An Arresting View of Juvenile Justice," *National School Safety Center Journal,* Spring 1992, pp. 13–17.

12. Samuel Walker, *The Police of America* (New York: McGraw-Hill, 1983), p. 133.

13. Karen A. Joe, "The Dynamics of Running Away, Deinstitutionalization Policies and the Police," *Juvenile Family Court Journal* 46:43–45 (1995).

14. The President's Crime Prevention Council, "Preventing Crime and Promoting Responsibility—50 Programs that Help Communities Help Their Youth" (Washington DC: President's Crime Prevention Council, 1995).

15. National Conference of State Legislatures, *A Legislator's Guide to Comprehensive Juvenile Justice, Interventions for Youth at Risk* (Denver, CO: NCSL, 1996).

16. John Wilson and James Howell, "Serious and Violent Juvenile Crime: A Comprehensive Strategy," *Juvenile and Family Court Journal* 45:3–35 (1995); James Howell, ed., *Guide for Implementing a Comprehensive Strategy for Serious Violent and Chronic Juvenile Offenders* (Washington, DC: OJJDP, 1995).

17. National Advisory Commission on Criminal Justice Standards and Goals, *Task Force Report on Juvenile Justice and Delinquency Prevention* (Washington DC: Law Enforcement Assistance Administration, 1976), p. 258.

18. Linda Szymanski, *Summary of Juvenile Code Purpose Clauses* (Pittsburgh: National Center for Juvenile Justice, 1988); see also, for example, GA Code Ann. 15; Iowa Code Ann. 232.2; Mass. Gen. Laws, ch. 119, 56.

19. Samuel M. Davis, *Rights of Juveniles—The Juvenile Justice System* (New York: Clark-Boardmen, rev. June 1989), Sec. 3.3.

20. National Council of Juvenile and Family Court Judges, *Juvenile and Family Law Digest* 29:1–2 (1997).

21. See Fourth Amendment, U.S. Constitution.

22. *Chimel v. Cal.,* 395 U.S. 752, 89 S.Ct. 2034 (1969).

23. *United States v. Ross,* 456 U.S. 798, 102 S.Ct. 2157 (1982).

24. *Terry v. Ohio,* 392 U.S.1, 88 S.Ct. 1868 (1968).

25. *Bumper v. North Carolina,* 391 U.S. 543, 88 S.Ct. 1788 (1968).

26. *Miranda v. Arizona,* 384 U.S. 436, 86 S.Ct. 1602 (1966).

27. *Commonwealth v. Gaskins,* 471 Pa. 238, 369 A.2d 1285 (1977); *In re E.T.C.,* 141 Vt. 375, 449 A.2d 937 (1982).

28. *People v. Lara,* 67 Cal.2d 365, 62 Cal.Rptr. 586, 432 P.2d 202 (1967).

29. *West v. United States,* 399 F.2d 467 (5th Cir. 1968).

30. *Fare v. Michael C.,* 442 U.S. 707, 99 S.Ct. 2560 (1979).

31. *California v. Prysock,* 453 U.S. 355, 101 S.Ct. 2806 (1981).

32. See, for example, Larry Holtz, "*Miranda* in a Juvenile Setting—A Child's Right to Silence," *Journal of Criminal Law and Criminology* 79:534–56 (1987).

33. Kenneth C. Davis, *Discretionary Justice: A Preliminary Inquiry* (Baton Rouge: Louisiana State University Press, 1969); H. Ted Rubin, *Juvenile Justice: Police, Practice and Law* (Santa Monica, CA: Goodyear, 1979).

34. Joseph Goldstein, "Police Discretion Not to Invoke the Criminal Process: Low-Visibility Decisions in the Administration of Justice," *Yale Law Journal* 69:544 (1960).

35. Victor Streib, *Juvenile Justice in America* (Port Washington, NY: Kennikat, 1978).

36. Herbert Packer, *The Limits of the Criminal Sanction* (Palo Alto, CA: Stanford University Press, 1968).

37. Black and Reiss, "Police Control of Juveniles"; Richard J. Lundman, "Routine Police Arrest Practices," *Social Problems* 22:127–41 (1974).

38. Nathan Goldman, *The Differential Selection of Juvenile Offenders for Court Appearance* (Washington, DC: National Council on Crime and Delinquency, 1963).

39. Irving Piliavin and Scott Briar, "Police Encounters with Juveniles," *American Journal of Sociology* 70:206–14 (1964); Theodore Ferdinand and Elmer Luchterhand, "Inner-City Youth, the Police, Juvenile Court, and Justice," *Social Problems* 8:510–26 (1970).

40. Paul Strasburg, *Violent Delinquents: Report to Ford Foundation from Vera Institute of Justice* (New York: Monarch, 1978), p. 11; Robert Terry, "The Screening of Juvenile Offenders," *Journal of Criminal Law, Criminology, and Police Science* 58:173–81 (1967).

41. FBI, *Crime in the U.S.: Uniform Crime Reports, 2000* (Washington, DC: U.S. Government Printing Office, 2001).

42. Douglas Smith and Christy Visher, "Street-Level Justice: Situational Determinants of Police Arrest Decisions," *Social Problems* 29:167–78 (1981).

43. Douglas Smith and Jody Klein, "Police Control of Interpersonal Disputes," *Social Problems* 31:468–81 (1984).

44. Goldman, *The Differential Selection of Juvenile Offenders for Court Appearance,* p. 25; Norman Werner and Charles Willie, "Decisions of Juvenile Officers," *American Journal of Sociology* 77:199–214 (1971).

45. Aaron Cicourel, *The Social Organization of Juvenile Justice* (New York: Wiley, 1968).

46. Piliavin and Briar, "Police Encounters with Juveniles," p. 214.

47. David Klinger, "Demeanor or Crime? Why 'Hostile' Citizens Are More Likely to Be Arrested," *Criminology* 32:475–93 (1994).

48. Richard Lundman, "Demeanor or Crime? The Midwest City Police–Citizen Encounters Study," *Criminology* 32:631–53 (1994); Robert Worden and Robin Shepard, "On the Meaning, Measurement, and Estimated Effects of Suspects' Demeanor toward the Police." Paper presented at the American Society of Criminology meeting, Miami, November 1994.

49. James Fyfe, David Klinger, and Jeanne Flaving, "Differential Police Treatment of Male-on-Female Spousal Violence," *Criminology* 35:455–73 (1997).

50. Dale Dannefer and Russel Schutt, "Race and Juvenile Justice Processing in Police and Court Agencies," *American Journal of Sociology* 87:1113–32 (1982); Smith and Visher, "Street-Level Justice: Situational Determinants of Police Arrest Decisions"; also, Ronald Weitzer, "Racial Discrimination in the Criminal Justice System: Findings and Problems in the Literature," *Journal of Criminal Justice* 24:309–22 (1996).

51. Dan M. Kahan and Tracey L. Meares, "The Coming Crisis of Criminal Procedure," *Georgetown Law Journal* 86:1153–84.

52. Randall Kennedy, *Race, Crime and the Law* (New York: Vintage, 1998).

53. Terence Thornberry, "Race, Socioeconomic Status, and Sentencing in the Juvenile Justice System," *Journal of Criminal Law and Criminology* 70:164–71 (1979); Dannefer and Schutt, "Race and Juvenile Justice Processing in Police and Court Agencies"; Jeffrey Fagan, Ellen Slaughter, and Eliot Hartstone, "Blind Justice? The Impact of Race on the Juvenile Justice Process," *Crime and Delinquency* 33:224–58 (1987).

54. Donna M. Bishop and Charles E. Frazier, "The Influence of Race in Juvenile Justice Processing," *Journal of Research in Crime and Delinquency* 25:242–61 (1988).

55. Ibid., p. 258; see also Melissa Sickmund, *Juvenile Court Statistics 1995* (Washington DC: OJJDP, 1998), p. 28.

56. National Council on Crime and Delinquency, *The Over-Representation of Minority Youth in the California Juvenile Justice System* (San Francisco: NCCD, 1992).

57. Merry Morash, "Establishment of a Juvenile Record: The Influence of Individual and Peer Group Characteristics," *Criminology* 22:97–112 (1984).

58. Meda Chesney-Lind, "Judicial Enforcement of the Female Sex Role: The Family Court and Female Delinquency Issues," *Criminology* 8:51–71 (1973); idem, "Young Women in the Arms of Law," in L. Bowker, ed., *Women, Crime, and the Criminal Justice System*, 2nd ed. (Lexington, MA: Lexington Books, 1978).

59. Christy Visher, "Arrest Decisions and Notions of Chivalry," *Criminology* 21:5–28 (1983); see also Darlene Conley, "Adding Color to a Black and White Picture: Using Qualitative Data to Explain Racial Disproportionality in the Juvenile Justice System," *Journal of Research in Crime and Delinquency* 31:135–48 (1994).

60. Donna Bishop and Charles Frazier, "Gender Bias in Juvenile Justice Processing: Implications of the JJDP Act," *Journal of Criminal Law and Criminology* 82:1162–86 (1992).

61. Douglas Smith, "The Organizational Context of Legal Control," *Criminology* 22:19–38 (1984); see also Stephen Mastrofski and Richard Ritti, "Police Training and the Effects of Organization on Drunk Driving Enforcement," *Justice Quarterly* 13:291–320 (1996).

62. John Irwin, *The Jail: Managing the Underclass in American Society* (Berkeley: University of California Press, 1985).

63. Darlene Conley, "Adding Color to a Black and White Picture: Using Qualitative Data to Explain Racial Disproportionality in the Juvenile Justice System," *Journal of Research in Crime and Delinquency* 31:135-48 (1994).

64. Robert Sampson, "Effects of Socioeconomic Context of Official Reaction to Juvenile Delinquency," *American Sociological Review* 51:876–85 (1986).

65. Ronald Weitzer "White, Black, or Blue Cops? Race and Citizen Assessments of Police Officers," *Journal of Criminal Justice* 28:313–324 (2000).

66. Thomas Priest and Deborah Brown Carter, "Evaluations of Police performance in an African American Sample," *Journal of Criminal Justice* 27:457–65 (1999); see also Matt De Lisi and Bob Regoli, "Race, Conventional Crime, and Criminal Justice: The Declining Importance of Skin Color," *Journal of Criminal Justice* 27:549–57 (1999.

67. Eric Fritsch, Tory Caeti, and Robert Taylor, "Gang Suppression through Saturation Patrol, Aggressive Curfew, and Truancy Enforcement: A Quasi-Experimental Test of the Dallas Anti-Gang Initiative," *Crime and Delinquency* 45:122–39 (1999).

68. Sherwood Norman, *The Youth Service Bureau—A Key to Delinquency Prevention* (Hackensack, NJ: National Council on Crime and Delinquency, 1972), p. 8.

69. Finn-Aage Esbensen and D. Wayne Osgood, *National Evaluation of G.R.E.A.T.* (Washington, DC: National Institute of Justice, 1997).

70. Finn-Aage Esbensen and D.Wayne Osgood, "Gang Resistance Education and Training (G.R.E.A.T.): Results from the National Evaluation," *Journal of Research in Crime and Delinquency* 36:194–225 (1999).

71. For an analysis of this position, see George Kelling and James Q. Wilson, "Broken Windows: The Police and Neighborhood Safety," *Atlantic Monthly* 249:29–38 (1982).

72. U.S. Department of Justice, "Community Policing," *National Institute of Justice Journal*, 225:1–32 (1992).

73. Robert Trojanowicz and Hazel Harden, *The Status of Contemporary Community Policing Programs* (East Lansing: Michigan State University Neighborhood Foot Patrol Center, 1985).

74. Peter Finn, "Block Watches Help Crime Victims in Philadelphia," *National Institute of Justice Reports,* December: 2–10 (1986).

75. James Q. Wilson, "Drugs and Crime," in Michael Tonry and James Q. Wilson, eds., *Crime and Justice—A Review of Research,* vol. 13 (Chicago: University of Chicago Press, 1990).

76. Susan Guarino-Ghezzi, "Reintegrative Police Surveillance of Juvenile Offenders: Forging an Urban Model," *Crime and Delinquency* 40:131–53 (1994).

77. The President's Crime Prevention Council, *Preventing Crime and Promoting Responsibility: 50 Programs that Help Communities Help Their Youth* (Washington, DC: U.S. Government Printing Office, 1995).

Chapter 13

1. Kelly Dedel, "National Profile of the Organization of State Juvenile Corrections Systems," *Crime and Delinquency* 44:507–525 (1998). Herein cited as National Profile.

2. Anne L. Stahl, *Delinquency Cases in Juvenile Courts, 1997* (Washington, DC: Office of Juvenile Justice and Delinquency Prevention, 2000).

3. *Powell v. Alabama* 287 U.S. 45, 53 S.Ct. 55, 77, L.Ed.2d 158 (1932); *Gideon v. Wainwright* 372 U.S. 335, 83 S.Ct. 792, 9 L.Ed.2d 799 (1963); *Argersinger v. Hamlin* 407 U.S. 25, 92 S.Ct. 2006, 32 L.Ed.2d 530 (1972).

4. Howard Davidson, "The Guardian *ad Litem*: An Important Approach to the Protection of Children," *Children Today* 10:23 (1981); Daniel Golden, "Who Guards the Children?" *Boston Globe Magazine,* 27 December 1992, p. 12.

5. Chester Harhut, "An Expanded Role for the Guardian ad Litem," *Juvenile and Family Court Journal* 51:31–35 (2000).

6. Steve Riddell, "CASA, Child's Voice in Court," *Juvenile and Family Justice Today* 7:13–14 (1998).

7. American Bar Association, *A Call for Justice: An Assessment of Access to Counsel and Quality of Representation in Delinquency Proceedings* (Washington, DC: ABA Juvenile Justice Center, 1995).

8. Douglas C. Dodge, *Due Process Advocacy* (Washington, DC: Office of Juvenile Justice and Delinquency Prevention, 1997).

9. James Shine and Dwight Price, "Prosecutor and Juvenile Justice: New Roles and Perspectives," in Ira Schwartz, ed., *Juvenile Justice and Public Policy* (New York: Lexington Books, 1992), pp. 101–133.

10. James Backstrom and Gary Walker, "A Balanced Approach to Juvenile Justice: The Work of the Juvenile Justice Advisory Committee," *The Prosecutor* 32:37–39 (1988); see also *Prosecutors' Policy Recommendations on Serious, Violent, and Habitual Youthful Offenders* (Alexandria, VA: American Prosecutors' Institute, 1997).

11. Leonard P. Edwards, "The Juvenile Court and the Role of the Juvenile Court Judge," *Juvenile and Family Court Journal* 43:3–45 (1992); Lois Haight, "Why I Choose to be a Juvenile Court Judge," *Juvenile and Family Justice Today* 7:7 (1998).

12. American Correctional Association, *Standards for Juvenile Detention Facilities* (Laurel, MD: ACA, 1991).

13. National Profile, p. 514.

14. Madeline Wordes and Sharon Jones, "Trends in Juvenile Detention and Steps Toward Reform," *Crime and Delinquency* 44:544–60 (1998).

15. Robert Shepard, *Juvenile Justice Standards Annotated: A Balanced Approach* (Chicago, IL: ABA, 1997).

16. Anne L. Stahl, *Delinquency Cases in Juvenile Courts, 1997.*

17. Snyder and Sickmund, *Juvenile Offenders and Victims—A National Report,* pp. 143–50.

18. Bohsiu Wu and Angel Ilarraza Fuentes, "The Entangled Effects of Race and Urban Poverty," *Juvenile and Family Court Journal* 49:41–51 (1998).

19. Edward J. Loughran, "How to Stop Our Kids from Going Bad," *Boston Globe,* 11 February 1990, p. 42.

20. Ira M. Schwartz and William H. Barton, eds., *Reforming Juvenile Detention—No More Hidden Closets* (Columbus: Ohio State University Press, 1994), p. 176.

21. James Maupin and Lis Bond-Maupin, "Detention Decision-Making in a Predominantly Hispanic Region: Rural and Non-Rural Differences," *Juvenile and Family Court Journal* 50:11–21 (1999).

22. Earl Dunlap and David Roush, "Juvenile Detention as Process and Place," *Juvenile and Family Court Journal* 46:1–16 (1995).

23. "OJJDP Helps States Remove Juveniles from Jails," *Juvenile Justice Bulletin* (Washington, DC: U.S. Department of Justice, 1990).

24. Community Research Associates, *The Jail Removal Initiative: A Summary Report* (Champaign, IL: Community Research Associates, 1987).

25. David Steinhart, "Status Offenders," *The Future of Children—The Juvenile Court,* 1996, p. 96.

26. Mark Soler, James Bell, Elizabeth Jameson, Carole Shauffer, Alice Shotton, and Loren Warboys, *Representing the Child Client* (New York: Matthew Bender, 1989), Sec. 5.03b.

27. *Schall v. Martin,* 467 U.S. 253, (1984).

28. Jeffrey Fagan and Martin Guggenheim, "Preventive Detention for Juveniles: A Natural Experiment," *Journal of Criminal Law and Criminology,* 86:415–28 (1996).

29. Anne L. Stahl, *Delinquency Cases in Juvenile Courts, 1997.*

30. Leona Lee, "Factors Influencing Intake Disposition in a Juvenile Court," *Juvenile and Family Court Journal* 46:43–62 (1995).

31. H. Ted Rubin, "The Emerging Prosecutor Dominance of the Juvenile Court Intake Process," *Crime and Delinquency* 26:299–318 (1980).

32. Edwin E. Lemert, "Diversion in Juvenile Justice: What Hath Been Wrought?" *Journal of Research in Crime and Delinquency* 18:34–46 (1981).

33. Don C. Gibbons and Gerald F. Blake, "Evaluating the Impact of Juvenile Diversion Programs," *Crime and Delinquency Journal* 22:411–19 (1976); Richard J. Lundman, "Will Diversion Reduce Recidivism?" *Crime and Delinquency Journal* 22:428–37 (1976); B. Bullington, J. Sprowls, D. Katkin, and M. Phillips, "A Critique of Diversionary Juvenile Justice," *Crime and Delinquency* 24:59–71 (1978); Thomas Blomberg, "Diversion and Accelerated Social Control," *Journal of Criminal Law and Criminology* 68:274–82 (1977); Sharla Rausch and Charles Logan, "Diversion from Juvenile Court: Panacea or Pandora's Box," in J. Klugel, ed., *Evaluating Juvenile Justice* (Beverly Hills, CA: Sage, 1983), pp. 19–30.

34. Arnold Binder and Gilbert Geis, "Ad Populum Argumentation in Criminology: Juvenile Diversion as Rhetoric," *Criminology* 30:309–333 (1984).

35. Mark Ezell, "Juvenile Diversion: The Ongoing Search for Alternatives," in Ira M. Schwartz, ed., *Juvenile Justice and Public Policy* (New York: Lexington Books, 1992), pp. 45–59.

36. Albert W. Alschuler, "The Prosecutor's Role in Plea Bargaining," *University of Chicago Law Review* 36:50–112 (1968); Joyce Dougherty, "A Comparison of Adult Plea Bargaining and Juvenile Intake," *Federal Probation* June:72–79 (1988).

37. Sanford Fox, *Juvenile Courts in a Nutshell* (St. Paul, MN: West, 1985), pp. 154–56.

38. See Darlene Ewing, "Juvenile Plea Bargaining: A Case Study," *American Journal of Criminal Law* 6:167 (1978); Adrienne Volenik, *Checklists for Use in Juvenile Delinquency Proceedings* (Chicago: American Bar Association, 1985); Bruce Green, "Package Plea Bargaining and the Prosecutor's Duty of Good Faith," *Criminal Law Bulletin* 25:507–550 (1989).

39. Joseph Sanborn, *Plea Negotiations in Juvenile Court* (Ph.D. thesis, State University of New York at Albany, 1984); Joseph Sanborn, "Philosophical, Legal, and Systematic Aspects of Juvenile Court Plea Bargaining," *Crime and Delinquency* 39:509–527 (1993).

40. Charles Puzzanchera, *Delinquency Cases Waived to Criminal Court, 1988–1997* (Washington, DC: Office of Juvenile Justice and Delinquency Prevention, February 2000).

41. Puzzanchera, *Delinquency Cases Waived to Criminal Court, 1988–1997.*

42. Ind. Code Ann. 31-6-2(d) 1987; Ill.Ann.Stat. Ch. 37 Sec. 805 (1988); Penn. Stat. Ann. Title 42 6355(a) (1982); Patrick Griffin et al., *Trying Juveniles as Adults in Criminal Court: An Analysis of State Transfer Provisions* (Washington, DC: OJJDP, 1998).

43. Joseph White, "The Waiver Decision: A Judicial, Prosecutorial, or Legislative Responsibility?" *Justice for Children* 2:28–30 (1987).

44. *Kent v. United States,* 383 U.S. 541, 86 S.Ct. 1045, 16 L.Ed.2d 84 (1966); *Breed v. Jones,* 421 U.S. 519, 95 S.Ct. 1179, 44 L.Ed.2d 346 (1975).

45. Barry Feld, "The Juvenile Court Meets the Principle of the Offense: Legislative Changes in Juvenile Waiver Statutes," *Journal of Criminal Law and Criminology* 78:471–534 (1987); Paul Marcotte, "Criminal Kids," *American Bar Association Journal* 76:60–66 (1990); Dale Parent et al., *Transferring Serious Juvenile Offenders to Adult Courts* (Washington DC: U.S. Department of Justice, National Institute of Justice, 1997).

46. Richard Redding, "Juvenile Offenders in Criminal Court and Adult Prison: Legal, Psychological and Behavioral Outcomes," *Juvenile and Family Court Journal* 50:1–15 (1999).

47. Ibid., p. 11.

48. Ibid.

49. Snyder and Sickmund, *Juvenile Offenders and Victims: A National Report,* p. 157; Eric Fritsch, Tory Caeti, and Craig Hemmens, "Spare the Needle But Not the Punishment: The Incarceration of Waived Youth in Texas Prisons," *Crime and Delinquency,* 42:593–610 (1996).

50. James Howell, "Juvenile Transfers to the Criminal Justice System: State of the Art," *Law & Policy* 18:17–60 (1996).

51. M.A. Bortner, "Traditional Rhetoric, Organizational Realities: Remand of Juveniles to Adult Court," *Crime and Delinquency* 32:53–73 (1986).

52. Puzzanchera, *Delinquency Cases Waived to Criminal Court, 1988–1997;* Jeffrey Fagan, Martin Forst, and T. Scott Vivona, "Racial Determinants of the Judicial Transfer Decision: Prosecuting

Violent Youth in Criminal Court," *Crime and Delinquency* 33:359–86 (1987); J. Fagan, E. Slaughter, and E. Hartstone, "Blind Justice: The Impact of Race on the Juvenile Justice Process," *Crime and Delinquency* 53:224–58 (1987); J. Fagan and E. P. Deschenes, "Determinants of Judicial Waiver Decisions for Violent Juvenile Offenders," *Journal of Criminal Law and Criminology* 81:314–47 (1990); see also James Howell, "Juvenile Transfers to Criminal Court," *Juvenile and Family Justice Journal* 6:12–14 (1997).

53. Anne L. Stahl, *Delinquency Cases in Juvenile Courts, 1997* (Washington, DC: Office of Juvenile Justice and Delinquency Prevention, 2000); Puzzanchera, *Delinquency Cases Waived to Criminal Court, 1988–1997*.

54. Barry Feld, "Delinquent Careers and Criminal Policy," *Criminology* 21:195–212 (1983).

55. Howard N. Snyder, Melissa Sickmund, Eileen Poe-Yamagata, *Juvenile Transfers to Criminal Court in the 1990s: Lessons Learned from Four Studies* (Washington, DC: Office of Juvenile Justice and Delinquency Prevention, 2000).

56. Frank Zimring, "Treatment of Hard Cases in American Juvenile Justice: In Defense of the Discretionary Waiver," *Notre Dame Journal of Law, Ethics and Policy* 5:267–80 (1991); Lawrence Winner, Lonn Kaduce, Donna Bishop, and Charles Frazier, "The Transfer of Juveniles to Criminal Courts: Reexamining Recidivism over the Long Term," *Crime and Delinquency* 43:548–64 (1997).

57. Robert Shepard, "The Rush to Waive Children to Adult Courts," *American Bar Association Journal of Criminal Justice* 10:39–42 (1995); see also Kevin Strom and Steven Smith, *Juvenile Felony Defendants in Criminal Courts* (Washington, DC: Bureau of Justice Statistics, 1998).

58. Institute of Judicial Administration, American Bar Association Joint Commission on Juvenile Justice Standards, *Standards Relating to Adjudication* (Cambridge, MA: Ballinger, 1980).

59. Joseph B. Sanborn Jr., "The Right to a Public Jury Trial—A Need for Today's Juvenile Court," *Judicature* 76:230–38 (1993).

60. Linda Szymanski, *Juvenile Delinquents' Right to Counsel* (Pittsburgh, PA: National Center for Juvenile Justice, 1988).

61. *In re Winship,* 397 U.S. 358, 90 S.Ct. 1068 (1970).

62. *McKeiver v. Pennsylvania,* 403 U.S. 528, 91 S.Ct. 1976 (1971).

63. See, generally, R. T. Powell, "Disposition Concepts," *Juvenile and Family Court Journal* 34:7–18 (1983).

64. Sanford Fox, *Juvenile Courts in a Nutshell* (St. Paul, MN: West, 1984), p. 221.

65. This section is adapted from Jack Haynes and Eugene Moore, "Particular Dispositions," *Juvenile and Family Court Journal* 34:41–48 (1983); see also Grant Grissom, "Dispositional Authority and the Future of the Juvenile Justice System," *Juvenile and Family Court Journal* 42:25–34 (1991).

66. Barry Krisberg, Elliot Currie, and David Onek, "What Works with Juvenile Offenders," *American Bar Association Journal on Criminal Justice* 10:20–24 (1995).

67. Anthony Platt, *The Child Savers: The Invention of Delinquency* (Chicago: University of Chicago Press, 1969); David Rothman, *Conscience and Convenience: The Asylum and the Alternative in Progressive America* (Boston: Little, Brown, 1980).

68. Joseph Goldstein, Anna Freud, and Albert Solnit, *Beyond the Best Interests of the Child* (New York: Free Press, 1973).

69. See, for example, *in Interest on M.P.* 697 N.E. 2d 1153 (Il. App. 1998); *Matter of Welfare of CAW* 579 N.W. 2d 494 (MN. App. 1998).

70. See, for example, *Matter of Willis Alvin M.* 479 S.E. 2d. 871 (WV 1996).

71. Simon Singer and David McDowall, "Criminalizing Delinquency: The Deterrent Effects of NYJO Law," *Law and Society Review* 22:Sections 21–37 (1988).

72. Washington Juvenile Justice Reform Act of 1977, Chap. 291; Wash. Rev. Code Ann. Title 9A, Sec. 1–91 (1977).

73. National Criminal Justice Association, *Juvenile Justice Reform Initiatives in the States, 1994–1996* (Washington, DC: U.S. Department of Justice, 1997).

74. Lynn Cothern, *Juveniles and the Death Penalty* (Washington, DC: Office of Juvenile Justice and Delinquency Prevention, 2000).

75. Victor Streib, *The Juvenile Death Penalty Today: Death Sentences and Executions for Juvenile Crimes, January 1, 1973–June 30, 2000* (Ada, OH: Ohio Northern University Claude W. Pettit College of Law 2000); idem., *Death Penalty for Juveniles* (Bloomington: Indiana University Press, 1987); Paul Reidinger, "The Death Row Kids," *American Bar Association Journal* April: 78 (1989); Victor Streib, *The Juvenile Death Penalty Today: Present Death Row Inmates under Juvenile Death Sentences* (Cleveland: Cleveland State University, 25 August 1992); see also, Sam Verhovek, "A Legislator Proposes Death Penalty for Murderers as Young as Eleven," *New York Times,* 18 April 1998, p. B10.

76. Steven Gerstein, "The Constitutionality of Executing Juvenile Offenders, *Thompson v. Oklahoma,*" *Criminal Law Bulletin* 24:91–98 (1988); *Thompson v. Oklahoma,* 108 S.Ct. 2687 (1988).

77. 109 S.Ct. 2969 (1989); for a recent analysis of the *Wilkins* and *Stanford* cases, see the note in "*Stanford v. Kentucky* and *Wilkins v. Missouri*: Juveniles, Capital Crime, and Death Penalty," *Criminal Justice Journal* 11:240–66 (1989).

78. Victor Streib, "Excluding Juveniles from New York's Impendent Death Penalty," *Albany Law Review* 54:625–79 (1990).

79. Paul Piersma, Jeanette Ganousis, Adrienne E. Volenik, Harry F. Swanger, and Patricia Connell, *Law and Tactics in Juvenile Cases* (Philadelphia: American Law Institute, American Bar Association, Committee on Continuing Education, 1977), p. 397.

80. J. Addison Bowman, "Appeals from Juvenile Courts," *Crime and Delinquency Journal* 11:63–77 (1965).

81. *In re Gault,* 387 U.S. 1 87 S.Ct. 1428 (1967).

82. *Davis v. Alaska,* 415 U.S. 308 (1974); 94 S.Ct. 1105.

83. *Oklahoma Publishing Co. v. District Court,* 430 U.S. 97 (1977); 97 S.Ct. 1045.

84. *Smith v. Daily Mail Publishing Co.,* 443 U.S. 97, 99 S.Ct. 2667, 61 L.Ed.2d 399 (1979).

85. Linda Szymanski, *Confidentiality of Juvenile Court Records* (Pittsburgh, PA: National Center for Juvenile Justice, 1989).

86. Ira M. Schwartz, *Justice for Juveniles: Rethinking the Best Interests of the Child* (Lexington, MA: D. C. Heath, 1989), p. 172.

87. National Institute of Justice Update, "State Laws on Prosecutors' and Judges' Use of Juvenile Records" (Washington, DC: Office of Justice Programs, 1995).

Chapter 14

1. Charles Murray and Louis B. Cox, *Beyond Probation* (Beverly Hills, CA: Sage, 1979).

2. Robert Shepard Jr., ed., *Juvenile Justice Standards, A Balanced Approach* (Chicago: ABA, 1996).

3. George Killinger, Hazel Kerper, and Paul F. Cromwell Jr., *Probation and Parole in the Criminal Justice System* (St. Paul, MN: West, 1976), p. 45; National Advisory Commission on Criminal Justice Standards and Goals, *Corrections* (Washington, DC: U.S. Government Printing Office, 1983), p. 75.

4. Ibid.

5. Jerome Miller, *Last One over the Wall: The Massachusetts Experiment in Closing Reform Schools* (Columbus: Ohio State University Press, 1998).

6. Bureau of Justice Statistics, *Report to the Nation on Crime and Justice* (Washington, DC: U.S. Government Printing Office, 1988), pp. 44–45; Peter Greenwood, "What Works with Juvenile Offenders: A Synthesis of the Literature and Experience," *Federal Probation* 58:63–67 (1994).

7. Robert Coates, Alden Miller, and Lloyd Ohlin, *Diversity in a Youth Correctional System* (Cambridge, MA: Ballinger, 1978); Barry Krisberg, James Austin, and Patricia Steele, *Unlocking Juvenile Corrections* (San Francisco: National Council on Crime and Delinquency, 1989).

8. Personal correspondence, Taneekah Freeman, executive assistant, January 3, 2001; "Roxbury Agency Offers a Map for Youths at the Crossroads," *Boston Globe,* 18 February 1990, p. 32.

9. Adapted from C. Puzzanchera, A. Stahl, T. Finnegan, H. Snyder, R. Poole, and N. Tierney, *Juvenile Court Statistics 1997* (Washington, DC: Office of Juvenile Justice and Delinquency Prevention, 2000).

10. Ibid.

11. In re J.G. 692 N.E. 2d 1226 (Ill.App. 1998).

12. In Re Michael D, 264 CA Rptr 476 (CA App. 1989).

13. *Morrissey v. Brewer,* 408 U.S. 471, 92 S.Ct. 2593, 33 L.Ed.2d 484 (1972); *Gagnon v. Scarpelli,* 411 U.S. 778, 93 S.Ct. 1756, 36 L.Ed.2d 655 (1973).

14. Patricia McFall Torbet, *Juvenile Probation: The Workhorse of the Juvenile Justice System* (Washington, DC: Office of Juvenile Justice and Delinquency Prevention, 1996).

15. Richard Lawrence, "Reexamining Community Corrections Models," *Crime and Delinquency* 37:449–64 (1991).

16. See Richard G. Wiebush, "Juvenile Intensive Supervision: The Impact on Felony Offenders Diverted from Institutional Placement," *Crime and Delinquency* 39:68–89 (1993); James Byrne, "The Control Controversy: A Preliminary Examination of Intensive Probation Supervision Programs in the United States," *Federal Probation* 50:4–16 (1986).

17. For a review of these programs, see James Byrne, ed., "Introduction," *Federal Probation* 50:2 (1986); see also Emily Walker, "The Community Intensive Treatment for Youth Program: A Specialized Community-Based Program for High-Risk Youth in Alabama," *Law and Psychology Review* 13:175–99 (1989).

18. James Ryan, "Who Gets Revoked? A Comparison of Intensive Supervision Successes and Failures in Vermont," *Crime and Delinquency* 43:104–118 (1997).

19. Richard Ball and J. Robert Lilly, "A Theoretical Examination of Home Incarceration," *Federal Probation* 50:17–25 (1986); Joan Petersilia, "Exploring the Option of House Arrest," *Federal Probation* 50:50–56 (1986); Annesley Schmidt, "Electronic Monitors," *Federal Probation* 50:56–60 (1986); Michael Charles, "The Development of a Juvenile Electronic Monitoring Program," *Federal Probation* 53:3–12 (1989).

20. Sudipto Roy, "Five Years of Electronic Monitoring of Adults and Juveniles in Lake County, Indiana: A Comparative Study on Factors Related to Failure," *Journal of Crime and Justice* 20:141–60 (1997).

21. Joseph Papy and Richard Nimer, "Electronic Monitoring in Florida," *Federal Probation* 55:31–33 (1991); Annesley Schmidt, "Electronic Monitors—Realistically, What Can Be Expected?" *Federal Probation* 55:47–53 (1991).

22. Dennis Mahoney, Dennis Romig, and Troy Armstrong, "Juvenile Probation: The Balanced Approach," *Juvenile and Family Court Journal* 39:1–59 (1988).

23. Gordon Bazemore, "On Mission Statements and Reform in Juvenile Justice: The Case of the Balanced Approach," *Federal Probation* 61:64–70 (1992); Gordon Bazemore and Mark Umbreit, *Balanced and Restorative Justice* (Washington, DC: Office of Juvenile Justice and Delinquency Prevention, 1994).

24. Gordon Bazemore, *Guide for Implementing the Balanced and Restorative Justice Model* (Washington, DC: Office of Juvenile Justice and Delinquency Prevention, 1998).

25. Anne L. Schneider, ed., *Guide to Juvenile Restitution* (Washington, DC: Department of Justice, 1985); Anne Schneider and Jean Warner, *National Trends in Juvenile Restitution Programming* (Washington, DC: U.S. Government Printing Office, 1989).

26. Gordon Bazemore, "New Concepts and Alternative Practice in Community Supervision of Juvenile Offenders: Rediscovering Work Experience and Competency Development," *Journal of Crime and Justice* 14:27–45 (1991); Jeffrey Butts and Howard Snyder, *Restitution and Juvenile Recidivism* (Washington, DC: Department of Justice, 1992).

27. Anne Schneider, "Restitution and Recidivism Rates of Juvenile Offenders: Results from Four Experimental Studies," *Criminology* 24:533–52 (1986).

28. Shay Bilchik, *A Juvenile Justice System for the 21st Century* (Washington, DC: Office of Juvenile Justice and Delinquency Prevention, 1998).

29. Peter Schneider, William Griffith, and Anne Schneider, *Juvenile Restitution as a Sole Sanction or Condition of Probation: An Empirical Analysis* (Eugene, OR: Institute for Policy Analysis, 1980); S. Roy, "Juvenile Restitution and Recidivism in a Midwestern County," *Federal Probation* 57:55–62 (1995).

30. Anne Schneider, "Restitution and Recidivism Rates of Juvenile Offenders," *Directory of Restitution Programs* (Washington, DC: OJJDP Juvenile Justice Clearinghouse, 1996). This directory contains information on more than 500 restitution programs across the country.

31. Greenwood, "What Works with Juvenile Offenders."

32. Mark W. Lipsey, "Juvenile Delinquency Treatment: A Meta-Analytic Inquiry into the Variability of Effects," in Thomas D. Cook et al., eds., *Meta-Analysis for Explanation: A Casebook* (San Francisco: Russell Sage Foundation, 1991); Carol Garrett, "Effects of Residential Treatment on Adjudicated Delinquents: A Meta-Analysis," *Crime and Delinquency* 22:287–308 (1985); Ted Palmer, *The Re-Emergence of Correctional Interventions* (Newbury Park, CA: Russell Sage Foundation, 1992), p. 69.

33. Barry Krisberg, Elliot Currie, and David Onek, "New Approaches in Corrections," *American Bar Association Journal of Criminal Justice* 10:51 (1995).

34. Ira Schwartz, *Juvenile Justice and Public Policy* (New York: Lexington Books, 1992), p. 217.

35. U.S. Department of Justice, *Children in Custody 1975–85: Census of Public and Private Juvenile Detention, Correctional, and Shelter Facilities* (Washington, DC: U.S. Department of Justice, 1989), p. 4.

36. For a detailed description of juvenile delinquency in the 1800s, see J. Hawes, *Children in Urban Society: Juvenile Delinquency in Nineteenth Century America* (New York: Oxford University Press, 1971).

37. D. Jarvis, *Institutional Treatment of the Offender* (New York: McGraw-Hill, 1978), p. 101.

38. Margaret Werner Cahalan, *Historical Corrections Statistics in the United States, 1850–1984* (Washington, DC: U.S. Department of Justice, 1986), pp. 104–105.

39. Clemons Bartollas, Stuart J. Miller, and Simon Dinitiz, *Juvenile Victimization: The Institutional Paradox* (New York: Wiley, 1976), p. 6.

40. LaMar T. Empey, *American Delinquency—Its Meaning and Construction* (Homewood, IL: Dorsey, 1978), p. 515.

41. Edward Eldefonso and Walter Hartinger, *Control, Treatment, and Rehabilitation of Juvenile Offenders* (Beverly Hills: Glencoe, 1976), p. 151.

42. Ibid., p. 152.

43. M. Rosenthal, "Reforming the Justice Correctional Institution: Efforts of U.S. Children's Bureau in the 1930s," *Journal of Sociology and Social Welfare* 14:47–73 (1987).

44. Bureau of Justice Statistics, *Fact Sheet on Children in Custody* (Washington, DC: U.S. Department of Justice, 1989); Barbara Allen-Hagen, *Public Juvenile Facilities—Children in Custody, 1989* (Washington, DC: Office of Juvenile Justice and Delinquency Prevention, 1991); James Austin et al., *Juveniles Taken into Custody, 1993* (Washington, DC: Office of Juvenile Justice and Delinquency Prevention, 1995).

45. National Conference of State Legislatures, *A Legislator's Guide to Comprehensive Juvenile Justice, Juvenile Detention and Corrections* (Denver: National Conference of State Legislators, 1996).

46. Ibid.

47. Hunter Hurst and Patricia Torbet, *Organization and Administration of Juvenile Services: Probation, Aftercare, and State Delinquent Institutions* (Pittsburgh: National Center for Juvenile Justice, 1993), p. 4.

48. Melissa Sickmund, *State Custody Rates, 1997 Bulletin* (Washington, DC: Office of Juvenile Justice and Delinquency Prevention, 2000).

49. Robert DeComo, et al., *Children Taken into Custody 1992* (Washington, DC: Office of Juvenile Justice and Delinquency Prevention, 1995).

50. Ira Schwartz, Marilyn Jackson-Beck, and Roger Anderson, "The 'Hidden' System of Juvenile Control," *Crime and Delinquency* 30:371–85 (1984).

51. Rebecca Craig and Andrea Paterson, "State Involuntary Commitment Laws: Beyond Deinstitutionalization," *National Conference of State Legislative Reports* 13:1–10 (1988).

52. Alan Breed and Barry Krisberg, "Is There a Future?" *Corrections Today* 48:14–26 (1986).

53. Barry Krisberg, Ira Schwartz, G. Fishman, Z. Eisikovits, and E. Gitman, "The Incarceration of Minority Youth," *Crime and Delinquency* 33:173–205 (1987).

54. Craig Fischer, ed., "Washington State Moves to End Juvenile Justice Race Disparity," *Criminal Justice Newsletter* 27:1–8 (1996).

55. Bartollas, Miller, and Dinitz, *Juvenile Victimization*, sec. C.

56. Christopher Sieverdes and Clemens Bartollas, "Security Level and Adjustment Patterns in Juvenile Institutions," *Journal of Criminal Justice* 14:135–45 (1986).

57. Several authors have written of this sexual double standard. See E. A. Anderson, "The Chivalrous Treatment of the Female Offender in the Arms of the Criminal Justice System: A Review of the Literature," *Social Problems* 23:350–57 (1976); G. Armstrong, "Females under the Law: Protected but Unequal," *Crime and Delinquency* 23:109–20 (1977); M. Chesney-Lind, "Judicial Enforcement of the Female Sex Role: The Family Court and the Female Delinquent," *Issues in Criminology* 8:51–59 (1973); idem, "Juvenile Delinquency: The Sexualization of Female Crime," *Psychology Today* 19:43–46 (1974); Allan Conway and Carol Bogdan, "Sexual Delinquency: The Persistence of a Double Standard," *Crime and Delinquency* 23:13–135 (1977); M. Chesney-Lind, *Girls, Delinquency and the Juvenile Justice System* (Pacific Grove, CA: Brooks/Cole, 1991).

58. Leslie Acoca, "Outside/Inside: The Violation of American Girls at Home, on the Streets, and in the Juvenile Justice System," *Crime and Delinquency* 44:561–89 (1998).

59. For a historical analysis of a girls' reformatory, see Barbara Brenzel, *Daughters of the State* (Cambridge, MA: MIT Press, 1983).

60. Ilene R. Bergsmann, "The Forgotten Few Juvenile Female Offenders," *Federal Probation* 53:73–79 (1989).

61. For an interesting article highlighting the debate over the effectiveness of correctional treatment, see John Whitehead and Steven Lab, "Meta-Analysis of Juvenile Correctional Treatment," *Journal of Research in Crime and Delinquency* 26:276–95 (1989).

62. National Conference of State Legislatures, *A Legislator's Guide to Comprehensive Juvenile Justice, 1996.*

63. Robert Shepard Jr., "State Pen or Playpen? Is Prevention 'Pork' or Simply Good Sense?" *American Bar Association Journal of Criminal Justice* 10:34–37 (1995); Howell, *Guide for Implementing the Comprehensive Strategy for Serious, Violent and Chronic Juvenile Offenders.*

64. Louise Sas and Peter Jaffe, "Understanding Depression in Juvenile Delinquency: Implications for Institutional Admission Policies and Treatment Programs," *Juvenile and Family Court Journal* 37:49–58 (1985–1986).

65. See, generally, William Glasser, "Reality Therapy: A Realistic Approach to the Young Offender," in Robert Schaste and Jo Wallach, eds., *Readings in Delinquency and Treatment* (Los Angeles: Delinquency Prevention Training Project, Youth Studies Center, University of Southern California, 1965); see also Richard Rachin, "Reality Therapy: Helping People Help Themselves," *Crime and Delinquency* 16:143 (1974).

66. Helen A. Klein, "Toward More Effective Behavior Programs for Juvenile Offenders," *Federal Probation* 41:45–50 (1977); Albert Bandura, *Principles of Behavior Modification* (New York: Holt, Rinehart & Winston, 1969); H.A. Klein, "Behavior Modification as Therapeutic Paradox," *American Journal of Orthopsychiatry* 44:353 (1974).

67. Larry Brendtero and Arlin Ness, "Perspectives on Peer Group Treatment: The Use and Abuses of Guided Group Interaction/Positive Peer Culture," *Child and Youth Services Review* 4:307–324 (1982).

68. Elaine Traynelis-Yurek and George A Giacobbe, "Communication Rehabilitation Regime for Incarcerated Youth: Positive Peer Culture," *Journal of Offender Rehabilitation* 26:157–67 (1998).

69. Bruno Bettelheim, *The Empty Fortress* (New York: Free Press, 1967).

70. California Youth Authority, "Ventura School for Juvenile Female Offenders," *CYA Newsletter* (Ventura, CA: author, 1988).

71. Thomas Castellano and Irina Soderstrom, "Therapeutic Wilderness Programs and Juvenile Recidivism: A Program Evaluation," *Journal of Offender Rehabilitation* 17:19–46 (1992); Troy Armstrong, ed., *Intensive Interventions in High Risk Youth: Approaches in Juvenile Probation and Parole* (New York: Willow Tree Press, 1991).

72. William J. Taylor, "Tailoring Boot Camps to Juveniles," *Corrections Today*, (July) 1992, p. 124.

73. Jerald Burns and Gennaro Vito, "An Impact Analysis of the Alabama Boot Camp Program," *Federal Probation* 59:63–67 (1995).

74. Ronald Corbett and Joan Petersilia, eds., "The Results of a Multi-site Study of Boot Camps," *Federal Probation* 58:60–66 (1995).

75. Margaret Beyer, "Juvenile Boot Camps Don't Make Sense," *American Bar Association Journal of Criminal Justice* 10:20–21 (1996).

76. Eric Peterson, *Juvenile Boot Camps: Lessons Learned* (Washington, DC: Office of Juvenile Justice and Delinquency Prevention, 1996); Michael Peters et al., *Boot Camps for Juvenile Offenders*

(Washington, DC: Office of Juvenile Justice and Delinquency Prevention, 1997).

77. Anthony Salerno, "Boot Camps—A Critique and Proposed Alternative," *Journal of Offender Rehabilitation* 20:147–58 (1994).

78. Joanne Ardovini-Brooker and Lewis Walker, "Juvenile Boot Camps and the Reclamation of Our Youth: Some Food for Thought," *Juvenile and Family Court Journal* 51:12–28 (2000).

79. Morton Birnbaum, "The Right to Treatment," *American Bar Association Journal* 46:499 (1960).

80. See for example, *Matter of Welfare of CAW* 579 N.W. 2d 494 (MN App. 1998).

81. *Inmates of the Boys' Training School v. Affleck,* 346 F. Supp. 1354 (D.R.I. 1972).

82. Ibid., p. 1343.

83. *Nelson v. Heyne,* 491. F. 2d 353 (1974).

84. *Morales v. Turman,* 383 F. Supp. 53 (E.D. Texas 1974).

85. *Pena v. New York State Division for Youth,* 419 F. Supp. 203 (S.D.N.Y. 1976).

86. *Ralston v. Robinson,* 102 S.Ct. 233 (1981).

87. Patricia Puritz and Mary Ann Scali, *Beyond the Walls: Improving Conditions of Confinement for Youth in Custody* (Washington, DC: Office of Juvenile Justice and Delinquency Prevention, 1998)

88. Snyder and Sickmund, *Juvenile Offenders and Victims: A National Report,* p. 177.

89. Michael Norman, "Discretionary Justice: Decision Making in a State Juvenile Parole Board," *Juvenile and Family Court Journal* 37:19–26 (1985–1986).

90. James Maupin, "Risk Classification Systems and the Provisions of Juvenile Aftercare," *Crime and Delinquency* 39:90–105 (1993).

91. National Conference of State Legislatures, *A Legislator's Guide to Comprehensive Juvenile Justice.*

92. David M. Altschuler, "Intensive Aftercare for High-Risk Juvenile Parolees: Overview" (Washington, DC: Office of Juvenile Justice and Delinquency Prevention, n.d.).

93. David M. Altschuler and Troy Armstrong, "Reintegrating Juvenile Offenders: Translating the Intensive Aftercare Program Model into Performance Standards." Paper presented at the American Society of Criminology meeting, San Francisco, November 2000.

94. See *Morrissey v. Brewer,* 408 U.S. 471, 92 S.Ct. 2593, 33 L.Ed.2d 484 (1972).

Glossary

abandonment: Parents physically leave their children with the intention of completely severing the parent–child relationship.

academic achievement: Being successful in a school environment.

active speech: Expressing an opinion by speaking or writing; freedom of speech is a protected right under the First Amendment to the U.S. Constitution.

addict: A person with an overpowering physical or psychological need to continue taking a particular substance or drug.

addiction-prone personality: The view that the cause of substance abuse can be traced to a personality that has a compulsion for mood-altering drugs.

adjudicatory hearing: The fact-finding process wherein the juvenile court determines whether there is sufficient evidence to sustain the allegations in a petition.

adolescent-limiteds: Delinquent youth who begin their offending career in their late teens and soon desist from crime.

advisement hearing: A preliminary protective or temporary custody hearing in which the court will review the facts and determine whether removal of the child is justified and notify parents of the charges against them.

aftercare: Transitional assistance to juveniles equivalent to adult parole to help youths adjust to community life.

age-graded theory: Identifies turning points (such as marriage and career) that can cause delinquents to reverse course and desist from further criminal behavior.

age of consent: Age at which youths are legally adults and may be independent of parental control. When an adolescent reaches the age of consent, he or she may engage in sexual behaviors prohibited to youths.

age of onset: Age at which youths begin their delinquent careers; early onset is believed to be linked with chronic offending patterns.

aging-out process (also known as desistance or spontaneous remission): The tendency for youths to reduce the frequency of their offending behavior as they age; aging out is thought to occur among all groups of offenders.

alcohol: Fermented or distilled liquids containing ethanol, an intoxicating substance.

Alternative Work Sentencing Program (Earn-It): A Massachusetts program that brings together the juvenile and the crime victim to develop an equitable work program to provide restitution to the crime victim.

anabolic steroids: Drugs used by athletes and body builders to gain muscle bulk and strength.

anesthetic drugs: Nervous system depressants.

anomie: Normlessness produced by rapidly shifting moral values; according to Merton, anomie occurs when personal goals cannot be achieved using available means.

appellate process: Allows the juvenile an opportunity to have the case brought before a reviewing court after it has been heard in juvenile or family court.

arrest: Taking a person into the custody of the law to restrain the accused until he or she can be held accountable for the offense in court proceedings.

at-risk youths: Young people who are extremely vulnerable to the negative consequences of school failure, substance abuse, and early sexuality.

authority-conflict pathway: The developmental path taken to delinquency that begins with stubborn and defiant behavior.

bail: Amount of money that must be paid as a condition of pretrial release to ensure that the accused will return for subsequent proceedings; bail is normally set by the judge at the initial appearance, and if unable to make bail the accused is detained in jail.

balanced probation: Programs that integrate community protection, accountability of the juvenile offender, competency, and individualized attention to the juvenile offender; based on the principle that juvenile offenders must accept responsibility for their behavior.

balancing-of-the-interest approach: Efforts of the courts to balance the parents' natural right to raise a child with the child's right to grow into adulthood free from physical abuse or emotional harm.

barrio: A Latino term meaning neighborhood.

battered child syndrome: Nonaccidental physical injury of children by their parents or guardians.

behaviorism: Branch of psychology concerned with the study of observable behavior rather than unconscious processes; focuses on particular stimuli and responses to them.

behavior modification: A technique for shaping desired behaviors through a system of rewards and punishments.

best interests of the child: A philosophical viewpoint that encourages the state to take control of wayward children and provide care, custody, and treatment to remedy delinquent behavior.

bifurcated process: The procedure of separating adjudicatory and dispositionary hearings so different levels of evidence can be heard at each.

bindover: *See* waiver.

biosocial theory: The view that both thought and behavior have biological and social bases.

blended families: Nuclear families that are the product of divorce and remarriage; blending one parent from each of two families and their combined children into one family unit.

boot camps: Juvenile programs that combine get-tough elements from adult programs with education, substance abuse treatment, and social skills training.

broken home: Home in which one or both parents is absent due to divorce or separation; children in such an environment may be prone to antisocial behavior.

capital punishment: Use of the death penalty to punish offenders.

chancery courts: Court proceedings created in fifteenth-century England to oversee the lives of high-born minors who were orphaned or otherwise could not care for themselves.

child abuse: Any physical, emotional, or sexual trauma to a child, including neglecting to give proper care and attention, for which no reasonable explanation can be found.

Children's Aid Society: Child-saving organization that took children from the streets of large cities and placed them with farm families on the prairie.

child savers: Nineteenth-century reformers who developed programs for troubled youth and influenced legislation creating the juvenile justice system; today some critics view them as being more concerned with control of the poor than with their welfare.

chivalry hypothesis (also known as paternalism hypothesis): View that low female crime and delinquency rates are a reflection of the leniency with which police treat female offenders.

choice theory: Holds that youths will engage in delinquent and criminal behavior after weighing the consequences and benefits of their actions; delinquent behavior is a rational choice made by a motivated offender who perceives that the chances of gain outweigh any possible punishment or loss.

chronic delinquent offenders: *See* chronic juvenile offender.

chronic delinquents: *See* chronic juvenile offender.

chronic juvenile offender (also known as chronic delinquent offenders, chronic delinquents, or chronic recidivists): Youths who have been arrested four or more times during their minority and perpetuate a striking majority of serious criminal acts; this small group, known as the "chronic 6 percent," is believed to engage in a significant portion of all delinquent behavior; these youths do not age out of crime but continue their criminal behavior into adulthood.

chronic recidivists: *See* chronic juvenile offender.

classical criminology: Holds that decisions to violate the law are weighed against possible punishments and to deter crime the pain of punishment must outweigh the benefit of illegal gain; led to graduated punishments based on seriousness of the crime (let the punishment fit the crime).

cliques: Small groups of friends who share intimate knowledge and confidences.

cocaine: A powerful natural stimulant derived from the coca plant.

cognitive theory: The branch of psychology that studies the perception of reality and the mental processes required to understand the world we live in.

college boy: Strives to conform to middle-class values and to move up the social ladder but is ill-equipped to succeed and fated to become frustrated and disappointed.

commitment to conformity: The strength of the ties of youths to conventional social institutions predicts their likely behavior; those with poor or negative ties are more likely to indulge in delinquent acts.

community policing: Police strategy that emphasizes fear reduction, community organization, and order maintenance rather than crime fighting.

community service restitution: The juvenile offender is required to assist some worthwhile community organization for a period of time.

community services: Local delinquency prevention services such as recreational programs and drug and alcohol information programs in schools that help meet the community's needs for youths.

community treatment: Using nonsecure and noninstitutional residences, counseling services, victim restitution programs, and other community services to treat juveniles in their own communities.

complaint: Report made by the police or some other agency to the court that initiates the intake process.

concurrent jurisdiction: More than one court has jurisdiction; the prosecutor then has the discretion of filing charges in either juvenile or adult court.

conditions of probation: The rules and regulations mandating that a juvenile on probation behave in a particular way.

confidentiality: Restricting information in juvenile court proceedings in the interest of protecting the privacy of the juvenile.

containment theory: Asserts that a strong self-image insulates youths from the pressure to engage in illegal acts; youths with poor self-concepts and low self-esteem are more likely to engage in crime.

continuity of crime: The idea that chronic juvenile offenders are likely to continue violating the law as adults.

control theories: Suggest that many forms of delinquent behavior are attractive to all teenagers, but only those who have few social supports (through family, friends, and teachers) feel free to violate the law.

control theory: Posits that delinquency results from a weakened commitment to the major social institutions (family, peers, and school); lack of such commitment allows youths to exercise antisocial behavioral choices.

co-offending: Committing criminal acts in groups.

corner boy: Not a delinquent but may engage in marginal behavior; eventually will marry a local girl and obtain a menial job with few prospects for advancement or success.

cottage system: Housing juveniles in a compound containing a series of small cottages, each of which accommodates twenty to forty children and is run by a set of cottage parents who create a home-like atmosphere.

Court Appointed Special Advocates (CASA): Volunteers appointed by the court to investigate the needs of the child and help officers of the court ensure a safe placement for the child.

covert pathway: The developmental path taken to delinquency that begins with sneaky, deceitful, and underhanded behavior.

crack: A highly addictive crystalline form of cocaine containing remnants of hydrochloride and sodium bicarbonate, which emits a crackling sound when smoked.

crack down: A law enforcement operation that is designed to reduce or eliminate a particular criminal activity through the application of aggressive police tactics, typically involving a larger than usual contingent of police officers.

criminal atavism: The idea that delinquents manifest physical anomalies that make them biologically and physiologically similar to our primitive ancestors, savage throwbacks to an earlier stage of human evolution.

critical criminologists: Analysts who review historical and current developments in law and order to expose the interests of the power elite and ruling classes.

crowds: Loosely organized groups who share interests and activities.

cultural deviance theory: Links delinquent acts to the formation of independent subcultures with a unique set of values that clash with the mainstream culture.

cultural transmission: Cultural norms and values that are passed down from one generation to the next.

culture conflict: When the values of a subculture clash with those of the dominant culture.

culture of poverty: View that lower-class people form a separate culture with their own values and norms, which are sometimes in conflict with conventional society.

custodial interrogation: Questions posed by the police to a suspect held in custody in the prejudicial stage of the juvenile justice process; juveniles have the same rights against self-incrimination as adults do when being questioned.

dark figures of crime: Incidents of crime and delinquency that go undetected by police.

degradation ceremony: Going to court, being scolded by a judge, or being found delinquent after a trial are examples of public ceremonies that can transform youthful offenders by degrading their self-image.

deinstitutionalization: Removing juveniles from adult jails and placing them in community-based programs to avoid the stigma attached to these facilities.

delinquency prevention programs: Programs developed by the police in cooperation with social services agencies to provide needed services to juveniles.

delinquent: Juvenile who has been adjudicated by a judicial officer of a juvenile court as having committed a delinquent act.

delinquent boy: Adopts a set of norms and values in direct opposition to middle-class society and resists control efforts by authority figures.

designer drugs: Lab-made drugs designed to avoid existing drug laws.

desistance: *See* aging out.

detached street workers: Social workers who go out into the community and establish close relationships with juvenile gangs with the goal of modifying gang behavior to conform to conventional behaviors and to help gang members get jobs and educational opportunities.

detention: Temporary care of a child alleged to be delinquent who requires secure custody in physically restricting facilities pending court disposition or execution of a court order.

detention hearing: A hearing by a judicial officer of a juvenile court to determine whether a juvenile is to be detained or released while juvenile proceedings are pending in the case.

determinate sentence: Sentence that specifies a fixed term of detention that must be served.

developmental process: At different stages of the life course a variety of factors can influence behavior; factors influential at one stage of life may not be significant at a later stage.

developmental theories: Assert that personal characteristics guide human development and influence behavioral choices but that these choices may change over the life course.

developmental view: The view that factors present at birth and events that unfold over a person's lifetime influence behavior; developmental theory focuses on the onset, escalation, desistance, and amplification of delinquent behaviors.

differential association theory: Asserts that criminal behavior is learned primarily within interpersonal groups and that youths will become delinquent if definitions they have learned favorable to violating the law exceed definitions favorable to obeying the law within that group.

differential reinforcement theory: A refinement of differential association theory that asserts that behavior is shaped by the reactions of others to that behavior; youths who receive more rewards than punishments for conforming behavior will be the most likely to remain nondelinquent.

disaggregated: Analyzing the relationship between two or more independent variables (such as murder convictions and death sentence) while controlling for the influence of a dependent variable (such as race).

discretion: Use of personal decision making and choice in carrying out operations in the criminal justice system, such as deciding whether to make an arrest or when to accept a plea bargain.

disorganized neighborhood: Inner-city areas of extreme poverty where the critical social control mechanisms have broken down.

disposition: For juvenile offenders, the equivalent of sentencing for adult offenders; however, juvenile dispositions should be more rehabilitative than retributive.

disposition hearing: The social service agency presents its case plan and recommendations for care of the child and treatment of the parents, including incarceration and counseling or other treatments.

diversion: Officially halting or suspending a formal criminal or juvenile justice proceeding at any legally prescribed processing point after a recorded justice system entry, and referral of that person to a treatment or care program or a recommendation that the person be released.

dramatization of evil: The process of social typing that transforms an offender's identity from a doer of evil to an evil person.

drift: Idea that youths move in and out of delinquency and that their lifestyles can embrace both conventional and deviant values.

dropouts: Youths who leave school before completing their required program of education.

drug courts: Courts whose focus is providing treatment for youths accused of drug-related acts.

due process: Basic constitutional principle based on the concept of the primacy of the individual and the complementary concept of limitation on governmental power; safeguards the individual from unfair state procedures in judicial or administrative proceedings; due process rights have been extended to juvenile trials.

early onset: The outbreak of deviant or delinquent behavior in preadolescence, which is generally viewed as a precursor of chronic offending in adolescence and which generally continues into adulthood.

egalitarian families: Husband and wife share power at home; daughters gain a kind of freedom similar to that of sons and their law-violating behaviors mirror those of their brothers.

ego identity: According to Erik Erikson, ego identity is formed when persons develop a firm sense of who they are and what they stand for.

electronic monitoring: Active monitoring systems consist of a radio transmitter worn by the offender that sends a continuous signal to the probation department computer, alerting officials if the offender leaves his or her place of confinement; passive systems employ computer-generated random phone calls that must be responded to in a certain period of time from a particular phone or other device.

equipotentiality: View that all people are equal at birth and are thereafter influenced by their environment.

evolutionary theory: Explaining the existence of aggression and violent behavior as positive adaptive behaviors in human evolution; these traits allowed their bearers to reproduce disproportionately, which has had an effect on the human gene pool.

excluded offenses: Offenses, some minor and others very serious, that are automatically excluded from juvenile court.

extravert: A person who behaves impulsively and doesn't have the ability to examine motives and behavior.

familicide: Mass murders in which a spouse and one or more children are slain.

family group homes: A combination of foster care and a group home in which a juvenile is placed in a private group home run by a single family rather than by professional staff.

Federal Bureau of Investigation (FBI): Arm of the U.S. Department of Justice that investigates violations of federal law, gathers crime statistics, runs a comprehensive crime laboratory, and helps train local law enforcement officers.

feminist theory: Asserts that the patriarchal social system oppresses women, creating gender bias and encouraging violence against women.

final order: Order that ends litigation between two parties by determining all their rights and disposing of all the issues.

focal concerns: The value orientation of lower-class culture that is characterized by a need for excitement, trouble, smartness, fate, and personal autonomy.

foot patrol: Police patrolling an area by walking around the community rather than driving about in patrol cars.

foster care programs: Juveniles who are orphans or whose parents cannot care for them are placed with families who provide the attention, guidance, and care they did not receive at home.

freebase: Purified cocaine crystals that are crushed and smoked to provide a more powerful high than cocaine.

free will: View that youths are in charge of their own destinies and are free to make personal behavior choices unencumbered by environmental factors.

gangs: Groups of youths who collectively engage in delinquent behaviors.

gateway drug: A substance that leads to use of more serious drugs; alcohol use has long been thought to lead to more serious drug abuse.

gender identity: The gender characteristics individuals identify in their own behaviors; members of both sexes who identify with "masculine" traits are more likely to engage in delinquent acts.

gender-schema theory: Asserts that our culture polarizes males and females, forcing them into exclusive gender roles of "feminine" or "masculine"; these gender scripts provide the basis for deviant behaviors.

general deterrence: Crime control policies that depend on the fear of criminal penalties, such as long prison sentences for violent crimes; aim is to convince law violator that the pain outweighs the benefit of criminal activity.

gentrified: The process of transforming a lower-class area into a middle-class enclave through property rehabilitation.

graffiti: Inscriptions or drawings made on a wall or structure and used by delinquents for gang messages and turf definition.

group autonomy: Maintaining subcultural values and attitudes that reinforce the independence of the group and separate it from other cultural groups.

group homes: Nonsecured, structured residences that provide counseling, education, job training, and family living.

group therapy: Counseling several individuals together in a group session; individuals can obtain support from other group members as they work through similar problems.

guardian *ad litem*: A court appointed attorney who protects the interests of the child in cases involving the child's welfare.

guided group interaction (GGI): Through group interactions a delinquent can acknowledge and solve personal problems with support from other group members.

hallucinogens: Natural or synthetic substances that produce vivid distortions of the senses without greatly disturbing consciousness.

hashish: A concentrated form of cannabis made from unadulterated resin from the female cannabis plant.

hearsay: Out-of-court statements made by one person and recounted in court by another; such statements are generally not allowed as evidence except in child abuse cases wherein a child's statements to social workers, teachers, or police may be admissible.

heroin: A narcotic made from opium and then cut with sugar or some other neutral substance until it is only 1 to 4 percent pure.

hot spot: A particular location or address that is the site of repeated and frequent criminal activity.

house arrest: An offender is required to stay at home during specific periods of time; monitoring is done by random phone calls and visits or by electronic devices.

House of Refuge: A care facility developed by the child savers to protect potential criminal youths by taking them off the street and providing a family-like environment.

identity crisis: Psychological state, identified by Erikson, in which youth face inner turmoil and uncertainty about life roles.

Illinois Juvenile Court Act of 1899: A major event in the history of juvenile justice, this act served as a model for other states, establishing the special status of juveniles and the emphasis on helping to treat rather than punish young offenders.

indeterminate sentence: Does not specify the length of time the juvenile must be held; rather, correctional authorities decide when the juvenile is ready to return to society.

index crime: *See* Part I offenses.

individual counseling: Counselors help juveniles understand and solve their current adjustment problems.

individualized treatment model: Each sentence must be tailored to the individual needs of the child.

inhalants: Volatile liquids that give off a vapor, which is inhaled, producing short-term excitement and euphoria followed by a period of disorientation.

inheritance school: An early form of biological theory that held that deviant behavior was inherited and therefore ran in families, being passed on from generation to generation.

in loco parentis: In the place of the parent; rights given to schools that allow them to assume parental duties in disciplining students.

intake: Process during which a juvenile referral is received and a decision is made to file a petition in juvenile court to release the juvenile, to place the juvenile under supervision, or to refer the juvenile elsewhere.

Intensive Aftercare Program (IAP): A balanced, highly structured, comprehensive continuum of intervention for serious and violent juvenile offenders returning to the community.

interactional theory: Asserts that youths' interactions with institutions and events over the life course determine criminal behavior patterns and that these patterns of behavior evolve over time.

interstitial group: Delinquent group that fills a crack in the social fabric and maintains standard group practices.

intrafamily conflict: An environment of discord and conflict within the family; children who grow up in dysfunctional homes often exhibit delinquent behaviors, having learned at a young age that aggression pays off.

judicial waiver: When the juvenile court waives its jurisdiction over a juvenile and transfers the case to adult criminal court.

jurisdiction: Every kind of judicial action; the authority of courts and judicial officers to decide cases.

juvenile court: Court that has original jurisdiction over persons defined by statute as juveniles and alleged to be delinquents, status offenders, or dependents.

juvenile court judge: A judge elected or appointed to preside over juvenile cases and whose decisions can only be reviewed by a judge of a higher court.

juvenile defense attorneys: Represent children in juvenile court and play an active role at all stages of the proceedings.

juvenile delinquency: Participation in illegal behavior by a minor who falls under a statutory age limit.

juvenile intensive probation supervision (JIPS): A true alternative to incarceration that involves almost daily supervision of the juvenile by the probation officer assigned to the case.

Juvenile Justice and Delinquency Prevention Act of 1974: This act established the OJJDP as an independent agency charged with developing and implementing programs to prevent and reduce juvenile crime.

juvenile justice process: Under the paternal (*parens patriae*) philosophy, juvenile justice procedures are informal and nonadversarial, invoked for the juvenile offender rather than against him or her; a petition instead of a complaint is filed; courts make findings of involvement or adjudication of delinquency instead of convictions; and juvenile offenders receive dispositions instead of sentences.

Juvenile Justice Reform Act of 1977: A Washington state statute that created mandatory sentencing for juvenile offenders based on their age, the crime, and their prior history as an offender.

juvenile justice system: The segment of the justice system including law enforcement officers, the courts, and correctional agencies, designed to treat youthful offenders.

juvenile officers: Police officers who specialize in dealing with juvenile offenders; they may operate alone or as part of a juvenile police unit within the department.

juvenile probation officer: Officer of the court involved in all four stages of the court process—intake, predisposition, postadjudication, and postdisposition—who assists the court and supervises juveniles placed on probation.

juvenile prosecutor: Government attorney responsible for representing the interests of the state and bringing the case against the accused juvenile.

***klikas*:** Subgroups of same-aged youths in Hispanic gangs that remain together and have separate names and a unique identity within the gang.

labeling theory: Posits that society creates deviance through a system of social control agencies that designate (or label) certain individuals as delinquent, thereby stigmatizing youths and encouraging them to accept this negative personal identity.

latchkey children: Children left unsupervised after school by working parents.

latent delinquents: Youths whose troubled family life leads them to seek immediate gratification without consideration of right and wrong or the feelings of others.

latent trait view: The view that a master trait, developed at birth or soon after, influences behavior across the life course. People who have this trait are crime prone throughout their lives.

law enforcement: The primary duty of all police officers to fight crime and keep the peace.

Law Enforcement Assistance Administration (LEAA): Unit in the U.S. Department of Justice established by the Omnibus Crime Control and Safe Streets Act of 1968 to administer grants and provide guidance for crime prevention policy and programs.

learning disability (LD): Neurological dysfunction that prevents an individual from learning to his or her potential.

learning theory: Posits that delinquency is learned through close relationships with others; asserts that children are born "good" and learn to be "bad" from others.

least detrimental alternative: Choosing a program for the child that will best foster a child's growth and development.

least restrictive alternative: Choosing a program with the least restrictive or secure setting that will benefit the child.

left realism: Asserts that crime is a function of relative deprivation and that criminals prey on the poor.

legalization of drugs: Decriminalizing drug use to reduce the association between drug use and crime.

liberal feminism: Asserts that females are less delinquent than males because their social roles provide them with fewer opportunities to commit crimes; as the roles of girls and women become more similar to those of boys and men, so too will their crime patterns.

life-course persisters: Delinquent youth who begin their offending career quite early and persist into their adulthood.

life-course theory: The view that people change as they mature and that the quality of their personal development shapes their behavior choices.

lifestyle violent juveniles: Juveniles who become more violent when exposed to more serious offenders in institutions.

longitudinal studies: A research design that entails repeated measures over time; for example, a cohort may be measured at several points over their life course to determine risk factors for chronic offending.

low-visibility decision making: Decisions made by public officials in the criminal or juvenile justice system that the public is not in a position to understand, regulate, or criticize.

mandatory sentence: Sentence is defined by a statutory requirement that states the penalty to be set for all cases of a specific offense.

marijuana: The dried leaves of the cannabis plant.

Marxist feminists: *See* radical feminists.

masculinity hypothesis: View that women who commit crimes have biological and psychological traits similar to those of men.

meta-analysis: An analysis technique that synthesizes results across many programs over time.

middle-class measuring rods: Standards by which teachers and other representatives of state authority evaluate students' behavior; when lower-class youths cannot meet these standards they are subject to failure, which brings on frustration and anger at conventional society.

milieu therapy: All aspects of the environment are part of the treatment, and meaningful change, increased growth, and satisfactory adjustment are encouraged; this is often accomplished through peer pressure to conform to the group norms.

minimal brain dysfunction (MBD): Damage to the brain itself that causes antisocial behavior injurious to the individual's lifestyle and social adjustment.

Miranda **warning:** Supreme Court decisions require police officers to inform individuals under arrest of their constitutional rights; warnings must also be given when suspicion begins to focus on an individual in the accusatory stage.

Missouri Plan: Sets out how juvenile court judges are chosen and specifies that a commission should nominate candidates, an elected official should make the appointment, and the incumbent judge should run uncontested on his or her record in a nonpartisan election, usually every three years.

monetary restitution: A requirement that juvenile offenders compensate crime victims for out-of-pocket losses caused by the crime, including property damage, lost wages, and medical expenses.

moral entrepreneurs: Interest groups that attempt to control social life by promoting their own personal set of moral values and establishing them as law.

multisystemic treatment (MST): Addresses a variety of family, peer, and psychological problems by focusing on problem solving and communication skills training.

National Advisory Commission on Criminal Justice Standards and Goals: Established in 1973, the commission's report identified major strategies for juvenile justice and delinquency prevention.

National Council of Juvenile and Family Court Judges: An organization that sponsors research and continuing legal education to help juvenile court judges master their field of expertise.

natural areas for crime: Inner-city areas of extreme poverty where the critical social control mechanisms have broken down.

nature theory: Holds that low intelligence is genetically determined and inherited.

near groups: Relatively unstructured short-term groups with fluid membership.

need for treatment: The criteria on which juvenile sentencing is based. Ideally, juveniles are treated according to their need for treatment and not the seriousness of the delinquent act they committed.

negative affective states: Anger, depression, disappointment, fear, and other adverse emotions that derive from strain.

neglect: Passive neglect by a parent or guardian, depriving children of food, shelter, health care, and love.

neuroticism: A personality trait marked by unfounded anxiety, tension, and emotional instability.

neutralization techniques: A set of attitudes or beliefs that allow would-be delinquents to negate any moral apprehension they may have about committing crime so that they may freely engage in antisocial behavior without regret.

neutralization theory: Holds that youths adhere to conventional values while "drifting" into periods of illegal behavior; for drift to occur, youths must first neutralize conventional legal and moral values.

nonresidential programs: Juveniles remain in their own homes but receive counseling, education, employment, diagnostic, and casework services through an intensive support system.

nuclear family: A family unit composed of parents and their children; this smaller family structure is subject to great stress due to the intense, close contact between parents and children.

nurture theory: Holds that intelligence is partly biological but mostly sociological; negative environmental factors encourage delinquent behavior and depress intelligence scores for many youths.

Office of Juvenile Justice and Delinquency Prevention (OJJDP): Branch of the U.S. Justice Department charged with shaping national juvenile justice policy through disbursement of federal aid and research funds.

orphan train: A practice of the Children's Aid Society in which urban youths were sent West on trains for adoption with local farm couples.

overt pathway: The developmental path taken to delinquency that begins with violent outbursts and bullying.

parens patriae: Power of the state to act in behalf of the child and provide care and protection equivalent to that of a parent.

parole guidelines: Recommended length of confinement and kinds of aftercare assistance most effective for a juvenile who committed a specific offense.

Part I offenses (also known as index crimes): Offenses including homicide and nonnegligent manslaughter, forcible rape, robbery, aggravated assault, burglary, larceny, arson, and motor vehicle theft; recorded by local law enforcement officers, these crimes are tallied quarterly and sent to the FBI for inclusion in the UCR.

Part II offenses: All crimes other than Part I offenses; recorded by local law enforcement officers, arrests for these crimes are tallied quarterly and sent to the FBI for inclusion in the UCR.

passive speech: A form of expression protected by the First Amendment but not associated with actually speaking words; examples include wearing symbols or protest messages on buttons or signs.

paternalism hypothesis: *See* chivalry hypothesis.

paternalistic family: A family style wherein the father is the final authority on all family matters and exercises complete control over his wife and children.

peacemakers: Assert that peace and humanism can reduce crime and offers a new approach to crime control through mediation.

petition: Document filed in juvenile court alleging that a juvenile is a delinquent, a status offender, or a dependent and asking that the court assume jurisdiction over the juvenile.

plea bargaining: The exchange of prosecutorial and judicial concessions for a guilty plea by the accused; plea bargaining usually results in a reduced charge or a more lenient sentence.

pledge system: Early English system in which neighbors protected each other from thieves and warring groups.

Poor Laws: English statutes that allowed the courts to appoint overseers over destitute and neglected children, allowing placement of these children as servants in the homes of the affluent.

Positive Peer Culture (PPC): Counseling program in which peer leaders encourage other group members to modify their behavior and peers help reinforce acceptable behaviors.

power-control theory: Holds that gender differences in the delinquency rate are a function of class differences and economic conditions that influence the structure of family life.

precocious sexuality: Sexual experimentation in early adolescence.

predatory crimes: Violent crimes against persons and crimes in which an offender attempts to steal an object directly from its holder.

predispositional investigation: An investigation usually carried out by a member of the probationary staff to acquire information about the child that will allow the judge to make a decision in the best interest of the child.

predisposition report: *See* social investigation report.

President's Commission on Law Enforcement and the Administration of Justice: This 1967 commission suggested that we must provide juveniles with opportunities for success, including jobs and education, and that we must develop effective law enforcement procedures to control hard core youthful offenders.

prestige crimes: Stealing or assaulting someone to gain prestige in the neighborhood; often part of gang initiation rites.

pretrial conference: The attorney for the social services agency presents an overview of the case and a plea bargain or negotiated settlement can be agreed to in a consent decree.

preventive detention: Keeping the accused in custody prior to trial because the accused is suspected of being a danger to the community.

primary deviance: Deviant acts that do not redefine the self- and public image of the offender.

primary sociopaths: Individuals with an inherited trait that predisposes them to antisocial behavior.

probable cause: Reasonable ground to believe the existence of facts that an offense was committed and that the accused committed that offense.

probation: Nonpunitive, legal disposition of juveniles emphasizing community treatment in which the juvenile is closely supervised by an officer of the court and must adhere to a strict set of rules to avoid incarceration.

problem behavior syndrome (PBS): Convergence of a variety of psychological problems and family dysfunctions including substance abuse and criminality.

Project D.A.R.E.: An elementary school drug abuse resistance education program designed to prevent teenage drug abuse by giving youths the skills they need to resist peer pressure to experiment with drugs.

prosecutorial discretion: Allowing the prosecutor to determine the jurisdiction by selecting the charge to be filed or by choosing to file the complaint in either juvenile or adult court.

pro-social bonds: The attachment a child has with positive elements of society such as schools, parents, and peers.

psychodynamic theory: Branch of psychology that holds that the human personality is controlled by unconscious mental processes developed early in childhood.

psychopathic personality (also known as sociopathic personality): A person lacking in warmth and affection, exhibiting inappropriate behavior responses, and unable to learn from experience.

psychotherapy: Highly structured counseling in which a skilled therapist helps a juvenile solve conflicts and make a more positive adjustment to society.

public defender: An attorney who works in a public agency or under private contractual agreement as defense counsel to indigent defendants.

radical feminists (also known as Marxist feminists): Hold that gender inequality stems from the unequal power of men and women and the subsequent exploitation of women by men; the cause of female delinquency originates with the onset of male supremacy and the efforts of males to control females' sexuality.

reaction formation: Rejecting conventional goals and standards that seem impossible to attain.

reality therapy: A form of counseling that emphasizes current behavior and that requires the individual to accept responsibility for all of his or her actions.

reflective role-taking: A process whereby youths take on antisocial roles assigned to them by others.

reform schools: Institutions in which educational and psychological services are used in an effort to improve the conduct of juveniles who are forcibly detained.

relative deprivation: Condition that exists when people of wealth and poverty live in close proximity to one another; the relatively deprived are apt to have feelings of anger and hostility, which may produce criminal behavior.

removal: *See* waiver.

representing: Tossing or flashing gang signs in the presence of rivals, often escalating into a verbal or physical confrontation.

residential programs: Placement of a juvenile offender in a residential, nonsecure facility such as a group home, foster home, family group home, or rural home where the juvenile can be closely monitored and develop close relationships with staff members.

restorative justice: Nonpunitive strategies for dealing with juvenile offenders that make the justice system a healing process rather than a punishment process.

retreatists: Gangs whose members actively engage in substance abuse.

review hearing: Periodic meetings to determine whether the conditions of the case plan for an abused child are being met by the parents or guardians of the child.

right to treatment: Philosophy espoused by many courts that juvenile offenders have a statutory right to treatment while under the jurisdiction of the courts.

role conflicts: Conflicts police officers face that revolve around the requirement to perform their primary duty of law enforcement and a desire to aid in rehabilitating youthful offenders.

role diffusion: According to Erik Erikson, role diffusion occurs when youths spread themselves too thin, experience personal uncertainty, and place themselves at the mercy of leaders who promise to give them a sense of identity they cannot develop for themselves.

routine activities theory: View that crime is a "normal" function of the routine activities of modern living; offenses can be expected if there is a motivated offender and a suitable target that is not protected by capable guardians.

rural programs: Specific recreational and work opportunities provided for juveniles in a rural setting such as a forestry camp, a farm, or a ranch.

school failure: Failing to achieve success in school can result in frustration, anger, and reduced self-esteem, which may contribute to delinquent behavior.

search and seizure: The U.S. Constitution protects citizens from any search and seizure by police without a lawfully obtained search warrant; such warrants are issued when there is probable cause to believe that an offense has been committed.

secondary deviance: Deviant acts that redefine the offender's self- and public image, forming the basis for the youth's self-concept.

secondary prevention (also known as special prevention): Psychological counseling, psychotropic medications, and other rehabilitation treatment programs designed to prevent repeat offenses.

secondary sociopaths: Individuals who are biologically normal but exhibit antisocial behavior due to negative life experiences.

sedatives: Drugs of the barbiturate family that depress the central nervous system into a sleep-like condition.

self-control: Ability to control impulsive and often imprudent behaviors that offer immediate short-term gratification.

self-fulfilling prophecy: Deviant behavior patterns that are a response to an earlier labeling experience; youths act out these social roles even if they were falsely bestowed.

self-labeling: The process in which a person who has been negatively labeled accepts the label as a personal role or identity.

self-reports: Questionnaire or survey technique that asks subjects to reveal their own participation in delinquent or criminal acts.

shelter care: A place for temporary care of children in physically unrestricting facilities.

skinhead: Member of white supremacist gang, identified by a shaved skull and Nazi or Ku Klux Klan markings.

situational crime prevention: A crime prevention method that relies on reducing the opportunity to commit criminal acts by (1) making them more difficult to perform, (2) reducing their reward and (3) increasing their risks

social bond: Ties a person to the institutions and processes of society; elements of the bond include attachment, commitment, involvement, and belief.

social capital: The positive relationships a person develops that help them succeed in life and avoid criminal behaviors.

social conflict view: Asserts that society is in a state of constant internal conflict, and focuses on the role of social and governmental institutions as mechanisms for social control.

social control: Ability of social institutions to influence human behavior; the justice system is the primary agency of formal social control.

social development model (SDM): An array of personal, psychological, and community-level risk factors that make some children susceptible to development of antisocial behaviors.

social disorganization: Neighborhood or area marked by culture conflict, lack of cohesiveness, a transient population, and insufficient social organizations; these problems are reflected in the problems at schools in these areas.

social disorganization theory: Posits that delinquency is a product of the social forces existing in inner-city, low-income areas.

social ecology: Theory focuses attention on the influence social institutions have on individual behavior and suggests that law-violating behavior is a response to social rather than individual forces operating in an urban environment.

social investigation report (also known as predisposition report): Developed by the juvenile probation officer, this report consists of a clinical diagnosis of the juvenile and his or her need for court assistance, relevant environmental and personality factors, and any other information that would assist the court in developing a treatment plan for the juvenile.

socialization: The process of learning the values and norms of the society or the subculture to which the individual belongs.

social learning theory: The view that behavior is modeled through observation either directly through intimate contact with others or indirectly through media; interactions that are rewarded are copied, whereas those that are punished are avoided.

social process theories: Posit that the interactions a person has with key elements of the socialization process determine his or her future behavior.

social structure theories: Explain delinquency using socioeconomic conditions and cultural values.

Society for the Prevention of Cruelty to Children (SPCC): First established in 1874, these organizations protected children subjected to cruelty and neglect at home or at school.

sociopathic personality: *See* psychopathic personality.

somatotype school: Argued that delinquents manifest distinct physiques that make them susceptible to particular types of delinquent behavior.

special prevention: *See* secondary prevention.

specific deterrence: Sending convicted offenders to secure incarceration facilities so that punishment is severe enough to convince offenders not to repeat their criminal activity.

spontaneous remission: *See* aging out.

status offense: Conduct that is illegal only because the child is under age.

stimulants: Synthetic substances that produce an intense physical reaction by stimulating the central nervous system.

strain theory: Links delinquency to the strain of being locked out of the economic mainstream, which creates the anger and frustration that lead to delinquent acts.

stratification: Grouping society into classes based on the unequal distribution of scarce resources.

stigmatized: People who have been negatively labeled because of their participation, or alleged participation, in deviant or outlawed behaviors.

subculture of violence: An identified urban-based subculture in which young males are expected to respond with violence to the slightest provocation.

subcultures: Groups that are loosely part of the dominant culture but that maintain a unique set of values, beliefs, and traditions.

substance abuse: Using drugs or alcohol in such a way as to cause physical harm to yourself.

subterranean values: The ability of youthful law violators to repress social norms.

suppression effect: A reduction of the number of arrests per year for youths who have been incarcerated or otherwise punished.

teen courts: Courts that make use of peer juries to decide non-serious delinquency cases.

TOP program: Police and community prevention effort in which teens are hired to patrol the city's parks and recreation areas.

totality of the circumstances doctrine: Legal doctrine that mandates that a decision maker consider all the issues and circumstances of a case before judging the outcome; the suspect's age, intelligence, and competency may be issues that influence his or her understanding and judgment.

tracking: Dividing students into groups according to their ability and achievement levels.

trait theory: Holds that youths engage in delinquent or criminal behavior due to aberrant physical or psychological traits that govern behavioral choices; delinquent actions are impulsive or instinctual rather than rational choices.

tranquilizers: Drugs that reduce anxiety and promote relaxation.

transfer hearing: Preadjudicatory hearing in juvenile court for the purpose of determining whether juvenile court should be retained over a juvenile or waived and the juvenile transferred to adult court for prosecution.

transfer process: Transferring a juvenile offender from the jurisdiction of juvenile court to adult criminal court.

transitional neighborhood: Area undergoing a shift in population and structure, usually from middle-class residential to lower-class mixed use.

trial de novo: A review procedure in which there is a complete retrial of the original case.

truancy: Staying out of school without permission.

truly disadvantaged: According to William Julius Wilson, those people who are left out of the economic mainstream and reduced to living in the most deteriorated inner-city areas.

turning points: According to Laub and Sampson, life events, such as marriage, that help a person desist from crime.

underachievers: Those who do not achieve success in school at the level of their expectations.

underclass: Group of urban poor whose members have little chance of upward mobility or improvement.

Uniform Crime Report (UCR): Compiled by the FBI, the UCR is the most widely used source of national crime and delinquency statistics.

utilitarians: Those who believe that people weigh the benefits and consequences of their future actions before deciding on a course of behavior.

victimizations: The number of people who are victims of criminal acts; young teens are fifteen times more likely than older adults (age 65 and over) to be victims of crimes.

victim service restitution: The juvenile offender is required to provide some service directly to the crime victim.

Violent Crime Control and Law Enforcement Act of 1994: This act made available increased funding for juvenile justice and delinquency prevention.

Violent Juvenile Offender (VJO) program: Specialized programs in small, secure settings where youths are gradually reintegrated into the community with intensive supervision.

waiver (also known as bindover or removal): Transferring legal jurisdiction over the most serious and experienced juvenile offenders to the adult court for criminal prosecution.

watch system: Replaced the pledge system in England; watchmen patrolled urban areas at night to provide protection from harm.

wayward minors: Early legal designation of youths who violate the law because of their minority status; now referred to as status offenders.

widening the net: Phenomenon that occurs when programs created to divert youths from the justice system actually involve them more deeply in the official process.

wilderness probation: Programs involving outdoor expeditions that provide opportunities for juveniles to confront the difficulties of their lives while achieving positive personal satisfaction.

writ of certiorari: Order of a superior court requesting that the record of an inferior court (or administrative body) be brought forward for review or inspection.

writ of habeus corpus: Judicial order requesting that a person detaining another produce the body of the prisoner and give reasons for his or her capture and detention.

zero tolerance policy: Mandating specific consequences or punishments for delinquent acts and not allowing anyone to avoid these consequences.

Name Index

Subject Index

Photograph Credits

This page constitutes an extension of the copyright page. We have made every effort to trace the ownership of all copyrighted material and to secure permission from copyright holders. In the event of any question arising as to the use of any material, we will be pleased to make the necessary corrections in future printings. Thanks are due to the following authors, publishers, and agents for permission to use the material indicated.

1 © D. R. M. News/CORBIS-Sygma; 3 © Bob Daemmrich/ The Image Works; 5 © Catherine Leroy/Sipa Press; 9 © *The Repository,* photo by Joy Newcomb; 11 The Pierpont Morgan Library/Art Resource, NY; 12 Stock Montage, Inc.; 15 © Sherman Zent/*Palm Beach Post;* 18 © Mike Mazzachi/Stock, Boston; 22 © Bruce Davidson/Magnum Photos; 24 AP/Wide World Photos; 31 © Catherine Leroy/Sipa Press; 35 AP/Wide World Photos; 37 © A. Ramey/Stock, Boston; 44 © Joel Gordon; 46 © Catherine Leroy/Sipa Press; 51 © Nick Lacy/Stock, Boston; 53 AP/Wide World Photos; 57 © Collection Viollet/ Liaison Agency; 63 © Frank Siteman/Stock, Boston; 69 Dimension Films/Shooting Star; 71 AP/Wide World Photos; 75 AP/Wide World Photos; 78 © Joel Gordon; 84 © Patrick Zachman/Magnum Photos; 85 © Mark Richards/Sipa Press; 86 © Dorothy Littell/Stock, Boston; 89 © Richard Hutchings/Photo Edit; 91 © Gregg Mancuso/ Stock, Boston; 95 © McLaughlin/The Image Works; 98 AP/Wide World Photos; 100 AP/Wide World Photos; 102 AP/Wide World Photos; 106 © Katherine McGlynn; 108 AP/Wide World Photos; 111 AP/Wide World Photos; 114 AP/Wide World Photos; 120 PhotoEdit; 122 AP/Wide World Photos; 126 © Joel Gordon; 128 AP/Wide World Photos; 130 © Bruce Davidson/Magnum Photos; 133 © Gale Zucker/Stock, Boston; 134 AP/Wide World Photos; 140 © Myrleen Ferguson/Photo Edit; 142 © Jeffry W. Myers/Stock, Boston; 147 © Lisa Quinones/Black Star;

149 © David Woo/Stock, Boston; 151 © Joel Gordon; 155 © Sadin/Liaison/Rapho; 159 AP/Wide World Photos; 162 © Joel Gordon; 167 American Humane Society; 173 © Denis LaCuyer/Liaison Agency; 177 © Joel Gordon; 180 AP/Wide World Photos; 182 AP/Wide World Photos; 184 © Bob Daemmrich/The Image Works; 186 © Robert Yager/Sipa Press; 190 © Michael Abramson/ Black Star; 196 © Nancy Siesel/Saba; 201 AP/Wide World Photos; 205 AP/Wide World Photos; 207 © Joe Rodriguez/Black Star; 212 © Joel Gordon; 214 AP/Wide World Photos; 218 AP/Wide World Photos; 219 AP/Wide World Photos; 226 © Joel Gordon; 227 AP/Wide World Photos; 233 AP/Wide World Photos; 237 © Gale Zucker/ Stock, Boston; 239 © Paul Milette/*Palm Beach Post;* 241 © Joel Gordon; 243 © AP/Wide World Photos; 248 © Joel Gordon; 252 © Joel Gordon; 258 © Joel Gordon; 261 AP/Wide World Photos; 264 American Correctional Association; 266 © Jim Alcorn/*New York Post* Pool/CORBIS; 270 Stock Montage, Inc.; 276 © 1998 Time, Inc. Reprinted by permission of TimePix; 282 © Glen Korengold/Stock, Boston; 285 AP/Wide World Photos; 286 AP/Wide World Photos; 291 © Joel Gordon; 295 AP/Wide World Photos; 299 © Kelly Wilkinson/ *Indianapolis Star*/Sipa; 301 © Joe Rodriguez/Black Star; 303 © Michael A. Dwyer/Stock, Boston; 308 AP/Wide World Photos; 311 © AP/Wide World Photos; 314 © Shelley Gazin/CORBIS; 317 © Joel Gordon; 323 © Rich Graulieh/*Palm Beach Post;* 327 © Joel Gordon; 331 AP/Wide World Photos; 285 AP/Wide World Photos; 337 © Tony Savino/The Image Works; 343 © Gale Zucker/Stock, Boston; 345 AP/Wide World Photos; 349 © Lee Celano/ Liaison Agency; 353 AP/Wide World Photos; 355 © Joel Gordon; 360 AP/Wide World Photos; 361 Dick Schmidt/*Sacramento Bee;* 362 © David Woo/Stock, Boston; 366 © A. Ramey/Stock, Boston; 368 © Jacques Brund/Design Concepts.